METHODS AND TOOLS FOR COLLABORATIVE NETWORKED ORGANIZATIONS

METHODS AND TOOLS FOR COLLABORATIVE NETWORKED ORGANIZATIONS

Edited By

Luis M. Camarinha-Matos
New University of Lisbon, Portugal

Hamideh Afsarmanesh
University of Amsterdam, The Netherlands

Martin Ollus
VTT Industrial Systems, Finland

 Springer

Editors

Luis M. Camarinha-Matos
New University of Lisbon
Campus de Caparica
Quinta da Torre
2829-516 Monte Caparica
Portugal
cam@uninova.pt

Hamideh Afsarmanesh
University of Amsterdam
Collaborative Networks Group
Kruislaan 419, MATRIX I
1098 VA Amsterdam
The Netherlands
hamideh@science.uva.nl

Martin Ollus
VTT Industrial Systems
Enterprise Network Management
Tekniikantie 12, Espoo
P.O. Box 1000, FI-02044 VTT
Finland
martin.ollus@vtt.fi

Methods and Tools for Collaborative Networked Organizations
Edited By: Luis M. Camarinha-Matos, Hamideh Afsarmanesh, and Martin Ollus

ISBN: 978-1-4419-4637-9   e-ISBN: 978-0-387-79424-2

springer.com

TABLE OF CONTENTS

REFEREES

The following people helped with the revision of the various chapters:
António Abreu
Josefa Arana
Eoin Banahan
Servane Crave
Ekaterina Ermilova
Nathalie Galeano
Filipa Ferrada
Iris Karvonen
Toni Jarimo
Simon Msanjila
Wico Mulder
Alexandra Pereira-Klen
Michel Pouly
Ricardo Rabelo
João Rosas
Iiro Salkari
Ingo Westphal

ECOLEAD REVIEW TEAM

The following members of the European Commission Review Team followed the development of the ECOLEAD project where this work was developed and provided very useful guidance for its improvement:
Jorge Grazina
Alberto Bonetti
Bernhard Koelmel
Jorge Pinho Sousa
Norman Roth

SPONSOR

ECOLEAD
European Collaborative Networked Organizations Leadership Initiative
IST IP 506958 project
www.ecolead.org

FOREWORD

Collaborative Networked Organizations nowadays represent one of the most relevant organizational paradigms in industry and services. During recent years, due to the recognition of the need and supported by the ICT advances, there are a large number of focused developments in this area. These developments in fact have turned Collaborative Networks into a pervasive phenomenon in all socio-economic sectors.

Complementarily to these developments, new advances are progressively emerging in different research initiatives worldwide. However, unfortunately most of the generated knowledge and experiences are often confined to the participants in those projects. Only fragmented aspects of these advances usually become publicly available, e.g., through conference papers.

The main aim of this manuscript is to provide a comprehensive set of reference material in a single book. The book is developed in the context of ECOLEAD, a large 4-year European initiative, involving 28 organizations (from academia, research and industry), from 14 countries (in Europe and Latin America) in which the editors had the leading responsibility. Various sections of this book represent a synthesis of the achievements in the focus areas of the project. This book is complemented by a second book "Collaborative Networks – Reference Modeling" that is devoted to the theoretical foundation and introduction of reference models for Collaborative Networks.

As a multi-author book, the contents and views expressed in each chapter and the applied styles are naturally the responsibility of their authors. Nevertheless, as all contributors are involved in the ECOLEAD initiative, and share the same strategic goals and culture, it is expected that the book presents a reasonable homogeneity.

Three main types of results from ECOLEAD are presented: (i) Conceptual frameworks and models, (ii) Methods and processes, and (iii) Software tools and systems. Furthermore, the experience and lessons learned with a number of large pilot implementations in real-world running networks of enterprises are also included as an indication of the assessment/validation of the project results.

The editors take this opportunity to thank the contributions of all authors, as well as the help of those colleagues that reviewed earlier versions of this manuscript. We expect this work to help those who are active in or entering the field of Collaborative Networks, and thus providing an effective contribution to the consolidation and progress of this area.

The editors

Luis M. Camarinha-Matos
New University of Lisbon, Portugal

Hamideh Afsarmanesh
University of Amsterdam, The Netherlands

Martin Ollus
VTT Industrial Systems, Finland

PART 1

INTRODUCTION

1. ECOLEAD AND CNO BASE CONCEPTS

L. M. Camarinha-Matos [1], H. Afsarmanesh [2], M. Ollus [3]

[1] *New University of Lisbon, PORTUGAL, cam@uninova.pt*
[2] *University of Amsterdam, THE NETHERLANDS, hamideh@science.uva.nl*
[3] *VTT, FINLAND, martin.ollus@vtt.fi*

Collaborative networked organizations represent an important paradigm to help organizations cope with the challenges of market turbulence. Under this scope, the ECOLEAD integrated project was launched with the aim of creating the necessary foundations and mechanisms for establishing an advanced network-based industry society. The main underlying concepts, research roadmap and achieved results of this initiative are briefly summarized.

1. INTRODUCTION

Participation in networks has nowadays become very important for any organization that strives to achieve a differentiated competitive advantage, especially if the company is small or medium sized. Collaboration is a key issue in addressing market demands, particularly in the manufacturing sector, through sharing competencies and resources. A new competitive environment for both manufacturing and service industries has been developing during the last few years, and this trend is forcing a change in the way these industries are managed. In order to be successful in a very competitive and rapidly changing environment, companies need significantly improved competencies in terms of dealing with new business models, strategies, organizational and governance principles, processes and technological capabilities. Thus companies are increasingly restructuring their internal operating and information systems and re-engineering production processes to both eliminate waste and lower the costs. Furthermore, they are changing the nature of their modus operandi by partnering with other companies in complex value chains and business ecosystems, which now extend globally (Myers, 2006).

In today's industry, collaborative networks manifest in a large variety of forms. Moving from the classical supply chain format, characterized by relatively stable networks with well defined roles and requiring only minimal coordination and information exchange, more dynamic structures are emerging in industry. Some of these organizational forms are goal-oriented, i.e. focused on a single project or business opportunity, such as in the case of virtual enterprises (VE). The same concept can be applied to other contexts, e.g. government and service sectors, leading to a more general term, the virtual organization (VO). A VE/VO is often a temporary organization that "gathers" its potential from the possibility of (rapidly) forming consortia well suited (in terms of competencies and resources) to each business opportunity. Other emerging collaborative networks are formed by human professionals who may collaborate in virtual communities and form virtual teams to address specific problems, such as collaborative concurrent engineering or development of a consultancy project.

Another case of collaborative network is the collaborative virtual laboratory (VL). Here a virtual experimental environment is provided for scientists and engineers to perform their experiments, enabling a group of researchers located in different geographical regions to work together, sharing resources, (such as expensive lab equipment), and results. In this case, and in addition to the network of involved organizations (e.g. research centers or research units of enterprises), there is an overlapping network of people. In a research activity most collaborative acts are in fact conducted by researchers that have a high degree of autonomy. Therefore, in this example, the necessity for tools to support human collaboration – advanced groupware tools, becomes evident. A typical VL involves scientific equipment connected to a network, large-scale simulations, visualization, data reduction and data summarization capabilities, application-specific databases, collaboration tools, e.g. teleconferencing, federated data exchange, chat, shared electronic-whiteboard, notepad, etc., application-dependent software tools and interfaces, safe communications, and large network bandwidth. A similar situation can happen in a virtual enterprise when engineering teams formed by engineers of different enterprises (virtual teams) collaborate on some engineering problem.

Many more examples can be found in different sectors. For instance, we can think of networks of insurance companies, networks of governmental institutions, networks of academic institutions forming virtual institutes for joint delivery of advanced courses, networks of entities involved in disaster rescuing, networks of care centers, healthcare institutions, and family relatives involved in elderly care, etc.

With the development of new collaborative tools supported by Internet and mobile computing and a better understanding of the mechanisms of collaborative networks, new organizational forms are naturally emerging. And yet all these cases have a number of characteristics in common (Camarinha-Matos, Afsarmanesh, 2006):

- Networks composed of a variety of entities - organizations and people – which are largely autonomous, geographically distributed, and heterogeneous in terms of their operating environment, culture, social capital and goals.
- Participants collaborate to (better) achieve common or compatible goals.
- The interactions among participants are supported by computer networks.

Therefore, the notion of collaborative network was established as a generic term to represent all these particular cases (Camarinha-Matos, Afsarmanesh, 2005):

A **collaborative network** (CN) is a network consisting of a variety of entities (e.g. organizations, people, machines) that are largely autonomous, geographically distributed, and heterogeneous in terms of their operating environment, culture, social capital and goals, but that collaborate to better achieve common or compatible goals, thus jointly generating value, and whose interactions are supported by computer networks.

Most forms of collaborative networks imply some kind of *organization* over the activities of their constituents, identifying roles for the participants, and some governance rules, and therefore, can be called manifestations of **collaborative networked organizations (CNOs)**. Other more spontaneous forms of collaboration in networks can also be foreseen. For instance, various **ad-hoc collaboration processes** can take place in virtual communities, namely those that are not business oriented – e.g. individual citizens contributions in case of a natural disaster, or simple gathering of individuals for a social cause (Camarinha-Matos, Afsarmanesh, 2008). These are cases where people or organizations may volunteer to collaborate hoping to improve a general aim, with no pre-plan and/or structure on participants' roles and how their activities should proceed.

Reinforcing the effectiveness of collaborative networks and creating the necessary conditions for making them an endogenous reality in the European industrial landscape, mostly based on small and medium enterprises (SMEs), is a key survival factor. If properly established and managed, collaborative networks can provide a basis for competitiveness, world-excellence, and agility in turbulent market conditions, they can support SMEs in identifying and exploiting new business potential, boost innovation, and increase their knowledge. The networking of SMEs with large-scale enterprises also contributes to the success of big companies in the global market.

Continued dedicated efforts on virtual organizations (e.g. through the Esprit, IST, and IMS initiatives), although fragmented, have led to a European critical mass and a culture of collaboration, giving early and systematic entry into the area. This "movement" is consistent with the process of European integration, which represents a push towards the "cooperation culture", while preserving the desire to leverage regional values and assets. In a time of very rapid technological evolution and socio-economic transformation, but also when other geographical regions (e.g. USA, Latin America, Australia, Japan, and China) are focusing their research strategies on this area, it is necessary to break with the tradition of fragmented incremental research, and aim at a sustainable breakthrough with large beneficial impacts on the society.

2. BASE ORGANIZATIONAL FORMS

Early projects and proposals, too much technology-driven, underestimated the difficulties of the Virtual Organization / Virtual Enterprise (VO) creation process and suggested very dynamic scenarios. However, the agility and dynamism required for VOs are limited by the difficult process of establishing common operational basis and building trust. Even if flexible support infrastructures become widely available, the aspects of trust building and the required reorganization at the enterprise level are hard to cope with in collaborative business processes. "Trusting your partner" is a gradual and long process. The definition of "collaborative business rules", contracts for VO or even common ontologies are challenging, especially when different business cultures are involved. In this sense, very dynamic organizations formed by enterprises without previous experience of collaboration might be limited to scenarios of simple commerce transactions (e.g. buy-sell).

The creation of long term clusters of industry or service enterprises represents an approach to overcoming these obstacles and can support the rapid formation of

VO inspired by business opportunities. The concept of cluster of enterprises, which should not be confused with a VO, represents an association or pool of enterprises and related supporting institutions that have both the potential and the will to cooperate with each other through the establishment of a long-term cooperation agreement. Buyer-supplier relationships, common tools and technologies, common markets or distribution channels, common resources, or even common labor pools are elements that traditionally bind the cluster together. In some cases they are formed around a special technology or product type, sometimes to support an OEM (original equipment manufacturer).

A more frequent situation is the case in which the cluster is formed by organizations located in a common region, although geography is not a major facet when collaboration is supported by computer networks. Nevertheless, the geographical closeness has some advantages for collaboration, as it may facilitate better adaptation to the local (cultural) needs and an easier creation of a "sense of community". But with the development of more effective communication infrastructures, such long-term associations are not necessarily motivated by geographical closeness. Cultural ties, even particular human relationships are also motivating factors in forming such associations which in fact represent VO **Breeding Environments** (VBE) for the dynamic formation of VOs. For each business opportunity found by one of the VBE members, acting as a **broker**, a subset of the VBE enterprises may be chosen to form a VO for that specific business opportunity. Thus:

> A **VO Breeding Environment** (VBE) represents an association of organizations and their related supporting institutions, adhering to a base long term cooperation agreement, and adoption of common operating principles and infrastructures, with the main goal of increasing their preparedness towards rapid configuration of temporary alliances for collaboration in potential Virtual Organizations. Namely, when a business opportunity is identified by one member (acting as a broker), a subset of VBE organizations can be selected to form a VE/VO (Afsarmanesh, Camarinha-Matos, 2005).

From a regional perspective, a well-managed VBE may offer the opportunity to combine the necessities of both "old" and "new" economies, and form a sustainable environment (local business ecosystem) while leveraging and preserving the regional assets and culture. The VO breeding environment can support the exploitation of local competencies and resources by an agile and fast configuration of the most adequate set of partners for each business opportunity. Furthermore, the local VBEs can gather and empower a unique set of competencies tailored to regional culture and local customers' preferences, allowing a concerted offer of cooperation to global companies. As a result, members of the local industry cluster for instance can play an important role in the customization and final assembly of products to local markets even though the basic components may be produced elsewhere. Therefore, in times of tough competition and market turbulence, the organization and effective management of the local industry or service enterprises, VBEs focused on the characteristics of SMEs, provide a promising approach for regional sustainability. In addition to the mentioned benefits of cooperation within dynamic VOs, there is also the opportunity to share experiences and costs in the learning process of introducing new ICT for instance, within an industry cluster, and to reduce the risk of big losses and failure.

Some researchers with a more theoretical perspective, often focused on very limited scenarios, advocating that it is better to consider VOs in a totally "open universe" context and thus consider VBEs as a too constrained approach. However, reality is proving the correctness of the approach as a large number of related initiatives and real world implementations have emerged during the past decade, namely in Europe (Afsarmanesh et al., 2004), (Flores et al., 2007), Japan (Kaihara, 2004), Brazil (Vargas, Wolf, 2006), Mexico (Flores, Molina, 2000), and USA (Goranson, 2004). Virtuelle Fabrik (Plüss, Huber, 2005) in Switzerland and south Germany is a well-known case of breeding environment with more than 70 active organization members. But the advances in information and communication technologies now bring new opportunities to leverage the potential of this concept, namely by providing the adequate environment for the rapid formation of agile virtual organizations.

Furthermore, current trends in mass customization have highlighted the need to take into account the preferences, specificities, and constraints as well as the assets of the target market regions. The current challenge is to enable *collaborative innovation* involving a network of SMEs (manufacturers, designers, etc.), interfacing different entities and customers. Therefore, VBEs are evolving to address the much more challenging scope of customer involved networked collaboration and co-innovation, as shown in Fig. 1 (Camarinha-Matos, 2007).

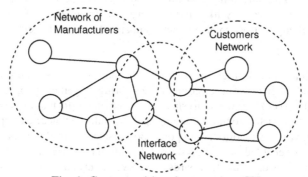

Fig. 1: Customers' involvement in a CN

The concept of **virtual enterprise** (VE), understood as a *temporary* consortium of enterprises that strategically join skills and resources, supported by computer *networks*, to better respond to a business opportunity, has emerged during the 1990s (Davidow, Malone, 1992), (Nagel, Dove, 1995).

Facing business globalization around the world, companies need to co-operate efficiently despite of their different infrastructures, business cultures, organizational forms, languages, and legal and fiscal systems. As a reaction to the highly dynamic market challenges, and taking advantage of the facilities offered by the advances in information and communication technologies, enterprises are increasingly operating in cooperative networked environments. Moreover, the business networks themselves are dynamic and constantly changing. In this setting the benefits from collaborative networking are usually considered to come from e.g. the following features:

- Business partners can quickly and easily come together to benefit from a business opportunity, fulfill the need and then disclose the collaboration.
- Increasing applications in early stages of product life cycle, speeding up and giving more efficiency to engineering and design.
- Increased customer collaboration and logistics enhance market understanding and reduce delivery times and times to market.
- Customer collaboration in after delivery networks enables new form of support activities over the life-cycle of the delivered product or service.
- Efficiency relies on capability for companies to co-operate despite different infrastructures, business cultures, organizational forms, and languages, legal or fiscal systems.
- Business networks themselves continuously change.

A virtual organization represents an extension of the VE concept by considering other possible kinds of members in addition to enterprises (Camarinha-Matos, Afsarmanesh, Ollus, 2005):

> A *virtual organization* (VO) is considered to be a set of collaborating (legally) independent organizations, which to the outside world provide a set of services and functionality as if they were one organization, supported by computer networks.

This definition, like many others, assumes that a virtual organization behaves and can be managed in some way like single enterprise. However, the features of a VO create new challenges to its management compared to the management of a single organization.

Virtual or online communities are important social structures emerging from an Internet-enabled society. These communities bring together people of similar interests in order to communicate, to share and exchange information, to have fun or just to fulfil the need for social belonging and empathy. Typical examples include communities involving emotional support, sports, science, professions, etc. Virtual communities are enabled and empowered by an increasing amount of internet technologies, such as e.g. bulletin boards, list servers, newsgroups, chat rooms, work spaces, document repositories. Such communities invent new social-relationships, resulting in new behavioural patterns and new ways of sharing and creating knowledge, which creates specific value from their activities. On the other hand, Communities of Practice (CoP) have been around for many years and are described as *"groups of people informally bound together by shared expertise and passion for joint enterprise (that) share their experiences and knowledge in free-flowing, creative ways that foster new approaches to knowledge"* (Wenger, Snyder, 2000). Leavitt et al. (2001) point out that CoPs have become more prominent and formalized in recent years because they develop critical organizational knowledge assets. Most communities are "boundary-spanning units in organizations, responsible for finding and sharing best practices, stewarding knowledge, and helping members work better".

When communities of practice adopt computer networks and most of the practices and tools of virtual communities, they become **Professional Virtual Communities** (PVC):

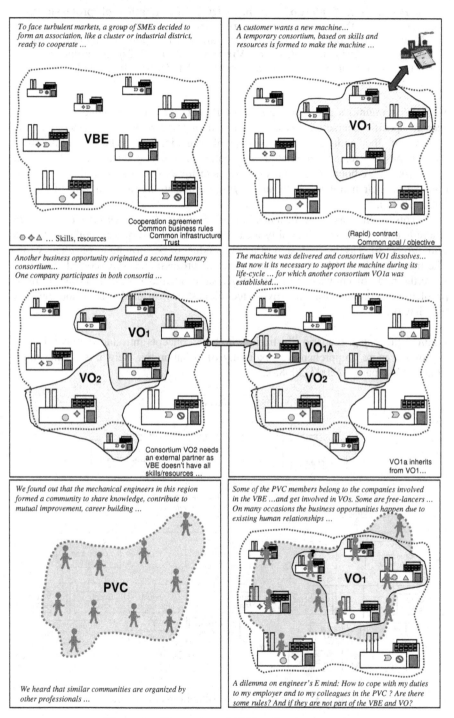

Figure 2 – Illustration of CNO-related concepts

A ***Professional virtual community*** is an alliance of professional individuals that aim at being prepared for collaboration under a business perspective, and provide an environment to facilitate the agile and fluid formation of **Virtual Teams** (VTs) to respond to business opportunities, similar to what VBE aims to provide for the VOs.

Virtual Communities and Communities of Practice are not new concepts but they acquire specific characteristics and increased importance when considered in the context of the collaborative networks of organizations. These communities, spontaneously created, promoted by companies, or induced by the work relationships, are bound to certain social rules resulting from the commitment (social bounds) of their members to the underlying organizations (new concept of *social-bound PVCs*).

This is the case, for instance, in *concurrent* or *collaborative engineering* where teams of engineers, possibly located in different enterprises, collaborate in a joint project such as the co-design of a new product or performing a consultancy job. The trend is followed by other communities of professionals (e.g. consultants) that share the body of knowledge of their professions such as similar working cultures, problem perceptions, problem-solving techniques, professional values, and patterns of behavior.

Figure 2 presents a scenario illustrating the base concepts introduced above. Figure 3 shows a more comprehensive taxonomy of collaborative networks (Camarinha-Matos, Afsarmanesh, 2007, 2008a).

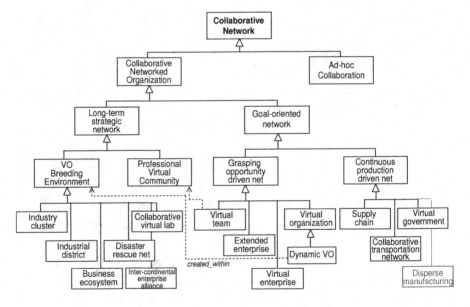

Figure 3 – A taxonomy of collaborative networks

3. A HOLISTIC APPROACH

During the last 10-15 years, and in parallel with the development and spread of Internet technologies, traditional collaborative networks have found new supporting tools and new collaborative business forms have emerged. In terms of research, there has been significant activity during the last decade especially in Europe in the area of Virtual Organisations. From the European Commission's funded activities a large number of projects can be identified, which are complemented by a large number of national initiatives. However, as verified by the VOSTER cluster network (Camarinha-Matos et al, 2005) and the VOmap roadmap projects (Camarinha-Matos et al., 2004), these initiatives corresponded to *fragmented* research and in most cases, due to the funding and assessment criteria, targeted very short-term objectives, focused on solving a specific problem, and were too biased by "fashionable" short-life technologies. Furthermore, there has been little cross-fertilization among these initiatives. This implies that a large number of developments were repeated over and over again in each project. This is particularly evident in terms of the development of horizontal infrastructures in these initiatives. In summary, the situation regarding these past initiatives could be characterized as follows:

- ❑ Research on VOs has created a critical mass and a European-wide *intuitive* understanding of the area.
- ❑ Required basic supporting infrastructures and relevant technologies are well identified, but the developments are often focused on particular needs and are based on ad-hoc experiments, hardly re-usable.
- ❑ Generic functions or harmonization of achievements are addressed only in few projects.
- ❑ To a large extent efforts on general plug-and-play architecture and interoperability are missing. Consequently, no generally accepted reference model or interoperability base is available.
- ❑ Although several disciplines are concerned, the main focus has been on the ICT infrastructure. Research on social/organizational aspects, including management, is mainly focused on best practice. Integration with technological development and impacts on organizational structures are not covered. In addition little research is focused on the social and organizational issues created by VOs.

Nevertheless there is a growing awareness that the CNO developments should be based on contributions of a multidisciplinary nature, namely from the information and communication technologies, socio-economic, operations research, organizational, business management, legal, social security, and ethical areas, among others.

In this context, the ECOLEAD project was launched with the aim to create the necessary strong foundations and mechanisms for establishing an advanced collaborative and network-based industry society. The guiding vision was that:

"In ten years from now most enterprises will be part of some sustainable collaborative networks that will act as breeding environments for the formation of dynamic virtual organizations in response to fast changing market conditions."

ECOLEAD was a 51-month initiative, running from Mar 2004 till Jun 2008, and involved 28 partners from industry and academia, from 14 countries (12 in Europe and 2 in Latin America), namely:

- Academic and research organizations:
    - VTT (Finland), project management
    - UNINOVA (Portugal), scientific direction
    - University of Amsterdam (Netherlands)
    - Federal University of Santa Catarina (Brazil)
    - Institute of Technology of Monterrey, ITESM / IECOS (Mexico)
    - BIBA / University of Bremen (Germany)
    - Jozef Stefan Institute (Slovenia)
    - Czech Technical University (Czech Republic)

- Industrial partners and other organizations:
    - TeS Teleinformatica e Sistemi (Italy)
    - Virtuelle Fabrik (Switzerland)
    - Grupo Formula (Italy)
    - Software AG (Spain)
    - TXT e-Solutions (Italy)
    - Enicma (Germany)
    - Certicon (Czech Republic)
    - Logica CMG (Netherlands)
    - France Telecom (France)
    - Siemens (Austria)
    - Comarch (Poland)
    - AIESEC (Netherlands)
    - ISOIN - Ingeniería y soluciones Informáticas S.L (Spain)
    - CeBeNetwork GmbH (Germany)
    - Swiss Microtech (Switzerland)
    - Supply Network Shannon Ltd. (Ireland)
    - ORONA EIC S. Coop. (Spain)
    - Joensuu Science Park (Finland)
    - Edinform SpA (Italy)
    - HSPI, Italy.

It should be mentioned that a number of these organizations (Virtuelle Fabrik, ISOIN, Supply Network Shannon, Joensu Science Park, Edinform, AIESEC, CebeNetwork, ITESM / IECOS), represented in fact end-user networks (VBEs and PVCs), providing real-world scenarios and validation cases for the project results.

The underlying rational of ECOLEAD was that efficient launching and operation of VOs requires preparedness, both in the VO environment and regarding the involved individuals. Thus the planned core research addressed three main focus areas (ECOLEAD pillars): **VO Breeding Environments (VBE)**, **Virtual Organizations,** and **Professional Virtual Communities (PVC)**, as well as their inter-relationships. These areas were complemented by research on **horizontal ICT** support **infrastructures** and **theoretical foundation** for CNOs (Fig. 4).

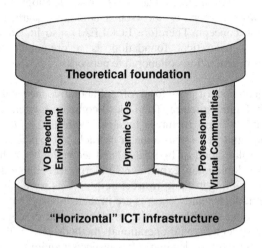

Figure 4 – The ECOLEAD focus areas

Long standing relationships - regional clustering being an example – when driven by the willingness to cooperate and anchored on common business practices, supporting *institutions*, and common infrastructures and ontology, form a business ecosystem where trust is incrementally built and where dynamic virtual organizations can be created whenever business opportunities arise. The need for such long-term sustainable networks is now widely recognized as the basis or breeding environment that can support the realistic emergence of true collaborative virtual organizations. The temporary nature of VOs, the inter-organizational processes needed, and the potentially diverging objectives of the participating partners require the development of a VO management system, which is based on the preparedness created in the VBE. The VO breeding environment is also the boosting element for the emergence of new *institutions* and mechanisms for accreditation and "life maintenance" in a turbulent business environment, where sustainability must build on both new approaches to cope with the partly contradicting individual calls for stability and the agility required by business needs.

The human collaborative relationships, namely based on common professional interests, approaches, and motivations, constitute the third area. Unlike some (not so successful) traditional virtual communities that have populated the web during last years, professional virtual communities have distinctive elements and are mobilized to face specific challenges. Their distinctive facets are not only due to the professional needs (e.g. infrastructures, tools, protocols). They cannot either be dissociated from the underlying business ecosystem of the society, due to their contractual links (social-bounds) with all the consequences at the intellectual property and life maintenance levels. Complementarily, PVCs are seen as one of the most relevant elements for keeping the business ecosystem "alive" and for launching and operating dynamic VOs in the future.

Ad-hoc approaches and poor understanding of the behavior of the collaborative structures and processes mainly characterize past developments in the area of collaborative networks. There is not even a commonly agreed definition of the virtual organization concept. Therefore ECOLEAD also included research on the establishment of a theoretical foundation as a pre-condition for the sound development of next generation collaborative networks.

Finally the implantation of any form of collaborative network depends on the existence of an ICT infrastructure. The lack of common reference architectures and generic interoperable infrastructures, together with the rapid evolution of the underlying technologies, represents a major obstacle to the practical evolution of the area. The rapid proliferation of Internet-related technologies, although creating the opportunity for developing new experiments in terms of collaborative processes, has also created the illusion that the infrastructure problems were solved. Nevertheless, most of these technologies and concepts are in their infancy, have a very short life-cycle, and require considerable effort to implement and configure comprehensive VO support infrastructures and operational methods. Even the most advanced infrastructures coming out of leading R&D projects require complex configuration and customization processes, hardly manageable by non ICT-oriented SMEs. The interoperability problem, although an old issue in systems integration, still remains in the agenda. The fact that most teams involved in VO projects lack strong software engineering expertise (e.g. various projects are dominated by experts in the application domain but with limited background in computer science) justifies the fact that almost all VO projects are mainly "followers" of the mainstream (new fashion) in ICT, rather than breakthrough contributors.

The fundamental assumption in ECOLEAD is that a substantial impact in materializing networked collaborative business ecosystems requires a **comprehensive holistic approach**. Given the complexity of the area and the multiple inter-dependencies among the involved business entities, social actors, and technologic approaches, substantial progress cannot be achieved with the incremental innovation in isolated areas.

4. RESEARCH ROADMAP

The implementation of a comprehensive research initiative such as ECOLEAD needs to be based on a focused strategic roadmap identifying the vision and major research actions for advanced collaborative, networked organizations. ECOLEAD adopted, as a starting basis, the results of a number of major European roadmap initiatives: VOmap (Camarinha-Matos et al., 2004), COMPANION, CE-NET, and ROADCON. Fig. 5 shows, in darker color, the components of the VOmap roadmap that were adopted in and addressed by ECOLEAD.

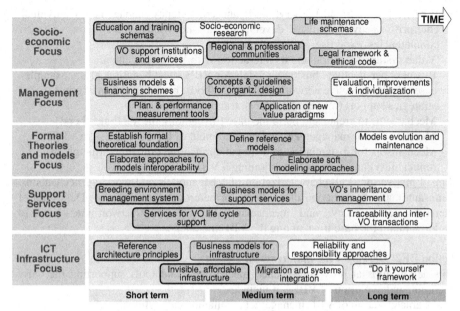

Figure 5 – VOmap roadmap, basis for ECOLEAD

Furthermore ECOLEAD approaches roadmapping as an important instrument for fine tuning of a research program, and as such, a continuously evolving activity. Therefore, ECOLEAD periodically updated its strategic roadmap and applied its findings and evolution into the project focus areas as a horizontal activity.

The following sections describe in detail different aspects of the ECOLEAD research roadmap.

4.1 VO Breeding Environment

The main aims of this focus area were to achieve substantial contribution on VBEs such that: the operating principles of VO breeding environments are understood and formalized, the infrastructures and services to support the full life cycle of these business ecosystems with a diversity of emerging behaviors are developed in a generic way, while also coping with regional and sector-based specificities and SME needs. For this purpose the following specific strategic research actions were planned for the VO breeding environments:

Action **BE1**: *Develop generic VBE models and mechanisms*
This action aims at addressing the challenges and providing the models and base mechanisms for breeding environments. It includes:
- Characterization of VBE establishment elements and features as well as VBE typology.
- Definition of working and sharing principles (responsibility, liability, as well as benefits), ethical code, and base general agreements; schema of incentives.
- Elaboration of common ontologies and ontology evolution support.

- Partners profiling and registry; skills and competency management (individual, enterprise, environment); developing a knowledge map on partners competencies, expertise, skills and tools.
- Value system definition and its interaction with VO management.
- Business perspective / business models for VBE - cost benefit analysis example cases; multi-objective network analysis methods; branding and marketing strategies support (models, structures, training needs).
- Mechanisms to create and build the base trust among the VBE members; Mechanisms for management and measurement of trustworthiness in VBEs.
- Mechanisms for instantiation to different application domains (principle of replicability) and support SMEs joining a VBE.

Aimed innovation: Full characterization of VBE models and working mechanisms. Semi-automatic construction of ontology for heterogeneous domains. Definition of members' competency; and mechanisms to measure trustworthiness and to build/maintain the base trust among the VBE members.

Action **BE2**: *Develop VBE management system*
This action aims at providing needed mechanisms and tools supporting the daily operation and evolution of VBEs. It includes:
- Characterization of VBE management elements and features.
- Mechanisms for competency management (members' competencies, VO competencies, and VBE competencies).
- Mechanisms for trust management.
- Mechanisms for structuring VBE members.
- Management of VBE Bag of Assets.
- Mechanisms to manage the VO configuration information, and its inheritance.
- Management of VBE ontology.
- Decision support mechanisms in VBEs.
- Mechanisms for VBE instantiation to different application domains (replicability).
- Performance catalogue and performance history management.

Aimed innovation: Competencies management at organization, VO, and VBE levels, trust management support, and dynamic VBE ontology creation and management.

Action **BE3**: *Develop VO creation framework*
This action aims at supporting the creation of the VOs within the VBE. It includes:
- Support and provision of practical guidelines for configuration and launching of VO.
- Identification of collaboration opportunity, brokerage and planning of VO.
- Provision of simple mechanisms for partners search and selection, based on their profiles, competencies, trust worthiness and past performance.
- Agreement negotiation and contract establishment support.
- Definition of operational rules and infrastructure parameterization, clarifying the transition between VO creation and VO management.

Aimed innovation: Simple and realistic matchmaking algorithms and negotiation support for VO creation in the context of a breeding environment.

4.2 Dynamic VO Management

The challenges on VO management come from the features of a virtual organization:
- Dynamic environment
  o Temporary nature of the VO and a need of fast reaction to changes on turbulent markets.
  o Management set-ups and structures can be VO-specific and dynamic.
- The organizations collaborating in the VO can have varying
  o Internal processes;
  o Organizational and business cultures;
  o Commitment and objectives.

In this environment, the VO management means differ from those ones in a single enterprise. Especially, the management has less management power and has also to rely on incomplete information.

The goal in this focus area was to develop business models to allow VO management under the described circumstances, namely to act in regards to planning, control, organization and leadership, taking into account the importance of social mechanisms in multi-interest collaboration networks, as well as the transitional nature of VO. For this purpose, the following strategic research actions were followed for the dynamic VO management:

Action **VO1**: *Definition of VO performance measurement approach and assessment mechanisms*
A common understanding of intra-VO shared benefits and costs (i.e. values) is elaborated to enable fair cooperation and common goal achievement. To get the needed understanding, a performance metrics with related measurement systems were developed. The metrics had to take into account multiple views and objectives, including:
- Definition of VO specific metrics based on process and type dependent key performance indicators, and development of a tool prototype.
- Development of rules and assessment procedures to measure performance and allocate values to processes and VO partners.
- Determination of individual (incremental) added-value and corresponding rewards.
- Interaction with VBE, PVC / Virtual Teams, and Theoretical Foundation in order to define a consistent framework.

Aimed innovation: Formal structure and systematic support for fair allocation of values in VO, enabling real competitiveness and increasing chances for SMEs.

Action **VO2**: *VO management, coordination, and supervision*
This action addresses the consolidation and necessary progress on VO management, and supervision. Management has to rely on comprehensive models of the VO processes. Issues addressed in this action are:
- Distributed business processes (DBP) modeling methodologies and tools (which come from multiple disciplines), including simulation models, management structures and interdependencies.

- Models and control methods for adaptive and pro-active management. Unlike past approaches, this perspective needs more emphasis that the distributed business processes topic alone.
- VO supervision including enactment, monitoring (including pre-warning and alarms), diagnosis and error recovery, based on key performance indicators.
- Identification, prevention, and handling of conflicts in VO.
- Multi-level, multi-modal access and visibility of information.

Aimed innovation: VO management methods for different VO categories, taking into account multi-objective and multi-cultural environments.

Action **VO3**: *VO inheritance management*

The outcome of the VO operation (generated knowledge, devised practices, developed products and processes, etc.), as well as liabilities, need to be handled after the VO dissolves. This "inheritance" relates to each VO partner and to further VOs that will continue the "processes" started by the VO being dissolved. It includes:

- Governing principles for joint knowledge management and ownership
- VO dissolution management, including procedure handbook, guidelines, legal contracts, in close interaction with VBE management.
- Collection and management of experiences, actions, etc. from the lifecycle of VO: Practices, Partners performances, Performance indicators.
- Collection and management of outputs and results created by the VO: Joint knowledge, intellectual property ownership, liabilities and enforcement mechanisms.

The VO inheritance is aimed to increase the "bag of assets" of the VBE by:

- Improving the preparedness of the VBE members and thus supporting a faster creation of VOs.
- Making the VOs more effective and reliable both in time and costs, and improving or ensuring the quality.
- Decreasing VO management efforts through increased trust and strengthened relationships.
- Supporting decision-making and tracking of VO problems or deviations.
- Increasing the value of the VBE for the members, e.g. by increasing their knowledge and market position.
- Supporting winning in competitive bidding, because of customer knowledge and closer customer relationships.
- Supporting the marketing of the VBE services to new customers by offering reference information.

Aimed innovation: Structured knowledge on VO inheritance, covering the dissolution and post-dissolution phases of the VO, collection of best practices and gathering of lessons learned.

Action **VO4**: *Develop generic business support e-services*

VO innovative services were developed to allow support of VOs. The services are based on a performance measurement based, real-time approach, allowing the VO management to have continuous access to the status of the VO through a dashboard. They include:

- VO specific definition of Key Performance Indicators and their measurement.

- A qualitative measurement approach, complementing the key performance indicators based measurement.
- Common dashboard for access to the performance of the VO and its partners
- Intelligent alerts on deviations and emerging problems.
- Simulation based decision support for evaluation of potential management actions before their implementation. The simulation is VO-oriented, i.e. local and global, simulation. Using the local approach, single VO partners can test and validate the impact of local changes within given boundaries. Global simulation covers the complete VO.

Aimed innovation: Toolbox of key generic services suited for different VO structures and application domains.

4.3 Professional Virtual Communities

The following strategic research actions were adopted to leverage the human centered management and exploitation of knowledge and value creation by Professional Virtual Communities (PVC), while ensuring member's motivation, commitment and welfare:

Action **VC1**: *Elaborate collaboration models and social forms*
Establishment of a conceptual framework for Professional Virtual Communities; identification of open legal and social issues; evaluation of viable approaches to the integration of PVCs into the market: workplace opportunities and direct interaction with market; identification of roadmap to best exploitation of PVC potential. It includes:
- Characterization and assessment of collaborative practices; Collaboration cultures.
- Governance principles of PVC – social, ethical, economic, and technological facets.
- Dynamic knowledge aggregation and intellectual property.
- Relationships to VO and VBE.
- Legal provisions and legal entities.
- Interfaces to existing professional bodies.
- Relationships to employers and unions.
- Roadmap for PVC exploitation.

Aimed innovation: Conceptual framework for professional virtual communities in interaction with VBE and VOs.

Action **VC2**: *Develop advanced collaboration space platform*
Analysis of mechanisms for collaboration among members with homogeneous and heterogeneous skills. Integrating methods to accommodate the constitution and deployment of virtual teams in support to specific projects, taking into account participation in VOs. It includes:
- Generic and integrated collaborative support services (e-collaboration spaces), including multi-modal interfaces.
- Identification of operational issues in PVC operation, with a specific emphasis on social, business, and knowledge capital evaluations.

- Community management and coordination services; member knowledge [expertise] profiling.
- Methods for knowledge elicitation and seeking.
- Secure identification and profiling; proof of delivery.
- Rapid method deployment systems (for VC members' collaborative working).

Aimed innovation: New ICT supported functionalities specific for individuals aimed at managing social, business, and knowledge capital.

Action **VC3**: *Business models for PVC exploitation*
Establishment of the business view for the exploitation of PVCs; development of methods for valuing knowledge, business, and social capital and associated capacity; analysis of the business infrastructure to support the PVC potential; development of methods and principles for interfacing PVCs to industry/service market. It includes:
- Analysis of exploitation scenarios in different domains: collaborative engineering, consulting, social service, scientific collaboration, etc.
- Identification, characterization, and support emerging value systems.
- Design and support "life maintenance" institutions in coordination with VBE and VOs.
- Knowledge capitalization and exploitation methods.
- IPR protection principles in PVCs.
- Harmonization of PVC membership with employment duties.
- Valuing Contribution to knowledge, social, and business capital.

Aimed innovation: Business view for exploitation of the PVC paradigm, characterization of exploitation scenarios, and model for life maintenance institutions.

Action **VC4**: *Develop collaborative problem solving methods*
Design and development of support tools for brainstorming, collaborative planning and for agreeing joint approaches to problem solving. It includes:
- Develop collaborative decision support methodology
- Brainstorming principles and tools
- Develop decision support models for particular decision making problems
- Collaboration measurement, certification and rewarding.

Aimed innovation: New generation of distributed, collaborative problem solving models and some support tools.

4.4 Theoretical Foundation

The following research actions are proposed for the theoretical foundation which aims to contribute to the establishment of Collaborative Networks as a recognized scientific discipline:

Action **TF1**: *Establish a formal modeling foundation*
As a starting point, promising theories, approaches, and models developed in other disciplines are collected and assessed regarding their applicability to, and modeling requirements of, the CNO. This action includes:
- Hands-on assessment of promising modeling approaches: formal languages, graph theory, multi-agent models, game theory, modal logics, etc.

- Identification and characterization of the necessary modeling *purposes*.
- Establish a map between needed modeling purposes and promising modeling tools ("shopping list").
- Perform modeling experiments applying promising theories to existing empirical knowledge based on selected representative cases.
- Promote education and increasing awareness for the need of a theoretical foundation.

Aimed innovation: Assessed shopping list of modeling approaches and illustrative example set.

Action **TF2**: *Elaborate reference models for collaborative networks*
The concept of "reference model" itself needs to be well established and the main business entities (breeding environment, virtual organization, and professional virtual community) need to be covered. This action thus includes:

- Consolidation of results from various focus areas of CNOs and their abstraction in terms of a general reference model (semi-formal and easily understandable by humans).
- Development of a modeling framework and engineering methodology for application to reference modeling.
- Dissemination and involvement of relevant actors in the CNO community seeking the endorsement of the reference model.

Aimed innovation: A comprehensive modeling framework and semi-formal reference models of key entities in collaborative networks.

Action **TF3**: *Develop soft models for collaborative organizations*
This action addresses the soft modeling needs in collaborative networks and elaborates on potential approaches to cover these needs. It includes:

- Combination of soft engineering models and social theories.
- Combination of causal networks, qualitative models and social networks.
- Development of soft reasoning models and decision-making support.
- Understanding of leadership, actors' roles, and social bodies roles.

Aimed innovation: More rigorous models of social actors and their integration into networked organizations.

Action **TF4**: *Define basis for combination of models*
As there is no single formal modelling tool / approach that adequately covers all modelling perspectives in CNOs (no "universal language" for all problems), interoperability of different modeling tools and approaches is needed. This action includes:

- Characterization of multi-level modeling perspectives.
- Devise approaches for models combination and integration, in order to enrich the reference models for CNOs.

Aimed innovation: Multi-perspective models for selected challenging problems in collaborative networks.

4.5 ICT Horizontal Infrastructure for collaboration

The following strategic research actions were proposed for the ICT infrastructure as a contribution to the development of an invisible, easy to use, and affordable enabler of collaborative behaviors in networked organizations:

Action **HI1**: *Elaborate infrastructure reference architecture principles for networked organizations*
Provides guidelines, principles, and ICT reference architecture to support organizations in developing applications and ICT infrastructures suitable for networked organizations. The results are described in conceptual and functional terms rather than specific technology prescriptions. It includes:
- Platform and technology independent ICT reference architecture for collaborative networks.
- ICT infrastructure reference framework for CNOs based on the Software-as-Service and Interoperability Service Utility paradigms, to be used as general guide for particular infrastructures derivations.
- Interoperability principles foundation, considering architectures and standards to solve different interoperability scenarios within the CNO scope.
- Baseline for the organization and management of on-demand and pay-per-use services via the concept of Services Federation.
- Approaches for enterprise applications integration, both at business level and intra-enterprise level.

Aimed innovation: Principles, guidelines, reference architecture and services federation structure regarding the ICT infrastructure applicable to CNOs.

Action **HI2**: *Devise new business models for the horizontal infrastructure*
Services-based infrastructures are a relatively new approach for CNOs. The comprehensive identification of the required business models to support services development, discovery, billing, availability, maintenance, and operation is an important need for sustainable and evolving ICT business infrastructures that relies on Software-as-Service and Interoperability Service Utility paradigms. It includes:
- Elaboration of suitable business models and characterization of stake holders in the "CNO infrastructure" business.
- Foundations for pay-per-use services and for the diversity of operation models, both of client applications and services providers.
- Assessment of models and methods based on CNO scenarios.
- Relationship of infrastructure business models to application services business models.

Aimed innovation: Approaches and assessed business models for services-based horizontal ICT infrastructures deployment, maintenance and operation.

Action **HI3**: *Develop generic security framework*
Lack of confidence due to insufficient security provisions is a major inhibitor for organizations to collaborate with each other. This action drives the development of a security framework for networked organizations. It includes:
- Configurable, multi-level security architecture and AAA (authentication, authorization and accounting) mechanisms.
- Infrastructure monitoring facilities.
- Dynamic security for allocation and revoking of access rights.
- Quality of protection.

<u>Aimed innovation</u>: Flexible and easily configurable multi-level security framework for distributed collaborative environments.

<u>Action</u> **HI4**: *Transparent inter-enterprise plug-and-play infrastructure*
Networked organizations need to be able to quickly define and set-up relations with other organizations, which requires a plug-&-play-&-do-business infrastructure. This being an area addressed by many activities and technology developments, supported by heavy resources, duplication of work needs to be avoided. Therefore this action focuses on the specific needs of CNOs, takes advantage of available / foreseeable results, and includes:
- Service-oriented framework for an ICT infrastructure for collaborative networks, which is platform independent.
- Standard-based support for interoperability among services deployed in heterogeneous SOA frameworks.
- Elaboration of inter-enterprise plug-&-play concept in line with current infrastructure trends.
- Assessment of emerging technologies (including technology watching) – e.g. SOA, MAS, GRID, semantic web, mobile computing - and related infrastructure developments.
- Federated information and resources management support.
- Web multi-channel accessibility.
- Support for legacy systems and corporate databases integration.

<u>Aimed innovation</u>: A contribution on concepts and technologies to configure applications and infrastructures for networked organizations as well as an extended collaboration model where services from CNO members can be shared.

5. KEY RESULTS

Aiming to address the application of the described research roadmap, ECOLEAD had to face a difficult exercise of combining (by contractual obligation) the need to reach innovative results and the extremely time-consuming requirement of implementing and assessing these results on real-world networks and comply with their actual requirements. As a consequence, the achieved level of innovation in some areas is perhaps lower that what would be desirable for a research project. However, the fact that these results were generated in interaction with and assessed by a large base of end-users represents a valuable achievement in itself. Nevertheless, in spite of the difficulties of the mentioned context, the project has achieved the following key results:

5.1 Main achievements

In the VBE area:
- <u>VBE reference framework</u> - Conceptual description and analysis of the VBE along its life cycle, including: a) Specification of the VBE concepts and their definitions, the VBE actors and roles, the base operations and processes along the VBE life cycle, and the working and sharing principles, b) Modeling and classification of VBE profiles and competency, c) Development of a generic VBE ontology.

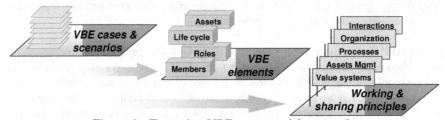

Figure 6 – Towards a VBE conceptual framework

- <u>Value system elements and characteristics</u>, including a set of metrics and elements characterizing past performance of collaboration processes, approaches and guidelines for VBE marketing and branding, characterization of the base for an ethical code and system of incentives.
- <u>Guidelines for creating a trust culture</u>, including measurement and management principles for organizations' trustworthiness.
- <u>VBE Management System</u> – software prototype including the following services: a) Management of VBE members' profiles, competencies, and trustworthiness levels and relationships, b) VBE structure and membership management, c)   Management of VO configuration and inheritance information, d) Management of VBE's decision support system, and e) Management of VBE's Bag of Assets.
- <u>VO Creation Framework</u>, including identification of relevant processes and the following support functionalities: a) Collaboration opportunities (CO) identification, b) CO characterization and VO rough planning, and c) Partners search and suggestion.
- <u>Agreement negotiation wizard</u>, including support for multiple virtual negotiation spaces and contract modeling.

In the VO management area:
- <u>VO operational governance models</u>, a framework defining the basis for the management of distributed collaborative organizations, including: a) Set of concepts and definitions, b) Performance management approach, supporting VO management partly configurable from a set of predefined indicators, c) Inclusion of qualitative performance measurement of the VO, d) Models for VOs on different organizational levels and in different tasks during its life-cycle, and e) Models of management styles and their impact.

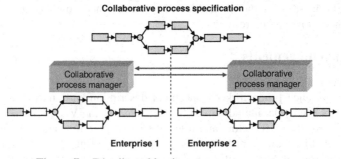

Figure 7 – Distributed business process management

- Guidelines for the set-up and operation of performance management of the VO.
- VO Management e-Services, containing most of the functionalities as e-services to support efficient VO-management. The developed functions are: a) A dashboard acting as the entry point to the management system; b) A modeling framework supporting the creation and operation of the VO management; c) A configurable set-up tool for the definition of the key performance indicators for the VO; d) A distributed measurement collection tool for catching real-time measurement in different environments and by different means, e) An alerting system supporting proactive VO management; and f) A simulation based tool for evaluation of alternative strategies in VO management.

In the PVC area:

- PVC Conceptual Framework, establishing the "Why" and "Who" aspects for these communities, through the identification of the environmental characteristics that justify the establishment of Professional Virtual Communities, the identification of stakeholders and of related value content offered by PVC, the dimensions (social, knowledge, and business) and value classes that are addressed in the PVC deployment, the PVC reference life-cycle and the governance and operation principles to be adhered to in the PVC life. The conceptual framework establishes the collaborative concept of PVCs and the motivational mechanisms founded on social, knowledge and business aspects, which sustain the aggregation of professionals through a PVC.
- PVC Business Model, addressing the general "What" aspect that is the reference objectives and mechanisms for value delivering and sustainability of PVCs. The Business Model is expected to characterize general PVCs, which individually would then develop own Business Plans and strategies to acquire and maintain a competitive edge towards other PVCs. The model is structured in accordance to a reference value proposition to customers and stakeholders, and includes the definition of mechanisms deployed to manage and grow the community assets and to deliver value to customers and stakeholders, as well as the identification of measurement based control methods to pursue operational effectiveness and efficiency (metrics).
- Advanced Collaborative Platform, the digital environment to support the management of relationships, competencies and value-added operations of PVCs. The platform therefore consists of an environment accommodating collaborative functions and services to support the Social, Knowledge, and Business pillars of the PVC. It allows for evaluating Social, Knowledge, and Business behavior of individual professionals and for promoting specific approaches to achieve PVC strategic positioning.
- Collaboration Support Services, addressing the problem-solving process that is required for the collaborative treatment of each PVC business opportunity along its life-cycle, with respect to issues in both internal management and governance, and in interaction of PVC entities with the external environment. It includes methods for the selection of professionals best suited to successfully cope with the identified problems, for the collaborative working of the constituted teams, and for the evaluation of individual and team performances.

In the ICT infrastructure area:
- ICT-I reference framework, conceptual design of the ICT-I architecture and reference framework, including: a) ICT-I reference framework, CNO requirements identification, ICT-I rationale, ICT-I architecture, reference framework and services specification; b) Global approach for interoperability, interoperability scope, ICT analysis and proposal of a global approach for dealing with interoperability problems in the scope of CNOs.

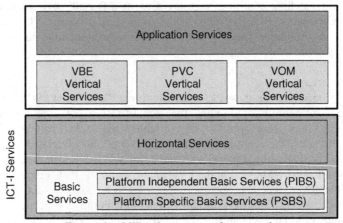

Figure 8 – ICT infrastructure framework

- ICT-I Business models, analysis and conceptual design of feasible business models to ICT-I clients (applications and developers) under the on-demand and pay-per-use models. It includes a set of business models and billing policies.
- Security framework, conceptual design of the generic security architecture and framework, including: CNO requirements identification from the security point of view, role of security in the ICT-I, security framework architecture and services specification, responsibilities and delegation policies, impact of the introduction of the security framework in SMEs as well recommendations to decrease this impact.
- ICT SOA-oriented infrastructure for collaboration, including the formal specification of services, their prototype implementation, deployment issues, interoperability standards, guidelines and examples for ICT-I access and use by client applications.

In the theoretical foundation area:
- Modeling foundation for Collaborative Networks, which includes: a) Portfolio of promising modeling theories and approaches, b) Examples of modeling cases, c) Mapping modeling needs – modeling tools.
- Reference model for CNs, including: a) Principles for a reference model for CNs, b) ARCON modeling framework, and c) Reference model for CNs.
- Soft modeling foundation for CNs, including: a) Motivation and approach for soft modeling in CN, and b) Experiments on soft modeling.

- Contribution to a theoretical foundation for Collaborative Networks, which synthesizes and integrates all results of the theoretical foundation and includes: a) Experiments of interoperability among models, b) A book on the theoretical foundation for CNs.

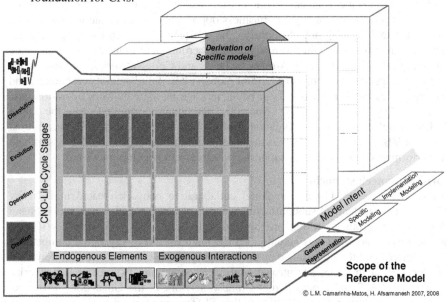

Figure 9 – ARCON reference modeling framework

The above results, except the theoretical foundation, are described in details in the following chapters of this book. The theoretical foundation results are included in a separate book (Camarinha-Matos, Afsarmanesh, 2008b).

5.2 Demonstrators

With the objective of performing a field assessment of the ECOLEAD results and also as an instrument for dissemination and impact creation, 9 demonstration pilots were implemented in real running business networks, eight functioning in Europe and one in Mexico, as follows:

IECOS scenario

IECOS (Integration Engineering and Construction Systems) is a Mexican enterprise that uses the VBE model integrating capabilities and competencies of its partners (mainly in metal-mechanic and plastic industry) to satisfy customer requirements. ECOLEAD demonstration activities within IECOS are oriented to the optimization of network management, which also will impact on partners (VBE members) performance. Therefore, the main end-user is the IECOS broker with the following objectives: improvement of the VBE member registration and characterization processes, formalization of the VBE performance management system, and semi-automation of the collaborative opportunity characterization to be matched against partners' competencies, used for search and selection of best fit partners for VO configuration.

HELICE/CeBeNetwork demonstration scenario

HELICE is the Andalusian aeronautic cluster, which operates under the VBE model to increase process efficiency and business opportunities while fostering innovation in a sustainable structure. Similarly, the CeBeNetwork represents a supplier network, mainly located in Germany, in the aeronautical industry and a strategic supplier to the main customer Airbus. HELICE and CeBeNetwork have joined their efforts to generate and coordinate a joint global VBE, in the area of aeronautics, and which applies ECOLEAD results to better manage the new network operation, and more fluidly creating VOs. Specific functionality applied by the joint Helice/CeBeNetwork is the dynamic management of the competencies and trust levels of VBE members, as well as the organization of the VBE's Bag of Assets, and its performance based decision support, and agreement negotiation wizard.

Swiss Microtech scenario

Swiss Microtech (SMT) is a regional collaborative network created in 2001 by SMEs of the mechanical subcontracting sector to address together new markets and develop new products which are beyond individual SME's possibilities if they would stay alone. SMT has actually 7 SME members. The very fierce competition on the prices and the importance of the emerging Chinese market led to the creation of DecoCHina in 2005, an international VBE combining two regional networks, namely the SMT and a new parent Chinese network in the Guangdong Province. ECOLEAD demonstration activities within SMT were oriented to the optimization of network management, which also impacts on its partners (VBE members) performance. Therefore, the main objectives were: the improvement of VBE competencies management, formalization of the VBE performance and added value and a more efficient creation of regional and international VOs, as well as reaching electronic agreements and signing contracts among the VO partners.

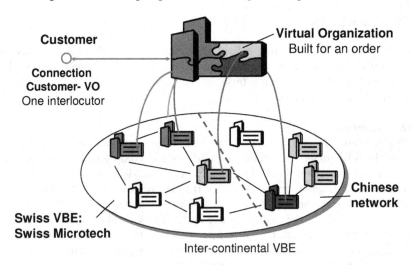

Figure 10 – The Swiss Microtech inter-continental VBE scenario

Virtuelle Fabrik scenario
The Virtual Factory (VF) is a network of industrial SMEs (operating as a VBE) in Switzerland and South Germany. The network provides a full range of industrial services and production to the customers. The network enables the SMEs to act in collaboration with other SMEs the same way as a very big industrial company. In ECOLEAD, the business case was part of the definition for a generic VO model. The application was focused on VO modeling, VO performance measurement, VO monitoring and integrated VO management supported by simulation.

Supply Network Shannon scenario
Supply Network Shannon (SNS) is an open network of companies in the Shannon region of Ireland, which provides a framework for companies to collaborate in joint marketing, training, development, and collaborative quotation development for participation in outsourcing networks. As such, SNS currently operates as a regional VBE with individual members currently creating sub networks on a global scale. The main application of ECOLEAD results was based upon the introduction of the structured VO management techniques to assist with the control and coordination of existing VOs in the network. This application includes the use of the VO-Model to maintain structured information about the VO, particularly in relation to the work breakdown structure, the individual management styles used in the network and the structured measurement of VO performance indicators.

ORONA / OIN scenario
ORONA stands as the Spanish leading company in the lift industry and belongs to the MCC, one of the leading business groups (made of 220 companies and entities) in Spain. The Orona Innovation Network (OIN), promoted by ORONA in 2002, is a research consortium supported by a network of experts (coming from universities, RTD Centers, companies in the sector, etc.) working in multidisciplinary and multi-company communities that centered their activity in: a) the discovery of new technological opportunities, b) the translation of these opportunities into innovative product ideas for short-distance transportation. In this scenario, OIN applied the ECOLEAD tools in two different cases, a) Virtual Organizations for Technology Platform Development and b) Virtual Organizations for New Product Development. Orona used the tools to a) formalize the network procedures, b) formalize and make easier the management of the network, and c) be prepared to increase the network with new external partners. All tools developed for VO management are thus relevant in this context.

AIESEC scenario
AIESEC is a non-profit, non-commercial, non-government global organization, run by students and recent graduates. AIESEC has offices in over 90 countries, with over 20.000 members globally. With ECOLEAD pilot, AIESEC aimed to build sustainable professional virtual communities for AIESEC alumni leveraging on the existing social ties and harvesting their economic potential. Therefore, this scenario focused on application of ECOLEAD results on PVC creation and life-cycle management, PVC governance, and virtual teams' creation.

EDINFORM / FEDERAZIONE demonstration scenario
Federazione Regionale Ordini Ingegneri Pugliesi is a regional Italian organization including all Apulian engineers – about 12.000. The objective for this scenario was

to organize a pilot panel of professionals selected among all the community members and composed of 100 units whose task was to test the proposed methodologies and ICT tools available from ECOLEAD and to provide a feedback about the benefits regarding the methodologies and tools for the professional activity they had.

Joensuu Science Park scenario
JSP is a technology park located in Eastern Finland. It is a regional development organization with global vision toward the development of the third generation of science parks which can evolve towards a combination of VBEs and PVCs. The main focus of the scenario was in the area of new collaborative working environments, namely support for PVC management and creation of virtual teams.

All these pilots were successful in demonstrating the usefulness of the various ECOLEAD results and also provided important feedback for future improvements and further research. Detailed descriptions of these results are included in other chapters of this book.

5.3 Training

Education plays a vital role in facilitating the dissemination and broad acceptance of collaborative networks. Therefore, ECOLEAD has organized several specialized training events for European industry as well as two summer schools oriented towards researchers and PhD students. A major outcome in the training area is a proposal for a "reference curriculum" for teaching Collaborative Networks at university level. This curriculum is based on the ECOLEAD consortium's experience in teaching and disseminating the corresponding concepts in the context of several international projects, as well as on the findings of a survey on this subject conducted worldwide (Klen et al. 2007). Guidelines for the application of the curriculum were also elaborated. A rich set of potential scenario cases and projects are also designed as a support for the accompanying hands-on lab work.

4. CONCLUSIONS

Collaborative networks are well recognized in the business context and society in general as a very important instrument for survival of SME organizations, especially in a period of turbulent socio-economic change. A growing number of diverse forms of collaborative-networked organizations have emerged as a result of advances in information and communication technologies, the market and societal needs, and the progress achieved in a large number of international projects.

Nevertheless most of the past initiatives have addressed only partial aspects, failing to address and properly support the various business entities and their inter-relationships in complex and fast evolving business ecosystems. The ECOLEAD project, as a large international initiative, has pursued a more holistic approach considering both the long-term and temporary organization alliances and collaboration among organizations and individuals. The extensive set of achieved results in ECOLEAD represents a basis for a new framework for advance collaborative networked organizations.

The implementation of a large number of pilot demonstrators in real business scenarios was a key element for the validation of the results and to elicit new challenges for future research.

Acknowledgments. This work was funded in part by the European Commission through the ECOLEAD project. The authors thank the contribution of their partners in the consortium.

REFERENCES

Afsarmanesh, H., Camarinha-Matos, L. M. (2005). A framework for management of virtual organizations breeding environments. In *Collaborative networks and their breeding environments*, Springer, pp. 35-48.

Afsarmanesh, H., Marik, V., Camarinha-Matos, L.M. (2004). Challenges of collaborative networks in Europe. In *Collaborative networked organizations – A research agenda for emerging business models*, Springer.

Camarinha-Matos, L. M. (2007). Collaborative Networked Organizations in manufacturing, (invited keynote), *Proceedings of IFAC Conference on Cost Effective Automation in Networked Product Development and Manufacturing*, Monterrey, Mexico, 2-5 Oct 2007.

Camarinha-Matos, L. M., H. Afsarmanesh (2005). Collaborative networks: A new scientific discipline. *J. Intelligent Manufacturing*, **16**(4-5), pp 439-452.

Camarinha-Matos, L.M.; Afsarmanesh, H. (2006). Collaborative networks: Value creation in a knowledge society, (invited keynote paper). In Proceedings of *PROLAMAT 2006, IFIP Int. Conf. On Knowledge Enterprise – New Challenges*, Shanghai, China, Jun 2006, Springer.

Camarinha-Matos, L. M., H. Afsarmanesh (2008a). Classes of Collaborative Networks. In *Encyclopedia of Networked and Virtual Organizations*, Edited by Goran D. Putnik and Maria Manuela Cunha (Idea Group), ISBN: 978-1-59904-885-7, Jan 2008.

Camarinha-Matos, L. M., H. Afsarmanesh (2008b). Collaborative networks – Reference modeling. Springer.

Camarinha-Matos, L.M.; Afsarmanesh, H.; Loeh, H.; Sturm, F.; Ollus, M. (2004). A strategic roadmap for advanced virtual organizations. In *Collaborative Networked Organizations – A research agenda for emerging business models*, chap. 7.2, Kluwer.

Camarinha-Matos, L. M., H. Afsarmanesh, M. Ollus (2005a). *Virtual Organizations: Systems and Practices*. Springer, Boston.

Camarinha-Matos, L. M.; Afsarmanesh, H., Ollus, M., (2005b). ECOLEAD: A holistic approach to creation and management of dynamic virtual organizations. In *Collaborative Networks and their Breeding Environments* (L.M. Camarinha-Matos, H. Afsarmanesh, Ed.s), pp. 3-16, Springer, Boston.

Camarinha-Matos, L. M.; Cardoso, T. (2004). Education on Virtual Organizations: An Experience at UNL. In *Virtual Enterprises and Collaborative Networks* (L. M. Camarinha-Matos, Ed.), pp 579-588, Springer: Boston.

Davidow, W.; Malone, T. (1992). The virtual corporation. Harper Business.

Flores, M., Boer, C., Huber, C., Plüss, A., Schoch, R., Pouly, M. (2007). The role of Universities developing new collaborative environments; Analysing the Virtuelle Fabrik, Swiss Microtech and the TENET group. In *Establishing the foundations of Collaborative networks* (L. M. Camarinha-Matos, H. Afsarmanesh, P. Novais, C. Analide, Ed.s), Springer.

Flores M., Molina A., "Virtual Industry Clusters: Foundation to create Virtual Enterprises", in *Advanced in Networked Enterprises - Virtual Organizations, Balanced Automation and Systems Integration*, L.M. Camarinha-Matos, H. Afsarmanesh, Heinz-H. Erbe (Eds.), Kluwer Academic Publishers, 2000, pp. 111- 120.

Goranson, T. (2004). Some American research concerns on VO. In *Collaborative networked organizations – A research agenda for emerging business models*, Springer.

Kaihara, T. (2004). A challenge towards the Japanese industry: Industrial cluster. In *Collaborative Networked organizations – A research agenda for new business models*, Springer.

Klen, E., Cardoso, T., Camarinha-Matos, L. M. (2005). Teaching Initiatives on Collaborative Networked Organizations, in *Proceedings of 38th CIRP - International Seminar on Manufacturing Systems*, May 16-18, Florianópolis-SC, Brazil.

Leavitt, Paige, Farida Hasanali, Darcy Lemons, Neil Peltier, Carla O'Dell, Cindy Hubert, and Richard McDermott, 2000, Building and Sustaining Communities of Practice, (American Productivity & Quality Center (APQC)). Available online at http://www.apqc.org/portal/apqc/ksn?paf_gear_id=contentgearhome&paf_dm=full&pageselect=detail&docid=100577

Nagel, R., Dove, D. (1995). 21st Century Manufacturing Enterprise Strategy. Bethlehem: Iaccoca Institute, Lehigh University.

Myers, J. (2006). Future value systems: Next generation economic growth engines & manufacturing. In: *Proc. of the IMS Vision Forum 2006* (B.-W. Choi, D. Nagy, Editors), pp 30-47. IMS International. Seoul, Korea.

Plüss, A., Huber, C. (2005). "VirutelleFabrik.ch – A Source Network for VE in Mechatronics. In *Virtual Organizations Systems and Practices*. Edited by L.M. Camarinha-Matos, H. Afsarmanesh and M. Ollus. Springer, pp. 255 – 264.

Vargas, R., Wolf, P. (2006). "Virtual Collaboration in the Brazilian Mould and Die Making Industry" in *Real-Life Knowledge Management: Lessons from the Field*, KnowledgeBoard. Abdul Samad Kazi & Patricia Wolf (Eds.), ISBN: 9525004724. April 2006, pp. 323 – 333.

Wenger, E. C., and Snyder, W. M. - Communities of Practice: The Organizational Frontier, Harvard Business Review. January-February: 139-145. 2000.

PART **2**

**VIRTUAL ORGANIZATIONS
BREEDING ENVIRONMENT**

VBE REFERENCE FRAMEWORK

Hamideh Afsarmanesh [1], Luis M. Camarinha-Matos [2], Ekaterina Ermilova [3]

[1]*University of Amsterdam, THE NETHERLANDS - hamideh@science.uva.nl*
[2] *New University of Lisbon, PORTUGAL - cam@uninova.pt*
[3] *University of Amsterdam, THE NETHERLANDS - ermilova@science.uva.nl*

Defining a comprehensive and generic "reference framework" for Virtual organizations Breeding Environments (VBEs), addressing all their features and characteristics, is challenging. While the definition and modeling of VBEs has become more formalized during the last five years, "reference models" for VBEs are yet to be established. Such models shall address the structural, componential, behavioral, operational, topological, cultural, and legal aspects of VBEs, among others. As such, identification/specification of the fundamental set of activities and functionalities associated with the VBEs, namely what needs to be supported by a VBE management system is also lacking. In the ECOLEAD project a first attempt contributing to the definition of a "reference framework" was made, addressing the fundamental elements of the VBEs. This framework was further validated through empirical trials by a number of international industry-based VBE networks involved in this project, as well as a few others outside. This chapter addresses the VBE reference framework and analyzes its fundamental elements, as classified into its characteristics and features, its reference modeling framework, its ontology, and addressing the VBE semi-typology that identifies an approach for its categorization.

1. INTRODUCTION

The Virtual organizations Breeding Environment (VBE) represents a long-term "strategic" alliance, cluster, association, or pool of *organizations* that provides the necessary pre-conditions for cooperation among its member organizations and facilitates the fluid establishment of Virtual Organizations (VOs) in response to the emerging collaboration opportunities in the market / society (Camarinha-Matos, Afsarmanesh, 2004a). Traditionally, earlier forms of VBEs, namely clusters / associations are established within given geographic regions, taking advantage of having common business culture and sense of community, and typically focused on one or a few specialty sectors of the region. Nowadays, the challenge is mainly directed to removing those restrictions, and finding solutions to extend and boost these associations with enhanced VBE "support-environments". These 2nd generation VBEs apply effective Information and communication infrastructures, tools and services to provide common grounds for organizations' interaction / collaboration, facilitate the configuration and establishment of VOs, assist with the needed evolution of VOs, introduce new approaches and mechanisms to build trust, define a collaboration business culture, establish the common value systems and working/sharing principles among independent organizations, and support multi-regional VBEs among others. In this chapter we consider the following definition for the 2nd generation VBEs:

"VBE is an association of organizations and the related supporting institutions, adhering to a base long term cooperation agreement, and adoption of common operating principles and infrastructures, with the main goal of increasing their preparedness towards collaboration in potential Virtual Organizations (Afsarmanesh, Camarinha-Matos, 2005)."

While the basic VBE characteristics can be observed and identified from the empirical observation of various case studies (e.g. Virtuelle Fabrik, Switzerland; IECOS, Mexico; CeBeNetwork, Germany; Helice network, Spain; NetworkA, Finland; Torino Wireless, Italy; Treviso region, Italy; etc.) (Afsarmanesh et al, 2007) and improved futuristic scenarios as addressed in Figure 1, a more systematic approach is needed for comprehensive modeling of VBEs. For this purpose, and considering the complexity of the general VBE environments, the development of a "reference framework" for VBEs, addressing the entire set of heterogeneous VBE characteristics is required. Some research in the last few years has focused on the definition of reference architectures for virtual enterprises (Tolle et al., 2003) (Zwegers et al, 2003), and to a much lesser degree also for the virtual organizations, nevertheless research on the reference modeling and a reference framework for their design and development is still at its early stages.

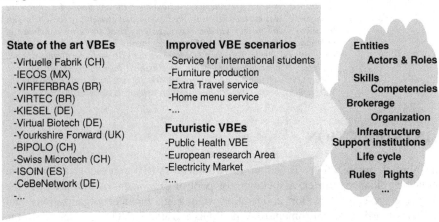

Figure 1 - Examples of studied VBEs

Generally, a *framework* is a conceptual structure used to approach and solve a complex issue. The *VBE reference framework* is therefore aimed to serve as a container of comprehensive concepts, entities, and functionalities needed both for establishing and managing VBEs. The VBE reference framework also provides guidelines for researchers and experts to model various aspects of VBEs, as a step towards developing the VBE management systems. Thus, to support modelers, designers and developers, the VBE reference framework consists of reusable guidelines and possible generic models that can assist such users with both understating of the existing components and concepts in VBEs, as well as how they operate.

Defining a comprehensive and generic "VBE reference model" is challenging. Nevertheless, based on the large amount of literature in this area and the initial empirical knowledge gathered from a large number of existing cases, it is realistic to systematically define a **"reference framework for VBEs"**, addressing its variety of aspects from the VBE topology, to its behavior and structure among many others.

In this chapter a VBE reference framework is presented, addressing the 2nd generation VBEs. For this framework, we first in Section 2 address the identified environment characteristics of a VBE, e.g. its actors and their rights / responsibilities, its life cycle and the main VBE functionalities related to different stages of its life cycle, etc., resulted from literature and empirical studies. We then in Section 3 present four near-orthogonal sub-spaces for the VBE paradigm grouping the endogenous VBE elements. Furthermore, in Section 4 we introduce an ontological representation of the various VBE knowledge concepts. Finally, in Section 5 we present a VBE semi-typology that is developed through the identification of a set of distinguishing characteristics for different kinds of VBEs.

2. VBE ENVIRONMENT CHARACTERIZATION

This section addresses the general VBE characterization. It first presents the motivation for the VBE creation as well as the advantages provided by the VBEs. It then defines the VBE actors and their roles in the VBE. Finally it addresses the VBE life cycle and main functionalities related to every stage of the life cycle.

2.1. Base VBE concepts

Some earlier research have assumed that partners for a new VO could be easily identified and simply selected from the wide *open universe* of available enterprises / organizations, and merged into a collaborative network. This assumption however overlooks a number of important obstacles in this process among which the following can be mentioned:

> *How to know about the mere existence of potential partners in the open universe and deal with incompatible sources of information? How to acquire basic profile information about organizations, when there is no common template or standard format? How to quickly establish an inter-operable collaboration infrastructure, given the heterogeneity of organizations at multi-levels, and the diversity of their interaction systems? How to build trust among organizations, which is the base for any collaboration? How to develop and agree on the common principles of sharing and working together? How to quickly define the agreements on the roles and responsibilities of each partner, to reflect sharing of tasks, the rights on the produced results? Etc.*

In order to support rapid formation of collaborative networks, e.g. a business consortium, as a basic rule, it is necessary that potential partners are *ready and prepared to participate* in such collaboration. This readiness includes common interoperable infrastructure, common operating rules, and common cooperation agreement, among others. Any collaboration also requires a base level of trust among the organizations. Therefore, the concept of breeding environment has emerged as the necessary context for the effective creation of dynamic virtual organizations. Figure 2 shows the vision of the next generation of VBEs and how the fluid creation of dynamic VOs can be enhanced through the pre-existence of VBEs.

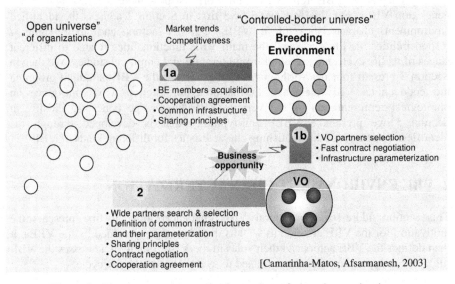

Figure 2 - Two approaches to the formation of virtual organizations

The concept of **breeding environment** (traditionally bound to a sector), has emerged as the necessary context for the effective creation of dynamic virtual organizations.

Cultural ties and particular human relationships are important motivating factors to start up and form such associations representing the VBE, as the support environment for dynamic formation of VOs.

Primarily VBEs constitute two categories of regional and global. While regional VBEs mainly involve organizations (of different sizes) from one geographical region, a global VBE incorporates the involvement of geographically distributed organizations. In this chapter, we address mainly global VBEs. Furthermore, both regional and global VBEs can be either single-sector, i.e. specializing in a single focus area, or multi-sector, i.e. covering a number of focus areas.

Generally VBEs aim at the transition from point-to-point connections among organizations, to a network structure, in order to increase the chances of their member organizations' involvement in opportunities for collaboration. Traditionally, breeding environments are established within one geographic region, in the tradition of industry districts, with the advantage of having common business culture and sense of community, as well as focusing on one specialty sector of the region. But, this restriction can today, in most cases, be overcome by VBEs.

The main purpose for the existence of the VBEs is the efficient creation of VOs. As such, the motivation for creation of VBEs primarily depends on identification / creation of opportunities for organizations' collaboration in certain sector(s). There are two kinds of opportunities pursued by a VBE, namely those that can be identified in the market / society, and those that can be created by the VBE for the purpose of innovation. The main actors in creation / identification of opportunities are either the VBE members who broker the VOs, or the VBE administrator who promotes the initiation of some VOs that seem to be beneficial for the market / society.

Establishment of VBEs provides the **advantages** listed and exemplified below (Afsarmanesh, Camarinha-Matos 2005), that are further addressed and described in this chapter:

- o *Agility in opportunity-based VO creation*: supporting reduction of needed efforts and complexity, flexibility for VO re-configurability, and cost effectiveness.
- o *Acquiring a(n apparent) larger size and negotiation power*, which contributes to better access to markets / opportunities and better (joint) purchasing conditions.
- o *Provision of base effective IC technology infrastructures for VBE members*: the common grounds for interoperability / inheritability / collaboration.
- o *The VBE bag of assets, providing properties of interest for its members*: general sharable information / knowledge (e.g. standardized product definitions and processes), software tools, lessons learned.
- o *Provision of mechanisms, guidelines, and assisting services to both motivate and facilitate configuration and establishment of VOs*: creating system of incentives, mechanisms to create positive reputation, and services for partners search, contract negotiation, etc.
- o *Proactive management of competencies and resources available in VBE*: assuring coverage of the needed competency / resources within the VBE.
- o *Provision of related consulting / life maintenance support for VBE members through its support institutions*: supporting insurance, branding, training, etc.
- o *Introduction of approaches / mechanisms to build trust among VBE members*: by recording the performance history, and definition of criteria for organizations' trust worthiness.
- o *Provision of general guidelines for collaboration*: constituting rules of conducts, working and sharing principles, value systems, collaboration ethics and culture, IPR protection, etc.
- o *Increasing the chances of VO involvement for VBE members, even from remote geographic regions*: through provision of members' profile in the VBE catalog, including their competencies, resources, products, services, etc.
- o *Improving the potential / capacity of risk taking by the VO planners*: due to the reduction of the VO setup efforts / time, availability of both a wide variety of competency / resources as well as indicators of the level of trust worthiness and past performance of the VBE members.

Nevertheless for VBEs to function properly and generate all these advantages there is a set of requirements that need to be met as some are addressed in (Afsarmanesh, Camarinha-Matos, 2005). The main requirements consist of the following:

- The VBE establishment itself needs to be supported by a strong ICT-based VBE management system, providing a set of tools to both support the administration of the VBE as well as the configuration and creation of new VOs.
- Active involvement from the VBE member organizations, including provision of up-to-date information about their capabilities, resources, capacities, costs, and conspicuities for the provided information.
- Proper establishment of a viable business model for the VBE establishment, covering the issues of VBE finances and how to survive in the market / society.
- Proper establishment of the management strategies, government rules and bylaws, addressing the working and sharing principles as well as contracting, rewarding and sanctioning.

2.2. VBE members

Structurally, a VBE is a regulated open, but *controlled-border* association of its members. It aims at improving the preparedness of its member organizations for joining potential future VOs, hence providing a cradle for dynamic and agile establishment of opportunity-driven collaborative networks. As represented in Figure 2, since a part of the needed tasks are already performed within the VBE for all VBE members prior to the establishment of any VOs, for creation of a new VO it is far less costly and much more effective to quickly build a VO in a breeding environment context (branch-1b) than through a generalized partners' search (branch-2). In other words, VBEs substantially contribute to the increase of the level of preparedness of their members for participation in potential collaborative processes.

A VBE does not need to be a closed organization; new members can join and adhere to the association but they must comply with the general operating principles of the association. For instance, a *loosely associated member* of the VBE may need to adhere to nothing more than a minimum level of organization "preparedness" that is necessary for getting involved in a VO, and to making some minimum information available to the VBE administration, e.g. about their activities related to the VO. At the same time, typically a *fully active member* of the VBE contributes to its promotion, growth, and the enrichment of its bag of assets, and can take an active role from brokerage and planning of VOs in a niche market, to being involved in the expansion of the VBE into new sectors, and initiating VOs towards innovation.

Therefore there may be different levels of membership defined and supported in a VBE, each complying with a different set of rights and responsibilities. In principle, these different levels may constitute a range, with a loose-membership on one end and a tight-membership on the other end of the range. Within this VBE structure, for the formation of a VO, while preference will be given to the VBE members (at different levels), in some cases for example related to the lack or insufficiency of the required skills of capacities within the VBE, it might become necessary to find an external partner. The identified external partner will then naturally have to adhere at least to the loosest level of VBE membership, e.g. including the common infrastructure and the VBE's cooperation principles. In this case, the external enterprise will be invited and/or coached to establish this loose membership with the VBE. This invitation and coaching will be either through the VBE administrator or the planners of the new VOs.

Further to the main VBE organizations, who aim at joining potential VOs, a VBE might include other kinds of organizations (such as research institutes, sector-associations, governmental support organizations, etc.) and even free-lancer individual workers e.g. consultants that represent a one-person small organization. The main purpose of including these other kinds of organizations in the VBE is to provide different services supporting the regular VBE members, and therefore they are referred to as support-institutions. Typical services / expertise required in VBEs may include legal services, marketing expertise, insurance, training, etc.

Therefore, three kinds of *organizations* can be identified as registered within the VBEs, including:

- *Business entities* providing products and services to the market that get involved in the VOs to gain quantitative profit, e.g. enterprises.
- *Non-profit institutions* that get involved in the VOs to gain qualitative profit, e.g. academic and research institutions.
- *VO Support institutions*, for example: legal and contractual service providers, companies supporting life maintenance to individuals (e.g. insurance and training companies), ministries, sector associations, chamber of commerce, environmental organizations, etc.

Within VBEs, organizations establish common ties with each other, as addressed before. VBE members shall comply with the general VBE rules and policies, e.g. adapting the common ICT infrastructure. At the same time, once joined the VBE, member organizations might benefit from the following available elements among others: common tools and technologies; common market and distribution channels; common resource and labor pool; common VBE cultural ties; facilities to share the cost of new experiences, e.g. to test new IT tool; facilities to share lessons learned.

A large variety of possibilities are offered to the VBE member organizations, some of which are mentioned below. For example, participants in a VBE can play the role of a broker, to establish a new virtual organization, for instance in response to a market opportunity or a new mission in the society, etc. Member organizations can be invited to join in new VOs due to their competencies and/or past performance records, or even to fulfill a skill gap in the running VOs. Every member can access a variety of necessary general information and knowledge available through the VBE, as well as sharing the costs for market research, advertisement, etc. Through the VBE, its members can have access and benefit from available necessary support services (e.g. legal, insurance, training, etc.) that are provided by the VBE support institutions, among many others. They can access the shared resources (software tools, information files, etc.) contributed to the VBE's bag of assets, which are either provided by the VBE administration or constitute contributions by other VBE members for common use. VBE members can also benefit from the experiences and lessons learned that are shared by other members in the common on-line space provided in the VBEs. Member organizations also receive a wider visibility and will have access to broader possibilities and markets.

Considering that the main goal of the VBE is the promotion and facilitation of effective VO formation, special support is provided in the VBEs for those member organizations that will act as the VO brokers. As such, the *Broker* of a new VO is a member of the VBE that starts the process of creating the VO, as a response to a new opportunity (e.g. for business or otherwise). Further to the above mentioned possibilities, the Broker within the 2nd generation VBE, can for instance benefit from a variety of VBE support services, for example the following:

- Access to the catalog of available variety of competencies provided by all VBE member organizations, and the costs associated with them;
- Access to the catalog of available variety of resources and their free capacities within the VBE;
- Support for finding suitable collaboration opportunities that can relate to the competencies in the VBE;
- Support for efficient search and selection of suitable partners for the VO;
- Possibility of evaluation / comparison of potential partners, in terms of their performance-based (rational) trust level;
- Support for planning the VO and task distribution among potential partners
- Access to an agreement/negotiation forum;
- Contracting assistance (using the provided templates and tools).

A variety of *roles* can be assumed by a large number of actors in the VBE (Mejia, Molina, 2002) (Molina, Flores, 2000), where a VBE actor represents either a VBE member organization, or an individual representing a VBE member organization. The following main roles are considered for the 2nd generation VBEs (as also represented in Figure 3):

- *VBE member*: this is the basic role played by those organizations that are registered at the VBE and are ready to participate in the VBE activities.

- *VO partner*: this is a basic role played by a VBE member in a VO.

- *VBE administrator*: the role performed by the organization responsible for the

VBE operation and evolution, promotion of cooperation among the VBE members, filling the skill/competency gaps in the VBE by searching and recruiting / inviting new organizations into the VBE, daily management of the VBE general processes, e.g. the assignment / re-assignment of rights to different actors in the VBE based in their responsibilities, the daily conflict resolution, the preparation of VBE's bag of assets, and the making of common VBE policies, among others.

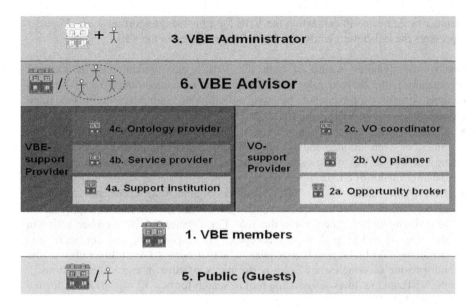

Figure 3 - The main roles in a VBE

• *Opportunity Broker* or simply *Broker*: a role performed by a VBE actor that identifies and acquires new collaboration opportunities (business opportunities or others), by marketing VBE competencies and assets and negotiating with (potential) customers. There is also the possibility of this opportunity brokerage role being played by an outside entity, as a service to the VBE.

• *VO Planner* or *business integrator*: a role performed by a VBE actor that in face of a new collaboration opportunity (designed by an opportunity broker), identifies the necessary competencies and capacities, selects an appropriate set of partners (VBE members and even outsiders in case there is not enough competencies and/or capacities inside the VBE), and structures the new VO. In many cases the roles of opportunity Broker and VO planner are performed by the same actor.

• *VO coordinator*: a role performed by a VBE actor that will coordinate a VO during its life cycle in order to fulfill the goals set for the collaboration opportunity that triggered the VO.

Furthermore, the wide variety of services and support tools and mechanisms that will be provided within the VBE, including both the base necessary services as well as the advanced assisting tools, will be provided by different actors, e.g. those providing the common VBE services (here called common service providers), or those providing the common VBE ontology (here called common ontology providers) within the VBE, that again each require assigning proper rights / responsibilities to these actors. Therefore, a number of other roles are also useful to be considered in a VBE, including: the *VBE advisor* (or an advisory board), the *VBE Services provider*, the *VBE Ontology provider*, the service provider through a support institution involved in the VBE, and the last but not least is the role of a VBE guest played by an organization outside the VBE that is interested in finding general promotion information about the VBE, either interested to become a VBE member or interested in contacting the VBE for a business opportunity, etc. Figure 3 represents these different kinds of roles to be considered in the VBE.

Due to the dynamic nature of both the VBE's environment and its member organizations, the defined roles and therefore the responsibilities / rights of VBE member organizations cannot be static. Following items represent the main characteristics of the VBE roles, rights, and responsibilities:

- Different roles can be assumed by a VBE member organization at different times, or even simultaneously. For instance, a VBE member can act as a VO broker for one VO, while either at the same time or at another time, it may act at the coordinator of another VO.
- Every role taken by a VBE member organization represents a set of responsibilities, a set of required rights / authorization, and further requires a set of assisting tools for the actor in this role. For instance, a VBE member, acting in the role of a VO broker, has accepted the responsibility to configure and negotiate a VO, for which it requires a set of access / visibility rights to the information on competency / past-performance of other member organizations in the VBE, and requires an assisting tool to search for best fit organizations for the required skills.
- Considering the responsibilities and rights that need to be associated with every role of an actor in VBE, it is necessary that VBE members inform the VBE administrator about every new role they plan to assume within the VBE (starting with becoming a VBE member organization) and to request that proper rights for the role are associated to them.

Considering this variety of roles for VBE actors and their associated responsibilities and rights, at a first step the classification of these roles became necessary. This includes the identification of what elements (information) they mainly need to access as well as the base assisting services (software tools) that they need to use to perform their responsibilities. At a second step, the scope of access / visibility / use rights (to the information and available service) associated with each role, as well as the propagation of these rights are classified. The results of these two steps are described below in more details.

Step 1: VBE roles identification
The Table 1 below represents the first classification of roles in the VBE into ten classes, and their example "main" requirements to access information and the need to use assisting tools / services.

Step 2: VBE rights propagation
Earlier it was addressed that with every role in the VBE, there are some associated responsibilities, for which the actors require sufficient access / authorization rights, e.g. for information visibility and/or for use of certain assisting tools / services to help them with performing their tasks. It was also described that the actors in the VBE shall request the VBE administrator to acquire a higher role (with more responsibilities) in the VBE. Once the request for a higher role is accepted, the associated access / authorization rights will be granted to the requesting actor.

Table 1 - Specification of VBE roles

1. VBE Member	– all needs of public (guests) – needs to access the VBE's internal assisting info / news, as well as the internal shared services / tools – requires tools to register and submit its competency info and to apply for potential broker position
2. VO support providers:	
2.1. Opportunity broker	– all needs of VBE members – need to access information about VBE capabilities – needs to access VBE members information and competencies – requires tools to publish new opportunities, search for competency/resource/product/services that can be made available in the VBE, and potentially to apply for the VO planner position
2.2. VO planner (Integrator)	– all needs of VBE members – needs to access the past performance of the VBE Members – needs to access information about new opportunities – requires tools to search for best fit VBE members to the VO requirements, and to create/negotiate VOs, and potentially to apply for VO coordination position
2.3. VO coordinator	– all needs of VBE members – needs to access the VO related information – requires tools to measure & submit VO (partners') performance
3. VBE Administrator (Manager/Coach)	– all needs of advisors – requires tools to register (from the provided info) VBE members / opportunity brokers / VO planer / VO coordinator, and all other kinds of roles in the VBE and tools to assign roles/rights to all members, and to run several software (Monitor usage / Evaluate system / Extract knowledge, etc.) and store the results in the VBE database
4. VBE support providers:	
4.1. Support institution assistance provider	– all needs of VBE members – needs the VBE Member info – requires tools to submit new information about available services
4.2. Common tools/services provider	– all needs of VBE members – needs system-evaluation results and usage monitoring results – requires tools to submit new services/tools
4.3. Common Ontology provider	– all needs of VBE members – needs the knowledge extraction/discovery results – requires tool to submit new model/meta-data definitions
5. Public (guest)	– needs access to the VBE's public information and services – requires tools to apply for VBE membership
6. VBE advisor (board)	– all needs of providers and organizers – requires tools to submit recommendations to the administrator
6. VBE Administration	– all needs of advisors – requires tools to register VBE members / opportunity brokers / VO planer / VO coordinator (from their provided info.), and all other kinds of roles in the VBE and tools to assign roles/rights to all members, and to run several software (Monitor usage / Evaluate system / Extract knowledge, etc.) and store the results in the VBE database

In this step, the classes of VBE roles were arranged in a semi-hierarchical diagram that defines the incremental propagation of access / authorization rights among different VBE roles. The incremental propagation of rights coincides with the increase in the VBE member's responsibility, associated with each role. The propagation of rights, as shown in Figure 4, also represents different degrees of sensitivity of each VBE role in comparison to the others, and the fact that clearly higher level decision making in VBE requires higher access / authorization to the existing more sensitive assets (proprietary information, models, etc.) and supporting tools in the VBE.

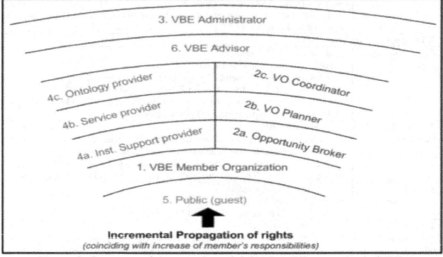

Figure 4 - Incremental propagation of rights for different roles in VBE

2.3. VBE life cycle and life cycle functionalities

The *life cycle of the VBE* (Figure 5) represents all stages that a VBE may go through during its life, from its creation stage, to its operation, and possible dissolution.

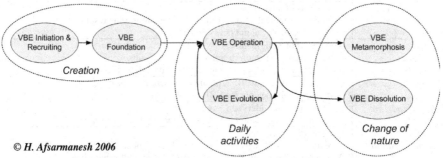

© *H. Afsarmanesh 2006*

- VBE Initiation & Recruiting – *planning and incubation*
- VBE Foundation – *constitution and start up*
- VBE Operation – *the "normal" phase of the VBE existence*
- VBE Evolution – *small changes in membership, daily operating principles*
- VBE Metamorphosis – *major changes in objectives, principles, membership and/or mergers, leading to a new form and purpose*
- VBE Dissolution – *when the collaborative entity ceases to exist, to preserve its valuable gained knowledge, typically this stage of VBE is replaced by the metamorphosis stage*

Figure 5 - VBE life cycle stages

In fact for a VBE, being a long-term alliance, the role that it plays in the market / society, and considering its valuable bag of assets that is gradually built up, its dissolution is a very unusual situation. Instead, it is much more probable that the VBE goes through another stage, our so called metamorphosis stage, where it can evolve and change its form and purpose, as it is also described later below. On the other hand, it is the case that only during the operation stage of a traditional VBE (e.g. an industry cluster), the VOs can be created. However, considering the overwhelmingly increasing variety of VOs, and the fact that usually VBEs serve specific sectors / domain and have specific aims, in the coming time there will be large numbers of different sector / domain-dependent VBEs, needed to be established. Therefore, it is very important to cover and support all stages of the VBE's life cycle in the reference framework, and not only focus on its operation stage.

Management of the VBE during all stages of its life cycle is at the heart of the 2nd generation VBE research and development area. But as mentioned before so far, there is still a lack of a common "reference models" for the VBEs that addresses its different aspects, including their behavior, structure, physical topology, cultural / legal framework, etc., as well as to support sensitive issues such as the value systems, IPR, trust, sanctions and rewards etc., so far there are no clear definitions of what exact activities are associated with the VBEs that need to be supported by their management system. However, several examples of VBEs can already be found in practice that are used as a source of inspiration for our work, e.g. the cases represented by Virtuelle Fabric (Switzerland), IECOS (Mexico), SMT (Switzerland), CeBeNetwork (Germany), and HELICE (Spain), and the potential next generation VBEs that we can learn from their practice and standards. Nevertheless, for research and development work related to the management of the VBE during its life cycle, we did not start from scratch. For instance, during our earlier studies in some other European initiatives, e.g. THINKcreative and VOmap (Camarinha-Matos, Afsarmanesh, 2004b), VOSTER (Camarinha-Matos et al, 2005), and PRODNET (Camarinha-Matos, Afsarmanesh, 1999), the main requirements for the VO environments are identified. Although, these results on VOs cannot be directly applied to the VBEs, they served as the base and a starting point in ECOLEAD. The remaining of this section presents the main identified *required functionality for the 2nd generation VBEs*, in relation to different stages of the VBE life cycle. For this purpose, we have applied three groups of life cycle stages, as defined in Figure 5, to group different VBE life cycle stages. As such the first group refers to *VBE's Creation* or the "Initiation and Foundation", the second group refers to *VBE's Daily activities* or the "Operation and Evolution", and the third group refers to *VBE's Change of nature* or the "Metamorphosis and Dissolution".

Figure 6 represents the base required functionality for VBEs, as divided into these three groups of its life cycle stages:
- *Base functionality supporting the VBE creation* – This phase includes two main steps: (1) initiation / recruiting, which requires the establishment and setup of a common base infrastructure, recruiting potential organizations to join the VBE, and establish some base ontology / thesaurus of the domain, to establish the vision and strategic objectives of the VBE are defined; (2) VBE foundation, requiring support for parameterization of the used systems, setting up the necessary links, creation of the necessary databases (with initial meta-data / ontology), and populating these information structures.

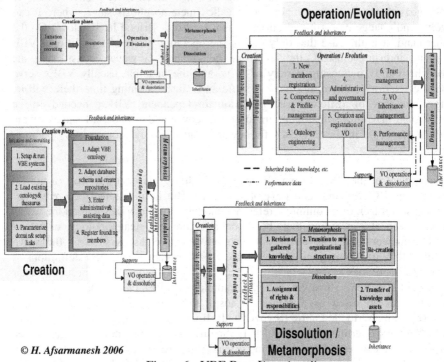

© *H. Afsarmanesh 2006*

Figure 6 - VBE Base Functionality

- *Base functionality supporting the VBE operation and evolution* – This phase requires support for: (i) Management of competencies and assets, (ii) Registration of new members (including profiling, characterization of competencies, products, services, etc.), (iii) Assisting VO creation, (iv) Incremental generation / evolution of meta-data / ontologies for the domain / sector, (v) Keeping records of past performance and collaboration processes, (vi) Assessment and assistance tools, (vii) Collaboration support (e.g. newsgroups, discussion forum, common information repositories, etc.), (viii) Management and evolution of working and sharing principles and rules, (ix) Acquisition and management of common knowledge and assets.

- *Base functionality supporting the VBE metamorphosis and dissolution* – This phase will require assistance for the design of the aimed new organizational structure, selection and reorganization of the information and knowledge collected during the VBE operation and that might be transferred to the new organization, analysis and adjustment to the new context, etc. In the case of VBE dissolution there is a need to plan the transfer of its collected knowledge, information, bag of assets to its members or another organization based on defined agreements.

Considering the life cycle stages of the VBEs, by nature VBEs represent self organizing environments and thus can be defined through the Chaordic graphs from the Chaordic system theory (van Eijnatten, 2003). Figure 7 represents the main stages of the VBE life cycles in a chaordic graph. As illustrated in this Chaordic graph, the normal operation phase of a VBE involves a number of small evolutions, where each small evolution in the VBE has itself a similar, though shorter life cycle. Furthermore, the combination of these smaller evolutions constitutes the operating stage of the dynamic VBEs.

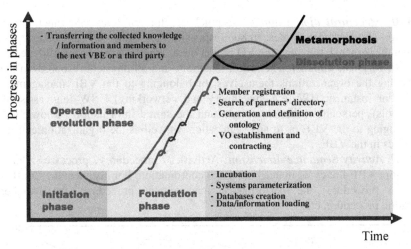

Figure 7 - Chaordic graph representation of VBE life cycle stages

3. NEAR-ORTHOGONAL VBE SUB-SPACES

Considering the complexity of VBEs, any attempt to formally define this paradigm and description of its supporting infrastructure, must carefully cover the *multiple perspectives and dimensions* of this system. With this aim in mind, identification of the multi-dimensions of this paradigm and its supporting system is of high importance.

These dimensions must together comprehensively, or at least as much as possible totally, cover all the *known features and aspects of the VBEs*, no matter how simple or how compound these features are. Different features and aspects of the VBEs that all need to be modeled and formally defined, are of completely different nature, ranging from the hardware resources at the level of one organization, or the generic working and sharing as well as conflict resolution policies, to the functionalities related to the configuration of a newly instantiated VBE or different goal-oriented activities related to different phases of the VBE's life cycle, and even the semi-automatic decision making processes for knowledge discovery, etc. These aspects among others shall all be covered by these dimensions.

As a first trial reference framework for VBEs, with its roots in an early work in the Data Base community (Afsarmanesh et al, 1985), we have identified four complementary near-orthogonal (*elements within different dimensions are bound to each other*) dimensions / perspectives for VBEs that can together represent the complexity of the variety of entities, concepts, and functionalities, and model different aspects of the VBE environments and needed support systems. The applicability and benefits of the introduction of these dimensions for the purpose of systematic classification and better modeling of multiple perspectives of the VBEs are further investigated. The ARCON reference model for collaborative networks, also developed within the ECOLEAD project, have adopted these four dimensions for modeling the *endogenous elements* of collaborative networks. A short description of these dimensions is presented in this section. Also Figure 8 represents these dimensions as *overlays* above the VBE.

1.   VBE Structural dimension: Conceptual structure of roles and functions of VBE actors. For instance: Roles, rights, responsibilities, duties etc. associated with each member organization, e.g. the VO broker's role, rights, and responsibility, etc.

2.   VBE Physical dimension: entities, materials, and all physical resources in the VBE, being the organizations themselves, or belonging to the VBE management system. For instance: HW (e.g. machinery and networking) / SW (e.g. assisting shared tools), personnel (human capital), and the stored information / knowledge, etc. belonging to the VBE or to an organization, as well as the organization entities themselves in the VBE.

3.   VBE Activity Sequence dimension: Activities / procedures / processes related to the entire VBE life cycle management and coordination. For instance: the Conflict resolution procedure, the performance management procedure, the member registration procedure, etc.

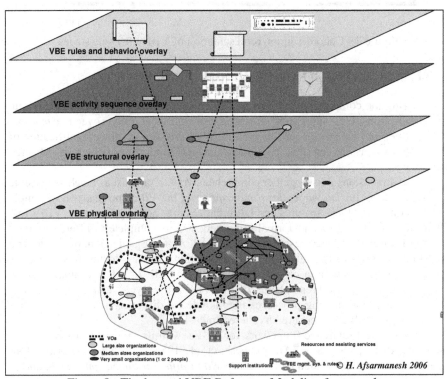

Figure 8 - The layered VBE Reference Modeling framework

VBE rules of Behavior dimension: Policies and governance rules. For instance: the Interoperability principles, Policies for code of conduct, Conflict resolution policy, Contract enforcement policy, etc.

Every dimension represents a specific aspect / perspective of the complex VBE environment and its needed support system. These specific four dimensions are chosen for the reason of their near-orthogonality, in the sense that elements in each dimension mostly belong together and are mainly inter-related with each other, and may only be weakly related to elements in the other dimensions. Namely, if elements in different dimensions are bound to each other, then changes in one dimension affect the elements of the other dimensions, weakly across some region of relevance. For example, there may be some relationships among elements of the physical and structural dimensions of the VBE.

Some example bindings between different dimensions follow:
- between the physical components (different organization) and the structural components (different roles and functions to be assumed by VBE member) there can be a relationship identifying the role of each organization;
- between the behavioral components (policies) and the life cycle related sequence of activities (procedure for measuring the performance of VBE members during the operation phase in a VO) there be a relationship that identifies the policy applied to every procedure.

Figure 8 addresses these dimensions and how they can be linked through the bindings. This defined reference framework is applied and validated for comprehensive modeling of all endogenous aspects of VBEs.

4. VBE ONTOLOGY

This section addresses an ontological representation of the VBE paradigm. Besides the contribution to the VBE reference framework, the VBE ontology - developed in the ECOLEAD project - aims to support the following challenging tasks related to the VBE instantiation and management:
1. Establishment of a common semantic subspace for VBEs.
2. Instantiation of VBE knowledge repositories for VBEs from different domains / business areas.
3. Automated processing VBE knowledge by software tools in dynamic VBEs.
4. Enabling inter-organizational learning & co-working.
5. Integrability of VBE knowledge with existing standards.

The main motivations for engineering the VBE ontology are to support the above tasks through providing the following:
– Adequate, formal and uniform representation of VBE knowledge / information.
– Unified and common semantic subspace for VBE knowledge / information.

4.1. Definition and scope of the VBE ontology

We define the VBE ontology as *a form of unified and formal conceptual representation for the heterogeneous knowledge within the VBE environments to be easily accessed by, and communicated between human and application systems, for analysis and evolution purposes (Afsarmanesh, Ermilova, 2007) (Ermilova, Afsarmanesh, 2008).*

As a first step for specification of the VBE ontology, the main conceptual groups of the heterogeneous VBE knowledge are identified mainly through focusing on and covering two of its characteristics, including:

- Variety of *owners/providers* of the VBE knowledge, such as: the VBE-self, VBE members / participants, and VO-self networks.
- Variety of *usage of VBE knowledge* in the VBE document repositories and in the sub-systems of the VBE Management, System (VMS) such as: VBE Bag of Assets repository, VBE Governance's document repository, Profile and Competency Management system, VBE Performance Measurement system, Trust Management system, and VBE Value system (Afsarmanesh et al, 2007).

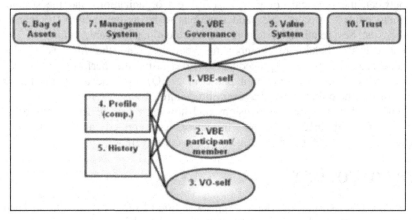

Figure 9 - Conceptual groups of the VBE knowledge

As a result, the following ten main disjoint, but inter-related **conceptual groups** of VBE knowledge were identified as illustrated in Figure 9:

(1) *VBE-self* knowledge that represents the general concepts about the VBE itself, e.g. the VBE life cycle stages concept.

(2) *VBE participant / member* knowledge that represents the main concepts related to the characteristics of VBE member organizations, e.g. the roles of VBE members.

(3) *VO-self* knowledge that represents the concepts about VOs that are configured within the VBE, e.g. the VO contract concept

(4) *Profile / competency* knowledge that represents those knowledge classes that need to be collected from different VBE entities related to their profile and competency definitions, e.g. the concept of capacity of resources owned by a VBE member.

(5) *History* knowledge that represents concepts related to the history of performance, collaboration and cooperation of VBE members, e.g. the VO inheritance concept.

(6) *VBE Bag of Assets* knowledge that represents the concepts addressing the Assets structure in VBEs, e.g. the concept of Lessons Learned.

(7) *VBE Management System* knowledge that represents those concepts related to the functionalities and services supporting the VBE management, e.g. the generic VBE service definition.

(8) *VBE Governance* knowledge that represents the concepts related to the VBE rules, bylaws and culture, e.g. the classification of VBE principles.

(9) *Value System* knowledge that represents the concepts describing VBE capitals and measures, e.g. the concept of performance indicator.

(10) *Trust knowledge* that represents the concepts of trust elements, as well as the kind of data for measurable elements that need to be collected for assessment of trust level of organizations, e.g. the concept of trust objective and criterion.

Additionally, the VBE knowledge categorized in each conceptual group is divided by their **levels of abstraction or usability / reusability** into:

(i) meta-knowledge, constituting the very small set of characteristics describing all other knowledge;

(ii) core knowledge, constituting the ten groups of knowledge addressed above, that are common to all VBEs, e.g. generic/unified model of the VBE competency;

(iii) domain knowledge, e.g. classification of general metalworking competencies;

(iv) application knowledge, e.g. concepts which are specific only to one VBE application from the above domain;

(v) real knowledge, e.g. the detailed competency description of a real VBE member.

4.2. VBE ontology structure and engineering approaches

The **structure** of the VBE ontology consists of four levels of abstraction and ten partitions constituting sub-ontologies of the VBE ontology, as also illustrated in Figure 10. The four levels of abstraction are introduced to reflect on reusability of the VBE ontology by the variety of VBE application environments. Namely, all VBE applications are supposed to share the ontology defined for the three above levels and differ only at the application level. The ten ontology partitions address the conceptual classifications of VBE knowledge as addressed in section 4.1 above. Please note that in Figure 10, the number / symbol inside parenthesis next to each ontology level represents the cardinality of instances of this VBE ontology level, namely there is only one VBE meta and one core ontology common to all VBEs, while N and M both represent "many", e.g. the fact that there are many different domains / business areas for VBEs and each VBE domain / business area may have many VBE applications.

Further, the decomposition of this ontology structure into levels and partitions supports the incremental development of the VBE ontology, while the developed parts of the ontology can be reused by different VBE management subsystems.

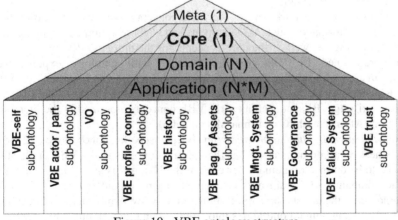

Figure 10 - VBE ontology structure

A description of the levels of the VBE ontology is addressed below, while an example of a constructed sub-ontology, namely the VBE profile / competency sub-ontology, is presented further in section 4.3.

1. *Meta level* represents the meta-concepts (such as "synonym" and "abbreviation") that are used to define other concepts of the VBE ontology.
2. *Core level* specifies the VBE concepts that are common to all VBEs, no matter to which domain it is applied (e.g. the specification of "VBE bag of Assets", "VO inheritance", "VBE member's competency", etc.), which will be then reused by different VBE applications. Therefore, the main objective of the core ontology is to present the common main types of information/knowledge that VBEs typically accumulate.
3. *Domain level* represents all VBE concepts related to different specific VBE domains (e.g. manufacturing, tourism, health care, etc.), that contains/extends the entire VBE core ontology. As such, it represents the customization and population of the VBE core ontology to the specific domain that it applies, for instance addressing specific competencies (e.g. "injection moulds fabrication"), or specific processes/activities (e.g. "welding", "milling", etc.) Therefore, the main objective of the domain ontology is to formally specify and organize the VBE domain knowledge.
4. *Application level* represents the VBE concepts that are common only for the members of the same VBE application, such as trust criteria or VBE value metrics, etc. for the specific food processing application of manufacturing canned food domain.

The **approaches for engineering** the VBE ontology for the meta and core levels differ from the domain and application levels as explained below. The main reason is that the domain and application level ontology of VBEs cannot be predefined and need to be created on demand during the operation stage of each specific VBE. Additionally, the domain and application levels evolve continuously during the VBE operation and evolution phases (e.g. when new VBE members bring new knowledge to the VBE). Below a summary of approaches for engineering different levels of VBE ontology are presented:

I. *For the meta and core levels:* the meta-concepts and meta-properties (e.g. semantic information such as "synonyms" and "abbreviations") for the unified VBE ontology as well as the core concepts for the unified VBE ontology shall be pre-defined by VBE experts together with ontology experts. The information / knowledge resources that can be reused for construction of the VBE ontology at the core level include the database schemas / data models from existing VBEs, as well as some VBE concepts presented in the literature, e.g. in (Afsarmanesh, Camarinha-Matos, 2005).

II. *For the domain and application levels:* the specific concepts to the VBE business area / domain as well as the specific concepts to the VBE application need to be defined on demand for each of the N domains and M applications in each domain. The main approaches that can be considered and applied for building up the domain and application ontology levels include: (1) Integration of all existing domain ontologies into a unified ontology (Pinto et al, 1999), (2) Semi-automated discovery of ontology concepts from text documents (Grobelnik, Mladenić, 2005) (Anjewierden at al, 2003).

4.3. Detailed overview of the VBE profile and competency sub-ontology

Engineering of the VBE profile and competency sub-ontology is fundamental for modeling, collection and processing of the information about VBE profiles and VBE competencies within the VBE, and namely within its **Profile and Competency Management System (PCMS)**, as also addressed in chapter 2.4 of this book.

First of all, in order to achieve the VBE's main goal, i.e. to prepare its member organizations for participation in VOs, it is necessary to collect and analyze the knowledge about all member organizations at the VBE level. We define a concept of the *VBE member organization's profile* to represent the knowledge about each organization in the VBE.

Additionally, in order to represent the qualifications of VBE members for collaboration in VOs, we define the *VBE member organizations' competencies*, as a fundamental element of their profiles. The initial purpose of introducing the "profile" and "competency" concepts is to present the knowledge about the VBE member organizations. We have introduced the *"VBE entity"* concept to represent all acting entities in the VBE context. For example, the VBE entities may include: VBE member organizations, VBE support-providing organizations, VBE customers, VO-self networks (for VOs formed in VBE), and the VBE-self network. The "VBE profiles" and "VBE competencies" represent the knowledge about all types of VBE entities. The VBE profiles and VBE competencies are defined as follows:

VBE profile consists of the set of determining characteristics (e.g. name, address, capabilities, etc.) about each VBE entity, collected in order to: (a) distinguish and compare each VBE entity with others, (b) analyze the suitability of each VBE entity for involvement in some specific line of activities / operations.

VBE competency is the main element of the VBE profile that provides up-to-date information about capabilities and capacities of each VBE entity, as well as conspicuous information about their validity, qualifying it for participation in some specific activities / operations within the VBE, and mostly oriented towards the VO creation.

The **generic VBE profile and competency model** (Ermilova, Afsarmanesh, 2007) represents the set of classes of VBE knowledge/information, as well as the relationships among these classes that needs to be collected and managed in the VBE. A high-level abstraction of the main elements of unified / generic model of the VBE profiles and VBE competencies is illustrated in Figure 11.

The core level of the VBE profile and competency sub-ontology, as well as an example of its domain level, was constructed in OWL (OWL, 2007).

The **core level of the VBE profile and competency sub-ontology** is a form of representation of the core / generic VBE profile and competency model. One example screen-shot from this core sub-ontology, constructed in the Hozo editor (Sunagawa at al, 2004), is partially illustrated in Figure 12. In this Figure, the ontology concepts, e.g. "VBE Profile", "Competency", "Resource", representing the elements in the core/generic profile and competency model, are illustrated as boxes. There are also three types of relationships among the concepts, including the "p/o" meaning "part of", the "a/o" meaning "attribute of", and the "is-a" meaning "is a kind of".

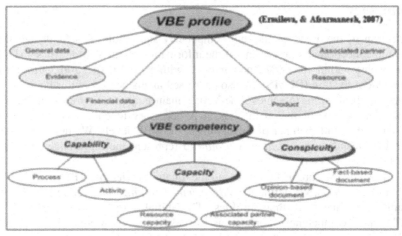

Figure 11 - A high-level abstraction of the model of VBE profiles and competencies

The *main purposes and usage* of the sub-ontology of the core VBE profile / competency in the VBE includes the following:

(1) Support of the R&D in the VBE field through providing means for the evolution of the VBE profile and competency models by being an extensive, uniform and sharable representation of these models.

(2) Support for the common understanding of the structure of the VBE profiles and competencies through providing the extensive definitions of the related concepts.

(3) Support for semi-automated design and development of the PCMS's database, or example using a methodology provided in (Guevara-Masis et al, 2004).

Support for structuring of the VBE profile and competency knowledge in the PCMS's GUI.

The **domain level of the VBE profile and competency sub-ontology** is a form of representation of the domain classes of profile and competency information/knowledge and their generalization hierarchies. The domain VBE profile / competency sub-ontology can be further partitioned into several specific "sub-sub-ontologies" depending on: a specific core concept (e.g. only for domain capabilities), or a specific domain / business area (e.g. only for metalworking domain). One example partial screen-shot from the sub-sub-ontology of practices and processes in the metalworking domain that is constructed in Protégé (Protégé, 2007) is illustrated in Figure 13 specifically depicting a part of domain-dependent classifications of practices and processes within an existing VBE from Mexico, called IECOS.

The *usage* of the domain VBE profile and competency sub-ontology in the VBE includes the following:

(i)   Support of the representatives of the VBE entities with the definition of their domain-specific profile and competency related data (e.g. identification of classes of the domain-specific business processes performed within a VBE entity).

(ii) Support for representation of the "standard names" and the "standard relationships" for the domain-dependent profile and competency knowledge/information that can be further facilitate the software-based matching/processing of the knowledge.

(iii) Support for structuring of the domain-dependent VBE profile and competency knowledge in the PCMS's GUI.

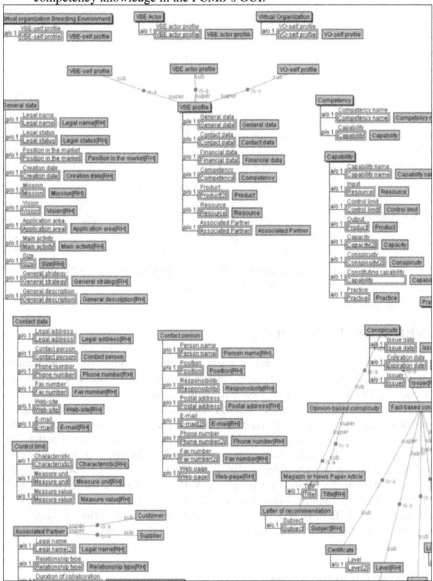

Figure 12 – Example Partial screen-shot from core profile/competency sub-ontology (in Hozo)

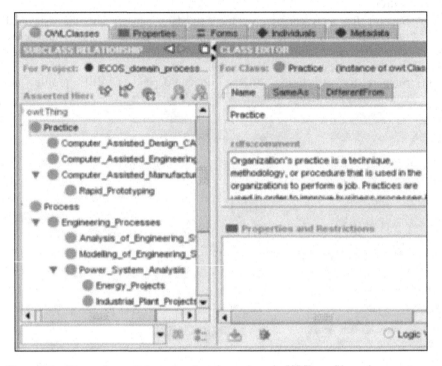

Figure 13 – Example partial screen-shot from domain VBE profile and competency
sub-ontology (in Protégé)

5. VBE SEMI-TYPOLOGY

A systematic study of the wide variety of existing and emerging VBEs can facilitate
both the modeling of their structural, componential, functional, and behavioral
aspects, as well as the creation of a base for their reference modeling. In this section
we aim to classify the VBEs and to identify their main "types", thus establishing the
base for future research on each type of VBE. Namely, to investigate the specific
needed components (e.g. actors, roles rights, and responsibilities), the functionality
(e.g. for managing their information/knowledge) and the behavior (e.g. to assist the
decision making in such networks) for each type of VBEs. In addition to the
literature study on the state of the art on VBEs, we have conducted in depth
investigation of six running European industry-based clusters / networks of SMEs
that operate as VBEs. Based on the achieved results, we define a systematic
approach for the specification of the VBE semi-typology (Afsarmanesh, Camarinha-
Matos, 2007).

5.1. Investigated networks

Prior to addressing the systematic approach for the definition of the VBE typology, below this sub-section summarizes our investigation results related to each of the six networks of SMEs. Please note, that in order to preserve the anonymity of these SME networks we refer to them as VBE-A, -B, -C, -D, -E, and -F.

1. *VBE-A* (Italy). This VBE is made up of 200 member companies that mostly constitute the information and communication sector in their respective district. This VBE is fully financially supported by the government. In its operation, the VBE administrator helps the member companies in finding business opportunities. Further to configuring VOs, this VBE in some cases also generates and configures new specialized VBEs, focused on certain regional specialties, and constituting organizations that know and trust each other. But also, sometimes, this VBE helps these generated sub-VBEs to merge into a larger VBE. The VBE administration does not get involved in VO coordination. Only partial overlap of competencies is allowed among organizations, and the VBE tries to avoid any competition.

2. *VBE-B* (Finland). This VBE consists of 12 member companies mostly in paper and automation industry ranging in size from big to small, and coming from close by regions. This VBE does not receive any financial support from the government. It is privately supported, by collecting a token fee of 100 Euros, charged to each member company. VBE management also does the brokerage of VOs, and in most cases making decisions about new business opportunities are also handled by the VBE management. However, once the VO is initiated, the VBE management does not provide any more support for the VO operation, which will be led by the VO coordinator. For this VBE, it was stated that a few software services may be helpful to assist with the VBE management tasks, but for the moment all activities are supported manually. This VBE avoids any possible competition between member companies (no overlap of expertise is allowed) in the network, believing that it is not good for trust establishment. Furthermore, in this VBE, there is an "oral" set of rules, and a number of "boards" of people in charge of different network activities, but there are no written rewards/sanctions rules to handle conflicts. Only some ethical rules in written form but even those they are not compulsory.

3. *VBE-C* (Germany). This VBE has 28 member companies from the aircraft industry, and it has been growing both in size and in making profit continuously. It has a single customer that is a major aeronautics company in Europe, which constantly gives them many opportunities for which they can configure VOs. In fact the motivation to create this network came from the fact that the aeronautics company decided to reduce the number of suppliers and therefore these companies had to join efforts in order to qualify as a supplier. Financially, the VBE administration depends on the actual profits made from opportunities/projects (it charges about 5% of the profit) made by the VOs that are configured in the VBE. In this VBE, the management does the marketing and brokerage, but other partners can also bring in opportunities. Member companies in this VBE trust each other and work together very well, not competing but some overlaps are allowed in case it is required to fulfill customer's orders. This VBE believes that more and more companies join in the network because the amount of the product/services demanded is high and no company alone can provide the products and the needed capacity in the required time. Furthermore, VOs can still be configured including non-member companies, but only when the capacity cannot be achieved within the VBE or the required expertise is not available within the VBE. Usually losses in a VO are taken by the VO partners, but this VBE also has a loss insurance contract for the sake of the VBE as whole.

4. VBE-D (Finland). This VBE is a one year old regional engineering and automation network consisting of 16 engineering companies as its members. Financially, it depends on small membership fees. In addition to brokerage of business opportunities, the VBE initiates the VO, and also supports the VO management. For easier searching of suitable partners and also management of the VBE at large, the VBE management believes that it needs to maintain and manage a competency/expertise matrix, and share knowledge and experience, promote cooperation, raise the image of companies, support collaboration in marketing activities, and making bigger and more international contacts.

5. VBE-E (Italy). The region around this VBE in Italy represents a very old collection of more than 10,000 manufacturing companies, from a wide variety of areas that includes from sport clothing to furniture, etc. but all focused on innovation and new products. The government supports establishment of self organizing clusters, a kind of VBE, in the area. Each cluster must have a minimum of 80 SMEs in order to qualify for funding. There are already about 40 clusters formed in this region. Organizations in the region represent a strong mix of competition. The tradition in the area governs the cooperation, and defines the rules. The aspects of time and fashion are the most important criteria for successful cases and projects. As it is, this VBE does not run any VBE management system.

6. VBE -F (Spain). This VBE has a strong consulting company associated with it. It has 23 member companies and 20 other associated supporting SMEs, mostly in the aeronautics industry. The consulting company is working as a supporting institution for the VBE, and mostly providing legal assistance. This VBE is supported financially both by the government and also through the token membership fees from its members that use some tools provided in the VBE for their VO internal operations. When a business opportunity is identified, it is presented to the VBE members, where several VBE members may plan some VOs and submit a proposal to the VBE administration. Depending on the case, the evaluation of these proposals is either done by the VBE administration to suggest to customer and/or together with customer itself to choose the best VO and start it. VBE management only configures and initiates VOs and does not coordinate it. Currently, the VBE management of the VBE has perceived the need for the following aspects in order to improve the VBE management functionalities: trust management measures and ensuring confidentiality issues; storage of the past history/performance of organizations, to ensure trustability / trustworthiness evaluation; better legal framework for non conformance and for conflict situations; competencies management.

5.2. A systematic approach to development of the VBE semi-typology

Due to the lack of a defined scientific approach for typology identification in formal sciences, and aiming to identify the main types of VBEs, we have partially followed a systematic stepwise approach, mimicking the case by case investigation (collection and observation) approach practiced in Beta-sciences (e.g. bio-diversity). In our study, both for the VBEs reported in the literature and the six clusters mentioned above, we followed a 3-step approach: The *first step* was to characterize different VBEs, in order to reach a *common set of characteristics for the VBE paradigm*. The *second step* was to use the common characteristics to classify different VBEs, and thus to reach the *main categorization of the VBEs*. The more challenging *third step* was to investigate if based on the main VBE classification results reached in second step we can *identify and generate a typology for the existing and emerging VBEs,* such that the attributes defining every type in the typology are true for all its members.

Table 2 - VBE Domain Categories

	Criteria	Potential network categories			Criteria impact
1.	Finances	Public support	Own support (Members' fee or % of turnover)		Level of VBE's autonomy
2.	Orientation / Value system	Profit	Non profit		Pressure from market or society
3.	Localization	Regional	Non regional		Legal and tax issues
4.	Customer	One or few	Many		Strong or weak customer's dependence
5.	Product / service	One or few	Large diversity of products/services		Product/service dependency
6.	Sector / domain	Single sector	Multi sector		Sector dependency
7.	Collaboration aim	Cost reduction	Innovation		Goal dependence
8.	Dynamism level	More Static	More dynamic		Stability
9.	Member Competences	Based on competence complementarities	Based on complementarities and competition		Trust issues
10.	Integrating new members	Loose alliance - limited term / condition alliance	Tight alliance - permanent full members		Role of actors, Membership level
11.	Origin	VBE with strong historical roots	New VBE		Strong impact on ICT tools
12.	Focus	Product / service oriented	Market / society oriented		Volatility
13.	Stage of VBE Life cycle	Creation	Operation	Evolution / Meta-morphosis	Needs in term of guidelines, methodologies, and ICT tools
14.	VBE size	Small: <20	Medium: <100	Large: <1000 / Very large: above	Role of the administration and needed ICT tools
15.	VBE role in VO operation	None		domination	Coordination and conflict resolution
16.	Current use of technology and ICT tools	Low	Medium	High	Level of ICT tools dependency
17.	Members types	Business companies only	Business companies + non-business organizations		More potential, less coherency
18.	Broker	Internal	External		Access rights and member roles

19.	**VO**	Recurrent		Formed with new members each time	Needs for VO creation tools
20.	**Profiles (management)**	Informal	Limited (Excel)	Database	Potential to be processed by ICT tools, trust, and access rights
21.	**Competencies (management)**	Informal	Limited (Excel)	Database	Potential to be processed by ICT tools, trust, and access rights

Below we address these three steps in details:

- **Step 1: Common set of characteristics for VBEs**

Based on our network analysis experience, the following set of questions represents the main criteria for investigating these networks: *How many sectors are involved in the VBE? How and which sources support the VBE financially? How does the VBE find VO opportunities? What is the frequency of VO configuration, namely the VBE members' involvement in VOs? How the VBE is managed, and are there formal governance regulations? What are the functions performed by the VBE administration? How is the VBE configured in terms of roles of its actors, permitted competition, location of VBE members, etc.? What kind of organizations can be included or are invited to join the VBE and how large is the VBE? Are VOs always configured of the VBE members, or also consisting some organizations from outside? And if so, under what conditions SMEs from outside can be involved in such VOs? What is the relationship between the VO customers and the VBE?*

In this step of our study and as a response to the above questions, we encountered a large number of distinguishing characteristics for VBEs that can in one way or another be further used as the purpose/criteria for VBE classification. The *main identified "distinguishing characteristics"*, which constitutes a subset of the identified common set of VBE characteristics, include: (1) Multiplicity of sectors/domains, (2) Variety of collaboration drivers, (3) Orientation (value system), (4) Level of dynamism, (5) Financial support mechanism, (6) Localization, (7) Size, (7) Nature of output results, (8) Mission categories, and (9) Application of ICT tools.

- **Step 2: Main classes/categories of the VBEs**

At this step, we used the set of VBE common characteristics as the means to reach some classification of different VBEs. Therefore, for each characteristic, we identified a number of potential classes. For example, two classes were identified for the Multiplicity of sectors/domains that included the single-sector and the multi-sector. For some other characteristics, a number of classes could be identified, e.g. for the size characteristic for example, as suggested by some of the network's representatives, we could identify Small (under 20), Medium (under 100), Large (under 1000), Very-Large (above 1000) number of members, etc. The following list shows some of the identified classes in our study for each of main VBE characteristics addressed above:

- Multiplicity of sectors/domains: Single sector, Multi-sector
- Variety of collaboration drivers: Customer induced, Capacity achievement, etc.
- Orientation (value system): Business orientation, social welfare orientation, etc.
- Level of dynamism: Dynamic pace (evolving), Static pace, etc.
- Financial support mechanism: Publicly supported, Privately supported, etc.

– Localization: Regional, Non-regional
– Size: Small (under 20), Medium (under 100), Large (under 1000), Very-Large (above 1000) number of members, etc.
– Nature of output results: Tangible output, Intangible output, etc.
– Mission categories: Profit-based, Non-profit-based, etc.
– Application of ICT tools: Base management services, advanced services, etc.

In order to summarize our findings, Table 2 is developed to represent: (1) the main criteria/characteristics for characterization and comparison of different VBEs, (2) for each characteristic, it provides the two main potential categories for the networks, and (3) a clue to the main impact of each characteristic/criteria on the network.

- **Step 3: A semi-typology for existing and emerging VBEs**
  Our third and more challenging aim was to investigate if based on the main VBE classification results we can *identify a typology for all existing and emerging VBEs,* such that the attributes that characterize every type in the typology are true for all of its members. As described / argued below, reaching this aim was quite challenging and we could finally achieve not one, but a number of *semi-typologies* for VBEs.

Typology is a classification of all elements in the domain, based on the definition of particular types or categories in that domain, where the members of each type or category are identified by postulating their specified attributes. Typically, *types/categories in a typology are: (1) mutually exclusive,* and *(2) collectively exhaustive.* For example in the biodiversity area, the taxonomy defined for the "limited", though large, collection of animals on earth, although it took a few centuries to establish, has followed a straightforward procedure to create the typology classifying them, as well as to identify the few exceptions where the defined types are not mutually exclusive. Considering the above definition, in our study, it became clear that defining a typology for a new "paradigm" such as the VBE, is a big challenge if at all possible. This is simply due to the fact that first the VBE paradigm is not a limited environment, although it already has a large variety of manifestations. Second, every VBE has distinctly unique "intangible" specificities. And third, there is a wide diversity of purposes and perspectives that can be considered through which the existing and emerging VBEs can be classified.

Therefore, prior to our efforts towards identification of a VBE typology, we became aware of the fact that we will not identify a set of *mutually exclusive types* to classify the VBEs. Consequently, we chose to aim at the identification of a *VBE semi-typology* to tackle the challenge of identifying *a number of types that can collectively exhaust both the existing and the forthcoming VBEs.* Such a semi-typology defined for VBEs, even though does not provide clear cut categorization of VBEs, as for instance exemplified above for the Bio-diversity area, is still valuable, since it provides an insight into the characterization / understanding, and thus better modeling of the VBEs. Furthermore, if one of our identified semi-typology has an "intuitive" appeal for categorization of VBEs, and gets adopted by the research and practice community in this paradigm, we have reached a *common base* for understanding and co-working among the researchers in this area.

For this purpose, we have identified three main perspectives as more dominant and intuitive in representing and classifying the VBEs, which are also validated by the networks involved in our study. Below, for every considered perspective, a list of references is also made to the rows in Table 2, which represent its related characteristics and classifications.

    I. *Domain categories* (1, 3, 4, 5, 6, 7, 8, 9, 11, 12, 13, 14, 15, 16, 19, 20, 21)

    II. *Main Collaboration Drivers* (1, 2, 3, 4, 5, 7, 9, 10, 11, 13, 14, 15, 16, 17, 20, 21)

    III. *Orientation/Value Systems* (1, 2, 3, 5, 7, 11, 12, 13, 14, 15, 16, 17, 20, 21)

In the following text, applying each perspective, a few types (and their main characteristics) are identified. For every perspective, the identified types collectively exhaust the categorization of the so far reported as existing or emerging VBEs. Please notice that as explained above, the typology defined for VBEs under each perspective may not present mutually exclusive VBEs; namely while an existing VBE may primarily be a member of one type, it may at a secondary stage be also a member of a second type in that typology. Therefore, at best these three provide a semi-typology for VBEs. Below the VBE semi-typology is identified for each of the three perspectives:

I. Domain categories – Based on the investigated characteristics (both in literature and in the field) and with the perspective of categorizing the main domains, this VBE typology identifies the following four types of VBEs. For each type of VBE, the SME networks (among the six mentioned above) that best fit each type are also identified below (also see Table 3).

    Type A1 - Stable products/services domain (e.g. VBE-C, VBE-B, VBE-D)

    Type A2 - Stable one-of-a-kind domain

    Type A3 - Emerging domain (e.g. VBE-F, VBE-A)

    Type A4 - Innovation driven domain (e.g. VBE-E).

The Stable products/services domain VBE type is primarily characterized by substantiated sectors or domains, business or social oriented, traditionally regional but nowadays more with a mix of regions, and constituting VBEs of different sizes (from large to small), and using some IT related tools (e.g. VBEs to support traditional manufacturing and services industry). Some general principles for this type of VBEs are already established both in research and in practice. In several business oriented domains some body of knowledge as well as practiced regulations are already created and instantiated, that provide a strong base for the current study of this type of VBEs. These VBEs are operation-based, meaning that their daily activities are known and repetitive, and thus do not require new or innovative solutions for each product and service (Bremer et al, 1999) (Mejia, Molina, 2002) (Pluss, Huber, 2005). Nevertheless, this type of VBE still lacks proper mechanisms and semi-automatic tools for the management of its competency and profile, establishing trust, developing generic ontology, and enhancing the potential of the VBE in responding to the market/society demands.

    The Stable one-of-a-kind domain VBE type – typically identified with substantiated sectors and domains focused on longer term VOs to develop one of a kind products/services - typically with a mix of business & possible social orientation, constituting medium size regional VBEs with a high trust level among the members from multi-sector and complementary organizations, using IT related tools (e.g. VBEs to support traditional construction industry, environmental cleansing of wastes). Similar to the stable products/services domain, also for the one-of-a-kind domain in some areas, e.g. construction industry, there is a rich body of knowledge and formal definitions of some general principles that can be used as the base. Despite the fact that these VBEs are well established, their products are always unique, e.g. a bridge, an airport, etc. Thus, they have a project-based working style where some unique ideas are necessary for every new product. Once developing proper IT tools for trust establishment among VBE member organizations, this type of VBE can benefit from extending its boundaries to include new non-regional members that may increase its level of competency.

The emerging domain VBE type is primarily characterized by the merge of organizations from several substantiated domains in order to respond to some new market/society demands. The VBE for emerging domain will constitute organizations from different sizes with complementary capabilities, established knowledge, culture, and practice tradition. A number of challenges rise due to the merge of these heterogeneous domains, e.g. the integration/inter-linking of their substantiated and formalized knowledge, developing rules of cooperation and establishing trust and recognition among the involved organizations. Examples of this type of VBEs include the merge between the housing and ambient intelligence domains to address the house of the future, merge between the broadcasting, mobile devices, and the entertainment industry to address the entertainment of the future, or the merge between the public safety and environmental scientists/engineers to address the environmental cleansing of the future.

Table 3 - Brief summary of the VBE typology according to the Domain categories

	Collaboration driver	Dynamism level	Degree of readiness	Customer	Finance	Typical VO's duration
Type A1	Ecosystem, capacity achievement, Customer induced cost reduction	Some static/ dynamic	Medium	One/Many	Self support	Medium
Type A2	Customer induced Complement competence	Static	Medium	One	Self support	Long
Type A3	Market induced Cost reduction	Evolving	High	Many	Need public support	Medium
Type A4	Innovation	Evolving	Very high	One/many	Need public support	Short

The Innovation driven domain VBE type – this classification of VBE mostly identifies with the establishment of its short term VOs to deliver innovation for the market or society's benefit, constituting a number of organizations potentially from different sectors with complementary competencies. The degree of readiness of the organizations in this VBE must be very high and typically, due to the role that these VBEs play in a region and the risks involved in innovation-based VOs, there is usually public support available to these VBEs. The new line of products in clothing, e.g. from Italy, and in computer hardware, e.g. from California, are examples of this type of VBEs.

Please notice that the following is considered for measuring the duration of the VOs: Short = some weeks to 6 months, Medium= between 6 months to 1 year, Long= longer than 1 year.

Table 4 - Brief summary of VBE typologies according to main collaboration drivers

	Membership	Overlapping of competencies	Support institutions	Market accesss
Type B1	Enterprises & others Highly selective	Possible	Limited	Extremely focused
Type B2	Organizations in same domain/sector	Mostly	Limited	Focused in one domain (general)
Type B3	May cover various sectors Basic adhesion rule	Possible, limited (regulated)	Limited	Generic (as much as possible)
Type B4	Specific sector (mostly) Regional basis	Possible	Strong	Generic with regional focus

II. Main Collaborative Drivers - If we put our perspective on the main collaboration drivers, a different VBE typology classification can be established including the following four classes (also see Table 4):

Type B1 - Customer induced VBE, when the alliance is formed to qualify as a supplier (e.g. VBE-C).

Type B2 - Capacity achievement driven VBE, formed to support high demands (e.g. VBE-F, VBE-D).

Type B3 - VBE oriented towards complementary competencies, formed to capture new markets, new products/services, or new dimension (e.g. VBE-B).

Type B4 - Regional ecosystem, formed to preserve local specificities, tradition, culture, benefiting from government incentives (e.g. VBE-E, VBE-A).

Table 5 - Brief summary of the VBE typologies according to the value system

	Main expected benefits	Membership	Outputs
Type C1	Economic (profit)	-Private organizations (enterprises)	-Products - Services
Type C2	-Social prestige -Coverage	-Public organizations -NGOs	- Services (mostly)
Type C3	-social prestige & -Economic sustainability	-Public & -Private organizations	-Services -Products (some)

III. Orientation/Value systems - With the perspective of the underlying value systems, another VBE typology classification may include the following three classes (also see Table 5):

Type C1 - Profit / market oriented – to produce economic profit (e.g.

manufacturing – VBE-C, VBE-B, VBE-D, VBE-F, VBE-A, VBE-E)
Type C2 - Social oriented – to support the society (e.g. environment support)
Type C3 - Hybrid market/social – (e.g. R&D on new source of energy).

6. CONCLUSIONS

The Virtual organization Breeding Environment (VBE) is an emerging challenging area of research. Most elements comprising VBEs are not yet properly defined, and so far there is a lack of suitable reference models and reference architectures addressing the constituting elements and behavior of the VBEs. The multi-disciplinarity of research on VBEs further adds to its complexity. Consequently, even discovery and identification of VBEs' requirements and proper definition of this problem area itself becomes challenging. Furthermore, to handle its wide variety of requirements, innovative approaches and mechanisms are required.

Nevertheless, in order to support the establishment of VBEs in the market / society, as well as the development of the supporting ICT-based VBE Management Systems, development of a comprehensive VBE "reference framework" is presented in this paper as a contribution to the VBE field of research, addressing the fundamental components so far identified for VBEs. Therefore, the chapter addresses the identification, definition, and classification of the VBE's main characteristics. Based on the case studies of several existing networks of organizations, and the related past research, we systematically approached and represented the VBE reference framework from different perspectives.

First, this chapter presents the VBE's basic characteristics, such as its actors and their roles, rights and responsibilities, its' life cycle and the life cycle functionalities, etc. Second, it approaches the VBE reference framework through the definition of four generic near-orthogonal sub-spaces to address different aspects of the VBEs. Third, it introduces an ontology-based framework for different types of VBE-related knowledge. Last, it approaches the VBE paradigm definition through the categorizations of its "distinguishing" characteristics for the purpose of identification / specification of a VBE typology.

Elements defined in the VBE reference framework further support the definition and development of components that are needed to support different stages of the VBE life cycle, and for proper management of the VBEs, as addressed in the other chapters of the Part 2 of this book. The next step in the research will extend/merge this framework with the VBE reference modeling research, which is the subject of another forthcoming book from ECOLEAD results.

Acknowledgement. This work was funded in part by the European Commission through the ECOLEAD project. The work on the VBE typology has also been contributed by Servane Crave (France Telecom) and Ana Ines Oliveira (New University of Lisbon / Uninova).

7. REFERENCES

Afsarmanesh, H., Camarinha-Matos, L.M. (2005): A framework for management of virtual organization breeding environments, in Collaborative Networks and their Breeding Environments, pp. 35-49, Springer, Boston.
Afsarmanesh, H., Camarinha-Matos, L.M. (2007): Towards a semi-typology for virtual organization

breeding environments, COA'07 – 8th IFAC Symposium on Cost-Oriented Automation, Habana, Cuba.

Afsarmanesh, H., Camarinha-Matos, L.M., Msanjila, S.S. (2007): Virtual Organizations Breeding Environment: Key Results from ECOLEAD. In the proceedings of the International conference on Cost Effective Automation in Networked Product Development and Manufacturing - IFAC-CEA'2007. Monterey, México.

Afsarmanesh, H., Ermilova, E. (2007): Ontology Engineering for VO Breeding Environments. In the Proceedings of the 9th International Conference on the Modern Information Technology in the Innovation Processes of the Industrial Enterprises – MITIP'07, pp. 124-137, Florence, Italy.

Afsarmanesh, H., Knapp, D., Mcleod D., and Parker, A. (1985): An approach to Engineering DesignDatabases with Applications to VLSI/CAD. In Proceedings of the 11th Int. Conference on Very Large Databases (VLDB)

Anjewierden, A., Wielinga, B.J., Hoog R. and Kabel S., 2003: Task and domain ontologies for knowledge mapping in operational processes. Metis deliverable 2003/4.2. University of Amsterdam.

Bremer, C.; A. Mundim, F. Michilini, J. Siqueira, L. Ortega (1999): A Brazilian case of VE coordination, in Infrastructures for Virtual Enterprises, Kluwer, Boston.

Camarinha-Matos, L. M., Afsarmanesh, H. (1999): Infrastructures for Virtual Enterprises – Networking Industrial Enterprises. Kluwer Academic Publishers, ISBN 0-7923-8639-6, Porto, Portugal

Camarinha-Matos, L. M., Afsarmanesh, H. (2003): Elements of a base VE infrastructure. *Computers in Industry*, 51(2).

Camarinha-Matos, L.M., Afsarmanesh, H., Ollus, M.(editors) (2005): Virtual Organizations: Systems and Practices, Berlin, New York: Springer Science

Camarinha-Matos, L.M.; Afsarmanesh, H. (2004a): The emerging discipline of collaborative networks, in Virtual Enterprises and Collaborative Networks (L.M. Camarinha-Matos, Editor), Kluwer Academic Publishers

Camarinha-Matos, L.M.; Afsarmanesh, H. (Ed.s) (2004b): Collaborative networked organizations – A research agenda for emerging business models, Kluwer Academic Publishers, ISBN 1-4020-7823-4

Ermilova, E., Afsarmanesh, H. (2007): Modeling and management of Profiles and Competencies in VBEs. Journal of Intelligent Manufacturing, Springer.

Ermilova, E., Afsarmanesh, H. (2008): A unified ontology for VO Breeding Environments. In proceedings of DHMS'08 international conference. Athens, Greece, 9-12 March.

Grobelnik, M. and Mladenić, D. (2005): Automated knowledge discovery in advanced knowledge management. Journal of knowledge management, vol 9, no 5

Guevara-Masis, V., Afsarmanesh, H, Hetzberger, L. O. (2004): Ontology-based automatic data structure generation for collaborative networks, in Proceedings of 5th PRO-VE'04 – Virtual Enterprises and Collaborative Networks, Kluwer Academic Publishers, ISBN 1-4020-8138-3, pp 163-174

Mejia, R.; A. Molina (2002): Virtual enterprise broker: Processes, methods and tools, in Collaborative business ecosystems and virtual enterprises, Kluwer, Boston.

Molina, A. and Flores M. (2000): Exploration of Business Opportunities: The role of the virtual enterprise broker, in E-Business and Virtual Enterprise. Managing Business Cooperation (Camarinha-Matos, L.M., Afsarmanesh, H., Rabelo, R, Eds) Kluwer Academic Publishers, Boston

OWL (2004): OWL Web Ontology Language Overview, W3C Recommendation 10 February 2004, http://www.w3.org/TR/owl-features. Viewed 29.08.2007.

Pinto, H.S., Gomez-Perez, A., Martins, J.P (1999): Some Issues on Ontology Integration. In Proceedings of the IJCAI-99 workshop on Ontologies and Problem-Solving Methods (KRR5) Stockholm, Sweden, August 2, 1999

Plüss, A.; C. Huber (2005): Virtuellefabric.CH – A source network for VE in mechatronics, in Virtual Organizations – Systems and Practices, Springer, Boston.

Protégé. http://protege.stanford.edu. Viewed 29.08.2007.

Sunagawa, E., Kozaki, K., Kitamura, Y., Mizoguchi, R. (2004): Organizing Role-concepts in Ontology Development Environment. AI Technical Report (Artificial Intelligence Research Group, I. S. I. R., Osaka Univ.), AI-TR-04-1.

Tolle M., Zwegers A., Vesterager J. (2003): Virtual Enterprise Reference Architecture and Methodology (VERAM), GLOBEMEN Jopint D412 & D43 deliverables

van Eijnatten, F.M. (2003): Chaordic systems thinking chaos and complexity to explain human performance management, in Proceedings of Business Excellence I (G. Putnik, A. Gunasekaran, Eds.), ISBN 972-8692-08-0, University of Minho, Portugal

Zwegers A., Tolle M., Vesterager J.(2003): VERAM: Virtual Enterprise Reference Architecture and Methodology, in Karvonen, I, et. al. (Eds.) Global Engineering and Manufacturing in Enterprise Networks, GLOBEMEN, VTT Symposium 224, VTT Information Service, pp. 17-38

VO BREEDING ENVIRONMENTS VALUE SYSTEMS, BUSINESS MODELS AND GOVERNANCE RULES

[1]David Romero, [1]Nathalie Galeano, [2]Arturo Molina
[1]CIDYT - ITESM Campus Monterrey, Monterrey, Mexico
david.romero.diaz@gmail.com, ngaleano@itesm.mx
[2]VIYD - ITESM Campus Monterrey, Monterrey, Mexico
armolina@itesm.mx

By defining important theoretical concepts like value systems, business models, and governance rules, a theoretical framework is be developed and described in this chapter to analyse the business logic behind value creation within VO Breeding Environments (VBEs). VBEs are long-term strategic collaborative networks that should have defined a priori its value system, business model and governance rules for its operation. Main questions to be answered then are how to create value for all network stakeholders as well as for the customer, how to measure the value created, how to manage the interests and concerns of all parties involved in a collaborative value-creation system, and which are the elements to define the business and governance models of the network.

1. INTRODUCTION

Digital (network) economy in present day markets demands a new logic for value creation, one different from the traditional industrial view in which value creation is a linear and additive process based-on the value chain model (Porter, 1985). The emerging view of a value creation model instead is synchronic and non-additive process, mobilizing constellations of resources and activities to respond a particular business opportunity. Therefore, *value* nowadays is co-created in a system based-on a networked model that integrates a number of stakeholders which work together to co-produce value (a product or a service). This new value creation model is known as the "value network" (Allee, 2000), and refers to the engagement of customers, suppliers, competitors, complementors and allies in rich and dynamic relationships and exchanges for tangible and intangible value flows: goods, services, revenues, knowledge and other benefits.

Under this new conceptualization of a value-creation system, an expanding holistic and systemic understanding, encompassing the role and contribution of multiple stakeholders in the value creation process is addressed by the definition of a *value system* according to the notion that "each product/service offered requires a set of activities carried out by a number of actors forming a value-creation system, that uses tangible and intangible resources for creating value for customers" (Parolini, 1999).

This chapter addresses three important theoretical concepts: *value systems, business models,* and *governance rules* in order to provide a theoretical framework for network managers to analyse and understand the business logic behind value creation within - VO Breeding Environments as long-term strategic collaborative networks (Camarinha-Matos & Afsarmanesh, 2006) - by trying to answer the questions of how to create value for all stakeholders as well as for the customer, and at the same time how managing the interests and concerns of all parties in a collaborative value-creation system.

Furthermore, *business models* have conventionally served to describe the way an organisation, or a network of organisations, aim to create customer value and wealth for all stakeholders; *value networks* represent a different logic in "value-creation systems", in opposition to the traditional value chain; and finally, *governance rules* look into how inter-organisational collaboration can be governed to allow autonomous, geographically distributed, and heterogeneous organisations - in terms of operating environment, culture, social capital, and goals - to work together as a more or less integrated firm.

2. VBE VALUE CREATION FRAMEWORK

Business environment is becoming increasingly dynamic and is changing rapidly; competition is becoming progressively more intense; and successful organisations are evolving towards more agile, dynamic and adaptive organisational structures that can make quick response to customer requirements and face market turbulent conditions. Therefore, a lot of organisations are redesigning their value-creation systems, and reviewing their business models & strategies in order to take advantage of new business opportunities that are often leading to collaborative endeavours.

In this sense, in order to develop a VBE value creation framework (see Figure 1), three building blocks will be addressed in the following sections: First, a conceptual model for defining a *VBE value system* (Romero et al, 2007a) considering the main elements that should be identified in a value network to manage the different strategies to jointly create and deliver value to customers (customer value) as well as to all network stakeholders in the value-creation system (mostly in the form of revenues). Also a proposal for defining a performance measurement system and an ethical code for a collaborative value-creation system will be presented. Secondly, a generic *VBE business model* (Romero et al, 2006) will be introduced describing the value proposition that a breeding environment could offer to its customers and stakeholders, and the infrastructure and organisational arrangements needed to deliver such value proposition in a way that generates profitable and sustainable revenue streams. Thirdly, *VBE governance model* (Romero et al, 2007b) will be depicted aiming to provide a set of operational rules, bylaws and principles as a set of guidelines for the value exchange among network actors that will govern their behaviour during VBE lifecycle.

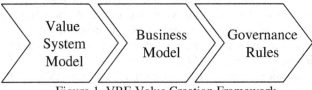

Figure 1. VBE Value Creation Framework

3. VBE VALUE SYSTEM AND ITS ELEMENTS

3.1 Value Systems Basic Concepts

Nowadays, value definition has an increasing interest to both academics and practitioners, mainly in two scientific disciplines: economy and sociology. As a result there are a large number of definitions for the term "value" according to its own definition and meaning context. Therefore, in order to have a better understanding of this fuzzy term, this chapter will focus on two main definitions referring to economic values and ethical/cultural values.

Economic values will be defined as "the worth of a product or service (often measured in terms of money) to someone", and used for making economic choices that involve tradeoffs in allocating resources given certain preferences and constrains; *Ethical values* will be defined as "the shared beliefs on moral/ethical principles that govern the behaviour of individuals and organisations in society", and used as moral principles concerning acceptable or unacceptable behaviours in respect for the law and fair practices in business environment (Macedo et al, 2006); and both definitions will serve to understand the value fundamentals in a value-creation system (e.g. a collaborative network) that creates, defines, measures, captures and sustains different tangibles and intangibles assets with the ability to create customer value (e.g. products/services) and stakeholders value (e.g. revenues).

Furthermore, considering these value fundamentals, a *value system* in a - sociologic perspective - can be referred as a set of ethical values well-defined and represented by a moral code (e.g. ethical code) that is held and applied by an individual or organisation; and in an - economic perspective - a *value system* can be understood as a production system integrating different actors and value activities to create or add value to a product or a service.

Moreover, a new integral perspective is proposed in this chapter combining both perspectives and conceptualizing a *value system* as a value-creation system (production system) creating, holding and exchanging in a sustainable way the economic (products, processes and services) and ethical (trust, loyalty and fairness) values of different actors (individuals or organisations) in an integrated whole (e.g. collaborative network) that balance both value types in the overall transactions among its constituents.

After introducing *value* and *value system* definitions, next concept to be tackle is *valuation*, and this term is strongly related to *performance measurement* as a systematic process continually monitoring and assessing whether progress is being made in a value-creation system towards the desired goals, according to a set of quantitative and qualitative measures (indicators) that provide critical information about activities performed, resources employed, and outcomes obtained.

Different valuation models and methods for *performance measurement* have been developed by several authors in the last decades, each one with different advantages and disadvantages, and different measuring approaches: direct intellectual capitals methods, market capitalization methods, return on assets methods or scorecard methods (Luthy, 1998; Williams, 2000; Sveiby, 2007). Sveiby (2007) research on this topic presents an extensive literature review on valuation models and methods studying 34 measuring models/methods according to its chronological order and measuring approach. What it can be concluded from this work is that in recent years most new valuation methods and models that have been developed represent modified versions, extensions or adaptations of classical models such as: Balanced Scorecard and its scorecards (Kaplan & Norton, 1992); Intangible Assets Monitor and its TANGO business simulation (Sveiby, 1997); Skandia Navigator and its Dolphin information system + IC-index (Edvinsson & Malone, 1997); and EFQM model and its RADAR logic + pathfinder card (EFQM, 1999).

From the classical valuation models and methods mentioned, *scorecard methods* like Balanced Scorecard and EFQM have become the more popular and employed by organisations today; both models offer a measuring approach based-on driver and outcome indicators to monitor and assess different perspectives in an organisation and allow an integral vision of the progress made towards strategic goals achievement.

Nevertheless these models/methods focus on one organisation's strategy and not in a collaborative strategy, so they should be adapted and/or extended to a collaborative network environment that copes with the emerging paradigm of value co-creation.

3.2 VBE Value Generation Objects: Capitals in Organisations

In a VBE context, a *value system* refers to the "identification, structure and measurement of a set of values that a VBE creates, holds and exchanges among and together with its stakeholders" (Romero et al, 2007a).

The *VBE value system* main purpose is to identify and measure, through a performance measurement system, the tangible (economic) and intangible (strategic and social) values and benefits generated by the VBE for its stakeholders: *economic benefits* are achieved from increasing revenues by collaborating in business opportunities that would not be possible if attempted individually; *strategic benefits* are accomplished through the integration and access to new knowledge, resources and complementary skills and capacities which allow each stakeholder to focus on its core competencies; and *social benefits* arise from the interaction between stakeholders that promotes a trustable environment for collaborative undertaken of business opportunities.

For the VBE value system identification and structure aims, a *capitals taxonomy* to recognize and classify the tangible and intangible values, also known as value generation objects, that VBE stakeholders (VBE members) and the VBE itself (VBE platform) hold. Plus the possible emerging ones (VBE system), result of combining different tangible and intangible values in a value creation opportunity (e.g. collaboration opportunity) to add value to an existing product, service or process, or create new value by manufacturing/offering new value propositions (products and/or services) to the market (e.g. VO customers), both through the creation of virtual organisations (Romero et al, 2007a). This value creation logic can be depicted in Figure 2, named VBE value creation strategy.

VBE Members		VBE Platform		Value Co-Creation
VBE Members' Capitals	**+**	VBE Platform Capital	**=**	VBE System Capital

Figure 2. VBE Value Creation Strategy

Furthermore, based-on the *capitals taxonomy*, VBE members, VBE platform and VBE system value generation objects can be categorized into tangible and intangible assets, and these at the same time, into a capitals classification where *financial capital* refers to those physical assets capable of producing tangible outputs, and *intellectual* & *social capitals* refer to those intangible assets capable of producing tangible and intangible outputs (Romero et al, 2007a) (see Tables 1 to 3):

Table 1. VBE Members' Capitals

Financial Capital	Intellectual Capital	Social Capital
• *Financial Capital*. It refers to the financial resources (e.g. cash, bank accounts, physical assets) that an organisation uses to achieve its objectives.	• *Human Capital*. It refers to the assets of knowledge (explicit or tacit) of the organisation staff useful to create value through their competences (skills, talent, capabilities and knowledge). • *Structure Capital*. It is the knowledge that an organisation materializes, systematizes and internalizes in the form of physical resources like: ICTs, production technologies, work processes, management systems, and quality standards. • *Innovation & Learning Capital*. It refers to the possibility to maintain the success of an organisation in a long term by developing or improving competences to increase and fortify the efficiency of the manufacturing processes or services development.	• *Relational Capital*. It refers to the relations and logistic channels that an organisation maintains with his clients, suppliers and other type of organisations. • *Identity Capital*. It refers to the mix of recognition and history of the organisation used to influence the perception and activities of employees, customers and other organisations. It has the ability to create the image of vision of the organisation as parts of its culture.

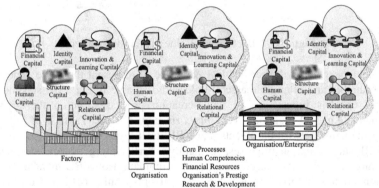

Figure 3. VBE Member's Value Generation Objects

Table 2. VBE Platform Capitals

Financial Capital	Intellectual Capital	Social Capital
• *Financial Capital*. It refers to the financial resources that a VBE as a platform uses to achieve its objectives.	• *Human Capital*. Composed by the VBE administrator, VO broker team (VO broker, planner & coordinator), VBE advisor, and VBE service providers with their skills, talent, capabilities and knowledge. • *Infrastructure Capital*. It includes the technologies, methods, processes and physical resources that support the VBE operation.	• *Culture Capital*. It refers to the working & sharing principles of a VBE represented in his strategies, philosophy, culture and ethical code.

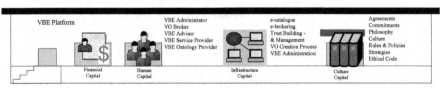

Figure 4. VBE Platform Value Generation Objects

Table 3. VBE Platform Capitals

Financial Capital	Intellectual Capital	Social Capital
• *Financial Capital.* It refers to the sum of VBE members' financial capital that will be shared in the VBE and invested in the VBE platform.	• *Expert Human Capital.* It is the result of sharing and combining the Human Capital competences of the VBE members' staff with other VBE member's or VBE staff. • *Integrated Infrastructure Capital.* It is the result of sharing and combining resources between VBE members to increment their capacity to develop new products or services.	• *Community Interaction Capital.* It refers to the VBE strategies focused on the exploitation of VBE members' relations and logistics channels. Also, it represents the relations and working & sharing principles of a VBE and its members that create a moral responsibility, positive intentions, understanding, respect and equity between the VBE and its members in collaborative opportunities.

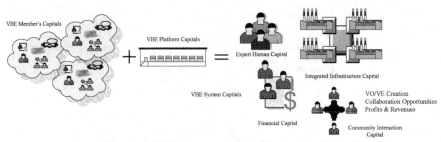

Figure 5. VBE System Value Generation Objects

VBE members' capitals (see Table 1 & Figure 3) represent the value generation objects (tangible and intangible assets) hold and available in the VBE stakeholders that will serve as inputs for all value-creation processes within the breeding environment (e.g. VO creation); *VBE platform capitals* (see Table 2 & Figure 4) stand for the value generation objects that VBE itself holds and serve also as inputs for the VBE value-creation processes, but mainly as "articulating" objects/mechanisms for aligning and allowing the exchange and combination of VBE members' value generation objects involved in a value creation opportunity (e.g. VO creation & management tools); and *VBE system capitals* (see Table 3 & Figure 5) represent the VBE value-creation processes outputs (e.g. VO products/services) (see Figure 6).

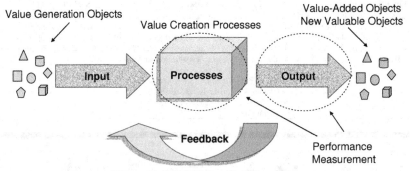

Figure 6. VBE Value Creation System

In summarize, Romero et al (2007a) approach allows the identification of the value generation objects available in each VBE stakeholder and the VBE itself towards the definition of value creation strategies (e.g. VO creation), based-on the inventory of available competencies, capabilities and capacities to answer to particular collaboration opportunities. In this sense, a successful VBE value creation strategy will represent the right combination of value generation objects (tangible and intangibles assets) to create specific value creation processes within VOs to respond to certain collaboration opportunities identified and deliver the output expected by the VO customer with the required quality, and within the required time- and cost-frame.

3.3 VBE Performance Measurement System

Once that all VBE value generation objects have been indentified, and most important ones supporting core-value creation processes recognized, next step is to unfold this *capitals taxonomy* in the form of a *strategic map* to monitor the contribution of each VBE stakeholder and value generation object to the achievement of the VBE strategic goals. The VBE value creation strategy should be developed starting from its current value-creation system state, and be measured & monitored through an *indicator system* showing the progress made towards the strategic goals established. Therefore, for the VBE value system measurement aim, different financial (financial capital) and non-financial (intellectual & social capitals) valuation methods and models could be used, and each organisation, or collaborative network, should select the most appropriate model to measure the value generated (new value or value-added) depending on its purpose, situation and audience (Sveiby, 2007).

The suggested measuring approach by the authors focus on *scorecard methods* like the well known and applied Balanced Scorecard (Kaplan & Norton, 2006) or EFQM (Hakes, 2007) models, since they offer a comprehensive picture of an organisation's health and can be easily applied at any level of an organisation. Considering this replicability advantage, these models could be adapted to a collaborative network environment, where they can be replicated at each network node, making of course some adjustments, towards a collaborative performance measurement system.

Scorecard methods advantages offer a closer measure to an event and a faster and more accurate reporting of the value generated than pure financial measures, but their disadvantages are that indicators are contextual and have to be customized for each organisation and each purpose, which makes sometimes difficult comparisons (Sveiby, 2007).

Managing and measuring performance in a collaborative network where individual contributions to value creation are much more difficult to determine implies the development of appropriate *performance measurement systems*, and further research is required in the nature of collaborative performance indicators.

A first intent to adapt the Balanced Scorecard model to become a collaborative performance measurement system for a breeding environment is addressed by Romero et al (2007a) and depicted in Figure 7.

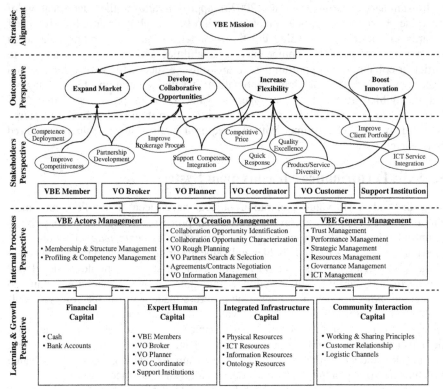

Figure 7. VBE Balanced Scorecard Model

The Balanced Scorecard is a model combining financial and non-financial performance measures derived from organisation's strategy, and connecting long-term objectives to short-term actions using cause-effect relationships to track the progress made towards the desired goals around four distinct perspectives: outcomes, stakeholders, internal processes, and learning & growth.

Using Balanced Scorecard as a *performance measurement system* will provide strategic information to the VBE stakeholders about how their different value generation objects are working together to co-produce value. The VBE mission will be translated into specific target outcomes and impacts in the VBE stakeholders and then VBE value-creation processes aligned to the objectives achievement, always looking for improvement opportunities in investment (Financial Capital), people (Expert Human Capital), systems & procedures (Integrated Infrastructure Capital), and strategic partnerships (Community Interaction Capital) to enhance the VBE value-creation processes.

Table 4 presents a proposal for an *indicator system* that aligns the indicators in each perspective providing relevant feedback as how internal processes are supporting goals achievement according to stakeholders' interests, and which adjustments have to be made to continuously improve internal processes towards the outcomes desired.

Table 4. VBE Balanced Scorecard - Indicator System

Perspective	Element	Indicator
Outcome	Expand Market	• VBE sales
	Develop Collaborative Opportunity	• VOs created
	Boost Innovation	• New products • New services
	Increase Flexibility	• Competencies available • Capabilities available • Capacities available

Perspective	Element	Indicator
Stakeholders	VBE Member	• Competence deployment
	VO Broker	• Opportunities identified
	VO Planner	• VOs created
	VO Coordinator	• VOs performance
	VO Customer	• Customer satisfaction
	Support Institution	• Support services provided

Perspective	Element	Indicator
Internal Processes	VBE Actors Management	• Business processes performance
	VO Creation Management	• Business processes performance
	VBE General Management	• Business processes performance

Perspective	Element	Indicator
Learning & Grow	Financial Capital	• Investments
	Expert Human Capital	• Training
	Integrated Infrastructure Capital	• New equipment • New technology
	Community Interaction Capital	• New VBE members (recruitment) • New Support Institutions

Another effort to adapt EFQM Excellence Model to become a collaborative performance measurement system for a breeding environment is presented in Figure 8.

The EFQM model is a framework based-on nine criteria, five "enablers" and four "results", describing what an organisation does to achieve its objectives, and what achievements are really attained according to the strategic planning.

Enablers include: (1) leadership - as leaders making the right decisions and performing the correct actions to support VBE mission; (2) people - as people deploying their knowledge and skills to perform VBE value-creation processes; (3) policy & strategy - as aligning relevant policies, plans, objectives, targets and processes to the VBE mission; (4) partnerships & resources - as external and internal resources supporting the VBE value-creation processes; and (5) processes - as well designed, managed and continuously improved set of activities creating value for the VBE stakeholders and allowing the VBE mission achievement.

Results include: (1) people results - as achievements in employees performance; (2) customer results - as achievements in customers satisfaction; (3) society results - as achievements in positive impact to society; and (4) key performance results - as achievements according to the strategic planning and VBE overall performance.

Employing EFQM model as a *performance measurement system* will allow identifying clearly VBE strengths and weakness areas in which improvements can be made since "results" are caused by "enablers" and "enablers" improved using feedback from "results".

The EFQM model RADAR logic (Results, Approaches, Deployments, Assessment and Reviews) and its pathfinder card depicted in Table 5 and Figure 9 represent a proposal for an *indicator system* that allows planning results (outcomes), developing action courses to achieve them, deploying these actions, and assess the results obtained to feedback the VBE strategy.

────────── Enablers ──────────▶ ────── Results ──────▶

Leadership	People	Processses	People Results	Key Performance Results
Deploy: • Working & Sharing Principles • Collaborative Planning • Collaborative ICT-Infrastructures • Supporting Tools & Methodologies Facilitate: • Comunication • Trust Building • Information Sharing • Resources Sharing	Human Capital: • VBE Administrator • VBE Member • VO Broker • VO Planner • VO Coordinator **Policy & Strategy** [Policy] VBE Governance • Principles • Bylaws • Rules [Strategy] VBE Strategy • Mission & Vision • Goals & Objectives **Partnerships & Resources** [Partnerships] Community Interaction Capital • Support Institutions • Service Providers • Third-Party Institutions [Resources] Financial Capital • Financial Assets Integrated Infrastructure Capital • Technologies • Methodologies • Processes • Physical Resources	VBE Actors Management: • Membership & Structure Management • Profiling & Competency Management VO Creation Management: • Collaboration Opportunity Identification • Collaboration Opportunity Characterization • VO Rough Planning • VO Partners Search & Selection • Agreements/Contracts Negotiation • VO Information Management VBE General Management: • Trust Management • Performance Management • Decision Support Management • Strategic Management • Marketing Management • Financial Management • Accounting Management • Resources Management • Governance Management • Bag of Assets Management • Value System Information Management • Ontology Management • ICT Management • Support Institutions Management	VBE Members Services: • VBE Membership Structure Services • VBE Competency Management Services • VBE Trust Building Services • VBE Shared Bag of Assets • VBE VO Creation Support Services • VO Management Support Services **Customer Results** VO Customers: • Products/Services Quality • On-Time Delivers • Customer Satisfaction • Customer Loyalty **Society Results** VBE Society Impact: • Employment Impact • Economic Sustainability • Investment Attraction	Expand Market: • Improve Competitiveness • Partnership Development • Competitive Price • Improve Client Portfolio Develop Collaboration Opportunities: • Competence Deployment • Partnership Development • Improve Brokerage Process • Support Competence Integration Increase Flexibility: • Improve Brokerage Process • Support Competence Integration • Competitive Price • Quick Response • Quality Excellence • Product/Service Diversity • Improve Client Portfolio Boost Innovation: • Product/Service Diversity • ICT Service Integration

◀────────── Innovation & Learning ──────────

Figure 8. VBE EFQM Excellence Model

Table 5. VBE EFQM Pathfinder Card - Indicator System

Results	0%	25%	50%	75%	100%
Trends	VBE strategy towards achieving sustainable competitive advantages and financial profitability.				
	No results or anecdotal information	Positive trends and/or satisfactory performance on some results	Positive trends and/or sustained good performance on many results over at last 3 years/months	Strongly positive trends and/or sustained excellence performance on most results over at least 3 years/months	Strongly positive trends and/or sustained excellence performance in all areas over at least 5 years
Targets	VBE objectives and goals achievement.				
	No results or anecdotal information	Favourable and appropriate in some areas	Favourable and appropriate in many areas	Favourable and appropriate in most areas	Excellent and appropriate in most areas
Comparisons	VBE performance vs. other VBEs vs. Best in industry (Benchmarking).				
	No results or anecdotal information	Comparisons in some areas	Favourable in some areas	Favourable in many areas	Excellent in most areas and best in class in many areas
Causes	VBE enablers supporting the breeding environment strategy.				
	No results or anecdotal information	Some results	Many results	Most results	All results - leading position will be maintained
Total	5 10	15 20 25 30 35	40 45 50 55 60	65 70 75 80 85	90 95 100
Scope	VBE drivers supporting the breeding environment strategy.				
	No results or anecdotal information	Some areas addressed	Many areas addressed	Most areas addressed	All areas addressed
Total	5 10	15 20 25 30 35	40 45 50 55 60	65 70 75 80 85	90 95 100
Overall Total	5 10	15 20 25 30 35	40 45 50 55 60	65 70 75 80 85	90 95 100
Approach	**0%**	**25%**	**50%**	**75%**	**100%**
Sound	VBE business processes supporting and delivering the results expected by stakeholders.				
	No evidence or anecdotal	Some evidence	Evidence	Clear evidence	Comprehensive evidence
Integrated	VBE governance principles, bylaws and rules affecting positively the breeding environment strategy.				
	No evidence or anecdotal	Some evidence	Evidence	Clear evidence	Comprehensive evidence
Total	5 10	15 20 25 30 35	40 45 50 55 60	65 70 75 80 85	90 95 100
Deployment	**0%**	**25%**	**50%**	**75%**	**100%**
Implemented	VBE strategy is implemented as planned.				
	No evidence or anecdotal	In about ¼ of relevant areas	In about ½ of relevant areas	In about ¾ of relevant areas	All relevant areas
Systematic	VBE strategy is deployed in a structured and systematic way.				
	No evidence or anecdotal	Some Evidence	Evidence	Clear evidence	Comprehensive evidence
Total	5 10	15 20 25 30 35	40 45 50 55 60	65 70 75 80 85	90 95 100
Assessment	**0%**	**25%**	**50%**	**75%**	**100%**
Measurement	VBE performance measurement is carried periodically, monitoring the progress made towards objectives established.				
	No evidence or anecdotal	Some evidence	Evidence	Clear evidence	Comprehensive evidence
Learning	VBE strategy receives continuously feedback for its tactical improvement.				
	No evidence or anecdotal	Some evidence	Evidence	Clear evidence	Comprehensive evidence
Improvement	VBE strategic results are continuously analyzed to discover improvement opportunities.				
	No evidence or anecdotal	Some evidence	Evidence	Clear evidence	Comprehensive evidence
Total	5 10	15 20 25 30 35	40 45 50 55 60	65 70 75 80 85	90 95 100
Overall Total	5 10	15 20 25 30 35	40 45 50 55 60	65 70 75 80 85	90 95 100

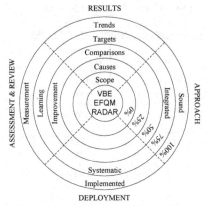

Figure 9. VBE EFQM RADAR Model

3.4 VBE Ethical Values

VBE ethical values stand for common working & sharing principles, creating a collaborative culture, where new ways of working are developed by excelling individual capabilities to better respond to collaboration (business) opportunities.

VBE ethical values represent a guide to stakeholders to consider right or wrong decisions when facing situations which pose a dilemma in action courses (Romero et al, 2007a; 2007b). Having an ethical code (see Figure 10) will help VBE stakeholders to regulate their behaviour and promote fairness in value exchanges among them (see VBE Governance Model - section 5 for more detail).

VBE Ethical Code		
Preamble: VBE Objectives & Strategic Statements		
Code Scope: VBE Actors Accepted Conduct Standards		
Values:		
Collaboration	Sharing Attitude	Fairness
Quality & Reliability	Competence	Innovation
... ...	... ...	... ...
General Issues:		
VBE Actors Own Ethical Code		
Responsibility to Clients	**Responsibility of VBE Actors** (Focus on VBE Admin. &Broker)	**Responsibility to VBE Actors** (Focus on VBE Members)
Responsibility to VBE Partners	**Responsibility to Society**	**Business Operation Issues**
... ...		

Figure 10. VBE Ethical Code (Template)

3.5 VBE Value System Ontology

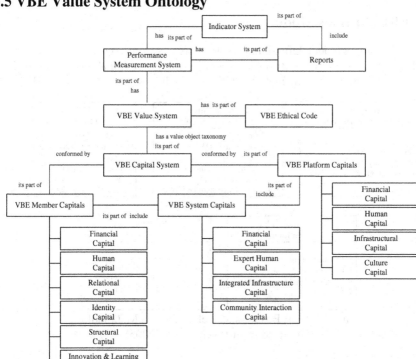

Figure 11. VBE Value System Ontology

Figure 11 presents a VBE value system ontology showing the relationships between the VBE value generation objects (section 3.2), the VBE performance measurement system (section 3.3) and the VBE ethical values (section 3.4) as the three components representing an innovative conceptual model for VBE value systems.

4. VBE BUSINESS MODEL

4.1. Business Models Basic Concepts

Business models are blueprints describing organisation's core logic for creating and delivering value to the customer in a sustainable and profitable way for its stakeholders. Business models components range from revenue models and value propositions to organisational infrastructures and arrangements for trading relationships. These components express *what* an organisation (or a network) offers to its stakeholders and customers, *who* it targets and through which channels with certain value propositions, *how* it creates and delivers such value propositions by attracting the right customers and establishing the right partnerships with other organisations with the necessary core competencies and resources to answer the first two questions, and *how much* an organisation can earn from investing and participating in a value network that makes it possible to answer the questions stated before (Osterwalder, 2004).

4.2. VBE Business Model

For VBE business model definition, two elements were considered:
(1) A "Methodology for Business Model Definition of Collaborative Networked Organisations" by Jimenez et al (2005), which was instantiated for VBEs, and

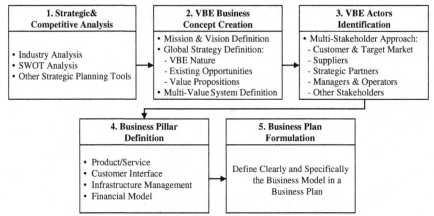

Figure 12. VBE Business Model Definition Methodology
(Adapted from Jimenez et al, 2005)

(2) Osterwalder's (2004) business model ontology, which was the basis for the fourth step of the methodology proposed by Jimenez et al (2005).

Table 6. VBE Business Model Ontology (Adapted from Osterwalder, 2004)

Pillar	Building Block	Definition
Product	Multi-value Proposition	Value offered to the stakeholder/customer (What).
Multi-Stakeholder Interface	Target Stakeholders	Target stakeholder/customer and target market (Who).
	Distribution Channel	Channels to reach the market and the customer/stakeholder.
	Stakeholders Relationship	Links and strategies to maintain customer/stakeholder relationship.
VBE Infrastructure Management	Multi-Value Configuration	Activities and resources arrangement necessary to create value for the customer (Value Configuration - How).
	VBE Capabilities	Capabilities will be integrated to underpin the VBE value proposition.
	Partnership	Strategic alliances, joint-ventures and long-term partnerships.
Financial Aspects	Cost Structure	Costs incurred in the creation, marketing and delivering of value.
	Revenue Model	Definition of the business model economic sustainability.

Following Osterwalder's (2004) ontological approach for business models, based-on four pillars & nine building blocks, and adapting it to a collaborative business rationality for a VBE business model; two main adjustments have been made in comparison to a single organisation:

- A "multi-value proposition" that can be understood through the VBE value system model explained in section 3, and
- A "multi-stakeholder" approach considering that a collaborative network joins complementary competencies, capabilities and capacities of several business allies in a value co-creation process where VBE actors play multiple

roles, have many interactions and provide different value generation objects to co-produce a product or a service for the customer as result of VO creation & operation processes.

Table 7 presents a generic VBE business model based-on Osterwalder's (2004) ontological approach describing:

(1) VBE Product (multi-value proposition) as a source network providing a bundle of services for the establishment of a common ground for interaction and cooperation between VBE members towards VO creation and other short-term coalitions;

(2) VBE multi-stakeholders interface as a pool of organisation with the interest to cooperate with each other, through the establishment of a base long-term cooperation agreement towards their preparedness to get involved in ad-hoc collaborations (e.g. VO creation);

(3) VBE infrastructure as a supporting ICT-infrastructure for collaboration, with cooperative business rules, acting as the enabler of interoperation among VBE members; and

(4) VBE financial aspects as an investment in a long-term strategic alliance to benefit from collaborative business opportunities, marketing possibilities, negotiation power as a network and access to new markets in multi-disciplinary sectors.

Table 7. VBE Business Model (Adapted from Osterwalder, 2004).

Pillar	Building Block	VBE Business Model Description	
Product (What)	Multi-Value Proposition	*Value proposition - Examples:* • VBE Membership Structure Services • VBE Competency Management Services • VBE Trust Building Services • VBE Shared Bag of Assets • VO Creation Support Services • VO Management Support Services	*Benefits - Examples:* • Financial • Productivity • Strategic • Social
Multi-Stakeholders Interface (Who)	Target Stakeholders	*Stakeholders - Examples:* • Small, Medium & Large Enterprises • Industrial Associations • Chambers of Commerce • Regional Development Agencies • Universities • Government Entities • Financial Institutions	*Stakeholders Roles:* • VBE Administrator • VBE Member • VO Broker • VO Planner • VO Coordinator • Support Institution • Service Provider
	Distribution Channel	*ICT-Infrastructure – Examples:* • VBE Management System • VO Management System	
	Stakeholders Relationship	*Relationship – Examples:* • Among VBE Members, or among VO Partners • Among VBE Member & VBE (Admin.) • Among VBE (Admin.) / VO (Coordinator) & its Customers	
VBE Infrastructure Management (How)	Multi-Value Configuration	*Value Exchanged – Examples:* • Financial • Technological • Knowledge • Social	
	Capabilities	*VBE Capabilities – Examples:* • Services for VBE Members: Brokering, Legal, MKT, Insurance… • Common Base ICT-Infrastructure • Cooperative Business Rules • Shared Bag-of-Assets • Support for VO Creation Process	

	Partnership	*Partnership – Examples:*
		• Support Institutions & Service Providers:
		  o Certification Entities o Logistics Entities
		  o Insurance Entities o Financial Entities
		  o Coaching Entities o Training Entities
		  o Research Entities	

Financial Aspects (How Much)	Cost Structure	Cost – Examples: • ICT Costs • Staff Costs • Billing Costs • Marketing Costs
	Revenue Model	Revenue Models – Examples: • VBE Membership Fees • VO Commissions • External Funding

Besides the elements mentioned in this section, the following issues should be considered when defining a VBE business models:

- VBE business model has to provide guidelines for creating a sustainable breeding environment using different mechanisms that will support the creation of dynamic virtual organisations;
- VBE business model should be oriented to enhance breeding environments establishment and management through an adequate framework, infrastructure and services to support the VO creation process in a dynamic way that copes with the short-term nature of business opportunities in a hypercompetitive market;
- VBE business model definition should include a business strategy considering the VBE typology (domain sector, collaboration drivers, value system) to achieve sustainable competitive advantages1;
- VBE business model should consider market dynamics (changing and turbulent conditions) to provide the business model with abilities to evolve over time in order to remain profitable by creating new value propositions, new capabilities, new strategic relationships, etc. to leverage the business network; and
- VBE business model should take advantage of network effects2 to support its value-added strategy.

4.3 VBE Business Planning Tools & Business Modelling

Following the Methodology for Business Model Definition of Collaborative Networked Organisations (Jimenez et al, 2005) a complete business planning exercise was developed, analyzing in general how a VBE can define its business model. During this exercise, the main analysis and results achieved were:

- The identification of strengths, weaknesses, opportunities and threats that a VBE may have, using the *SWOT analysis.*
- The identification of *sustainable competitive advantages* as the elements that support the VBE survivability/competitivity and form a strong network over a long time period.
- The *critical success factors analysis* identifying the important elements for the VBE success.
- The identification of VBE *business concept elements* such as: mission, vision and strategy.
- The identification of existing market opportunities for VBEs and the VBE added-value benefits for VBE members and stakeholders.
- The definition of VBE *business model pillars* and its elements.

---

[1] Sustainable competitive advantage, it refers when an organisation possess a value-creation process and position that can not be duplicated/imitated by other organisations that lead its value creation above normal rents/incomes (Porter, 1985).
[2] Network effects, it refers to the increase of product(s) value as the number of users or complementary layers of the product or service increases (Katz & Shapiro, 1985).

Furthermore, after the identification of all this elements, an exercise for modelling a VBE business model was developed using *value maps*. A VBE generic value map was developed using Gordijn's e³value tool (Gordijn & Akkermans, 2001) to give a practical idea to the VBE stakeholders involved in a breeding environment about their value exchanges and benefits from collaboration (Romero et al, 2006).

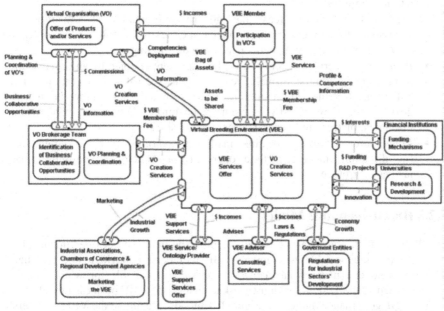

Figure 13. VBE Value Map using e3value (Romero et al, 2006)

Figure 13 depicts a generic VBE value network highlighting four value flows: goods, services, revenues & knowledge - representing the value exchanges (what is received vs. what is offered) among the VBE stakeholders, and allowing to create a sustainable business model in where all VBE stakeholders benefit from win-win situations.

5. VBE GOVERNANCE MODEL

5.1 VBE Governance Basic Concepts

Collaboration needs to be governed in order to look over the fairness between individuals, groups and/or organisations in collaborative endeavours and value exchanges to avoid opportunistic behaviours. Governance models are aimed at defining how collective actions where several actors negotiate and collaborate to achieve a common and compatible goals. Governance models intend to provide a set of guidelines to adapt, coordinate and safeguard autonomous actions collectively working in a jointly plan where risk, resources, responsibilities and rewards are shared among actors to achieve a mutual goal.

Governance refers to the act of affecting government and monitoring (through policy) the long-term strategy and direction of an organisation (Graham et al, 2003). Good organisation governance structures encourage organisations to create value (through entrepreneur, innovation, development and exploration) and provide accountability & control systems commensurate with the risk involved (Kumar, 2005).

Three main elements are defined when described the governance model of an organization as follows:

- *Principles* are the values that govern individual's or organisation's behaviour. There are some important principles to be followed in order to assure the value creation, maintenance and developing.
- *Bylaws* are generally understood as the document adopted by an organisation to regulate its affairs; formally referred to as the rules of operation. Since bylaws are the rules and regulations adopted by a corporation for its internal governance, they usually contain provisions relating to shareholders, managers, officers and general corporate business.
- *Rules* refer (formally or informally) to various types of guidelines (i.e. direction, standard, method, operation) or standard (i.e. definition, fact, law, code, truth, etc.).

5.2 VBE Governance Model

In a VBE context, a governance model refers to the definition of operational rules, bylaws and principles that will govern VBE members' behaviour, and will help to define who can make what decisions, who is accountable for which effects, and how each of the VBE actors must work to sustain the VBE business model.

The VBE governance model (see Figure 14) intends to facilitate the VBE members' collaboration in business opportunities, as well as guaranteeing the effective performance of all VBE stakeholders involved in the business network. A generic VBE governance model should include the following definitions (Romero et al, 2007):

- *Principles* as the values that govern VBE behaviour, constituting the personal guidelines for stakeholders to behave within a VBE.
- *Bylaws* as formally declare operation rules which will regulate VBE stakeholders' behaviour.
- *Rules* divided in two groups related to:
    - *Behavioural Rules* as rules for good acting and conducting, including ethical behaviour (e.g. ethical code) and culture.
    - *Functional Rules* that support both operational and administrative procedures along the VBE lifecycle stages - creation, operation, evolution, metamorphosis and dissolution.

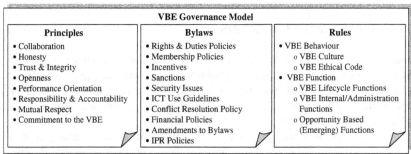

Figure 14. VBE Governance Model

VBE principles are strongly linked with the VBE vision, where the breeding environment objectives were depicted. Some basic principles that a VBE should follow are: collaboration, honesty, trust & integrity, openness, performance orientation, responsibility & accountability, mutual respect, and commitment to the VBE.

VBE bylaws establish the roles and duties of VBE actors, the timing and procedures for participating in collaborative opportunities, and the manner for conducting the VBE administration. General bylaws are related to: rights & duties policies, membership policies, incentives, sanctions, security issues, ICT use guidelines, conflict resolution policy, financial policies, amendments to bylaws, and intellectual property rights policies.

VBE behavioural rules are related to breeding environment social values, ethical code, and culture (see Figure 10).

VBE functional rules are related to VBE manager's decision-making, negotiation and resources allocation policies between parties involved and taking actions to optimize VBE functionalities, relationships and performance. Figure 15 details a classification proposed for these rules according to different process part of the VBE management.

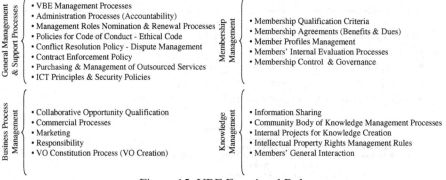

Figure 15. VBE Functional Rules

Main recommendations for defining a VBE governance model are:

- It should be defined by the VBE administrator together with VBE members and written down in document available for all VBE stakeholders;
- VBE rules and bylaws definition will depend on the VBE specific sector; and
- VBE creation and inclusion of new rules should be clearly defined in the VBE bylaws.

5.3 VBE Governance Guidelines

Designing and managing an effective corporate governance structure for a VBE is a challenging process. VBE rules and bylaws definition will depend on many criteria such as VBE typology and management style among others. Nevertheless in order to support the definition of VBE governance elements authors had proposed some guidelines as explained in this section.

In order to identify these guidelines, the analysis of different examples of real VBE was developed. Table 8 summarizes the study cases analyzed and its governance structure.

Table 8. VBE Governance Structure Examples

VBE case	Size	Region	Governance Structure
IECOS	30	Mexico	General Director that manages three main groups: Engineering, Brokerage and Technology.
Virtuelle Fabrik	90	Switzerland and Germany	Five Working Parties (formed by representatives of each company). Executive Committee (formed by 5 members and headed by a chairman).
Swiss Microtech	7	Switzerland and China	A Registered Association with lucrative goals, with a Steering Committee (President, Vice-President and one member) and a General Assembly.
CeBeNetwork	35	Germany, France, UK	CeBeNetwork Group is formed by 5 companies: CeBeNetwork Engineering & IT, CeBeNetwork Services, CeBeNetwork France, CeBeNetwork UK, Werucon Automation GmbH
Virfebras	12	Caxias do Sul, Brazil	Directory Board composed by a President, a Vice-President and a Financial Responsible. Statute and Ethical Rules are also defined.
VEN	~ 250	Yorkshire, UK	Advisory Board is the final accountable body, with the power to hire and fire VEN service providers, and sanction or dismiss VEN members.
Supply Network Shannon	25	Shannon Region of Ireland	Steering Committee (9 members and 2 development agencies). 4 Sub-Committees: Marketing, Environment, Training and Projects.
Torino Wireless	~ 47	Turin and Piedmont, Italy	Torino Wireless Foundation (Administrative Committee, President, Vice-President, Reviewers College, Ordinary Assembly).

Three main guidelines and templates were developed for supporting a VBE to define the governance elements:

- VBE Ethical Code template (see Figure 10).
- Guidelines for VBE Bylaws (see Figure 16).
- Guidelines for VBE operational rules (see Figure 17).

Figure 16. VBE Bylaws Guidelines (Extract)

GENERAL MANAGEMENT AND SUPPORT PROCESS		
Type	**Rule**	**Description**
[illegible]	[illegible]	[illegible]
BUSINESS PROCESS MANAGEMENT		
Type	**Rule**	**Description**
[illegible]	[illegible]	[illegible]
MEMBERSHIP MANAGEMENT		
Type	**Rule**	**Description**
[illegible]	[illegible]	[illegible]
KNOWLEDGE MANAGEMENT		
Type	**Rule**	**Description**
[illegible]	[illegible]	[illegible]

Figure17. VBE Functional Rules Guidelines (Extract)

6. CONCLUSIONS

This chapter presents a VBE value creation framework as a set of guidelines for defining a VBE Value System, Business Model and Governance Rules.

The *VBE value system* model supports the identification of the value generation objects (or capitals) that a VBE and its members create, hold and exchange. The VBE performance measurement system complements part of the VBE Value System by supporting the VBE value generation objects measurement in the value-creation processes.

The *VBE business model* considers a multi-value system characterization and a multi-stakeholder perspective that support the definition of the elements that will maintain the VBE operation in the long-term. The use of value maps helps the VBE stakeholder to understand the VBE rationale and the different values exchange among its actors.

The *VBE governance model* supports the management of an effective corporate governance structure in a collaborative environment. The research results of this work developed in ECOLEAD project present different templates and guidelines that support the VBE governance elements.

Acknowledgments. The information presented in this document is part of the results of the ECOLEAD Project (European Collaborative Networked Organizations Leadership Initiative), funded by the European Community, FP6 IP 506958.

7. REFERENCES

1. Allee, V. (2000). Reconfiguring the Value Network, in Journal of Business Strategy, Volume 21, No. 4, pp. 36-39.
2. Camarinha-Matos, L.M. and Afsarmanesh, H. (2006). "Collaborative Networks: Value creation in a knowledge society" in K. Wang et al (Eds.), Knowledge Enterprise: Intelligent Strategies in Product Design, Manufacturing and Management, International Federation for Information Processing (IFIP), Vol. 207, pp. 26-40, New York: Springer Publisher.
3. Edvinsson, L. and Malone, M. (1997). "Intellectual Capital: Realizing your Company's True Value by Finding Its Hidden Brainpower", in Harper Business Press, New York, NY.

4. EFQM - European Foundation for Quality Management (1999). "EFQM Excellence Model", URL: http://www.efqm.org/

5. Graham, J.; Amos, B. and Plumptre, T. (2003). "Principles of Good Governance in 21st Century", in Policy Brief, IOG Canada.

6. Gordijn, J. and Akkermans, J.M. (2001). "e³-Value: A Conceptual Value Modelling Approach for e-Business Development", in K-CAP Proceedings 2001, First International Conference on Knowledge Capture, Workshop Knowledge in e-Business, pp. 29-36.

7. Hakes, C. (2007). "The EFQM Excellence Model to Assess Organizational Performance - A Management Guide", in Van Haren Publishing.

8. Jimenez, G.; Galeano N.; Nájera, T.; Aguirre, J.M.; Rodríguez C., and Molina, A. (2005). "Methodology for Business Model definition of Collaborative Networked Organizations", in Collaborative Networks and their Breeding Environments, Camarinha-Matos L.M., Afsarmanesh, H., Ortiz, A. (Eds.), in International Federation for Information Processing (IFIP), pp. 346-354, New York: Springer Publisher.

9. Kaplan, R. and Norton, D. (1992). "The Balanced Scorecard: Measures that Drive Performance", in Harvard Business Review 70, No. 1, pp. 71-79.

10. Kaplan, R. and Norton, D. (2006). "Alignment: Using the Balanced Scorecard to Create Corporate Synergies", in Harvard Business School Press.

11. Katz, M. and Shapiro, C. (1985). "Network Externalities, Competition and Compatibility", in American Economic Review, Volume 75, No. 3, pp. 424-440.

12. Kumar, P. (2005). "Driving Globalisation without its Discontents - Roles of Corporates Proceedings of Corporate Governance challenges in a disparate world". (pp 26-32) 2005. London, England.

13. Luthy, D. (1998). "Intellectual Capital and its Measurement", URL: http://www3.bus.osaka-cu.ac.jp/apira98/archives/htmls/25.htm

14. Macedo, P., Sapateiro, C., Filipe, J. (2006). "Distinct Approaches to Value System in Collaborative Networks Environments", in Network-Centric Collaboration and Supporting Frameworks, Camarinha-Matos, L.M., Afsarmanesh, H., and Ollus, M. (Eds.), in International Federation for Information Processing (IFIP), Volume 224, New York: Springer Publisher, pp. 111-120.

15. Osterwalder, A. (2004). "The Business Model Ontology a Proposition in a Design Science Approach", PhD-thesis, in Lausanne University, Switzerland. http://www.hec.unil.ch/aosterwa/PhD/

16. Parolini, C. (1999). "The Value Net Tool for Competitive Strategy", in John Wiley & Sons Ltd Publisher.

17. Porter, M. (1985). Competitive Advantage: Creating and Sustaining Superior Performance, Free Press: New York.

18. Romero, D.; Galeano, N.; Giraldo, J. and Molina, A. (2006). "Towards the definition of Business Models and Governance Rules for Virtual Breeding Environments", in Network-Centric Collaboration and Supporting Frameworks, Camarinha-Matos, L.M., Afsarmanesh, H., and Ollus, M. (Eds.), in International Federation for Information Processing (IFIP), Volume 224, New York: Springer Publisher, pp. 103-110.

19. Romero, D.; Galeano, N. and Molina, A. (2007a). "A Conceptual Model for Virtual Breeding Environments Value Systems", in Establishing the Foundation of Collaborative Networks, Camarinha-Matos L.M., Afsarmanesh, H., Novais, P. and Analide, C. (Eds.), in International Federation for Information Processing (IFIP), Volume 243, New York: Springer Publisher, 2007, pp. 43-52.

20. Romero, D.; Giraldo, J.; Galeano, N., and Molina, A. (2007b). "Towards Governance Rules and Bylaws for Virtual Breeding Environments", in Establishing the Foundation of Collaborative Networks, Camarinha-Matos L.M., Afsarmanesh, H., Novais, P. and Analide, C. (Eds.), in International Federation for Information Processing (IFIP), Volume 243, New York: Springer Publisher, 2007, pp. 93-102.

21. Sveiby, K. (1997). "The New Organizational Wealth: Managing and Measuring Knowledge Based Assets", in Berrett Koehler, San Francisco, CA.

22. Sveiby, K. (2007). "Methods for Measuring Intangible Assets", in Sveiby Knowledge Associates, URL: http://www.sveiby.com/Portals/0/articles/IntangibleMethods.htm

23. Williams, M. (2000). "Is a Company's Intellectual Capital Performance and Intellectual Capital Disclosure Practices Related? Evidence from Publicly listed Companies from the FTSE 100", in McMasters Intellectual Capital Conference, Hamilton, Ontario.

INTER-ORGANIZATIONAL TRUST IN VBEs

Simon Samwel Msanjila, Hamideh Afsarmanesh

University of Amsterdam, THE NETHERLANDS, *msanjila@science.uva.nl, hamideh@science.uva.nl*

Understanding conceptual modeling, assessment and establishment of inter-organizational trust in collaborative networks is challenging. Traditionally, the concept of trust has been addressed at the individuals' level. It is also mostly assumed to be a phenomenon that naturally emerges rather than being created. However, today the concept of trust has become an amenable factor for smoothening inter-organizational collaboration and thus has raised the need to address trust from a new angle. However, the traditional approaches and mechanisms for both assessing the trust level of individuals and/or applying such results for creation of trust are inadequate for analyzing inter-organizational trust. This chapter contributes to the support for understanding the concepts and needs of trust among organizations involved in collaborations. The chapter characterizes inter-organizational trust, presents three modeling formalisms for trust and exemplifies them with some trust models that can be applied for different purposes related to inter-organizational trust in Virtual organization Breeding Environments (VBEs).

1. INTRODUCTION

Establishing trust relationships among organizations in a VBE is a pre-condition for their smooth cooperation. Furthermore, considering that effective creation of Virtual Organizations (VOs) is the main aim of the VBEs, the measurement of trust level of organizations provides fundamental information for establishing trust relationships among organizations. While in a small-size VBE e.g. with 20 to 40 members, organizations may have a good chance to get to know each other, and can therefore have a subjective judgment of the trustworthiness of others, in medium and large-size VBEs, trust analysis of other organizations is a main obstacle for VO creation and a big challenge. Design and development of rational (fact-based) approach for assessing the trust level of organizations is of particular importance for large and very large VBEs, where usually their member organizations may not even be totally known to each other. In this chapter we address trust among organizations. Based on survey on reported research on inter-personal trust, the chapter addresses the aspects of inter-organizational trust. It then presents three trust modeling formalisms.

The remainder of the chapter is structured as follows: Section 2 presents the base concepts of inter-organizational trust and also addresses the motivation and problem description. Section 3 focuses on reported research results on trust in different disciplines. Section 4 addresses the emerging practices and research results on inter-organizational trust in VBEs. Section 5 addresses the main aspects related to inter-organizations trust. Section 6 focuses on modeling trust and trust relationships among organizations. Lastly, section 7 concludes the chapter.

2. BASE CONCEPTS TRUST AND RESEARCH MOTIVATION

This section addresses the base concepts of inter-organizational trust and presents the research motivation.

2.1 Definition of trust and emerging base concepts

In this section we present the base concepts of trust among organizations.

2.1.1 Diversities among definitions of trust

There is no consensus yet in the literature on the definition of trust and what constitutes the management of trust among different entities. Researchers have recognized its importance in smoothing interactions and co-working among individuals as well as organizations (Camarinha-Matos & Afsarmanesh, 2006). They have differently defined trust for the purposes of providing common understand in specific domain or application environment.

Regardless of the attempts to define it in research and the difficult to reach consensus among researchers, the word "trust" as used daily by individuals refers to the opinion of somebody about another person. It is not only an estimation of another's intention but also the possible competencies of others that are needed to establish trust relationships among people. Gambetta (Gambetta, 1988) provided a definition of trust, which has been widely used, *"as the subjective probability by which an individual "A" expects another individual "B" to perform a given action on which A's welfare depends"*. Furthermore, the three following definitions are among the dominant ones in current research works:

- *Trust is the willingness of a trustor to be vulnerable to the actions of another party based on the expectations that the trustee will perform a particular action important to the trustor irrespective of the ability to monitor or control the trustee (Mayer, et al 1995).*
- *Trust is the belief in the competency of an entity to act dependably, securely and reliably within a specified context (Grandison & Sloman , 2000).*
- *Trust is a psychological condition comprising the trustor's intention to accept vulnerability based upon positive expectation of trustee's intentions and behavior (Rousseau, et al 1998).*

The diversity among these definitions (and others) and the difference among their identified elements makes it difficult to properly characterize trust as it needs to be addressed today. As we have pointed out earlier there are many theories on trust, some of which diverge from each other only in their identification of the grounds on which they are based (Settle, 1998). Despite the difficulties in solidifying the definition of trust, in practice the concept of trust is applied daily as a base for cooperation and collaboration among individuals as well as among organizations. Research on CNOs had reported that the effectiveness of the VBE establishments as well as the VO creation depends on the balance of trust level of the organizations.

Therefore, while this work can benefit from the general past research on trust relationships among individuals, their results cannot be directly applied. Trust among organizations in VBEs is a more complex subject, which must be addressed considering the interdisciplinarity among the domains, the heterogeneity and contradiction among interests and goals of involved organizations (Msanjila & Afsarmanesh, 2007a). In our study, *identification and tuning of trust elements, modeling of trust relationships, assessment of trust level, and establishment and promotion of trust relationship* constitute the main focus of the management of trust among organizations in VBEs. The following trust definition is applied in this work:

We define trust among organizations, as it is applied in VBEs, as the objective-specific confidence of a trustor organization to a trustee organization based on the results of rational (fact-based) assessment of trust level of the trustee organization (Msanjila & Afsarmanesh, 2007c).

Therefore, fact-based trust creation refers to the process of creating trust among organizations based on the results of the rational (fact-based) assessment of their trust levels. Only measurable elements (numeric data) are applied for the assessment and the resulted trust levels can be supported with formal reasoning (i.e. mathematical equations) applied during the rational assessment of trust level, which in turn supports reasoning about the results (Msanjila & Afsarmanesh, 2007a).

2.1.2 Base concepts of trust among organizations in VBEs

The following definitions of base concepts of trust among organizations are applied in this work (Msanjila & Afsarmanesh, 2007a).

Trust actors	Refer to the two organization parties involved in a specific trust relationship. The first party is the organization that needs to assess the trustworthiness of another and is referred to as the trustor. The second party is the organization that needs to be trusted, and thus its trust level will be assessed and is referred to as the trustee.
Trust objective	Refers to the purpose for which the trust relationship establishment among the involved organizations is required. Examples of trust objectives include the following: for inviting an organization to join a VO, for selecting an organization as the VO coordinator, for an organization to decide joining a VBE, etc.
Trust perspective	Represents the specific "point of view" of the trustor on the main aspects that must be considered for assessing the trust level of the trustee. Trust perspective guides trustor organizations making decision on what information about trustees should primarily, secondarily, etc., be made available to them to enable them create the required trust level.
Trust criteria	Represent the measurable trust elements that characterize a respective trust requirement. Therefore, for each organization, the values of its trust criteria (related to a requirement) can be used to make a rational (fact-based) judgment on whether the respective requirement is met. Each trust criteria constitutes a value structure that defines the acceptable structure for its data, such as scalars, vectors, arrays, list of strings, etc. Furthermore, the value structure defines the metric that is applied to scale the specified data.

2.2 Motivation and problem area description

In this section we describe the motivation for the research reported in this work by analyzing the existing trust challenges using three example cases.

2.2.1 Example cases for the need of inter-organizational trust in VBE

In order to properly analyze challenges related to the management of trust among organizations we present three example cases showing different levels of complexity faced by trustor organizations while assessing trust level of trustee organizations.

Case I: Virtual organization to deliver expensive and delicate products (VO-CDP)

Consider that a broker has acquired a business opportunity in a market. The opportunity is about delivering expensive and delicate products, such as flat screen

LCD TV, laptops, etc., to the market. The deliverance should meet the large demand of the geographically distributed market. The organizations that shall be involved should be capable of both covering pre-investment such as hiring transport means, and covering all losses that may occur while transporting products.

The broker then decides to appoint a VO planner with the help of the VBE administrator. One important task for the VO planner is to select suitable VO partners among the VBE member organizations. In this case the VO planner must select the most trustworthy organizations for this specific trust objective of inviting them into the VO. Since the main requirements in this VO is that the potential partners must be capable to cover the costs needed for the pre-investments and losses that may occur during the operation phase of the VO, such as damage to the products, the VO planner might primarily prefer to assess the *economical trustworthiness*. Thus the *capital and financial stability* might be considered as the trust requirements (section 4.2.1) that must be met by all potential VO partners. In this case trust criteria whose values must be provided by organizations might include: *cash capital, physical capital, profits on past VOs, operational capital,* etc.

Case II: A virtual organization for providing support to street children (VO-SCS)
In developing countries the problems related to street children (children who are homeless and thus live in streets without proper support of foods, shelters, clothes, etc.) is becoming seriously challenging. Consider an international organization that wants to configure a VO that shall constitute the following two kinds of partners: (1) Organizations capable of providing fund for acquiring resources necessary to support the provision of services to street children in some cities in one country, and (2) Organizations in local cities to deliver services to the designated children.

In such a network, the international organization that then assumes the role of the VO planner takes the social life of these children of importance. Thus the potential VO partners should also have the same perception on the problem. Specifically, taking social support to people to be primarily important than the daily business of the respective organizations must be proved by some rational (fact-based) data. This means that *primarily* the VO planner might assess the *social trustworthiness* of the potential partners. Therefore, factors such as community service provision, community standards commitment (e.g. child labor rules), etc., (section 4.2.2) will be considered for the assessment of their trust levels.

Furthermore, the VO planner prefers that the local partners should be capable of using internal resources, such as employees to deliver the required services. Thus the number of employees, personnel experts, number of branches/offices, organizational competencies, etc., for the local organizations might be secondarily important for the VO planner to apply to the trustworthiness evaluation. Thus the *structural trustworthiness* will *secondarily* be assessed. Lastly, each organization especially the local ones should be able to financially support itself on the activities that are not directly related to the service delivery. For example, when their employees visit the centers where the children are hosted, their traveling costs should be met by the respective organizations. In this case the economical stability of the local partners is needed and thus their *economical trustworthiness will be assessed.*

Case III: A virtual organization for building a parliament house (VO-BPH)
A parliament is a legislature, especially in those countries whose system of government is based on the Westminster system which was modeled after that of the

United Kingdom. The name is derived from the French *"parlement"*, the action of *"parler"* (to speak): a *parlement* is a talk, a discussion, hence a meeting (an assembly, a court) where people discuss matters. A parliament constitutes representatives of different groups of people or organizational representatives and among others they include: government leaders, regional commissioners, province representatives, etc.

The construction of parliament houses is now being addressed very careful in many aspects such as security, facilities, privacy, etc. Configuring a VO to build such house is a challenging task and especially when it comes to selecting potential trustworthy partners to invite into such VO. Such construction not only costs a lot of money but also touches the interests of the entire public in the country and is now demanding modern and complex technologies for both ensuring the security and providing high quality facilitative tools.

Fundamentally, to be selected to join the VO the image of potential partners to the entire public in the country is basically important. Traditionally, the image of an organization is represented by the image of its managerial, both internally and externally. Thus the issues related to the management of organizations, such as experience, stability, past opportunistic behavior, corruption scandals, etc., will be considered to evaluate the *managerial trustworthiness* of potential partners (section 4.2.3). However, since privacy and security of the building must be ensured the technology to be applied must be available and proven. Thus experience and owning the technology within an organization are fundamental factors. This concludes that *primarily* the VO planner may assess both *the managerial and the technological trustworthiness* of potential partners.

Moreover, if an organization has a bad social image to the community, such as failing to meet some community standards, e.g. involved in illegal exporting or importing products, waste water avoidance, industrial waste disposing, etc., is invited to the VO then this may also cause a bad implication in relation to the future of the entire project. Thus social image then becomes second fundamental aspect for the required specific trustworthiness of the potential partners. Furthermore, the construction of such houses is confidentially handled. Despite signing the contract the VO planner might need to show some assurance concerning the issue of keeping the knowledge, such as the security mechanisms of the building, within the involved organizations only. Thus availability of personnel experts, competencies, etc., within an organization also becomes important. Hiring temporary employees from other organizations for the purpose of providing the expertise needed in the project is quite discouraged. Therefore, the specific trustworthiness of potential organizations shall also be assessed in relation to their internal structure. In this case, *secondarily* the VO planner will evaluate both *social and structural trustworthiness* of the potential partners. Lastly, the potential partners must be capable to invest a priori to the first payment. Thus they also need to be financially stable, especially in relation to operational capital. Thus lastly the VO planner might prefer to assess *the economical trustworthiness* of potential partners.

2.2.2 Problem analysis and research focus

The trustors as described in the three example cases above prefer different aspects for evaluating the trustworthiness of potential partners, as summarized in Table 1.

Table 1: Summary of preferences of trustor organizations in the three cases

	VO-CDP	VO-SCS	VO-BPH
Economical trustworthiness			
Social trustworthiness			
Technological trustworthiness			
Managerial trustworthiness			
Structural trustworthiness			

Primary	Secondary	Ternary	No interest

Considering the three cases presented above, a number of open issues must be addressed to support tasks related to the management of trust among organizations. Some open issues include those addressing the:

(a) Difference among preferences of aspects that are considered by trustor organizations to assess trust level of trustee organizations

(b) Variation of requirements and purposes for the assessment of trust level of organizations which in turn influences the perceptions of trust of trustor organizations

(c) Identification of trust elements and development of their related models to support any emerging preference of trustor organizations

(d) Management of fact-based data/values for trust criteria in the VBE for all organizations

(e) Mechanisms to dynamically support the rational assessment of trust level of organizations taking into account such variation of selection of trust criteria

(f) Automation of fundamental processes related to the management of trust among organizations, such as assessing trust level, establishing trust relationships, etc.

(g) Provision and presentation of the trust level of organizations which must be as understandable as possible to all stakeholders regardless of their expertise.

This chapter addresses the trust aspects referred in (a), (b), (c) and (d).

3. TRADITIONAL PRACTICES ON TRUST

Trust is a subject which in recent years has been increasingly getting attention and addressed in both research and practice. The challenges related to trust among individuals has been stated to be of history and in line with the start of human life. In this section we survey existing and reported research work in relation to trust among individuals as well as among organizations.

3.1 Inter-personal versus inter-organizational trust

Many researchers have pointed out that trust is an important issue in smoothing inter-personal and inter-organizational relationships (Hagan & Choe, 1998). However, the research work conducted to address inter-organizational trust, have been focusing on the theoretical standpoint (Currall & Judge, 1995). Nevertheless, in the current information society there are some studies that are addressing trust from practical standpoint and they are producing fundamental empirical evidence on the creation of trust among actors (Smith & Barclay, 1997; Karahannas & Jones, 1999). However, until today there is still no agreement on the exact nature and definition of the trust considering its conceptualization, perception, preference and measurement.

In order to properly: address the trust subject in research, understand the effects of trust in different types of partnerships, and enable produce acceptable results for all stakeholders however; it requires involvement of the communities and other institutions from heterogeneous domains (Smith & Barclay, 1997).

Basically, a certain level of trust is required for smoothing the inter-organizational cooperation (Dibben, 2000). An established climate of trust that is internalized in organizational behavior and supported by mutual belief is necessary for collaborative efforts between partner organizations (Dodgson, 1993). Optimal gains of a network can be achieved through collaboration facilitated by inter-organizational trust, such as reduced costs, greater achievement speed, and improved ability to handle complexity (Arrow, 1974). Furthermore, trust influences organization's long-term strategic plans and orientations, collaborative market performance, loyalty (Chow & Holden, 1997), relationships, commitment, cooperation, functional conflict, uncertainty, the propensity to leave, and acquiescence (Doney & Cannon, 1997). The difficulty in the conceptualization of trust among organizations is in relation to extending what is inherently at an individual-level phenomenon to the organizational level (Zaheer *et al.*, 1998). The confusion and thus an open question is how inter-organizational trust is actually created. Furthermore, the antecedents of inter-personal and inter-organizational trust differ (Msanjila & Afsarmanesh, 2007d). Inter-personal trust is defined at the level of the individual, and represents the extent to which a person places trust in another person. Table 2 presents the summary of comparisons of complexity of trust among individuals and among organizations.

Table 2: Complexities of trust among individuals and among organizations

Trust among individuals (subjective)	Trust among organizations (rational)
Trust creation is traditional and proven	The creation of trust is emerging and unproven
Mechanisms for assessing trust level are known and informal. The assessment applies opinions of others	There is lack of mechanisms for assessing trust level and formal ones are needed. The assessment is based on rational data
The trust related data and their sources are known and are proven	The trust related data and their sources are difficult to define and need verification
Does not necessarily need automated tools for supporting related processes	Needs tools due to the urgency for processing large amount of data
Trust criteria are mostly known and static	Specific criteria are not known & are dynamic
Less interferences in establishing trust relationship	Other stakeholders must be involved while establishing trust relationships

3.2 Trust among individuals

The theory on origins of inter-personal trust (Cosimano, 2004; Lahno, 2004; Lewicki & Tomlinson, 2003) has mainly proceeded along three main fronts of: (1) explaining differences among the individual propensity to trust, (2) understanding diverse dimensions of trustworthy behavior, and (3) suggesting different levels of trust development, as we address below.

* *Individual propensity to trust:* Trust among individuals is regarded as a generalized expectancy that people can be relied on. This expectancy is a function of the degree to which trust has been honored by that individual's history of past social

interactions. Recent work has suggested that both the characteristics of the trustees involved in trust relationships and their trust level vary with time (Gill, et al 2005).

✦   *Dimensions of trustworthy behavior:* Trust among individuals can be grounded into the evaluation of three main specific characteristics, namely: their ability, integrity, and benevolence (Cosimano, 2004). Namely, the more the trustor observes/identifies these three characteristics in trustee, the more it is likely that the level of trust in that trustee grows for the trustor (Msanjila & Afsarmanesh, 2007a).

✦   *Different stages of trust development:* Early theories on trust have described it as a uni-dimensional phenomenon that simply increases (or decreases) the magnitude and strength of a relationship (Ishaya & Mundy, 2004). However, more recent approaches to trust suggest that trust builds along continuous and sequential stages (Lewicki & Tomlinson, 2003). Thus with time, trust may grow to 'higher' levels (or diminish to lower levels), moreover it can become stronger and more resilient, and it can change its characters.

3.3 Trust in different practice disciplines

Trust is a key concept addressed by research in different disciplines and has increasingly gained importance in the emerging info-society. In Table 3 we list the perceptions of trust in some disciplines (Msanjila & Afsarmanesh 2007a).

Table 3: Perceptions of trust

Discipline	Perception
Sociology	Reputation and interactions
Economic	Decision about risky choices
Psychology	Beliefs
Politics (government)	Truth telling
Computer science	Security, reputation, & privacy

4. CHARACTERIZATION OF TRUST IN VBEs

In this section we address the emerging practices and achieved research results on trust among organizations involved in VBEs.

4.1 Main challenges of trust studies in VBEs

In relation to trust studies in VBEs, we have identified three main challenges that must be well addressed in order for trust to be realized and met by the VBE member organizations, VBE administration and external stakeholders as follows:

✦   *Causality:* A main challenge in trust studies is its causality. The future trustworthiness of a VBE member organization is "causally" related to its role and behavior at present, and actions it has performed and events it has caused in the past. Therefore, a part of trust engineering in VBEs is intended to support the decision-making about present and future trustworthiness of a member organization, while the information needed for this estimation mostly belongs to the past.

✦   *Transparency and fairness:* One more challenge in assessment of trust level for VBE member organizations is the transparency and fairness to all stakeholders. Each step taken for entire process of assessing trust level must be clear and transparent to all involved VBE member organizations. For fairness, the steps taken and the approach used for trust level assessment must be accompanied with some (formal) reasoning, and also the information used for the assessment must be accredited/certified to avoid personal (subjective) judgment and biases.

* **Complexity**: Another challenge in trust study in VBEs is the handling for the complexity of multi-objective, multi-perspective, and multi-criteria nature of inter-organizational trust in VBEs. Trust is not a single concept that can be applied for all cases and for trust-based decision making. Trust level measurements are subjected to both the purpose of the trust relationship, and specific actors involved. Every case is different and needs specific trust criteria to apply for assessing trust level.

4.2 Boundary characteristics of rational (objective) and subjective trust

Subjective trust is the most popular form of trust that has been adopted and practiced for smoothing interactions among individuals. However, nowadays collaboration among organizations has become a fundamental approach for co-working in business, such as joining initiatives and efforts for the purpose of enhancing competitive power in the market. In this aspect applying subjective trust concept is difficult as it lacks the reasoning approach and mechanism on the results of the assessment of trust level of organizations (Msanjila & Afsarmanesh, 2007a). Thus rational trust analysis is now becoming popular (Castelfranchi & Falcone, 2000).

Subjective trust is created based on qualitative data and is an opinion-based. Some fundamental sources of information for creating subjective trust among parties include: experience and knowledge of the trustor on the trustee, recommendations of third parties on the trustee, previous interactions, reputation of the trustee, etc.

Rational trust is created based on quantitative data and is a fact-based. The main source of trust related data is the organizational performance which is accumulated in the past from different activities participated, both in collaboration with other partners, and also, as an individual organization. Rational approaches for assessing trust level of organizations apply formal mechanisms, such as mathematical equations, which in turn provide some formal reasoning on the resulted trust level (Msanjila & Afsarmanesh, 2007a).

In addition to the difference in approaches for assessing trust level and their sources of data (see Table 1 and (Msanjila & Afsarmanesh, 2007d), subjective and rational trust also differ in relation to the *"boundaries"* to which they apply. The challenging aspect is related to where do trust boundaries start and end for daily interactions among actors for both rational and subjective trust.

Boundaries for subjective trust
Boundaries for subjective trust can be addressed in relation to the transitivity and propagation nature of trust among the involved actors. Subjectively, trust transitivity means, for example, that if "Alice" trusts "Bob" and "Bob" trusts "Eric" then "Alice" trusts "Eric". This assumes that Bob actually tells Alice that he trusts Eric, which is called a *recommendation*. In social and individual interactions, in which subjective trust is mostly practiced, trust can be assumed as transitive. This is because trust among individuals participating in these interactions is mostly created based on opinions from others. The opinions from others who trust the specific individual are used to create trust to a new trustor. Thus subjective trust is transitive.

It is common to collect advices from several sources in order to be better informed when making decisions. In other words, it is also common to collect several recommendations in order to convince the trustor, such as for job application, on the trustworthiness of the trustee. When the trustor has different sources of recommendations from which he/she can create trust to the specific trustee a specific characteristic of trust transitivity namely *parallelism* emerges.

Since subjective trust is transitive the complex issue is at which point does the propagation ends? The point at which trust propagation ends defines the trust boundary and it is not clear which factors will indicate it. As such even the trust boundary itself is subjective from one trustor to another.

Assume E is an entity representing an actor such that E_1 trusts E_2; E_2 trusts E_3; ... E_j trusts E_{j+1}. Assume also TR refers to trust relationship and TL refers to trust level of trustee. Trust boundary TB for E_1 can be represented in mathematical logics as:

$$\forall \left(E_1, E_j, E_{j+1} \right) \in E, \exists TR \left(E_1, E_{j+1} \right) \Leftrightarrow$$

$$\left\{ \exists TR(E_1 E_2) \wedge \exists TR(E_2 E_3) \wedge \dots \wedge \exists TR \left(E_j, E_{j+1} \right) \right\} \wedge \left\{ TL_{E_2} \leq TL_{E_3} \dots \leq TL_{E_{j+1}} \right\}$$

Boundaries for rational trust

It can be shown that trust is not transitive for objective specific collaborations and transactions for which rational trust is mostly practiced. For example, the fact that Alice trusts Bob to look after her child, and Bob trusts Eric to fix his car, does not imply that Alice trusts Eric for looking her child, or for fixing her electric lamp. This is because the trust objectives in the two cases differ. Rational trust is created based on facts and applying formal mechanisms in which different cases will have different preferences. As such the value of trust level in this case is not absolute and cannot be transferred to different cases. This is the reason why rational trust fits better than subjective trust for smoothing organizations' objective specific collaborations. Thus rational trust is not transitive.

Rationally, trust boundary does not exist since trust is created based on the preferred perspective. Different trustor can prefer different perspectives to trust the same trustee. When the same set of trust criteria is preferred for all trustors then at the end the same trust level shall be achieved independent of the trustor. Therefore, rational trust does not propagate among involved actors and thus all trustors shall trust their respective trustee based on their own preferred perspective. *The open question is what happens when the same trustor changes its preference on trust and thus changes the trust perspective. Can transitivity exist between two perspectives when the same trustor changes its preferences?*

4.3 Main concepts related to inter-organizational trust

Trust is related to different concepts and these relations either complement (such as trust and security, reputation, co-working) or contradict (such as trust versus risks, privacy, etc.) its perceptions among actors. In this section we address trust in relation to five concepts.

4.3.1   *Trust versus risks*

Risk is a concept that denotes a potential negative impact to an asset or some characteristics of a value that may arise from some present processes or future events. In everyday usage, "risk" is often used synonymously with the probability of a known loss. Many definitions of risk depend on specific application and situational contexts. Frequently, risk is considered as an indicator of threat. It can be assessed qualitatively or quantitatively. Qualitatively, risk is considered proportional to the expected losses which can be caused by an event and to the probability of this event. The harsher the loss and the more likely the event, the greater the overall risk. Measuring risk is often difficult; the probability is assessed by the frequency of the past similar events, which in fact is difficult to link to real future.

Trust and risk are negatively related. When there is a high chance that certain risks can arise in an environment it is very hard for an organization to trust others in the environments. Moreover, when organizations trust each other they tend to relax and rely on each other with the feeling that risks may not arise which in fact increases the chance of risks arising due to less caring. The relation between the concept of trust and risks is further addressed in (Msanjila & Afsarmanesh, 2007d).

4.3.2   Trust and security
The inter-play of trust and security can be looked at from different aspects. The two most popular ones that are also addressed here are: first in respect to the management systems, and second in respect to the technologies owned by and available to organizations.

❖ *Trust and security for management systems*
Until a few years ago, enhancing security of systems that are used for the management of information, resources, stored knowledge, available skills, etc., was the fundamental approach to enhance trust among collaborating organizations. Since then and even currently the situation has changed dramatically: new security regulations, significant security, privacy incidents, etc. are not enough to assure smooth operations for business organizations in the current market which faces continuously increasing turbulent conditions (Grandson & Sloman, 2000). Thus the involvement of both business organizations and ICT industries in finding the solution and the balance between trust and security in relation to the ICT systems and the facilitated businesses is now fundamental.

From business aspects, security is mostly about managing risks, and in this case related to ICT facilitative tools. The current market is characterized with turbulent conditions, such as among others: scarce resources, lack of knowledge and skills, volatile business opportunities, changing and emerging unique customer requirements. Thus enhancing security of the ICT systems and managing the related risks do not fully guarantee organizations' success and survival in such market.

An ICT system can provide the right level of security whether or not it keeps the risks for business at an acceptable level. What counts for each risk, are the potential losses due to malicious acts by disgruntled employees, hackers, unauthorized users, etc. Whether a risk is acceptable or not is a business decision and is not only influenced by the state of the ICT system but also with many more different factors, such as behavior of other partners, changes of business requirements, etc., in relation to the system (Msanjila & Afsarmanesh, 2007c). To describe the security level and to demonstrate that an ICT system meets that level is a fundamental challenge in computer science, and specifically in relation to management of trust among organizations. It is more challenging today when organizations must collaborate to together acquire and respond to opportunities. This collaboration needs geographically distributed supports from ICT systems. *What level of security is enough to support the creation of inter-organizational trust in such environment?*

Security of ICT system alone is not enough to smoothen the cooperation and collaboration among organizations, and thus guaranteeing the needed successes and survivability. As a result, the security boundaries among organizations are quickly becoming less and less strict. Thus trust propagation based on security of ICT system is decreasing and becoming rationally specific. Applications that used to run on dedicated servers now are running on virtual environments, sharing infrastructure with others, using physical resources that are widely distributed (Rabelo, et al 2006). This makes the process of creating inter-organizational trust applying system security even more difficult.

Because of the amplification of problems related to: security of ICT systems, risks associated with businesses which are supported with ICT systems, market turbulences, etc., some other approaches for smoothing the co-working environments, such as VBEs, are needed and must be looked upon. Managing trust among organizations, by applying rational mechanisms for assessing trust level and creating trust, has emerged to be one of the promising approaches for providing the required smoothing (Msanjila & Afsarmanesh, 2007a). In our approach systems – Trust Management systems - are suggested to support organizations perform the tasks related to creating their trust to others. A number of processes need to also be automated to provide the required semi-automatic services for management of trust among organizations as addressed in (Msanjila & Afsarmanesh, 2007e).

✦ *Trust and security in relation to owned and experienced technologies*

There has been a misconception about trust and security, and the role that technology plays in this binomial for setting/facilitating collaboration. Most people tend to believe that trust is merely the result of security - when it is secure, actors can trust each other - but researchers have observed that this is not the complete picture (Rousseau, et al 1998). Trust is a wider concept and its link with security is not linear (Msanjila & Afsarmanesh, 2007c). Technology can effectively provide security, for example, every step of an online transaction has one or more procedures for transmitting users' data safely, such as using cryptography, protocols, etc., technologies. This does not mean trust though. Security driven approaches for creating trust among organizations have led to a bias that is named "*the double illusion of 100% safe*" (Ulivieri, 2004).

It is said that technology is always deceptive: it is safe until it is violated. Every secure environment will soon become insecure, because technical innovation works both on the good side of security protocols and on the bad side of hacking processes. Technology can only make this breaking moment as far in time as possible (Grandison & Sloman, 2000). Organizations that assume the security of the environment, which is enhanced by the technology, as the only means to trust others might face difficult when unexpected problems occurs, such as hacking of software (Msanjila & Afsarmanesh, 2007c). This is the first illusion.

Consider a moment that a secure environment is obtained. Organizations can act freely and confidently because they are protected by technology. However this is not a trust building atmosphere because the importance of trust increases when there is a chance of some risks happening (Rousseau, et al 1998). An environment depicted with hard technology protection deteriorates trust building: organizations feel the security but not necessarily the trust. This is the second illusion.

4.3.3   Trust versus privacy

At individual level, privacy can be seen as a fundamental human right. Similarly, organizations are now facing the problem of privacy and specifically, in relation to confidential data and strategies. Different mechanisms have been proposed to protect the privacy of organizational data in the world of computers, both legislative and technological, depending on whether privacy is seen as a right, which should be protected by laws; or a need, which should be supported by devices (Msanjila & Afsarmanesh, 2007c). From the privacy point of view and considering the co-working among organizations, there is an inherent conflict between trust and privacy: the more knowledge a first entity gains about a second entity, the more accurate will be the result of trust level assessment. But the more knowledge is gained about the second entity, the less privacy is left to this entity (Seigneur & Jensen, 2004). Due to this contradiction enhancing trust level of organizations while enhancing their privacy is a challenge for further research.

4.3.4   Trust and reputation

Reputation is the general opinion (more technically, a social evaluation) of the public toward a person, a group of people, or an organization. It is an important factor in many domains, such as business, online communities or social status. Reputation is known to be a ubiquitous, spontaneous and highly efficient mechanism of social control in natural societies. It is a subject which is being studied in social, management and technological sciences. Furthermore, reputation acts on different levels of agency, individual and supra-individual. At the supra-individual level, it focuses on groups, communities, collectives and abstract social entities (such as firms, corporations, organizations, countries, cultures and even civilizations). It affects phenomena at different scales, from everyday life to relationships between nations. There are two kinds of reputation namely witness reputation and certified reputation (further addressed in (Msanjila & Afsarmanesh, 2007d)).

Individual's reputation management involves recording a person's actions and the opinions of others about those actions. These records can then be published in order to allow other people (or agents) to make informed decisions about whether to trust that person or not. A reputation management system, especially as applied in multi-agent technologies and which uses pre-programmed criteria for reputation management, automates the process of encouraging cooperative behaviour over selfish behaviour. Reputation has been applied in different disciplines to study the relations among entities and their trustworthiness.

4.3.5   Trust and organizational virtual co-working

The emerging economy is knowledge-based and without borders, where the competition is among organizations - local and international – on how to learn faster and organize more flexibly to take advantage of "technology-enabled" market (Fowler & Wackerbarth, 1980). Within this new economy, the ICTs are ubiquitous. They have transformed geographically separated locales into a "global village" for information sharing, organizational interactions, and exchange of economical value. Technology, in particular, ever-expanding digital bandwidth, has resulted in creation of new economy forms of intangible, knowledge-based capital, the value of which now exceeds that of the physical capital that dominated old economies (Afsarmanesh & Camarinha-Matos, 2005). Whereas business models for old economy emphasized tasks and roles organizationally, business models for the new economy focus on self-organizing: teams, companies, and industry-based clusters, or CNOs. Organizations have now realized that by virtually co-working, such as in CNOs, they can enhance their chance to jointly meet continuous changing requirements of "innovation-demanding" opportunities more effectively (Camarinha-Matos & Afsarmanesh, 2006). There are three questions that need to be addressed when thinking about technology in relation to virtual co-working (Msanjila & Afsarmanesh, 2007c): (1) What are the distinguishing factors, which separate ICT-enabled collaboration in physical from virtual settings? (2) Can previous findings on physical collaboration help us to understand the characteristics of emerging virtual collaborations? (3) How does the creation of trust differ for physical collaborations and for virtual collaborations?

Innovative organizations that employ technology to facilitate collaborative projects are the hallmark of the new economy (Camarinha-Matos & Afsarmanesh, 2006). Such collaborations can range from arms-length information sharing to highly inter-dependent and geographical dispersed joint projects. In large VBEs, organizations cooperate/collaborate with others that sometimes are physically unknown to them. These organizations must trust each other in order to effectively work together. Basically, in the current innovative-based economy trustees must possess the technology which can facilitate the virtual co-working.

Moreover, the current economy demands ability to acquire and possess competitive information and knowledge. Technologies are playing a great role in efficiently achieving such organizations' goals. The number of domains where technical artifacts are filtering communications and relationships is increasingly growing: computer supported interactions, computer supported co-work, e-commerce, or even e-mails are just few examples of this trend. The importance of trust, considering the technology side, is twofold: (1) it can be seen as trust towards the technical system (i.e. in electronic payments), and (2) trust in the technology as a mediator of interactions among actors. Therefore, when setting-up technologically related collaboration, organizations that possess required technologies are assessed technologically trustworthy.

5. ASPECTS OF ORGANIZATIONAL TRUSTWORTHINESS

Most reported research results have addressed trust among organizations considering few aspects and in most cases applying a single point of view. In our research we have identified five trust perspectives that can be preferred by trustor organizations. These trust perspectives are technological, structural, economical, social, and managerial, (Msanjila & Afsarmanesh, 2007c). The *technological perspective* is in detailed addressed in (Msanjila & Afsarmanesh, 2007c) and the *structural perspective* is thoroughly addressed in (Msanjila & Afsarmanesh, 2007a). This section briefly describes the technological and structural aspects and then in detail addresses economical, social and managerial aspects of inter-organizational trust.

The technological aspects of inter-organizational trust

The current new economy is a knowledge-based economy without borders, where competition, in addition to winning business, is now in acquiring and owning technology for both communication and delivery of products/services. The technology in this case can play two roles: (1) facilitating the collaborations among organizations in a collaborative consortium, acting as communication infrastructure, and (2) applied in production being used as resources (e.g. machines, computers, etc.). Thus the organizations possessing technologies which thoroughly address these two aspects will be assessed technologically trustworthy. As stated above the technological perspective is further addressed in (Msanjila & Afsarmanesh, 2007c). The trust criteria subordinated to technological perspective are shown in Table 4.

The structural aspects of inter-organizational trust
As an organization grows: in size, in geographical scope (coverage), and in abilities (competences and expertise), etc. which are key elements of structural perspective, it improves its structural performance. Thus, it enhances its capability to transform, collaborate and cooperate, and so its structural trustworthiness is raised. As stated earlier the structural perspective is further described in (Msanjila & Afsarmanesh, 2007a). Trust criteria subordinated to structural perspective are shown in Table 4.

The economical aspects of inter-organizational trust
The today's technologies and the volatility of opportunities have encouraged organizations to start investigating and deploying the values of trust that can be achieved through the economical successes. With the current advances of information and communication technologies (ICTs), it is difficult for organizations to keep information about their business strategies and investment plans confidential. Simultaneously, government policies have been encouraging collaboration among organizations (Assimakopoulos & Macdonald, 2002), which in turn requires extensive sharing of economical data. While organizations are not willing to let their competitors access their potential business data and thus are only looking for advanced mechanisms to enhance their privacy, the emerged forms of collaborative networks, such as VBEs, VOs, etc., encourage openness and sharing. The challenging issue is related to selecting the trustworthy partners to share such strategic economical information. The dilemma remains on what information to open and at what level of openness will be acceptable to all stakeholders. One crucial economical advantage of inter-organizational trust is the reduction of transaction costs for organizational collaborations and specifically related to the need of extensive management (Dyer & Chu, 2003). The following are the key counts of economical aspects for creating trust among organizations in VBEs (Msanjila & Afsarmanesh, 2006a):

(1) Collaborative *economical success and survival* of organizations in VBE is dependent on the trust among them,
(2) The possibility of finding *scarce resources and lacking knowledge* owned by other partners depends on the intensity of trust among involved organizations,
(3) Trust among organizations reduces the frequency of occurrence of *financial risks* such as by discouraging opportunistic behavior,
(4) Trust among organizations enhances the *interoperability* among business processes at different organizations.

Based on economical perspective, trustors need to access economical data for assessing trust level that will persuade them to trust the trustees. The trust criteria of this perspective (Table 4) are addressed in (Msanjila & Afsarmanesh, 2007c).

The social aspect of inter-organizational trust

A precise definition of social trust is difficult to pin down, but it has been encapsulated as an ongoing motivation for social relations that form a basis for interactions. At individual level, social trust can entail perceived honesty, objectivity, consistency, competency, and fairness, all of which foster relationships among individuals that must be maintained by the sustained fulfillment of these elements (Boslego, 2005). It has been described by several trust experts that decision to trust based on social perspective is a "risk judgment:" a form of cooperation that has no immediate payoff or benefit and gambles that the trusted party will act as expected (Good, 1988). The aspects of social trust are not universal, but vary in cultures, contexts, countries, etc.

Basically, people may trust their relatives, co-workers, classmates, friends, and even their friends' friends, but the puzzle of social trust is the idea of trusting strangers. The difficult for a person to trust a stranger is similar to that an organization faces when need to trust another organization that it had never interacted with it before and thus is completely unknown. The only basis for whether to socially trust other organizations is their social performance and status, which may be influenced by their ethnic or cultural group, the characteristics and values of the society in which they were registered and they are currently operating, and their past experiences and interactions, and more broadly the historical tradition of their society (Msanjila & Afsarmanesh, 2006a). *A practical challenge is what to do when social trust has fallen? Should organizations with many racial, religious, and ethnic problems resign themselves to low level of trust, or can trust be somehow re-engineered?* Social trust is a public good that should be maximized and thus it is non-excludable, non-competitive, and does not result in direct profit but benefits organizations and society indirectly. It must be re-engineered with time and must be at the optimal level whenever needed.

In VBEs, organizations must enhance their trust to the society in which they are operating. Social trust of an organization is very important to enable it keep moral acceptance to the market and society in which it is operating its business. For social trust, the internal achievements of the organization get little weight than its external social achievements. Trust criteria for social perspective are shown in Table 4 and further addressed in (Msanjila & Afsarmanesh, 2007c).

The managerial aspect of inter-organizational trust

The need for agile and responsive organizations has been widely publicized in today's technologically enabled and competitive market. This has driven the shift to new organizational structures and processes to support this agility. The organizations of this century cannot remain static. They must constantly respond to the dynamic environments. Even more, they must also learn to take a proactive stance, sometimes even creating changes. To be in a static mode may very well mean an organization will be left in the dust of their competitors when the market and technology advance (Msanjila & Afsarmanesh, 2007c).

Changes, uncertainties and complexities that are characterizing the greatest challenges in today's world and especially the virtual world, also present challenges to managers in all levels. Responding to changes in the external environments requires ever-vigilant managers. Managers must be agile themselves in order to effectively promote agility in their organizations. The required agilities include:

flexibility in managing and competing for VBE rewards, ability to flexibly and collaboratively plan, flexibility in collaborative problem solving, technological agility, and flexibility in addressing VBE politics (Msanjila & Afsarmanesh, 2006a).

Table 4: Trust elements for organizations

Perspective	Requirements	Criteria
Structural	Structural strength	Size
		Competences
		Personnel expertise
	Business strength	Geographical coverage
		Joint ventures
		Centres
		Workload allocation
Social	Community participation	Activities participated
		Service contribution
	Community compliance	Standards complied
Economical	Capital	Cash
		Physical
		Material
	Financial stability	Cash in
		Cash out
		Profit/Loss
		Operational costs
	VO financial stability	Cash in
		Cash out
		Profit/Loss
	Financial standards	Auditing standards
		Auditing frequency
Technological	ICT- Infrastructure	Network speed (Broadband)
		Interoperability
		Availability
	Technology standards	Protocol supported
		Software standards
		Hardware standards
		Security standards
	Platforms	Operating systems
		Programming languages
	Platform experience	Applied in VOs
		External project applied
		Duration held
Managerial	Stable management	Years in power
		Management structure
		Frequency of power change
	VO-Collaborative behaviour	VO opportunistic behaviour occurred
		VO successful collaborations
		VO leadership history
	Reliability	Quality
		Adherence to delivery dates

Although the palpability of trust is known to organizations in the VBE, but it still proves difficult to create. Management cannot be successful without acquiring trust to those who they are managing whether at the level of the organization or at the level of the VBE. There are two possibilities from which a trustor organization can create trust to a trustee organization based on managerial aspects:

- The trustor organization can trust the trustee organization only focusing on the current tasks or roles, and specifically on aspects of managerial *competency* to fulfill those particular roles or tasks. This kind of trust is referred to as *situational-based rather than relational-based*. For example, business organizations do trust credit card companies that they can handle the financial transactions taking place all over the world via their cards. However, these business organizations can hardly trust those organizations to train their employees on financial management. This *competence-based trust* is rationally developed and need authorized evidence. It can emerge quickly and it does not require previous interactions.
- The trustor organization can also trust the trustee organization by assessing and evaluating its *motivations*. This kind of trust takes much longer time to develop because both actors must be able to *understand and experience each other's intentions*. The difficulty is that managers might have self- interests that might lower the trustworthiness of their organizations. This kind of trust needs rational data based on previous performance of managers.

For some purposes, a trustor organization may consider managerial history of the trustee organization as the primary aspect when assessing its trust level. In this manner, the trust assessment is based on how well the trustee professionally behaved and how well it used its power when it gets into the management position in past networks such as in VOs. Trust criteria for managerial perspective are shown in Table 4 and further addressed in (Msanjila & Afsarmanesh, 2007c).

6. APPROACHES FOR MODELING TRUST RELATIONSHIPS

The support for understanding of trust and trust relationships among trust actors must be properly addressed considering their key role in VBEs. In this section we address modeling of trust and trust relationships among organizations which can assist with conceptual and common understanding of the concepts related to trust among organizations. Section 6.1 presents a survey on related research on trust models and section 6.2 addresses modeling of trust among organizations in VBEs.

6.1 Related research on trust modeling

This section addresses four existing trust models that although they seem to be applied in different environments than VBEs, each one addresses specific aspects that are related to VBEs.

i)   A trust model for inter-organizational network effectiveness

This trust model is proposed to support and provide guidelines (act as a driver) to organizations involved in collaboration or cooperation as a means for enhancing the chance of achieving their common or compatible goals, and thus raising the effectiveness of their collaborative network. The focus of this model is on how inter-organizational networks can benefit from and influence the strategic resource acquisition (Figure 1) (Wever, et al 2005).

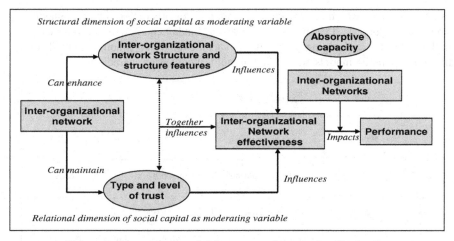

Figure 1: Conceptual model for trust and network effectiveness

This proposed model addresses factors that are related to the structural and relational dimension of social capital built among organizations in a network. Based on this model organizations can analyze the effectiveness of their networks considering the following aspects:

+ How collaboration among organizations influences the possibility to achieve common goals?
+ How do achievements of common goals enhance network's effectiveness?
+ How trust affects organizations' collaboration especially in relation to sharing and exchanging information, resources, etc.?
+ What are the relations between network performance and organizations' performance?

Figure 1 shows the influences among a number of factors addressing the above questions. It also shows how those factors influence the network performance.

ii) Taxonomy-based trust model to assist understanding in multi-agent systems
There have been a significant growth and experience in the field of multi-agent systems in both research and practice in the recent years. As applied in collaborative networks, an agent represents an organization rather than an individual or a system. A challenging issue in this field is related to the provision of support which is needed to facilitate cooperation among different agents and fundamentally is related to the computation of their reputations. Several researchers have addressed this challenge and a number of reputation models have appeared in literature offering solutions to this problem. However, most solutions use their own concepts, terminologies to represent reputation models, and manipulation mechanisms (Figure 2). Consequently, it is difficult to achieve a common understanding of reputation evaluation among agents using different reputation systems.

Pinyol (et al 2007) proposes a trust model based on ontology, which aims at assisting agents with achieving common understanding and specifically related to their mechanisms applied to computing reputations. A number of characteristics are considered and included in the ontology as visualized in Figure 2 (Pinyol, et al 2007). The key elements considered in the model are the belief of an agent and its social evaluation, which are affected by a number of other subordinate elements as shown in Figure 2. The model proposes a fundamental solution that can be implemented for exchanging the results of social evaluations among agents that use different reputation models are applied in multi-agent system paradigm.

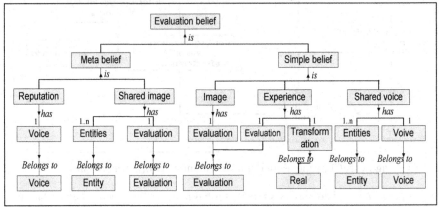

Figure 2: The taxonomy, membership relations, and components of evaluation of belief

iii) *Federation of Identity and Cross- Credentialing Systems (FiXS)*

This trust model defines the underlying foundation to guide common operating rules and legal procedures for the Federation of Identity and Cross- Credentialing Systems. It facilitates all participants and advisors to maintain their existing security systems and policies intact while strengthening their credentialing processes to achieve a balanced trust level in a shared infrastructure. The model is based on the concept of community trust and brokered trust (Figure 3) (Fix, www.fix.org).

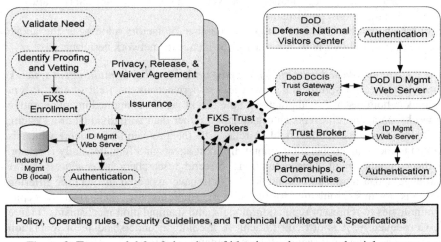

Figure 3: Trust model for federation of identity and cross-credential systems

iv) *An integrated model of trust for e-commerce applications*

In order to study trust in electronic commerce relationships, Kini and Choobineh (1998) developed a theory that provides a strong theoretical foundation for evaluating factors that influence its behavior. The model consists of four dimensions

as shown in Figure 4, namely based on the: (1) Assumption that trust in an on-line system is a function of the characteristics of the person making the transaction, (2) On-line system itself which is supporting the required transactions, (3) Task for which the system is being used, and (4) Information and its source environment.
All four dimensions, as shown in Figure 4, influence the creation of trust among the involved partners in the e-commerce transactions and as well to the system.

In their study Kini and Choobineh (1998) proposed that *personal* characteristics of an individual determine his/her readiness to trust. Trust of an individual is dependent on her/his *Tendency to Trust* (TTT). It is shown that when confronted with novel situations, people with a high TTT are more willing to trust others. To further understand the TTT in a certain specific transactions it is important to study the kinds of *task* that need trust among involved partners and to focus on means of fostering and developing trust in these tasks in order to ensure that *electronic commerce systems* can be developed for a wide range of applications.

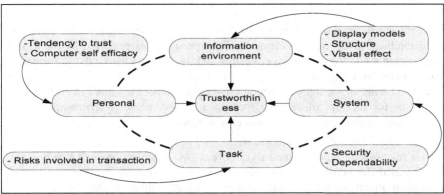

Figure 4: An integrated model of trust for E-commerce application

The characteristics of the system with which the user interacts are critical in developing and maintaining trust among participating partners in e-commerce based transactions. Security, dependability and reliability are the important fact for the trustworthiness of the system.

The *information environment* can be seen as two different entities, namely: the environment presented by the system, and the external environment that might influence the perception of users to the system, (e.g. news media). The environment presented by the system should be correctly perceived and understood by the user. In this aspect, presentation and organization of the information are critical issues that must be taken into account in order to successfully adopt the technology.

The external environment influences trust creation among actors by providing the knowledge or the information about various aspects of the Internet, and contributes to the overall perception about the trustworthiness of the system.

6.2 Modeling inter-organizational trust in VBEs

In order to precisely model trust relationships among organizations, and their related components, we have chosen to define models based on three formalisms, namely: *record-based formalism, object-based formalism, and ontology-based formalism*

(Msanjila & Afsarmanesh, 2007b). A priori to modeling trust one challenging task is in fact selecting and classifying the aspects and factors that must be included in a model. Another challenge is ensuring that the model incorporates and covers all concepts as perceived in the targeted domain or by the users of the model.

Main parameters applied to modeling trust:
We have classified the modeling parameters that must be included in models for trust relationships among organizations into three groups as addressed below.

   i) *Trust relationship actors: Trustor and Trustee*
The two parties of the trust relationship, namely: the trustor organization and the trustee organization are very important for defining, modeling, and creating trust between them. Generally, a variety of factors might be required by different trustor organizations for assessing trust level of the same trustee organizations, even with the same "trust objective". Therefore, it is important that both trustor organization and trustee organization are represented in the trust relationship model distinctively.

   ii) *Trust elements: Trust perspectives*
Some models defined here include trust elements at high-level while other considers all hierarchical levels of trust elements. Trust perspectives preferred by the trustor organization guide the process of collecting and deciding on the kind of information that it prefer to apply for assessing the trust level of the trustee organization. As described earlier in section 4.2 there are five trust perspectives that can be preferred by trustor for the aim of creating trust to a trustee, namely: *Structural, Social, Economical, Technological and Managerial perspectives.*

   iii) *Time: Past, Present and Future*
A trust relationship (and its intensity) between two organizations is a timely issue, which may differ considering yesterday, today, and tomorrow. In other words, trust level of an organization is not static and may vary depending on changes in the trust criteria applied, the values of the trust criteria, involved organizations, specific ratings, etc. All these factors that might influence the changes of the trust level of organizations are time sensitive. Thus time is an important factor, and must be properly addressed in modelling trust relationships among organizations in VBEs.

6.2.1   Object-based formalisms
Object-oriented modeling (OOM) has become the de-facto standard in the early phases of a software development process during the recent years. The current state-of-the-art is dominated by the existence of the Unified Modeling Language (UML), the development of which has been initiated and pushed by industry (Finkelstein, 2000). In this modeling approach, modelers can develop three kinds of models namely: *static models, structural models, and transitional models.* In our research we apply the concepts for developing static models (Figure 5).

   The main aim for developing the trust model by applying object-based formalism is to represent the trust elements as objects, which will provide us with proper way of studying their cardinality relations among these trust elements. Thus in object-based formalism, trust elements are modeled as objects and their cardinalities are indicated to show the relations among the objects for trust elements and also to represent relevant details necessary to define the trust relationship model. Figure 5 shows an objective-based trust relationship model.

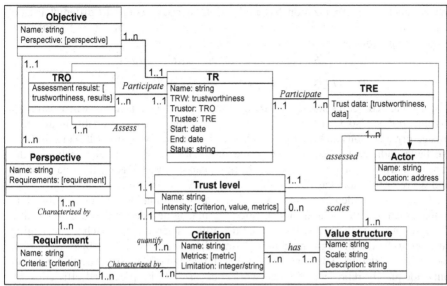

Figure 5: Object based model for trust relationship among member organizations

6.2.2   *Record-based formalisms*

Using this formalism we model trust relationships as record (e.g. relational data model) of their components. Equation (i) shows general representation of a single trust relationship between the trustor and the trustee. In this model and others presented here, **TR** refers to trust relationship, **TRO** refers to trustor organization, **TRE** refers to trustee organization, **TL** refers to trust level and **constr** refers to constraints. The **status** indicates whether the TR is past, present or future.

$$TR = [TRO, TRE, TL, start\_date, status];$$
$$TL = [Perspective, (requirements, (criteria))];$$
$$Criteria = [value\_constr, value\_metric] \quad\text{.....................(i)}$$

When the respective trustor organization has multiple trust relationships to the same trustee organization the attributes: *TL, start-date* and *status* of *TR* record become repeating attributes. The repeating attributes are closed by parentheses. The repeating attributes representation takes into account the fact that although the actors are the same but it is possible for each trust relationship between the trustor organization and the trustee organization there might be different trust level. While the records for *TL* and *criteria* remain the same, the *TR* record changes as in (ii).

$$TR = [TRO, TRE, (TL, start\_date, status)] \quad\text{..................(ii)}$$

Furthermore, it is possible for a trustor organization to have many trust relationships to different trustee organizations (equation iii). A single trustee can also have many trust relationships to different trustors (equation iv). Moreover, these TR can have dissimilar intensity due to different trust levels of the participating actors.

$$TR = [TRO, (TRE, TL, start\_date, status)] \quad\text{................................(iii),}$$
$$TR = [TRO, (TRE, (TL, start\_date, status))] \quad\text{................................(iv)}$$

When the trustee organization has multiple trust relationships to different trustor organizations, the inverse of the records in equation (iii) and (iv) become the required equations as shown in equations (v) and (vi).

$$TR = [TRE, (TRO, TL, start\_date, status)] \quad\quad\quad\quad\text{.................(v)},$$

$$TR = [TRE, (TRO, (TL, start\_date, status))] \quad\quad\quad\quad\text{.................(vi)}$$

The formalized representation of trust relationships among actors when a trustor organization is also a trustee organization at the same time and probably to different trustee organizations and trustor organizations respectively is difficult. For this case, we have addressed it using an example of record based trust relationship model represented in a diagrammatic form. In this example we focus on the relationships and we refer the model as relationship-based model, as shown in Figure 6.

One most challenging but key task towards automating processes related to management of trust among organizations is managing needed data for supporting the assessment of their trust level. Traditionally, a scientific approach for managing structured data is through maintaining some databases. The main objective of data modeling in relation to databases is providing a design of data structure that does not only adequately represents the real world but also can be processed efficiently by database management systems. As it is desired to automate processes related to management of trust among organizations, similarly applies to the management of trust related data. Thus trust related data must be also managed using some automated systems in order to enhance its exploitation's effectiveness.

Most existing databases and database management systems follow relational approach. To enhance the interoperability and the sharing of the trust related data managed by the TrustMan system, and also to ease the access to the database the design and implementation of its database adopted relational approach. In relational database, data is represented in terms of records. Thus with the record-based trust models the schemas for relational database can in fact be generated. Therefore, in our design and implementation of the system for management of trust related data of organizations we apply the record-based trust models to define relational database schemas detailing the required records (types) and respective attributes (columns). Based on the classification of trust elements as presented in (Msanjila & Afsarmanesh, 2007e) we have designed three different schemas, namely: *scheme for trust element data, schema for general organizational data, and schema for organizational trust related data* (Msanjila & Afsarmanesh 2007e).

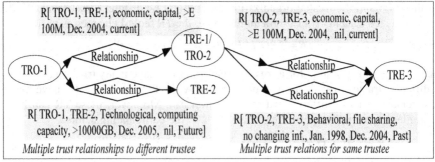

Figure 6: Relationship based model for multiple participations of organizations

6.2.3 Ontology-based formalisms

In information sciences and engineering, an ontology refers to 'an explicit specification of conceptualization', 'a theory or a system of concepts/vocabulary used as building blocks for information processing systems', 'the representation for the semantics of terms and their relationships'. VBEs environments are known by their dynamic characteristics, such as in their environments, objectives, member organizations, etc. New ontologies will continue to emerge and the existing ones will also be evolving and thus ontology will also evolve (Figure 7).

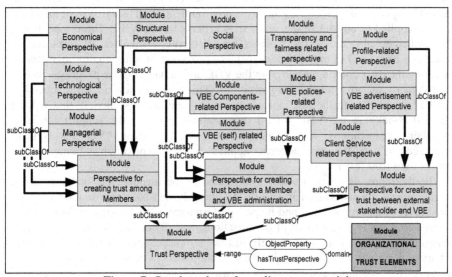

Figure 7: Ontology-base formalism trust model

The effectiveness of assessment of trust level of organizations and acceptability of the results will be influenced by the common understanding among involved parties, including trustor organizations, trustee organizations, VBE administrators, and other stakeholders. One approach for supporting common understanding is providing them with an ontology which shall describe the concepts and terms applied for various elements, features, principles, approaches, mechanisms and software tools (Afsarmanesh & Ermilova, 2007a). Specifically for supporting the common understanding we have developed ontology for classifying the taxonomical relations among trust elements (Msanjila & Afsarmanesh, 2007b). For the VBE environment and specifically for the needed understanding to semi-automatically facilitate the cooperation and collaboration the ontology is in detail described and included in the *Ontology Discovery and Management System* (ODMS) (Afsarmanesh, et al 2007).

7. CONCLUSION

This chapter addresses trust among organizations when they are involved in collaborative/cooperative activities. Five fundamental aspects related to rational trust measures of organizations which have been used in different practices are addressed, namely: the technological, structural, social, managerial and economical aspects. The chapter also presents main concepts related to inter-organizational trust.

Furthermore, the chapter introduces the modeling formalisms that can be applied to model inter-organizational trust, namely: an object-based formalism, a record-based formalism and an ontology-based formalism. Example models are presented for each modeling formalism.

For management of trust among organizations the VBE administrator and other actors can apply the approach presented in this chapter. The fundamental contribution of the addressed approach include: (1) the possibility to reflect the aspect of specific importance in the VBE environment, such as value system, which can be applied to customize the set of trust criteria for the VBE. These aspects can be applied to also define the weights for trust criteria involved in formulas for assessing trust level of organizations, (2) The provision of transparency in VBEs on defining the trust criteria measured in the VBE and in handling the processes related to balancing the trust level of organizations. This transparency can be practiced in VBEs by announcing the common elements of "rational trust model" that will be applied equally in the VBE for all organizations, and (3) the support for VBE member organizations to understand this step of their "VO involvement preparedness" and the main concepts applied to the system which is being used to assess their trust level.

Furthermore, three main challenges related to the management of trust among organizations are introduced in section 4.1, namely: (1) causality relation between trust level of an organization and its past performance, (2) transparency and fairness related to assessing trust level of organizations, and (3) complexity of trust and its measurement. This chapter has mainly addressed the challenge related to complexity of trust. Rational trust of organizations is addressed as a multi-objective, multi-perspective, and multi-criteria aspect. Trust level measurements are subjected to both the purpose of the trust relationship, and the specific actors involved. Furthermore, every case is different and needs specific trust criteria to be applied for assessing trust level of organizations.

To clearly analyze the causality relations between trust level of an organization and its past performance, real data needs to be collected in a relatively long period of time, and get analyzed to capture the actual causalities. The collected data and the results from a number of trust analysis works can be used to examine the applicability and validity of our suggested approaches in capturing causalities. The approaches and tools proposed in this chapter and also in our past publications are now put to practice in several industry-based VBE networks. The causal analysis applied to the trust criteria in our current trust assessment formulas are rooted in the general published results in the area of economy and social science. Nevertheless, taking advantage of the validation results from VBE networks provides us a chance for further research on the causality challenge, which will be reflected in future publications.

The presented trust model addresses a large set of trust elements that may be applied to assess trust level of organizations. This model however shall be customized by the VBE administrator to address the requirements and preferences of each specific VBE to which it is applied. The acceptability of the customized model and its relation to addressing its transparency and fairness for all organizations in the VBE need to be further addressed in future research.

Acknowledgement: This work was supported in part by the ECOLEAD project funded by the European Commission. The authors acknowledge contributions from partners in ECOLEAD.

8. REFERENCES

Ahuja, G. (2000). Collaboration networks, structural holes, and innovation: A longitudinal study. In Administrative Science Quarterly, Vol. 45, pg. 425–55.

Afsarmanesh, H. & Ermilova, E. (2007). Ontology Management for VO Breeding Environments. In the proceedings of 9th International conference on the Modern Information Technology in the Innovation Processes of the Industrial Enterprises., pg. 124-137.

Afsarmanesh, H., Camarinha-Matos, L. & Msanjila, S.S. (2007). Virtual organizations breeding environments: key results from ECOLEAD. In the proceedings of International conference on Cost Effective Automation in Networked Product Development and Manufacturing - IFAC-CEA'2007. Monterey, Mexico.

Arrow, K. J. (1974). Limits of Organization. New York: W.W. Norton.

Barber, S. & Kim, J. (2001). Belief Revision Process Based on Trust: Simulation Experiments. In the proceedings of the fourth workshop on Deception, Fraud and Trust in Agent Societies. Canada.

Castelfranchi, C. & Falcone, R. (2000). Trust Is Much More than Subjective Probability: Mental Components and Sources of Trust. In proceedings of the 33rd Hawaii International Conference on System Sciences.

Chow, S. & Holden, R. (1997). Toward an understanding of loyalty: the moderating role of trust. In the Journal of Managerial Issues, Vol. 9, No. 3.

Cosimano, T. F., 2004. Financial institutions and trustworthy behavior in business transactions. In the Journal of Business Ethics, Vol. 52, pg. 179–188

Currall, S. C. & Judge, T. A. (1995). Measuring trust between organizational boundary role persons. In Organizational Behavior and Human Decision Processes, Vol. 64, No. 2.

Dasgupta, P., (1988). Trust as a commodity. In Trust: Making and Breaking Cooperative Relations. Basil Blackwell: New York. pg. 49–72.

Dibben, M. R. (2000). Exploring Interpersonal Trust in the Entrepreneurial Venture. London: Macmillan.

Doney, P. M. & Canon, J. P. (1997). An examination of the nature of trust in buyer-seller relationships. In the Journal of Marketing, Vol. 61.

Dodgson, M. (1993). Learning, trust, & technological collaboration. Human Relations, Vol 46, No. 1.

Dyer, J. H., Chu, W., (2003). The role of trustworthiness in reducing transaction costs and improving performance: Empirical evidence from the United States, Japan, and Korea. Organization Science 14 (1), 57–68.

Falcone, R. & Castelfranchi, C., (2001). Social trust: a cognitive approach. In Trust and Deception in Virtual Societies. Kluwer Academic Publishers: Norwell, MA., pg. 55–90.

Finkelstein, A. (2000). The Future of Software Engineering. In ACM Press. ISBN 1-58113-253-0.

Fowler, G. D., & Wackerbarth, M. E. (1980). Audio teleconferencing versus face-to-face conferencing: A synthesis of the literature. Western Journal of Speech Communication, Vol. 44, pg. 236-252.

Gill, H., Kathleen Boies, K., Finegan, J. & McNally, J., (2005). Antecedents of trust: establishing a boundary condition for the relation between propensity to trust and intention to trust. In the Journal of Business Psychology, Vol. 19, pg. 287–302.

Good, D., (1988). Individuals, interpersonal relations, and trust. In Trust: Making and Breaking Cooperative Relations. Edited by D.G. Gambetta, Basil Blackwell: New York.. pg. 31–48.

Grandison, T. & Sloman, M., (2000). A survey of trust in Internet applications. In the IEEE Communication Survey Tutorial, Vol. 3, pg. 2–16.

Grover, S.L., (2005). Trust and distrust in organizations: dilemmas and approaches. In the Personal Review.. Vol. 34, pg. 507–509.

Hagan, J. M. & Choe, S. (1998). Trust in Japanese inter-firm relations: institutional sanctions matter. In Academy of Management Review, Vol. 23, No. 3.

Ishaya, T. & Mundy, D.P., (2004). Trust development and management in virtual communities. In Trust Management. Springer: Berlin, pg. 266–276.

Karahannas, M. & Jones, M. (1999). Inter-organizational systems and trust in strategic alliances. In Proceedings of the 20th International Conference on Information Systems, North Carolina,.

Kini, A. & Choobineh, J. (1998). Trust in electronic commerce: definition and theoretical considerations. In the proceedings of the 31st Annual Hawaii International Conference on System Sciences, Kohala Coast, Hawaii, pg.51–61.

Lahno, B. (2001). On the emotional character of trust. In the Journal of Ethics Theory Moral Practice, Vol. 4, pg. 171–189.

Lewicki, R.J. & Tomlinson, E.C., (2003). Trust and trust building. In Beyond Intractability, (Burgess, G., Burgess, H. - editor), Conflict Research Consortium, USA,.

Mayer, R. C. Davis, J. H., Schoorman, F. D. (1995). An integrated model of organizational trust. In Academy of Management review. Vol 20 No. 3, pg 709-734.

Msanjila, S. S. & Afsarmanesh, H. (2007a). Trust Analysis and Assessment in Virtual Organizations Breeding Environments. In the International Journal of Production Research, ISBN (print) 0020-7543, Research, Taylor & Francis., Vol. 46, No 5. pg. 1253-1295.

Msanjila, S.S. & Afsarmanesh, H. (2007b). Modeling trust relationships in Collaborative Networked Organizations. In international Journal of Technology Transfer and Commercialization, ISBN (print): 1470-6075, Inderscience, Vol. 6, No. 1, pg. 40-55.

Msanjila, S. S. & Afsarmanesh, H. (2007c). HICI: An approach for identifying trust elements – The case of technological perspective in VBEs. In proceeding of International conference on availability, reliability and security (ARES-2007), , Vienna, pg. 757-764

Msanjila, S.S. & Afsarmanesh, H. (2007d). Towards establishing trust relationships among organizations in VBEs. In establishing foundation of collaborative networks - Proceedings of PRO-VE 2007, IFIP, Vol. 225, Springer, , pg. 3-14.

Msanjila, S.S. & Afsarmanesh, H. (2007e). Specification of the TrustMan system for assisting management of VBEs. In lecture notes of computer science series, LNCS 4657, Springer, pg 34-43.

Msanjila, S. S. & Afsarmanesh, H. (2006a). Assessment and creation of trust in VBEs. In proceedings of PRO-VE 2006 conference, IFIP, Vol. 224, Network-Centric Collaboration and Supporting Frameworks (Camarinha-Matos, L., Afsarmanesh, H. & Ollus, M.-editors), , Springer, , pg. 161-172.

Msanjila, S. S. & Afsarmanesh, H. (2006b). Understanding and modeling trust relationships in collaborative networked organizations. In Business, Law and Technology: Present and Emerging Trends, (Kierkegaard, S.M. –editor), Vol. 2, ISBN87-991385-1-4, , IAITL, pg 402-416.

Pinyol, I., Sabater-Mir, J. & Cuni, G. (2000). How to talk about reputation using a common ontology: from definition to implementation. In the proceedings of 6th International joint conference on Autonomous Agents and Multi-agent Systems – W20: Trust in Agent Societies,. Hawaii, pg 90-101.

Rousseau, D.M., Sitkin, S.B., Burt, R.S. & Camerer, C. (1998). Not so different after all: a cross-discipline view of trust. In Academy of Management Review, Vol. 23, pg. 393–404.

Seigneur, J.M. & Jensen, C.D. 2004. Trading privacy for trust. In Proceedings of Second Trust Management International Conference, UK, , pg. 93–107.

Settle, J. (1998). The element of 'trust' in mediation: practice pointers drawn from theory. In the ADR Report, Vol. 2, pg. 5–7.

Smith, J. B. & Barclay, D. W. (1997). The effects of organizational differences and trust on the effectiveness of selling partner relationships. In the Journal of Marketing, , Vol. 61.

Ulivieri, F. (2004). Naïve approaches to trust building in web technologies. In ISTC-Technical report, vol. 15426B,

Wever, S. de, Martens, R. & Vandenbempt, K. (2005). The impact of trust on strategic resource acquisition through inter-organizational networks: Towards a conceptual model. In the International Journal of Human Relations. ISBN – 1523-1543. SAGE Publications, , Vol. 58, No. 2.

Zaheer, A., McEvily, B. & Perrone, V. (1998). Does trust matter? Exploring the effects of inter-organizational and interpersonal trust on performance. In Organization Science,. Vol. 9, No. 2.

VBE MANAGEMENT SYSTEM

Hamideh Afsarmanesh[1], Simon Samwel Msanjila[1], Ekaterina Ermilova[1],
Stefan Wiesner[2], Walter Woelfel[3], Marcus Seifert[2]

[1]University of Amsterdam,
[2]Bremen Institute of Industrial Engineering and Applied work Science
[3]Siemens

Possibility of rapidly forming a virtual organization (VO), triggered by a business collaboration opportunity and specially tailored to the requirements of that opportunity, is the emerging solution, specially for SMEs, and a survival mechanism in face of market turbulence (Camarinha-Matos, et al 2005). The same approach is however spreading and also becoming appealing in non-business oriented domains and contexts. Nevertheless, agility in configuration of VOs as a mission/goal-oriented collaboration networks, necessitates a-priory preparedness of organizations, which takes time and effort, and is nowadays supported within a pre-existing network called the VO breeding environment (VBE). For VBEs to properly operate and facilitate their actors, it is necessary to provide a set of automated functionalities and services supporting the necessary activities and processes that can ultimately assist with the agile/fluid creation of VOs within the VBE, namely the existence of a VBE management system (VMS). This chapter addresses a number of services/functionalities that are fundamental for the VMS. Among others, they include services for supporting the management of the VBE ontology and specially the management of the organizations' competencies, assessment and management of trust among the organizations, the structuring of VBE memberships, the management of VBE's Bag of assets, and the processes related to decision making in VBE environment.

1. INTRODUCTION

Effective management of a VBE is bound to the objective of preparing VBE members and maintaining their preparedness for collaboration in VOs. Organization preparedness is therefore strategic and requires time and effort to be established and maintained throughout the entire VBE life cycle (Afsarmanesh & Camarinha-Matos, 2005). As such establishing and efficiently managing a VBE helps to reduce the VO's set-up time and efforts. This is in contrast to selecting best-fit enterprises at the emergence of new opportunities from an "open universe" of enterprises, where the organizations that may be brought together by a broker have no familiarity with each other and there is no commonality among them since they did not collaborate with each other before. Collaboration Opportunities (COs) can be captured much more efficiently in terms of time and effort and the selection of best-fit organizations can be much more reliable when using the means supported by the VBEs and specifically through its VMS.

Keeping organizations prepared for collaboration requires the management of various kinds of information in the VBEs. A set of core functionality are required to support the administration of the VBE members, including their registration, roles & right management, etc. Furthermore, as identified and emphasized in previous publications (Afsarmanesh & Camarinha-Matos, 2005), a number of advance functionalities are fundamental to guarantee the added value of the VBEs, including the management of the VBE memberships and VBE's Profile/Competency, management of rational (objective) Trust establishment among the members, the management of VBE's Bag of Assets and the VO information, and the Decision support mechanisms assisting the operational stage of the VBE. The VBE management system (VMS) addressed in this chapter is designed to support the management and processing of information/knowledge needed to effectively create, operate, and evolve VBEs, as well as all their needed functionality for proper running of the VBEs.

1.1 VMS base concepts and motivation

Collaborative network (CN) has been established as an emerging new scientific discipline (Camarinha-Matos & Afsarmanesh, 2005). A number of specific forms of CNs can now be observed being practiced in daily business and society. As new forms of CNs are also emerging, innovative solutions are required to address many challenges facing collaborating partners.

A number of VBE networks (or at least with some characteristics common to VBEs) now exist world-wide, such as the SwissMicroTech (Switzerland), HELICE (Spain), CeBeNetwork (Germany) IECOS (Mexico), etc. The management activities of these VBE networks can be facilitated with some semi-automated tools and services. These services aim to enhance the efficiency of performing VBE activities (such as reducing the required resources, time and costs). However, the existing management systems at the running VBEs do not properly capture the characteristics of VBEs, such as the involvement of independent organizations that are heterogeneities in many aspects, e.g. their structural, componential, functional and behavioral aspects, and autonomous in their decision making, systems of values, and aims and interests in the market and society (Afsarmanesh, et al 2007). Furthermore, a good VBE administration is the one practicing transparency.

A number of sub-systems are developed in the VMS, as further addressed in section 1.2. Briefly, the VMS is developed to assist the VBE administration with performing the following:

- Collecting / managing information on performance of organizations in the VBE
- Managing profiles and competencies related to the VBE member organizations, VOs, and the VBE itself
- Assessment, managing and balancing the trustworthiness of the member organizations in the VBE
- Supporting the acquisition of new members and managing the VBE structure
- Managing the collected bag of assets and the VO information management in the VBE
- Supporting the processes related to decision making in the VBE

1.2 VMS sub-systems

VMS is designed to assist the VBE administration with performing its tasks related to enhancing the VBE and its successful operation towards achieving its objectives. As characterized and developed in ECOLEAD, the VMS constitutes a number of subsystems as shown in Figure 1, and further summarized briefly in paragraphs below, as an introduction to the subsystems addressed in this chapter. Figure 1 also indicates the needed interactions among these subsystems. Please notice that the box in the center of this diagram reflects a number of specific components related to the creation of VOs in the VBEs that are developed in the ECOLEAD project. The VO creation components are further addressed in Chapter 2.5 and not as a part of the VMS subsystems.

Furthermore, please notice that the need for addressing these specific VMS components in ECOLEAD, as opposed to others, was identified through the roadmapping work performed during the EC-funded project VO-map (Camarinha-Matos, Afsarmanesh, 2003). The fundamental R&D steps identified in this roadmapping activity were achieved together, and in consensus with, a large group of field experts involved in this roadmapping initiative, and were further validated and approved by the CN community of experts including academic, research and industry visionaries.

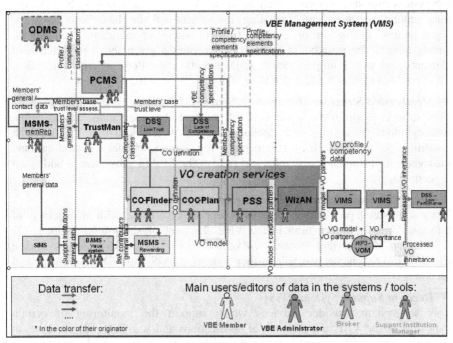

Figure 1- Global view of the VMS subsystems and their related interactions

✦ *Ontology discovery management system (ODMS)*
This subsystem provides services which assist different VBE actors with achieving the following objectives: (1) support the common understanding of the VBE-related

concepts, (2) facilitate the reusability of knowledge accumulated in one VBE with other VBEs, (3) provide formal classification of the knowledge represented in the Profile and Competency Management System (e.g. competency) in order to facilitate the knowledge processing at VBE by other software, and (4) support the knowledge interoperability both intra-VBE (to support varied forms of collaboration), and inter-VBEs (through sharing the unified models of PCMS information/knowledge). The ODMS subsystem is addressed in section 2.

✦ *Profile and competency management system (PCMS)*

This sub-system provides services which support the creation and maintenance of profiles of VBE member organizations, of the VBE itself, and of VOs registered within the VBE. The VBE competencies represent a specific part of the profile descriptions of the VBE entities, aimed at providing the main characteristics that are directly / indirectly needed to evaluate organizations for VO creation. A unified profile and competency model is designed and applied to the development of PCMS. The PCMS subsystem is addressed in section 3.

✦ *Trust Management system (TrustMan)*

An important intangible enabler of organizations' collaboration is trust among them. In preparing VBE member organizations for collaboration in a VO it is important to know whether partners trust each other enough to facilitate their co-working. This sub-system provides services which assist the VBE administration with managing trust among organizations, including assessment of the base trust level of organizations, evaluation of specific trustworthiness of member organizations, among others. The assessment of trust level applies a given set of preferred trust elements such as certain perspective, requirements, and criteria for trust evaluation. The TrustMan system is addressed in section 4.

✦ *Membership Structure Management System (MSMS)*:

This subsystem provides services which support the integration, accreditation, disintegration, rewarding, and categorization of members within the VBE. It constitutes of functionalities for member registration, member rewarding, and management of the members' roles and rights. The MSMS subsystem is addressed in section 5.

✦ *Set of supporting information management systems*

These subsystems provide services which support VBE actors with management of different kinds of information in the VBE. This set of subsystems include: *VO Information Management System (VIMS),* and *Bag of Assets Management System (BAMS).* In this chapter we will further address BAMS and VIMS as covered in section 6.

✦ *Decision Support System (DSS)*

This sub-system provides services which support the monitoring of certain indicators in the VBE and issuance of notifications and warnings. For example, in the case of low performance level, or diminishing trust level of VBE members, as well as in cases that the required VBE competencies are insufficient to satisfy the Collaboration opportunities in the market. The DSS subsystem is addressed in section 7.

✦ *VO creation services*

These are services which are designed and implemented to support the VO planner and other actors to semi-automatically configure a VO. VO creation services includes services provided by: Collaboration Opportunity (CO) finder system (CO-Finder), CO characterization and rough planning system (COC-Plan), Partner search and suggestion system (PSS) and Contract negotiation wizard (WizAN). These services and their related systems are further addressed in chapter 2.5.

2. ONTOLOGY DISCOVERY AND MANAGEMENT SYSTEM

In Chapter 2.1 of this book, the **VBE ontology** is defined and specified, and the need for the VBE ontology is justified. As such, the VBE ontology aims to support the following challenging tasks related to the VBE instantiation and management:

1. Establishment of a common semantic subspace for VBEs.
2. Instantiation of VBE knowledge repositories for VBEs from different domains / business areas.
3. Automated processing VBE knowledge by software tools in dynamic VBEs.
4. Enabling inter-organizational learning & co-working.
5. Integrability of VBE knowledge with existing standards.

The Ontology Discovery and Management System (ODMS) (Afsarmanesh & Ermilova, 2007) (Ermilova, & Afsarmanesh, 2008) is a fundamental components of the VMS that aims at *providing advanced functionalities to support VBE Knowledge Modelling and Management* based on the VBE ontology.

2.1 ODMS functionalities

Being a fundamental VMS component, the ODMS supports the VBE through its entire life cycle (i.e. from the VBE creation stage to the VBE dissolution stage). The functionalities of the ODMS for each of these stages are addressed in Figure 2.

Twelve main functionalities are identified for the ODMS. These are divided into two groups, namely the *VBE ontology maintenance (OM)* functionalities and the *ontology-based functionalities for VMS support (VS)*, which are addressed further in this section.

The ***VBE ontology maintenance functionalities*** aim at maintaining the VBE ontology itself, as addressed in OM1 to OM6 below. They are applied right after the common VBE ontology meta and core levels are loaded to the ODMS. The maintenance functionalities address the discovery and evolution of the VBE ontology that takes place through the entire life-cycle of a running VBE.

- **OM1. Discovery of domain and application levels of the VBE ontology.** Ontology discovery and customization needs to be performed periodically during the VBE operation and evolution stages. It is activated after new domain or application knowledge appears in the VBE in forms of structured (e.g. members' database schemas), semi-structured (e.g. companies' HTML-pages) or unstructured (e.g. organizations' brochures) sources. This functionality supports the VBE ontology developers and VBE experts with semi-automated discovery of ontology elements (data/knowledge) for the VBE domain ontology from different sources.

- **OM2. Integration of VBE members' ontologies into the VBE ontology.** This functionality is required at the VBE creation stage after VBE members start joining the VBE. In case some of the VBE members offer their domain ontologies to the VBE, these ontologies can be semi-automatically integrated into the VBE ontology domain as well as the application levels.

- **OM3. Editing of the domain and application levels of the VBE ontology.** This functionality provides a user-friendly interface for authorized VBE actors and members to manually edit the VBE ontology. Through this interface, users can for instance add new VBE concepts and introduce their definitions, synonyms, abbreviations, properties, associations and inter-relationships. The VBE sub-ontologies can be represented in a textual format, and visualized in form of graphs and diagrams.

- **OM4. Evolution of the domain and application levels of the VBE ontology.** The ontology evolution functionality supports monitoring the evolution of the VMS sub-systems (e.g. through monitoring of their related repositories) and after that suggests and semi-automatically performs the related changes in the VBE ontology.

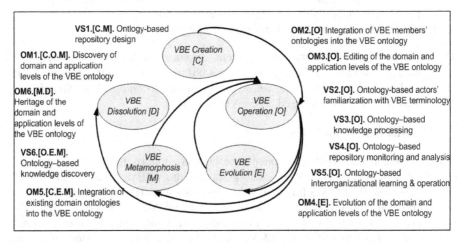

Figure 2 - ODMS's life cycle functionalities

- **OM5. Integration of existing domain ontologies into the VBE ontology.** This functionality is required mainly at the VBE creation stage. It supports integration of the general domain / business area knowledge to the VBE ontology, thus results in the creation of the VBE ontology domain level. Such ontologies can be the inherited from other VBEs from the same domain or from the representation of domain knowledge created for other purposes. In this case, this ODMS's functionality provides means for semi-automated integration of the external ontologies to the existing VBE ontology.

- **OM6. Heritage of the domain and application levels of the VBE ontology.** This functionality allows the other VBE networks to reuse existing VBE domain and application level ontologies after the VBE dissolves. Since some of the VBE ontology data can be of a high level of confidentiality this functionality semi-automatically extracts the "public" part of the VBE domain and application levels ontology for further distribution.

The ***ontology-based VMS support functionalities*** aim to support the core VMS functionalities, such as competency management, VO creation, trust management, etc., by means of the VBE ontology, as addressed in VS1-VS6 below.

- **VS1: Ontology-based repository design.** This functionality supports the design of VMS's repositories needed at the VBE creation stage. Particularly, it maintains the consistency among the main entities of VMS's repository and the main classes of VBE information as specified in the VBE ontology.
- **VS2: Ontology-based actors' familiarization with VBE terminology.** This functionality provides a user-friendly interface for all VBE actors to familiarize themselves with the VBE terminology. Through this interface, users search for different VBE concepts and investigate their definitions, synonyms, abbreviations, properties, associations and inter-relationships. The VBE sub-ontologies are represented in the textual format and visualized in the form of graphs and diagrams.
- **VS3: Ontology-based knowledge processing.** This functionality supports data processing for different VMS functions by using the ontology's knowledge classifications, e.g. using competency classification for matching members' competencies needed to support the VO partners search and suggestion process.
- **VS4: Ontology-based repository monitoring and analysis.** This function supports the VBE administration and ontology experts with a tool to monitor and analyze of the VBE domain knowledge by using the reasoning facilities of the VBE ontology encoded in the OWL, e.g. to identify competency gaps.
- **VS5: Ontology-based inter-organizational learning and operation.** This functionality supports the semi-automated capturing of the ontology elements from the VBE ontology domain and application levels that represents the business area concepts related to a specific VBE member. Thus, the VBE members can learn about the area of expertise of each other through the ODMS.
- **VS6: Ontology-based knowledge discovery.** This functionality supports the VBE administration and supports VBE experts with semi-automated discovery of knowledge about the VBE through mining the text-corpora made available by the VBE members and actors. The related VBE domain sub-ontologies are used as the base to discover new concepts in order to introduce them in different VMS's components (e.g. discovery of competency knowledge for the PCMS subsystem of VMS (Ermilova & Afsarmanesh, 2007).

2.2 State of the art work in the ODMS

The following related "state of the art" works on the ontology maintenance and management are applied for the implementation of the ODMS prototype:

a. Ontology registry.
The VBE ontology represents a set of complimentary partitions / sub-ontologies. Each sub-ontology can be further partitioned into a set of "sub-sub-ontologies". For example, the "VBE domain profile and competency sub-ontology" can be partitioned depending on the number of the VBE profile elements, into a specific

"VBE domain competency sub-ontology", a "VBE domain resource sub-ontology", etc. Similarly, the "VBE domain resource sub-ontology" within one VBE can be partitioned for example into a specific "VBE metalworking domain resource sub-ontology" and "VBE plastic manufacturing domain resource sub-ontology". In order to organize and monitor all VBE sub-ontologies and VBE sub-sub-ontologies, a special "VBE ontology registry" is needed. In (Ding & Fensel, 2001) (Simoes, et al, 2007) the concept of an Ontology Library System (OLS) is addressed. The OLS is defined as "an important tool in grouping and re-organizing ontologies for further re-use, integration, maintenance, mapping, and versioning". In our ODMS's design and development, we integrate the OLS as a fundamental component of the ODMS.

b. Ontology editing and viewing.
In (Afsarmanesh & Ermilova, 2007) we have identified requirements for the ontology editing/viewing environments for the ODMS that include (1) friendly user interface (including possibilities of visualization), (2) complete OWL (refer to OWL reference) support (i.e. exporting and importing of OWL files, as well as complete OWL features support, e.g. the annotation properties support) and (3) collaborative ontology editing support. The survey of ontology editing/viewing tools by Michael Denny (Denny, 2004) represents 94 ontology editors. However none of those editors respond to all three requirements. Therefore, currently we are partially applying (reusing) the two following ontology environments: *Hozo* (Sunagawa, et al, 2004) enables viewing and editing of OWL ontologies in the form of diagrams. However it supports only restricted set of OWL features and does not support collaboration. *Protégé* (Protégé, 2007) supports the complete OWL specification and collaborative work (Tudorache, 2007), however it does not yet have facilities for editing ontologies in the form of diagrams. Another main disadvantage of most existing ontology editing/viewing environments is their complex user interface, since they are developed to support work of competent and experienced ontology experts and software engineers. While reusing these complex environments for the ODMS's "OM3" functionality is reasonable, reusing them for the ODMS's "VS2" functionality is not suitable, because VS2's users are mostly non-ICT people. Thus, simplification of existing ontology environments for VS2 or even development of a new environment is required for ODMS.

c. Ontology merging and integration.
Ontology integration is addressed in the literature (Pinto, et al, 1999) either as building of a new ontology reusing other available ontologies or as merging different ontologies on the same subject into a single ontology that "unifies" all of them. Ontology integration is challenging (Spivack, 2006). The main reason for this is that each ontology has its own naming conventions, philosophical orientation and design biases. The OWL (OWL, 2007) currently is not expressive enough to support mapping among all ontologies. However ontology merging is an issue addressed by many theoretical and practical works (Pinto, et al, 1999) (Denny, 2004). We have applied several approaches, such as those reported in (Calvanese, et al, 2001) (Pinto, et al, 2001) (Noy, 2003), to the implementation of the ODMS's functionalities "OM2" and "OM5". For example, the approach defined in (Pinto, et al, 2001) addresses a set of steps for ontology integration, such as: identification of integration possibilities, identification of resulting ontology top-level blocks and modules,

identification of assumptions and ontological commitments, identification of the knowledge for representation in each module, study and analysis of candidate/source ontologies, applying the integration operations, and analyzing the resulting ontology.

d. Ontology evolution.
In (Stojanovic, 2004) the ontology evolution process is defined as the "timely adaptation of an ontology to the arisen changes in the consistent propagation of these changes in the dependent artefacts". This process consists of two steps; the knowledge changes discovery step and the semantic ontology changes step. For our purposes we apply the semantic approach for ontology evolution addressed in (Stojanovic, 2004) to the ODMS's functionality "OM4".

e. Ontology-based repository design and monitoring.
Modern approaches for data structure generation include among others the approaches for transformation of abstract ontologies to valid schemas for database systems. These transformation approaches solve the problem when the developers are proficient on database languages, but lack sufficient knowledge in the application domain. They also automate and speed up the database development. For the ODMS's functionality "VS1" we apply the approach addressed in (Guevara-Masis, et al, 2004). This approach includes a series of transformation steps for translating an object-oriented ontology to a relational schema, starting with the specification of mapping rules between the object oriented model and the relational schema. While applied to the database design, the approach is also suitable for further database monitoring, i.e. ODMS's functionality "VS4", applying the mapping rules

f. Knowledge discovery and ontology discovery.
Knowledge discovery (Grobelnik, et al, 2005) facilitates many information management systems by automatically obtaining knowledge. Knowledge can be discovered from a variety of sources, including sources that are structured (e.g. database and XML schemas), semi-structured (e.g. HTML-pages), or unstructured (e.g. plain text) documents (OntoBasis, 2007). Knowledge discovery approaches apply ontologies in order to set up and annotate the vocabulary and thesaurus needed for semantic discovery. For the ODMS's functionality "VS6" we apply the approach called TOKO addressed in (Anjewierden, et al, 2003). TOKO supports ontology-based knowledge discovery from text corpora such as HTML-pages and MS Word documents. It also supports the selection of concepts in text-corpora and introducing them in the original ontology, and thus it can be also used for the ODMS's functionality "OM1".

2.3 ODMS implementation and validation

As a proof of concepts, the ODMS prototype is implemented in Java and validated by three industry-based VBEs involved into the ECOLEAD project, namely SMT (Switzerland), IECOS (Mexico), and HELICE (Spain).

Figure 3 illustrates a part of the VBE core ontology viewed through the web-based GUI, developed for the ODMS functionality "VS2 - Ontology-based familiarization with VBE terminology". Using this GUI during the PCMS validation step, the VBE representatives viewed the core VBE ontology and familiarized themselves with the VBE core/common terminology. As such, the "VS2" functionality provides a simplified ontology editor and viewer with an easy understandable and user-friendly GUI for searching and viewing VBE ontology concepts. The "VS2" GUI includes 3 main areas: (1) the concepts catalogue (on the left), (2) the selected concepts characterization (on the right), and (3) the search area (the pop-down menu on the right).

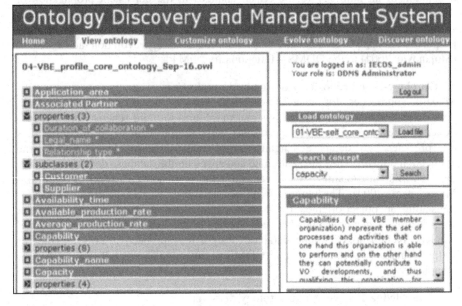

Figure 3 - Example screen-shot from VS2 - Ontology-based familiarization with VBE terminology

3. PROFILE AND COMPETENCY MANAGEMENT SYSTEM

In Chapter 2.1 of this book the **VBE profiles** and **VBE competencies** (Ermilova & Afsarmanesh, 2006) (Ermilova & Afsarmanesh, 2007) are defined and specified, and the need for them is justified. As such, the VBE profiles and VBE competencies are defined as follows:

VBE profile consists of the set of determining characteristics (e.g. name, address, capabilities, etc.) about each VBE entity, collected in order to: (a) distinguish and compare each VBE entity with others, (b) analyze the suitability of each VBE entity for involvement in some specific line of activities / operations.

VBE competency is the main element of the VBE profile that provides up-to-date information about capabilities and capacities of each VBE entity, as well as conspicuous information about their validity, qualifying it for participation in some specific activities / operations within the VBE, and mostly oriented towards the VO creation.

The Profile and Competency Management System (PCMS) aims at ICT-based collection and processing of VBE profiles and competencies. The main motivation for the design and development of the ICT-based representation and the ICT-based management of the VBE profiles and competencies include the following:
– In medium and large VBEs (i.e. with more than 20 members) as well as in geographically distributed VBEs, the only way for all VBE entities to get the up-to-date information about each other is the computer-based representation and distribution of their profiles and competencies.
– Due to the dynamism of VBEs caused by the daily changes of the customer's demands in the market and society, the VBE must rapidly analyze the VBE members' competencies. In medium and large VBEs, the VBE administration is not able to obtain and analyze the up-to-date knowledge about all members with such a high level of dynamism. Thus, there is a need for the ICT-based submission and processing of the members' profiles that shall facilitate the VBE's dynamism.

The following *requirements* were also identified for the PCMS:
- support for continuous (e.g. daily) updating of profile and competency data,
- handling the confidentiality of profile and competency data,
- support for adaptability of the PCMS to the wide varieties of VBE applications,
- support for sustainability of the PCMS in dynamic and expanding environments,
- support for replicability of the PCMS.

The following set of technical *challenges* was identified for the design and development of the PCMS:
- common understanding of profile and competency models by all VBE members,
- cataloguing of competencies,
- naming of competencies,
- formal representation of profile and competency data in order to further process it semi-automatically, and
- semantic integration of the description of VBE members' expertise submitted to the PCMS.

3.1 PCMS functionalities

The PCMS supports VBEs through their entire life cycle (i.e. from the VBE creation stage to the VBE dissolution stage). At each stage of VBE's life cycle, the PCMS is required to support certain functionalities. For this purpose, twelve main functionalities are identified for the PCMS as illustrated in Figure 4. All functionalities are activated at different VBE life cycle stages. In Figure 4, these activation times are indicated next to each functionality's name (e.g. "(C)" indicates the VBE creation stage, etc.). Detailed description of the PCMS's functionalities is addressed below in this section. Please note, that most of PCMS functionalities are supported by the VBE ontology (as addressed in Chapter 2.1).

1. **Uploading of core profile/competency model.** This functionality supports the uploading and installation of the core profile/competency model (e.g. in the form of the VBE core profile/competency sub-ontology) to the PCMS and adaptation of the PCMS's database to this model.

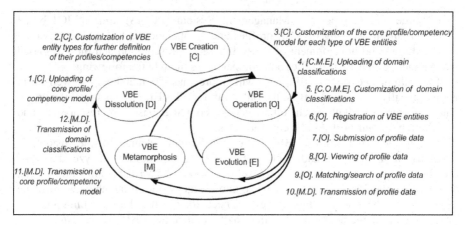

Figure 4 - PCMS functionalities

2. **Customization of the VBE entity types.** This functionality supports adding /deleting the VBE entity types (e.g. the VBE member organization, the VO-self network and the VBE-self network) that have profiles/competencies in the PCMS.

3. **Customization of the core profile/competency model for each type of VBE entities.** This functionality supports assignment of the core profile/competency knowledge classes to specific VBE entity types.

4. **Uploading of domain classifications.** This functionality supports the uploading and installation of specific generalization hierarchies of domain classes to PCMS (e.g. in the form of the VBE domain profile/competency sub-ontology).

5. **Customization of domain classifications.** This functionality supports updating of generalization hierarchies of domain classes, for example through adding new domain-dependent profile knowledge classes needed in a specific VBE application.

6. **Registration of VBE entities.** This functionality supports registration of real VBE entities in the PCMS and thus creation of their profiles.

7. **Submission of profile data.** This functionality supports uploading of profile/competency data related to each VBE entity.

8. **Viewing of profile data.** This functionality supports viewing profile / competency data accumulated in the VBE. The viewing scope can address both: a single profile and the aggregated competency data of the entire VBE (also see Figure 5).

9. **Matching/searching of profile data.** This functionality supports both: the search for specific profile elements and the matching of the profile/competency descriptions of a group of VBE member organizations against the detailed descriptions of the new collaborative opportunities arisen in the VBE.

10. **Transmission of profile data.** This functionality supports the transmission of VBE profile data to a special format in order to support its inheritance by other VBEs or external institutions and thus its usage as a valuable asset for further VBE-related activities in the market and society.

11. **Transmission of core profile/competency model.** This functionality supports transmission of the customized core profile/competency model of one VBE to a special format (e.g. ontology) to support its usage by the R&D organizations working on the evolution of the generic/core VBE profile/competency models.

12. **Transmission of domain classifications.** This functionality supports transmission of customized generalization hierarchies of domain classes of one VBE to a special format (e.g. ontology) in order to support its inheritance by other VBEs from the

same domain or by the R&D organizations working on the evolution of these domain classifications.

Figure 5 - Example screen-shot from the PCMS's functionality "8 - Viewing of profile data"

3.2 PCMS implementation and validation

As a proof of the designed concepts the PCMS system is implemented in Java and being applied to the four industry-based VBE networks of: IECOS (Mexico), CeBeNetwork (Germany), HELICE (Spain), and SMT (Switzerland).

An example screen-shot of the PCMS running at SMT is provided in Figure 5. This Figure illustrates the "aggregated competency catalogue", implemented for the PCMS's functionality of "Viewing of profile data". On the upper level, this catalog represents a list of competency classes that are collectively owned by all VBE members. For each competency class, the PCMS provides an aggregated list of related competency components, e.g. its capabilities (see Chapter 2.1 for more details). This functionality is used mainly by the SMT customers who require an aggregated overview of all competencies owned by the VBE.

4. TRUST MANAGEMENT SYSTEM

In the past, in order to assess trust level of other organizations and to apply the results to the establishment of their trust relationships, organizations have been using approaches that in most cases were supported with ad hoc and manual processes. For agile creation of VOs, the need to establish fact-based (rational) trust relationships with other organizations in VBEs is now evident but challenging (Msanjila & Afsarmanesh, 2007c). Creating trust among organizations requires the careful identification of trust assessment criteria. This section addresses the automation of processes related to the management of trust among organizations in the VBE.

The implementation of TrustMan system adopted the web service technology thus its functionalities are here referred to as services. Web service technology was adopted for the design and implementation of the system to enhance its platform and application independence (Msanjila, et al 2005).

4.1 Main purpose of TrustMan system

The main purpose of TrustMan system is to assist the VBE administration with performing tasks related to support the management of inter-organizational trust in the VBE. The system supports five main kinds of users namely: VBE member organizations, VBE administrator, Trust experts, External stakeholders, and VO planner. Table 1 summarizes the requirements of each user on TrustMan system.

Table 1: User and their requirements for TrustMan system

User	User requirements
VBE administrator	- Customize the system in the given VBE environment. - Assess the base trust level of VBE member applicants. - Assess and manage the base trust level of VBE members. - Update the list of base trust criteria. - Support the VO planner to evaluate the trustworthiness of VBE members.
VO planner	- Select specific trust criteria for trustworthiness evaluation. - Evaluate the trustworthiness of members to invite them to a VO.
Trust experts	- Support the administrator to customize the system in a given VBE environment. - Support the administrator and VO planner during assessment of trust level. - Support the VBE administrator to defined new trust criteria.
Member	- Access its base trust level records. - Access allowed base trust level records of other VBE members. - Update its values for trust criteria.
Applicants	- Submit information for the assessment of its base trust level for the application.
External stakeholders	- Create trust to the VBE for providing a business opportunity. - Create trust to the VBE before deciding to join the VBE.

To address these users' requirements a number of services are implemented in TrustMan system as further addressed in section 4.3.

4.2 Mechanisms for assessing trust level of organizations

Perceptions of trust have been in line with the nature of purposes for its applications as well as involved actors. Thus purposes for establishing trust differ among the practices. For each specific practice in which a particular group of actors is involved trust is differently interpreted and perceived as compared to others. In our research, we classify trust aspects into five perspectives: Technological (Tech), Social (Soc), Structural (Str), Managerial (Man), and Economical (Eco) (Msanjila & Afsarmanesh 2007c). Furthermore, to address variation of trust perceptions, a *rational* trust level assessment approach is required to support measuring trust level of organizations and reason on the results. Thus measurable trust elements are needed. We hierarchically characterize trust elements into: perspectives, requirements and measurable criteria.

To "*rationally*" assess trust level of organizations a series of fact-based trust criteria can be applied. With the empirical study of co-innovation networks as well as survey of the past research, we have identified a good number of measurable criteria that act as indicators of inter-organizational trust analysis (Msanjila & Afsarmanesh 2007c). However, we have also identified that the influence of a trust criterion on the trust level can be either positive or negative depending on its behaviour. Furthermore, the behaviour of each trust criterion changes in time, and causally influences others. Causal influences can be studied by applying concepts from system dynamics (Kirkwood, 1998). Results of causal analysis can be represented in a so-called "*causal diagram*". Results can also be translated into mathematical equations reflecting inter-relations of trust criteria (Msanjila & Afsarmanesh 2007c). The formulated equations comprise the base for our designed mechanisms for assessment of trust level of organizations (Msanjila & Afsarmanesh 2007a). Basically, mechanisms developed for TrustMan system implement three forms of equations. The first form of equation is applied to calculate the final comparative scores of trust level of organizations as an average of weighted scores of all perspectives (equation 1). This equation is represented as the average of weighted scores for all trust perspectives achieved by the organization (see in equation 1).

In the three equations: **TL** represents trust level, **S** represents score, **per** represents trust perspective, **IF** represents intermediate factor, **W** represents weight, & **Avg** represents average.

$$TL = Avg[(W_{Tech} * S_{Tech}), (W_{Soc} * S_{Soc}), (W_{Str} * S_{Str}), (W_{Man} * S_{Man}), (W_{Eco} * S_{Eco})] \dots\dots(1)$$

The score for each trust perspective is calculated as weighted average of score for all intermediate factors as shown in equation (2) which represents the second form.

$$S_{per} = \frac{1}{n} \sum_{i}^{n} W_{IF_i} * S_{IF_i} \dots\dots\dots\dots\dots\dots(2)$$

The score for intermediate factors is calculated as a function of trust criteria and known factors as shown in equation (3) which represents the third form.

$$S_{IF} = f[trust\_criteria, known\_factors] \qquad Where \, 0 < W_i < 1, and \sum_{\forall i} W_i = 1 \dots\dots(3)$$

4.3 Functionalities and services provided by TrustMan system

The TrustMan system implementation adopted the web service technology standards. Thus it provides web functionalities for human user as well as web services for system users. The specified functionalities are here referred to as services. Seven main services are implemented as shown in Table 2 (Msanjila & Afsarmanesh, 2007a).

Table 2: Services provided by TrustMan system

Service for	Description of the service
Assessing base trust level of organizations	When customizing the TrustMan system, in a specific environment, the VBE administrator selects a minimum set of trust criteria here called *"base trust criteria"*. The results of the assessment that applies this set are referred to as *"base trust level"* of organizations. This service is implemented to support the assessment of trust level for organizations based on these base trust criteria. There are two kinds of assessment supported by this service, namely: *Periodic assessment of base trust level for member organizations, and one-time assessment of base trust level for a membership applicant.*
Evaluating specific trustworthiness of organizations	This *service* aims at measuring how trustworthy an organization is for a specific trust objective, i.e. inviting a VBE member to participate in a VO, appoint a VBE member to become a VO coordinator or VBE administrator, etc. A priori to the evaluation, the trustor organization selects the specific set of trust criteria and then applies for the evaluation of trustworthiness. The evaluation of specific trustworthiness can be done at a certain point in time such as current time. Also, the evaluation can be applied to forecast trustworthiness for future collaborations.
Establishing trust relationships among organizations	The approach suggested to facilitate *establishing trust relationships* among organizations is through measuring their historical data for both their trust records and performance records. While establishing trust relationships among them the participating organizations can be provided with relevant information queried from the data stored in the TrustMan system, which will enable them trust others.
Managing trust related data	This service supports three users of the system, namely: VBE membership applicants, VBE member organizations, and the VBE administrator. The VBE membership applicant will use this service for submitting their trust related data to facilitate the evaluation of their application towards joining the VBE. The submitted data is used to assess their base trust level to support the VBE administrator for deciding whether to accept their application. The VBE member organizations will use this service to update their trust related data. And finally, the VBE administrator will use this service to manage all the trust related data in the system i.e. ensuring it is updated, valid, etc.
Creating trust to the VBE	This service supports external stakeholders (the invited organizations for becoming members, and the customers) to create trust to the VBE. These external stakeholders need to access information that will assist them with trusting the VBE in relation to their businesses. The service will thus guide each stakeholder to access specific information which fits its purpose and perception of trust.
Managing the assessment	As described in section 4.2 the equations applied for the development of mechanisms for assessing trust level of organizations incorporates some

Service for	Description of the service
mechanisms	weights for the applied parameters. These weights are changed with time when it is needed, using the services.
Analyzing *history of trust level for organizations*	Trustors such as VBE administrators are sometimes interested not only the current trust level of respective trustees but also their trust level evolution. Thus they will be interested on analyzing how the trust level has been evolving in a certain period of time in the past. This might also involve using the past trust level history to predict the future trustworthiness behavior by assuming certain scenario. This service supports such users to track the needed history. The service has a mechanism which in specific schedule (such as in six month period) triggers the service for assessing base trust level for all organizations in the VBE. Then the service stores the results into the TrustMan database. The user can retrieve trust level history of specified organizations for given range of period of time including some analyzes such as partial results for each period.

4.4   Human and system interfaces supported by TrustMan system

TrustMan system is designed and implemented to provide different users with services which will assist them with performing their trust management related processes. The main users and their respective requirements are detailed in Table 1. There are two kinds of interface, namely: *administrative interface and member interface*. Upon login through common interface the system automatically redirects the specific user to required interface based on the provided information (username, password and role). Figure 6 shows a login interface customized for IECOS.

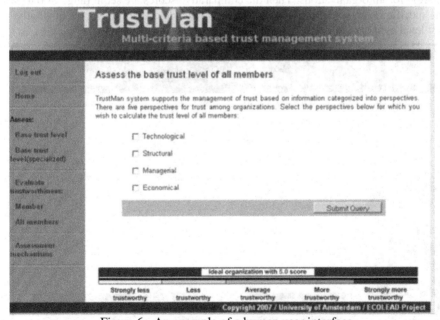

Figure 6 - An example of a human user interface

The administrative interface is designed to support the VBE administrator with handling the administrative duties related to management of trust in the VBE. Such duties include assessing trust level of organizations, managing trust related data, managing mechanisms for assessing trust level, etc. Other users which temporary get administrative rights such as trust experts, VO planer, etc. can also access specific administrative functionalities in this interface, such as for evaluating specific trustworthiness. The member interface supports organizations to access their trust level records and manage their own trust related data.

TrustMan system also provides services that can be invoked by other systems (Msanjila & Afsarmanesh, 2007b). Thus system interface based on standards for invocation of web services is implemented. The only interface for service invocation is through the WSDL component of the system. This component provides details on how a specific service can be invoked including: target name space (address), port type, request parameter, response parameter, etc.

4.5 Computation and interpretation of trust level of organizations

Trust level of an organization is not an absolute value that can be measured once and applied in any case. It is a comparative value depending on a number of factors, among others, including: set of trust criteria, applied data, involved organizations, and specific ratings of trust level set by the trustor organization. Thus trust level of an organization is measured for each specific case and is valid for that case.

The manipulation of values of trust criteria as addressed earlier applies mathematical equations. While computing the trust level each value of trust criterion of every involved organization is compared to most optimal value of each trust criterion for all organizations. Then the comparative scores are set in range of 0 to 5. The specific range is then used by the trustor to decide on sub-ranges for qualitative trust level as shown in Figure 7.

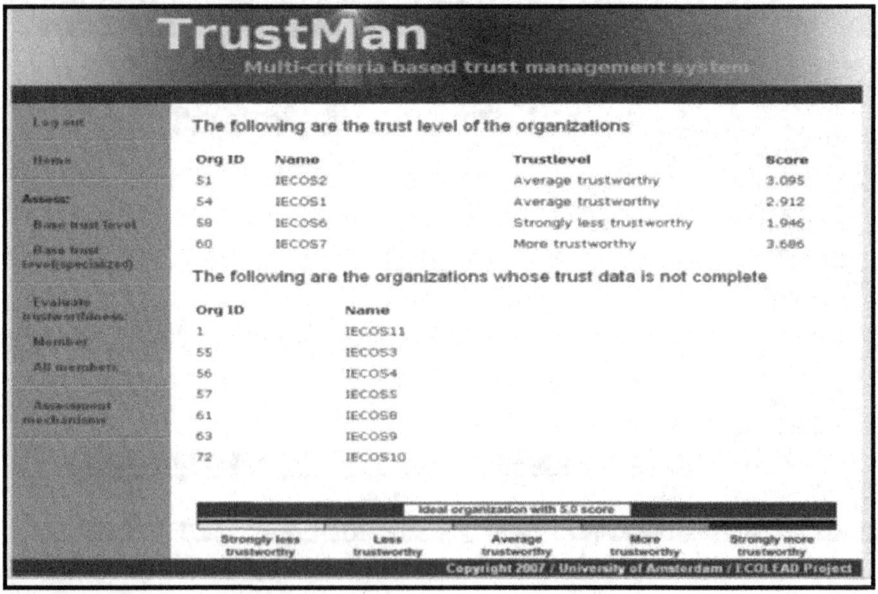

Figure 7 - Results of the service for assessment of base trust level for organizations

For example, in Figure 7 the score of 3.095 means that considering all IECOS2's values of trust criteria applied in the equations as compared to those values of all involved organizations, the IECOS2 scored 3.092 out of 5. According to the specific preferred rating in this case its trust level is "Average trustworthy".

5. MEMBERSHIP STRUCTURE MANAGEMENT SYSTEM

Membership and Structure Management System (MSMS) supports the VBE administrator, the VBE members, and those organizations that want to become members, through providing functionalities to submit, store, access, delete, and modify the member's company and contact information. Management of the structure of the VBE, and the company-related information about its members is a crucial cornerstone for supporting performing fundamental VBE related activities. Primary functions of VBE membership management are to register and delete members to and from the MSMS database; to reward members in case of proactive and positive behavior, and to manage the rights, roles, and responsibility of the VBE members.

The functionalities for the management of VBE members therefore include the registration of new VBE members, the rewarding of appropriate and proactive behaviour within the VBE, and the management of the member's rights and roles. Figure 8 shows the needs and provided functionalities for VBE structure and membership management.

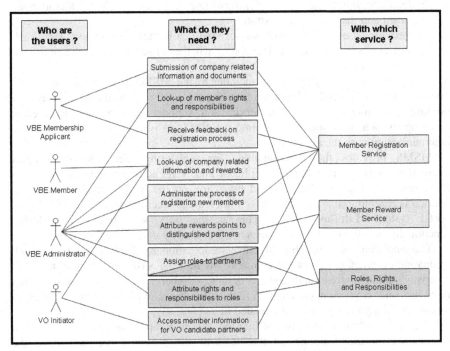

Figure 8- Membership and Structure Management Functionalities

The MSMS will mainly be used by enterprises applying for membership in the VBE (VBE Membership Applicant), the VBE Members, the VBE Administrator, and the VO Initiator. The membership applicant will use the system to initiate the process of entering the VBE by providing all the information necessary for registration, and get notification on the approval or denial of the request for membership. VBE Members will use the system mainly for retrieving information on whether they have earned awards. The VO Initiator will make use of the system for gathering basic information on candidate members for VO being configured. The VBE Administrator will be responsible for adding new members to the database, for awarding members that behave proactively and beneficial to the VBE overall strategies and objectives, such as for technically maintaining the databases and services within the system.

5.1 VBE Member Registration

Registration of new members to the VBE and its Management System (MSMS) is a fundamental step in VO creation and evolution. Objective of the registration process is to get a comprehensive picture of the company applying for membership, including first assessments on trustworthiness (based on multi-criteria trust model (Msanjila & Afsarmanesh 2006)), and an estimation on how good the competencies offered by the applicant fit into the required / unoccupied competencies the VBE seeks (Ermilova, & Afsarmanesh, 2006). Consequently, the registration process has the following two objectives:

1. To facilitate initial exchange of information between the VBE Membership Applicant and the VBE Administrator.
2. To provide the VBE Administrator with all the information the VBE Management needs to make a decision on whether to accept the applicant as new VBE partner or not.

In the process of registering a new member to the MSMS two actors are mainly involved: the VBE membership applicant, and the VBE administrator. The primary purpose of the member registration service is to support a new member in entering its company- and user-specific data into the VMS, as well as the administrator in communicating with the applicant.

MSMS provides the functionalities for registering members and support interactions between membership applicant and VBE administrator. The Member Registration Service can be accessed by a link on the VBE website. When this Service is entered, the applicant is asked to create an account to access the LifeRay portal system (LifeRay, 2007). This is the only step based on LifeRay functionalities. All other functionalities are provided by independent portlets.

The applicant is then able to enter basic company data to allow a quick evaluation on whether or not the company fits into the VBE. Information raised is company name, address and contact details, number of employees, last annual turnover, and core competencies. A person-in-charge will be granted rights to modify the company and user data related to its company.

The VBE administrator is notified on the new applicant by email, and a notification on the desktop. On the basis of the provided company data, the administrator performs a basic credibility check of information and evaluates whether the primary activity of the applicant fits into the VBE scope.

If the applicant is accepted for the second stage of transmission of company information, the applicant uploads accreditation information to the MSMS. Mandatory information are: accreditation, certificate, and financial rating; optionally, the applicant can also provide letters of recommendation, licenses and patents the company achieved, articles in newspapers and magazines on it, such as awards it won. This information will allow a precise statement on whether to accept or reject the applicant. Through integration with the TrustMan system, the trust level of the member applicant based on the accredited information which is submitted by the applicant can be assessed.

Based on all information gathered, the VBE administrator decides on acceptance / rejection of applicants based on four fundamental information inputs: (i) basic information validation; (ii) base trust level; (iii) validity of evidence information; (iiii) compliance of competency. This information is provided by VMS services and made visible on the registration portlet (administrator's view).

5.2 VBE Member Rewarding

Virtual organizations Breeding Environments are constituted with enterprises co-operating on common visions, strategies, and objectives. By joining the individual enterprises' competencies the VBE comprises a pool of competencies necessary to quickly respond to Collaboration Opportunities (CO) in a specific industrial or service sector. The response takes place by quickly joining VBE members' competencies and creating a Virtual Organization (VO) out of the subset of members providing the required competencies. The state of VBE members being able to quickly join competencies and collaborate with others in a VO is called preparedness. Leveraging preparedness and acquiring CO's are crucial enablers to the main objective of VBE operations – the creation of economically beneficial VO's. Each VBE member has the opportunity to both enhance preparedness and to open sources for new Collaboration Opportunities. This can be done by:

- *Leveraging of members' competencies and skills:* Competence and skills can mainly be leveraged by any kind of training. For instance, project management training may enable members to act as VO managers or provide valuable contributions to VO planning. Members can either publish information on external training events, or organize and announce training events.
- *Enhancing name-recognition of the VBE:* Enhancing name-recognition of the VBE means effectively market the VBE – and to increase the number of potential sources for Collaboration Opportunities. This can be done by placing articles in newspapers and magazines, by organizing workshops or industrial fairs, or by gaining patents and licenses that provide a unique market position to the VBE.
- *Providing Collaboration Opportunities:* Collaboration Opportunities can come to be either by direct contacting potential customers, or by responding to calls-for-tenders.

Contributions to all the three aspects increase the wealth of the VBE and its members. Vice versa, pro-activeness of members is required to gather those contributions. Not every member providing such contribution receives direct economic value out of it: in case a member acquires a Collaboration Opportunity that leads to a VO in which it is not involved, others would gain economic benefit for the contribution provided. Ensuring mechanisms for rewarding beneficial contributions is an important means of motivating members to contribute regardless of whether they directly get economic benefit or not.

Contributions supporting the strategic objectives of the VBE can be uploaded by partners into the VBE bag-of-assets. Consequently they enrich the VBE amount of assets. Providing benefits to the members contributing to the bag-of-assets is an important incentive to pro-active behaviour. This can be done by means of a member rewarding system. There are already several existing rewarding systems in various industries, mostly with the objective to make a customer spend more money on items and services which a company offers, but also on helping to lower costs, or raise attractiveness as business partner. Typical examples are airline bonus miles (e.g. Sky Team (KLM, 2007) or the eBay evaluation system (eBay, 2007)).

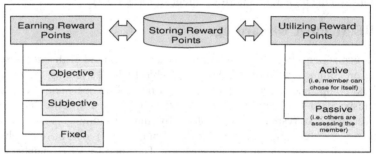

Figure 9 - Earning and utilizing points in Rewarding Systems

By looking at existing rewarding systems, characteristic elements and commonalities clearly show. First, an actor can earn reward points by investing on a number of issues or at least by showing certainty on behaviour. Attribution of points can either be objective (according to a certain algorithm), or subjective (based on personal assessment). Second commonality is the utilization of accumulated points. This can either be done actively or passive: Actively utilizing reward items means to choose what to do with those points. Passively utilizing reward points means being estimated by others according to the number of points a member has accumulated (Lauer, 2004). Points are hereby maintained, not being reduced or spent through the act of assessment by others. Figure 9 shows the general mechanisms of earning and utilizing reward points.

The Member Rewarding Service creates the possibility to reward and encourage proactive behaviour of VBE members. VBE related contributions that can be rewarded are listed in the Table 3:

Table 3: Possible actions that can lead to rewarding a member

Item	Description	Reward	VBE Benefit
Announce Training Event	A VBE member gets notion of a training events and posts an announcement in the bag-of-assets.	Evaluated	Increased Competencies
Organize Training Event	A VBE member is organizing a training event and announces it in the bag-of-	Evaluated	Increased Competencies

Item	Description	Reward	VBE Benefit
	assets for other members to participate.		
Bringing new member to the VBE	A member brings a new member into the VBE closing competency gaps	Fix	Increased Competencies
Articles in the press	Press-releases on the VBE spread the name of the VBE throughout the public leveraging name-recognition of the VBE	Evaluated	Increase Name Recognition
Patent Achievement	A VBE member gains a patent for a specific item or service.	Fix	Increase Name Recognition
License Achievement	A VBE member is offering licenses	Fix	Increase Name Recognition
Announcing Industrial Fairs	A VBE member gets notion of an upcoming industrial fair relevant to the VBE. It posts announcement to the BAMS	Evaluated	Increase Name Recognition
Organizing an Industrial Fair	A member takes the part of organizing an industrial fair in the VBE industrial sector. This provides lots of contacts and business opportunities to the VBE	Fix	Increase Name Recognition
Announcing Industrial Workshop	A member gets notion of an upcoming industrial workshop relevant to the VBE posting the announcement to the BAMS	Evaluated	Increase Name Recognition
Organizing Industrial Workshop	A member is organizing an industrial workshop, providing several contacts to the VBE.	Fix	Increase Name Recognition
Winning an industrial award	Industrial awards leverage the name recognition of the one winning it, simultaneously leveraging the attractiveness of the company.	Evaluated	Increase Name Recognition
Providing a Call-for-Tenders	Calls for Tenders open-up the doors towards collaboration opportunities. The VBE can write a proposal on this, and maybe achieves a new CO	Evaluated	Collaboration Opportunity
Acquiring a Collaboration Opportunity	A member can directly convince one of its partners to give an order to the VBE. This is providing direct benefit to the VBE	Fix	Collaboration Opportunity

Taking a look at the third column (reward) of Table 3 it is indicated that two options for attributing reward points to contributions: Fixed and evaluated. Attributing fixed points to items is simple for the present value of a partner's reward points is just increased by the fixed number of points. Having to evaluate partner's contributions to figure out the amount of points to be attributed proves to be more complicated: the VBE admin has to access the item, study it, and assign reward points according to specific criteria. Using the Member Rewarding Service, the VBE administrator can assess the documents by four criteria:

1. Relevance for the VBE: Different contributions may have different relevance for the VBE.
2. Overall quality of the contribution: Is the content well structured, understandable, become relevance and expected benefit for the VBE clear from the representation of contents in the document.
3. Timeliness: Does the contribution leave the VBE enough time to react. In case this is a call-for-tenders ("collaboration opportunity"), with an insufficient proposal preparation time, the contribution is useless, despite of possible high relevance, good quality, and a good expected benefit.
4. Potential Impact to the VBE: The benefit the contribution is expected to provide to the VBE.

To each of those criteria a maximum score can be attributed. Actually achieved scores are subjectively attributed by the VBE administration evaluating the contribution. The achieved value is given in absolute and relative numbers. Adding the achieved points, giving them in percentages of the maximum score, and multiplying those percentages with the number of maximum possible points for the kind of contribution delivers the number of reward points the member is awarded for its contribution. The Member Rewarding course of actions is as follows:

Entries to the bag-of-assets cause an alert on the administrator's screen. This alert shows the name, the category of contribution, such as the date is was entered. Clicking on the respective message, the administrator can now access the document and evaluate it. Accessing the new contribution, the administrator can read it and attribute reward points to it. For each of the four criteria a maximum number of points can be assigned by the VBE administrator and are accumulated to an aggregate value. The newly awarded points are attributed to the partner.

On earning rewards points, the VBE member can trade these points against incentives that provide direct value to strategic contribution by this partner. Therefore the VBE member accesses the list of pre-defined incentives and makes his choice. Reward-points required to "buy" this incentives are automatically deducted from the member's reward account. The VBE administrator is notified by the partner selecting this incentives and initiates further steps for providing the member with the incentive's benefit. The VBE member is notified that its selection of incentive is accepted.

The ability to configure the list of incentives leverages flexibility of the rewarding system. This is done by the VBE administrator accessing the list of incentives. Then the administrator enters incentives and points required to "buy" this incentive and confirms. Alternatively, the VBE administrator accesses a specific existing incentive, modifies the incentive's properties and stores modified dataset.

In case the process of attributing reward points to the member that earned them turns out dissatisfactory to the member, the VBE member can claim points missing. Missing points can result from a forgotten / delayed attribution of points, or from an "unfair" assessment of the partner's contribution. Initially, the VBE member gets notified on the number of points it is attributed. If the member organization is not satisfied with the number of points, it opens the "reward claim" portlet and leaves a message to the VBE administrator justifying the claim. The VBE administrator is notified about the incoming complaint, reads it and, if necessary, initiates further actions, and decides on how to manage the problem. The number of reward points may be corrected and the VBE member is notified about the updated number of reward points.

5.3 VBE Members Roles, Rights and Responsibility Management

The actors of the VBE who become users of the VMS have different roles and rights in the VBE. Therefore, they will also have different rights and responsibilities that need to be adapted and supported by MSMS. Each member's participation in a VBE is related to a specific role, equipping the member with a set of rights and responsibilities. The member roles, rights, and responsibility functionalities provide the VBE administrator with opportunities to assign the related information to each VBE actor.

The Members Roles, Rights and Responsibility Management is based on the Liferay user administration functionalities. VBE members can thus be assigned to a pre-defined role, giving them specific access to different functionalities of the MSMS. Examples for roles in MSMS are Membership Applicants, VBE Members, the VBE Administrator and the VO Initiator. An example of use would be Member Registration. An applicant can not login into the system unless he is accepted by the VBE administrator. This is guaranteed by the authentication which is role based.

6. SUPPORT FOR INFORMATION MANAGEMENT

This section addresses two systems designed and implemented to provide services for supporting the management of information in the VBE, namely the VIMS and BAMS.

6.1 VO Information Management System (VIMS)

As easily to be seen from the underlying concepts of Virtual Breeding Environments and Virtual Organizations, it is beneficial for the VBE to incorporate experiences from previous VO's into the creation of new ones. Developing thorough processes and guidelines on how to use this information in the process of VO Creation is dependent on the VO Creation Framework, but the management and provision of VO related data is subject to the VIMS. Consequently, the functionalities for management of VO information provide mechanisms for storing information on created VO's in the VMS data-structure such as structuring, storing, and providing inheritance information to the VO Creation process.

VO related information will be needed by the VO Initiator as repository of experiences with certain partners and combinations of partners in the past. The VO initiator will need this information as input to the decision on which of two or more competing partners to engage in the VO. The VO Information Management System comprises the functionalities of (i) Registration of Created VOs Service, and (ii) Management of VO Inheritance Information. In more detail:

- *Registration of created VO's:* Created VO's need to be registered in the VMS, specifically in the VBE profile. Registration of created VO services provides features to retrieve VO data from the corresponding VO services, and to update the VBE profile.

- *Inheritance Management:* VO's create various kinds of assets. These assets need to be properly managed to be of sustainable benefit to the VBE. VO Inheritance Management has the objective to retrieve inherited information from the VO, to store them in the VBE Bag-of-Assets and to make them available to related processes that require inherited information as input (for instance VO creation).

Registration of created VOs

Registering created VO's in the VBE Management System will be an automated process triggered by a set of data provided by the VO Creation Framework. Triggered by an incoming notification on a newly created VO, the dataset is structured according to the VIMS database structure and stored in the VIMS. The Registration of created VO's is therefore implemented as a web-service, providing an interface for submitting the VO related data to the VIMS. Additionally, a portlet provides a GUI to notify the VBE administrator about newly created VO's and the VO members. Other existing VO's and their members can also be displayed.

Management of VO Inheritance Information

Every Virtual Organization creates a lot of immaterial assets facilitating the process of creating and running new VO's out of a VBE. Consequently, inheritance management is a function of knowledge management to ensure the sustainability of results from one VO. After dissolution of a VO, the VO related information is stored within the VMS for utilization in the VO Creation Process. The Inheritance Information is being pushed from the VO Management System to the VMS before the VO dissolves. Information must be classified (flagged) into: *Confidential* – restricted to VO Partners (will NOT be submitted to VIMS), *Restricted* – restricted to a defined group of VBE actors (will be stored as part of VIMS bag of assets), *Public* – publicly available (will be stored as part of VBE bag of assets). The interface to push information from the VO to the VMS is realized as a web-service. It includes methods for updating the VO contract and agreement data, for providing the members past performance information and all other VO related information. The VO Inheritance Information can be accessed using the Bag-of-Assets (BAMS) according to the classification of the documents. While confidential information is not submitted to the VIMS, restricted information can only be accessed by a group of VBE actors defined by their role mapping. Public information may be accessed by every member.

6.2 Bag of Assets Management System

The **VBE Bag of Assets,** as also addressed in Chapter 2.1 of this book, refers to all valuable elements that different VBE actors use and share with others. Some of the assets can also be the property of the VBE administrators which are added to Bag of Assets for access/use by VBE member organizations. In a VBE the following potential document assets are identified:

- "Lessons learned" contributed by VBE member organizations enable the knowledge gained from past experiences to be applied to the current and future projects. Its intention is to avoid the repetition of past failures as well as the ability to share observations and best practices.

- General policies in the form of documents, books, leaflets, to help member organizations to easily follow the guidelines of a VBE.
- Information of interest which is specific to the sector.
- Sample contracts to speed up the contracting and negotiation phase while creating VOs.
- General legal documents related to the sector.
- For the first step of implementation, historic performance information can also be managed through the bag-of-assets.

The Bag of Assets Management System (BAMS) (Afsarmanesh, at al, 2007) provides services which supports VBE member organizations to publish and share information within VBE. It provides services which address the automated management of VBE structural information such as guidelines, bylaws, value systems guidelines, incentives information, etc. It also support the interchanging of experiences and business information related to assets items, information about support institutions, VO inheritance and historic performance information, etc. Bag of Assets provides a number of elements that are fundamental and useful for VBE member organizations (and for VBE as a whole) including: the general sharable information provided in some documents, software tools, lessons learned, etc.

The BAMS aims at supporting actors in the VBE in sharing common data. Thus one crucial aspect of the BAMS is to enhance understanding of both the concepts related to the assets stored and their respective representations in the system. Figure 10 shows an ontology based model representing the common structure of BAMS. As such this model represents a partial architecture of the BAMS.

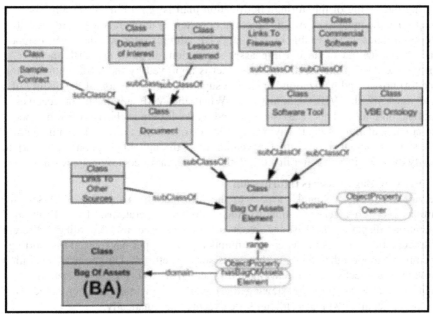

Figure 10: Ontology of Asset items

BAMS has been implemented as a Content Management System (CMS), thus its main functionality aims at supporting both: publishing information and conducting workflows (i.e. approval processes). Furthermore, BAMS supports dynamic definition of different types of structured documents, while it also provides storage for regular file-base documents, such as PDF files, MS-Word files, graphical files, etc. Additionally, the semantic search functionality for full-text is provided in BAMS to facilitate users in their search for the needed information. One example screenshot from the BAMS of IECOS (a VBE from Mexico) is addressed in Figure 11. This Figure specifically illustrates the process of submission of a new article to the BAMS's document library.

The developed BAMS is primarily used by the VBE members, who provide the VBE consortium with relevant supporting information, e.g. lessons learned, software tools, etc. Furthermore, it is used by the VBE Administrator during the Member Rewarding process for checking if members collaborate in the VBE through submitting the relevant documents and best practices to the BAMS.

The following specific functionalities/services are implemented for the BAMS:

1. Publishing Bag of Assets information
Service supports the collection of new valuable information of different types (e.g. documents, lessons learned, software tools, and links to other sources) from VBE members. This service consists of the following operations: The "Creation of a new asset" operation supports the creation of a new "asset" through a special "asset form". In this form, the VBE member enters all data for the selected asset type by using an rtf-editor (i.e. a "rich text field" editor developed for entering text, formatting, attaching files, and inserting web links). The meta-data fields of a certain asset type are represented individually, and have to be filled in by VBE members. During the saving of this form, a notification mail is sent to the VBE administrator to approve the new asset. At this time, the new item is temporary added to the list of proposed items and is visible only to the VBE administrator and the VBE member. The "Modification of an existing asset" operation supports the VBE member to change the data in the asset, until the asset is approved by the VBE administrator. The "Approval and realization" operation supports the evaluation of the quality of a new asset by the VBE administrator. When the VBE administrator receives a notification mail and also sees the new (red marked) item in the asset list, he checks the content of this asset. If any ambiguities or questions arise, VBE administrator can start communication with the vendor (e.g. through mail, phone, or chat) to clarify the open issues. After that the VBE administrator decides on approval.

2. Viewing Bag of Assets information
Service facilitates a "quick" access to the information in the Bag of Assets for further use. This service supports the following operations: The "Browsing" operation displays the list of asset items that set up according different characteristics, such as the asset type, number of assets per page, etc. The "Sorting" operation supports the changing the assets sorting settings. The "Search" operation provides the selection of all items matching search criteria. The "View specific asset item" operation support the viewing the content of an asset in a formatted way. Furthermore, all downloads and links are executed automatically.

3. Subscribing / unsubscribing
Service supports the informing of the subscribed VBE members about new emerged assists via e-mail.

Figure 11 - Example screen-shot from BAMS' document library of the IECOS VBE

4. Support of Member Rewarding

Service provides quantifiable information needed for the VBE rewarding mechanisms. This service consists of the following operations: The "Feedback (Rating)" operation supports the rating of the usefulness of asset items provided by VBE members. The "Commenting / discussion" operation supports commenting on asset items. The "Accessing from Member Rewarding service" operation provides all necessary information according all asset items of a certain VBE member to support rewarding mechanism conducted by the VBE administrator. Specifically, following types of data about asset items are processed: title, rate, comments, and access.

The Bag of Asset is used to manage different kinds of information which can be classified into twofold: *Structured textual information:* representing documents and knowledge stored as free text data to be read by humans. This category includes organizational guidelines, asset items, textual part of the VO inheritance and historic performance data, etc. *Structured data:* representing numerical and other sorts of well thought-out data used for further calculations. This category includes for example numerical values from the VO inheritance and historic performance information. The management of the structured data of the BAMS is done separately from the CMS. The data is stored in the specific database reflecting the required structure and data types. From the user point of view, structured data is interlinked with the textual information and usually presented in the tabular format. At the same time, the data can be accessed and used by other modules of the VMS in calculations such as an input to functionalities of Decision Support and TrustMan systems.

7. DECISION SUPPORT SYSTEM

The *Decision Support Subsystem (DSS) assists* the VBE Administrators and VBE members with a performance and competency analysis in the VBE. This system provides services which enable actors of the VBE to make informed decision about a number of issues. The system provides services that basically apply two approaches for assisting users in their decision and management process:

- *Data analysis:* processing the data stored in the VBE Management system and providing user with the results that are easy to understand.
- *Pro-active notification:* the DSS can automatically perform selected data analysis regularly and notify user by email when the results of analysis require user attention.

Based on these approaches, the DSS provides services, which support users to make decisions, namely the three services of: (1) Controlling and alarming on the lack of performance of organizations, (2) Analyzing and capturing the VBE competency gaps, and (3) Controlling and alarming on the low trust level of organizations

7.1 Service for controlling and alarming on lack of performance

This service, also called "lack of performance warning", supports analyzing the progressive performance of an organization and provide a warning or notification when it is falling. It is a security precaution for ensuring the wealth of organizations in terms of their performance in the VBE. Based on the input data from other subsystems of VMS, such as VIMS, etc., the performance indicators are calculated for the different areas and activities of the VBE and its member organizations. The results presented in form of graphs and traffic lights helps users understand how well the VBE and its members do perform in achievement of both internal and external goals. Active monitoring and notification is supported by this service. An email notification is sent to the appropriate organizations when their performance level falls below the threshold. Figure 12 shows a global view of the service.

The functionality of the "lack of performance warning" service is based on the concept of the **Balanced Score Cards (BSC)** developed by Robert S. Kaplan and David P. Norton (Kaplan & Norton, 1992) and implemented through integration and extension of an existing BSC tool called **Siemens Succeed** (Siemens Succeed_URL). The BSC should not be regarded as an information system with a new type of key performance indicators or ratios, but rather as a strategic management system or leadership instrument. Apart from the well-known financial indicators, other perspectives (customer, internal process, learning and growth) are being considered as well in order to gain a more balanced picture of an organization's situation.

The VBE's special aspects, e.g. its organizational structures, business strategies, business models, and collaboration issues, have to be taken into account, when defining a strategic management system such as DSS. After analyzing the VBE value systems and metrics (Romero, et al, 2007), a base set of *performance indicators* for the VBE-self, VBE members, and VOs, considered for perspectives of Financial, Productivity, Strategic, and Social, are identified. As an example, the VBE member's performance indicators from the financial perspective are addressed in Table 4. These "performance indicators" are adopted for measurement of performance in the "lack of performance warning" service.

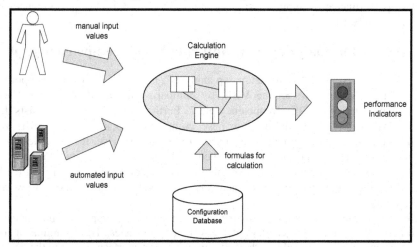

Figure 12 - Manipulation of data for performance analysis as supported by DSS

Table 4: Example performance indicators for VBE members

	VBE Member
Financial	1. Annual profits derived from VO participation
	2. Annual incomes derived from VO participation
	3. Increase in annual sales as result of VO participation
	4. Increment in profits as result of VO participation

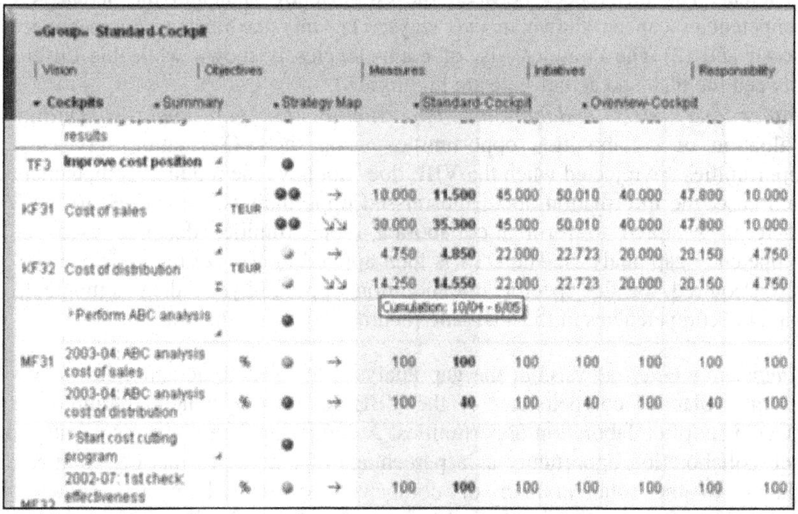

Figure 13 - An example screen-shot from the "lack of performance warning" service

The "lack of performance warning" service, implemented on the base of Siemens Succeed tool, supports the following operations: (1) definition and configuration of "scorecards" (i.e. objectives, measures and key performance indicators), (2) manual/automatic collection of planned and actual data, and (3) publishing of the results. One example screen-shot of the services provided by the DSS to support the "lack of performance warning" illustrating the evaluation of a set of performances is shown in Figure 13.

7.2 Service for analyzing and capturing VBE's competency gaps

This service, also called "competency gap analysis", is used to discover weak points and missing competencies in the VBE, by comparing the available in the VBE competencies with the VBE "competency plan". Furthermore, this service assists the VBE administrator with defining a new competency plan for the VBE by determining the missing competencies discovered by this service, for example when evaluating business opportunities, or when VO creation failed due to lack of competencies. The general overview of this service is addressed below in Figure 14. Basically, the "competency gap analysis", service provides the following functionality:

- *Basic definition of the strategic competency plan:* Strategic competency plan is used to describe a future, desired state of the VBE competencies. The definition of the competency plan is entered into the DSS through a user interface similar to the one of PCMS. However, the specification of competencies in the plan is simplified, for example the organizations' resources are not taken into account. Initially, the complete set of VBE competencies is copied into the plan. After all the desired competencies in the VBE are specified in the DSS, the plan is set. A number of different competency plans can be specified.

- *Show differences between the planned and actual competencies:* The differences can be of two types, namely, either (i) the capability is missing or (ii) the capacity is not sufficient. The differences between the competency plan and the actual state of competencies can be shown in two ways: (1) Only the missing competencies are shown and (2) The complete list of competencies is shown while the differences between the plan and actual state are highlighted.

- *Gather and select collaboration opportunities for gap analysis:* During the evaluation of collaboration opportunities using the VO creation services some opportunities are rejected when the VBE does not have the required competencies. In such case, the information about the missed opportunities is provided to the VMS where it is stored to form a collaboration opportunities database used for the competency gap analysis. The DSS is then applied to analyze the competencies that were required for the specific collaboration opportunity. It then compare to the available competencies in the VBE and identify those missing ones.

- *Competency Gap analysis:* In the gap analysis, the system actually shows how the current / planned competencies of the VBE cover competencies required for the selected set of collaboration opportunities. A competency gap index is calculated for each collaboration opportunity as a percentage of number of missing competencies relative to the total number of competencies required by the collaboration opportunity. User can display the index for each individual collaboration opportunity. The user can also view the total competency gap index calculated as an average of the individual indexes.

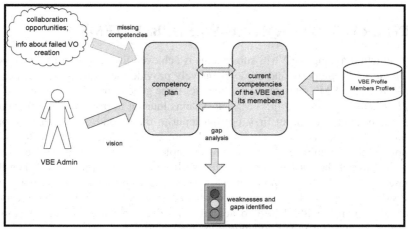

Figure 14 - Process of competency gap analysis

- *Analyze impact of newly acquired or lost members:* A competency gap analysis can be also used for evaluating the impact of acquiring new or losing existing members of VBE. User can either define competencies of potential member organizations, or select actual membership applicants or existing VBE member organizations. Then, the user can see how the competencies of the VBE would change when acquiring or losing those member organizations. The user can also create a derived copy of the competency plan where the competencies of new member organizations are added and competencies of lost members are removed. The derived competency plan can be then used for further analysis against the collaboration opportunities.

7.3 Service for controlling and alarming on the low trust level of organizations

This service, also called "low trust level warning", supports VBE administrator to analyze and monitor the progressive base trust level of member organizations. Based on the results of analysis, the administrator can send a warning notification to the organizations whose trust level has fallen below given threshold. The service supports the administrator in the following analysis steps:

- *Configure schedule:* VBE administrator specifies the schedule for performing periodic trust level assessment. Several different schedules can be specified either for a single member organization, subset of members or all members. The administrator can select a set trust level criteria when a specialized trust level has to be analyzed.
- *Perform check:* This action is done automatically by the system. In the configured periods, system calculates the base trust level of the specified VBE member or set of members. If the resulting base trust level has fallen below the defined threshold then the system sends an email notification to the VBE administrator and/or to the corresponding VBE members.
- *Process warning:* The notification email message will contain URL link that will forward user to the VBE portal page showing the detailed results of the base trust level analysis and the reason why the warning was issued. The graphical user interface of the TrustMan system is used for this purpose.

8. INTERACTIONS AMONG VMS SUBSYSTEMS

The interaction among the VMS subsystems is achieved through a set of developed web services. To properly and comprehensively provide the required services each subsystem of the VMS interacts with others for three general purposes, namely:

(1) *For acquiring input data:* VMS subsystems interact to pass to each some data that may either be output first tool but input to the second one. Sometime one tool sends some data to another tool to be processed and gets back results as its input while providing its services. For example TrustMan system interacts with MSMS to get the trust related data for VBE membership applicants. When the base trust level of the applicant is assessed the results are then used by the MSMS to support the decision on the acceptance. Similarly, VO creation services interact with PCMS to acquire related competencies of organizations needed for specific VO or collaboration opportunity.

(2) *For providing services to others:* Some VMS subsystems need to invoke a number of services provided by others in orders either gets the results or integrate those services with the local services. For example, three VMS subsystems are identified, which invokes TrustMan services, namely: MSMS, DSS and VO creation services. The MSMS invokes the service for assessing base trust level of membership applicant for the aim of analyzing whether the applicant organization meets the specified minimum level of trust in the VBE. Furthermore, in order to analyze the deteriorating trust level of the organization the DSS invokes the services provided by TrustMan system for assessing base trust level of organizations. Moreover, while selecting potential VO partners among the VBE members for inviting them into a VO the TrustMan services are invoke for the evaluation of their trustworthiness.

(3) *For supporting human access:* Some subsystems need to interact with others in order to use their specific user interface. For example, while DSS provides notification on the falling trust level, the respective organization is redirected to TrustMan system to view the details of its trust level through the web.

However, it should be noted that the developed VMS sub-systems although they interoperate for different purposes they are independent systems. Thus each sub-system can be installed as a stand alone system to provide its intended services.

9. CONCLUSION

This chapter addresses the specification of the VBE management system (VMS) and its constituted subsystems. The VMS is designed and implemented to provide the fundamental services needed for assisting the VBE administration and other VBE actors with automated and/or semi-automated handling of a number of their tasks. As such, the VMS supports the management of the VBE during its entire life cycle. In specific, the chapter addresses services for: management of competency and profiles of organizations, management of trust among organizations, managing member registration and VBE structure, management of the VBE's bag of assets and the VO information as well as supporting the decision making processes in the VBE.

As indicated in Figure 1, the VMS subsystems can be accessed in two different ways, namely: through web interfaces for human users of each subsystem, and through service invocation for supporting subsystem interactions. Web interfaces of all subsystems that are presented in this chapter have been addressed in their respective sections, e.g. Figure 3 illustrating the web-interface for the ODMS. Furthermore, interactions among subsystems are facilitated through web services' invocation as briefly introduced in section 8, thorough research needs to be performed to extend support for needed interactions among VMS subsystems as well as to develop the needed components to automate those interactions.

Current design and development of the VMS reflects and properly supports the requirements and characteristics of its subsystems of the level that they are currently identified in research and practice on VBE networks. However, it is expected that in future new or evolved requirements and characteristics shall emerge. Therefore, the VMS subsystems shall enhance and extend accordingly if and when needed, to capture new or changing requirements. Consequently, besides customizability of the subsystems, they also need to be adaptable and scalable to the new changes in the environment, with some semi-automated features. For instance, ODMS has already partially addresses these requirements. These aspects point to our future progressive research in this area.

Acknowledgement: This work was supported in part by the ECOLEAD project funded by the European Commission. The authors acknowledge contributions from partners in ECOLEAD.

9. REFERENCES

Afsarmanesh H., & Camarinha-Matos L.M. (2005). A framework for management of virtual organization breeding environments, in Collaborative Networks and their Breeding Environments, Springer, pp. 35-49, ISBN 0387282599.

Afsarmanesh, H., Camarinha-Matos, L., Msanjila, S.S. (2007). Virtual organizations breeding environments: key results from ECOLEAD. In the proceedings of International conference on Cost Effective Automation in Networked Product Development and Manufacturing - IFAC-CEA'2007, Monterey, Mexico.

Afsarmanesh, H., Ermilova, E. (2007). Ontology Engineering for VO Breeding Environments. In the Proceedings of the 9th International Conference on the Modern Information Technology in the Innovation Processes of the Industrial Enterprises – MITIP'07, pp. 124-137, Florence Italy.

Anjewierden, A., Wielinga, B.J., Hoog R. and Kabel S. (2003). Task and domain ontologies for knowledge mapping in operational processes. Metis deliverable 2003/4.2. University of Amsterdam

Calvanese, D., Giuseppe, D.G., Lenzerini, M. (2001). Proceedings of the 2001 Description Logic Workshop (DL 2001).

Camarinha-Matos L., Afsarmanesh H., & Ollus M. (2005). ECOLEAD: A holistic approach to creation and management of dynamic virtual organizations, in Collaborative Networks and their Breeding Environments, Springer, pp. 3-16

Camarinha-Matos, L. M., Afsarmanesh, H. (2003). A roadmap for strategic research on virtual organizations, in Proceedings of PRO-VE'03 – Processes and Foundations for Virtual Organizations, Kluwer Academic Publishers, Oct 2003.

Camarinha-Matos, L.M. Afsarmanesh, H. (2005). Collaborative networks: A new scientific discipline, Journal of Intelligent Manufacturing, vol. 16, N° 4-5, pp. 439-452, ISSN: 0956-5515.

Denny, M. (2004). Ontology Tools Survey. http://www.xml.com/pub/a/2004/07/14/onto.html. Viewed 29.08.2007.

Ding, Y., Fensel, D. (2001): Ontology Library Systems: The key to successful Ontology Re-use, in Proceedings of the First Semantic Web Working Symposium

eBay, www.ebay.com (access Nov. 6th, 2007)

Ermilova E., Afsarmanesh, H, (2008). An ontology based approach for development and operation of Virtual Organization Breeding Environments, In Proc. of IASED SE'08 conference, Austria, Innsbruck

Ermilova, E., Afsarmanesh, H. (2006). Competency and profiling management in Virtual Organization Breeding Environments. In IFIP International Federation of Information Processing, Volume 224, Network-centric collaboration and Supporting Frameworks, eds. Camarinha-Matos L., Afsarmanesh H., Ollus M., (Boston: Springer), pp. 131-142.

Ermilova, E., Afsarmanesh, H. (2007). Profiling and competency management in Virtual organization Breeding Environments, in Int. J. Intelligent Manufacturing.

Grobelnik, M. and Mladenić, D., (2005). Automated knowledge discovery in advanced knowledge management. Journal of knowledge management, vol 9, no 5, pp 132-149.

Guevara-Masis, V., Afsarmanesh, H, Hetzberger, L. O. (2004). Ontology-based automatic data structure generation for collaborative networks, in Proceedings of 5th PRO-VE'04 – Virtual Enterprises and Collaborative Networks, Kluwer Academic Publishers, ISBN 1-4020-8138-3, pp 163-174, 23-26.

Kaplan R. S. and Norton D. P. (1992). The balanced scorecard: measures that drive performance. Harvard Business Review Jan - Feb pp71-80.

Kirkwood, C. W. (1998). System Dynamics Method. Ventana System Inc.

KLM, (2007). www.klm.com (access November, 2007)

Lauer, T. (2004). Bonusprogramme – Rabattsysteme für Kunden erfolgreich gestalten, Springer

LifeRay, (2007). www.liferay.com (access November 2007)

Msanjila, S.S. & Afsarmanesh, H. (2007a). Specification of the TrustMan system for assisting management of VBEs. In the lecture notes of computer science series, LNCS 4657, Springer

Msanjila, S.S. & Afsarmanesh, H. (2007b). On architectural design of TrustMan system applying HICI analysis results. In the International Journal of Software. Academy Publisher. Issue 6.

Msanjila, S.S. & Afsarmanesh, H. (2007c): Towards Establishing Trust Relationships among Organizations in VBEs. In Establishing the Foundation of Collaborative Networks. pg 3-14,

Msanjila, S.S., Afsarmanesh, H. (2006). Understanding and Modeling Trust Relationships in Collaborative Networked Organizations, in Proceedings of international conference on Business, Law & Technology present and Emerging Trends, Volume 2, ISBN 87-991385-1-4, IAITL, pp 402-416, Copenhagen, Denmark , 5-7 December 2006.

Msanjila, S.S., Tewoldeberhan, T.W., Janssen, M., Block-Bockstel, W. & Verbraeck, A. (2005). E-supply chain orchestration using web service technologies: a case using BPEL4WS. In the Proceedings of Information Resource Management Association Conference, San Diego. pg. 282–285

Noy, N.F. (2003). What do we need for ontology integration on the Semantic Web (Position Statement). In Proceedings of the Semantic Integration Workshop, CEUR Workshop Proceedings, vol. 82.

OntoBasis project, (2007). http://wise.vub.ac.be/ontobasis/index.html . Viewed August, 2007.

OWL 2004. Web Ontology Language Overview, W3C Recommendation , http://www.w3.org/TR/owl-features. Viewed 29.08.2007.

Pinto, H.S., Gomez-Perez, A., Martins, J.P (1999). Some Issues on Ontology Integration. In Proceedings of the IJCAI-99 workshop on Ontologies and Problem-Solving Methods (KRR5) Stockholm, Sweden, August 2, 1999.

Pinto, H.S., Martins, J.P. (2001). A Methodology for Ontology Integration. In Proceedings of K-CAP'01, October 22-23, 2001, Victoria, British Columbia, Canada.

Protégé. (2007). http://protege.stanford.edu. Viewed 29.08.2007.

Romero, D., Galeano, N., Molina, A. (2007). A conceptual model for Virtual Breeding Environments Value Systems. Accepted for publication in Proceedings of PRO-VE'07 - 8th IFIP Working Conference on Virtual Enterprises (Springer).

Siemens Succeed, (2007). http://www.pse.siemens.at/apps/sis/en/pseinternet.nsf/CD_Index? OpenFrameset&Bookmark&/view0/PK24050336D7EA234BC1257230002AB267 (access Dec. 12th, 2007)

Simoes, D., Ferreira, H., Soares, A.L. (2007): Ontology Engineering in Virtual Breeding Environments, in proceedings of PRO-VE'07 conference, pp. 137-146

Spivack, N. (2006). The Ontology Integration Problem http://novaspivack.typepad.com/nova_spivacks_weblog/2006/08/the_ontology_in.html. Viewed 29.08.2007.

Stojanovic, L. (2004): Methods and tools for ontology evolution, Ph.D. Thesis, University of Karlsruhe, Germany.

Sunagawa, E., Kozaki, K., Kitamura, Y., Mizoguchi, R. (2004). Organizing Role-concepts in Ontology Development Environment. AI Technical Report (Artificial Intelligence Research Group, I. S. I. R., Osaka Univ.), AI-TR-04-1.

Tudorache, T., Noy, N. (2007). Collaborative Protege. In Workshop on Social and Collaborative Construction of Structured knowledge, 16th Int. World Wide Web Conf. (WWW 2007), Canada.

VO CREATION
ASSISTANCE SERVICES

Luis M. Camarinha-Matos [1,2], Ana Inês Oliveira [2],
Damjan Demsar [3], Michele Sesana [4], Arturo Molina [5],
Fabiano Baldo [6], Toni Jarimo [7]

[1] *New University of Lisbon, PORTUGAL, cam@uninova.pt*
[2] *UNINOVA, PORTUGAL, aio@uninova.pt*
[3] *Jozef Stefan Institute, SLOVENIA, damjan.demsar@ijs.si*
[4] *TXT e-Solutions, ITALY, michele.sesana@txt.it*
[5] *Tecnologico de Monterrey,MEXICO, armolina@itesm.mx,*
[6] *Federal University of Santa Catarina, BRAZIL, baldo@gsigma.ufsc.br*
[7] *VTT Technical Research Centre of Finland, FINLAND, toni.jarimo@vtt.fi*

The concept of virtual organization (VO) appears particularly well-suited to cope with very dynamic and turbulent market conditions. The underlying rational the possibility of rapidly forming a consortium triggered by a business opportunity and specially tailored to the requirements of that opportunity. Implicit in this idea is a notion of agility, allowing rapid adaptation to a changing environment. In order to make this possible, a VO creation process is designed in the context of a virtual organization breeding environment context. A framework for VO creation is thus introduced and a set of assistance services are designed and tools developed.

1. VO CREATION IN A VBE CONTEXT

The effectiveness of the virtual organization (VO) creation process is a critical element in collaborative networks. Early works on VO creation assumed that partners could be quickly identified and selected from the *open universe* of existing enterprises / organizations, and engaged into a collaboration network. This assumption however overlooks a number of important obstacles in this process among which the following can be mentioned (Afsarmanesh & Camarinha-Matos, 2005; Camarinha-Matos & Afsarmanesh, 2003; Camarinha-Matos et al., 2005b):

- How to know about the mere existence of potential partners in the open universe and deal with incompatible and limited sources of information?
- How to acquire basic profile information about organizations, when there is no common template or standard format?
- How to quickly and reliably establish an inter-operable collaboration infrastructure, given the heterogeneity of organizations at multi-levels, and the diversity of their interaction systems?

- How to build trust among organizations, which is the base for any collaboration?
- How to quickly develop and agree on the common principles of sharing and working together?
- How to quickly define the agreements on the roles and responsibilities of each partner, to reflect sharing of tasks, the rights on the produced results, etc.?

The situation is not too critical in the case of long-term collaboration processes not limited to a single business opportunity, such as in the case of supply chains (case A in Figure 1). In this case the costs (and time) of preparation for collaboration are affordable given the long term perspectives.

On the other hand (case C in Figure 1), for some specific niche sectors in which all actors share the same or compatible tools, business culture and practices, it is possible to quickly form a consortium even for a short-term single opportunity.

For the other cases the situation is much more critical. Particularly when the window of opportunity is short, in order to support rapid formation of collaborative networks it is necessary that potential partners are ***prepared and ready to participate*** in such collaboration. Preparedness includes common interoperable infrastructure, common operating rules, and common cooperation agreement, among others. Any collaboration also requires a base level of trust among the organizations. In this case a working solution is the creation of a long-term association of entities that prepare themselves to cooperate whenever an opportunity arises. This association is a **VO Breeding Environment** (VBE) (Afsarmanesh & Camarinha-Matos, 2005; Camarinha-Matos & Afsarmanesh, 2003; Camarinha-Matos et al., 2005b) for the creation of dynamic VOs (case B in Figure 1).

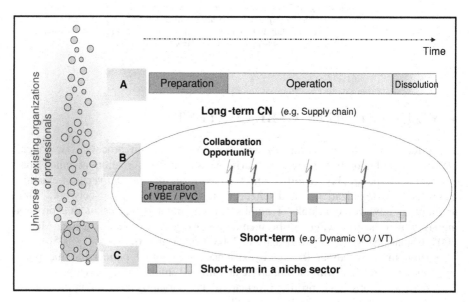

Figure 1 - VO creation in different contexts

The ECOLEAD project focus on VO creation process as that happen in the context of a VO Breeding Environment (VBE) (Camarinha-Matos & Afsarmanesh, 2003; Camarinha-Matos & Oliveira, 2005; Rabelo et al., 2000). This long term collaborative association is composed of organizations that are prepared to collaborate and thus may rapidly respond to a collaboration opportunity.

VBE makes it possible to collect and maintain data of the profile of VBE members. Furthermore, this enables the use of more sophisticated selection criteria, including aspects such as trust and historical collaboration performance. This would not be possible in an "open universe", since there is no practical means for collecting the necessary data.

As illustrated in Figure 2, it shall be noted that VBE creation and VO creation are different processes, triggered by different motivations. A VBE is created as a long term "controlled border" association and its members are recruited from the "open universe" of organizations according to the criteria defined by the VBE creators or administrators. A VO is a temporary organization triggered by a specific business / collaboration opportunity. Its partners are primarily selected from the VBE members. In case there is a lack of skills or capacity inside the VBE, organizations can be recruited from outside.

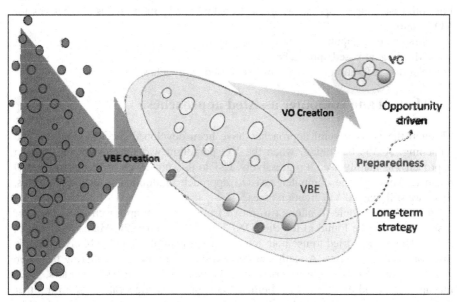

Figure 2 – VO creation in a VBE context

It is therefore necessary to develop an approach and a supporting framework to facilitate the VO creation process in order to make it effective. This chapter describes the approach developed by the ECOLEAD project for the concepts of VO creation within the context of VBE and introduces a set of developed services in the form of tools to support the various steps of the VO creation process.

2. BRIEF HISTORIC PANORAMA

A large number of R&D projects have addressed some specific aspects of the VO creation process, as found out by the VOSTER study (Luis M. Camarinha-Matos et al., 2005).

From a methodological point of view two main situations in VO creation can be considered:

- <u>Designed VO</u> – once a collaboration opportunity is detected by a VBE member playing the role of opportunity broker, a top-down process is launched for the VO design and creation coordinated by the VO planner (which can be the same organization that performs the role of opportunity broker).
- <u>Emergent VO</u> – in this case the broker would announce the collaboration opportunity to the VBE members and then would simply wait for the emergence of potential candidate consortia. In the end, the opportunity broker and/or the VO planner, or the customer, would choose the most suitable consortium.

For both cases, three approaches are so far addressed in the R&D as alternatives for VO creation:

- Manual or computer-assisted approaches
- Multi-agent based approaches
- Service-federation or service market based approaches.

2.1 Manual and computer assisted approaches

Through the years several approaches have been developed for VO planning and launching. At the beginning, when the VO paradigm was introduced, the manual approach was mainly used. Progressively, ICT tools were developed to assist the VO planner. Although the computer assisted approach predominates in today's VOs, there are still manual VO creation cases.

An earlier example of attempt to move from a manual approach to a computer assisted one can be found in the PRODNET project (Camarinha-Matos & Cardoso, 1999). This project tried to use both internal lists of suppliers and publicly available directories of enterprises. A methodology involving a preliminary filtering based on profiles and required characteristics, followed by a call for tenders, bids management, and tools-assisted human decision, was elaborated. Several other works invested on matching algorithms to find partners whose competences best fit the requirements of a business opportunity.

In the last decade a considerable effort has been put in the so-called electronic procurement. The main objectives in this area include the definition of "normalized" procedures for public announcement of business offers, reception, and management of bids.

In parallel with the progress of the technological infrastructures and standards for information exchange, more advanced assistance mechanisms have been proposed, as illustrated in Figure 3 (Camarinha-Matos et al., 2005).

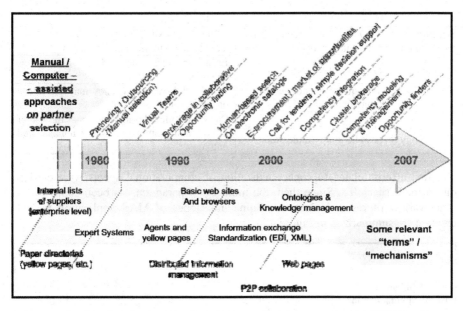

Figure 3 – Evolution of manual/computer-assisted approaches for VO creation

2.2 Multi-agent based approaches

Agents are autonomous software entities designed to operate and interact in distributed environments. They can handle sophisticated interactions due to their social abilities and also timely respond to changes in their environment (Jennings & Wooldridge, 1998). A multi-agent system (MAS) shows, at an abstract level, many similarities with a collaborative network. Therefore, a natural motivation to use MAS as a modeling and implementation support for the VO creation process has been present in many research works (e.g. Camarinha-Matos et al., 2005). Examples of such similarities are illustrated on the table below.

Table 1 – VO creation requirements vs. multi-agent based mechanisms

VO creation requirements	MAS mechanisms
Members are autonomous entities	Autonomous operation of agents
Different levels of cooperation	Scalability and multiple configuration options
Composed of distributed, heterogeneous and autonomous components	Easily mapped into a MAS
Flexible management and decision making	Coordination and distributed problem solving
Need for rapid reactions in execution and supervision of distributed business processes	Having agents representing each organization, it is possible to distribute tasks and use agent's communication to facilitate supervision
Market characteristics and negotiation needs	Ability to interact with other agents and several negotiation and auction protocols

	available
Structure of VO might need some reconfiguration during its life-cycle	Allows a flexible modeling as MAS can quickly adapt to new circumstances
Dynamic change of roles of its members	Easily mapped into MAS, namely as behaviors
Need to handle the requirements of autonomy vs. cooperative behavior	Federated MAS approaches may provide a balanced solution
Need for an unambiguous and precise terminology that can be jointly understood	Can be fulfilled through means of the use of a common communication language and ontology

The first efforts related to conceptualization of computational agents were carried out in the earlier 80's. Since then, the multi-agent paradigm has been applied to a large variety of research domains. Some milestones of MAS application to VO creation are summarized in Figure 4.

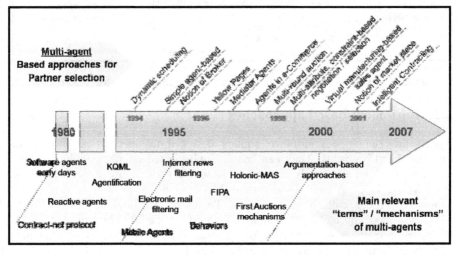

Figure 4 – Multi-agent based approaches for partner selection

A growing number of research prototypes applying multi-agent systems and market-oriented negotiation mechanisms for the VO formation are being developed. An early example is the work of (Rocha & Oliveira, 1999) that introduced a <u>virtual market place</u> where geographically distributed and autonomous enterprises are represented by agents. The work described in (Li et al., 2000) follows a similar approach. (Rabelo et al., 2000) developed a multi-agent-based architecture to support partners' selection in the context of a cluster of twelve enterprises in the moulds and die sector.

Various negotiation protocols have been elaborated for partners selection and coalition formation. <u>Auction mechanisms</u> became popular in agent-based consortia formation due to its simplicity and well predefined rules, as can be found in (Norman et al., 2004). There are several action mechanisms (Wurman, 2001), and the most used one is perhaps the combinatorial auction approach. This is a sophisticated type of auction where multiple units of multiple (potentially inter-related) items are traded simultaneously.

Given so, a multi-agent based approach can be very suitable in this domain since there are a number of characteristics that can fulfill the VO requests.

2.3 Service market based approaches

According to the service federation approach, companies (potential members of the virtual organization) are considered as "service providers", i.e. the potential collaborative behavior of each company is "materialized" by a set of services (Camarinha-Matos et al., 2005). The approach assumes the existence of one entity that keeps a catalog of services where service provider companies publish their service offers. This entity is sometimes called a "service market", a "service promoter node", or even "service portal". Regardless the different implementation approaches the general three major functions of service oriented architectures – publish / advertise, discover, invoke – are usually considered.

In this case, standard technologies should be used for service description, communication and data formats. In the case of web services such standards include, for instance, WSDL (for service description), UDDI (for repository organization), SOAP (for service invocation), etc.

This approach reflects an indirect partners' selection – what is selected is the service (not the provider), i.e. the immediate task is the composition (or orchestration) of complex services based on simpler ones, not the consortia. Partners are implicitly selected via the specific services that are chosen. It is nevertheless possible to include partners' characteristics in the service search query. The processes of service publishing, discovering, selecting, invoking and binding provide an alternative to the provision and management of organization competencies, selection of partners and negotiation to configure the VOs in a VBE.

Figure 5 shows a brief historic overview of the development of the service technologies and their adoption in VO creation. One early example of the service-based approach applied to the tourism sector can be found in (Afsarmanesh & Camarinha-Matos, 2000), which has introduced service-oriented approaches to VOs for the tourism sector called federated Web-based Tourism Information System (WTIS). Another example is given by the OSMOS project (Rezgui 2005), which was focused on the construction industry and followed a service-based approach for the design and development of its ICT infrastructure. OSMOS platform federates services inside a common framework, and allows their use and collaboration.

Besides the "popularity" of the web services paradigm which gives this approach considerable relevance, there are still a number of limitations in the current service model when we envisage applications that go beyond simple transactions, including: Are services always available? What is the level of commitment of the provider? Which underlying business model and how is the workload balanced? What is the level of awareness of the service provider? What are the levels of visibility and access to services? Are there dependencies between services? Can all skills be represented as services? Does it make sense to consider specific services for the partner search / negotiation phase?

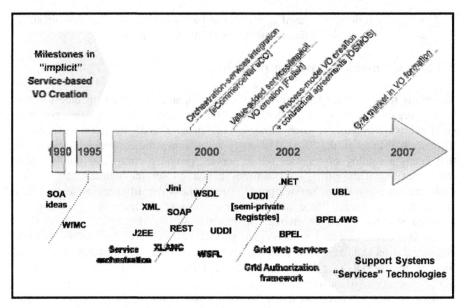

Figure 5 - Service federation based approaches in VO creation

3. VO CREATION PROCESS

According to the approach adopted by ECOLEAD, when creating a new VO, partners are primarily selected from the VBE members, nevertheless, in case there is lack of skills or capacity inside the VBE, other organizations can be recruited from outside the VBE boundaries.

However, partners' selection is not a single step operation. Furthermore, choosing the adequate partners for the VO (consortia formation) is not the only task that needs to be performed. There are other topics that need to be taken care of such as preparation and finalization phase. Figure 6 illustrates the main phases of the VO creation process for a given collaboration opportunity.

The **preparatory planning** phase includes:
- Collaboration Opportunity Identification and Characterization: a step that involves the identification and characterization of a new Collaboration Opportunity (CO) that will trigger the formation of a new VO. A collaboration opportunity might be external, originated by a customer and detected by a VBE member acting as a broker. Some opportunities might also be generated internally, as part of the development strategy of the VBE.
- Rough VO planning: determination of a rough structure of the potential VO, identifying the required competencies and capacities, structure of the task to be performed as well as the organizational form of the VO and corresponding roles. At this stage it is important to define the partnership form which is typically regulated by contracts and cooperation agreements.

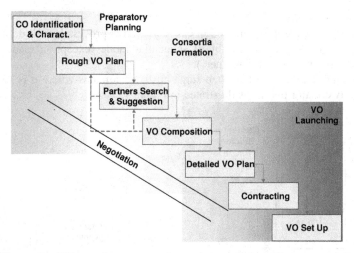

Figure 6 – VO creation process for a given collaboration opportunity

The **consortia formation** phase departs from the previous characterization and rough planning and mainly includes:

- Partners' search and suggestion: perhaps one of the most addressed topics in past research, this step is devoted to the identification of potential partners, and their assessment and selection.
- VO composition: in which the detailed organizational structure is defined and the assignment of roles to VO members is made.
- Negotiation: is an iterative process to reach agreements and align needs with offers. It can be seen as complementary to the other steps in the process and runs in parallel with them as illustrated in Figure 6.

The **VO launching** phase includes:

- Detailed VO planning: once partners have been selected and collaboration agreements are reached, this step addresses the refinement of the VO plan and its governance principles.
- Contracting: involves the final formulation and modeling of contracts and agreements as well as the contract signing process itself, before the VO can effectively be launched. In other words, this step is the conclusion of the negotiation process.
- VO set up: the last phase of the VO creation process, i.e. putting the VO into operation, is responsible for tasks such as configuration of the ICT infrastructure, instantiation and orchestration of the collaboration spaces, selection of relevant performance indicators to be used, setting up of the VO governance principles, assignment and set up of resources / activation of services, notification of the involved members, and manifestation of the new VO in the VBE.

Basically with the consortia formation phase but also spreading to the other phases there is a very important step: Negotiation. The negotiation steps might also include the "contracting" activity.

The previous sequence is applied in cases where the process is well defined and phases can be performed in an almost sequential mode (exception made for the negotiation with the suggested partners).

On the other hand, there are often some business domains where it is necessary to consider two major phases as illustrated in Figure 7.

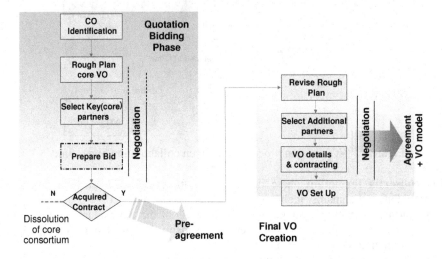

Figure 7 – VO creation process for quotation/bidding

These two phases are:

Quotation / bidding – when a collaboration opportunity is found it is necessary to prepare a bid / quotation in order to try to get a contract with the customer. For the preparation of this bid, it is necessary to make a rough plan of the foreseen VO and to also select the core partners. The bid is often prepared by this initial consortium. In case the bid is unsuccessful, the core consortium dissolves; otherwise we move to the next phase.

Final VO creation – In case the bid is successful, the VO's rough plan needs to be revised, based on the specific conditions of the contract with the customer, new additional partners might be necessary, and the VO will be finally detailed and launched.

As a result of the interactions with industry end-user networks and in order to correspond to the two processes illustrated above, four tools were designed and developed in ECOLEAD for the VO creation framework: collaboration opportunity finder (coFinder); CO characterization and rough planning (COC-Plan); partners search and suggestion (PSS); and agreement negotiation wizard (WizAN).

Although these tools attempt to assist and facilitate the entire process of the VO creation, the assumption when designing these tools was that the decisions are always responsibility of human actors. Figure 8 illustrates the main interactions among the four tools of the VO creation framework as well as the actors involved in the process. As VOs are created in a VBE context, it is also necessary to interact with the VBE management system that will provide critical information such as members' profiles and competencies, previous performance record, trustworthiness levels, etc.

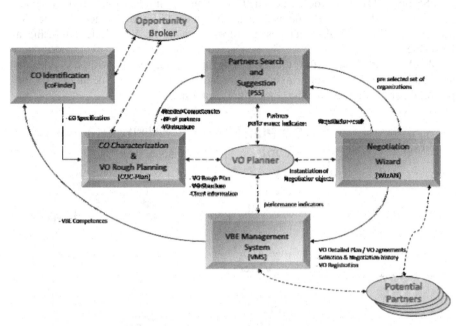

Figure 8 – Main interactions among the VO creation framework tools

3.1 Interoperability among VO creation tools

A global <u>VO Model</u> data structure provides the "vehicle" for data flow among the various tools. This solution enables to simplify and solve all the issues related to integration: any tool can work with its own architecture, database tables, servers, etc. The only interface is at the data model which means that any tool will save and add part of the VO creation model during the execution of its activities. This solution is justified by the huge number of dependencies that may arise for performing the integration at the application level: all modules will have its own database structure, with different tables, different user GUI, and different programming languages. Creating a unique integrated environment may require a great effort. For this reason the solution to leave its own architecture to the modules and performing integration only at VO model level can simplify and solve the above problems.

The VO Model was designed as an XML file aimed to allow data sharing among all VO creation tools (see Figure 9). According to the COC-Plan tool design specifications, the tool is required to interoperate with the Collaboration Opportunity Identification (CO-Finder) tool and the Partners' Search and Suggestion (PSS) tool:

COC-Plan tool and CO-Finder tool: The information of a collaboration opportunity identified and described in the CO-Finder tool is saved in a XML file and sent as an input to the COC-Plan tool. The XML file is included into the VO

Model file and the manipulation of data is done through the VO Model Web-services.

PSS and COC-Plan tool: Once the COC-Plan tool information is processed, all its data is stored in an XML file made available to the PSS tool and added to the VO Model. The PSS tool also includes its information in the VO Model file using a XML file.

WizAN and PSS: After the PSS tool update the XML with the relevant information, the WizAN tool can use it in order to collect the significant data on the potential parters to negotiate the consortium creation.

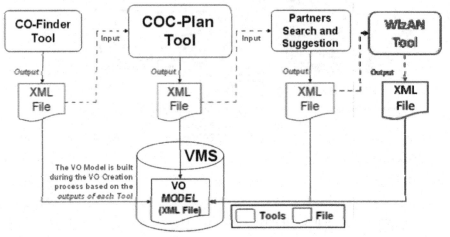

Figure 9 – VO Creation Tools Interoperability

In the following sections the first three tools (coFinder, COC-Plan and PSS) are described whereas, WizAN is described in chapter 2.6 of this book (*Agreement Negotiation Wizard*).

4. CoFinder TOOL

The coFinder tool is aimed at facilitating the work of a VO broker. It uses the same approach that is usually carried out manually by the broker: comparing potential collaboration opportunities (CO), identified from Calls for Tenders (CfTs), with the actual competencies of the VBE, stored in the Profiling and Competency Management System (PCMS, which is part of the VBE Management System VMS) (Ermilova & Afsarmanesh, 2007). In order to automate this process, the coFinder tool needs comparable structure of information contained at both sides. These structures can then be aligned and matched with each other in order to detect similarities and consequently detect possible collaboration opportunities. The matching in the coFinder tool is based on the comparison of textual descriptions of CfTs and VBE competencies. Like the broker, the tool is able to browse public CfTs available on the web and extract CfTs' descriptions from the relevant web pages. Similarly, competencies are also described in web pages or can be manually entered in text format within the coFinder tool, and collected from PCMS. Once the CfTs' descriptions and competencies have been provided, coFinder is able to compute their similarity in order to estimate the interestingness of CfTs and identify the most promising ones, and finally to propose them to the broker as potential collaboration opportunities.

4.1 coFinder System Overview

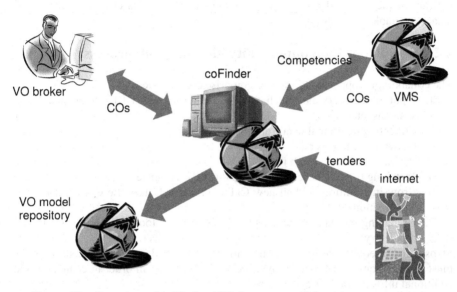

Figure 10 – Overview of coFinder (CO denotes a collaboration opportunity)

The overview of coFinder and its interactions are shown in Figure 10. The tool is accessed through a web interface by the VO broker. The coFinder tool accesses internet to collect the data from specified CfT servers. It also accesses the VMS (PCMS) to gather the competencies data, it stores the selected COs in the VO model repository and makes the COs in its internal database available to the VMS tools for further analysis (e.g. analysis of needed competencies).

Implementation-wise, coFinder is a set of PhP tools around a local MySQL database. The most important tools are crawler, parser, browser, and the CfT server template set up tool. The CfT server template set up tool is used to help the user to set up a template, which is used to separate CfTs from other web pages and collect the information from CfT web pages. Additional simple tools are used to collect other information needed to run coFinder.

Some of the tools like CfT server template set up tool are used only during the set up, other tools run on a regular schedule (like crawler and parser), and the rest are used as an interface between the user and the database (for browsing and searching the data) while web service clients and server access and provide data from and to other tools.

The initial set up data (along with the addresses of the CfT servers and templates for each of the servers) is stored in the database. Additional to the initial set up data the information about VBE competencies is regularly collected from PCMS. The data about servers is then collected by the crawler and used to gather all new information (web pages) from each of the CfT servers. Web pages are again stored in the database, from where they are collected by the parser. Parser uses the templates to sift out the CfT web pages from the rest and to extract the information about the CfT. This information (in an XML form), along with the calculated similarity to the VBE's competencies, is stored in the database. The users are notified of the best collaboration opportunities (or CfTs) via e-mail. All collected data is available for browsing by users.

4.2 The collaboration opportunity identification process

The collaboration opportunity process comprises several steps:
1. Input of necessary data, such as list of tender servers' URLs, templates, XML schemas, etc,
2. Collecting additional data from PCMS,
3. Crawling CfT servers,
4. Parsing the crawled web pages,
5. Matching the CfT descriptions with the VBE competencies,
6. Browsing, editing, adding new CfT data and selecting the CfTs suitable for VO creation, and
7. Uploading the data about selected CfTs to other tools (using the VO model repository).

Steps 1 and 6 require user interaction, while steps 2-5 and 7 are automated. Step one must be taken only once, but can be accessed at any time in order to change or add additional information (for example new servers).

In step 1, the user has to provide some information such as a list of CfT servers that he intends to use for finding potential collaboration opportunities. In addition, for each server, the user must create a template that is used to help the system identifying CfTs' descriptions inside the HTML pages. Indeed, the HTML format itself does not provide any semantics to access this information directly; therefore a template is needed to detect the CfT structure and its contents within the HTML page. Usually, the CfT pages on the same server are generated automatically from data stored in a database and thus share the same structure to represent CfTs. And a template makes it possible to match different parts of CfT HTML pages to their corresponding fields in the CO description part of the VO model.

The template is usually created by comparing different CfT web pages on the same server. Since they are generated automatically, they have the same structure but different contents. Only the contents, not the form, should change from one CfT to another. This makes it possible to figure out where are the variable parts of the page. The meaning of the variable parts is defined by the user by matching the parts of the web pages to fields in the XML schema for the output of collaboration opportunities (the CO schema). The template is stored along with the server data in a local database.

Another input needed is the competencies of the VBE. Competencies are entered manually by the broker in a textual format as well as collected automatically and periodically from PCMS (in step 2). Textual competencies are organized in two categories: general competencies and specific competencies. While data collected from PCMS is also in two categories: available competencies and processes.

In step 3, the coFinder tool crawls all the servers specified by the user and gathers CfT pages. This step usually runs regularly on a schedule.

The next, step 4, is to parse CfT pages. The template built previously is used here to extract CfTs' descriptions from their web page. The information is then stored in the database using the CO XML schema.

Step 5: Once the CfTs' description have been extracted and structured, it is possible to identify potential collaboration opportunities by matching CfTs' description with the competencies available. The interestingness factor is computed for each CfT. This measure is a weighted sum of the similarity between textual fields describing the CfT and fields describing the VBE competencies.

Step 6: To limit the number of potential collaboration opportunities, a threshold is used for the interestingness measure. This threshold is set by the user at the beginning of the process. The VO broker will be notified by an e-mail only about the potential collaboration opportunities that are above this threshold.

It is also possible to browse and search through all the collected CfT data, select the CfTs suitable for VO creation, or just select the data to be send by an e-mail to the VO broker. Since all needed data is not always available in the CfT data supplied by the server, the system offers the possibility to include some data that the VO broker may collect using other methods (phone calls, email correspondence, etc.). Such data can be useful in further steps of VO creation. In this step broker can also select CfTs that are suitable for VO creation

In strep 7, coFinder sends the data about the selected CfTs to the VO model repository and thereby makes data available to other VO creation tools.

The coFinder structure and data flow is shown in Figure 11. CoFinder first crawls each website from the list of servers and stores the web pages in the local database. Then it parses the collected web pages using CfT templates. For the resulting CfT data the interestingness measure is calculated, and finally the VO broker is notified. The VO broker then checks and possibly edits the data and selects the CfTs which are suitable as a basis for potential VO creation. The selected CfTs (which can now be called collaboration opportunities) are then delivered as the output of coFinder.

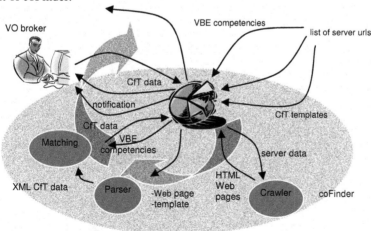

Figure 11 – coFinder working procedure

The whole process is meant to automatically find the structured web pages (from specified servers) that best match the data we have (VBE competencies) and thereby reduce the need to manually search and extract the data available on the web.

4.3 An example of use

In this section we show an example of the use of coFinder. When the tool is used for the first time, initial data has to be set up. Most of that data is a simple text like VBE competencies, the e-mail addresses for notification, and the URL addresses of CfTs servers. The most important part of the setup is the definition of CfT server templates. The template is usually generated from two or more CfTs on the server, using a tool in coFinder. This tool compares the web pages of CfTs and asks the user to define the meaning of the differences. The tool in use can be seen in Figure 12, a CfT provided as an input to the tool in Figure 13, and the final template in Figure 14.

After the initial data has been set up, coFinder crawls the specified servers, parses the collected web pages and puts the information about the collected CfTs into the internal database. All CfTs are compared to the VBE competencies as they were set up at the beginning as well as additionally collected from the PCMS and interestingness factor is calculated. A notification by e-mail is then sent to the specified address, giving information about the best CfTs found on the servers (those that are above the pre-specified interestingness threshold).

Figure 12 – An example of template generation tool in coFinder

The user/broker can use coFinder to browse and search through the collected CfTs (Figure 15). Both, the complete data of the selected call for tender (Figure 16), as well as the original web page can be inspected. The data can also be edited in order to add additional information collected by the broker (e.g., through e-mail, phone calls or other methods) and thereby enrich the data needed during further steps of the VO creation process. To start the process, the broker selects the appropriate CfTs, and selects them as appropriate for VO creation. coFinder then uploads the data about the CfTs to the VO model repository, making it available to subsequent tools that plan the process needed in VO, suggest the partners, help with negotiation...

The selected CFTs and all other CfT data is also available to VMS tools using web services in order to analyze the competencies gaps and other possibilities of VBE improvement.

Bidding Type	International Competitive Bidding
Project Name	CAIRO NORTH COMBINED-CYCLE POWER PLANT PROJECT (THE EGYPTIAN ELECTRICITY HOLDING COMPANY (EEHC), A JOINT STOCK COMPANY ESTABLISHED BY LAW NO. 164 YEAR 2000 (FORMERLY EGYPTIAN ELECTRICITY AUTHORITY), HAS SECURED A LOAN FROM THE ARAB FUND FOR ECONOMIC AND SOCIAL DEVELOPMENT AND HAS REQUESTED THE PARTICIPATION OF THE EUROPEAN INVESTMENT BANK (EIB) TO FINANCE THE PROCUREMENT OF MATERIALS AND ASSOCIATED SERVICES FOR SEVERAL PACKAGES OF THE CAIRO NORTH COMBINED-CYCLE POWER PLANT PROJECT)(
Financier	
Tender Notice No.	Not Provided
Description	DESIGN, FABRICATION, FURNISHING, DELIVERY, INSTALLATION, TRAINING, TESTING, START-UP AND COMMISSIONING FOR 2 X 250 MW (ISO) GAS TURBINE GENERATORS AND AUXILIARIES (TWO 250 MW (ISO) COMBUSTION TURBINE GENERATORS, AND ONE 250 MW (NOMINAL) STEAM TURBINE GENERATOR), INCLUDING ALL MECHANICAL AND ELECTRICAL WORK REQUIRED FOR A COMPLETE OPERATIONAL SYSTEM.
Estimated Project Cost	Not Provided (**Currency Converter**)
Document Cost	Not Provided (**Currency Converter**)
Submission Deadline	Not Provided
Earnest Money / Bid Security	Not Provided
Updates	

Figure 13 – An example of Call for Tender from the TerndersInfo.com server

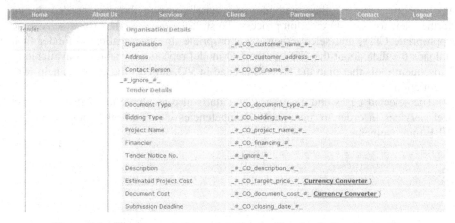

Figure 14 – The generated template for the TendersInfo.com server

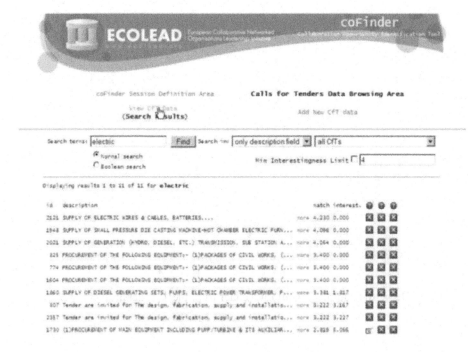

Figure 15 – Searching through collected CfTs

```
CO_customer_country    egypt
CO_CF_name
CO_CF_phone
CO_CF_fax
CO_CF_email            mktg@tendersinfo.com
CO_title               DESIGN, FABRICATION, FURNISHING, DELIVERY, INSTALLATION, TRAINING, TESTING, START-UP AND COMMISSIONING of gas turbines
CO_language            english
CO_description         DESIGN, FABRICATION, FURNISHING, INSTALLATION, TRAINING, TESTING, START-UP AND COMMISSIONING FOR 2 X 250 MW
                       (ISO) GAS TURBINE GENERATORS AND AUXILIARIES (TWO 250 MW (ISO) COMBUSTION TURBINE GENERATORS, AND ONE 250 MW (NOMINAL)
                       STEAM TURBINE GENERATOR), INCLUDING ALL MECHANICAL AND ELECTRICAL WORK REQUIRED FOR A COMPLETE OPERATIONAL SYSTEM.
CO_project_name        CAIRO NORTH COMBINED-CYCLE POWER PLANT PROJECT (THE EGYPTIAN ELECTRICITY HOLDING COMPANY (EEHC), A JOINT STOCK COMPANY
                       ESTABLISHED BY LAW NO. 164 YEAR 2000 (FORMERLY EGYPTIAN ELECTRICITY AUTHORITY), HAS SECURED A LOAN FROM THE ARAB FUND
                       FOR ECONOMIC AND SOCIAL DEVELOPMENT AND HAS REQUESTED THE PARTICIPATION OF THE EUROPEAN INVESTMENT BANK (EIB) TO
                       FINANCE THE PROCUREMENT OF MATERIALS AND ASSOCIATED SERVICES FOR SEVERAL PACKAGES OF THE CAIRO NORTH COMBINED-CYCLE
                       POWER PLANT PROJECT)(
CO_sector              energy
CO_document_type       ="68%" class="rowbg"> Events
CO_bidding_type        International Competitive Bidding
CO_contract_type
CO_target_price        Not Provided (
CO_objectives          DESIGN, FABRICATION, FURNISHING, DELIVERY, INSTALLATION, TRAINING, TESTING, START-UP AND COMMISSIONING of 2 gas
                       turbines
CO_duration            one time
CO_issuing_date
CO_opening_date
CO_due_date            1.1.2008
CO_closing_date        Not Provided
CO_closing_time
CO_product_description
```

Figure 16: coFinder parsed data from the call for tender shown in Figure 13

5. COC-PLAN TOOL

The Collaboration Opportunity Characterization &VO Rough Planning (COC-Plan) tool consists of two modules: a) One component, described in Section 5.1, supporting the COC process with the aim of assisting the *opportunity broker* – in designing the VO and deciding which roles and partners best fit with the VO structure; and b) a second component, described in Section 5.2, supporting the VO-RP process with the aim of assisting the *VO planner* and/or *VO coordinator* with the mapping of the tasks to be carried out during the VO operation phase (Camarinha-Matos et al, 2005).

5.1 Collaboration Opportunity Characterization

The CO-Characterization process refers to the identification of the main features of a collaboration opportunity to be developed, in terms of a product and/or project to be manufactured or executed from its most complex items (assemblies/activities) to the simplest ones (component/sub-activities), plus the specification of collaboration opportunity competency-related information (per item) required to carry out partners' search and selection (Concha et al, 2008).

Once the collaboration opportunity has been identified (e.g. using coFinder), the *opportunity broker* or the *VO planner* should describe the business opportunity as a product and/or a project as part of the CO-Characterization process. **Figure 17** presents product and project definitions under a decomposition context of their items:

- Products can be defined by components, sub-assemblies and assemblies. A *component* is the smallest part of a product. In some cases, many components are integrated in a special order forming a *sub-assembly* or an *assembly* (depending on the complexity of the product) to fulfil a specific requirement.

- Projects are defined as temporary endeavours undertaken to create a unique service. As in the product decomposition, projects decomposition has lower levels: activities and sub-activities. An *activity* is a component of work performed as a *task* that has an estimated duration, cost and resources requirements to turn inputs into products and/or services. Depending on the complexity of a project, an activity can be divided into as many sub-activities / tasks as it is needed to execute the project.

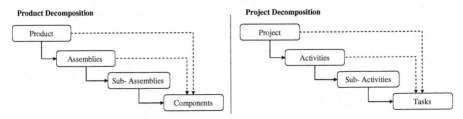

Figure 17 – Product and Project Decomposition

Products and projects have their own attributes which are inherited by their lower items in the decomposition process; there are no limitations to the number of levels that can be defined (see **Figure 18**).

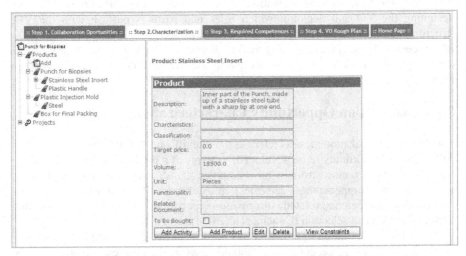

Figure 18 – CO Characterization in the COC-Plan

After a collaboration opportunity has been described as a product and/or a project and its items decomposed, the next step in the CO-Characterization process is the competency requirements definition in terms of the necessary processes, resources and standards for future matching the potential VO partners that posses them. Each item of a product and/or a project decomposed in the first step has to include the specification of the necessary competency to accomplish their production or execution. A *competency* as defined by Ermilova & Afsarmanesh (2005) is understood as the organisation's capability to perform (business) processes (in collaboration with partners such as suppliers), having the necessary resources (human, technological, physical) available, and applying certain standards, with the final aim to offer certain products and/or services to the customer (see Figure 19); furthermore a *capability* is the potential ability to perform a process; a *process* is a structured, measurable, manageable and controllable set of interrelated and interacting activities that use resources to transform inputs into specified outputs; *resources* are classified into: human resources (e.g. engineers, technicians), technological resources (e.g. software) or physical resources (e.g. machines). For the development of some products or services it is necessary to have formalized techniques, methodologies and/or procedures that are frequently used in organisations to perform specific processes known as *standards*.

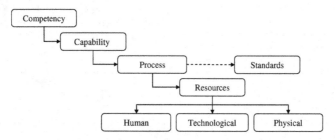

Figure 19 – Competency Definition
(Adapted from Ermilova & Afsarmanesh, 2005).

The COC module will simplify the collaboration opportunity decomposition by presenting the decomposition as a tree, making easier the navigation through the resulting items (the leaves), and allowing to find and access the information related to a specific item (a leaf) in a faster way thanks to the tree hierarchical view. The CO decomposition hierarchical structure represents a similar schema to the Bill of Materials (BOM), term used in manufacturing processes to describe the components needed to complete in a product. As in the CO decomposition, the BOM decomposition presents different levels of a product (assemblies, sub-assemblies and raw materials) necessary to manufacture a product.

Figure 20 shows the COC-Plan tool competency definition template, where a product is described by its minimal components and decomposed in terms of competencies (as a set of capabilities defined by processes, resources and standards).

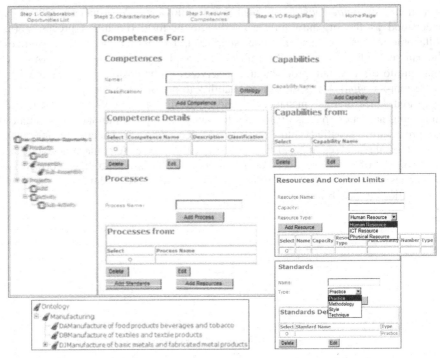

Figure 20 – COC-Plan Tool Competency Definition Template

5.2 VO Rough Planning

VO Rough Planning (VO-RP) represents the second module of the COC-Plan tool. The tasks supported in this module and carried out by the *VO planner* and/or *VO coordinator* are: *collaboration opportunity modality* identification and VO *rough plan* design. The following sections describe these tasks in detail.

5.2.1 Collaboration Opportunity Modalities

When the CO-Characterization process is finished, it is necessary to classify the collaboration opportunity under a *collaboration modality* in order to facilitate the creation of a VO rough plan. Four modalities have been defined (Camarinha-Matos et al 2005) for this purpose:

1) *Collaborative Business Process modality*, representing a set of heterogeneous activities normally distributed in cross-organisational sub-processes;

2) *Collaborative Project modality* aimed to support the performance of multi-projects through the definition of a work breakdown (WBD) structure. This structure is composed by projects, activities, tasks and resources that belong to multi-organisations;

3) *Collaborative Problem-Solving modality*, describing a specific situation or problem (AS-IS situation) that wants to be improved or modified. The desired scenario (TO-BE scenario) should be defined and modelled and working groups should also be identified; and

4) *Ad-hoc Collaboration modality,* designed for organisations that are not used to work under collaboration schemas and join their efforts to quickly respond to a specific external request.

5.2.2 VO Rough Planning Process Definition

The VO-RP module supports the process of determining a rough structure for the potential VO in accordance to each *collaboration modality,* and by considering the competencies and capacities required from VO partners to respond to a specific collaboration opportunity. Thus, VO-RP objective is to determine possible VO configurations as WBDs, and associate competencies and capacities required from each VO partner to execute the tasks corresponding to its roles and competency domain during VO operation phase.

In the COC-Plan tool, the VO-RP module is accessed through an editor, with enhanced and innovative features for importing/exporting files from both proprietary and open-source project planning tools. Figure 21 shows the VO-RP module template, which allows creating and removing tasks to/from the BOM and its further presentation in a project Gantt diagram.

Figure 21 – VO-Rough Planning: Tasks Creation and Gantt diagram.

5.3 COC-Plan tool technical characteristics

5.3.1 System Architecture

Figure 22 presents the COC-Plan tool architecture. Users access the VO framework Web-server through a client machine (a PC or a laptop). COC-Plan tool modules can be accessed through the CO-Characterization module that will invoke the related server, and also the VO-RP module (CO-Plan editor) that resides on top of the COC-Plan tool and can be used by a Java Web start. Both modules store their information at the VO model repository.

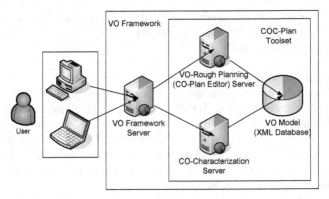

Figure 22 – COC-Plan System Architecture

5.3.2 Database Schema

The database model describes the interactions between the objects (classes) that take part in the CO-Characterization process. Figure 23 presents the relations among the most important elements in the COC module database.

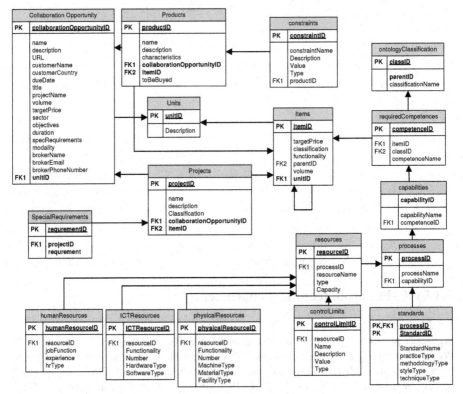

Figure 23 – COC module Database Schema

5.3.3 Development Platform

To guarantee the integration and optimal data transfer (interoperability) among the

VO creation tools, the following development platform was built-up using the following technologies and software tools.

Table 2 - Development Platform.

Design	UML Tool	Microsoft Office Visio 2003
		Enterprise Architecture
Development	Language	J2EE (Java 2 Enterprise Edition)
	IDE	Eclipse + plug-in (MyEclipse)
	Libraries	Apache - Axis
	Serviettes Container	Tomcat v5.5.15
	Portal	Liferay 3
	Objects Persistency	Hibernate 3.1
	Application Framework	Struts
	Code Documentation	Javadoc (installed with J2SE)
	Code Building	Ant (installed with MyEclipse)
Data Storage	Database	PostgreSQL 8.1
	Mapping Tool (object - Relational DB)	Hibernate Framework

6. PSS TOOL

6.1 Purpose

The purpose of the partners' search and suggestion (PSS) tool is to assist the VO Planner in the selection of the most suitable members for a VO regarding the requirements of a given collaboration opportunity (CO). These requirements are received from the previous VO creation phase "CO characterization and rough planning" (COC-Plan), which provides a VO macro structure, concerning the CO work breakdown structure, the tasks assigned to each CO part as well as the competences and resources necessaries to fulfill each task.

The output of the PSS tool is a list of potential VO configurations, including the configurations' expected performance with respect to the specified criteria. These possible VO configurations are presented to the VO Planner for a further decision making and final VO composition.

Partners are suggested based on a set of criteria that, besides traditional elements like price, delivery date and quality level, includes also performance indicators. These criteria are applied both in the searching (filtering inadequate organizations) and in the suggestion (electing the ones that better fit the desired indicators) steps in order to achieve faster and potentially better results.

6.2 Functionalities

The PSS tool is composed of three functionalities responsible to perform the partners' search and suggestion process. These three functionalities are described as follows and Figure 24 depicts the interrelationship among them, highlighting the control and information flows:

- **Suggestion Criteria Identification**: As the main purpose of the PSS tool is to suggest partners, first it is necessary to identify the criteria that will be taken into account to compare the potential candidates. This comparison is important to ensure that the suggested organizations are the best ones among the potential candidates.

- **Partners' Search**: The partners' search looks for potential partners that have the required competences / processes as well as resource availability to be part of the new VO.
- **Generation and Analysis of Suggested VOs**: With the potential partners already identified, this functionality generates optimized arrangements of organizations. Using a suitable GUI, the user can see additional information regarding each arrangement and thus select the most appropriate one.

Besides the three PSS functionalities, Figure 24 also presents two entities that play an important role during the partners' search and suggestion process: the VO Creation (Supporting) Services and the VBE supporting services (VMS). The former represents the services used to integrate all the tools that are part of the VO Creation framework and its main purpose is to intermediate the VO Model exchange among the VO Creation tools. The latter represents the services provided by VBE and used to integrate the VBE tools with the other ECOLEAD tools (e.g. VO Creation framework, VO management tools). Especially concerning PSS tool, these services are used to have access to the competences information and trustworthiness information.

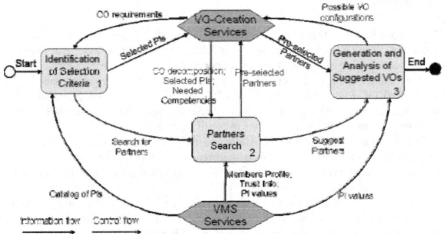

Figure 24 – PSS tool functionalities

6.2.1 Suggestion Criteria Identification

To identify the most suitable Performance Indicators (PIs) to be used to compare and afterwards suggest the proper potential partners for a new VO, a methodology that aids the human user to easily identify these PIs was developed. This methodology is composed of two parts. One that runs just once, called *configuration phase*, and another one that runs whenever a new VO needs to be created to fulfill a certain CO, called *operation phase*. Figure 25 shows the whole methodology which is briefly described below.

Configuration phase:
1. Acquisition of the information related to the PIs (from a catalog of PIs) that will be used to measure the organizations' processes and activities. It means, collect information, such as PI name, PI description, PI type, etc.
2. Application of a semantic annotation technique, combined with an ontology that describes PIs, to create annotations in the PIs' information gathered in the previous step. A semantic annotation links a concept stated in an ontology to a piece of information inside a text (Kiryakov *et al.*, 2003).

Operation phase:
a. Acquisition of the preferences and constraints' list that the VO needs to fulfill. This list is required to create a VO that performs the envisaged CO.
b. Identification of the CO performance requirements based on the match between the preferences and constraints list and the CO ontology. These performance requirements comprise a list of keywords that will be taken into account for filtering the set of PIs.
c. Search for the proper PIs based on the keywords selected previously. In this step, information retrieval techniques are used to search for PIs indexed in the preparatory phase.

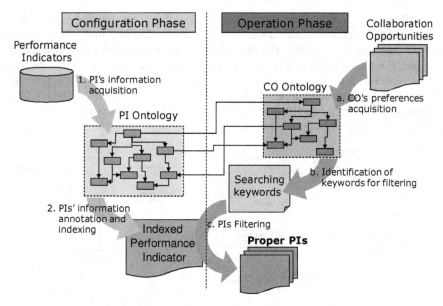

Figure 25 – Performance Indicators Identification Methodology

Ontology:
The ontology conceived here aims at describing every concept related to PIs and COs as well as the relationships between them. Nevertheless, it is important to mention that this ontology was developed following such recommendations (Missikoff *et al.*, 2002):

- It has been verified that there is no other ontology specified for this domain.

- Several sources of information to understand this domain have been used. Some of these are: performance measurement systems, benchmarks, etc.
- Some domain experts have been consulted to realize which concepts should be cover. These experts were either business consultants or economic researchers.

The most important questions that this ontology can provide answers include:

- What is a PI?
- What is a CO?
- Which aspects are relevant to classify a PI?
- Which are the correlations between a CO and a PI?

Two statements that express what this ontology stands for are:

– A PI, in general terms, has the purpose to measure *something*, with an *objective*, considering a specific *perspective*, applied to a *domain*, using a *calculation rule* and providing results in a certain *measurement unit*.
– A CO is an entity that provides an *outcome*, considering some *technical specifications*, classified according to a *modality* and that has some *requirements*. More specifically, the *performance requirements* imply performance of *something*, delimited into a *perspective*, having as target an *objective*, comprising a *specific domain*.

Figure 26 shows the top level of the PI and CO ontology. The ontology is basically used to organize the knowledge about the PIs and COs. Besides that, it is also used to refine the search of proper PIs through the contextualization of what is being searched. For example, instead of searching for PIs that are related to "flexibility", it can be searched PIs that are related to the <u>perspective</u> of "flexibility" with the <u>objective</u> of "order fulfillment". It means that this ontology characterizes both "flexibility" and "order fulfillment" as instances of different concepts as well as many other instances of other concepts.

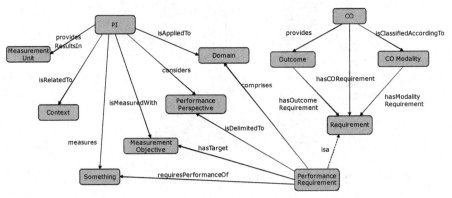

Figure 26 – PI and CO Ontology Top Level

6.2.2 Partners' Search

The partners search is divided into two steps. First, the search for the potential partners is performed. It means, all the VBE members that have some competences required for the new VO that is being created will be selected as potential partners. The second step is to classify the potential partners in groups of similar competencies. In fact, it is expected that more than one VBE member has the same competences and thus will dispute for the same position in the VO. In order to identify which members are the proper ones to be invited to participate in the VO, it is necessary to compare them using a common set of criteria. For this purpose the PIs identified in the previous functionality are used. Using such PIs, the VO planner can make a more precise decision about which are the more suitable VBE member to be part of the new VO. As PIs are measured periodically, it is possible to always compare the potential partners with up to date information.

The partner search process can be roughly understood as the matching of required competencies from the CO decomposition with the competencies provided by the VBE members. An organization's competency constitutes the triple of organization's "capability-capacity-conspicuity" (Ermilova et al., 2007). An organization's *capability* represents the set of *processes* and *activities* that an organization is able to perform and can potentially contribute to the development of the VO (Ermilova et al., 2007). An organization's *capacity* represents the availability of resources that can be applied within the new VO. An organization's *conspicuity* can be given by a number of different documents that can add different levels of validity to the organizations' claims.

Based on these concepts, in order to figure out if an organization can be a potential partner it is necessary to verify if it fulfills the following constraints:

1. It has the capability to perform a certain process required by the CO;
2. It has the capacity to satisfy the demand of the CO. To declare that an organization has capacity regarding a process, the process execution rate (number of times that the process runs within a specific period) must be greater than or equal to the CO process demand (number of outputs required within the same period). This aspect ensures that the VO execution flow can be fulfilled;
3. It has availability of resources (human and physical) that can be allocated to attend the CO. To declare that an organization is available to perform such process, the amount of resources available in a period of time must be greater than or equal to the total of outputs required by the CO for this period.

Bellow, the process of identifying the potential partners is presented in more details.

Let $M = \{1,...,m\}$ denote the set of organizations belonging to a given VBE and $N = \{1,...n\}$ the tasks that should be performed by organizations in order to fulfill one specific CO. Let us also consider other important information elements used in the partners' search process:

C_i – the set of competences that an organization $i \in M$ has.

Cr_j – the set of competences that a task j requires to be performed.

X_{mxn} – the matrix where each element $x_{i,j}$ represents whether or not the organization i has the whole set of competences to perform the task j. So that,

$$x_{i,j} \begin{cases} 0, & if \ \ Cr_j \not\subset C_i \ \ \ \forall \, i \in M \wedge \forall \, j \in N \\ 1, & if \ \ Cr_j \subset C_i \ \ \ \forall \, i \in M \wedge \forall \, j \in N \end{cases}$$

and

R_i – the set of resources that an organization i has.

Rr_j – the set of resources that a task j requires to be performed.

So, an organization i has the required resources to fulfill a specific task j whether

$f_{i,j}$ is not a empty set, as follow:

$$f_{i,j} \begin{cases} \emptyset, & \text{if } Rr_j \not\subset R_i \quad \forall\, i \in M \wedge \forall\, j \in N \\ Rr_j, & \text{if } Rr_j \subset R_i \quad \forall\, i \in M \wedge \forall\, j \in N \end{cases}$$

Therefore, an organization $i \in M$ can be considered a candidate partner for a task $j \in N$, if it satisfies the following restriction:

$$x_{i,\,j} g(f_{i,\,j,\,k}) \geq g(Rr_{j,\,k}) \quad \forall\, k \in Rr_j$$

where,
g(w) – amount of resources assigned to w.

6.2.3 Generation and analysis of suggested VOs

This functionality finds and evaluates feasible VO configurations with respect to user-defined criteria. The feasibility of a configuration is defined through its ability to perform the requirements of the CO. These requirements are described by tasks, each of which requires a specific competence. In addition, work-loads (e.g. person month) can be attached to the tasks.

The functionality formulates the VO partner selection as a work-allocation problem, which is approached by multi-objective mixed integer linear programming (MILP, Jarimo and Pulkkinen, 2005). This approach has been chosen for two reasons. First, a reasonable size MILP model is computationally solvable using well known algorithms. Computational experiments suggest that the MILP models are tractable for problems of reasonable size and consequently potentially useful for VO decision making. Second, MILP models are flexible to modifications. The multi-objectivity is captured by goal-programming techniques (e.g. Taha, 1997) or additive value functions (MAVT, Keeney and Raiffa, 1993). Heuristic algorithms are used to find Pareto-efficient solutions.

The approach accounts for a large variety of selection criteria. First, total costs include fixed and variable work costs and transportation costs. Second, stochastic risk measures are applied to model risks of failure, delays, or capacity shortfall. Third, network interdependencies, such as collaboration history or total number of partners can be taken into account.

Using this functionality, a decision-maker (DM, e.g. VO planner) can identify a set of Pareto-optimal configurations, of which the DM can manually select the preferred one. In other words, it suggests several alternatives that are "good" in respect of different preferences over the selection criteria. Hence, the DM does not need to explicitly weight the criteria, but instead can identify configurations that reflect different preferences.

The inputs for this module are as follows. There are n tasks with a work-load (e.g. person month) attached to each of them. The tasks also have a relational work sequence, and information on possible transportation needs between tasks. For each task j, there are m_j candidate partners, the total number of candidates being $m = \Sigma_j$ m_j. Each candidate has a capacity, and fixed and variable costs for working on the tasks to which it is a candidate. The data is easily represented by matrices, where the rows and columns represent the candidates and the tasks. A candidate can have a probability distribution over its capacities, reflecting the uncertainty on the true capacity. Moreover, each candidate can have a fixed cost for working on the project, a geographical location, a collaboration history with other candidates, etc. Also the selection criteria that will be used in partner selection are to be defined for each case.

Its output is a set of Pareto-efficient work allocations, i.e. VO configurations. The constituents of this set depends on how the DM has expressed his/her preferences over the selection criteria. The DM can then manually select the most preferred configuration.

The scores of the identified configurations on the selection criteria are also given. Hence, in addition to the partners in Pareto-efficient configurations, the DM can compare the expected performance of the configurations.

Bellow, the computational model behind the generation and analysis of suggested VOs is described in more detail.

Computational multi-criteria model:

Let $M = \{1,...,m\}$ denote the set of partners candidate. The project is divided into tasks, denoted by $N = \{1,..., n\}$. Each task $j \in N$ has a work load w_j, which describes the amount of work required (e.g. person months) in order to perform that task. The information gathered from candidates includes the following parameters:

$c_{i,j}^k$ — capacity, or amount of work that member $i \in M$ can perform on task j (e.g. person months), with probability $p_{i,j}(k)$

$p_{i,j}$ — probability measure on set $C_{i,j}$, which includes $c_{i,j}^k$'s for given i and j

$v_{i,j}$ — variable costs of member $i \in M$ working on task j (e.g. €/person month)

f_i — fixed cost of member i becoming part of the VO, i.e. working on at least one task of the project

$f_{i,j,k}$ — performance of member i starting to work on task j, according to performance indicator k.

λ_k — weight of the relative importance of performance indicator k.

The actual decision variable is the work-allocation matrix $X_{m \times n}$, whose element $x_{i,j}$ denotes the amount of work that VBE member i performs on task j. In addition, we define the following dummy variables, whose values depend completely on x's.

First, let

$$y_i = \begin{cases} 0, & \text{if } x_{i,j} = 0 \, \forall j \in N \\ 1, & \text{if } x_{i,j} > 0 \text{ for at least one } j \in N. \end{cases}$$

That is, y_i is binary, denoting whether any work in the project is allocated to VBE member i. Furthermore, let

$$y_{i,j} = \begin{cases} 0, & \text{if } x_{i,j} = 0 \\ 1, & \text{if } x_{i,j} > 0. \end{cases}$$

In words, binary $y_{i,j}$ denotes whether any work on task j is allocated to i.

The objective function sums fixed and variable costs and other performance indicators:

$$\min_{X,Y} \underbrace{\lambda_{cost} \sum_{i=1}^{m} f_i y_i}_{(I)} + \underbrace{\lambda_{cost} \sum_{j=1}^{n} \sum_{i=1}^{m} v_{i,j} x_{i,j}}_{(II)} + \underbrace{\sum_{k=1}^{l} \lambda_k \sum_{j=1}^{n} \sum_{i=1}^{m} f_{i,j,k} y_{i,j}}_{(III)},$$

where X is m×n matrix consisting of x's and Y is m×(n+1) matrix of y's. Interpretation of the sum terms is the following:
  (I) Sum of fixed costs for adding a new member to VO
  (II) Sum of variable costs of each member's work on tasks
  (III) Weighted sum of performance indicator data.
It should be noted, however, that the model is flexible in the sense that some costs can be ignored if considered irrelevant. On the other hand, the model allows accounting for completely new criteria.

The constraints of the optimization problem assure the requirements of the CO are met. First the work load of each task has to be covered:

$$\sum_{i=1}^{m} x_{i,j} \geq w_j \quad \forall j \in N.$$

Second, the work allocation may not exceed expected capacities:

$$x_{i,j} \leq \sum_{k=1}^{|c_{i,j}|} p_{i,j}(k) c_{i,j}^k \quad \forall i \in M, j \in N.$$

Third, work loads are non-negative:

$$x_{i,j} \geq 0 \quad \forall i \in M, j \in N.$$

Optimization Results:
The above multi-criteria optimization model is linear, thus it can be solved with normal binary programming algorithms, such as simplex and branch-and-cut. Since it is unreasonable to expect that the decision-maker would give point estimates for the relative importance of the selection criteria, we solve the problem with a set of weights. Hence, the solution is a set of Pareto-efficient VO configurations, in which the performance of the configuration with respect to any criterion can not be increased without compromising another criterion.

The generation of the Pareto-efficient VO configurations enables the use of different sensitivity analyses and finally the manual selection of the most preferred VO configuration. Comparing the expected performance of whole VO configurations instead of sole individual partner candidates gives the decision maker a better view on the overall performance of the VO. Moreover, the comparison of whole VO configurations enables the incorporation of inter-organizational dependencies, such as collaboration history or geographical distance, in partner selection.

6.3 PSS tool technical characteristics

6.3.1 System architecture

The PSS system architecture, presented in
Figure **27**, is composed of the following elements:
  - Three portlets that are the GUIs where users can interact with the PSS tool.
  - KIM Platform (www.ontotext.com/kim/) used to semantically annotate, index and retrieves the PIs' information.
  - One database management system that stores and manages the information.
  - One portal that contains the three portlets aforementioned.
  - One web server that contains the web portal.

- One client web service used to exchange the VO Model file and thus realize the integration.

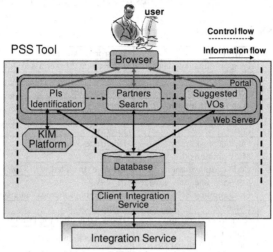

Figure 27 – PSS System architecture

6.3.2 Database Schema

The information used by PSS tool needs to be stored in order to be used and reused whenever necessary. To store all the information required by PSS a database schema was designed. Figure 28 presents the most important information that is stored.

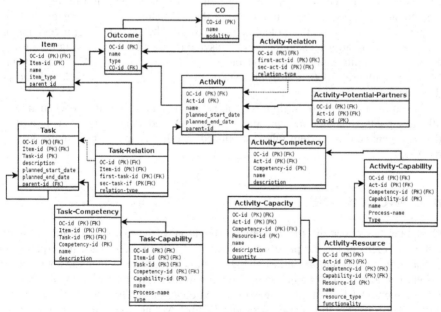

Figure 28 – PSS tool database schema

6.3.3 Development Platform

Table 3 presents the tools and technologies used to implement the PSS tool.

Table 3 – PSS development platform

Design	UML tool	Enterprise Architecture
Development	Programming language	J2EE (Java 2 Enterprise Edition)
	IDE	Eclipse + Lomboz plug-in
	Script language	JSTL and JSP
	Web service libraries	Apache – Axis
	Web application container	Tomcat v5.5.15
	Portal	Liferay 3
	Objects persistency	Hibernate 3.1
	MCV framework	Struts
	Code documentation	Javadoc (installed with J2SE)
	Mixed Integer Linear Programming Solver	lp_solve (http://groups.yahoo.com/group/lp_solve/)
Data Storage	Database	PostgreSQL 8.1
	Reverse engineering	JBoss Tools: Eclipse Plugins
	Mapping tool (object - Relational DB)	Hibernate Framework

7. FURTHER STEPS

The process described in previous sections is simplified and incomplete. In fact, the results of the PSS tool are based on the available information about potential candidates. But in reality, the actual engagement of an organization in the VO will depend on a successful negotiation between the VO planner and this organization or among all members of the potential consortium. The negotiation process might imply several iterations, changing conditions and trying alternative configurations.

In order to facilitate the negotiation process, another tool – WizAN (Camarinha-Matos & Oliveira, 2006; Camarinha-Matos et al., 2007) – was developed and is described in another chapter.

When finally a VO consortium is established and an agreement is reached among all participants, the outcome represented in the VO model data structure is passed to the VO management system (also introduced in other chapters) to actually launch the VO.

8. CONCLUSIONS

Computer assistance in the process of creation of virtual organizations is an important element for the possibility of having truly dynamic VOs, in response to collaboration opportunities in fast changing market contexts. A realistic approach to materialize agility in VO creation is defined with the assumption of a VO Breeding Environment (VBE) that guarantees the preparedness of its members to quickly get engaged in collaboration processes. The ECOLEAD approach to VO creation is developed under such assumption, and proposes a detailed process covering all required steps from the identification of the collaboration opportunity till the actual launching of the VO that will exploit that opportunity. A set of tools are proposed to support an iterative decision-making process in which the final decisions are made by the broker / VO planner. These tools were specified in interaction with end user networks.

Acknowledgements. This work was funded in part by the European Commission through the ECOLEAD project.

9. REFERENCES

Afsarmanesh, H., & Camarinha-Matos, L. M. (2000, 19-20 June). Future smart organizations: A virtual tourism enterprise. Paper presented at the WISE 2000 -1st ACM/IEEE International Conference on Web Information Systems Engineering, Hong Kong.

Afsarmanesh, H., & Camarinha-Matos, L. M. (2005, 26-28 September). A Framework for Management of Virtual Organization Breeding Environments. Paper presented at the 6th IFIP Working Conference on Virtual Enterprises, Valencia.

Camarinha-Matos, L. M., & Afsarmanesh, H. (2003). Elements of a base VE infrastructure. J. Computers in Industry, Vol. 51(Issue 2), pp. 139-163.

Camarinha-Matos, L. M., Afsarmanesh, H., & Ollus, M. (2005a, 26-28 September). ECOLEAD: A Holistic Approach to Creation and Management of Dynamic Virtual Organizations. Paper presented at the 6th IFIP Working Conference on Virtual Enterprises, Valencia.

Camarinha-Matos, L. M., Afsarmanesh, H., & Ollus, M. (2005b). Virtual Organizations: Systems and Practices. Boston: Springer.

Camarinha-Matos, L. M., & Cardoso, T. (1999). Selection of Partners for a Virtual organization, Infrastructure for Virtual Enterprises (pp. 259-278): Kluwer Academic Publishers.

Camarinha-Matos, L. M., Silveri, I., Afsarmanesh, H., & Oliveira, A. I. (2005). Towards a Framework for Creation of Dynamic Virtual Organizations. In L. M. Camarinha-Matos (Ed.), Collaborative Networks and theirs Breeding Environments (pp. pp. 69-80): Springer.

Concha, D., Romero, T., Romero, D., Galeano, N., Jimenez, G., and Molina, A. (2008). "Analysis & Design of a Collaboration Opportunity Characterization Tool for Virtual Organisations Creation", submitted to 17th IFAC World Congress Proceedings, Seoul, Korea.

Ermilova, E.; Afsarmanesh, H.;(2007). Modeling and Management of Profiles and Competencies in VBEs, for the Journal of Intelligent Manufacturing on Modeling Frameworks for Collaborative Networks, Springer.

Ermilova, E. and Afsarmanesh, H. (2006). "Competency and Profiling Management in Virtual Organisation Breeding Environments", in Network-Centric Collaboration and Supporting Frameworks, Camarinha-Matos, L.M., Afsarmanesh, H. and Ollus, M. (Eds.), International Federation for Information Processing (IFIP), New York: Springer Publisher, 2006, pp. 131-142.

Jarimo, T., Pulkkinen, U. (2005). A Multi-Criteria Mathematical Programming Model for Agile Virtual Organization Creation. In Collaborative Networks and their Breeding Environments, editors L. M. Camarinha-Matos, H. Afsarmanesh, A. Ortiz, Springer, pp. 127–134.

Jennings, N. R., & Wooldridge, M. J. (1998). Agent Technology - Foundations, Applications, and Markets: Springer.

Keeney, R. L.; Raiffa, H. (1993). Decisions with Multiple Objectives: Preferences and Value Tradeoffs. Cambridge University Press.

Kiryakov, A.; Popov, B.; Ognyanoff, D.; Manov, D. (2003). Semantic Annotation, Indexing, and Retrieval. In: In 2nd International Semantic Web Conference (ISWC2003: 20-23 Oct. 2003: Florida, USA). Proceedings. Springer-Verlag. p. 484-499.

Li, Y., Huang, B., Liu, W., Wu, C., & Gou, H. (2000, 21-25 August). Multi-agent system for Partner Selection of Virtual Enterprise. Paper presented at the 16th IFIP World Computer Congress, Beijing, China.

Missikoff, M.; Navigli, R.; Velardi, P. (2002). The Usable Ontology: An Environment for Building and Assesing a Domain Ontology. In: International Semantic Web Conference (ISWC: Sardinia, Italy.). Proceedings

Norman, T. J., Preece, A., Chalmers, S., Jennigs, N. R., Luck, M., Dang, V. D., Nguyen, T. D., Deora, V.,

Shao, J., Gray, W. A., & Fiddian, N. J. (2004). Agent-based formation of virtual organisations. Retrieved 12 April 2004, 2004, from the World Wide Web: www.sciencedirect.com

Plisson J, Ljubič P, Mozetič I, Lavrač N. (2007). An ontology for Virtual Organization Breeding Environments. To appear in IEEE Trans. on Systems, Man, and Cybernetics.

Rabelo, R. J., Camarinha-Matos, L. M., & Vallejos, R. V. (2000). Agent-based Brokerage for Virtual Enterprise Creation in the Moulds Industry, E-business and Virtual Enterprises (pp. pp. 281-290): Kluwer Academic Publishers.

Rezgui, Y. (2005). OSMOS: Open system for inter-enterprise information management in dynamic virtual enterprises, in Virtual Organizations: Systems and Practices, Springer.

Rocha, A. P., & Oliveira, E. (1999). An Electronic Market Architecture for the Formation of Virtual Enterprises, Infrastructures for Virtual Enterprises. Boston: Kluwer.

Taha, H. A. (1997). Operations Research: An Introduction. Prentice-Hall International.

Wurman, P. R. (2001). Dynamic Pricing in the Virtual Marketplace. IEEE Internet computing, 36-42.

AGREEMENT NEGOTIATION WIZARD

Ana Inês Oliveira[1], Luis M. Camarinha-Matos[1,2]

[1]UNINOVA, PORTUGAL, aio@uninova.pt
[2]New University of Lisbon, PORTUGAL, cam@uninova.pt

Negotiation is a critical activity that encompasses all stages of the virtual organization (VO) creation process. Particularly, negotiations are needed during the selection of partners, determination of their roles and task allocation, definition of the operating conditions of the VO, etc. A synthesis of the results of the negotiation activity can be represented by an agreement among the partners that will participate in the VO. In order to reach such agreement, a negotiation wizard is proposed. Assisted by this wizard, users will be able to access an environment which allows them to negotiate the specific topics of the new VO, either in a safe bilateral way or in a multiparty context.

1   INTRODUCTION

In a simplified perspective, the virtual organization (VO) creation process can be considered structured into three main phases (L. M. Camarinha-Matos et al., 2005):

- Preparatory Planning: Process of identification and characterization of the Collaboration Opportunity (CO) and draft planning of the VO to fulfill the CO needs;
- Consortia Formation: In order to get the proper set of partners (competences / capacities / services) for the new VO, a process of partners' search and selection and its corresponding negotiation is then needed;
- VO Launching: To finalize the VO creation, it is necessary to refine the VO plan and its governance principles, to formulate and model contracts and agreements and to put the VO into operation.

For these three phases, four tools were developed in the ECOLEAD project in order to perform: CO identification (coFinder); CO characterization and rough planning (COC-Plan); partners' search and suggestion (PSS), and negotiation wizard (WizAN). More information on these tools can be found in the previous chapter (2.5 – "VO Creation Assistance Services") and also in (L. M. Camarinha-Matos et al., 2007).

Figure 1 illustrates the main steps of the simplified VO creation process and the tools that cover some of them.

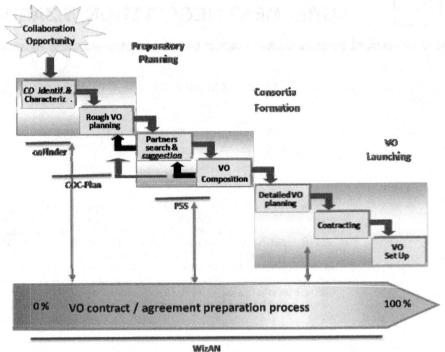

Figure 1 – VO creation framework

The main actors involved in this process are the Opportunity Broker and the VO Planner in the initial phases. Potential partners participate in the last phase of the process. The Opportunity Broker is the one that is responsible for finding the collaboration opportunity whereas the VO Planner is the one responsible for setting up the VO, i.e. responsible for the characterization and planning of the CO, finding the suitable partners, and coordinating the process of reaching the final agreements between all parties involved. Creating a new VO is not only a matter of planning and selecting partners. In fact, the final structure of the VO will depend on the agreements reached among all participants during a negotiation process. Negotiation is, therefore, an activity that encompasses all other stages of the VO creation process.

A synthesis of the results of the negotiation activity is represented by an agreement among the partners that will participate in the VO. The preparation of this agreement, namely in terms of collecting the necessary information, spans along the full VO creation process.

Although Figure 1 might give the impression that the VO creation is a linear / sequential process, in fact several iterations and parallel activities may take place. At every phase of the VO creation process, there is a flow of information that passes from each phase of the process; and in parallel with the entire process, the tasks of creating the internal VO agreement are spawned. As a result various iterations might be needed. The negotiation phase is an iterative process to reach agreements and align needs with offers. It is typically seen as complementary to the partners' selection process and might in fact require going back to the previous step(s) if a solution cannot be found with the current configuration of partners.

Important issues to consider at the negotiation stage include: Determination of the objects of negotiation; Negotiation protocols; Decision making process and corresponding parameters; Representation of agreements; etc. business process (BP) negotiation, i.e. BP refinement and assignment to partners may also be considered at this stage. The main roles intervening in the negotiation process are the VO planner role, and the VBE member role.

In this context, an Agreement Negotiation Wizard (WizAN) tool is proposed, which aims to assist the user in the possible steps that a negotiation among candidate partners for a VO might need, being the main outcome of this negotiation a contract / agreement that will govern the behavior of the various actors involved in the future VO.

2 RELATED WORK ON NEGOTIATION & CONTRACTING

Agreements and contracts and the way they are established are being challenged by new technology, such as: new communication channels, artificial intelligence, intellectual property rights, even the emergence of electronic legal entities, etc. The negotiation process can follow various paradigms: auctions, game theory, intelligent agent mechanisms, etc (Rocha & Oliveira, 1999). Nevertheless, its automatization is a rather difficult process and according to (Angelov & Grefen, 2002), the efforts in this direction did not yet produce any context-independent solution; only partial and very specific prototypes are available.

Similarly to the traditional business relationships, the virtual organization also relies on the notion of contract and cooperation agreement among its members. Standard paper-based contracting is often slow and requires involvement of human actors in all contracting phases (Grefen & Angelov, 2002). In order to enable a fast contracting process, an electronic representation of contracts is required (Angelov & Grefen, 2002). To (Rocha et al., 2004) the electronic contract describes the rights and duties of the virtual organization partners, as well as penalties to apply to those that do not satisfy the agreement. E-contracting is expected to be faster and cheaper than standard contracting and to offer new opportunities to partners. According to Angelov and Grefen (2002) an e-contracting process consists of a number of e-contracting phases: information, pre-contractual, contracting, and enactment phases (Angelov, 2006).

An electronic contract can have both a machine readable and/or human readable representation. The existence of a human readable representation of the contract is required if the contract creation and management involves the participation of human beings. Grefen and Angelov (2002) divide the contract content into three general parts:
- The first part describes the participating parties and mediators.
- The second part provides the rights and obligations of the parties. This part contains the service (payment) description, its delivery process, legal and technical provisions, etc.
- The third part gives definitions required for the contract enactment. These

definitions can range from the business context of the contract to different terms and formulae used in the contract. The definitions aim at establishing an identical understanding about the contract among all participating parties.

Some important concepts to be taken care in negotiation and e-contracting are:
- Contract Models: templates that enable enterprises to specify contracts that can be monitored / enforced by a contract framework.
- Contract Framework: comprehends the environment on which a contract, for a certain business opportunity, is created / specified, executed and monitored (Xu, 2003, 2004; Xu & Vrieze, 2007).
- Electronic Institutions: a framework that enables, through a communication network, automatic transactions between parties, according to sets of explicit institutional norms and rules. Thereby, the electronic institutions ensures the trust and confidence needed in any electronic transaction (Rocha et al., 2004).
- Digital Signature: are methods to authenticating digital information using cryptography techniques.

From the legal point of view, the European efforts to deal with new technologies used for commercial communication and contracting led to the directives 97/7/EC, 2000/31/EC and 93/13/EEC. Internationally, requirements for e-contracting are given by the OECD Recommendation concerning Guidelines for Consumer Protection in the context of Electronic Commerce and UN Draft Convention on electronic contracting. Also, in order to certify the consent to the contracting terms, in e-contracting, the notion of digital signature becomes relevant. The directive 1999/93/EC of the European Parliament and of the Council on a Community framework for electronic signatures provides clarification regarding the use of digital signatures. However, not all problems of digital signing have been resolved. Digital signatures are used to certify that the original document content has not been changed and that the document was sent from the genuine person. This means that digital signatures can also be used during the exchange of non-legally binding documents between parties. As a result, legally binding digital signatures have to be differentiated from non-legally binding digital signatures. A possible solution to this problem is provided in the ebXML standard (Waldt & Drummond, 2004). Another issue about digital signatures is that a signature has to be connected to a human being.

With the purpose of re-enforcing users' trust, there are Certification authorities that are responsible to ensure the privacy of information exchanged when users connect to a web server on the Internet, particularly if they plan to exchange private information and they want to be sure that the persons who are responsible for that server are indeed who they say they are. The method used to do this involves complex encryption with public and private keys, and independent verification of the server's owner or manager.

According to Angelov and Grefen (Angelov & Grefen, 2003) two types of e-contracting can be considered: Deep and shallow e-contracting, differing in the grade of automation of each of them. Deep e-contracting can show in 5 forms: 1) Micro-contracting, giving the possibility of customizing the contract to the client or supplier, 2) Just-in-Time-contracting, giving the opportunity to design the contract in a short period of time, 3) Precision-contracting, allowing contract specifications to be automatically defined and verified for consistency against internal and external requirements, 4) Enactment-contracting, allowing the information technology supporting the contract establishment process to be linked to the information technology supporting the enactment process, and 5) Management-contracting, linking the contract establishment process to the contract management process.

Although much work is still necessary in this area, several approaches and initiatives are being carried out in order to solve (or at least reduce) the difficulties faced in the contracting / agreement establishment process by enterprises that want to work together. Some of these concepts and techniques are described below and the most relevant milestones related to e-contracting research are summarized in the time line of the Figure 2.

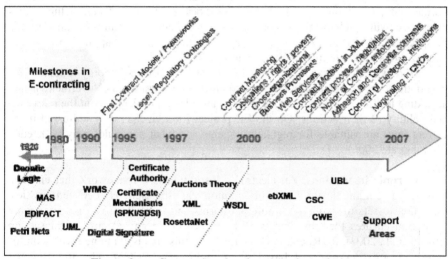

Figure 2 – e-Contracting development through time

Some related and relevant current research topics in negotiation and contracting include:

Contract representation. On the theoretical side, Deontic Logic is being tried to describe contract models specifying obligations, permissions, and forbiddances for a specified business process which works in an extremely ideal process. Some works in this area can be found in (Quirchmayr et al., 2002), as well as (Xu, 2004) that make use of deontic logic for the representation of the contract clauses but the results are still far from practical applicability. From a more pragmatic perspective various efforts have been put in the representation of contracts in XML (Angelov & Grefen, 2002; Carter et al., 2001).

Trust. The work of (Dimitrakos et al., 2004) through the TrustCom European Project, among other objectives, tried to focus on the provision of trust services to support the management of electronic contracts, the incorporation of guarantees to facilitate trustworthy collaboration, and performance assessment at the enactment of electronic contracts.

Legal Issues. Legal issues, especially about VO legal personality and contract with third parties (B2C e-contract), have been studied mainly in the ALIVE project. According to (Shelbourn et al., 2002), a VO needs a legal personality that will allow it to be seen as a legally independent entity in the country in which the contract has been incorporated. This requirement is however a subject of controversy as many definitions of VO claim that it does not have a legal entity. In fact, in many cases the contract with the client is signed by a single member of the VO. The other partners sign contracts with this member.

In the eLegal European project (Carter et al., 2001) the main goal was to develop solutions to legal issues related to VEs in the area of civil construction. Nevertheless, this framework would be prepared specifically for each project. Furthermore, (Shelbourn et al., 2005), describes the legal and contractual issues associated with each of these contracts / agreements, concentrating on the ICT perspective. An example of how e-contracting can be applied to virtual organizations can be found in (Xu & Vrieze, 2007).

Moreover, the usage of software agents is also commonly adopted for negotiations to set up a VE and for contracting VE partners. Nevertheless, and according to (Cevenini et al., 2007), agents raise legal problems about the relevance and validity of their actions. On the EC project LEGAL-IST, it is addressed if the current laws are suitable for regulating agents and what new rules may be needed (Sartor et al., 2006).

Electronic institutions. An electronic institution is a framework that enables, through a communication network, automatic transactions between parties, according to sets of explicit institutional norms and rules. Thereby, the Electronic Institution ensures the trust and confidence needed in any electronic transaction (Rocha et al., 2004). In (Rocha & Oliveira, 1999) this area is combined with a multi-criteria negotiation protocol based on a multi-agent system. The implemented approach is based on a traditional architecture representing enterprises by agents and introducing into the community a market agent that plays the role of coordinator in the electronic market and whose main goal is the virtual enterprise formation when consumer's needs are identified. In fact the notion of electronic market used here is a primitive form of VO breeding environment. The negotiation protocol is defined through the multi-agent systems (MAS) paradigm. Also on this topic (Cardoso & Oliveira, 2004) have been working on the validation of contracts according to a normative framework and their monitoring and enforcement. Further developments in various projects try to establish the notion of e-notary. Moreover, there are several cases where a trusted third party is mandatory in trading markets. (Conrad et al., 2007) proposed a framework that provides legal certainty, according to European regulations for distributed market platforms.

Supportive Frameworks. For the support of electronic contracts and negotiation some tools have been suggested such as "Contract wizards" offering a clauses library, contract editors, and Virtual Negotiation Rooms. A Clauses Library is the knowledge base of the Wizard (Shelbourn et al., 2002; Shelbourn et al., 2005), the Contract Editor uses this knowledge base to electronically produce contracts and the Virtual Negotiation Room (VNR) can be used by the different parties to collaborate, choose the different terms of the contracts and download the current version of the contract. However, in terms of implementation such concepts are at a very primitive stage. For instance, some implementations of the VNR are just a document management system and do not offer negotiation support.

In (Andreoli & Castellani, 2001, 2004) is reported a framework based on multi-agent systems to let partners engage into flexible negotiation. The negotiation mechanism is an extension to the Contract Net protocol and it exploits the coordination mechanisms provided by CLF/Mekano that consists in a middleware platform designed to integrate negotiation and transaction aspects in distributed systems. The framework is based on unidirectional "announce/collect/decide" paradigm, but intends to go towards a multi-directional "announce/refine/decide" paradigm allowing flexible refinement of the negotiation terms.

3   NEGOTIATION WIZARD REQUIREMENTS

Through interaction with various end-users networks, i.e. VO breeding environments (VBEs) involved in the ECOLEAD project, various critical negotiation activities were identified:

- Reaching agreements concerning coordination aspects: For instance, who will be responsible for the VO.
- Reaching agreement concerning the sharing of risks among the involved partners. It also relates to the amount of impact that a problem in a task performed by one partner can cause in the whole VO. Moreover, agreement about the amount of budget retained to cope with possible problems is needed.
- The contract should follow a basic set of standard templates: It is important to depart from common templates, selected for each kind of CO, and extend the selected template to cope with the detailed agreement specifications using "add-on" clauses.
- Reaching agreements on the detailed activities and scheduling.
- Information exchange agreement: i.e. how should information be exchanged among partners, and also which kind of information should be exchanged. These agreements have also a close relationship with the detailed scheduling of activities; detailed costs agreement, i.e. discuss and agree with each partner the value of the part that it will produce or the service it will perform.
- Support for privacy of proposals, where only the involved partners have access to the information being negotiated.

Having into account this list, it is evident that these types of agreements require fundamentally decision making by human actors rather than fully-automated decision-makers. In this case, what is addressed is not a complex e-contracting process where the system is capable of automatically generate, interpret, execute, and manage a contract, but to a certain extent, the system should store and receive inputs into an electronic source for later interpretation, guiding the user through the process.

Regarding the VO creation environment, there are two different situations where negotiation might be required: i) to select the right partners to compose the VO, and ii) to reach agreements on the details of the VO. The proposed negotiation wizard (WizAN) is intended to provide facilities for both situations, being the main result of it an agreement where all the related issues of the VO are covered.

Usually contracts are used to regulate the exchange of values (e.g. money, knowledge), and mainly its provisions are for protection of parties in case that something does not go according to what was planned, and to describe what was agreed in the case that any party forgets it. In business relationships, a contract might be established among two single parties, but it can also be established among several parties (multi-party contract). In the case of the contract / agreement produced with the help of WizAN it can be either bilateral or multi-party depending on what is being negotiated.

4   WizAN

4.1 Purpose of the tool

The agreements' negotiation wizard (WizAN) runs in parallel to the other tools of the VO Creation Framework, and is aimed at assisting human actors during negotiation processes towards the VO establishment. The full negotiation process involves a number of elementary negotiations in order to reach the necessary agreements with the purpose of accomplishing a VO internal agreement. Given so, the internal consortium agreement is the result or synthesis of all agreements established among the participants of the VO being created and that will regulate their collaboration.

The main inputs for WizAN are collected along the various steps of the VO creation. These inputs shall come from the other tools of the VO creation framework. For instance, the coFinder tool will provide WizAN with the CO identity, the "client" and other relevant data about the CO; the COC-Plan tool provides WizAN with the structure of the process, the suggestion of the needed competencies, etc.; finally, the PSS tool provides WizAN with a suggested list of the most suitable configuration of partners to fulfill the CO requirements.

Table 1 summarizes the main inputs for the WizAN tool that besides the information manually introduced by the VO planner, shall be received from the other tools of the VO creation framework (Luis M. Camarinha-Matos & Oliveira, 2006).

In WizAN, the VO agreement is the "assemblage" of all relevant information about the VO that was agreed by the involved participants. This information is divided into several sections according to their categories. For example, there is a section related to the partners involved in the VO; a section with the scheduling of the entire VO; a section specifying the tasks where certain parties are involved as well as their obligations and rights; etc. All these topics that are matter of negotiation are here called "negotiation objects".

Independently of the negotiation content, the negotiation object shall also contain information about the involved participants, when the negotiation started, when it was agreed, etc.

Table 1 – Inputs to WizAN

VO Creation Tools	COfinder	COC-Plan	PSS
Description	Support in detection of collaboration opportunities	Characterization of the CO and preparation of a rough structure of the VO and needed processes	Recommendation of potential VO configurations and details of task assignment
Inputs to WizAN	CO identity, "customer" and other relevant data	-Collaboration modality -Process structure / VO logical structure -Suggestion of needed number of partners and the competences they shall have -Definition of main processes to be carried out by each partner (according to competencies).	-Suggested list of most suitable partners (with corresponding competences, criteria and performance indicators) to fulfill the CO requirements.

During a specific negotiation, only the involved parties shall have access to the corresponding exchanged information. Therefore, with the purpose of supporting the process of negotiation for each needed negotiation object, a temporary virtual negotiation room (VNR) shall be created. So it is through the utilization of VNRs that partners will be able to privately discuss about subjects that must be agreed. Only the involved organizations will be invited to take part in the discussion of each specific subject.

4.2 Implemented functionalities

The WizAN functionalities can be divided into four main modules: Contract Editor, Virtual Negotiation Room, Electronic Notary, and Assisted Contract Elaboration. In the following subsections, these four modules are described.

4.2.1 Contract Editor (CE)

The WizAN Editor is the main editor of the information that regards the agreements being established among the VO partners. It allows the VO planner to initiate, conduct, and monitor the VO creation. It deals with the general part of the agreement that is being established.

In this editor there are four distinct levels of entities: *General Information; Supporting Documents; Negotiation Topics*; and *signing of the final agreement,* as is illustrated in Figure 3 that represents the CE GUI.

This editor provides different functionalities to its users according to their role, since different roles might have different permission / visibility access to the VO information.

If the user is playing the role of <u>planner</u>, then the available functionalities are:

- **Add partners to the VO**: according to the results provided by the PSS tool for a given CO, or just add partners from the set of VBE members according to the preferences of the planner;

- **Add / read / edit documents that refer to the general part of the VO**: the planner is able to edit the documents that are attached to the general part of the agreement of the VO. Each time a document is modified, the system keeps a record with document versioning control. Only the VO planner can delete/remove these attached documents;

- **Create new Virtual Negotiation Room (VNR)**: the planner is the only member that is allowed to create a new VNR whenever a new topic requires discussion among some / all partners;

- **Produce the final document**: when all negotiations are closed and there is no need for further discussion, the VO planner can generate the document that represents a synthesis of the VO agreements.

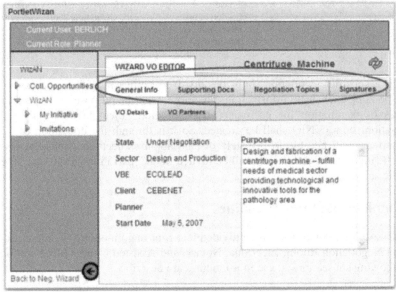

Figure 3 – Example of WizAN Contract Editor GUI

If the user is playing a role of <u>potential partner</u>, the offered functionalities are:

- **Participation acceptance**: whenever a VBE member receives an invitation to participate in a VO, it can accept or reject it in the editor;

- **See general conditions of the VO**: through this editor, the potential VO partner can have access to the general conditions of the VO being created;

- **See involved partners in the VO**: it is also possible to have access to the information regarding the other participants of the VO being created;

- **Read / add documents to the general part of the VO**: playing the role of partner, the user can read all documents that are related to the general agreement of the VO, but can only edit the ones that were created by himself/herself. When adding a new document version, a history track is kept;

- **Have access to the VNRs**: the partner will have access to a list of all VNRs to which it has been invited to participate (partners will not be able to visualize VNRs where they have no participation);

- **Signing functionality**: when all the discussions are already closed and the VO planner has already generated the VO agreement, each partner has to accept and sign it, with the help of the eNotary.

4.2.2 Virtual Negotiation Room (VNR)

When the VO planner wishes to discuss any specific topic with certain members, he / she creates a virtual sub-space inside the VO negotiation space, i.e. a new virtual negotiation room. Given so, the VNR is the virtual "place" where the negotiation takes place. Through the VNRs the participants can access the various negotiation topics and can discuss in order to reach agreements. For each negotiation topic there will be one corresponding VNR.

In Figure 4, the instantiation of the negotiation objects for evaluation and discussion by the invited potential VO partners are illustrated.

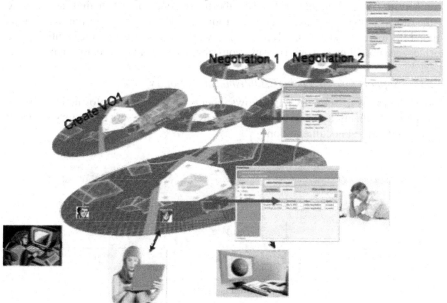

Figure 4 – Virtual spaces in WizAN

Each VNR can be divided into two distinct parts: one for edition of the negotiation topic characteristics and associated documents, and another for enabling discussion among the partners involved in the negotiation topics.

The **edition** part of the VNR provides functionalities for the VO planner such as:

- **Add partners to the room (negotiation topic)**: choose from the partners already invited to the VO, the ones that are directly involved in the discussion of a certain topic;
- **Choose the topic agreement modality**: each topic might have different agreement modalities depending on what it concerns. The topics might be

agreed by: unanimity (when all partners must agree), majority (when only the majority of partners have to agree), or informative (when there is no need for partners to agree);

- **Add / read / edit documents that refer to the VNR**: manage the associated documents;
- **Open discussion area**: with the functionalities of chat and forum. In the case of the forum, the partners will only have access to the topics where they have a direct participation;
- **Close VNR**: manage partners' commitments.

On the other hand, the <u>partners</u> involved in the negotiation have some restrictions regarding the use of these functionalities, namely in what concerns:

- Adding partners to the VNR;
- Editing associated documents;
- General management.

Moreover, the **discussion** functionality of the forum enables the involved members to discuss subjects related to the negotiation topic that they are dealing with. At each time that a user enters the room, he/she has access to the discussions around the topics he/she is involved in. As a way to provide some confidentially, the partners are not allowed to view discussions about subjects they are not involved in.

4.2.3   Support for Agreement Establishment – eNotary

The e-Notary is a module that allows clients to exchange information with a warranty of authenticity and validity as well as providing a safe repository for them to save and request documentation.

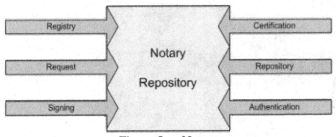

Figure 5 – eNotary

This module was developed as a web service allowing its clients to use the following facilities:

- **Registry**: any user who wants to use this service will be obligated to prior registration. As the service works based on asymmetric key cryptography this is the moment in which the service and the user exchange keys. If the user doesn't have a key yet, one can be assigned;
- **Request documents**: any registered user can request documents that are available for him/her to sign or just for consultation. When a user requests the available documents, the service will return a list of documents and the actions associated with them;
- **Signing**: the notary is the entity responsible for validating each user's signature for each document. This functionality allows the user to digitally sign a document;

- **Certification**: this means that a user can submit a document to the notary to be certified. The certification of a document means that the document is valid and is indeed signed by the people/entities it claims to be signed by;
- **Repository**: every document that is in any way submitted to the notary's appreciation will be saved both for future consultation and to provide means of certification;
- **Authentication**: provide ways for a user to guarantee its identity before any other entity.

4.2.4 Assisted Contract Elaboration System – ACE

This component provides participants in the VO creation with the ability to write and sign digital contracts based on rules, clauses and categories. This is accomplished in a simple way and taking advantage of reusable components. To fulfill these requests there are editors to build the contract's structure and template and to instantiate the variable components ("variables") with the results from negotiation. The contract's correctness is validated by a number of checkers that work based on user defined rules. In this way, virtually anyone is able to write a contract and submit it to negotiation and signature by other members knowing it is structurally correct.

The contract's construction process can be divided into four phases:
1. Building/editing the contract's skeleton;
2. Building/editing the contract's template;
3. Instantiating the contract's variables with the negotiated objects; and
4. Submitting the contract to the online notary to be signed and saved for consultation.

Along this pathway nine different components are involved:
- **database**: to provide information persistence;
- **editor of rules, categories and collaboration types**: to provide a way to create or edit a new rule, category or collaboration type (depending on the type of consortium that this contract is being created, e.g. explicit consortium (L. M. Camarinha-Matos et al., 2005)) and all of the associated properties;
- **editor of rules and clauses**: to make it possible for the user to create new clauses, inserting text, variables and rules associated to that clause;
- **editor of the contract's skeleton**: to allow a user to create areas in a new document that will be placeholders for clauses;
- **repository of the contract's skeleton**: to provide facilities for contract skeletons list viewing, associated properties viewing and saving and loading of a contract skeleton;
- **editor of the contract's template**: to provide lists of available clauses for each placeholder based on the type of placeholder and, if sufficient information exists, suggests some for each area;
- **repository of the contract's template**: to provide a list of contract templates viewing and all its associated properties, and saving and loading of a contract template;
- **editor of the contract's variables**: to provide the user with the ability to replace the variables in a contract with concrete values;

- **repository of contracts**: where the contracts are stored.

Table 2 presents a summary of the four functionalities formerly described as well as the outputs of each of them and the involved actors.

Table 2 – WizAN's main functionalities

Functionality	Description	Outputs	Actors
Contract Editor (CE)	Uses the CRT repository and agreed negotiation objects to add clauses to contracts	Contracts	VO Planner
Virtual negotiation room (VNR)	Virtual "place" where the negotiation participants can access the various negotiation objects and can "discuss" in order to reach agreements	Agreed negotiation objects	VO Planner and all possible partners
Support for agreement establishment (eNotary)	Set up facilities for contract signing and notification to relevant parties, and repository/archive for its storage	Repository with signed contracts	VO Planner and all partners involved
Assisted Contract Elaboration System (ACE)	Collection of contract templates and negotiation object templates to support the contract creation	"Skeletons" of contracts	VO Planner

4.3 Phases and use cases

In this process there are clearly two important levels: creation of the general agreement of the VO and, in parallel, the generation of specific negotiation rooms for each topic that might need discussion. Therefore, the phases of the VO creation and VNR usage can be divided as illustrated in Figure 6 and
Having into account the functionalities previously described, the table below illustrates the use cases when a VO is successfully created.

Table 3.

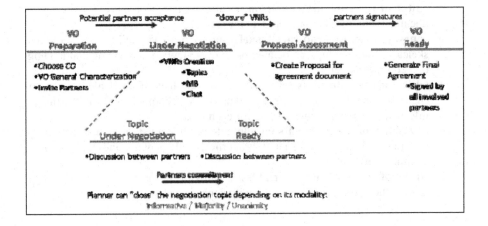

Figure 6 – VO and VNRs phases

Having into account the functionalities previously described, the table below illustrates the use cases when a VO is successfully created.

Table 3 – VO and VNRs Life phases

Life Cycles of VO and VNR		Description
VO Preparation		When the broker / planner choose a CO and make the general characterization of the CO and the rough planning of the VO. Also at this stage, the planner can invite the adequate partners.
VO Under negotiation	**Topic Under Negotiation**	While the topic is being discussed among partners
	Topic Ready	Once partners agree (depending on topic modality) the planner can close the Topic.
VO Proposal Assessment		After all negotiation topics are closed, the planner produces the final agreement document to be signed by all partners.
VO Ready		When all partners have agreed upon the final agreement and signed it. Hereafter, the VO can be registered in the VBE management system (VMS) and put into operation.

The "VO Under negotiation" / Description column also notes across both topic rows: "Phase where the topics are being discussed between the necessary partners involved."

Table 4 – Use case for a VO creation

UC – Create New VO (successful case)		
Primary Actor; VO Planner	**Scope: VBE –VO creation**	**Level: short summary**
Actors/ Actions		

- <u>VO planner</u> – intends to create a new VO to fulfill the requirements of a collaboration opportunity.
- <u>Possible partners</u> (VBE members) – will be invited to participate in the VO and negotiate its terms.

Precondition

System already with the information about all VBE members (the potential partners to the VO).

Main Success Scenario

1. The VO planner starts a new VO using the WizAN tool;
2. The VO planner collects the information regarding the VO topology and general characteristics (this can be collected through the information provided by the coFinder

and COC-Plan tools);
3. The VO planner creates the general part of the agreement based on the general VO characteristics;
4. The VO planner chooses the most suitable partners to compose the VO and invites them to participate in the VO (information on the right partners can be obtained through the PSS tool);
5. The invited partners accept to participate;
6. The VO planner creates the necessary VNRs and adds the required partners to them;
7. Negotiation rounds take place;
8. After all partners agree on their correspondent negotiation topics, the VO planner can create the document that comprises the relevant information of the VO that is being created;
9. The VO planner registers the document on the eNotary and sends its hash (i.e. digest) to all VO partners;
10. All partners of the VO accept the general terms and digitally sign the document on the eNotary;
11. The VO creation is ready.

Sequence Diagram

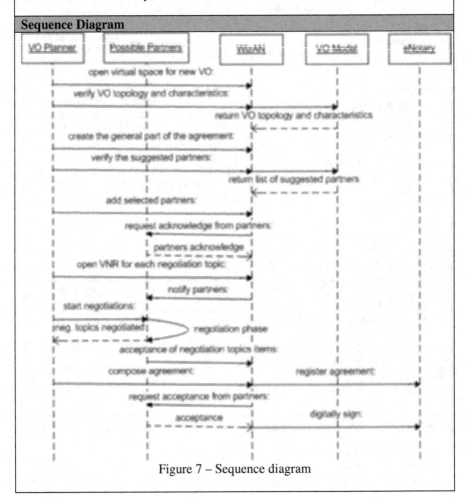

Figure 7 – Sequence diagram

4.3.1 Implementation architecture

The WizAN implementation architecture is based on a set of technologies that were combined to develop the designed functionalities. As illustrated in Figure 8, this architecture is based on the interactions of portlets (deployed in the Liferay portal), with the human actors and with the databases.

The eNotary was developed in the Java programming language and deployed as a web service resorting to the Apache Tomcat Servlet Container and Apache Axis. To be able to accomplish the planned services, the eNotary was supported on some existing cryptography algorithms, such as MD5 synthesis and PKI (Public Key Infrastructure).

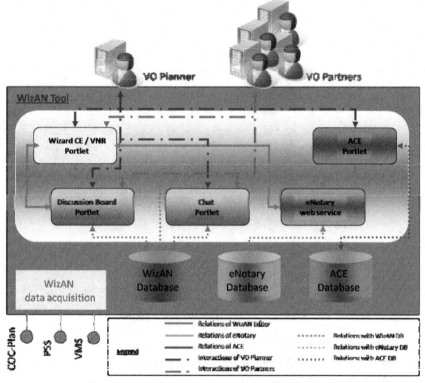

Figure 8 – WizAN implementation architecture

4.3.2 Database schema

With the purpose of storing the essential information to be used by the WizAN tool a database was built. This database also contains the information that will be later on utilized to build the VO agreement.

The main classes of information are (Figure 9):

- Participant – information on the VBE members that can participate in the VOs that are going to be created;
- Contact_Information – contact information of the VBE members, as well as of the clients;
- VBE – information about the VBE where the VO is being created;

- Client – includes the client's information;
- VO_Agreement – where the general part of the agreement of each VO that is being created is stored;
- Negotiation_Object – information on a specific negotiation topic (the information created in each VNR);
- Supporting_Documents – information on the documents that have been created either at the VO or VNR context;
- VO_Participants – includes all the involved participants in a certain VO;
- NO_Participants – includes all the involved participants in a certain VNR.

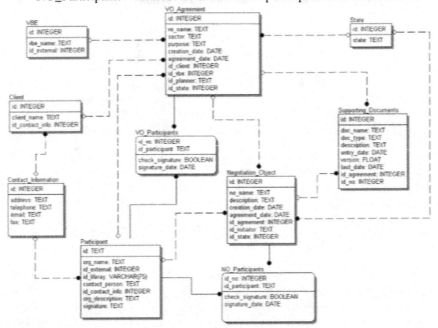

Figure 9 – WizAN database schema

4.3.3   Development platform

Technologies and tools used in the WizAN developments are:

- JAVA programming language;
- Sun Java Studio Creator 2, an integrated development environment that can be used for visual JavaServer Faces web application and portlet development;
- Liferay Portal were the developed portlets can be deployed;
- Apache Tomcat, a web container developed by Apache Software Foundation (ASF) that implements the servlet and the JavaServer Pages (JSP) specifications;
- Postgresql, a free software object-relational database management system (ORDBMS).

The tool can be accessed through any web browser, but preferentially the Microsoft Internet Explorer.

The following figure illustrates an example of the outcome of the WizAN developments using the above tools and technologies.

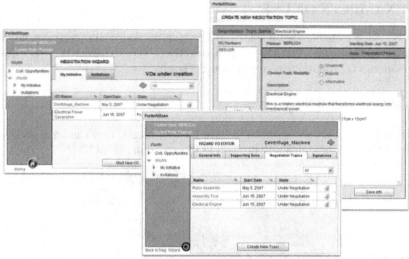

Figure 10 – Example of WizAN user interfaces as portlets that are deployed in the Liferay portal

4.4 Interaction with other VO creation framework tools

The necessary information for the creation of a VO can be inserted manually in the WizAN tool or it can be imported from the other tools of the VO creation framework, namely coFinder, COC-Plan and PSS. This integration is done through a VO model that can be accessed by all tools via web services. The interfaces where the integration is considered are illustrated below.

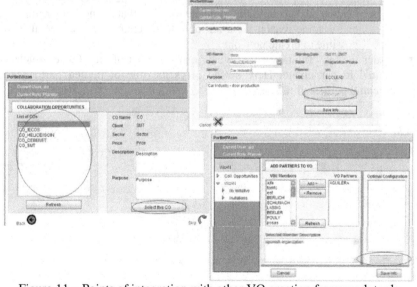

Figure 11 – Points of integration with other VO creation framework tools

5   EXAMPLES OF USE

The following examples are intended to illustrate the four main phases of the VO creation through the WizAN tool perspective: *VO Preparation, VO under negotiation, VO proposal assessment,* and *VO ready.*

5.1 VO preparation

As all VBE members are assumed to have Internet access, they can have access to the *WizAN Editor* through a web browser as illustrated in Figure 12.

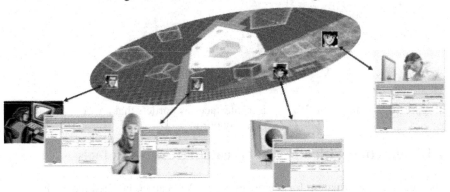

Figure 12 – VBE members access to WizAN editor

On the wizard there are two main tabs:
- "My Initiative": where the user is able to see the list of all VOs that he/she has created, i.e., regarding which he/she plays the role of VO planner.
  - On this tab it is possible to delete the VOs that are no longer important or for some reason were not able to be created. Moreover, it is also possible to create new ones.
- Under the tab "Invitations", the user can see a list of all VOs to which was invited to participate. Here he/she plays the role of invited partner, so a potential partner of the new VO.

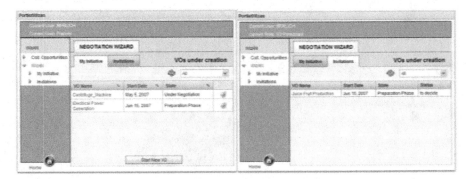

Figure 13- WizAN Editor for VO planner / VO partner

5.1.1   *VO preparation in WizAN*

When a VBE member takes the initiative of creating a new VO, for a given CO, it plays the role of planner. For that it must fill in the necessary information on the WizAN VO editor.

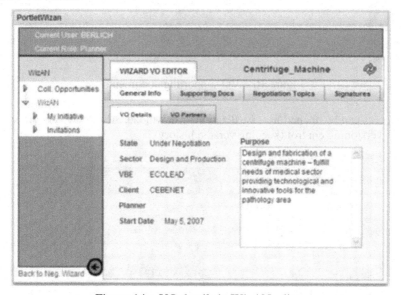

Figure 14 – VO details in WizAN editor

After filling in the initial information, it can invite other partners to participate in this VO. The invited partners, if willing to participate in the VO, will have to accept this invitation in their WizAN editor.

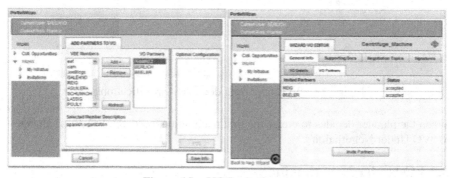

Figure 15 – VO Invited partners

The planner can also add the necessary supporting documents to this general part of the VO.

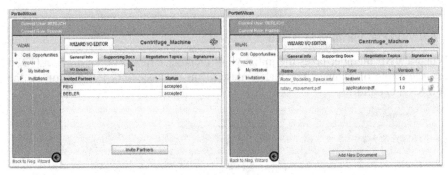

Figure 16 – VO supporting documents

The documents can be opened for visualization or download. Also, new versions can be added with versioning control (keeping version history).

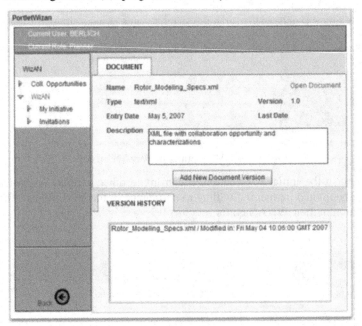

Figure 17 – VO supporting document specifications

When the planner decides to create the first negotiation topic, the VO phase changes to "VO Under Negotiation".

5.2 VO Under Negotiation

In order to start new negotiation topics, the involved partners have to previously accept to participate in the VO. Otherwise it will not be possible to create a new negotiation topic.

To create new topics (planner side) there is the "Negotiation Topics" option on the "Wizard VO Editor" where the necessary data shall be introduced.

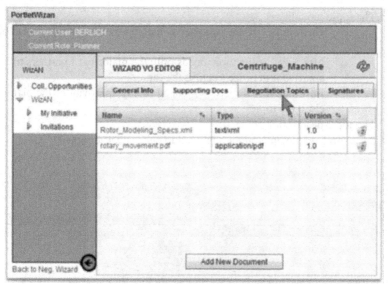

Figure 18 – VO Negotiation Topics tab

5.2.1   VO under negotiation in WizAN

In the picture below a list of two negotiation topics that were already created can be seen.

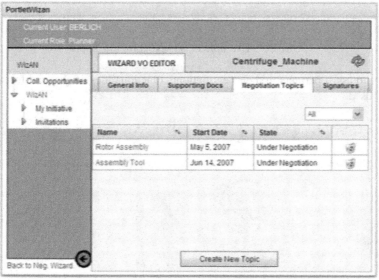

Figure 19 – VO Negotiation Topics

For each negotiation topic the planner has to introduce some information, such as:
   ⇨ Topic name
   ⇨ The VO partners that will participate (not all partners are necessary – only the ones that are directly related with the topic)

⇨ The topic modality:

    o   Unanimity – if the topic needs the approval of all partners to be agreed

    o   Majority – if the topic needs only the majority of partners to approve it in order to close the topic

    o   Informative – if there is no need of any approval for the planner to close the topic

⇨ The topic description

⇨ Also some documents might be added to each specific topic.

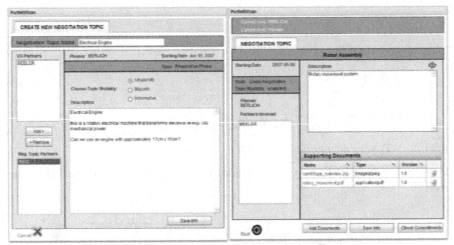

Figure 20 – Example of VO Negotiation Topic

In order to assist partners in their negotiations, functionalities of chat and forum can also be used.

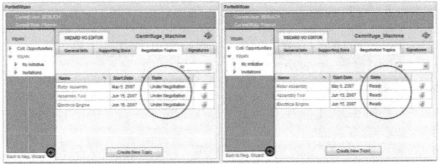

Figure 21 – VO Negotiation Topics state

After all negotiation topics are agreed – closed, the VO planner can generate the global agreement as a representation of all the topics negotiated.

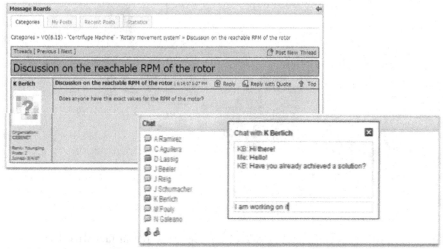

Figure 22 – Forum and Chat Functionalities

At this stage, the VO moves into the "VO Proposal Assessment" phase.

5.3 VO Proposal Assessment

After all negotiation topics are closed, the VO planner can create the agreement. This agreement shall be signed by all partners involved.

5.3.1 Agreement proposal creation in WizAN

When all negotiation topics are in the ready state, the final agreement can be created. For that, the planner creates a proposal for partners to accept.

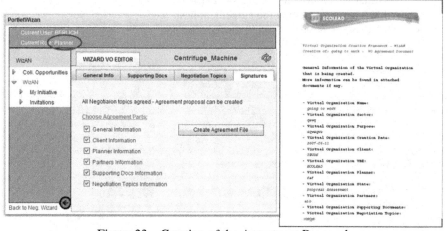

Figure 23 – Creation of the Agreement Proposal

In order to digitally sign the agreement, each participant has its own digital key that was assigned to them when they first used the WizAN editor.

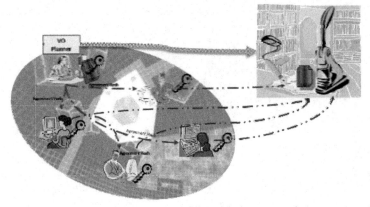

Figure 24 – eNotary example

The entire process is completely hidden from the users, but in fact what happens is that the planner sends the document that represents the agreement to the eNotary, generating a hash of the document that can also be understood as a digest signature or stamp. Subsequent to this, the generated hash is sent to all partners. Only with that hash of the document, partners will be able to request the exact document from the eNotary and through their private key digitally sign it (Figure 24 – eNotary example).

In the following example it is illustrated how the VO partners digitally sign the agreement document through the WizAN application.

5.3.2   *Generation of the final / signed agreement in WizAN*

The most important steps in this phase are:

1. The VO planner places / registers the VO agreement in the eNotary with information about who are the VO partners

2. All VO partners receive the agreement hash

3. All VO partners digitally sign the agreement.

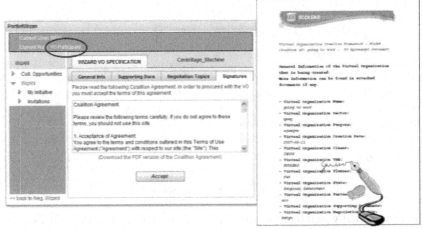

Figure 25 – Partners Signing the VO agreement.

5.4 VO Proposal Assessment

Only after all VO partners digitally sign the agreement, it becomes valid and the VO passes to the **VO Ready Phase**. Then, the VO can be registered in the VBE management system and put into operation.

6 CONCLUSIONS

The establishment of collaboration commitments, represented by contracts or agreements, is a crucial step in a virtual organization creation process. For that purpose, iterative negotiations need to take place and an environment that facilitates the establishments of such commitments is needed.

Using the proposed wizard, users are able to compose an agreement document that represents a synthesis of all VO partners' commitments that have been reached during the negotiation phase. Moreover, the environment allows the usage of collaboration tools, for instance discussion forum, associated to each specific topic of negotiation and only for the involved partners. As such, it is possible to guarantee confidentiality. Also for ensuring authenticity, an eNotary was introduced so that the agreement documents remain authentic and can be digitally signed by all partners.

Nevertheless, there are two major areas of remaining research challenges, namely:

- **ICT Challenges:**
  - o Definition and formalization of a negotiation protocol: definition of the actors, roles and phases of negotiation, defining taxonomy and a language for negotiation rules. Definition of the negotiation process as an exchange of negotiation objects followed by a phase of agreement formation, supporting the automation of the negotiation process, and making the process more efficient;
  - o Security, privacy and trust management: Further support security mechanisms and protocols that enable participants to do business in a trusted way. So, the communication is kept private in a secure, trustworthy environment;
  - o Data and Resources Modeling, Discovery and Allocation. It covers all subjects related to semantic definition, languages and schemes to discover, share and allocate data and resources (i.e. negotiation object consolidation), such as intelligent agents, Web Services, Data Mining, Grids, etc.
- **Social and Organizational Challenges:**
  - o The Negotiation Rooms can be seen as multidisciplinary/multicultural environmental that bring together people and organizations with different business practices, languages, objectives and terminology. Better support for this diversity is needed.
  - o The trust management of distant organizations, which may not have previous joint business experiences, is a challenge.
  - o As the negotiation process is dynamic, the wizard should be adaptable to this changing situation.

Acknowledgements. This work was funded in part by the European Commission through the ECOLEAD project.

7   REFERENCES

Andreoli, J. M., & Castellani, S. (2001, 5 September). *Towards a Flexible Middleware Negotiation Facility for Distributed Components*. Paper presented at the DEXA'2001 - Workshop on E-Negotiation, Munich, Germany.

Andreoli, J. M., & Castellani, S. (2004, 1-3 July). *Constraint-based decision makers in negotiation processes*. Paper presented at the The 2004 IFIP International Conference on Decision Support Systems (DSS 2004), Prato, Tuscany, Italy.

Angelov, S. (2006). *Foundations of B2B Electronic Contracting*. Unpublished PhD, Technische Universiteit Eindhoven, Eindhoven.

Angelov, S., & Grefen, P. (2002). An Approach to the Construction of Flexible B2B E-Contracting Processess. University of Twente, Computer Science Dept., The Netherlands.

Angelov, S., & Grefen, P. (2003). The 4W framework for B2B e-contracting. *Int. J. Networking and Virtual Organizations, Vol. 2*(No. 1), pp. 78-97.

Camarinha-Matos, L. M., & Oliveira, A. I. (2006, 18-20 September). *Contract Negotiation Wizard for VO Creation*. Paper presented at the 3rd International CIRP Conference on Digital Enterprise Technology - DET'06, Setúbal.

Camarinha-Matos, L. M., Oliveira, A. I., Ratti, R., Baldo, F., & Jarimo, T. (2007). A Computer-Assisted VO Creation Framework. *Establishing the Foundation of Collaborative Networks*, pp. 165-178.

Camarinha-Matos, L. M., Silveri, I., Afsarmanesh, H., & Oliveira, A. I. (2005). Towards a Framework for Creation of Dynamic Virtual Organizations. In L. M. Camarinha-Matos (Ed.), *Collaborative Networks and theirs Breeding Environments* (pp. pp. 69-80): Springer.

Cardoso, H. L., & Oliveira, E. (2004). *Virtual Enterprise Normative Framework within Electronic Institutions*. Paper presented at the ESAW'04.

Carter, C., Hassan, T., Mertz, M., & White, E. (2001). The eLegal project: specifying legal terms of contract in ICT environment (Special Issue - Information and Communication Technology Advances in the European Construction Industry ed., Vol. ITcon Vol. 6, pp. 163-174).

Cevenini, C., Contissa, G., & Laukyte, M. (2007). Agent-Based Contracting in Virtual Enterprises. *Establishing the Foundation of Collaborative Networks*, pp. 225-232.

Conrad, M., Funk, C., Raabe, O., & Walhorst, O. (2007). A Lawful Framework for Distributed Electronic Markets. *Establishing the Foundation of Collaborative Networks*, pp. 233-240.

Dimitrakos, T., Golby, D., & Kearney, P. (2004). Towards a Trust and Contract Management Framework for dynamic Virtual Organisations: eChallenges Workshop.

Grefen, P., & Angelov, S. (2002). *On t-, u-, p-, and e-contracting*. Paper presented at the CAiSE Workshop on Web Services, e-Business, and the Semantic Web (WES2002), Toronto, Canada.

Quirchmayr, G., Milosevic, Z., Tagg, R., Cole, J., & Kulkarni, S. (2002). Establishment of Virtual Enterprise Contracts. In R. Cicchetti & e. al. (Eds.), *DEXA 2002* (pp. 236-248): Springer-Verlag.

Rocha, A. P., Cardoso, H. L., & Oliveira, E. (2004). *Contributions to an electronic Institution supporting Virtual Enterprises' life cycle*. Paper presented at the Virtual Enterprise Integration: Technological and Organizational Perspectives.

Rocha, A. P., & Oliveira, E. (1999). An Electronic Market Architecture for the Formation of Virtual Enterprises, *Infrastructures for Virtual Enterprises*. Boston: Kluwer.

Sartor, G., Cevenini, C., Laukyte, M., Contissa, G., & Rubino, R. (2006). *Legal Issues in Software Agents*. Paper presented at the eChallenges.

Shelbourn, M., Hassan, T., & Carter, C. (2002). *Legal and Contractual Framework for the VO* (IST-1999-20570): eLegal Project.

Shelbourn, M., Hassan, T., & Carter, C. (2005). Legal and Contractual Framework for the VO. In L. M. Camarinha-Matos & H. Afsarmanesh & M. Ollus (Eds.), *Virtual Organization Systems and Practices*: Springer.

Waldt, D., & Drummond, R. (2004). *EBXML The Global Standard for Electronic Business*.

Xu, L. (2003). *Monitorable Electronic Contract*. Paper presented at the IEEE International Conference on E-Commerce (CEC'03).

Xu, L. (2004). *Monitoring Multi-Party Contracts for e-Business*. Unpublished PhD., Faculty of Economics and Business Administration of Tilburg University, Tilburg.

Xu, L., & Vrieze, P. d. (2007). Fundamentals of Virtual Organization e-Contracting. *Establishing the Foundation of Collaborative Networks*, pp. 209-216.

PART 3

VIRTUAL ORGANIZATIONS MANAGEMENT

GOVERNANCE AND MANAGEMENT OF VIRTUAL ORGANIZATIONS

Kim Jansson[1], Iris Karvonen[1], Martin Ollus[1], Ugo Negretto[2]

[1]VTT – Technical research Centre of Finland
e-mails: name.surname@vtt.fi
[2]Enicma Gmbh
e-mail: ugo_negretto@enicma.com

A Virtual Organization (VO) consists of independent organizations collaborating for a common goal. Towards the customers and the outer world, they are assumed to look and behave as they were a single organization. Proper governance principles and operative management are needed in order to achieve the objectives. The focus is on the enforcement of the collaboration between independent partners with their own internal aims and own internal processes and management means. The paper presents results and solutions to support the management of virtual organizations in a dynamic environment.

1. CHALLENGES IN VO MANAGEMENT

Virtual Organizations (VO) consist of a wide range of typologies in structure, topology, time span and life cycles (Karvonen et al., 2005). Depending on the categories of the VO, the behavior is usually supported by dedicated methods and tools. Examples are the so called supply chains and extended enterprises. However, the "Management" of generic Virtual Organizations, by coordinated activities towards target achievement, is less systematically studied and remains as a challenge.

A VO consists of independent organizations, which have agreed to collaborate towards a common goal. Towards the customers and the outer world, it can in many senses be assumed to look and behave as it was a single organization. However, the partner organizations have their own objectives, internal processes and business cultures. As an implication of this fact, a VO cannot necessarily be managed like a single organization. The management means are not the same ones as in a single organization (Toelle, 2004), nor does the manager of a VO have similar power as a manager in a single company.

The main challenges for VO management come from the characteristics of virtual organizations, the temporary nature and the distribution of operations in independent but interdependent organizations with their own aim, behaviour and culture. The VO management must relay on co-ordination to reach the objectives of the VO

- With little or no power, because all partners are independent actors

- Through creating trust and a collaborative atmosphere
- By considering risks and
- Relying on incomplete information.

The focus of this chapter is on the models needed for governing and managing dynamic Virtual Organizations under the described conditions. It explains the approaches taken in the ECOLEAD project to cope with these challenges.

The temporary nature of the VO implies that the VO is dissolved after the achievement of its goals. This feature creates challenges related to the sustainability of results and experiences. To cope with this fact, an inheritance approach has been developed in relation to the VO management. This feature can transfer important experience and knowledge about the VO and the performed tasks to more sustainable environments, like the Virtual Breeding Environment.

2. CONCEPTS

2.1. Governance

According to Plumtre, the founder of the Institute on Governance (http://www.iog.ca/), the word "governance" was almost unknown in English until the last few years of the 20th century and there are still debates about the definition. He suggests the following definition: *Governance is the process whereby societies or organisations make important decisions, determine whom they involve and how they render account.* This definition contains the idea that governance differs from "management" as it deals with important or strategic decision making about how to achieve important goals. It is a set of ideas and approaches about directing human activities to any form of collective actions, but formal management procedures do not have to be involved. Also Oxford Dictionary (Oxford, 1987) relates the term "governance" to standards and principles for control.

We have taken the same approach by using the governance term to denote basic principles and processes needed to support the achievement of the aims of the VO. The aspect of governance is used to understand the implication of power and the connected ability to suggest or force changes upon the operations of the VO. By governance, we understand the principles, the structure and the processes and their relationship supporting an efficient achievement of the aims of the VO. The governance of a VO is closely related to "project governance" (Renz, 2007). Project governance can be considered to:

- Outline the relationships between all internal and external groups involved in the project
- Describe the proper flow of information regarding the project to all stakeholders
- Ensure the appropriate review issues encountered within each project
- Ensure that require approvals and direction for the project is obtained at each appropriate stage of the project.

Like a VO, a project usually also consists of different organizations working towards a common aim. Consequently, similar understanding of the basic terms is natural.

O''Donovan (2003) defines corporate governance as 'an internal system encompassing policies, processes and people, which serves the needs of shareholders and other stakeholders, by directing and controlling management activities with good business savvy, objectivity and integrity. Sound corporate governance is reliant on external marketplace commitment and legislation, plus a healthy board culture which safeguards policies and processes'.

The VO governance principles are in the first place established in the underlying Virtual Organisations Breeding Environment (VBE) from which the VO is created. The VO is by definition temporary and thus the base governance principles are established already in the VBE. Participation in a VBE is driven by long term objectives and by joining a VBE the participating organisation agrees on certain rules and principles, one of them being the concept of trust (Afsarmanesh and Camarinha-Matos, 2005). Part 2 of this book goes into more detail on the establishment, management and governance of VBEs. In chapter 2.1, the basic roles and principles are defined, and chapter 2.2 deals with the governance of the VBE.

Because of the limited duration of a VO, the VO Manager has to adopt certain governance principles. The principles vary depending on the characteristics of the VO and the personal style of the VO Manager. The aspect of management styles are elaborated in ECOLEAD (Karvonen et al., 2005). Some identified VO management styles are e.g. "Encouraging", "Self-organizing", "Time-dominated" or "Multi-organizational management" (Pereira-Klen and Klen, 2005).

In order to act, the VO Manager needs a certain level of power and authority. Management decisions can only be put in place, if the VO manager has the corresponding power. Therefore, also the difference in power levels associated to management roles has to be considered. The distribution of power may have different reasons, like business environment, economical situation, relationship to the customer, owning a brand, carrying the risk etc. and the distribution has to be taken into account in the selection of governance approach (Karvonen et al., 2005).

2.2. Management

In this context, we relate the term management to the operative co-ordination of the common activities. The management rely on the governance approach and rules agreed for the specific VO. An early definition of management was given by Mary Parker Follett in the early twentieth century: *"the art of getting things done through people"* (Graham, 1995). Other definitions consider the management to deal with *"directing and controlling a group of one or more people or entities for the purpose of coordinating and harmonizing them towards accomplishing a goal"*. The management can consist of several dimensions, like human, financial, technological, etc. resources.

In a dynamic environment, both the structures (governance) and the operations (management) vary in different environments and situations. The approach in ECOLEAD is developed to allow adaptability in both areas.

The fact, that a VO consists of independent entities collaborating towards the goal, implies that governance and management activities are devoted to the collaboration, not to internal processes in the entities. Hence, the VO Management is considered as the management of business processes going over and across the VO members. It does not cover the management of the constituent members themselves.

In a study of previous research, no single form for Virtual Organizations in general was found, nor could it be developed out of the analyzed methodologies, scenarios and cases (Karvonen et al., 2005). Virtual Organizations have been structured in categories, topologies and contingency factors (Katzy et al., 2005). However, no single model for VO Management (VOM) could be derived. Identified groupings support the creation of common management support templates. Proposed models, methods and tools mainly support networked organizations with fairly stable processes.

In the ECOLEAD project, a real-time, performance measurement based VO management was developed. This approach supports the VO manager to be continuously aware of the status of the VO. In addition, it actively alerts the manager about possible anomalies and emerging problems via simulation based alerting. Similar techniques are also used for supporting decision making via scenario analyses and evaluation of possible management actions.

In this context, we define the VO Management to contain "the organisation, allocation and co-ordination of resources and their activities as well as their inter-organisational dependencies to achieve the objectives of the VO within the required time, cost and quality frame" (Ollus et al., 2007, 2007b). VO Management can be seen as the control of the VO life-cycle, interacting with the VO operational or customer service processes. Mainly, the concepts are based on linking some additional processes to available intra-organizational methods and tools. Because the VO consists of independent organizations, the VO management has very restricted possibilities to intervene into partners' internal processes. The VO management also has to rely on measurements available at the interfaces to the partner organizations.

An efficient collaboration in the described sense means that internal resistances against collaboration have to be minimized. Many of these ones are related to the environment, especially the breeding environment, in which the VOs are created and operate. Such ones are e.g. trust and rules for information sharing, but also competing positions or the quality of contracts have to be handled appropriately.

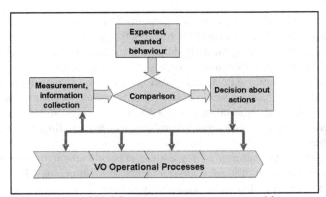

Figure 1 - VO Management seen as a control loop

The temporary nature of the VO implies that the life-time of the VO corresponds to the delivery time of the product or service the VO is created for. Consequently, all set-up procedures will serve only this specific case. An efficient creation and start-up of the VO does not allow complicated implementation and application actions. A modularized parameterized approach, where predefined actions can be configured for a specific VO, can reduce the set-up time and increase the efficiency of the VO operations (Jansson et al., 2005).

In Figure 1, the VO management is presented as a control loop. For the management of the VO data and information of the status of the VO operation are needed. Actions are based on the comparison of the actual achieved or estimated behaviour with the wanted behaviour. The actions are supposed to be proactive in order to avoid also emerging deviations from the expected outcome. In a dynamic environment this approach requires the development of a real-time VO Management approach.

3. VO MANAGEMENT VISION AND APPROACH

To efficiently manage virtual organizations, a broad scope is necessary, which also can be seen in the definition of VO Management. As stated, the main challenges in the management come from the temporary nature of a VO and the distribution of operations to several organizations. In addition, the VO is aimed to respond to fast changes in its environment, i.e. a dynamic management is needed, which also may include restructuring of the management approach or even the VO configuration.

The required dynamic management implies that needs of management actions are identified in real time. Consequently, an efficient performance measurement system should also be in place to give reliable, real-time indicators about the performance of the VO (Jansson et al., 2005, Westphal et al., 2007).

The virtual organisation is created to fulfil a certain task. The outcome of the virtual organisation is its fulfilment, i.e. keeping expected costs, time and quality. In order to manage the VO efficiently, we have to have control its efficiency. The efficiency can be divided into three different categories, which all can be interrelated:

1. The task fulfilment efficiency, i.e. keeping expected costs, time and quality
2. The efficiency of the VO and the collaboration
3. The efficiency of the management approach and management methods.

Figure 2 –The management of the VO focuses on efficient fulfilment of the tasks, e.g. a business opportunity (Ollus et al., 2006).

Most of the VO management actions are devoted to ensure an efficient task fulfilment. This fact is indicated by the main questions of concerns for the VO management shown in Figure 2. (All VOs are not financial profit oriented, and the questions can different accordingly. If e.g. the aim of the VO is to rescue people due to accidents or natural disasters, relevant questions could be "are we saving lives" and "are we acting fast enough").

Actions to maintain or enhance this task fulfilment are usually devoted to coordination of activities among the partners in the VO taking into account the challenges coming from the features of the VO.

The efficiency of virtual organisations depends heavily on the performance of the partners and their collaboration. This performance may, in addition to the task, depend on the configuration of the VO. The relationship between partner performance and the task fulfilment is not easy to model, nor are there obvious measurements available. Some of them are also qualitative and perhaps even subjective. However, the virtual breeding environment (VBE) would benefit from information about some indicators or measurements. Such information is essential in the creation of new VOs and is assumed to be collected during the VO dissolution phase and inherited by the underlying VBE (Westphal et al., 2007).

3.1 VO management Vision – The ideal VO management

Having gained the insight that no known models are suited to cover all cases of VO management, an ideal Vision of VO management will be addressed in this section. It is based on the question: What are the expectations and what is the vision on a future VO Management in 5 to 10 Years from now? The Vision is intimately related to business cases and is intended to communicate the fundamental 'why's and what's' related to VO management and is a gauge against which all future decisions should be validated.

Hence:

- The Vision sets development targets based on a perspective view of a Business Case, founded on market considerations. The Vision is driven by two things: the value provided to the final users and the market environment where they will exert this value.
- The Vision makes assumptions about what technological solutions the users will want, and will probably get – either from us or from competitors.
- In the VOM case, the term Vision is yet more appropriate since:
- The target scenario is set much farther in the future than for normal industrial development projects. Chances that the vision will prove wrong are high. On the other hand, chances to "reinvent the wheel" would be higher still, if we looked for inspiration into current industrial practices.
- The VO concept itself is not yet mature and does not rely on consolidated best practices or reference technological platforms like, e.g., the ERP concept. The following reflects the view of how the concept will be implemented, but this will not necessarily be the only view nor the only implementation.

3.2 VOM Vision in the business context

The following assumptions describe the vision of a future business environment. The VO management approach is expected to be a consolidated and feasible practice accepted by networked organizations world-wide.

CHARACTERISTICS of COLLABORATION

> Organizations will consider joining in a network of partners a viable and efficient solution to scale new businesses and to deliver new products and services. Viable means that there will be no internal resistances due to:
> - Trust issues,
> - Contracts inadequacy,
> - Competing positions,
> - Information sharing,
> - Enterprise-centric business models.
>
> *Efficient* means that "it can be done" without:
> - Redesigning internal business processes,
> - Acquiring new management competencies,
> - Colliding with internal functional barriers,
>
> Partner relationships can be built from scratch.

<u>*Justification:*</u> In a mature environment, VOs will not be pinpointed as the exception to the usual way to do business. Entrepreneurs will not have to be convinced, and then to be trained to join forces with each other to win an objective. While fierce competition and growth by acquisitions will remain the rule in mature sectors, market dynamism will force the smallest players to run VOs alongside their regular single-company businesses.

CRITICAL ASPECTS related to VOM

> From a VO management perspective, the most crucial aspects are cost, time, resources and governance. Independently of the business scenario and goals, the VO is a temporary construct. This simply means that its life-time corresponds to the amount of time required to deliver the VO result. Independently of the result nature (a new product, a construction project, a manufacturing order, a configured team service, etc.), the VO success will depend on how well the crucial aspects are administered.
>
> When a VO has been established to respond to a business opportunity and the customer is waiting, there will be:
> - No time or money to implement a shared application platform for VO operations management.
> - No time to negotiate contractual terms and policies among the partners.
> - Little time for the partners to provide feedback information to VO Management.

<u>*Justification:*</u> The mentioned critical aspects time, cost, resources and governance are equally critical in traditional businesses known so far. The major differences to Virtual Organizations are the temporary nature of a VO, the involvement of independent entities (governance) and not least the profitability of the whole VO

against that of single organisations (cost and resources). At the bottom line VO management is about delivering given results in a given time, as is traditional business management. Due to the mentioned differences though, VO management necessarily has a different perspective and different means to achieve its goals.

It can be stated that timeliness in information retrieval and exchange are the major supporting factors for VO management. Especially time wasted, or time spent in activities not directly related to the results, will impact on profitability for all the VO partners. In addition, most sectors are developing at a higher speed than in the past, and in the next years this trend will put even more emphasis on time-effective management.

CUSTOMER OF A VO

> The VO will be constituted having in mind the final customers who will benefit of the products and services delivered. VO members will have, none excluded, a direct role in providing value to the final customers. This means basically two things:
> - Value produced (and paid for by the Customer) will be the primary performance indicator for the VO and for the individual partners.
> - The partners will share risks and responsibilities towards the final Customers.

Justification: VOs will be created for doing together what the individual company is not capable of. In a context of increasing global competition, this means facing together the challenge of new markets, new competitors and new, ever demanding, customers. For the VO to work all the partners must face these challenges and assume responsibilities towards the customer, in proportion to their share of the VO budget.

COMMON BUSINESS OPERATIONS ARE STANDARDIZED

> Ordinary business activities like, e.g., production planning and monitoring, purchasing, shipping and receiving, will reach a high level of standardization across the VO members. This will allow for:
> - Consistent operations monitoring across the different VO members,
> - Shared performance measurement approaches,
> - Consistent semantics for the different partners' operative data.

Justification: The last decade has seen the formalization and diffusion of best practices in the basic enterprise areas like, e.g., accounting and logistics management. Ever more companies will adopt standards, either formal or "de facto", under the impulse of:
- Diffusion of enterprise information systems, which at the operative level are rapidly consolidating around few products with similar functionalities.
- Commoditization of operative business processes that, not being a competitive factor, will be standardized and often outsourced to lower costs.

3.3 Approaches for VO management

Although several approaches are addressing specific needs or typologies of CNOs and Virtual Organizations none of those was, so far, found to be suited as an umbrella on-size-fits-all Model covering all the identified needs of VO management. The reasons for that are manifold, one main aspect being the claim of considering an extensively wide range of Virtual Organization (production, service, emergency, etc.) coverage. Focussing on the structural differences analyzed and depicted the following can be stated:

Each model will vary according to the VO:
- topology
- lifecycle,
- governance structure

and may be represented according to different views, perspectives and dimensions (i.e. organization, structure, physical, functional, behavioural, information,…)

Inverting the perspective, it could be also reasoned that:
- each VO (in its particular instantiation) is unique,
  which means that
- each VO has its own VOM model,
  which means that
- there is no single VOM model.

From both reasoning streams the consequence is that:

Each VO should adopt a customized management approach

What are the constraints allowing or hindering to achieve this approach? Sheer economies of scale do not allow development of a specialized VOM environment for each particular VO. Besides costs and resources, the time constraint dos not allow long preparation times to set up the management of a VO.

To overcome this balancing act of combining the two controversial goals, the ECOLEAD project proposes to define a set of configurable respectively parameterised services for the VO management and a common operational runtime environment suited to support the functioning and interaction of the configured services. In this way the VO manager (broker, captain, team, etc.) can select the best suited "tools", configure them for the particular VO and use the runtime environment to support the management task. In detail the envisaged solution encompasses:

I. The adoption of a sensitive management approach/methodology for all VO model:

A real-time & performance measured-based management approach

and

II. The fine tuning of the management approach for each VO according to the following methodology:

1. *For each different VO underlying model. Its processes, activities and management can be defined, specified and supported by a set of (orchestrated) services.*

2. *A framework of VO specific services will be developed out of which, for each specific instantiation of a VO, a set of single or composed services is configured to serve the related needs.*

3. *The composition will be done by configuring the available or adapted services in a particular and logical sequence to follow and support the VO management process*

4. *Ideally the composition of a specific supporting environment for a VO instance is to be supported via an automatic or interactive user guiding environment*

To support this representation, the identified and needed VO management functions have been transformed into generally applicable components with a suited level of granularity. The identification of functions has been done by analysing the VOM "cases", their general goals and requirements. The decomposition or transformation has resulted first in building blocks (i.e. application supporting functions) and further in components (Jansson et al., 2005). A list of services have been specified, developed and evaluated together with end-user networks. The services are described in chapter 3.3 of this book. The evaluation and implementation activities are presented in chapter 6.3 "VO management cases".

4. VO DISSOLUTION AND INHERITANCE

4.1 Introduction

As described above, a VO is a temporary organization with the creation, operation & evolution and dissolution lifecycle phases. It is created for a specific task, most often to create value (product/ service) to a customer and after performing the task it is dissolved. The VO duration may vary from very short term tasks (max days) to extensive deliveries (years). Even if the VOs may repeat with similar tasks and structures they always have a start and an end. At the closing phase, it is typically not known if and when there will be a similar task to be performed. The customer product and the participants in the new VO are not necessarily the same as in the previous one. Thus the dissolution phase breaks off the concrete collaboration.

Projects are conceptually close to VOs. PMBOK (1996) defines projects as temporary endeavours undertaken to create a unique product or service. Projects share the same challenging characteristics, namely temporal limitedness and subsequent time and resource pressures. In fact many projects are performed as VOs, even if the project definition does not assume participation of different organizations. Projects also have the problem of discontinuity and transferring the knowledge from one project to future use.

In PMBOK (1996) the project closing phase (corresponding to VO dissolution) is described very briefly. The inheritance is handled mainly by "lessons learned" term but there is no definite guidance how to do this. Schindler and Eppler (2003) view the learning from project experiences through two groups of methods: process-based methods and documentation-based methods. Also in some specific fields of projects the re-use of information has been discussed, like for engineering projects (Fiatech

2001). These approaches focus on data, information and knowledge, not on other types of assets.

Thus, while creating the value for the customer, the VO partners have also increased their knowledge, gained valuable experience and strengthened mutual relationships. This experience and knowledge needs care to survive; otherwise it is distributed and lost. The gained experience can be used to improve the preparedness of the breeding environment (network). Thus in addition to the value created to the customer, the VO can create value also to the breeding environment. After the task has been fulfilled and the VO is dissolved, the increased knowledge, experience and other assets should be returned, "inherited" to the breeding environment (network), feeding to the "VBE bag of assets". The increased bag of assets improves the preparedness of the VBE for business opportunities, and supports the effectiveness and reliability of future VOs.

To make the activity visible, a term "VO inheritance" has been defined:

VO inheritance is the practice of storing and passing on the experience and other non-proprietary assets created through collaboration in a VO.

Additionally, a specific concept of VO heritage (the contents of VO inheritance; what is inherited) can be given:

VO heritage comprises of the different assets which are inherited from a VO to the VBE.

VO inheritance management considers the whole process:

VO inheritance management takes care of gathering, storing, refining, integrating and re-using experience and other non-proprietary assets created through collaboration in distinct VOs of the VBE.

To be successful, the VO inheritance management has to be followed up within the VBE management, as the VO itself is dissolved. VO inheritance management cannot be considered to be successful if, for example, experience data is stored and passed to the VBE, but never used in the VBE or in a new VO.

The VO product/service going to the customer will be the property of the customer after the VO dissolution and is thus not part of VO heritage. That is why the object of inheritance (what is inherited) excludes the assets which belong exclusively to only one partner. Assets with restricted IPR are usually not considered as part of the VO heritage. This does not, however, imply that the entire VO heritage is open for all VBE members.

The VO model (described above) and the information included in it can be utilized as part of VO heritage. One part of the VO heritage is also the VO performance measurement data described in chapter 3.2. The heritage contents are, however, not restricted to experience, data, information or knowledge, but include also other types of assets. The relationship of VO inheritance management to VBE Knowledge Management can be characterized as follows:

- Management of VO inheritance knowledge and information is a specific case of Knowledge Management, but

- VO inheritance management is not only about managing knowledge or information, but also of other types of (for example relational) assets. Thus VO inheritance is not only Knowledge Management.

4.2 Benefits of VO inheritance

VO inheritance is aimed to increase the VBE "bag of assets". The term VBE asset (as defined in chapter 2) has a wide meaning: it includes all the elements that have potential to give value or benefit to the VBE or its single members when VOs are created from the VBE. This benefit may be realized through:

- Improving the preparedness of the VBE: VOs can be created and started faster,
- Making the VOs more effective and reliable both in time and costs, and improving or ensuring the quality,
- Decreasing VO management efforts through increased trust and strengthened relationships,
- Supporting decision-making and tracking of VO problems or deviations,
- Increasing the value of the VBE for the members, for example by increasing their knowledge and market position,
- Supporting winning in competitive bidding because of customer knowledge and closer customer relationships,
- Supporting the marketing of the VBE services to new customers by offering reference information. References and reputation created can be used externally to convince the customers.

4.3 VO inheritance process

The main phases of VO inheritance and their location in the VBE and VO lifecycle are presented in Figure 3. The phases include:
- VO inheritance creation: VO inheritance is generated in the operational experience. This takes place during the whole VO lifecycle, starting from VO creation, through VO operation, evolution & management to VO dissolution. Also potential actions needed after the VO dissolution, because of VO liabilities, may be considered to create VO inheritance.
- VO inheritance storage "as it is" during the VO lifecycle in any format: in different forms: databases, documents, notebooks, systems, relationships, people's minds etc.
- VO inheritance analysis during the VO: this may be done to utilize the information already in the same VO, in its later phases.
- VO inheritance transfer to VBE storage. This phase may include combining different sources, pre-processing, definition of user rights for future etc.
- VO inheritance integration with previous inheritance / knowledge, processing, refinement and reinforcement: this may be performed in the VBE, where the inheritance of previous VOs is available.
- VO inheritance utilization: in the utilization phase the inheritance of a single VO is necessarily not separated. The utilization may take place either in the VBE or in the subsequent VOs.

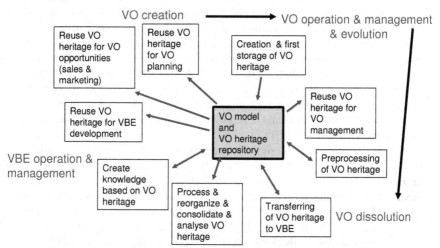

Figure 3 - Inheritance phases

Additionally, VO inheritance management is needed. It should cover both the VBE operation phase and the whole VO life cycle. VO inheritance management takes care of the implementation of the VO inheritance phases. It also defines the rules for inheritance collection, use and access.

4.3 Components of VO inheritance

VO inheritance increases the common VBE Bag of Assets. These assets are not as concrete and visible as the product created to the customer, and thus often the VBE does not even become aware of their existence. To identify the different forms of VO heritage the categorisation of VBE bag of assets can be used. Romero et al. (2007) identify three main types of assets:

- Financial capital: financial resources and values (cash, accounts, physical assets), risky elements
- Intellectual capital: data, information and knowledge, both in tangible and intangible (human) form
- Social capital: also called relational assets; relationships with customers, suppliers and other organizations.

Financial capital is typically owned by the independent organizations. However, in principle it is possible that part of the profit created in a VO would be inherited to the VBE. This could be used to pay for the common infrastructure services, development of common procedures and possibly as a reserve fund to reimburse expenses of potential customer complaints.

When discussing inheritance, an important point to solve is also how to take care about the potential risky or negative outcome of the VO: warranties of the customer product, other liabilities and realized risks. These post-VO liabilities may cause financial expenses and may thus be considered as negative financial heritage. They may require additional work, resources or costs, cause a delay of the customer payment or decrease the payment.

The intellectual capital includes all the VO data, information and knowledge, both in databases and documents and in human minds. The information may be both plans and experience about their realization, both of quantitative (for example performance measures) and qualitative type. As it is easier to collect and save quantitative data, in many cases there is a lack of restored qualitative information; for example of reasons behind decisions. A VO model (as described before) and VO performance measurement repository are useful sources for VO heritage. They may either be transferred as a whole package to the VBE or the information in them could be first pre-processed. The content of the intellectual capital is described more in Karvonen et al (2007).

Social / relational VO heritage is nearly linked to the increased knowledge of the collaborating organizations. However, the relational assets do not consist of the knowledge, but of the relationships. It is clear that having even all the knowledge about the relationship has not the same value as having the "living" relationship.

- Social and relational capital originates from collaboration. Thus VOs, where the partners collaborate for a common objective, are important contributors to the VBE social capital. Two different types of VO relational inheritance can be distinguished:

- The increase of relational capital between the VBE members: Operating in a VO makes the partners to know each other better both at the personal and organizational level. This means that they know the capabilities, strengths and weaknesses of each other, which makes it more effective to collaborate in the future VOs, and increases the VBE preparedness. VOs also produce tested configurations of partners for specific tasks. Collaboration increases the trust between the partners and contributes to the creation of a VBE "culture". Especially successful VOs increase the motivation of partners to work together.

- The increase of relational capital with the customers: Working with the customers contributes to improved customer relationship and understanding the customer needs which is very useful for future business and identification of new business opportunities. Also improved personal relationships and knowledge of customer practices support the preparedness to work for the customer in future. Successful VO deliveries to the customer increase the customer's trust to the VBE. The achieved market position and the references may also be considered as part of VO relational heritage and they are typically very important in order to gain also new customers.

Collaboration is not always successful and all the social relationships do not improve in every VO. It is even possible, that the overall social VO heritage is sometimes negative. In some cases it may even danger the sustainability of the VBE. Thus also mechanisms how to handle these cases, disagreements and disputes need to be considered.

4.4 VO inheritance methods and mechanisms

According to Schindler et al. (2003), the key success factors of project learning consist of developing and integrating of process and documentation based methods, for example continuous project learning instead of a single review and institutionalization of the lessons learned process to the project phase model. In the context of VOs this could mean that VO management process should support continuous learning and VO heritage collection. Examples of the process-based methods include reviews, audits and controls.

One process-based mechanism to support VO inheritance is briefing and debriefing. These techniques are applied in many areas, for instance aeronautics and training courses. Loss et al. (2007) apply the techniques for learning CNOs. In VO briefing process general information about the VO is shared to all VO actors and in the VO debriefing process feedback and cross-check with the briefing phase is provided.

Model-based VO management (RAVO concept presented chapter 3.3) supports the collection and storage of VO information. In the beginning of the VO the VO model is instantiated from a meta model and filled with the needed information of the specific VO. During the VO operation real time data is collected either to the VO model directly or to distributed storages available through the model and the supporting tools. For example performance data of the partners is stored by the VOPM system. The VO model can be considered as a "draft smart container" of a VO. Smart containers have the advantage of "knowing about themselves", both about the content, and how it should be interpreted and handled (FIATECH 2004). For example, a VO model knows about the context of the VO. Smart containers of single VOs, could perhaps be aggregated to more comprehensive smart containers.

In the field of one-of-a-kind manufacturing some development has been made to support product knowledge creation in a network (Välikangas & Puttonen 2003). They present a Knowledge Creation Environment (KCE) for collecting and classifying tacit knowledge, and the evolution of the knowledge to more explicit format. The environment utilizes mind mapping as a method for collecting and structuring the information. KCE assumes a role of a knowledge engineer who can analyse the data and even create rules for expert systems from it. The tool also enables concurrent and collaborative work in a network to evaluate and analyse the information. Even if the KCE was mainly designed to create and manage product data, the concept could be applied also for other types of VO information.

Different collaboration tools, like discussion forums, problem solving spaces, exception handling tools etc. may also accumulate VO experience information. VO dictionary organized in the "wiki-type" and complemented with additional comments could be an interesting tool. Their specific feature could be the accumulation of "soft" information which otherwise may be difficult to save. Intelligent data mining and search functions may be needed to be able to utilize this kind of sometimes unstructured information.

In specific business tasks, the setup of a VO should be performed very fast. This is the case for example in after-sales or maintenance services (Karvonen et al. 2002). A solution proposed is to maintain the VO in a "stand-by state". After the VO task is completed, the VO is not totally dissolved but it is transformed to a stand-by mode. In case of a new similar customer need the VO is again activated. This requires specific deactivation and activation processes and support tools. The deactivation/ activation allows the inheritance of not only the VO information, but also the whole system, including existing relationships and consortium, VO structure and plan, supporting tools and infrastructure etc. It is most applicable for repetitive, pre-planned maintenance.

In addition to the intellectual and information assets VO also affects the VBE social or relational capital or social networks, on one hand between the VBE partners and on the other hand, towards the customer. To save and maintain the social interest social forms can be used, for example social events, like "VO closing celebration" or "VBE yearly festival" internally in the VBE, or "contact forums" towards the customers.

4.5 Inheritance summary

VO inheritance aims to bridge the gap between the impermanent VOs. Transforming the VO discontinuity to continuous learning and improvement in the VBE is not an easy task. It requires attention to both the VBE and VO level. In VBEs the rules for the inheritance must be agreed, who is inheriting what, what are the user rights and information openness levels and responsibilities for the inheritance management. Methods and tools to identify the important information or to drag out knowledge from a mass of data or information should be developed. Also best practices to preserve the relational and structural assets of VOs should be found and implemented.

Management of experience, as VO inheritance in CNOs, is commonly recognized as an important activity, and the main challenge is to make it happen. The barriers that have been identified for re-use of information are technological, work process, and cultural (FIATECH 2001). The different actors (the VBE partners and the customers) should understand the potential benefits. The required resources to implement VO inheritance should be in balance with the achieved benefit. Too heavy or too complex inheritance processes and mechanisms do never work in practise.

5. CONCLUSIONS AND FUTURE CHALLENGES

The main challenges in the management of Virtual Organizations come from the temporary nature of a VO and the distribution of operations to several independent organizations, which are expected to collaborate towards a common goal. In addition, the VO is aimed to respond to fast changes in its environment, i.e. a dynamic management is needed, which also may include restructuring of the management approach, or even the VO configuration, during the operation of the VO (Ollus, 2005).

The efficiency of virtual organisations depends heavily on the performance of the partners and their collaboration. This performance may, in addition to the task, depend on the configuration of the VO. The relationship between partners' performance and task fulfilment is not easy to model, nor are there obvious measurements available. Some of the measurements are also qualitative and sometimes even subjective. In addition, they may contain sensitive and confidential aspects. One major challenge for the management of Virtual Organizations is to create a measurement approach for collection of intangible, qualitative features of virtual organizations and their partners. Interesting features to understand and measure are:

- Collaboration performance

- Collaboration spirit
- Motivation
- Communication and communication ability

From the management point of view, the impact of intangible features on the tangible outcomes of the virtual organization, e.g. time, cost and quality, is also an important issue. There are still needs to create models for describing these relationships.

A third challenge is related to the management means for impact on the mentioned qualitative features by the VO manager. To meet these challenges, a broad multidisciplinary approach is required.

Acknowledgements. The information presented in this document is based on work performed in the project ECOLEAD (FP6-IP 506958; www.ecolead.org) funded by the European Community within the IST-Programme of the 6th Framework Research Programme. The authors also thank the ECOLEAD consortium for the support.

6. REFERENCES

1. Afsarmanesh, H., Camarinha-Matos, L.M. (2005): A framework for management of virtual organization breeding environments. In: Collaborative Networks and their Breeding Environments, Springer, 2005, pp. 35-49.
2. Camarinha-Matos, L, and Afsarmanesh H (2003). Elements of a base VE infrastructure. J. Computers in Industry, Vol. 51, pp. 139-163.
3. Camarinha-Matos L, H Afsarmanesh H (Ed) (2004). Collaborative Networked Organizations – A Research Agenda for Emerging Business Models. ISBN 1-4020-7823-4. Kluwer Academic Publishers, Norwell.
4. Camarinha-Matos L, Afsarmanesh H, Löh H, Sturm F, Ollus M (2004). A Strategic Roadmap for Advanced Virtual Organisations. In: Collaborative Networked Organizations – A Research Agenda for Emerging Business Models. (Camarinha-Matos L, Afsarmanesh H (Ed)) ISBN 1-4020-7823-4. Kluwer Academic Publishers, Norwell.
5. Camarinha-Matos L, Afsarmanesh H, and Ollus M (Ed) (2005). Virtual Organisations – Systems and Practices. ISBN 0-387-23755-0. Springer, New York.
6. European Commission (2004). FP5 resource book.
7. FIATECH (2001). Guidelines and Drivers for Achieving Plant Lifecycle Data Management. The owner – operator forum. January 2001. http://www.fiatech.org.
8. FIATECH (2004) FIATECH Roadmap Element #9. Integrated Data & Information Management. http://www.fiatech.org
9. FIATECH (2006). Vision. www.fiatech.org, visited 6.9.2006
10. Filos E. (2006). Smart Organizations. In: Integration of ICT in Smart Organizations. (Mezgár I. (Ed)). ISBN: 1-59140-390-1. Idea Group.
11. Graham P (ed.) (1995). Mary Parker Follett: Prophet of Management. Harvard Business School Press. ISBN: 0-87584-736-6.
12. Graser F, Westphal I, Eschenbaecher J (2005). Roadmap on VOPM Challenges on Operational and Strategic Level. ECOLEAD deliverable D31.1. www.ecolead.org.
13. Graser F, Jansson K. Towards Performance Measurement In: Collaborative Networks and their Breeding Environments. (Camarinha-Matos L, Afsarmanesh H, Ortiz A (Ed)). Springer. New York.
14. Institute on Governance (http://www.iog.ca/)
15. Jansson K, Karvonen I, Ollus M, Paganelli P Stewens R, Negretto U (2005). Real Time Virtual Organisations Management. In: Innovation and the Knowledge Economy - Issues, Applications, Case Studies. (Cunningham P, Cunningham M (Ed)). ISBN 1-58603-563-0. IOS Press. Amsterdam.
16. Karvonen, I. & Jansson, K. & Ollus, M. & Hartel, I. & Burger, G. & Anastasiou, M. & Välikangas, P. & Mori, K (2002). Inter-enterprise eCollaboration in Sales and Service of one-of-a-kind products.

In: Stanford-Smith, B. & Chiozza, E. & Edin, M. (Ed.). Challenges and Achievements in E-business and E-work, IOS Press / Ohmsha, Berlin, Germany; 1388-1395.

17. Karvonen I, Salkari I, Ollus M (2005). Characterizing Virtual Organizations and Their Management. In: Collaborative Networks and their Breeding Environments. (Camarinha-Matos L, Afsarmanesh H, Ortiz A (Ed)). Springer. New York.

18. Karvonen, I., Salkari, I., Ollus, M (2007). Identification of forms and components of VO inheritance. In IFIP International Federation for Information Processing, Volume 243, Establishing the Foundation of Collaborative Networks; eds. Camarinha-Matos, L., Afsarmanesh, H., Novais, P., Analide, C.,; (Boston, Springer), pp 253-262.

19. Katzy B., Zhang C., Löh H: Reference Models for Virtual Organizations (2005). In: Virtual Organisations – Systems and Practices. ISBN 0-387-23755-0. Springer, New York, pp 45-58.

20. Loss, L., Pereira-Klen, A.A., Rabelo, R (2007). Towards Learning Collaborative Networked Organizations, In IFIP International Federation for Information Processing, Volume 243, Establishing the Foundation of Collaborative Networks; eds. Camarinha-Matos, L., Afsarmanesh, H., Novais, P., Analide, C.,; (Boston, Springer), pp. 243-252.

21. O'Donovan G. (2003). A Board Culture of Corporate Governance. In Corporate Governance International Journal, Vol 6, Issue 3.

22. Ollus M (2005). A Holistic Approach towards Collaborative Networked Organizations. In: Innovation and the Knowledge Economy - Issues, Applications, Case Studies. (Cunningham P, Cunningham M (Ed)). ISBN 1-58603-563-0. IOS Press. Amsterdam.

23. Ollus M, Jansson K, Karvonen I. (2006). On the Management of Collaborative Networked Organizations. In Conference Proceedings from IST-Africa 2006. (Cunningham P, Cunningham M (Eds)). IIMC International Information Management Corporation.

24. Ollus M, Jansson K, Karvonen I. (2007). On the management of collaborative SME networks. In the proceedings of COA'07 – 8th IFAC Symposium on Cost-Oriented Automation, Habana, Cuba.

25. Ollus, M, Jansson, K, Karvonen, I. (2007b). Approaches for the Management of Virtual Organizations; Results from ECOLEAD. IFAC Conference on Cost Effective Automation in Networked Product Development and Manufacturing. October 2-5, 2007. Monterrey, Mexico.

26. Oxford Dictionary of Current English (2007). Oxford University Press. Oxford.

27. Pereira-Klen A.A., Klen E.R (2005). Human Supervised Virtual Organization Management. In: Collaborative Networks and their Breeding Environments. In: Collaborative Networks and their Breeding Environments, Springer, pp. 229-238.

28. PMBOK Guide (1996). A guide to the project management body of knowledge. PMI Standards Committee. Upper Darby, PA, USA: Project Management Institute.

29. Renz P. S. (2007). Project Governance: Implementing Corporate Governance and Business Ethics in Nonprofit Organizations. ISBN-10: 3790819263. Physica-Verlag Heidelberg.

30. Romero. D., Galeano, N., Molina, A (2007). A conceptual model for virtual breeding environments value systems, In IFIP International Federation for Information Processing, Volume 243, Establishing the Foundation of Collaborative Networks; eds. Camarinha-Matos, L., Afsarmanesh, H., Novais, P., Analide, C.,; (Boston, Springer), pp. 43-52.

31. Schindler M., Eppler M., 2003. Harvesting project knowledge: a review of project learning methods and success factors. International Journal of Project Management 21 (2003), pp 219-228. Elsevier Science Ltd and IPMA.

32. Sennheiser A (2004). Determinant based selection of benchmarking partners and logistics performance indicators. PhD-Thesis, ETH Zürich.

33. Stich V, Weidemann M, Sennheiser A Glaubitt K, Schnetzler M (2005). Performance Measurement. In: Virtual Organizations: Systems and Practices. (Camarinha-Matos L, Afsarmanesh H, Ollus M (Ed)). Springer, New York 2005.

34. Toelle M (2004). Management and Engineering of Virtual Enterprises. Ph.D. Dissertation, Technical University of Denmark, Department of Manufacturing Engineering and Management.

35. Välikangas, P., Puttonen, J., : Knowledge Creation and Virtual Enterprises in Power Plant Construction, in Karvonen et al. Global Engineering and Manufacturing in Enterprise Networks (GLOBEMEN), VTT Symposium 224, 2003, p. 245-259.

36. Westphal I., Thoben K-D., Seifert M. (2007). Measuring Collaboration Performance in Virtual Organizations. In IFIP International Federation for Information Processing, Volume 243, Establishing the Foundation of Collaborative Networks; eds. Camarinha-Matos, L., Afsarmanesh, H., Novais, P., Analide, C.,; (Boston, Springer), pp 33-42.

SUPERVISION OF COLLABORATIVE PROCESSES IN VOs

Ingo Westphal[1], Wico Mulder[2], Marcus Seifert[1]

[1]*BIBA*, Bremen Institute for Production and Logistics, *GERMANY, win@biba.uni-bremen.de, sf@biba.uni-bremen.de*
[2]*LogicaCMG, THE NETHERLANDS, wico.mulder@logicacmg.com*

VO managers need a sound information basis to fulfil their management tasks. Hence, performance measurement is one of the key processes in the management of Virtual Organisations (VOs). In case VOs are complex in terms of dimensions, interactions or the level of heterogeneity, information retrieval and performance measurement becomes a demanding task and causes high efforts. A defined methodology that guides the VO manager through the process and support by means of ICT services can help to obtain the needed information basis in an efficient way.

The constraints and characteristics of the networks imply that the applied methodologies and services must be able to cope with distributed, dynamic, heterogeneous environments. They also require a performance measurement approach that is tuned towards the behaviour of the network as a whole, which might differ from traditional approaches that are used in single organisations or static cooperation such as supply chains.

This chapter is about the need and the challenges of a collaborative performance measurement approach and the requirements of its corresponding tool support, aligned to the specific conditions of VOs and relevant aspects for VO management.

1. INTRODUCTION

One of the key elements of VO management is the supervision of the collaborative processes in the VO. A VO manager determines performance indicators that provide information about the status and operation of the network or its entities and gathers the data that is necessary to measure the value of these indicators. The systematic approach to plan and conduct the collection of data regarding the accomplishment of tasks and the corresponding objectives is called *Performance Measurement* (PM). PM is part of *Performance Management.* Performance Management comprises planning, measurement, monitoring and assessment, improvement and rewarding of performance. The *supervision* of collaborative processes comprises the planning of performance, the performance measurement and the monitoring and assessment of the obtained performance data. The supervision provides input for improvement measures and rewarding, which are also VO management tasks. Figure 1 shows this schematically.

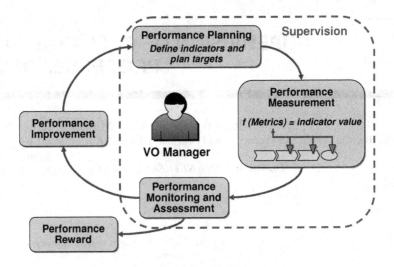

Figure 1: Supervision processes

In short-term VOs with a small number of partners the PM is often done "manually" or in an ad-hoc way; the VO manager uses telephone, fax or e-mail to get the needed data from VO members. According to practical experiences of collaborative networks this causes in many cases significant effort. VO managers describe this as an "annoying" procedure for both the VO manager and the VO members, in particular when the data has to be updated frequently. As a consequence there is a tendency to concentrate the PM in VOs on a limited set of indicators. To limit the effort, these indicators are often the same as in regular business when the companies work on their own. Typical examples are cost deviation from plan, work progress and quality issues. Experiences in these areas show that performance measurement and the considered indicators are not aligned appropriately to the specifics of collaboration in VOs.

As long as the VO Manager and most of the VO members have a sufficient informal overview over the activities and the relations, this ad-hoc PM will fulfil.

However, VOs can be complex with tasks that require a broader variety of competences and more resources. Correspondingly a bigger number of more diverse partners are involved. In addition, complex VOs can cover a longer time-span, be more dynamic, and may have to deal with a higher degree of uncertainty. In these cases ad-hoc, "manual" performance measurement comes to the bounds of feasibility and do not provide the VO management with the needed information in an adequate way. In these cases the VO manager needs a structured approach for PM in VOs and supporting services. For example, a system that supports the selection and retrieval of information might relieve a VO-manager from the unnecessary complexity of specifying, searching and obtaining the information that is relevant for getting overviews and taking decisions.

Research has provided several approaches for PM and some are well established in practice. However, this work was traditionally focused on intra-organisational PM or on inter-organisational PM in static cooperation like supply chains. There are no approaches and tools that were specifically developed for PM in dynamic VOs with its distributed, independent, and heterogeneous VO members. Therefore it has to be analysed what the particular requirements upon PM in VOs are, how existing PM approaches meet these requirements and how they have to be adapted or completed to meet the requirements.

2. CHALLENGES FOR PERFORMANCE MEASUREMENT IN VIRTUAL ORGANISATIONS

VOs have certain characteristics that differentiate them from traditional, single organisations and static cooperation like supply chains. These differences could also influence the structure and processes of PM. Therefore it should be analysed in this section what the main challenges for PM in VOs are and how existing PM approach and tools can deal with these challenges.

As there no universal understanding and unvarying use of the term "Performance Measurement" it is necessary to describe the basic understanding of PM that forms the underlying concept for the considerations. This provides a basis to identify the challenges for PM in VOs that are caused by the characteristics of VOs.

The purpose of PM is to evaluate the business performance with different perspectives and a variety of uses. Bititci, Carrie and Turner summarise the following reasons why companies measure their business performance [Kellen 2003, p. 4]:

- To monitor and control.
- To drive improvement.
- To maximise the effectiveness of the improvement effort.
- To achieve alignment with organisational goals and objectives.
- To reward and to discipline.

To achieve this, PM has to provide values for *Performance Indicators (PI)*, which are defined variables that assess the state of an object in scope, e.g. cost figures, the output of a production process or the responsiveness of a partner. PI could be as well quantitative as qualitative measures. *Key Performance Indicators (KPI)* represent essential or critical components that have highest impact on the organisation's overall success.

To obtain values for PI corresponding data has to be measured. *Measurement* should be understood in a broad sense as general collection of data. This could be done by asking responsible persons (in some cases even for estimations), obtaining data from a gauge like a counter, or by accessing electronic databases. The variables that are measured are called *Metrics*. Some PI values are calculated from several metrics, e.g. an indicator "lead-time" can be calculated from the date values for the metrics "start-date" and "end-date".

The PI values are provided to the *Customers of PM*. Main customer is usually the management of the concerned organisational unit. But there can also be additional customers like the employees of the organisational unit, customers of the unit, investors or other stakeholders. They can use the indicator values for further processing and analysis, e.g. time-series, control charts, tend-analysis etc.

In this chapter the term Performance Measurement is used in a broader sense. It should not only cover the gathering of data but also the identification of suitable indicators and the provision of data for further use. This leads to a partial overlapping with performance planning and performance monitoring/assessment but provides a more complete picture of PM challenges in VOs.

Based on the concept of PM as it was described above it has to be analysed how PM in VOs is affected by the specific characteristics of VOs and what are the resulting differences in comparison to intra-organisational PM respectively PM for static cooperation. The main characteristics of VOs were described in the previous chapters of this book. This leads to the main challenges for PM in VOs.

Independency of VO members: VO members are generally independent from each other. This has two main consequences for the VO. First the companies have their own business outside the VO and their own objectives, planning, structures and processes for this business. On the one hand this means that there could be a kind of competition between activities in the VO and other activities that are not related to the VO. On the other hand there is in many cases the possibility that the VO Members become competitors for other business opportunities. The second consequence is that the common VO has limited opportunities to control partners beyond their contractual obligations.

This has following implications for the PM:

- The PM on VO level has to be connected to the internal processes of the different VO members. There is a chance to make use of existing values for PIs or Metrics from the organisations' internal PM. However, there could also be a need for addition measurement. This produces additional effort to the already existing PM activities, which could cause problems regarding acceptance.
- The provision of needed data for PM depends on the trust level between the VO members and their commitment for collaboration in the VO.
- Usually, the VO members can not be forced to make their data sources accessible or to provide certain data if this is not defined in the contract. In particular when a need for additional PI occurs during the operation phase of the VO the "good will" of the VO members is needed. Therefore PM has to be done collaboratively.
- For many organisations it is important to keep local control of the measurement and the provision of data.
- The PM has to cover the aspect of collaboration, which means contributions and commitment beyond the contractual obligations. This is not only important for the value creation processes but also for supporting functions like the PM itself.

Heterogeneity of structures, processes and cultures: VO members are usually not only independent organisations but are covering different complementary areas of competences that are required to fulfil the VO's task. In addition they can be located around the globe. Therefore they have different organisational and ICT structures, processes, internal cultures, national laws and legislations and regional cultures.

This has following implications for the PM:

- A very clear definition of the indicators, the corresponding measurement and responsibilities is required to avoid misunderstanding and misinterpretation. While in a single company there are often standards and knowledge about the general structures of internal processes different VO members could have, for example, different understandings about start and

the end of processes or about quality issues and on-time-delivery.
- The PM has to be flexible to regard the specific conditions of the different VO members.
- It is likely that there are heterogeneous data sources. There could be different ICT systems and standards. Some VO members, in particular the small ones, may even have no ICT tools besides standard office application and internet access. This requires various different interfaces to make the data available for PM in the VO.

Distribution of partners: The VO members can be located in a distributed way, even in different countries and on different continents. This means that "face-to-face" coordination on the spot and transfer of physical documents causes higher effort than in a single company.

This has following implications for the PM:
- Again clear definitions are needed to avoid the necessity of on the spot coordination.
- The PM has to be based on ICT, which enables electronic data transfer and distributed access for the different VO members.

Impermanence and uniqueness: VOs are temporary limited. They are created for a certain collaboration opportunity and dissolute when their task is fulfilled. The life-time of VO can be from a few weeks to several years. As a consequence of this temporary limitation each VO is unique, when it is dissolved it will not be created in exactly the same way again.

This has following implications for the PM:
- The PM hast to be set-up new for each VO. This causes new effort for each new VO.
- As the PM is set up new for each VO there is no historic database that can be continued, like in established single companies and static networks.
- The set-up has to be adapted to the lifetime of the VO. When the life span of a VO is very short this set up has to be done very fast to make results available before the task is finished.
- As the PM vanishes with the dissolution of the VO the effort for the set-up and operation of the PM has to be limited to ensure a positive "return rfon investment". In other organisations the PM or parts of it can usually be re-used or further developed for other tasks.
- Generally it has to be ensured that provision of indicator values is synchronised with the lifespan of the VO. Short-term VOs with critical process, for example, may need almost real-time provision of data.

The challenges concern both the content of PM as well as the methodology. There is only one challenge regarding the content, which is the consideration of collaboration performance. On the other side there are several challenges regarding the methodology for set-up and operation of PM in VOs. They can be summarised as follows:
- PM in VOs has to be done collaboratively by the VO members. This means there should be common objectives and commitment for supporting the PM.
- More distinctive need for clear definitions to reach common understanding between the VO members.
- Need for flexibility to reduce or limit expenditure for setting-up and

operating the PM according to the available time and resources. A rapid set-up must be possible.

- PM must be adaptable to the processes and structures of the VO members and is has to be connected to their internal PM activities.
- Local control has to be enabled to avoid that a lack of trust obstructs the active participation in the PM and prevents the provision of data.
- PM in VOs have to be strongly ICT based to make it efficiently accessible for the distributed VO members.

Existing Approaches in Performance Measurement

Performance measurement approaches consist of mainly two parts: ***Performance perspectives and indicators*** and a ***performance measurement concept***. The suggested performance indicators describe the content to be measured for assessing the performance of a business process. Some approaches suggest performance perspectives that summarise performance indicators that consider the same area of content, e.g. a perspective "finance" can comprise various indicators for costs, revenues or involved capital. The performance measurement concept that describes how to set-up and conduct the PM. The concept may include a process model, rules to execute the measurement or guidelines to identify relevant business challenges. Literature and practice provide several frameworks in the context of business performance measurement. Some are offering pre-defined sets of performance indicators, some provide just the concepts and some are holistic methodologies with integrate a concept with concrete performance indicators. The following graphic gives an overview over this structure and example for existing performance measurement frameworks.

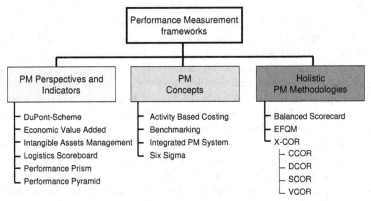

Figure 2: Existing performance measurement frameworks

See for example Kaplan; Norton [1992], Stewart [1999], Klingebiel 2001, Kellen [2003], Jana [2007], or the overviews of Sandt [2005], Graser et al. [2005] and Seifert [2007].

The existing and in some cases well established approaches offer a wide scope of performance perspective and indicators: Financial aspects, process performance, quality, relationship to suppliers and customers as well as value related aspect like intellectual capital and brand value. In addition there are various suggestions for the handling of PM, e.g. comparison with other organisations, reference models, deriving indicators from strategic objectives or analysing the dependency between PI.

However, none of the existing approaches is aligned explicitly to collaborative business between independent partners. Neither there is a performance perspective the covers collaboration nor a process for collaborative PM. The gap of a missing performance perspective for the interaction between cooperation network partners was already identified and discussed by several research works [e.g. Gunasekaran 2001, Leseure 2001, Hieber 2002, Zhao 2002, Sivadasan et al [2002], Simatupang and Sridharan [2004], Schweier [2004], MacBeth 2005]. Many of these research works considering cooperation in supply chains. They suggest Performance perspectives like equity, flexibility, reliability, responsiveness, partnership, collaboration efficiency, generic cooperation performance, absorption of complexity in collaboration, information sharing, decision synchronisation or incentive alignment (sharing of risks, costs and benefits). Leseure for example developed an approach for meta-performance on network level, which comprises the two dimensions of aggregated performance and equity. Simatupang and Sridharan introduced three dimensions to characterise collaboration: Information sharing, decision synchronisation and incentive alignment. More recent works like from Höbig [2002] or Seifert [2007] are looking at the performance of interactions between partners from the viewpoint of assessing a company's capability and preparedness for cooperation.

Nevertheless a consistent PM approach for Virtual Organizations is still missing. Hence, to provide VO manager with guidance and support a framework for VOPM is needed that comprises a concept how to handle PM in VOs as well as a framework of performance perspectives that includes collaboration performance.

3. PERFORMANCE MEASUREMENT IN VIRTUAL ORGANISATIONS

Performance Measurement provides essential input for the management of VOs. To ensure effectiveness PM has to take care of VOs' specific characteristics. Approaches that were developed for single organisations and static cooperation need adaptations and extensions to meet the requirement in VOs. This means tha VO manager can not do PM in VO as in other organisation. A PM framework that is aligned to the requirement of VOs can support the VO Management in its PM tasks. It should offer a basis for common understanding in the VO and guidance in the process of PM. A conceptual framework for Virtual Organisation Performance Measurement (**VOPM**) is developed in this section.

VOPM can be defined as the systematic approach to plan and conduct the collection of quantitative and qualitative data for performance indicators that assess the status of a VO.

VOPM is one of the VO management functions and therefore part of VO Management. The VO managers have to define what PIs should be measured and monitored as well as the target values or permissible corridors.

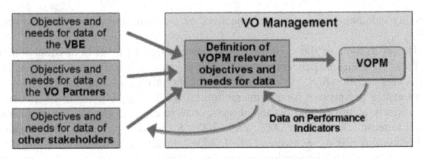

Figure 3: VOPM is part of overall VO Management

PIs and targets can be derived from the VO tasks, contractual obligations and the objectives defined for the VO. The VO management has to define a consistent set of objective that is a synthesis of the different objectives of the VO members, the Virtual Organizations Breeding Environment (VBE, this concept is described in detail in Part 2 of this book) as well as from other stakeholders.

Customers and objectives of VOPM: The objectives can be derived from the requirements of the different customers of VOPM. The customers of the VOPM are the recipients and users of the performance data provided by the VOPM. From this perspective VOPM has to serve different customers.

The following graphic shows how VOPM customers are provided with performance data.

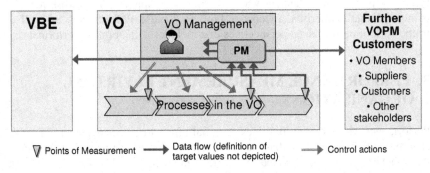

Figure 4: Customers of VOPM

Main customer is the VO Management that uses the data to monitor the accomplishment of the VO's objectives and to control the processes in the VO. In addition the performance indicators constitute a communication tool for the VO Management. In particular in VOs with heterogeneous partners, clearly defined performance indicators, e.g. for on-time-delivery, could help to avoid misunderstanding. Another important aspect for the VO Management is the effect on awareness and motivation caused by the performance indicators, especially in non-hierarchic VOs. Performance data can also support VO Management in trust-building as it creates transparency for the VO members.

The organisational units and employees that are involved in the VO activities can be also customers of the VOPM if they are using the data to monitor and control their work.

Therefore VOPM has to meet following objectives:

- Provide a transparency about the status of the VO and the accomplishment of its tasks as a basis for controlling.
- Provide a basis for communication inside the VO between VO Management and VO members.
- Create awareness and motivation, support trust-building through transparency.

In the ECOLEAD model VOs are created from a VBE. Since the VBE needs a feed-back for its work this organisation is another important customer of the VOPM. The VBE's main objectives regarding VOPM are:

- Provide feed-back regarding the effectiveness of VO creation, e.g. about suitability of initial planning or partner fit.
- Getting input for future VOs, in particular data regarding the performance of VO members for partner selection and data regarding needed resources for planning tasks.

Further customers could be the VO members as independent whole companies, external partners like supplier and customer or public/governmental institutions.

Levels of VOPM: Not every measurement activity of a VO member is automatically part of VOPM. As illustrated in the graphic below VOPM concentrates on the network level. It deals only with PIs that are relevant for the network, which means for more than only one member. On the other side this implicates that VOPM does not replace the members' individual PM. They have to define and measure appropriate PI to control their internal processes themselves.

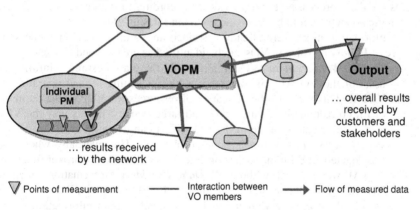

Figure 5: VOPM concentrates on network level

The network level includes a VO level and a VO member level.
On the *VO level* two types of indicators are measured:

- Output Indicators. They consider the overall results achieved by the VO. This output is received by the customer, the VO members or stakeholders, e.g. delivered products or revenue for the members. The accomplishment of defined overall objectives is also a kind of output.
- Indicators to assess the interactions between the VO members. Important aspects are effectiveness and efficiency of collaboration. Soft aspects like satisfaction of VO members in the VO can contribute to this assessment.

The second level is the *VO member level.* It considers the contributions of a single VO member to the VO, e.g. the output of a sub-process that is received as input by other VO members or the overall cost produced by the corresponding VO member. Hence, the PM on the VO member level concentrates on the interface between the VO member and the rest of the network. PI for the internal processes of a VO member are generally not regarded if they are not needed as data input for other VO members.

As shown in the graphic above some data can be obtained from the internal PM of the partners. Usually the VO members want to provide only the data that is relevant for the network level. Data concerning VO activities but is not relevant for other VO members and data corners activities outside the VO has to be kept usually inside the company. Therefore the VO member has to extract and process data for the VOPM.

An important aspect is the handling of confidential data that requires a restricted accessibility within the network. This requires an isolated VOPM with different roles and corresponding access rights.

Roles in VOPM: According to Vervest et al. [2005] essential roles for performance measurement are the information creator, the information broker and the information user. The source if information is the information creator that actively measures required data or records data that is produced during the activities in the VO. The creator can process this data and provides it to the user or the broker. The user receives this as input for his decisions and activities. If the information is not exchanged directly between the creator and the user there could be a broker that receives the data, processes it and provides it according to the demand of the user. This generic concept should be related to the main roles in VOs.

The information users were already described above in section "customers and objectives". Following roles in VOs can be identified as creators and brokers:

- The ***VO Management*** (VOM) is not only the main customer (information user) of the VOPM it is also responsible for setting-up and operating the VOPM. This includes the allocation of resources for VOPM, the definition of PI, corresponding data sources and target values. In this way the VOM acts as information broke in the VO. VOM can delegate operation VOPM work to a ***"VOPM officer"***, second broker role. However, also when work is delegated VOM remains responsible for VOPM and the broker function.

- VOPM won't work without PI ***Data Providers*** (information creators). Generally the data has to be provided by the VO members. Responsible are usually the ***process/task owners***. They can act as both information creator and information broker. The management of the involved organisational units has to decide, which data can be provided to the VOPM, which has to be treated confidentially and which is too confidential to make it transparent for other VO members. The practical provision of data is usually done by the employees involved in the tasks and by people from ICT departments.

VOPM process: To obtain results from the VOPM there has to be a process of designing, implementing and operating it. Various research work has been done on processes of performance measurement [e.g. Kaplan et al. 1992, Neely et al. 1996, Bitici et al. 2001, Andersen et al., 2002, Mendibil et al. 2002, Borst et al. 2005]. The processes shown in the graphic below were derived from these considerations, adapted and extended to the specific conditions of VOs. They should provide a guideline for set-up and operation of VOPM.

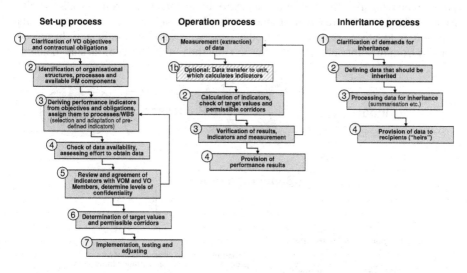

Figure 6: VOPM processes

The collaborative character of VOPM is in particular visible in the set-up process. For the clarification of objectives and conditions as well as for the agreement of indicators to apply all VO members have to be involved. In the operation process the data transfer between the distributed partners with the heterogeneous structures has to be regarded.

A VO-specific process is the inheritance of performance data when the VO dissolves. An important recipient of inherited data is the VBE. In many cases it will be necessary to process data first to obtain an utilizable format instead of transferring all available raw data. Typical processing is the calculation of means, maximum and minimum values as well as standard deviations. The number of measured values and the target values improve the picture.

Performance Indicators: An essential step in the VOPM process is the definition of indicators that should be considered.

Like single companies VOs have to fulfil the requirements of their customers upon quantities, cost, time and qualities. The base set of indicators can be derived from these contractual obligations. The subsequent step is to identify indicators to control the value creation and supporting processes that produce the overall output for the customers. While the value creation processes contribute directly to the output, e.g. assembly of a product, the supporting processes provide necessary conditions and input to the value creation process, e.g. the ICT environment, the procurement of goods or the management of human resources. Processes, output and the corresponding points of measurement for the different types of indicators are illustrated in the following graphic.

Output, value creation and supporting processes are comparable to single companies. For example the steps of an assembly processes will be more or less the same if a production line is doing that for an internal order or integrated in a VO. Therefore the corresponding indicators in VO are comparable to the indicators in single companies. Hence, the VO manager can use existing frameworks of indicators (e.g. SCOR or the Performance Prism of Neely). Some frameworks even provide benchmarks for particular standard indicators (e.g. from SCOR or Six Sigma). This can be relevant if one of the VO's objectives is to compare its capabilities to other organisations. In the same way additional indicators has to be derived from the other objectives of the VO and the requirements of its stakeholders.

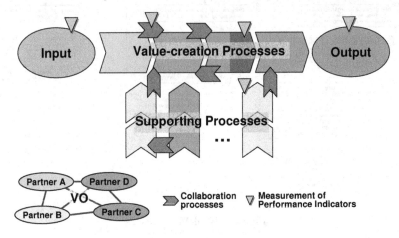

Figure 7: Types of VOPM indicators

Essential differences in comparison to single companies or static, hierarchical networks are the collaborative processes that are also shown in the graphic above. The VO manager has to consider the effectiveness and efficiency of interactions between the independent VO members when they merge their processes to accomplish the common task in non-hierarchic way. This *collaboration performance* is described in more detail in the following section.

4. MEASURING COLLABORATION PERFORMANCE

A very specific challenge for VOs is the measurement of collaboration performance. Collaboration is a kind of "lubrication" or "catalyst" for the value creation and supporting processes in the VO. A high collaboration performance ensures that all VO members can contribute to the VO according to their full potential.

The need for collaboration performance is caused be the characteristics of VOs: Independency of partners, heterogeneity of structures, processes and cultures, and the impermanence of the VO.

Generally it is almost impossible to regulate all issues and all potential situations when a project is set-up or cooperation is created. In VOs this is amplified by the temporary character of a VO and the heterogeneity. The effort for such regulations has to be limited to ensure that there is an amortisation within the limited lifetime of the VO. On the other side the heterogeneity increases the number and variance of interfaces and situations that have to be regulated. Consequently, unforeseen and not regulated problems will occur during the operation phase of a VO. This gap in agreed regulation has to be filled by the VO members with new agreements and actions, in many cases under tough time constraints. But there are not only unforeseen problems that need collaboration performance. In some VOs creative solutions have to be developed to fulfil the contractual obligations and reach the objectives. Creativity, giving impulses, sharing ideas can hardly be regulated in contracts when the VO is created. However the partners are independent and can not be forced to actions that are not regulated in contracts. There is a need for "good will" and motivation so that all VO members can make full use of their general capabilities to accomplish the defined tasks according to the defined objectives. Without effective collaboration the overall success of a VO could be jeopardised.

Collaboration performance focuses on efficiency of interaction and emergent behaviour within the VO.

To obtain corresponding data for the management of the VO the aspect of collaboration performance has to be integrated into the VO Performance Measurement (VOPM). As analysed in the chapters above existing PM approaches do not offer a concept of collaboration performance that fit for VOs. Therefore the provided frameworks for performance indicators have to be extended. It is proposed to regard collaboration performance as an own performance perspective that summarises different indicators that assess the effectiveness and efficiency of interaction between VO members. This is an addition to traditional performance perspectives that are also applicable in VO (e.g. cost, quality and time). The background of this new performance perspective is illustrated in the graphic below.

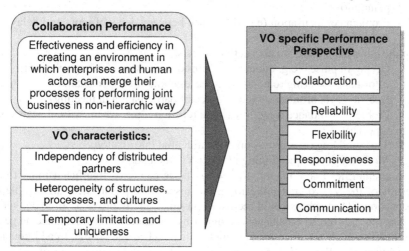

Figure 8: Perspective of Collaboration Performance in VOPM

The sub-perspectives derived from the characteristics and requirements of VOs.

For example, the involvement of distributed independent VO member leads to a dependency between the contributions of the different members. Therefore one essential aspect of collaboration performance is the reliability of the members. In the process perspective the reliability could be evaluated with indicators that measure if materials, information or resources are delivered in the agreed quantity, quality and time. In the financial perspective it is analysed if this also take place for agreed cost.

On the other hand there are additional aspects of reliability, which are related to trust, e.g. information is kept confidential and decisions are stable.

Performance indicators for reliability, flexibility, responsiveness and communication occur already in other approaches, e.g. SCOR or Höbig [2002]. However, they were used with another intention than measuring collaboration performance, they only cover only a part of the aspects (e.g. the aspect of confidentiality was not regarded in the perspective of reliability) and there was no consistent overall concept for this performance perspective. Nevertheless, these sub-perspectives should not be described in detail in this place.

In contrast the perspective of commitment is a specific core element of collaboration performance in VOs. It summarises the aspects of collaboration performance that are strongly related to the attitude towards the VO and the interaction with other VO members. Commitment considers contributions to the VO that are not formally defined but come from the motivation of partners. At first sight, commitment seems to be a "soft" aspect of collaboration performance that is difficult to measure. However, if commitment is divided into further sub-perspectives its meaning becomes clearer and potential performance indicators become perceptible.

On the one hand there are re-active aspects that describe how the VO members react on critical situations or problems:

- Problem and conflict solving (e.g. number of problems that require escalation to VO management).
- Willingness for compromise (e.g. degree of accepted adaptations in new planning).
- Problem compensation (e.g. difference between delay of input and delay of output).

On the other hand there are also active aspects:

- Giving impulses (e.g. number of realised suggestions for improvement).
- Information sharing (e.g. provided accessibility to documents).
- Decision synchronisation (e.g. degree of participation in meeting).
- Problem avoidance (e.g. provided reaction time when critical status is reported).
- Trust building (e.g. provision of confidential information).
- Motivating (e.g. questioning of other VO members).

This exemplifies that collaboration performance can have significant impact on the results of the VO (output indicators). For instance responsiveness and problem compensation VO members could reduce cycle times and improve on-time delivery to the customer. If the VO manager is monitoring collaboration performance he gets alerted before effects on process and output indicators became visible. In addition an active control of collaboration performance can improve the satisfaction of the VO members. Because even if the VO delivers the results as planned the VO members can be unsatisfied with the cooperation inside the VO and will not participate in comparable VOs again. Therefore the controlling of collaboration is a vital task for VO managers.

5. ICT SUPPORT FOR VOPM

In case a VO becomes more complex in terms of its size, dynamics or level of heterogeneity, PM needs to be supported by ICT tools that relieve a VO-manager from the unnecessary and time consuming tasks. ICT support should also reduce the complexity of specifying, searching and obtaining the information that is relevant for getting overviews and managing the VO.

There are many products and solutions for management support being developed. Large ICT oriented organisations, such as SAP, IBM, HP, Microsoft, Tibco, Cisco and Oracle provide software and approaches that support management and monitoring processes in organisations. Although their solutions have evolved from monolithic systems towards centralized, homogenous network systems, they are often focused on support within the boundaries of a single organization, and therefore not directly applicable in network organisations.

In line with the mentioned elements of the PM approach described above, examples of ICT support of VOPM are:

- VO Ontology management
  Tools that support common terminology and relationships
- VO Topology, KPI and WBS management
  Tools (databases) containing the information about the members,management indicators and workbreakdown structure
- Distributed information provisioning
  Tools that provide a secure and reliable mechanism for data retrieval
- Monitoring and alerting support
  Tools that help assessing and analysing the performance information
- Planning and decision support
  Tools that support in task planning, and simulation of alternatives

The challenges for VOPM, as mentioned at the beginning of this chapter, have their influence on the design and implementation of the supporting ICT tools. For example, measurement needs to be carried out in the various member environments dealing with diverse communication protocols and changing information streams. Furthermore, to allow proper usage by the VO manager, different kinds of supporting tools must be able to cooperate and integrate their information, while hiding the complexities of the underlying technical environments.

The requirements needed to meet these challenges can be grouped in three categories:

- dealing with heterogeneous ICT environments
- dealing with communication and ways of accessing local information
- dealing with semantics

In the process of data fetching each individual organisation has its own preferences and possibilities to reply to the fetching requests. For some organisations it is possible to use direct links to their local systems, enabling the performance measurement tool to fetch the values automatically. Other organisations prefer to key in the requested values by means of email, excel sheets, or electronic forms. One of the technical challenges is therefore to design and manage a flexible and extensible way of fetching that can perform the data fetching in a local environment and communicate the result to the network.

In this communication one has to deal with two other challenges; the first one is security. Apart from the encryption of the data that is send and shared by the network, also the content itself and the level of detail is often subject to careful design. Organisations want to be in local control of this information flow and often want to prevent automated fetching mechanisms to access their core information systems. A second challenge at the level of communication is the housekeeping about the topology. A distributed information retrieving mechanism must be aware about the locations of the individual fetching parts, and vice-versa, these parts, in sharing the results must be able to access each other as well as the address of the original data-requesting parts to which they should send the retrieved results.

The third kind of challenge lies in the area of semantics. The meaning, entity definition and unit-definition of the information that is requested needs to be defined and -if necessary- translated into various forms. On one hand organisation might use different names and descriptions for the same entity, and on the other hand different units might be used. Manual translations, open message formats, and the use of ontology rise up to be of important relevance here.

As VOs are temporary, and usually created in dynamic environments, the supporting tools must be very flexible in order to be able to adapt quickly to specific needs. The technical architecture must therefore be based on a modular, service oriented approach. It is here where technology and trends of service orientation (SOA) and software as a service (SAAS) find their application in the area of VOPM. Further more, in line with the concepts and trends of service orientation, tools that provide this support can be best described in terms of their end-user usage, i.e. in terms of services they offer for the VO manager.

Instead of supporting ICT tools, we then talk about *supporting ICT services* or VO Management eServices. While chapter 3.3 contains more details, we provide here a short introduction with respect to the aspects of PM.

The term service has a broad scope in its definition. Business process engineers, information annalists and computer engineers have a different understanding of what a service is. In our context, a *service is understood as conceptual building block in the provision of value in terms of support or delivery to the VO Manager*.

Services can be seen from both, a business perspective as well as an technical perspective; The ownership of the service may –in line with the VO thoughts- belong to different organisations. In their technical realisation and implementation, they often appear in the form of web services.

With respect to PM we can think of services in terms of 'monitoring service', 'information retrieval service' or 'alerting service'. As mentioned before, information and indicator management is one of the important elements of VOPM. Regarding this from a service perspective, allows us to design a systems that meets the requirements in a feasible and natural way.

Distributed information provisioning [Mulder et. all 2006] can be done by means of data fetching and information services in the individual member environments. They combine the individual results in predefined, summarized formats, (based on KPI definitions) and share it with other services or inform the VO Manager directly. The figure below sketches this approach.

The ECOLEAD project has developed a set of services that support in various aspects of VO Performance management. They are part of a so-called VO Management toolkit.

The ECOLEAD-VOM toolkit is a distributed system consisting of several independent services that can be configured to integrate and share information with each other. This means that the components are in principle self-contained, supporting in some particular management aspects, but can work together, forming a set of collaborating services supporting VO management processes. The components form a toolset, and are interconnected by defined functionalities and interfaces.

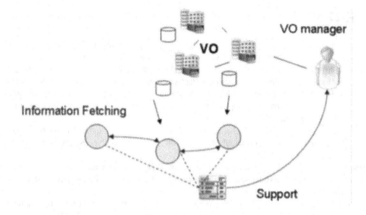

Figure 9: Information services supporting data retrieval in VOPM

6. CONCLUSIONS

This section if focussed on Performance Measurement in Virtual Organisations. VOPM is an essential part of VO Management that provides necessary data input for the supervision of processes in the VO. The challenges for PM in VOs and the differences between VOPM and PM in traditional organisations were identified. Although many PM approaches are provided by research and applied in practice they still leave some challenges when applied to VOs. As the existing approaches are mainly developed for single companies or static hierarchic networks the performance perspective of collaboration is not provided. In addition the suggested concepts for PM are not aligned to a temporary limited network of independent distributed partners. Necessary coordination steps and the inheritance of VOPM data when the VO dissolves can not be found in those approaches.

The proposed approach and framework for VOPM intends to fill these gaps and provide VO Managers with necessary support and guidance. Important elements are collaboration performance indicators and ICT support for VOs that are complex in term of their size or degree of interaction. The framework, developed by the ECOLEAD project, supports the performance measurement process. Amongst others it provides services for indicator management and distributed performance monitoring. The concepts and services do not claim a universal and unrestricted applicability to all kinds of VOs. As well as they do not demand a complete application of all elements. Rather, they are meant as an offer to the VO managers. They can make use of the concepts and service by selecting and applying those elements that facilitate their work in a particular VO best. Even though not all elements will be applied without any adaptation in every VO, the comprehensive consideration of PM in VOs should provide on overall picture of relevant aspects that helps the VO managers to orientate.

Acknowledgements: This work was funded in part by the European Commission through the ECOLEAD project (FP6-IP 506958; www.ecolead.org).

7. REFERENCES

1. Andersen, Bjørn; Fagerhaug, Tom: "Performance Measurement Explained: Designing and Implementing Your State-of-the-Art System". ASQ Quality Press, Milwaukee, 2002.
2. Bititci, U.; Turner, T.; Bourne, M.: "Performance Measurement: the comparison between a process and a model approach". In: Int. J. Business Performance Measurement, Vol. 3, Nos. 2/3/4, 2001.
3. Borst, Irma; Baaijens, Joan; Meijer, Geleyn: "Network analysis of terrorism defence organizations – A network approach for developing performance indicators". Proceedings of the PRO-VE Conference in Valencia, 2005.
4. Graser, Falk; Jansson, Kim; Eschenbächer, Jens; Westphal, Ingo; Negretto, Ugo: Towards Performance Measurement in Virtual Organisations - Potentials, Needs, and Research Challenges. In: Proceedings Pro-VE 2005.
5. Gunasekaran, A.; Patel, C.; Tirtiroglu, E.: Performance measures and metrics in a supply chain environment. International Journal of Operations & Production Management, Bradford, Vol. 21, Iss. 1/2, pg. 71, 2001.
6. Hieber, Ralf: Collaborative performance measurement in logistics networks : the model, approach and assigned KPIs. In: Logistik-Management, Nürnberg, Vol. 4, No. 2, 2002.
7. Höbig, Michael: Modellgestützte Bewertung der Kooperationsfähigkeit produzierender Unternehmen. Fortschritt-Berichte VDI Reihe 16 Nr. 140, VDI Verlag, Düsseldorf 2002
8. Jana, Prabir; Narag, A.S.; Knox, Alistair: Measuring Efficiency of a Supply Chain; December 2007
9. Kaplan, Robert S.; Norton, David P. The Balanced Scorecard - Measures that Drive Performance, Harvard Business Review, January-February, 1992
10. Kellen, Vince: Business Performance Measurement; Chicago 2003
11. Klingebiel, Norbert (Ed.): Performance Measurement & Balanced Scorecard. Verlag Vahlen, München 2001.
12. Leseure, M.; Shaw, N.; Chapman, G.: Performance measurement in organisational networks: an exploratory case study. In: International journal of business performance management. - Milton Keynes, Genève, Vol. 3, No. 1, 2001.
13. Macbeth, D.-K. (2005) Performance Measurement in Supply Chains. Presentation of the IMS-NOW SIg Meeting in Glasgow on Feb 24, 2005.
14. Mendibil, Kepa; Turner, Trevor J.; Bitici, Umit S.: "Measuring and improving business process reliability". In: Int. J. Business Performance Measurement, Vol. 4, No. 1, 2002.
15. Mulder, W., Meijer, G.R., Distributed information services supporting collaborative network management 2006, in IFIP International Federation for Information Processing, Volume 224, "Network-Centric Collaboration and supporting frameworks", Proceedings PROVE06, p. 491-498, Springer, ISBN 0-387-38266-6
16. Neely, Andy D.; Mills, John F.; Gregory, Mike J.; Richards, Huw A.; Platts, Ken W.; Bourne, Mike K.: "Getting the Measure of your Business". Findlay, London, 1996.
17. Sandt, Joachim: Performance Measurement – Übersicht über Forschungsentwicklung und –stand. In: Zeitschrift für Controlling & Management, Volume 49, No. 6, 2005.
18. Schweier, Hendrick: Aspekte eines Controlling logistischer Netzwerke. In: Gericke, J.; Kaczmarek, M.; Neweling, S.; Schulze im Hove, A., Sonnek, A.; Stüllenberg, F.: Management von Unternehmensnetzwerken. Verlag Dr. Kovač, Hamburg, 2004.
19. Seidl, Jörg: Business Process Performance; in: HMD Praxis der Wirtschaftsinformatik Heft 227, p.27-35; October 2002
20. Seifert, Marcus: Unterstützung der Konsortialbildung in Virtuellen Organisationen durch prospektives Performance Measurement; Bremen 2007
21. Simatupang, T.M.; Sridharan, R.: A benchmarking supply chain collaboration: An empirical study. In: Benchmarking, An International Journal, Vol. 11, No. 5, 2004.
22. Sivadasan, S.; Efstathiou, J.; Frizelle, G.; Shirazi, R.; Calinescu, A.: An information-theoretic methodology for measuring the operational complexity of the supplier-customer systems. International Journal of Operations & Production, 22, 80-102., 2002.
23. Stewart, T.A.: Intellectual Capital: The new wealth of organizations. Currency Doubleday, London 1999
24. Vervest, Peter; Preiss, Kenneth; van Heck, Eric; Pau, Louis: The Emergence of Smart Business Networks. In: Smart Business Networks, Springer, Berlin 2005
25. Wettstein, Thomas: Gesamtheitliches Performance Measurement; Freiburg 2002
26. Zhao, Fang: Performance Measures for Inter-organisational Partnerships. Presented at the 7th International Conference on ISO9000 & TQM (7-ICIT), 2002,

3.3

VO MANAGEMENT SOLUTIONS
VO Management e-Services

Ugo Negretto[1], Jiří Hodík[2], Luboš Král[3], Wico Mulder[4],
Martin Ollus[5], Lorenzo Pondrelli[6], Ingo Westphal[7]

(1) Enicma Gmbh, ugo_negretto@enicma.com
(2) Czech Technical University, Prague, Faculty of Electrical Engineering,
hodik@labe.felk.cvut.cz
(3) CERTICON Corp., Applied Research, kral@certicon.cz
(4) LogicaCMG Netherlands, University of Amsterdam, wico.mulder@logicacmg.com
(5) VTT, Martin.Ollus@vtt.fi
(6)HSPI, lorenzo.pondrelli@hspi.it
(7) BIBA, Bremen, win@biba.uni-bremen.de

A virtual organization is usually considered to be a set of co-operating independent entities, which to the outside world provides a set of services and functionality as if they were one organization. Virtual organization management denotes the organisation, allocation and co-ordination of resources and their activities as well as their inter-organisational dependencies to achieve the objectives within the required time, cost and quality frame. Collaboration and management therefore have to be tackled by provision of adequate methods and services for the single users involved, in dependence of their roles and profiles within the network. Based on the outlined results described in the previous 2 Chapters the following chapter concentrates on the description of e-Services as Solutions for Virtual Organization management.

1. VIRTUAL ORGANIZATION MANAGEMENT SOLUTIONS

1.1 Introduction

As outlined previously in this book Virtual Organisations encompass a wide range of typologies in structure, topology, time span as well as life cycle phase coverage (Karvonen *et al.*, 2005). Even though specific categories of VOs are more and more understood (i.e. supply chains, extended enterprises and other types of Networks) and systematically supported by dedicated methods and tools, the "Management" of their operations in terms of fostering the coordinated target achievement is still in its beginnings. Although several projects like THINKcreative (www.thinkcreative.org) and Globemen (http://globemen.vtt.fi) produced concepts such as e.g. VERAM (Toelle M, 2004) and sometimes ICT platforms, still the Management of generic VOs is seldom systematically researched and tools for a coordinated support of operation initiation and monitoring are not available off the shelf. VO Management is not about the management of the constituent Members themselves.

The real challenge for VO Management resides in the ability to handle distributed operations in independent but interdependent organizations with their own aim, behaviour and culture. This means that the VO Management must relay on co-ordination to reach the objectives of the VO

- Without forcing power (at least as a normal rule)
- Through creating trust and considering risks
- Often acting on incomplete information.

The inter-organizational supervision, control and coordination of the activities and resources in a VO are the main tasks of the Manager. The ability of supervising the behaviour of a single business process enables synchronization and orchestration of the VO by adapting and optimizing the complete distributed business process. VO Management receives data and information of the status of the VO operation. Actions are based on comparison of the actual achieved or estimated behavior compared to the wanted behavior. The actions are supposed to be proactive in order to avoid also emerging deviations from the expected outcome. In a very dynamic environment this requires the development of an set of dedicated supporting services running on a common platform accessible from every partner of the network.

The previous chapters (3.1 and 3.2) described results from Virtual Organizations (VO) management achieved both from conceptual, as well as methodological side. This chapter concentrates on achievements reached in the development of e-Services and tools based on the presented concepts and methods. In the context of prototype development, a suite of VO management tools was developed within the ECOLEAD project. This suite supports the VO manager in managing the VO throughout its lifecycle *Instantiation – Operation – Evolution – Dissolution*.

Several processes and activities related to management, occurring from the instantiation until the dissolution of a VO, could be addressed, as is shown in Figure 1. It will be shown that a comprehensive transformation from previously elaborated methodologies into tools and e-Services was accomplished. Moreover, an integrative platform was defined and developed, open to accommodate additional services in the future. This openness relies on the use of common standards and on the foreseen integration options of the VO management tools. This chapter provides an overview of solutions for VO management taking the business and user view as main guideline.

To support the business related view, usage oriented descriptions of e-Services covering business processes are provided.

1.2 VO Management e-Services

The elaboration and definition of concepts and methods was targeted to allow a holistic VO management. Having succeeded in the theoretical approach, the aim was to proof these concepts by developing an integrated set of software tools supporting VO management tasks.

The development has reached a stage of completion, whereby most of the elaborated methods have been transformed into working prototypes, validated in pilot networks. The platform, as it is, consists of different tools providing specific functionalities for the VO management. The tools can be configured to collaborate and exchange data to fulfill higher needs of the VO management. Based on the needs, VO specific configurations can be applied and described as business oriented VO management e-Services. They support collaboration between stakeholders in different situations and related to different processes. Using the integrated VO platform and its dashboard, they are configured for the individual VO from a set of tools realized as web services.

The e-Services are independently deployable in different VO contexts and they can cover different VO management aspects. The e-Services and their realizations are described within this chapter explaining the business context and the use of the services in this context. In Figure 1, the basic VO management processes are given, those supported by the developed tools are indicated in green, and the processes in yellow need further development. The provided e-Services are aligned to these processes.

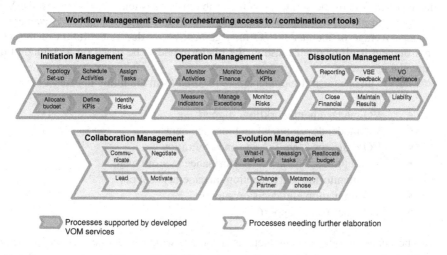

Figure 1: The VO management Processes

As shown in Fig. 1, the services within the block "Collaboration Management" is an area for further work, especially, in the area of managing and supporting collaboration between people. At the present stage of VO management Solutions, the collaboration support was based on tools available on the market (VoIP, groupware, etc.) or developed in the context of complementary work described in other chapters of this book, e.g. the agreement negotiation wizard (chapter 2.6).

2. FUNCTIONALITY OF VO MANAGEMENT SERVICES

In the previous chapter 3.1 of this book, a performance measurement based, real-time management approach was suggested and in chapter 3.2, the related performance measurement was described. The VO manager should be supported in the task of managing a specific case or instance, of a virtual organization. A common operational runtime environment is proposed for that purpose. In this environment, individual management services can be configured to fit VO specific needs from a set of parameterized and configurable services.

The developed solution encompasses:

- A common management approach/methodology for all VOs and
- The configuration of the operational environment for each VO instance

Despite the diversity of the cases in task complexity, participant's cooperation skills, ICT integration etc., the provided platform proved to be suited to accommodate the needs of different networks used as pilots.

In some cases, the configuration task only needs some basic features and a simple instantiation process, without customization or integration with an own environment. It is proven that adoption of supporting mechanisms highly depends on the adequateness of the solutions to the problem in question. In these cases, the VO management platform would provide simple and basic process support. However, to ensure coverage of increasing VO management needs due to evolution of the VO environment itself or other reasons, the platform had to be based on a common but expandable concept.

The VO management functions are configured from the following services:

- VO management workflow support
- VO model development and management
- VO Indicator Identification and Definition
- VO automatic integrated performance measurement
- VO monitoring and exception management support
- VO simulation and decision support
- VO inheritance support

The center for the management is a model, which is defined as the common representation of the VO and its management approach. To allow setting up the VO Model and the supporting environment for the manager, a web user interface was developed, the VO-Mod Wizard. It provides a single entry point for the VO manager and other stakeholders to import, define and modify relevant data. It also allows them to instantiate the specific VO model, to configure parameters for monitoring and management and to support and manage the VO operation.

In the following subsections, the functionality of the services is described and section 3 gives descriptions of their realization.

2.1 VO Management Support

2.1.1   e-Service: VO management workflow support

The workflow for the tasks to be performed by the VO forms the basis for the VO management (Jansson et al, 2005, Hodik et al., 2007). Macro-processes and specific activities have been defined and developed as starting point for the identification of the correct workflow. The VO *management workflow support* aims at giving a comprehensive solution to the VO manager to monitor and supervise all activities throughout the entire VO lifecycle.

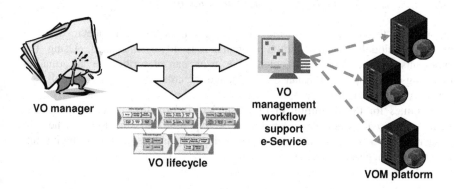

Figure 2: VO management workflow supports e-Service business context

A central user interface, the VO-Mod Wizard, was developed to provide both support for the initiation phase as well as a govern centre to enter dedicated e-Services and toggle in between them at managements need. Figure 3 shows the user interface to the VO management process. The user can navigate via the interface and access either all or only specific tools needed for the activity in course. Single activities with similar functionalities are collected in macro-processes representing the main phases of the VO lifecycle.

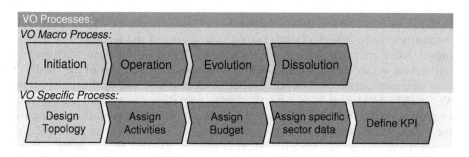

Figure 3: VO-Mod Wizard interface for following the VO lifecycle

The VO-Mod Wizard also provides links to external components:

- The VO model library to allow the management of different models simultaneously
- The VO-Mod Web service framework used to publish to external tools VO models information
- The performance measurement functions in order to share information about the VO performance indicators during the definition of Key Performance Indicators (KPIs) for the specific VO in question

2.2   Initiation Management

2.2.1   e-Service: VO model development and management

Supported by the VO-Mod tool, the VO manager uses this e-Service in order to define VO models of the Virtual Organizations to be managed. Using the components of the VO management, the user can describe the information concerning each single VO instance and manage the collection of these models in a coherent and flexible structure.

Guidelines for the definition of the basic VO information using a VO model schema are provided for the user. Figure 4 explains the workflow of the VO manager, who has to collect information from the VO partners in order to both setup the VO and manage the operations.

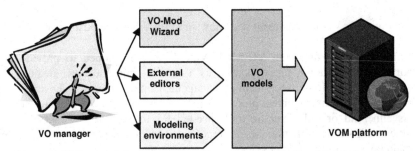

Figure 4: VO model development and management e-Service business context

In this context, the VO model management e-Service provides the VO manager with the instruments to collect VO information in a structured and reusable way, and to import data from external tools and applications. The main component involved in this service is the VO-Mod framework. It is composed by schemas of the main VO concepts, user interfaces for dealing with the instantiation and modification of the VO models, as well as Web services interfaces to allow information sharing with external systems. The main user of the environment is the VO manager, who can use the VO-Mod Wizard to perform the instantiation of the VO models and the management of the VO models library. If needed, external tools can be used to customize the models.

The Wizard provides support for the definition of the basic VO information:

- VO topology
- Work Breakdown Structure
- Budget
- Specific information can be added to this basic structure in order to cover the needs of a particular VO.

In relation to Fig.1 this e-Service covers:

2.2.2 e-Service: Identification and Definition of VO-indicators

The VO-Mod Wizard provides a simple option to allocate Performance Indicators to be considered in the specific VO. Whenever a need for more advanced definitions of performance indicators is requested, a service supports the VO manager in identifying the most appropriate performance indicators, specifying measured metrics, measurement frequencies, calculation rules, provision rules etc. The service also supports the definition of the operational procedures for automated measurements.

The support is based on a catalogue of pre-defined indicators, in which the VO manager can search for indicators that match the specific requirements of a specific VO and select them. The catalogue service can be used either by accessing the corresponding web page with a browser or via web service access. According to given application parameters, the web service provides a suggestion of potentially suitable pre-defined indicators.

Another service to support the initiation management is the configuration of selected generic indicators. To define and configure these indicators for the application in a particular VO, two possibilities are available:

- To select a particular indicator from the catalogue and assign it to a particular Work breakdown structure (WBS) tasks in the configuration function of the service
- To select certain indicators as standard indicators that should be considered for all WBS tasks. The provided auto-generate function creates these VO indicators for all WBS tasks and pre-configures them.

Information regarding VO members, WBS and KPI needed by the services is gathered and exchanged with the VO-Mod Web services framework.

In relation to Fig.1 this e-Service covers:

2.3   Operation Management

2.3.1 e-Service: VO Automatic Integrated Performance Measurement

To fulfill required management functions, the VO manager needs a sound information basis providing relevant information. The VO performance measurement service takes care of an essential part of this task.

In the instantiation phase, the relevant and valuable KPIs were defined. During the operational phase, the corresponding data has to be measured and calculated to determine the defined indicators. The experience from several networks shows, that "measurement" information in many cases is collected via telephone calls and mails. However, this is both time consuming and error prone for all involved parties. Therefore, a service for integrated measurement of data for VOs has been developed.

The measurement collection service is based on the measurement configuration, which defines metrics, measurement points, measurement frequency, calculation rule, provision rule for the data etc. Figure 5 indicates the measurement activities from measurement set-up to operative automatic measurements.

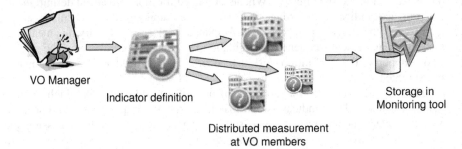

VO Manager

Indicator definition

Distributed measurement
at VO members

Storage in
Monitoring tool

Figure 5: Automated measurement of VO indicators

The VO manager uses the measurement services via the monitoring services to have an overview of the status and to manage the VO.

In relation to Fig.1 this e-Service covers:

Measure
Indicators

2.3.2   e-Service: VO monitoring and exception management support

The context of Virtual Organizations adds complexity to the common management activities due to the fact that the VO manager has to deal with multiple environments, different backgrounds and several frameworks at the same time. In this context, the control requires a clear view on the actual status. Consequently, the status monitoring of the VO is a key service needed to manage the VO and to identify and handle possible exceptions during the entire VO operational phase.

Most of the effort, spent in the set-up of the VO modeling and configure specific performance indicators, is devoted to the VO monitoring activities. Several components of the developed tools are, involved in the VO monitoring e-Service.

Figure 6 shows the context in which the VO manager can use the VO monitoring and exception management e-Service. An active monitoring support is provided to the VO manager by a complete set of tools, called the MAF platform, which is able to provide specific instruments for collecting raw performance data directly from the VO partners to be joined with management status information from the VO manager, in order to obtain a complete overview of the actual VO situation. This global overview feeds a proactive monitoring system, which supports actively the VO manager in the monitoring activities.

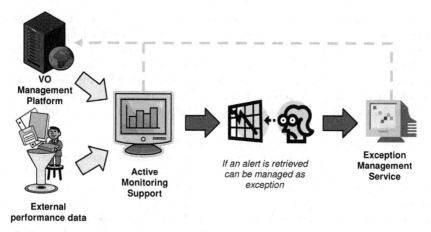

Figure 6: The VO monitoring and exception management e-Service

All alerts and warnings are collected in a coherent way and have been used to increase the knowledge base about each single VO and to engage automatically the partners involved in these problematic situations. The joint usage of these tools is driven by the VO-Mod Wizard, which guides the VO manager in all the steps needed to accomplish the model alignment and the alerts check.

In relation to Fig.1 this e-Service covers:

2.3.3 *VO Qualitative monitoring*

The VO manager may wish to establish a procedure for monitoring the internal state of the VO. VO qualitative monitoring is the collection and analysis of qualitative aspects which affect the performance of a VO. These qualitative factors include items like VO partner satisfaction, commitment and motivation. They do not typically have an immediate influence on the VO performance, but the effects develop gradually and can be seen in the quantitative performance measurements only in delay.

In relation to Fig.1 this e-Service covers:

2.4 Evolution Management

2.4.1 *e-Service: VO simulation and decision support*

For a long time, modeling and simulation have been used to support organizations in their value-adding activities e.g. for scheduling and rescheduling, optimizing the production plan before the production itself is started and for finding solutions during the operation when the original plan cannot be kept (Haifeng and Yushun, 2003). This e-Service provides the VO manager with simulation of possible future performance of the VO by comparing various events and behaviors of the VO members. Such simulations and what-if analyses support the VO manager in judging possible needs for rescheduling or reconfiguration of the VO. The analyses also support discovering potential bottlenecks and help in search for possibilities of their removing.

The simulation contains two partially independent levels: the VO manager level, where the global schedule of the VO is created, and the VO members' level, where members' local schedules are created. Such architecture copies structure of VOs, which consists of one VO manager and team of, by that leader, coordinated members. The simulation is based on the state of the system as it is and the simulation provides the state how it could be. The decision making process uses the simulation to generate various possible futures, which are generated according to configured constraints. The simulation consists of three main processes, which are:

- Process of the Simulation Configuration
- Process of the Simulated VO Performance
- Process of the Simulation Evaluation

During the first process, the simulation is configured. It consists of collecting actual operational data of the VO and set of various events and behaviors of the VO members to be simulated defined by the VO manager. Then the simulated rescheduling is executed as many times as required and finally the simulation results are collected and evaluated. The final decision about the VO schedule and configuration adaptations are up to the VO manager

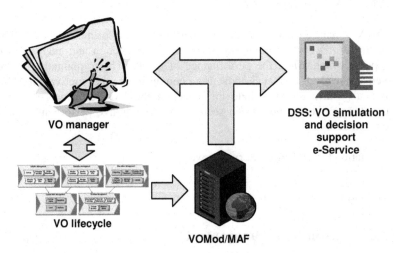

Figure 7: Business context of VO simulation and decision support e-Service

The figure 7 displays the information flow in case of application the e-Service of VO simulation and decision support. The actual VO operation data are collected at run-time (Hodík et al., 2007) and processed by the developed Decision Support System -DSS (Hodík and Stach, 2008, Hodík et al., 2007). The results are presented to the VO manager, who decides about needed interventions on the VO.

In relation to Fig.1 this e-Service covers:

2.5 Dissolution Management

2.5.1 e-Service: VO inheritance support

Because a VO is created from a VBE, there is in many cases needs to have a feed-back about the performance and the success of the VO. The feed-back information could be used by future VOs for marketing purposes, for partner selection, as a basis for planning or for other tasks, where it is important to regard previous experiences of VOs.

To facilitate this performance feed-back, services to support inheritance have been developed. The VO manager can use them to transfer VO model data, as well as VO indicator data, to the VBE. The service for the VO indicator values is realized in two steps. First the VO manager has to define in the indicator management which VO indicators data should be transferred to the VBE. Based on these definitions, the inheritance procedure can start and collect all stored values of the corresponding indicators and calculates the relevant data that is provided to the VBE, as is illustrated in figure 8.

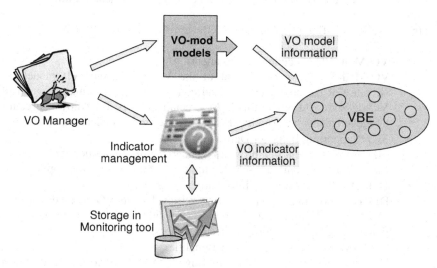

Figure 8: Inheriting model and performance data from VO to VBE

In relation to Fig.1 this e-Service covers:

3.   REALIZATION OF VO MANAGEMENT e-SERVICES

3.1   Main components of the VO management services

The VO management support is realized as a distributed system consisting of several, partially independent, services and modules specialized for various tasks in order to fulfill the functions specified in the previous sections. The developed services and modules and their relationship are illustrated in figure 9.

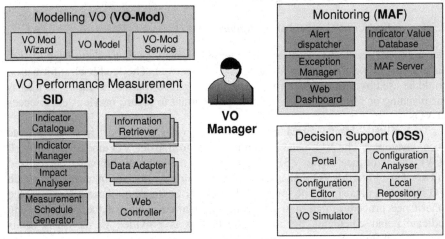

Figure 9: Component diagram of VO management toolkit

In the figure 9, the different components in the toolset are also indicated:

- VO-Mod (VO Modeling Environment)
  VO-Mod is a core component of the VO management. It models the structure of the contracted VO and contains all the information about the VO definition (e.g. VO topology, a detailed Work Breakdown Structure, budget elements, measurements of key performance indicators, etc.).
- SID (Supporting Indicator Definition)
  SID is a component that provides a catalogue of pre-defined indicators and functionality to configure selected indicators for case-specific application.
- DI3 (Distributed Indicator Information Integrator)
  DI3 is responsible for information retrieval from VO member locations according to VO management demands. It fulfills the measurement process that provides data for performance indicators.
- MAF (Monitor and Finance Functionalities)
  MAF is a set of tools for monitoring of the VO performance during its entire lifecycle.
- DSS (Decision Support System)
  DSS provides simulated (re)scheduling and (re)configuration of the VO.

To give a better understanding on how the VO manager is supported in his daily tasks the following sections gives an outline in the typical tasks and situations a VO manager is confronted with and needs to solve. First the set up of a VO is described and in the following the operational management of running VOs is shown.

3.2 Activities and support of the VO manager for the VO set up

The basic initiation procedure was explained in the previous section 2.2. In addition to this the VO Manager might have to adapt or define the basic parameters used by the monitoring eService. This has to be done specifically to each VO instance since what could be considered an exception in one case could be a normal value in another case. Of course when tasks and network settings do not vary much from one VO to the other the necessity to change alerting levels or rules might not be necessary.

The need for the VO Manager is to retrieve not only single measurements of the selected KPI's but "sensible" information about the actual status of the VO (Westphal et al., 2007). Therefore alerting rules and thresholds have to be defined by the VO manager (see Fig. 10). These alerting rules will trigger warning messages during the pro-active monitoring and support a management-by-exception driven approach.

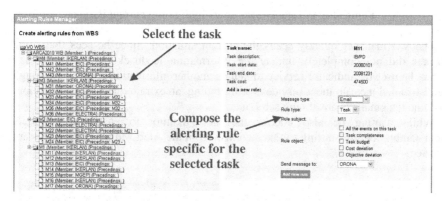

Figure 10: Creation of alerting rules and thresholds

3.3 Activities and support of the VO manager for the VO operation

The likely first task of the VO Manager when arriving at the office is to check the status of the VO (or more VOs if he manages more than one simultaneously). Therefore he starts the VO management environment: the MAF Web Dashboard. This Dashboard provides a general overview of the VO status, as shown in Fig. 11. In a single window the possible problems and the deviations from the planned KPIs, the budget and the completeness for all running tasks is displayed. The VO manager clearly understands the overall situation immediately by using the green/yellow/red traffic light system. In case more detailed information is needed the GUI allows drilling down and retrieving more accurate knowledge about possible issues and alerts.

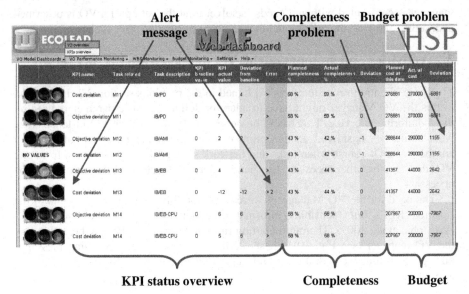

Figure 11: VO status overview highlighting current issues

The VO manager quickly scans the current situation. Since he sees that some partners did not completely update the information feedback requested the day before, he uses the indicator service to launch another information request. Although the distributed measurement service is still running, an extra request for information, this time via emails is now being send out.

While waiting he also checks the alert monitor to ensure a complete understanding before starting to take actions. From the Alert Monitor two issues are reported.

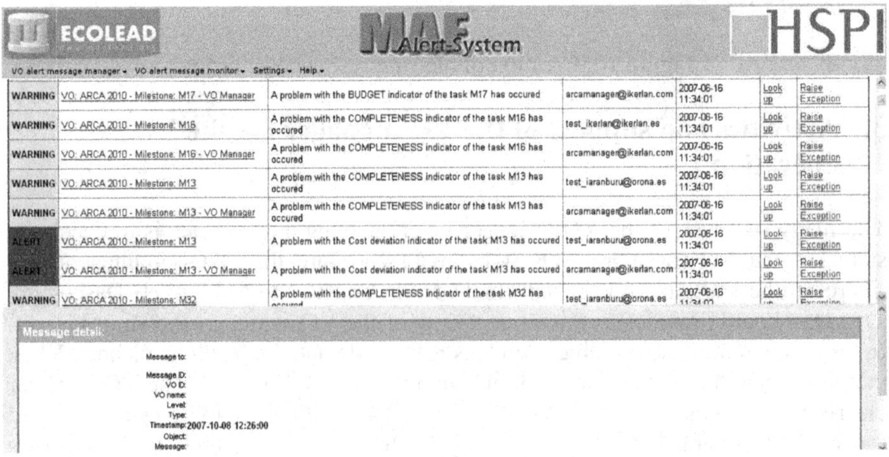

Figure 12: Alert monitor

After some time the single VO members answer to the request and the results are displayed to the VO manager.

Finally it is clear that one value exceeds the expected limit. The VO manager calls the partner asking for the reason of the issue. The partner reports serious problems and that he is not able to accomplish the task. The VO manager has now the problem to find an alternative production path and/or a suitable VO member.

For that he invokes the e-Service of VO simulation and decision support. To start reasoning about alternatives first the actual VO status is loaded (Fig. 12).

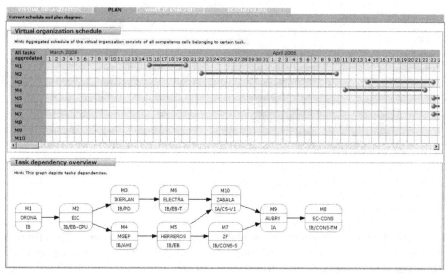

Figure 12: DSS-plan

The VO manager may choose to try manual adaptation of the VO configuration or schedule, semi-automated rescheduling of actual VO configuration, or simulation of future performance including injection of simulated events influencing the VO performance.

In all these cases the VO manager may manually modify resources of VO members dedicated to the VO as well as include new VO members into the consortium (Fig. 13). Doing that the VO manager may prove if alternative resources not used for the VO would help in its performance. Such resources could either be those contractually foreseen from the VO members as well as estimations of the VO manager, which would need a check of feasibility before really being considered. After simulation as well as during manual or semi-automated adaptation of the VO schedule and configuration the VO manager may evaluate actual modified state of the VO according to real state of the VO

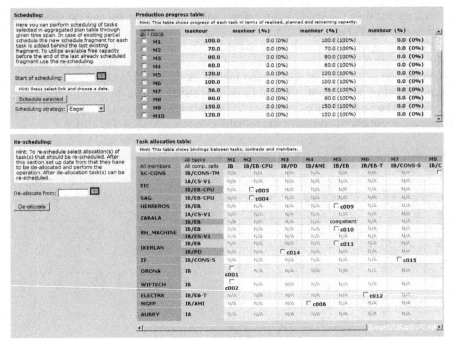

Figure 13: DSS-resources

The evaluation consists of three components. The first component provides a simple graphic overview of the original and final schedule. The second component concentrates to changes of overall VO start and end dates, if the modified schedule is fully covering all the requests for resources, and if they are provided in an appropriate time. This component also provides an overview of each task schedule and each VO member involvement. For the tasks the respective start and end dates are compared as well as an efficiency of the assigned time slot utilization. The member involvement overview presents a list of tasks in which they participate and their workload and day load over the all VO.

3.4   First application cases

The developed tools for the VO management have been evaluated in real business cases in three SME networks, which are partners in the ECOLEAD project. The results of this effort are reported separately. In this context the cases are only shortly described.

The *Virtual Factory* is a network of industrial SMEs. The network provides a full range of industrial services and production to the customers. The network enables the SMEs to act in collaboration with other SMEs in the same way as a very big industrial company. The "Backbone" of the Virtual Factory is a coordinated organization and information infrastructure; this is an obligatory standard for all groups. Thus VF brings knowledge and information in place – timelessly and purposefully to the application. Success in the market is realized by the activities of every individual partner of the Virtual Factory. The network aims to show the impact for VO management in terms of efficiency, speed and overview of the progress of all relevant data of a VO.

Supply Network Shannon (SNS) is an open network of companies in the Shannon region of Ireland. SNS provides a framework for companies to collaborate in joint marketing, training development and collaborative quotation development for participation in outsourcing networks. As such SNS currently operates as a regional VBE with individual members currently creating sub networks on a global scale. Presently these networks are formed using ad hoc processes, which are very much dependent on the networking companies' own structures. This leads to unstructured and ad hoc VO management, which again is closely linked to the participating VO member's normal operating procedures. The main SNS implementation activities for the ECOLEAD project are based upon the introduction of the structured VO management techniques to assist with the control and coordination of existing VOs in the network. This will include the use of the VO-Model to maintain structured information about the VO, particularly in relation to the work breakdown structure, the individual management styles used in the network and the structured measurement of some VO performance indicators.

ORONA stands as the Spanish leading company in the lift industry and belongs to the MCC, one of the leading business groups (made of 220 companies & entities) in Spain. OIN, promoted by ORONA in 2002, is a research consortium supported by a network of experts (coming from universities, RTD Centers, companies in the sector, etc.), working in multidisciplinary and multi-company communities that centered their activity in:

- the discovery of new technological opportunities,
- the translation of said opportunities into innovative product ideas for short-distance transportation.

The final objective is to guarantee its independence and its position close behind the leaders of the sector through the promotion of the technological capacity and the competitiveness of the own product innovation. ORONA aims to use the VO management tools to monitor and manage the performance of the activities in the research consortium OIN.

4. CONCLUSIONS

The area of real time VO management has been tackled by developing comprehensive e-Services, based on a methodology and a supporting set of tools. In this chapter the functionality and the realization of these services have been described.

The proof-of-concept was done via iterative validation steps involving finally three SME partner networks as target user group. The tools and e-Services have reached a good prototype state and include also sound and tested user interfaces. The development of the individual tools is completed, although integration efforts, failure debugging and user friendliness efforts still continue.

Each e-Service for VO Management was developed based on the common concept outlined in Chap. 3.1 and following state of Art technology.

Single innovative aspects were integrated in each single service. The main innovation relies in the comprehensive set of e-Services dedicated to VO Management, encompassing the main functions to be supported and at the same time being based on a common conceptual and data model. Especially to be noted is the scalability and configurability of each service. This enables the capability to support simple VOs with simple management and monitoring means and more complex VOs with more sophisticated rules and functions for the VO manager.

The ongoing proof of concept within the partner networks will be used to communicate results and take-up options to other SME networks. Through the performed work, a foundation has been laid to allow and foster further exploitation both in a commercial as well as in the research arena.

Acknowledgements. The work is (part-)funded by the European Commission's FP6 programme within the project ECOLEAD (contract NO. FP6 IP 506958). Any opinions expressed in this paper do not necessarily reflect the views of the European Community. The Community is not liable for any use that may be made of the information contained herein.

5. REFERENCES

1   Haifeng J. Yushun F. (2003) Dynamic scheduling based on simulation of workflow. In Proceedings of The Third International Conference on Electronic Commerce (ICeCE2003), pages 224-227.

1.   Toelle M (2004). Management and Engineering of Virtual Enterprises. Ph.D. Dissertation, Technical University of Denmark, Department of Manufacturing Engineering and Management.

2.   Hodík J, Mulder W, Pondrelli L, Westphal I, Hofman R. (2007). ICT services supporting virtual organization management. In D.T. Pham, E.E. Eldukhri, and A.J. Soroka, editors, Innovative Production Machines and Systems: Third I*PROMS Virtual International Conference, 2-13 July, 2007 [in print]. Whittles Publishing, 2007

3.   Hodík J, Stach J. (2008). Virtual organization simulation for operational management. Accepted for 2008 IEEE International Conference on Distributed Human-Machine Systems, 2008.

4.   Hodík J, Vokřínek J,,Hofman R. (2007). Decision support system for virtual organization management. In D.T. Pham, E.E. Eldukhri, and A.J. Soroka, editors, Innovative Production Machines and Systems: Third I*PROMS Virtual International Conference, 2-13 July, 2007 [in print]. Whittles Publishing.

5.   Jansson K, Karvonen I, Ollus M, Paganelli P Stewens R, Negretto U (2005). Real Time Virtual Organisations Management. In: Innovation and the Knowledge Economy - Issues, Applications, Case Studies. (Cunningham P, Cunningham M (Ed)). ISBN 1-58603-563-0. IOS Press. Amsterdam.

6.   Karvonen I, Salkari I, Ollus M (2005). Characterizing Virtual Organizations and Their Management. In: Collaborative Networks and their Breeding Environments. (Camarinha-Matos L, Afsarmanesh H, Ortiz A (Ed)). Springer. New York.

7.   Westphal, I Thoben K-D, Seifert, M. (2007). Collaboration performance in IT-intensive enterprise networks. In the Proceedings of the MITIP - 9th. International Conference on the Modern Information Technology in the Innovation Process of the Industrial Enterprise. pp 150-155.

8.   Karvonen I, van den Berg R, Bernus P, Fukuda Y, Hannus M, Hartel I, Vesterager J. (eds) (2002). Global Engineering and Manufacturing in Enterprise Networks (GLOBEMEN). VTT Symposium 224, ISBN 951-38-7539-5.

9.   VOMap http://www.vomap.org/

10. THINKcreative http://www.thinkcreative.org/

PART 4

PROFESSIONAL VIRTUAL COMMUNITIES

PROFESSIONAL VIRTUAL COMMUNITIES REFERENCE FRAMEWORK

R. Santoro, A. Bifulco

ESoCE-Net, ITALY (rsantoro@esoce.net, abifulco@esoce.net)

This chapter presents the conceptual framework of a new emerging business entity the "Professional Virtual Community" PVC, an association of individuals identified by a specific knowledge scope with an explicit business orientation, aimed at generating value through members' interaction, sharing and collaboration. PVCs are intended to empower individuals, communities of practice and social networks to realize their Knowledge Business and Social (KBS) potential.

1. INTRODUCTION AND MOTIVATION

In the current industrial context, the rapid evolution of technology has moved the focus from efficiency to creativity, for delivering suitable products and services to the economy. Furthermore, global challenges, such as environment, resources, competition, etc., are imposing new and harder constraints. With these challenges to face, the human capital is considered as an essential competitive advantage of business entities, being those individuals, enterprises or communities.

Despite this situation, individual human potential is scarcely realized within current organizational business entities and inter-organization business relationships. Best in class corporations are currently perceiving that they are approaching a limit of the possible improvements actually achievable in the exploitation of knowledge workers' human capital within current organizational structures. In addition to that, the European systemic innovation (i.e. societal changes determined by the introduction of technological infrastructures) promised by the developments of the Information and Communication Technology has been realised to a very limited extent, as compared to its potential, and the multicultural diversity, peculiarity and potential richness of Europe, is not generally used as a competitive advantage by the economic system. All the above evidenced situations are contributing to the fact that the European industrial competitiveness and growth is lagging behind with respect to other regions.

In response to the more and more dynamic market conditions, there is also a tendency of companies in expelling permanent expert knowledge resources to outsource them. This for the sake of economic efficiency, as well as of the fast-changing "knowledge" necessities. Among other causes, this situation is also activating a trend towards the increase of the percentage of Individual Professionals, which already constitute a considerable share of the total EU work force, as opposed to the Corporate Professionals' one.

Knowledge workers' main causes of dissatisfaction are the occupational precariousness, the poor recognition and reward of their professional achievements, and the restriction of their social interactions within the boundaries of very small communities during the working time (which is becoming greater and greater with respect to the available free time).

A new organizational arrangement, referred to as Professional Virtual Community (PVC), is now emerging as the evolution of previous organizational associative schemes (Virtual Communities, Community of Practices, Professional Communities) in order to address the objectives of increasing, at the same time:

- the European Industrial competitiveness,
- the Knowledge workers' quality of life.

The analysis of the two major objectives, passing through the identification of the corresponding challenges and potential solutions, as well on the base of specified assumptions, led to the identification of the overall PVC characteristics, as outlined in the Tables 1 and 2 below. The assumptions are made of basic observations of existing social networks carried out by the authors and represent an intuitive resolution of the underlying issues. Furthermore some of those assumptions have been also elaborated and investigated in the literature (e.g. see *Fleming*, *Kimble et al.* and *Ludford et al.* for the assumptions related to human interaction).

Table 1 – PVC characteristics addressing competitiveness

Objective	Current challenges	Potential solutions	Assumptions	The PVC Solution (PVC characteristics)
Increase the European Industrial competitiveness	European economic growth is lagging behind with respect to other regions.	Increase of business entities competitive advantage through **"innovation"**	Peer human interaction enhance creativity and innovation People cultural diversity is a key factor for innovation	The PVC (peer multicultural community) is an organizational form more suited for generating innovation in its interaction with other organizational forms. ICT means allow massive multi cultural interaction
	Classical enterprise "static" organizations, aimed at optimizing efficiency and productiveness, are inadequate to face dynamic markets (characterized by ever-transient	Increase of business entities **"flexibility"**	Individuals accept large degree of flexibility in work conditions, if mechanism are in place to guarantee the occupational security.	The PVC (stable, business oriented organization) provides: • to individuals, diversification of working opportunities (complementary to and co-existent with classical occupational forms)

conditions).			• to companies, an economically efficient availability of knowledge resources or knowledge-based solutions.

Table 2 – PVC characteristics addressing quality of life

Objectives	Current challenges	Potential solutions	Assumptions	The PVC Solution (PVC characteristics)
Increase Knowledge workers' quality of life	Knowledge workers increased precariousness, due to the companies' trend of outsourcing expert knowledge resources (or alternatively hiring on a temporary base)	The enlargement of the scope of individuals' working opportunities increases the **"stability"** of knowledge workers	The perceived "stability" is based on the individual perception of own knowledge exploitability	The PVC is an organizational form that makes explicit and fosters the personal knowledge "employability" (i.e. the business exploitation of personal knowledge) through the formation of Virtual Teams of members in response to business opportunities ICT means allow for an extensive market reach
	Knowledge workers' dissatisfaction for their working conditions (poor recognition and reward, scarce social networks developed at work)	Increase workers **"recognition"** and **"social interaction"**	Fair recognition of individual knowledge, business and social merits is assured by bottom up self-organized peer organizations	The PVC, through peer assessment and self organization approach provide individuals with a sense of fairness in attribution of personal recognition. The PVC implicitly introduce social dimension (networking and relationships) in working environments.

It is worth noting that the PVC organisational form is not conceived as an alternative to existing ones (for-profit companies, VOs, VBEs, research centres, universities, etc.), but rather is intended to interact with those forms, with the aim of optimally addressing the above mentioned objectives.

Real cases of PVCs have been implementing the PVC ECOLEAD framework and are described as well in this book in chapter 6.4.

2. THE CONCEPTUAL FRAMEWORK FOR "PVC"

2.1 The PVC definition

The Professional Virtual Community is a human-centric business entity, which has been designed to maximize the realization of knowledge workers and to best support innovation cycles within the related socio-economic environment.

The PVC is an association of individuals identified by a specific knowledge scope with an explicit business orientation, aimed at generating value through members' interaction, sharing and collaboration. This interaction among the members is optimized by the synergic use of ICT-mediated and face-to-face mechanisms.

The PVC generated value consists of:

- Advanced Knowledge (i.e. the creation of new knowledge relevant to the community knowledge scope)
- Professional services (i.e. the collaborative business activities performed by the members exploiting the community knowledge)
- Social cohesion (i.e. the social relationships among the members that enable their collaboration readiness - namely the effort reduction to start collaboration - and foster knowledge sharing and co-creation)

The epiphenomenon of the human cohesion realized in the PVC is the generation of higher functional abilities which can be referred to as "collective intelligence".

The PVC business activities are performed by Virtual Teams (temporary aggregation of PVC members for addressing specific business opportunities). Those activities consist of professional knowledge services (consultancies, studies, etc.) typically exploiting the "frontier" knowledge developed by the community (original applications of state-of-the-art knowledge, first implementations of emerging innovative methodologies, etc.).

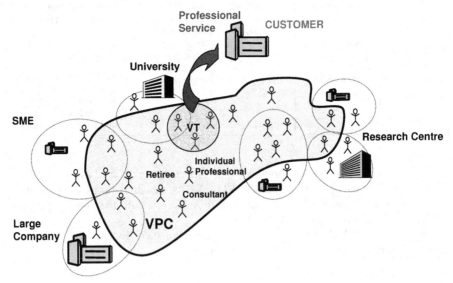

Figure 1 – The PVC model

The general principle ruling the PVC members' participation is that it is up to the members to decide the type and the extent of their individual involvement in the community activities, which is complementary to and co-existent with their normal working occupational forms. The PVC members are not PVC employees.

The PVC members can be individual professionals, free-lances, company employees, researchers (from university or research centres), retired knowledge workers, and even common people. The PVC composition depends on its specific typology and on the socio-economic environment in which the PVC is established.

2.2 The foundational principles of the PVC concept

The PVC concept is rooted on:
- the alignment of collective objectives to the individual's ones,
- the harmonization of the Knowledge, Business and Social value system of knowledge workers, and on
- the composition of the seemingly contradictory collaboration and competition drivers.

2.2.1 The "holographic" nature of the PVC business entity
Traditional for-profit business entities are pursuing business objectives that are eventually aimed at satisfying needs and expectation of their shareholders. Knowledge workers are used as resources for the execution of company value creation processes and are rewarded mostly in a mere economic way. As a result, the objectives of the individuals are necessarily not coincident with the company objectives, or at least are only partially satisfied. This can also be true for not-for-profit business entities, which generally are pursuing societal objectives relevant to certain categories of stakeholders and are not directly aimed at the knowledge workers' overall satisfaction.

The aimed coincidence of the objectives of its individual members to the ones of the PVC itself, differentiates the PVC business paradigm from the one typical of traditional companies and results in the holographic nature of the PVC, in which the Part (the Individual) represents the Whole (the community) and the Whole itself is aligned to the Parts.

2.2.2 The "KBS" principle
The fundamental principle on which the PVC is built on is that the "collective intelligence" (i.e. the full professional capability for individuals) can emerge only if three fundamental dimensions are simultaneously addressed in a comprehensive and balanced way. The three fundamental dimensions are:
- Knowledge
- Business
- Social

The balance of the three fundamental dimensions is considered the key to the full deployment of knowledge workers creativity and productivity. According to the PVC holographic nature, the KBS principle (Knowledge-Business-Social) equally applies to the community as a whole, which is deemed to be sustainable, motivated and durable only if a comprehensive and appropriate inclusion of the three dimensions is addressed. As a matter of fact, the absence of the business dimension would result in a limited activity scope, putting at risk the PVC sustainability and members' viability to spend significant time in the community activities. The lack of the social element, ensuring trusted relationships among the members, would limit the readiness to approach business opportunities and impair the free share of knowledge among members. Not addressing the knowledge development element would limit the usefulness of the community for the build-up of the knowledge society, reduce motivation of the knowledge worker and impairs his aspiration to obtain higher recognition and even economical reward.

The KBS principle infers a tri-dimensional value system for the PVC which can be represented in the "KBS Chromo-Framework", which takes advantage of the analogy of the three fundamental dimensions with the three fundamental colors (Blue for the Knowledge, Green for the Business, and Red for the Social dimension). Each KBS entity is then represented by a specific blending of the three basic colours, resulting in one determined chromatic integration.

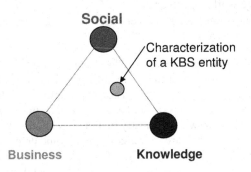

The KBS chromo-framework

© *A. Bifulco R.Santoro PRO-VE 2005*

Figure 2 – The KBS Chromo-framework

2.2.3   The PVC "oxymoronic" interactions

The collective intelligence aimed at by PVCs is enabled by the seemingly contradictory interactions among opposite elements:

- **Knowledge diversity within the same specified scope**. Though the knowledge scope of the PVC is specified, membership is open to diverse disciplines (even generic unstructured knowledge) and aims to allow interactions among members with different age, culture, expertise, etc.
  It has been proven (Lee Fleming, Perfecting Cross-pollination. Harvard Business review September 2004) that the diversity of team member's disciplinary knowledge increases the probability of breakthrough innovation. The PVC enables the interaction of diverse knowledge within a focused community environment (same principles, same values, same intent, etc.)
- **Connectivity among separated environments (multiple belonging)**. The members belong to the community and, at the same time, belong to other

business organizations, even in the sense that they may be employed by an traditional corporate organization and are allowed to spend independent time within the community. The ability of the team to exploit members knowledge diversity is enhanced by team members' simultaneous participation in multiple professional and social networks (Violina Ratcheva, Sheffield University, 2005)

- **Collaboration among conflicting interests**. The value generation within the PVC is generated collectively (higher value generated by the interaction of multiple individuals) and occurs through members' interaction in sharing and creating of value objects.

  The collaborative principle implies a joint intent among the individuals and their autonomous decision to participate in the activity.

  This collaboration is also competitive in the sense that:
  - within the same collaborative team, the members compete to gain knowledge rights' allocation
  - several collaborative teams compete to access business opportunities
  - members compete to become "hubs" of social relationships with others

  Co-creation is enhanced by competition (individual intent increases motivation and creativity).

2.3 The PVC Business strategy

The business strategy of the PVC business entity consists in being a market "Front Runner" characterised by:

- High adaptability to market conditions (i.e. being able to provide the new services satisfying the emerging needs of the market) through a flat self-adaptive organisation.
- Provision of Top Quality services

The PVC professional services are designed to address the market area that is not optimally covered by any of the traditional actors involved in supporting innovation processes (Universities, Research centres, Consultancy firms). The PVC positions itself at the intersection of the traditional actor's value proposition, with whom the PVC is intended to collaborate instead of competing.

An exemplary PVC professional service consists in supporting first implementations of an emerging innovative methodology, so characterised by "Innovation driven knowledge creation" (i.e. the Virtual Team develops ad hoc new knowledge to produce innovation).

Because of the knowledge sharing and collaborative knowledge creation mechanisms the PVC provides also a "lifelong learning" service to its members, implicitly through their participation to the PVC activities.

2.4 PVC Business model principles

A business model is a theoretical abstraction explaining the rationale behind the "logic of earning money" (or, for the non-for profit organizations, the logic of being sustainable) of the business and organizations. The identification of the business model for an organisation follows the definition of its business strategy and precedes the definition of the relevant operational processes (which define in detail how the elements identified by the business model are actually exchanged and accrued along the organisation operations).

The basic distinctive characteristics of generic PVC business models are:

The multi-dimensionality of its value system, according for the inclusion of Business, Knowledge and Social dimensions.

- The business dimension entails values such as "money", "working time", "business activities" etc.
- The knowledge dimension entails values such as "access to information", "execution of training sessions", "new knowledge generated" etc.
- The social dimension entails values such as "trusted links to other persons", "social relationships", etc.

A **multi-stakeholder perspective** in determining and assessing the viability of the Value Proposition.

2.5 The PVC governance Principles

The main Governance Principles characterizing a Human-centric organization, as the ECOLEAD Business oriented PVC is intended to be, can be defined as follows:

- **Empowerment.** All decisions and responsibility must be taken, as far as possible, at the lowest hierarchical level. As a result, for instance, the PVC business activities are fully endorsed by the VT members (the contract is between VT and the client, the PVC itself carrying out a brokerage function)
- **Self-commitment**. The members' participation to PVC activities, in terms of both quantity (which percentage of their working time) and typology (which kind of activities, such as research, industrial application, internal projects etc.), is decided by the member itself on a voluntary basis. The PVC member is not a PVC employee.
- **Self-organising leadership**. The organisation of PVC collaborative activities is left, as much as possible, to the actors actually performing those activities.
- **Peer assessment**. Any time there is the necessity for subjective evaluation (e.g. project selection and award, prize award, quality control, subjective performance metrics) this is done by assembling an ad –hoc peer committee which is empowered to take the decision.

These governance principle results in a PVC organisational structure which is:

- As flat as possible,
- Dynamic, in the sense that, by design, is not a-priori defined. Leaderships and the related hierarchical relationships are created depending on the specific context and for the duration of the specific activity
- Straightforward, linking directly the organisational entities which are asked to add value along the relevant process (so avoiding the non-adding value interposition of hierarchical intermediaries).

2.6 The KBS chromo strategic management system

The strategic management of the PVC is realised through the application of the KBS principle to:

- Members behavioural estimation, to assure the respect of the PVC ground rules corresponding to the shared value system , as well as to support their enactment;

- Members' self-assessment for managing personal improving actions;
- PVC assessment in terms of community capability and performance, necessary for managing improving actions
- Metrics for evaluating the satisfaction of all PVC stakeholders

The Chromo-Management system is used to set the strategic targets for both individuals and PVC. For individuals the Chromo-Management system is aimed at:

- Setting the desired status for individual KBS satisfaction,
- Comparing it with the current status as measured by relevant indicators, and
- Activating enablers to acquire the capabilities necessary to achieve the target.

For the PVC community, the chromo management system is aimed at steering the direction of the PVC toward the desired target of all the individuals (the collective target).

This figure shows the PVC strategic management model which correlates Values, Enablers and Results and provides a tool for guiding the individual to reach its personal excellence objectives (My-Mirror) and another tool for observing the overall community path toward excellence.

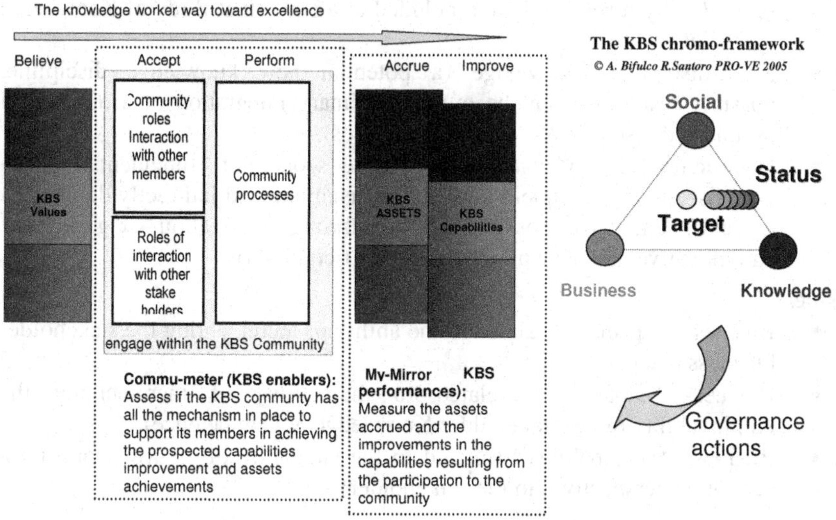

Figure 3 – The PVC chromo-management system

3. THE METHODOLOGICAL APPROACH FOR "PVC" IMPLEMENTATION

This section provides the approach to identify the appropriate type and characteristics of a PVC to be established, which satisfies the expectations of the PVC's stakeholders.

3.1 PVC Stakeholder needs

Depending on the context in which the PVC it is intended to be established, it is important first to identify the PVC stakeholders, which are the actors directly and indirectly involved in the KBS activities addressed by the PVC. Typical PVC stakeholders are:

- Citizen
- Knowledge worker
- Enterprise
- Research centre
- VBE
- Public Institution

3.2 Stakeholder needs

Needs and expectation relevant to the PVC can be systematically derived for each stakeholder by analyzing those against the three PVC characterizing fundamentals, in turn sub-structured in their major elements:

Knowledge
- Single Discipline Knowledege (well established knowledge disciplines, for which general principles and their relationships are already identified, scientifically formulated, and included in a consistent Body of Knowledge – e.g. "acoustics")
- Multi-discipline Knowledge (a potential new knowledge discipline, possibly resulting from the multidisciplinary integration of a number of established disciplines – e.g. bio-photonics)
- Unstructured Knowledge (a knowledge scope not coincident with an established or an incipient knowledge discipline and indirectly defined by a specific challenge, possibly for breakthrough innovation – e.g. develop an innovative new way of generating artificial light)

Business
- Business "capacity" (related to the ability of incrementing the stakeholder business reach)
- Business "capability" (related to the ability of incrementing the employability of the stakeholder Knowledge & Competence)
- Business "sustainability" (related to the capability of assuring long term economic perspectives to the stakeholder)

Social
- Social reach (related to the stakeholder capability of accessing and activating social interactions)
- Social capital development (related to the capability of generating social assets through the exploitation of social interactions)
- Social stability (related to the capability of assuring balance between stakeholder individual interests and freedom as compared to the limits imposed by the social compromises).

The combination of those two dimensions (PVC stakeholders and PVC main characterizing issues) provides a grid for the identification of specific needs/expectations.

3.3 The PVC typologies

The PVC typologies are defined along three dimensions:
- Knowledge/innovation scope (ranging from incremental innovation within defined disciplines to breakthrough innovation from unstructured knowledge bases)
- Business legal entity (ranging from not-for-profit "de facto" association to for-profit corporation with identified shareholders)
- Socio-economic settings (ranging from stand-alone PVC offering services to the open market, to PVC fully entangled to VBE serving VBE strategic objectives)

One type is defined by a specific value associated to these KBS dimensions.

PVC Knowledge/ Innovation scope	PVC Business legal entities	PVC related Socio-economic settings	
Incremental innovation from defined disciplines	Not-for-profit entity fostering profitable businesses for its members	Stand-alone community serving the open market	**From**
...	...	...	
Breakthrough innovation from unstructured knowledge	For-profit entity enabling capitalization of KBS assets for PVC owners and members	Entangled to Sectoral end/or Regional Industrial settings	**To**

Figure 4 – The PVC typologies

3.4 The PVC operational model

The PVC Value system (which can be structured in its Knowledge, Business and Social parts) gives an identity to the PVC and includes all the ethical values that the members shall "believe" in. It is the base for the social compromise among the members and influences the definition of the way in which the members behave and operate within the PVC. So the PVC Value system allows the constitution of the PVC as a social constituency, as well as influences the definition of the business processes and the relevant organisation.

The PVC's value system is then the base for the development of the rules (addressing both the relationships among themselves and with other stakeholders) that the PVC's members will "accept" through the acceptance of dedicated Agreements, as well as of the PVC value-adding processes that the PVC members will "perform" when actually engaging in the PVC community.

Through their operations within the PVC, the members will "accrue" Knowledge, Business and Social assets, as well as they will "improve" their capabilities in acquiring them. Dedicated Metrics will be aimed at assessing the PVC and the members' capabilities, as well as the performances actually achieved.

Other metrics will measure the compliance of the members' behaviour to the values included in the Value system (to support the social compromise), while a third category of metrics will support the PVC strategic management system (stakeholder satisfaction and processes effectiveness/efficiency).

The PVC has been designed as the enabler of members' realisation. A member joining the PVC should then:

- Increment his/her KBS assets
- Improve his/her KBS capabilities (the ones that support the achievement of KBS assets)

The figure below shows a synoptic graph describing the example key members' capabilities identified.

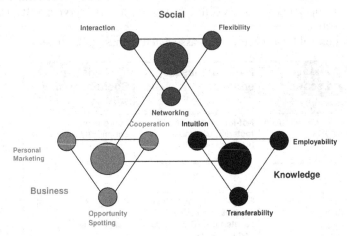

Figure 5 – The KBS capabilities

3.5 PVC Rules and agreements

The reference "rules" of the PVC are based on the PVC Value system and formalised in the PVC agreements. The agreements are divided into internal and external agreements.

Internal agreements

- PVC Member Agreement, defining the members' benefits and dues, the rules for members' qualification, evaluation and membership management, the PVC deontological code, the processes for initiating and conducting business or knowledge development activities, the processes for members interaction, the rules for the assignment of internal projects, general IPR management principles etc.
- Non disclosure agreement related to the access of emerging approaches in the PVC knowledge internal markets
- PVC Virtual Team Agreement, defining the assignment of the roles in a Virtual team, the work, profit and liability sharing among the VT members, project generated IPR partition and protection measurers etc.
- PVC Contract for Internal projects template, template contract between the PVC and a Virtual Team of its members, ruling internal projects for the PVC knowledge development

External agreements

- PVC Article of Association. The PVC Article of Association (also referred to as bylaw, or statute) is the foundation document of the PVC that shall state in unambiguous and synthetic terms the legal nature, scope, mission and the objectives of the Community, along with information regarding the internal organisation and management structure (e.g. directive council, members' assembly power and election mechanisms) .

- PVC Agreement with members' organisations, defining the general rules of members' participation and behaviour in PVC activities, with reference to the members obligations toward their employer (or professional order in case of individual professionals). This agreement include for instance confidentiality constraints, IPR management principles etc.
- PVC standard Contract clauses for External projects, template of standard clauses to be included in the contract between the External client and Virtual Teams

3.6 Reference processes and organizational structure

The "PVC business processes and organisational elements of the PVC operational model address the mechanisms put into action in the actual operation of PVCs.

3.6.1   *PVC organisational entities*

The organisational entities are PVC internal organisational settings aimed at managing and operating specific functions. The minimal institutional structure to enable the legal recognition for economic activity is the PVC Directive Council, which holds the legal responsibility of the association, elected by the general assembly of members. It includes the President of the Association, chairing the Directive Council and in charge of all executive activities on its behalf. Te board also takes care of administrative and external acquisition processes (PVC economic balance, payroll, economic transactions, taxes, membership management, acquisition of external services etc.).

All other organizational elements are intended to offer services to the members and are formed by the member themselves through peer self-organisation and election:

- PVC Marketing and communication. Organisational entity taking care of PVC overall marketing and communication processes
- PVC Steering Board. The organisational entity in charge of setting the PVC overall strategy, assuring the alignment of all PVC activities (Knowledge, Business and Social) with the defined scope and objectives, managing the updating/ evolution of the PVC rules, governing the PVC general management processes.
- PVC Technical committee. Organisational entity constituted by all the Technical Area leaders in charge of managing the PVC roadmapping activities. The technical area leaders, elected by the members general assembly, are the responsible for the main technical areas in which the community knowledge roadmap is partitioned (this partition is decided by the Steering board)
- Event Committees. Organisational entity nominated by the Steering Board aimed at the organisation and execution of PVC physical events.
- Virtual Teams. Organisational entity constituted through the self-

aggregation of PVC members for exploiting a specific business opportunity or working for a PVC internal project. The Virtual Team leader takes the role of the project manager.

- Peer Evaluation committees. Organisational entities constituted through the self-aggregation of PVC members for addressing a subjective evaluation process. This might be the case, for instance, of the member qualification process, the quality control of internal PVC project results, and all other cases where a subjective judgement shall be exerted for assessment.

3.6.2   *PVC value-adding and management business processes*
The processes of a generic organisation can be differentiated in:
- Value-adding processes (i.e. the processes by which the organisation produces the values needed for the accomplishment of its mission)
- Management system processes (the processes needed to govern the organisation in such a way to allow the realisation of its mission and to assure incrementing quality of the produced values)

Value-adding Processes
Since in the PVC case the values generated are threefold (knowledge, business and social values), the value adding processes can be analysed separately, and the totality of the PVC processes related to the PVC operation phase can be structured as follows:
Knowledge processes
- o Knowledge sharing (the advanced mechanisms by which the members' knowledge is exchanged among them. Those mechanism are necessarily based on personal interaction. The pure information sharing, the one that does not deserve interaction among members, is considered only a basic support function for the interaction mechanisms)
- o Knowledge creation (the interaction mechanisms among members used to produce new knowledge, from the conception of new ideas up to the support for large scale implementations. This new knowledge is at the base of innovative competences for practical applications or innovative products/services. "Base" research uncorrelated to practical application domains is out of the scope).
- o Research Roadmapping, (the processes aimed at developing Research Roadmaps and Studies to support the strategic decisions of all the stakeholders of the Research in the field, and in particular the relevant policy makers)
Business processes
- o Marketing (the processes followed by each member for generating PVC business opportunities with external clients. These processes are performed independently by the PVC members and are based on the list of available incipient services (i.e. the totality of professional services that the PVC as a whole is able to provide). These processes address also the elicitation of needs and expectations from potential clients.
- o VT constitution (all the processes related to the constitution and dissolution of Virtual Teams for the exploitation of an actual business opportunity, such as profile matching, legal agreement, VT agreement among members,

IPR agreement with the relevant owners, etc.)
- o VT operation (all processes regarding the execution of a contract signed by a VT with an external client for the provision of a PVC service, including both VT management and value adding processes)

Social processes
- o Networking (the processes aimed at supporting the continuous establishment of new social links and relationships among PVC members, as well as the promotion of the PVC to prospective members. These processes are intended to be performed by the members themselves)
- o Events (the processes related to the organisation and execution of physical and virtual events)
- o Facilitation (the community facilitation processes aimed at fostering the development of community social capital. These processes are intended to be performed by appointed "facilitators")

Management system Processes
- o Evaluation (individual and aggregated estimations of the quality of the "enabling mechanisms". Measurement of members capabilities and assets, evaluation of individual and collective performance etc. "My-mirror", "Commu-meter", etc.)
- o Administration (management of members' lifecycle from registration to subscription, management of internal currency and relevant internal cash flows. External and internal orders management. Budgeting and balance, Tax obligations etc.)
- o Marketing and communication (management of marketing and communication activities at PVC level)
- o Decision making (members qualification, acceptance of deliverables, strategic management, regulate internal money inflation, re-invest surplus in internal projects, etc.)

4. THE "PVC" ELEMENTS OF INNOVATION

The PVC can be seen as a radical evolution of "Community of Practices" to overcome their limits due to the lack of an explicit business dimension. As a matter of facts, the absence of such a dimension:
- jeopardizes members' motivation and even viability to spend significant time in the community activities
- reduces the scope of community activities
- impedes a deep sharing and an actual co-development of knowledge and competences
- induces mistrust because of hidden Companies' or members' business interests
- Prevent individuals and their companies to accrue the economic value which is actually generated through the community activities.

So the need to evolve towards a "balanced KBS entity", which is in itself the main characteristic and the substantial innovation element of the PVC. As a consequence of the balanced KBS principle the PVC includes innovative forms of:

- Business strategy and positioning (collaboration at the crossroads of traditional organization operating in research, business and education)
- Business model (multi-stakeholder and multi-value)
- Management system processes: chromo management system of individuals (my mirror) and community strategic management (Commu-meter)
- Value adding processes
  - o knowledge creation (garden of ideas)
  - o Business teams lifecycles (Self organising leadership)
  - o Social connections among organizations through individuals (social entanglements).

5. TRENDS AND RESEARCH AREAS FOR "PVC"

PVC trends. Several new social and industrial phenomena are acquiring a growing relevance in the knowledge society, and have aspects and/or causes which may result in strong favour of the adoption of PVCs at large.

An important phenomenon is the continuous increase in population life expectancy, where for example gains in life expectancy estimated in Canada[1] is 11 years over the 50-year period between 1989 and 2040.

An even more important metric is the increase in life expectancy for population aged 65, i.e. after the standard retirement age, which in US shows an increase of nearly 1 year per decade in the last 30 years.

Such condition is associated to a global improvement of health status in the retired population, with an increasing number of aged people seeking for flexible part-time professional work and for social opportunities, which would be the exact offering of emerging Professional Virtual Communities.

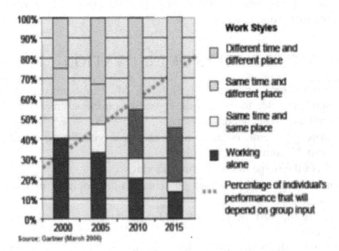

Figure 6 – Evolution of working styles

---

[1] Sarah Hogan and Jeremey Lise, Health Canada, "Life Expectancy, Health Expectancy, and the Life Cycle"

From a social point of view, there is furthermore a clear trend to increasing socialisation approaches through the web, with an evolution from the simple chat environments to increasingly address professional life, as in an increasing number of blogs dedicated to scientific and professional subjects, or through growing professional communities which are devoted to the facilitation of contacts among qualified people (the linkedin initiative).

With respect to industrial trends, most recent studies show an evident trend towards new characteristics of workers in the most advanced economies. McKinsey 2005 report evidences a growing importance of knowledge workers, capable of complex and dynamic interactions and of complex decisions, while leveraging knowledge, judgement, experience and instinct.

With 41% of US labour market and 70% of new US jobs created since 1998, the new knowledge worker profile is the evolution of employees in front of a stable propensity to outsourcing and in-sourcing of transactional services.

At the same time, a 2006 study by Frost & Sullivan shows a growing importance of collaboration, counting for 36% of overall corporate performance, and in particular for 36% on labour productivity, 30% on product development, and 30% on Innovation, while a study by Gartner Group in March 2006 (fig. 6) highlights a significant positive trend in the percentage of individual's performance that will depend on group input up to some 70% in 2015.

Such trends and the highlighted extreme importance of knowledge workers and of collaborative mechanisms in the industrial framework, is considered to put higher relevance to the development of PVCs, which can actually offer an organisational solution (combined with adequate technological tools) to the needs of better exploiting knowledge workers in future industrial environments.

Research challenges. The main research challenges which need to be addressed to support future deployment of the emerging PVC paradigm are listed below:
- Identification of open legal and social issues;
- Evaluation of viable approaches to the integration of PVCs into the market: workplace opportunities and direct interaction with market;
- Identification of roadmap to best exploitation of PVC potential. It includes in details:
    - Characterization and assessment of collaborative practices;
    - Collaboration cultures
    - Dynamic knowledge aggregation and intellectual property
    - Relationships to VO and VBE
    - Legal provisions for new forms of legal entities
    - Interfaces to existing professional bodies
    - Relationships to employers and unions.

6. CONCLUSIONS

This chapter has presented the fundamental principles and the practices defining the Professional Virtual Community PVC paradigm. The PVC is intended as an innovative organizational structure allowing the individual to full exploit its Knowledge Business and Social potential. Such an organisation is supposed to realise a "collective intelligence" out of all the individual intellectual capabilities involved in innovation processes, able to attain higher level capabilities.

This thesis is not demonstrated in this chapter, but its feasibility is envisioned by the authors, on the base of the observation of the effectiveness of human interactions, in terms of creativity, capability of understanding and intellect capabilities at general, when motivated self-organized teams aggregate to pursue a common goal.

The introduction of PVCs in the business environment and their envisioned structured interplay with traditional business entities and other emerging networked organizations such as VBEs and VOs, is thought to enable a breakthrough in the way "Innovation cycles" are managed, by removing organisational barriers to human interaction which currently impede the full exploitation of human potential. Further research and experimentation in real business contexts is needed to consolidate the theoretical framework of PVCs as well as the implementation and operational processes described in this chapter.

Acknowledgments. This work was funded in part by the European Commission through the ECOLEAD project.

7. REFERENCES

Andrea Bifulco, Roberto Santoro, A Conceptual Framework for "Professional Virtual Communities", IFIP International Federation for Information Processing, Volume 186, Jan 2005, Pages 417 - 424

Leavitt et al. – Building and sustaining Communities of Practice, http://old.apqc.org/ pubs/summaries/ CMKMCOP.pdf, 2001.

Wenger, E. C., and Snyder, W. M. - Communities of Practice: The Organizational Frontier, Harvard Business Review. January-February: 139-145. 2000.

Wenger, E. - Communities of Practice: Learning, Meaning and Identiy. Cambridge University Press. 1998.

Gongla, P. , and Rizzuto, R. – Evolving Communities of Practice: IBM Global Services experience, IBM Systems Journal, Vol 40, n.4, 2001.

Lee Fleming, Perfecting Cross-pollination. Harvard Business review September 2004

Chris Kimble and Paul Hildreth, Dualities, distributed communities of practice and knowledge management, Journal of Knowledge Management, Vol. 9 No. 4 2005, pp. 102-113

Pamela J. Ludford, Dan Cosley, Dan Frankowski, Loren Terveen, Think Different: Increasing Online Community Participation Using Uniqueness and Group Dissimilarity, CHI 2004, April 24–29, 2004, Vienna, Austria.

BUSINESS MODELS FOR PVC:
CHALLENGES AND PERSPECTIVES

Servane Crave
FRANCE TELECOM ORANGE LABS, FRANCE, servane.crave@orange-ftgroup.com

Volodja Vorobey
AIESEC volodja@vorobey.net

Defining Business Models for a Professional Virtual Community (PVC) includes both using traditional business modelling approaches and application of the methods designed for valuing intangible assets. Whilst traditional business modelling approaches could be applied to PVC by analyzing its business model both from the prospective of its individual members and from the prospective of PVC (as a collective of members) customers, there is a need to consider PVC goals of creating and sustaining intangible assets. Identifying the right business modelling methodology, aligning the selected models with the PVC long-term organizational goals and embedding the business model in the specific context is a fine balancing act.

1. INTRODUCTION

The overall objective of this chapter is to provide a Business Modelling approach suitable for supporting the implementation of PVC business models.

In order to achieve this overall objective, the following preparatory activities were executed in the frame of ECOLEAD:

- *Identification of a theoretical framework for analysing the business model of the ECOLEAD business oriented Professional Virtual Communities*: This activity was based on the examination of the state-of-the-art business model ontology/taxonomies and their corresponding methodologies for Business Model implementation. State-of-the-art business modelling techniques were analysed for investigating their suitability to the specific characteristics of the emerging PVC paradigm, by evidencing for each of them the business model elements applicable to PVC. This analysis provided also the identification of the research needs for specific topics. The overall result of this analysis was that no established business modelling methodology was suitable in its entirety for being applied to the PVC paradigm, whilst some specific elements of the analysed methodologies were considered very relevant to it.

-    *An in depth analysis of the business approach pursued by existing communities which showed sustainability/profitability in their historical tracks:* this activity was based on the observation of the value offer to the community subscribers of several on-line communities. The business elements coming out of such an empirical analysis have given additional contributions to the establishment of the PVC business modelling approach described in the following chapters.

Because of the inadequacy of current consolidated business modelling approaches in addressing the peculiarities of business oriented PVC, as well as the impossibility within the context of this research to develop a new business modelling methodology, a pragmatic approach was chosen for addressing the development of PVC business models. On the base of the results of the state-of-the-art analysis, a number of specific elements and characteristics belonging to different business modelling approaches were used to define the reference characteristics of the business model for generic PVC, as well as the basic principles for developing an actual business model for specific PVC, starting from the reference elements.

2. LITERATURE REVIEW ON BUSINESS MODELS

Apart from the literature review on the business modelling approaches (2.1.), this chapter also presents overview of the theories related to the value of intangibles (2.2.) as this concept is deemed as crucial to the PVC business model design. Analysis of a related case is also presented (2.3.)

2.1. Related Theories

A Business model is somehow a buzzword with no commonly agreed meaning.
Research in this domain shows a thin line between the business model and strategy concepts. Nevertheless, in the last years a significant body of knowledge on business models has emerged: definitions, taxonomies, identification of components, representation tools, ontological models, change methodologies and evaluation measures for business models. Overall, research in the area of business modelling, especially in its applicability to virtual networks and e-business overall, could be divided into two types (Krüger et al. 2003): (1) The description of specific business models, (2) The defining and analysing of the special components of a business model. Several theoretical constructs emerged: value chain, value shops, value networks, value constellations, business webs.

Osterwalder (2004) specifies that a business model is a conceptual tool containing a set of objects, concepts and their relationships with the objective to express the business concept of a firm. It is a simplified description and representation of the business idea of a company – how it will make money. It is a description of the value a company offers to one or several segments of customers and the architecture of the firm and its network of partners for creating, marketing and delivering this value and relationship capital, in order to generate profitable and sustainable revenue streams.

Business	**Model**
The activity of buying and selling goods and services, or a particular company that does this, or work made to earn money	*A representation of something, either as a physical object that is usually smaller than the real object, or as a simple description of the object which might be used in calculations*

Figure 1: an interpretation of the "business model" definition based on Osterwalder's approach (2004).

According to Osterwalder (2004], the business model rationale is located between the strategic planning activities and principles, and the business processes activities as shown in Figure 2 below:

Planning level	Strategic layer	Vision, goals & objectives
Architectural level	Business model layer	Money earning logic
Implementation level	Process layer	Organization & workflow

Figure 2: Relationship among business model, strategy and business processes. (Osterwalder 2004)

The literature review identified several suitable approaches for PVC developed y the following scholars: Weill and Vitale (2001), Leimeister and Krcmar (2004), Stähler (2001), Gordijn (e3 value tool, 2004), Osterwalder (2004), Bouwman and Haaker (2005), Joyce and Winch (Triple Flow Construct, 2005). Pateli et al (2004) provide an overview of other approaches to business modelling and emerging research agendas.

Weill and Vitale (2001) suggested eight types of business models (atoms), from which a business model could be constructed either by using single atoms or a complex arrangement (molecule). The models are defined in terms of the actors in the structure of the firm - customers, complementors, and suppliers - and the inter-linkages between them. The links include the movement of product, money and information.

Leimeister and Krcmar's Virtual Community (VC) business model framework (2004) consists of five embedded partial models: the *External Framework* model (mainly legal and technical conditions as well as market and competition conditions), the *Actor Model* (definition of the value proposition, participants involved within the VC, trust building and maintenance. This model is based around notions of community acceptance and attraction.), the *Product and Service Model* (distinguishes between information as a product, products in general and services: the value creation in VC strongly depends on the quality of the information which is made available to its members), the *Revenue Model* (tracks the origin of each revenue which can be direct/indirect and also identifies cost structure) and lastly the

Strategy Model in term of Strategy Development (strategic positioning of the VC either against or within value chains, as well as the strategic intention of the community). Four of these partial models belong to the external framework as they belong to the environment of a VC and are therefore identical, non-controllable variables for all competitors. Clients are considered as essential part of the VC (as "prosumers", producers and consumers of information within a VC) and thus not part of the external environment.

Stähler (2001) came up with a definition of business models, which comprises three main components: (1) Value Proposition, (2) Value Architecture and (3) Revenue Model.

The *e3-value* methodology developed by Gordijn (2004) provides modelling concepts for showing, which parties exchange things of *economic* value with whom, *and* expect *what* in return. More formal of all reviewed, it operates with *terms actor, value object, value port, value offering, value interface, value exchange, market segment.*

Bouwman and Haaker (2004) see a business model as a blueprint of how a network of organizations co-operates in creating and capturing value from technological innovation (Chesbrough & Rosenbloom, 2002; Faber et al., 2003). They distinguish four common components of business model: (1) s*ervice domain;* (2) t*echnology domain*; (3) o*rganization domain*; (4) *finance domain*. They then suggest a Business Blueprint Method (BBM) based on these domains. The process is modelled as subsequent phases and iterations – each phase consisting of a divergent (generating ideas) and a convergent (choosing and detailing ideas) part (Buijs, 1984; Buijs & Valkenburg, 1996). Steps in iterations include *Quick Scan, Test against Critical Success Factors, and Further Elaboration.*

Triple flow construct of Joyce and Winch (2005) is based on the fact that all business transactions are components of a supply chain fulfilment system comprising three flow processes: (1) Information flows, primarily the demands, (2) money flows, payments for goods or service, (3) delivery of goods or services to fulfil the customer's demands. Using the stock-flow diagramming convention of System Dynamics (SD), *business process models* can indeed be mapped onto specific *business models* from the Weill and Vitale (2001) classification. Joyce and Winch 2005 have shown that triple pair flow concept could be utilized for visualizing business models

2.2. Value of Intangibles

PVC are peculiar in the sense that the output of a PVC is not merely the delivery of an expertise under the form of a report but it goes beyond in the sense Social and Knowledge pillars of PVC are of equal importance to the Business pillar as presented in previous chapter. Thus, any of the business modelling tools used for PVC should take into account social and knowledge dimensions. As both knowledge-creation and social processes are intangible, it is useful to consider methodology developed for measuring intangible assets and similar concepts.

Notions of intellectual capital, intangibles are as important for PVC as they are for traditional companies. Effective management of knowledge was seen as the main source of competitive advantage (Prahalad and Hamel - 1990). Knowledge intensive processes have developed both within the company and within the network value creation process (Dunning, 2000). During the 90s, there has been an active debate on the nature and impact of intellectual capital in company value creation. Scholars studying Intellectual Capital (IC) such as Brooking (1997), Edvinsson and Malone (1997), Sveiby (1997), have generally adopted a three-part framework for understanding IC. These include ideas of human capital, organisational capital or internal structural capital, and customer or external structural capital as the three main component s of corporate IC:

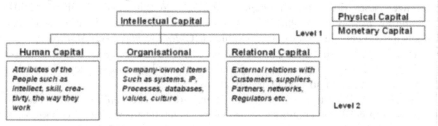

Figure 3: Categories of intellectual capital (Roos, 1997 & 1999)

Intangibles are closely linked to value creation processes. According to Holland (2001) corporate value creation processes normally include three common elements, involving hierarchical, horizontal, and alliance or network value creation. Albeit these three elements being primarily applied to organisations, they are of interest and can be applied to PVC.

Hierarchical value creation contains the primary drivers of overall corporate value creation: top management qualities, coherence and credibility of strategy, management remuneration schemes, developing employees human capital, R&D effectiveness, product innovation, brand power, brand management skills, financial management skills, etc. In application to PVC, hierarchical value creation process could mean management qualities (robustness and effectiveness of PVC governance, experience of PVC leaders), coherence and credibility of strategy (internal and external support for PVC strategy), performance systems for PVC, intensiveness of knowledge creation within PVC, PVC brand etc.

Horizontal value creation deals with a simpler process model of "input ===> process ===> output". This involved many core tangibles and intangibles as value drivers at middle management, employee, and operational levels. Within this process many companies exploit structural capital such as brands, quality of distribution systems, R&D systems, innovation for new products, technological skills, customer and supplier relations and many other intangibles distributed throughout the business. In application to PVC, this could mean how products and services are delivered within PVC (PVC supply chain), how confident and competent are PVC members in using supply chain tools (knowledge of IT platform and other IT infrastructure).

Network value creation processes involves sharing of both tangible and intangible value drivers via alliances, suppliers, and distributors and matching these to weak points in the internal value creation process, especially in the boundary areas. Applied to PVC, this would mean managing extensive networks of individuals and their relationships with external suppliers, distributors. As a result, in a PVC network value creation process could work through the strategy for recognition at the market, e.g. which portals recommend or advertise PVC etc.

Several **measurement tools** have emerged based on classifications IC and value creation processes. Scandia's *IC Navigator* reporting model included five areas of focus (financial, customer, process, renewal and development, and human capital) with over 100 metrics. *IC-Index* is based on subjective selection of IC criteria to be integrated into IC-Index (Roos et al. 1997). IC-Index tracks changes in the IC stock flows that can examine firms as organizational learning systems, which try to minimize stock-flow misalignment (Bontis, Crossan and Hulland, 2001). *Technology Broker's IC audit tool* (Brooking, 1996) offers three measurement models to help calculate the financial value of IC. *Intangible Assets Monitor* (Sveiby, 97) lists specific indices for each of three *growth and renewal*, *efficiency*, and *stability measurement* indicators used to assess each category of intangible assets of a knowledge organization.

Some other IC literature concepts of importance are *sources* and *sinks* with *sources* being net value creators and *sinks* – net value destroyers (Roos, G., Jacobsen, K., 1999). Another set of terms is *capitalizers* and *expensers (IASB, 2004)*. Stemming from accounting, the terms denote approach taken by the companies towards valuing their software expenditure with expensers writing off their expenses on software development to the expenses while capitalizers add such expenses to their capital for a long-term write-off. Identifying sinks and sources as well as selection approach towards valuing IT infrastructure of PVC could constitute final stages of the business model development or a cross-reference indicator (i.e. shall there be many sinks in PVC process based on a particular business model, the business model will have to be re-designed).

Another concept of interest to PVC business model is one of *social capital*. According to the Social Capital Assessment Tool (Grootaert, C., van Bastelaer T. 2001) of World Bank, three types of proxy indicators used for measuring social capital – (1) *membership in local associations and networks*, (2) *indicators of trust and adherence to norms, and (3) an indicator of collective action.* For PVC, social capital measures could mean respectively (1) membership in PVC and second level of membership (how many PVC members are members of other associations), (2) trust among PVC members (embedded mechanisms), (3) measures on how effective are collective virtual actions.

2.3. Related Cases

Linking the literature review on business models to Virtual Communities with an explicit business orientation leads us to provide a case study of LinkedIn (http://www.linkedin.com). The basic business idea of this network is to provide a *business networking service* by means of a social networking software that connects friends to friends of friends for business purposes. With LinkedIn, the members are supposed to find the people, jobs or business services they may need through the people they know and trust, while strengthening and extending their existing contacts' network. This value proposition doesn't address the knowledge dimension whilst there is an explicit business focus within a wider social setting. As a result, the value proposition is composed of two elements: (1) **increased business opportunities:** personal business opportunities (find a job, find a job candidate, find a partner, find a customer, find a supplier etc.) are increased by the enlarged networking and the mechanism of trusted introduction and a specific Value proposition is also underlined for value-added business networking services (such as recruitment search support) and (2) **increased networking capital:** business contacts' list (potential clients, employees, sales leads, business partners, industry experts) amended with a possibility of establishing relationships with people in the list, through the introduction of trusted members.

Regarding the business approach, the LinkedIn business logic is not known in detail, neither can be observed in its entirety, because its business life-cycle is still in the growing phase, where investment are made and revenue streams are just envisaged. However one can observe that *freemium* business model has been recently adopted: the *freemium* business model works by offering basic services for free, while charging a premium for advanced or special features.

From what is publicly declared by the Company management and what it visible in the community portal, the business model consist in leaving free the basic networking services for the majority of the community members and collecting revenue streams from a small percentage of members belonging to a certain segment (for instance the Employers) which are expected to be very active in the community and for which specific value added services will be designed. Other additional options could be: selling of context aware advertisements, by just leveraging the massive human presence in the portal cyberspace; selling at a very small price the general networking services (free at the moment).

From the moment of initial review of the LinkedIn's case, to the moment of this chapter preparation, we can already observe moves by LinkedIn to cover the knowledge dimension in their PVC (introduction of community questions etc.) as well as further reliance on *freemium* business model.

Cases of the ESoCE-NET, SourceForge, SAP development community have also been analyzed within the ECOLEAD project.

3. DESIGN OF BUSINESS MODELS FOR PVC

Based on the literature review and analysis of practical examples of the PVCs, a PVC business modelling framework is presented (3.1.), with the business modelling elements explained (3.2.) and contextualized in the specific PVC typology (3.3.).

3.1. PVC Business Modelling Framework

The wide availability of theories, terminology and methods on business models in general and of virtual communities in particular, provides a good platform for the suggested PVC business modelling framework. The suggested framework does not intend to replace the business models developed in the field but provides a framework on how to apply existing models to PVC case. The framework consists of 3 stages. An example of hypothetical PVC in the area of human resource management and talent management (HR PVC) is used to illustrate each stage. This PVC has experienced HR managers from companies, recruitment consultants, trainers etc. as members and can either provide advisory services to third parties (customers) as a PVC or provide access to collective knowledge repository to non-mebers against the fee.

Stage 1: *Business Model Definition from PVC Member Perspective* (short- and medium-term prospective of a PVC member). This step includes re-iteration of 5 steps (table 1) to identify several viable business models for PVC (competing, overlapping or complimentary). In essence this stage represents a structured brainstorming.

Table 1: Business model definition from PVC member perspective

Step in the Process	Applied Methodology	Results of the Step
1. Define initial business idea for PVC	Types of Weill and Vitale (2001) Other typologies	Suggestions for business models
2. Define components of the business model	Components of Weill and Vitale (2001) Components of Stähler (2001) Components of Leimeister and Krcmar 2004) Osterwalder's building blocks (2004)	Detailed outline of a business model
3. Conduct value analysis	Identifying business webs, value shop, value constellation, value network, etc. Value offerings and value interface of e3-value method	How value is created Analysis if components create value
4. Visualize business model	Visualize components through triple pair flow of Joyce and Winch (2005) Visualize value exchange as in e3-value methodology	Model is visually mapped (at least partly)
5. Viability check	Compare with other business models developed in steps 1-4 Compare with critical success factors as per Bouwman and Haaker (2005)	Decision if model is viable and to be considered

It is of importance to note that this stage covers business model definition both towards the PVC member and towards its customers. The later refers to the value of the services and products provided by the PVC as a collective of its members.

In the example case of HR PVC, several reiterations of business modelling using different methodologies can result in identification of several viable business models (with several others failing viability check), e.g. charging membership fee unless turnover target for PVC advisory services is achieved (*model 1*), re-distribution of income from PVC advisory services to members based on their contribution to the services' delivery (*model 2*), fee-based membership with income from the PVC services (both advisory and access to knowledge repository for third parties) re-invested into the knowledge resources acquisition (*model 3*).

Stage 2: *Business Model Definition from the PVC Organizational Prospective.* At this stage business models identified at stage 1 are judged from the overall PVC long-term prospective (contributing to the long-term goals of the PVC). Some of the business models from stage 1 are de-prioritized at this stage.

Table 2: Business model definition from the PVC organisational perspective

Steps in the Process	Applied Methodology	Results of the Step
1. Define metrics for intangibles assets and social capital of PVC	Use IC Navigator, IC Index, Intangible Assets Monitor Social Assessment Tool	What will make this PVC sustainable What are critical intangible

	for social capital	assets of PVC
2. Benchmark business model against metrics for intangible assets of PVC	Identify sinks/sources	Detailed outline of a business model

In the case of HR PVC it might appear that *model 2* undermines long-term social capital of the PVC by creating potential conflict situations around exact estimation of the individual PVC members contribution to the delivery of advisory services. Thus, *model 2* is eliminated at this stage from further consideration. *Model 1* can have a potential sink by stressing importance of short-term income generation activity, undermining incentives for members to share and create knowledge together (i.e. destroying value of collective knowledge in the PVC).

Stage 3: *Business Model Improvements' Mapping.* Based on long-term considerations, some of the business models from stage 1 are improved.

Table 3: Business model improvements' mapping

Steps in the Process	Applied Methodology	Results of the Step
Business Model Innovation	Apply Stähler business innovation methodology Use new approaches	Improve business models resulted from previous steps with new elements New business models' ideas

In our case of HR PVC such mapping can lead to incorporation of certain elements of the *model 1* into *model 3*, e.g. by eliminating fee for those members who contributed to the advisory services' delivery (i.e. either contribute to income-generation activity within PVC or pay a membership fee).

3.2.PVC Business Modelling Elements

One of the recommended methodologies during the stage 1 of the business modelling process are the overall business characteristics of the emerging PVC paradigm which are defined through the PVC Vision, Mission, Business Strategy and Shared Values. All of these elements satisfy the following criteria:

- The **multi-dimensionality** of PVC's value system, incorporating Business, Knowledge and Social dimensions
- A **multi-stakeholder** perspective in determining and assessing the viability of the Value Proposition
- The design objective of assuring an average **positive net value** gain (including tangible and intangible value objects) for all the PVC stakeholders corresponding to the PVC related activities

This leads to the identification of the following PVC basic business model constitutive elements:

- PVC **stakeholders'** classes (such as PVC members, PVC entity, Virtual Team, Companies as VT customers, Company as PVC members' employers, VBE, VO, etc.)
- **Knowledge, Social and Business Value objects**, intended as the objects (classifiable for the three dimensions) are of value for one or more PVC stakeholders, which can be actually exchanged among them.

- **Mechanisms for Value Objects exchange** (both acquisition and delivery when applicable) among all the PVC stakeholders
- **Equivalence relationships between different Value Objects** (needed for evaluating the net value gain for each PVC stakeholder)

3.3.PVC Context

While designing a business model for a PVC, it is essential to anchor the specific PVC to a particular typology, i.e. to define what this PVC is addressing, and what it is explicitly not addressing. Without contextualizing the PVC, a risk appears of using non-adequate methodologies (presented in 3.1.) or different interpretation of the PVC business modelling elements (3.2.).

The work presented in this chapter focuses primarily on the *Established Discipline PVC* typology. According to the PVC reference framework, others are *Multi-discipline* and *Unstructured* PVC typologies (as per knowledge pillar of the PVC) (Bifulco and Santoro 2005). Such PVC is addressing a specific knowledge domain for which general principles and their relationships are already identified, scientifically formulated, and included in a consistent *Body of Knowledge* for guiding the discipline implementation in different application domains. This PVC typology somehow extends the experts' mission of developing, structuring, consolidating and disseminating specialized knowledge, by embracing both theoretical and practical experiences. The PVC members are called to build up *the pyramid of knowledge and competences* related to their specific discipline.

This PVC typology best addresses its members' *human* expectations of continuously enhancing knowledge and competences at the core of their profession. Under this PVC type, members increase their individual economic gains and social security in a way proportional to the growth of their professional knowledge and accrual of additional competences.

These types of PVC are expected to serve the scientific community, enterprises and virtual organisations as recognized *reservoirs* of best of breed specific competences, accessible in an easy and economically efficient way. The sharing of PVC experts among different business actors would also induce the improvement of relationships at a corporate level.

VBE and political institutions for socio-economic development would benefit from the establishment of PVC with a particular scope, e.g. a VBE, a region, a district, a country etc. Such PVC will aim to provide the reference socio-economic environment with a competitive advantage, by capitalizing and leveraging the knowledge of the relevant disciplines of excellence.

4. CONCLUSION

The review of the state-of-art approaches in business model design and their application to the case of the established discipline PVC has provided foundations for the PVC business modelling framework. This framework has been presented in the chapter and an example of the PVC in the area of human resources and talent management was used to showcase the framework.

Moreover, the process of creating the framework has helped identifying inter-disciplinary approaches that could be further explored in relation to the business modelling for PVC. For instance, application of models used to study value of intangibles in conventional companies could help overcoming difficulty in adapting dynamic perspective in business modelling. Also recent developments in the research on virtual worlds could provide useful insights, for instance on such phenomena as *virtual organizational capital* (e.g. game items that can no longer be seen as trivial and entirely subject to the discretion of the developer) or *gold harvesting* (harvesting important virtual assets for the purpose of selling them to other virtual world members/avatars), that can enhance or, vice versa, decrease value of the intangibles. Having a clear anchor in maximizing value of the PVC consisting of value of all three dimensions (business, knowledge and social) is a suitable check on validity of the business model in its evolution process. There are also striking similarities between PVC business models and those used in cooperative movement and micro crediting. PVC could be considered as a virtual cooperative with members of the PVC being simultaneously owners of the PVC or, alternatively, as a credit union with members all having loans from PVC and thus having stake in its overall sustainability. Analysis of value creation, value distribution and value maximization processes in cooperative enterprises and micro credit financial institutions (especially taking into consideration low level of defaults on micro credit loans) could result in replicable models for PVC.

Existing business modelling approaches provide a fertile ground for constructing the business modelling framework necessary for a PVC business modelling. Carefully selecting a methodology best suited for a particular case, clearly defining constitutive elements, several viable business models, filtering such models through the tools related to intellectual capital measurement and adjusting those selected with a help of business model innovation tools, will help in selecting an ultimate robust business model for a PVC.

Acknowledgments. The authors would like to thank the European Commission for funding the ECOLEAD Integrated Project and the following partners in the ECOLEAD consortium: Andrea Bifulco and Roberto Santoro for their valuable contributions to key concepts for the PVC paradigm.

5. REFERENCES

1. Bifulco, A.; Santoro, R.; 2005. A Conceptual Framework for Professional Virtual. Communities in PRO-VE 2005 proceedings, pp 417-424
2. Bontis, N. (2000) ASSESSING KNOWLEDGE ASSETS: A Review of the Models Used to Measure Intellectual Capital, Michael G. DeGroote School of Business, McMaster University
3. Bontis, Nick. (1996). "There's a Price on your Head: Managing Intellectual Capital Strategically", Business Quarterly, Summer, 40-47.
4. Bontis, Nick, Crossan, M. and J. Hulland. (2001) "Managing an Organizational Learning System by Aligning Stocks and Flows", Journal of Management Studies.
5. Bouwman H., Haaker T., de Vos H. (2005) Designing Business Models: a practical and holistic approach, https://doc.telin.nl/dscgi/ds.py/Get/File-49778/bledpaper.PDF
6. Brooking A (1997),' Intellectual Capital', London : International Thomsom Press.
7. Buijs, J. (1984) Innovation and Intervention. Deventer: Kluwer
8. Buijs, J. & R. Valkenburg (1996). Integrale productontwikkeling (Integral Productdevelopment) Utrecht: Lemma.

9. Chesbrough, H. & R.S. Rosenbloom (2002) The role of the business model in capturing value from innovation: evidence from Xerox corporation's technology spin-off companies, derived from http://www.hbs.edu/research/facpubs/workingpapers/papers2/0001/01-002.pdf

10. Dunning J (2000), 'European Business in the global network', 1st Keynote address, EIBA, Maastricht, Dec 10-12, 2000,

11. Edvinsson L, and Malone M S, (1997), 'Intellectual Capital', London; Piatkus.

12. Edvinsson, L., and Malone, M.S. (1997). Intellectual Capital: Realizing Your Company's True Value by Finding its Hidden Brainpower. HarperBusiness, New York.

13. Gordijn, J. (2004), "e-Business Model Ontologies", book chapter contribution to "e-Business Modelling Using the e3value Ontology", Wendy Curry (editor), pages 98-128, Elsevier Butterworth-Heinemann, UK.

14. Grootaert, C., van BastelaerT. (2001), Understanding and Measuring Social Capital: A Synthesis of Findings and Recommendations from the Social Capital Initiative, The World Bank, Social Development Family, Environmentally and Socially Sustainable Development Network, April 2001

15. Holland, J. (2001) Corporate Value Creation, Intangibles, and Disclosure, Working Paper 2001/3, Department of Accounting and Finance, University of Glasgow, Working Paper Series

16. International Accounting Standards Board (IASB), International Accounting Standard (IAS) 38 Intangible Assets (ISBN 1-904230-53-9), 2004 revision

17. Joyce P., Winch G.W., (2005) An eBusiness Design and Evaluation Framework Based on Entrepreneurial, Technical and Operational Considerations," International Journal of Electronic Business.

18. Krüger, C. C., Swatman P.M.C., van der Beek K. (2003), Business Model Formation within the Online News Market: The Core + Complement Business Mode Framework, paper presented at 16th Bled Electronic Commerce Conference on eTransformation, Bled, Slovenia, June 9 - 11, 2003

19. Leimeister, J.M., Krcmar, H. (2004) Revisiting the Virtual Community Business Model. In: Proceedings of the Tenth Americas Conference on Information Systems (AMCIS), S. 2716-2726. Association for Information Systems, New York.

20. Lev, B. (2005) "Intangible Assets: Concepts and Measurements," Encyclopedia of Social Measurement, Elsevier Inc., 2005, Vol. 2, pp.299-305

21. MacInnes I. (2004), The Implications of Property Rights in Virtual Worlds, School of Information Studies, Syracuse University, Proceedings of the Tenth Americas Conference on Information Systems, New York, New York, August 2004 2727,

22. Mowbray M. (2002). What can virtual business communities learn from microcredits?, HP Labs Bristol, Presentation at the International Conference on Virtual Communities 2002, originally published on InformIT.com

23. Osterwalder, A., (2004) The Business Model Ontology (Ph.D. thesis 2004) a proposition in a design   science   approach,   Lausanne   University,   Switzerland,   2004 http://www.hec.unil.ch/aosterwa/PhD/

24. Ovans A. (2000), Can you patent your business model?, Harvard Business Review, vol. July – August 2000 p. 3-3.

25. Pateli, A. G., Giaglis, G. M. (2004), A Research Framework for Analyzing Business Models, European Journal of Information Systems (2004) 13, 302–314

26. Prahalad and Hamel (1990), ' The core competence of the corporation', Harvard Business Review, pp 79-91

27. Roos, G., Jacobsen, K., (1999), Management in a Complex Stakeholder Organisation, Monash Mt. Eliza Business Review, July, pages 82-93.

28. Stähler, P. (2001): Business Models in the Digital Economy, original title: „Geschäftsmodelle in der digitalen Ökonomie", Lohmar, Köln: Eul.

29. Stopford, J. (1997). Global Strategies for the Information Age', Opening session Address to EIBA Conference, Stuttgart, 'Global Business in the Information Age', December 15th.

30. Sveiby, K E (1997), 'The new organisational wealth: Managing and measuring knowledge based assets', Berret-Koehler, San Franscisco'.

31. Weill, P. and Vitale M. (2001) From Place to Space: Migrating to eBusiness Models, Harvard Business School Press, Cambridge, MA USA.

A COLLABORATION
PLATFORM FOR PVC

Alex Conconi, Sergio Gusmeroli, Roberto Ratti

TXT e-solutions, ITALY - {alex.conconi, sergio.gusmeroli}@txt.it

This chapter addresses the needs of Professional Virtual Communities for ICT solutions that effectively support new paradigms of collaborative work. An analysis of the most innovative and missing aspects of existing collaborative solutions is introduced. Building upon this analysis guidelines and motivations are derived for designing novel collaboration platforms. The outcome of this research is the Advanced Collaboration Platform (ACP) developed in the ECOLEAD project. The ACP integrates in a comprehensive environment the social, knowledge and business workspaces which provide a real innovation in the field of Professional Virtual Communities. First the ACP as a whole is introduced then its main features are presented in detail. An outline of the technical implementation is also provided.

1 INTRODUCTION

As described in Chapter 4.1, Professional Virtual Communities (PVC) are *Associations* of individuals (knowledge workers) identified by a specific *Knowledge* scope with an explicit *Business* orientation (Santoro, 2005). A PVC is a peer-based, self-organising community in which the Knowledge, Business and Social (KBS) dimensions coexists. Members of a PVC interact face-to-face as well as through ICT-mediated mechanisms; in this chapter we focus on the latter. The rationale for setting up a PVC collaboration solution in a community is to make better use of the knowledge held by its members and to facilitate exchange of this knowledge in collaborative work. PVC collaboration is thus taking up fundamental ideas from knowledge management but puts more emphasis on the processes, in which knowledge is applied, shared, and exchanged (Camarinha-Matos, 2005). Due to this social aspect of PVC collaboration, there is some overlap with the application area social software. Since collaboration is a complex process and PVC collaboration software aims at optimizing this process there is also a connection to the area of business process management.

From an ICT standpoint PVC collaboration is an application area combining collaboration technology from portals, groupware and personal information management (PIM). Its main purpose is to provide all functionality needed for business collaboration within and across enterprise boundaries in an integrated manner. Most solutions available today focus on particular aspects of collaboration, as opposed to a unified, comprehensive approach. Furthermore, they do not capture all of the three dimensions (Knowledge, Business and Social) at the same time.

This chapter focuses on need of Professional Virtual Communities for ICT solutions that effectively support new paradigms of collaborative work. Section 2 reviews the main aspects of existing collaborative solutions as well as their major shortcomings, and proposes principles and motivations for designing novel collaboration platforms tailored on PVC. Building upon such analysis, Section 3 introduces the ECOLEAD Advanced Collaboration Platform (ACP); the ACP integrates under a unique entry point the social, knowledge and business workspaces which provide a real innovation in the field of Professional Virtual Communities. Sections 4, 5 and 6 present in detail the individual features of the ACP in the Business, Social and Knowledge domains respectively. Section 7 outlines the PVC administrative features in the ACP. An overview of the ACP deployment as well as notes on the implementation and the major technical choices is given in section 8. Section 9 summarises the topics of this chapter and the user feedback received from the trial evaluation of the ACP.

2   ITC TOOLS FOR COLLABORATIVE WORK

2.1   Existing Collaborative Software

Collaborative software, also known as **groupware**, is application software that integrates work on a single project by several concurrent users at separated workstations (see also Computer supported cooperative work). In its modern form, it was pioneered by Lotus Software with the popular Lotus Notes application running in connection with a Lotus Domino server; some historians argue that groupware was anticipated by earlier monolithic systems like NLS.

Software becomes more valuable when more people use it and thus Metcalfe's law applies. For example, calendaring becomes more useful when more people are connected to the same electronic calendar and choose to keep their individual calendars up-to-date. The more general term social software applies to systems used outside the workplace, for instance, online dating services and social networks. The study of computer-supported collaboration includes study of the software and social phenomena associated with it.

Collaboration, with respect to information technology, seems to have many definitions. Some are defensible but others are so broad they lose any meaningful application. Understanding the differences in human interactions is paramount to ensure that the appropriate technologies are employed to meet interaction needs.

There are three primary ways in which humans interact; conversational interaction, transactional interaction, and collaborative interaction:

1. *Conversational interaction* is an exchange of information between one or many participants where the primary purpose of the interaction is discovery or relationship building. There is no central entity around which the interaction revolves but it is a free exchange of information with no defined constraints. Communication technology such as telephones, instant

messaging, and e-mail are generally sufficient for conversational interactions.

2. *Transactional interaction* involves the exchange of transaction entities where a major function of the transaction entity is to alter the relationship between participants. The transaction entity is in a relatively stable form and constrains or defines the new relationship. One participant exchanges money for goods and becomes a customer. Transactional interactions are most effectively handled by transactional systems that manage state and commit records for persistent storage.

3. In *collaborative interactions* the main function of the participants' relationship is to alter a collaboration entity (i.e., the converse of transactional). The collaboration entity is in a relatively unstable form. Examples include the development of an idea, the creation of a design, and the achievement of a shared goal. Therefore, real collaboration technologies deliver the functionality for many participants to augment a common deliverable. Record or document management, threaded discussions, audit history, and other mechanisms designed to capture the efforts of many into a managed content environment are typical of collaboration technologies.

An extension of groupware is *collaborative media*, software that allows several concurrent users to create and manage information in a website (e.gi wikis).

Groupware can be divided into three categories depending on the level of collaboration—communication tools, conferencing tools and collaborative management tools.

1. *Electronic communication tools* send messages, files, data, or documents between people and consequently they facilitate the sharing of information. Examples include e-mail, faxing, voice mail, Web publishing .

2. *Electronic conferencing tools* also facilitate the sharing of information, but in a more interactive way. Examples include: data, video and voice conferring, forums, chat rooms, electronic meeting systems (EMS).

3. *Collaborative management tools* facilitate and manage group activities. Examples include online calendars, project management systems, workflow managers, knowledge management systems, social networks systems.

Collaborative software can be either web or desktop based (such as CVS or RCS).

2.2 Designing a Collaboration Platform for PVC

2.2.1 *Knowledge, Business and Social Dimensions*

As described in (Ollus, 2007) the set of main features that a Collaboration Platform for PVC is expected to provide in order to cover the knowledge, business and social aspects is as follows:

- **Social & Networking Functionalities**. Members are allowed to build and maintain personal and professional relationships among them strengthening the social interaction in the PVC.
- **Human Competency Management and Team Building**. The functionality supports the creation of virtual teams tailored on specific needs and objectives through comparative assessments of competencies of potential members.

- **Collaboration rewarding.** Collaborative behaviours of a PVC member can be rewarded by his or her peers at individual, team and community levels.
- **Governance**. This function allows the PVC administrators to track the evolution of the PVC, examining the degree of collaboration in any of the three KBS dimensions, as well as tracking individual performance of members.
- **Knowledge IPR management**. Identification and tracking of the knowledge exchanged inside the PVC and related tools to enforce the associated Intellectual Property Rights.

In light of the above requirements, it is clear that a major shortcoming in Collaborative Software, as described in the previous section, is the lack of a unified approach addressing the Business Knowledge and Social dimensions. Most existing solutions are usually too biased towards one of the KBS dimensions. Business oriented products fail to encompass the social aspects of collaboration. On the other hand emerging Web 2.0 technologies and social networks do not appear to be fully suitable for business, besides they do not provide pervasive knowledge and IPR management. While it is possible that the dynamic of a PVC could make it evolve mainly in just one of the three KBS dimensions, all the three of them should be present, though with different weights. Failure to capture all the three dimensions would limit the growth and the flourishing of the PVC. In light of this, a Collaboration Platform designed to support PVC shall provide ICT tools that support a seamless blending of the KBS dimensions.

2.2.2   *Collaborative Problem Solving*

Collaborative Problem Solving (CPS) is a general formulation for describing a large quantity of methodologies and tools aimed to solve numerous different problems. A high level of detail description is necessary for a clearer interpretation of the CPS approach, highlighting its peculiarities and parameters (Biasci, Bifulco, and Fantoni, 2006). Several modalities can be described and analyzed in the field of collaboration, but most of the existing ones could be grouped into three main branches, namely: *planned, mediated* and *ad-hoc* collaboration.

A **Planned Collaboration** supports the creation, running and dissolvement of collaborative projects, where members are collaborating in a structured way to achieve a common goal. The typical scenario of this collaboration modality occurs whenever a project goal has to be achieved through a well defined GANTT. For this reason the project has a clear and fixed structure where responsibilities, tasks and deadline are defined and decided at creation time.

A **Mediated Collaboration** supports the creation, running and dissolvement of collaborative problem solving sessions where the relevant problem class requires the application of unstructured interactions among members mediated by a moderator. The typical scenario of this collaboration is a problem-solving process that requires to be managed, e.g. a tender-bidder process which requires a kind of negotiation between involved parties.

An **Ad-hoc Collaboration** supports the creation, running and dissolution of ad-hoc Virtual Teams. A typical scenario of such collaboration occurs whenever a quick team building process should be performed as a response to an emergency or whenever it is necessary to take a very important decision quickly. For this reason the selection of team members takes into account not only their knowledge and expertise with respect to the topic, but also their immediate availability.

2.2.3   Seamless integration

A major shortcoming in most commercial solutions is that they are available as standalone tools only: information sharing among heterogeneous collaboration components is far from being straightforward and seamless. Since basic technology needed for PVC collaboration is already available, the main challenge is to provide a platform seamlessly integrating all this functionality. Such an integrated platform would offer several advantages

- Single sign-on: using standalone tools for collaboration means that the user has to sign on for each tool separately. An integrated collaboration solution, on the other hand, allows a single sign on requiring the user to provide her access data only once and thereby obtaining access to all functionality integrated.

- Availability of information: in an integrated platform, information is available across collaboration components. Thus, when setting up a web conference the meeting information will become immediately visible on calendars.

- Unified search and archiving: the integration of collaboration functionalities allows the support of unified information processing tools, e.g. for search and archiving. It will be possible to use a single search interface to retrieve data from emails, instant messages, blogs, or documents.

- Enforcement of policies: using an integrated platform for PVC collaboration can help to enforce policies. This is achieved through well-defined workflows implemented in the platform. On the other hand, a centralized configuration of aspects such as archiving, security, or access rights guarantees that these policies are respected regardless of which collaboration component is used.

- No duplication of information: currently, information is often duplicated since it is needed in various collaboration tools. Contact information, for example, is stored both in the address book used by a mail tool and the contact list used by an IM tool. Within an integrated platform, information has to be maintained at one central place without the need to duplicate it.

- Centralized personalization: similarly, an integrated platform allows a centralized approach to personalization, instead of performing personalization on the individual tool level. For example, topics of interests can be chosen and used to filter emails, blog entries and documents.

- Reduced administration overhead: a key advantage of any integrated solution is that it reduces the administration overhead. Instead of several software products only a single product has to be maintained. In particular, access rights have to be managed once only.

In order to achieve those benefits, standardized interfaces have to be developed for the individual collaboration components. In addition, information shared by components has to be standardized as well, e.g. calendar information, address information, and access rights. The most appropriate solution is to use a central data model for such information, which is centrally managed and accessed by the individual collaboration components.

However, even if these technical challenges are met, a major challenge to all collaboration solutions remains the disciplined adoption by the end user. If end users do not enter their appointments into their electronic calendars, scheduling meetings does not become any easier. In general, the potential of PVC collaboration can only be fully leveraged if users are willing to invest a small individual overhead by using the tools appropriately. This overhead is then compensated by a significant reduction of coordination overhead.

3   THE ECOLEAD ADVANCED COLLABORATION PLATFORM

3.1   Overview

We introduce our Advanced Collaboration Platform (ACP), a suite of ICT tools that we developed to support Professional Virtual Communities, addressing their definition as *associations of knowledge workers identified by a specific knowledge scope with an explicit business orientation.* The key idea underlying Professional Virtual Communities collaboration support is to integrate a wide range of collaboration functionality to offer users a single, unified solution in which information can be easily shared between the various collaboration components (Gusmeroli and Ratti, 2007). The Advanced Collaboration Platform developed in ECOLEAD follows this approach by integrating the Business, Knowledge and Social oriented tools in a unified environment.

Section 4 of this chapter introduces the ACP Business modules: Competencies evaluation, Virtual Team constitution, and Collaborative Problem Solving. Section 5 describes the ACP Social modules: Chat, Who's online, and Forum. Section 6 presents the Knowledge modules: Document management and K-IPR protection. Section 7 outlines the PVC administrative features in the ACP, namely Governance and Collaboration rewarding tools.   Section 8 gives an overview of the ACP implementation and deployment from a technical standpoint, reviewing the major technical choices.

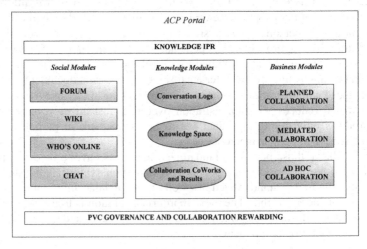

Figure 1: ACP overview

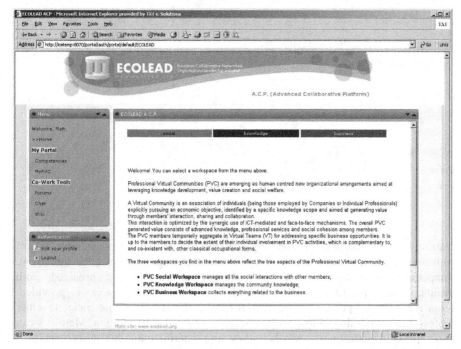

Figure 2: ACP Home page

4 BUSINESS DIMENSION IN ECOLEAD ACP

The Business dimension that makes ECOLEAD PVC an innovative community provides functionalities for team building, governing and supporting. This is the key factor which is missing in most of the existing groupware solutions and which has been requested by the end-users: to have an integrated solution able to handle not only social and knowledge interactions but also the business dimension.

4.1 Competencies evaluation

The ECOLEAD ACP supports the process of creating a Virtual Team starting from both self and peer evaluation of members' competencies. PVC Members competencies are modeled through an ontology maintained by the PVC Administrator through a dedicated tool.

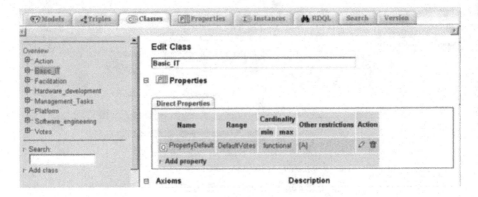

Figure 3: Definition of competencies

Starting from the competencies ontology defined for PVC, any user can rank himself with a skill and a level. Competencies' evaluation ranges are modeled directly in competencies ontology too, and application is automatically synchronized. Both qualitative and quantitative evaluation of professional competencies is provided. From a qualitative point of view a professional can assign competencies to other professionals according to its past joint experiences and collaboration. Members can also express in a quantitative way how they are mastering individual competencies.

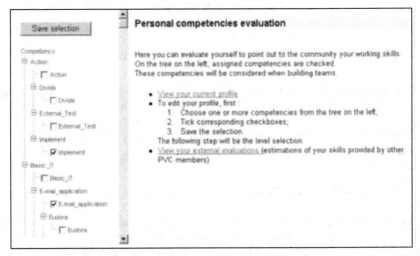

Figure 4: Personal competencies evaluation

4.2   Virtual Team constitution

The main feature provided by this module is the Virtual Team (VT) constitution. An user can create several teams, specifying the required competencies and their associated level. After selecting the competencies and their level, the system provides a list of candidate PVC members ranked by a matching value. Candidates are retrieved by comparing value of every requested skill both with self evaluated and external evaluated competencies.

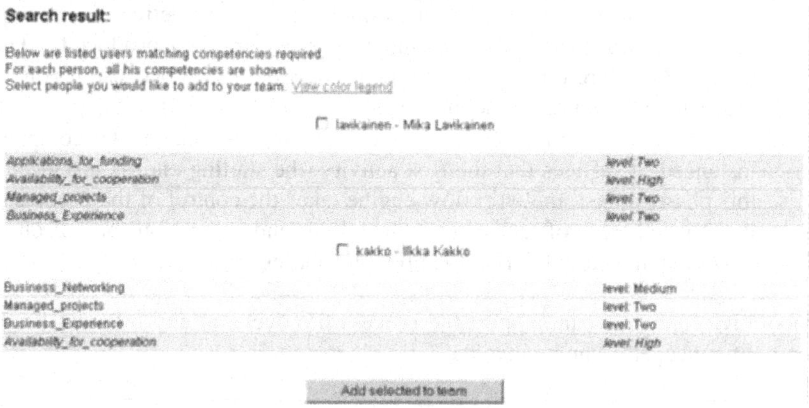

Search result:

Below are listed users matching competencies required
For each person, all his competencies are shown
Select people you would like to add to your team. View color legend

☐ lavkainen - Mika Lavkainen

Applications_for_funding	level: Two
Availability_for_cooperation	level: High
Managed_projects	level: Two
Business_Experience	level: Two

☐ kakko - Ilkka Kakko

Business_Networking	level: Medium
Managed_projects	level: Two
Business_Experience	level: Two
Availability_for_cooperation	level: High

Add selected to team

Figure 5: Team constitution process

Furthermore, the VT constitution tool is integrated with the Collaborative Problem Solving functionalities: this allows a VT leader to select and involve members within a collaboration session.

4.3 Collaborative Problem Solving

4.3.1 Planned Collaboration Tool

The Planned Collaboration Tool is a web-based and distributed platform for project management in collaborative environments. It includes a useful Workflow design module and uses some collaborative functions like conferencing, project management, and agenda. The platform architecture is modular: each component is independent from the others and they communicate through the services that each of them offer.

The modules composing the tool are made by:
- Process Definition Tool;
- Project Management Tool;
- Document Manager;
- Workflow Management System;
- Event / Notification Engine.

The process life cycle is divided into three levels: definition, instantiation and execution:
- The *definition* consists in the creation of the process schema. At this level there is the activities description (including the user's roles needed for their execution and the input and output document type) and transitions creation (enactment rules) that affect control and data flow between the activities, expressed with the Event-Condition-Action paradigm.
- The *instantiation*, instead, consists in the insertion of additional information into the activities such as start and end dates, users assignment to activities, names (template) of the document type to be produced. At this level the project manager can modify the process without limitations, according to

the particular case needs, by for example adding or deleting, for example, activities, transitions or document types to be produced. These modifications are not reported to the process definition because it is totally independent from its single instances.

- The *execution* of the process does not require the latter to be completely instanced; it suffices that the first activity (the starting one) is instanced. In this phase, at last, the workflow engine takes the control of the process and it is in charge of activities scheduling and execution based on the information inserted during the previous phases

Collaborative functions can support the process life cycle: at any moment the IM, Video-conference, etc., can be invoked.

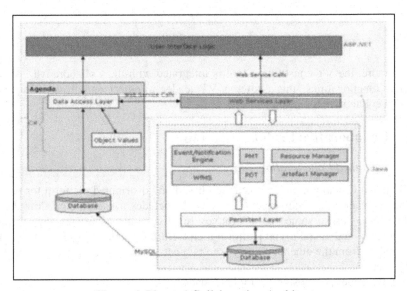

Figure 6: Planned Collaboration Architecture

4.3.2   *Mediated Collaboration Tool*

This section introduces the Mediated Collaboration Tool, a problem-solving modeling and execution environment where professionals are able to work in a team. The generated knowledge shall be protected using the mechanisms already provided by the K-IPR tool (Biasci et al., 2006). The main difference between the mediated and the planned collaboration is in the structure. The planned collaboration has a detailed decomposition of a project in activities and sub activities; relationships between them, scheduled start and end dates, etc. The mediated collaboration is more iterative: there is no activities definition, but rather a process of collecting and evaluating contributions. The main role is played by the moderator, who is responsible for defining the problem as well as scheduling and collecting contributions, and evaluating their quality.

The moderator is also the responsible for compiling the solution form, taking into account the experts suggestions, deciding which contributions shall be included in the solution, and rewarding the best contributors:

- *Problem definition*: the moderator shall define the problem to be solved, using a form. This may require the usage of the domain ontology, because the problem can be strictly related to the defined concepts. This feature requires filling in a problem form, attaching documents, adding notes, etc.
- *Required competencies selection*: the problem manager shall model a Virtual Team using the Human Competencies Evaluation Tool, and use it to initiate a collaboration. By selecting the competencies from the ontology, the system shall provide a rank list of users matching the required profile. The used algorithm is the same as for all the other collaboration modalities.
- *Virtual team creation and notification*: once the best candidates are selected, they should be notified and prompted for collaboration:
- *CBR technique*: the system can provide also a feature for searching similar problems occurred in the past. CBR is a technique that looks inside closed problems which are similar to new ones and calculates a similarity percentage. The higher this value, the greater the chance to have already a similar solution.
- *New / Modify / Remove collaborative problem-solving processes*: the module shall provide the possibility to create new problems, modify running ones, and remove those not yet started.
- *Search Problem*: another important feature is to search in the problem-solving repository for existing problem.
- *Contribution Provision*: the module shall provide a feature for offering contributions to a problem, namely addition of new documents and comments, as well as the opportunity to interact with the problem manager for asking clarifications.
- *View contribution*: a problem manager should be able to view the provided contributions and see all the available details.
- *Contribution evaluation*: the above feature is necessary for evaluating the received contributions; evaluation of a contribution means the possibility to see the provided documents, notes and description, and to establish how pertinent the contribution is for the solution.
- *Publish final documents and solution*: when a solution is reached, the problem manager shall describe it by taking the contributions that were important for the solution, and by filling in a form containing the information about the generated solution.

This collaboration modality is a web based application deployed in a portlet running on the default portal server container. It works with its own database, linked with the users table of the portal server. Problems are stored into XML format in a dedicated table: the decision to use XML has been based on the possibility to compare problems defined with a common schema; this is especially useful for the CBR feature. A user may have different roles in different projects: for this reason it shall be considered and managed by the module. The *Roles* and *Role* tables are responsible for storing such information.

4.3.3 Ad-Hoc collaboration Tool

This section presents the Ad-hoc Collaboration Tool, a module that supports on the fly creation of virtual team and collaboration among team members, i.e. virtual meeting facilities. Selected members are part of the teams generated using Human Competencies Evaluation tools, exactly like in Mediated Collaboration. The main idea is to provide a project manager with a tool for sharing agendas between suitable members of the virtual team, selecting them in accordance with their competencies and availabilities and then performing a collaborative real time session, where documents or decision can be promptly taken and implemented.

This module offers three main features:

1. Members selection for virtual team constitution;
2. Sharing Agenda;
3. Instant messaging or video conference set up.

The first item has been already described in section 4.2. In particular members are selected from the selection of required competencies taken from the ontology. Users are then ranked in a list according to the matching index provided by either the self or external evaluations. Then the project manager can select the best candidates and propose them a set of feasible date for the virtual meeting. After that the meeting occurs and the generated knowledge is protected thanks (once again) to the usage of the K-IPR tool.

5   SOCIAL DIMENSION IN ECOLEAD ACP

5.1   Chat

A chat server and client are included in the ACP. Members can join chat rooms on any topic at any time, inviting participants and keeping records of the conversation. The chat server also stores the log files generated during collaborative sessions. The log file is parsed by the K-IPR tool in order to recognize and protect the knowledge generated in collaborative chat sessions. The following figure shows an example of chat session.

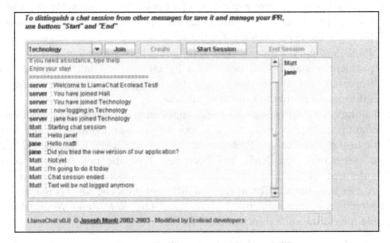

Figure 7: Chat session in the ACP

5.2 Who's online?

A specific page is dedicated to display online users. In this way any professional can check who is online and view the details. The system provides also the possibility to start an instant messaging session with the online users.

Currently Online Users		
UserName	**Location**	**Login time**
jane	Viewing home page	20/12/2007 12.17.41
ben	Using chat	20/12/2007 12.23.00
mark	Managing documents and Knowledge IPR	20/12/2007 12.23.21

Figure 8: Who's online panel

5.3 Wiki

A wiki system is provided in order to create a unique type of website, specifically one which allows anyone visiting the site to add, remove and edit all content, quickly and easily, without the need for registration. This makes it particularly well suited for collaborative writing. Furthermore, each PVC member is provided by default with a personal page on the wiki, which is read-only for the other members. This page can be used also as a personal presentation as well as a blog.

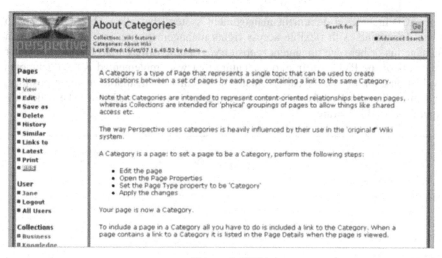

Figure 9: Wiki

5.4 Forum

A forum system is included; users can create new topics or join existing ones. The forum is integrated with the other collaboration tools and workflows.

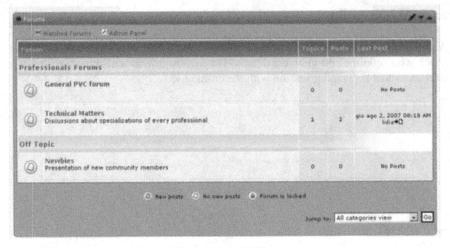

Figure 10: ACP Forum

6   KNOWLEDGE DIMENSION IN ECOLEAD ACP

6.1   Document management

The ACP includes a document management system that allows PVC members to share documents with flexible access rights management, i.e. any professional can manage his or her own document repository, granting different access leves to other members of the PVC. An important feature that was implemented is the documents evaluation ranking. Users can evaluate the documents available in the repository, and this affects the crediting system for the user who uploaded it. The following figure shows this feature.

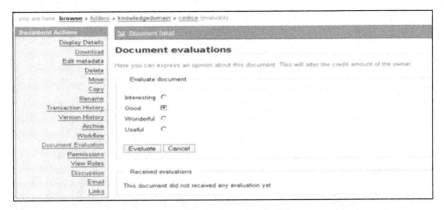

Figure 11: Ranking values loaded from ontology

Another significant feature is the integration of the document management system with the competencies ontology as well as the collaborative problem-solving tools.

In fact the generated knowledge of the business space is automatically organised in dedicated folders of the knowledge repository, by applying users' rights set during the execution of a collaborative session. This is an advanced feature which exploits K-IPR in an automatic and efficient way.

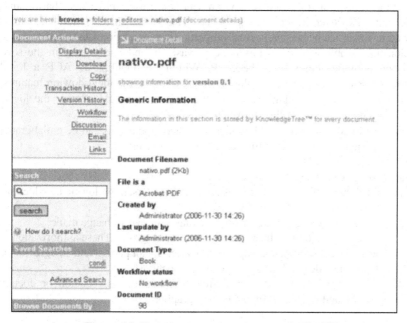

Figure 12: Document manages automatically IPR

Documents are stored in folders, where any user can set also the access rights and permissions (see figure below).

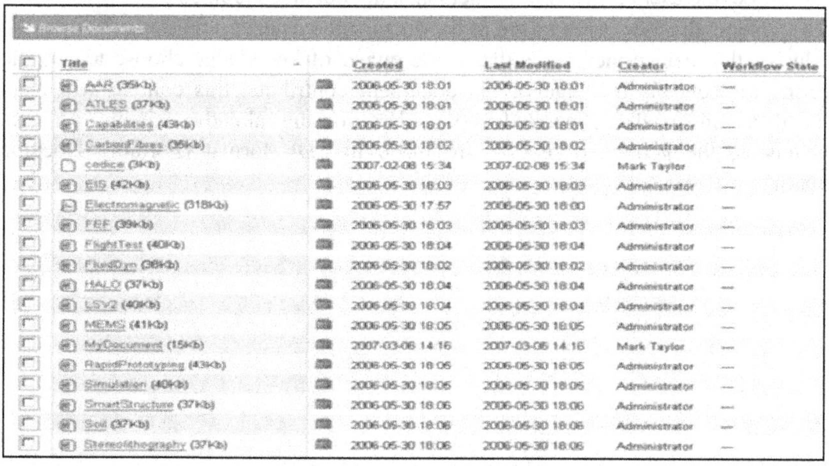

Figure 13: Knowledge repository

6.2   K-IPR protection

One of the goals of a collaborative environment is to foster knowledge sharing among participants. However, while knowledge is meant to be shared, its owner shall be allowed to retain his or her intellectual property rights. It emerges the need for an ICT solution that is able to address this issue pervasively and horizontally in the several tools and activities composing the ACP. Within the ECOLEAD ACP a K- IPR (Gusmeroli, Ratti, Serina 2007) a solution was developed with the following features:

- An automatic tracking activity which will capture and manage the log files coming from the collaborative chat sessions, and
- An intelligent web based application where documents can be collaboratively created and at the same time user rights are preserved.

The approach is based on four main phases:

1. Tracking: which tracks for instance the conversations log or the documents changes;
2. Owning: to identify the owner of messages, or every change made;
3. Accessing: to define the access rights of every group. These authorizations can be set on each single message by its owner, by all participants in agreement, or they can be decided for every document sections.
4. Protecting: to generate a group-related report of conversation or document with related watermarking and cryptography.

Regarding to Accessing phase, four kind of authorization can be set:

- Read: the user can download the knowledge with no restrictions;
- NoCopy: the user can download an encrypted version of knowledge, with no faculty of copy and print;
- See: the user can view only metadata, not document content;
- None: the user is not aware of the document existence.

One of the main principles is that if the owner of knowledge choose to not allow someone to view his message or his document contribute, this content will not be included at all in the generated report. For reusing already existing protection mechanisms, the generated reports are made in PDF format (Portable Document Format).

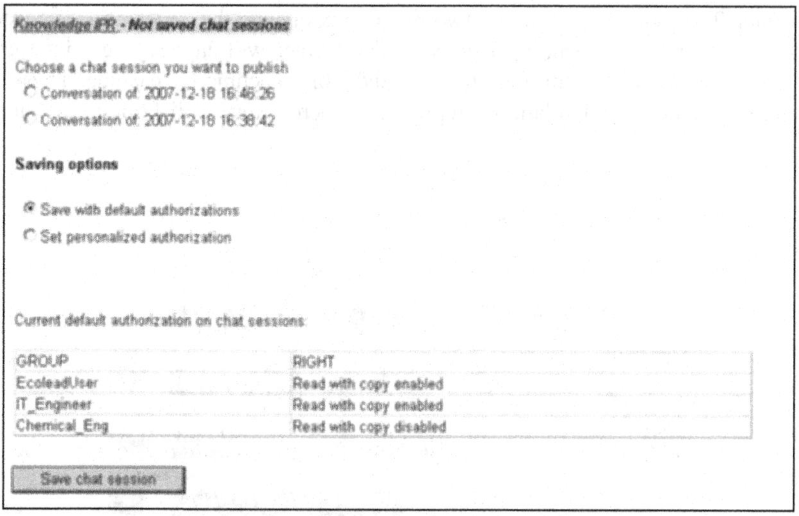

Figure 14: Chat session K-IPR protection

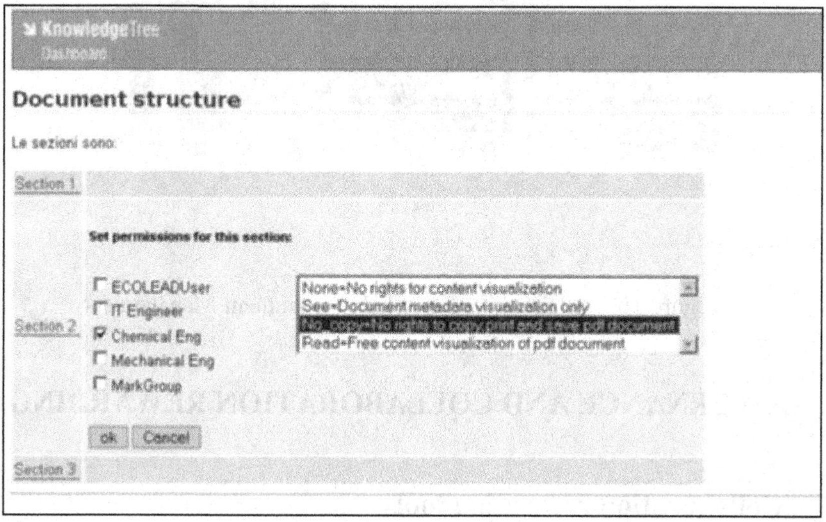

Figure 15: Documents K-IPR protection

IPR has to work as a real "metadata bag" which is associated to a document, granting us to track both the document history and the users who have contributed to its generation and realization, and making them real owners for the provided contents. For this reason, an XML metamodel has been proposed. It reproduces the document structure and allows the Professional Virtual Community technological tools to gain the biggest number of functional information for intellectual property management.

This metamodel is characterized by a versioning organization; in turn, each version embodies a section organization. Each section contains those interesting intellectual property elements which are distinctive for a particular document type. For example, "Track changes", comments, images and text are proper to Microsoft Word processing documents. The module is made by two main components: the Tracking Log System, and the Intelligent Document Management. The former will capture every interaction from users to machines, from users to users and from machine to machine. These will be stored in a dedicated relational repository where every collaborative session is tracked by users.

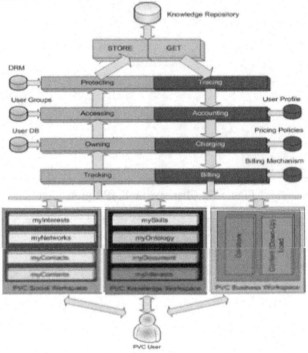

Figure 16: Collaborative Knowledge Document Management

7   GOVERNANCE AND COLLABORATION REWARDING

7.1   Collaboration rewarding tools

The crediting mechanism is important for defining the level of collaboration among PVC members. Credits may be earned either from active participation in collaborative activities as well as from peer based evaluations. In fact, any user can provide his or her evaluation of other users' behavior in the PVC. The system keeps track of this feedback and prevents incorrect usage by the member (the administrator can check at any time the evaluation process). The PVC administrator can also give credits to members adding also a comment on the evaluation.

Two main functionalities are provided by the Collaboration Rewarding tool: to assign credits to other users, and to check the received evaluations. Any user can at any time check how her credit portfolio is proceeding and see the evaluations she has received. A user can see the list of credits, and these can be managed at three separate levels:

- *Individual*: evaluation and credits are assigned to a single user;
- *PVC*: evaluations and credits can be managed at overall PVC level;
- *Virtual Team*: evaluations and credits can be provided as an output of Virtual Team collaboration.

The user can check his current rank of credits using the same instruments available to the PVC administrator and described below in Section 7.2: data extracted from the database are filtered and shown in graphical way.

Another feature is the detailed list of the activities which gained credit to the user, in order to have a diary of performed collaborations, as shown in the picture below. Like every ACP rewarding tool, information can be filtered by workspace and time.

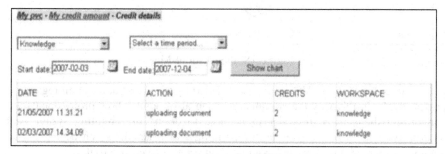

Figure 17: Credit details

7.2 Governance

The governance module is a tool that allows the PVC administrator to monitor the PVC status and evolution. It is responsible for the management of credits in the three dimensions: social, knowledge and business. Moreover this module provides a set of indicators for controlling the global behavior of the PVC, e.g. finding the more collaborative professionals, or which competencies are most requested but not present in any professional. This tool is an important module for the PVC administrator: by using such features it can monitor the PVC activities and compare the actual behavior with the expected one. In the following sections the major functionalities are reported.

7.2.1 The Commu-Meter

The most intuitive way for controlling PVC current trend is by checking the so called *Commu-Meter*. This tool is a graphical representation of the three PVC dimensions (Social, Knowledge and Business), and is shown in the picture below. It is a dynamic representation of the Chromo-framework proposed in (Bifulco and Santoro, 2005).

When the central ball in the Commu-Meter visualization is dragged, the tool suggests what actions shall be pursued in order to shift the PVC behavior towards the desired direction. The suggested actions can increase credits in one or more of the three dimensions.

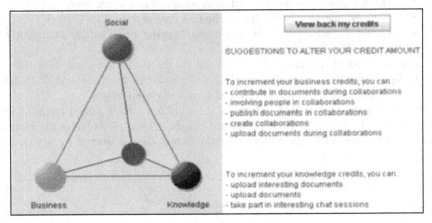

Figure 18: the Commu-Meter

The overall value of PVC credits is provided by the aggregation of all registered professionals: in this way the administrator can also monitor how professionals are committing themselves. In order to be able to define the crediting system, the module provides a set of features for defining which activities can be monitored automatically by the system, and associates due credits to each activity.

7.2.2   *Credits trends monitor*

The ACP also includes another governance tool to monitor credit trends in the PVC. This tool allows several graphical representations, e.g. pie or bar of different timeframes (last week, last month, or any given range).

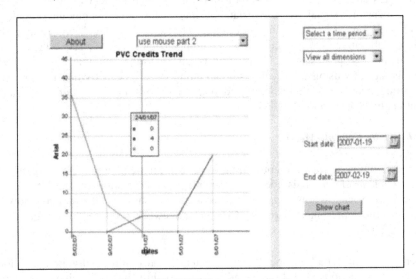

Figure 19: PVC Governance Indicators

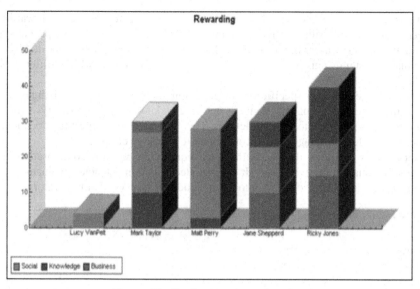

Figure 20: Credits bar chart visualisation

7.2.3 Competencies searches report

Another useful feature for the PVC administrator is the ranked report of competencies requested when building a team.

Collaboration rewarding - Competencies search

Here you can see how many times competencies have been requested from users in the process of virtual team creation. Click on each single competency for details.

Competency	Searched Times	Found
E-mail_application	24	lidia
Internet_browsing	10	mark
Basic_IT	3	halonen
Implement	3	lidia
XSL	3	not found

Figure 21: Competencies searches report

This allows the PVC administrator to monitor which skills are most required by members and act in consequence, for example by refining the ontology corresponding to the most required competencies, as well as seeking new PVC members providing the required skills. This reporting feature is therefore a valuable tool for orienting the growth of the PVC.

7.3 Ontology management

By using the integrated ontology management tool, PVC Administrator defines three ontologies: social, knowledge and competencies. The ontology management system allows to define and to associate crediting mechanism to concepts defined in the ontology. These credits will be used by the system for applying rewarding mechanism during collaborative sessions. In this way any user can provide an evaluation of other users based on the collaboration experience and supported by an automatic system. This is the evaluation of social features, which differ from technical competencies.

Knowledge ontology specifies knowledge domain of PVC, and this is integrated with the document management system: the knowledge repository reflects (automatically) the ontology structure. This is done by ordering documents according to their metatags, which correspond to ontology classes.

Competencies ontology defines both skills required to perform collaboration and range of evaluation for every skill. It is integrated with competencies evaluation tool and automatically updated when ontology is modified by PVC Administrator.

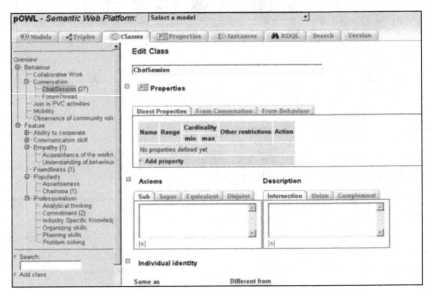

Figure 22: Ontology definition

8   ACP IMPLEMENTATION AND DEPLOYMENT

8.1   Portal framework

The ACP platform is a portal application, and every module is run inside a portlet complaint to the standard for Java Portlets JSR-168 (Sun Microsystems, 2003). This approach provides the required flexibility to integrate existing PVC-dedicated tools and to add new functionalities under the same environment in future developments. The main portal server features are the deployment of applications and the user management. Since the ACP was designed as a SOA, common features are accessible by any module thanks to the usage of web services. For instance, a web service is dedicated to the synchronization of central users data with single applications data.

An integrated PVC platform, composed by portal server and web services, offers single sign on, so that, the user logs in just once in the portal, and then accesses individual tools without the need for another sign on. A shared token carries the user identity: in this way every tool is able to recognize the user and to show his or her data. Information is collected and shared pervasively among components: for example, collaboration credits are gained acting in different environment but their total amount is visible in governance and rewarding tools, or built teams starting from competencies evaluation are directly usable in problem solving environment. Integrated functionalities include business tools in order to implement an environment covering all aspects of a PVC: social, knowledge and business.

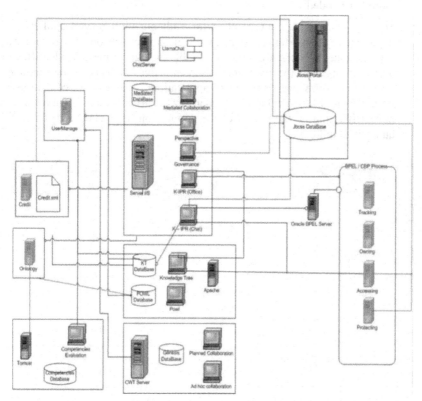

Figure 23: ACP deployment

The ACP portal was deployed in two portal servers: JBoss and Liferay. Both are Java-based open source portal servers, and they were to supply the PVC functionalities under the JSR-168 portlet standard. The reference architecture does not change in the two versions: thanks to their flexibility, it was possible to adapt all modules to another platform with minimal changes.

Liferay was installed and configured as an alternative to JBoss mainly for following reasons:

- Flexibility: whilst JBoss hosts just one portlet per page, Liferay can host several portlets for different purposes. In the current release, one portlet is visible by default, and others can be added by the user according to specific authorizations. A number of pre-built portlets is provided by default in Liferay, e.g. calendar and RSS feed aggregator.

- User Interface: portlets dimensions are automatically adapted to match different browsers and monitor resolutions. Graphic themes are interchangeable and workspace is larger.

- Permissions managements: the portal administrator can set different permissions on portlets (basically change and view) with a simple graphic interface, whereas in JBoss the portlet visualization and management is more hard-coded.

- Security management: a CAS (Central Authentication Server) application is deployed in the portal, in order to permit single-sign on in a secure way. This is done by storing a session variable at logon time that identifies the user, for instance the username ("screen name" in Liferay terminology). This variable is shared between all applications, and does not contain user's permissions, but only identity: when access to a module contained in a portlet is required, the portlet or the application itself checks if the user is authorized to log in.

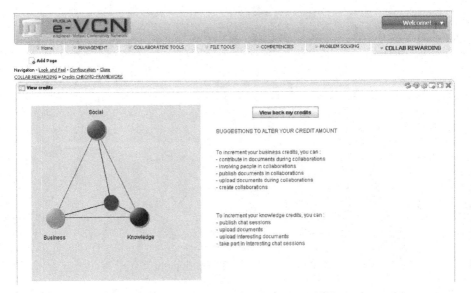

Figure 24: The ACP deployed in LifeRay

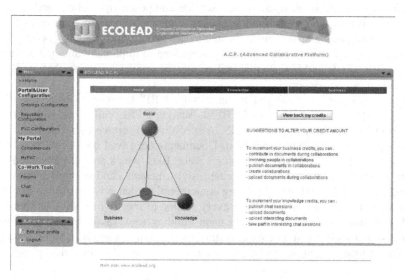

Figure 25: The ACP deployed in JBoss

8.2 Individual modules

All ACP integrated modules originate either from customised open source tools or from prototypes developed by the ECOLEAD project.

The document management system is based on Knowledge Tree, designed for teams and small and medium-sized organizations. It provides, besides an extensive and community supported documentation, a modular and well commented source code, with specific APIs to develop plug-ins. The following plug-ins were developed for the ACP:

- documents evaluation;
- authorization requesting;
- a plug-in to distinguish behavior of knowledge-dedicated folder and collaborations folder;
- permissions management on single documents (by default it is on folders only).

The ontology management system is based on Powl, which permits the PVC Administrator to model ontologies using an intuitive web editor. Ontologies are saved in a mySQL database and after ripped in a single OWL file. OWL (Ontology web language) is the w3c recommended language to specify ontologies; more precisely, this file is in OWL-DL standard, so named due to its correspondence with description logics. Powl was customized in order to save automatically the OWL file of each ontology: in this way a dedicated web service can pick it from the repository and let other ACP modules to access to it, for example to render competencies tree for evaluations, or team building.

Both Knowledge Tree and Powl are written in PHP, run on Apache server and store data in a mySQL database, hence their deployment is light and simple.

The chat server is an open source service composed by a client and a server developed in java language applying SocketConnection libraries. The server listens on a specific port, and the client is integrated into a user-friendly applet that is rendering the chat rooms. Modifications were done to implement automatic logging of messages and to add buttons that isolate specific conversations, so that the K-IPR mechanism can be applied.

The K-IPR tool is deployed as an extended BPEL process (using the iBPM service), and it runs under Oracle BPEL server. BPEL calls four web services written in c# language, running on IIS. A specific web service uses OpenOffice for sections tracking and PDF generation. Documents are saved by OpenOffice in the form of compressed archives containing several files, which are then extracted with 7-Zip. There is a dedicated file for content, style, metadata and settings: sections are distinguished and identified by parsing content.xml so that it is possible to render in the web interface of Knowledge Tree every section to specify its authorizations.

The competencies evaluation and team building tool was internally developed, since it is a completely new feature. It runs under a Tomcat server, it stores data in a mySQL database, and it exchanges data with other ACP modules using web services.

Rewarding, governance and problem solving tools were developed from scratch in C#. A collection of web services takes care of tracking credits matured in any collaborative workspace, and storing business documents concerning individual collaborations in the document repository.

8.3   Interactions with ICT-I services

ICT Infrastructure (ICT-I), described in Part 5 of this book, is a collection of services developed within the ECOLEAD project. Those services support the ACP as well as several other applications, and they are designed following a Service Oriented Architecture (SOA) approach. They are instantiated as web services and exploit existing tools adapted to fit ECOLEAD purposes. The collection of services is organized in Horizontal services and Basic services. Basic services are domain-independent services that are used mainly by other services. They represent the core of the ICT-I, and include the framework for service discovery, selection and orchestration, as well as security. Horizontal Services are higher level services that support the requirements of several ECOLEAD vertical applications (e.g. VOM, VBE and ACP). The ACP in particular exploits ICT-I services for the the K-IPR configuration and execution and for user sign on.

The K-IPR horizontal service automates the process of defining and executing intellectual property mechanisms. The PVC administrator can access the horizontal service and use it for modeling the whole process, in terms of configuring the manual and automatic activities. The generated process will be registered through the invocation of the registry service. After this configuration activity, the execution of the horizontal service will occur during every collaborative session, for instance while uploading a document inside the PVC ACP knowledge repository. This will automatically perform the execution of the modeled business process, inside the PVC portal. This integration is the simplest one because of the nature of this horizontal service. This service is used as a stand-alone tool for modeling extended business processes. It is encapsulated in a portlet included in the ACP portal server as ACP governance functionality; the portlet then takes care of downloading the Java application. After having configured and modeled the service, this is automatically registered as a web service in the ICT-I registry.

The second use case of ICT-I services usage in ACP regards security, and access control in particular. Security is guaranteed by the DRACO Security Framework developed in ECOLEAD and described in Chapter 5.2 The ACP login page is automatically redirected to the user management section of the DRACO console, where all the PVC users are registered. After that, any application or module loaded by a user in the ACP will be automatically monitored and authorized by the security platform. Since Security Framework mechanism works with public key cryptography, a private key and its associated certificate must be generated and installed (e.g. with openSSL). Tomcat is configured to use the private key to encrypt outgoing data and the public key to decrypt incoming data. The application is then registered in the DRACO Console, along with the public key and its users and passwords. As an example, when a PVC member enters the ACP address in the browser she is asked to accept the ECOLEAD security certificate, and upon acceptance the browser is automatically redirected to the DRACO console login page. If the user is recognized as authorized to access the ACP portal, her browser is automatically redirected to the PVC home page.

9 CONCLUSIONS

In this chapter we focused on the identification of the innovative and missing aspects of existing collaborative solutions, and we explained how this analysis inspired the development of a novel collaboration platform in the ECOLEAD project. The core idea underlying Professional Virtual Communities collaboration support is to integrate a wide range of collaboration functionality to offer users a single, unified solution in which information can be easily shared between the various collaboration components. The Advanced Collaboration Platform we introduced follows this approach by integrating Business, Knowledge and Social oriented tools in a unified environment, and provides a real innovation in the field of Professional Virtual Communities. Preliminary results and the feedback from end users demonstrations activities have shown a real need for a novel ICT solution for collaboration such as our ACP.

To conclude this chapter we wish to comment on our experience in the ACP evaluation. As stated before a major challenge for any solution aimed at collaborative working is the disciplined adoption by the end user. The potential of PVC collaboration can only be fully leveraged if users are willing to invest a small individual overhead in using the tools appropriately. In order to capture the user' interest and to motivate him or her to adopt a collaborative solution such as the ACP it is of paramount importance that the benefits *for the user* (and not only for the organisation) are clearly stated. Furthermore, the user should be properly trained to use the ACP, not only by a strictly ICT oriented standpoint. In other words, the user should be taught how to map his or her use cases onto the corresponding processes in the ACP. This is necessary because the user cannot be expected to be familiar with research in the PVC domain, and with the formalisation of several different collaboration modalities. In our experience once the user has discovered the potential benefits and has become familiar with the processes, he or she becomes keener on adopting the collaboration tools, and invites his or her colleagues to do the same, igniting a virtuous circle that allows the PVC to grow.

At an organisation level the benefits of adopting the ACP are easy to recognise. Fostering the collaboration among members improves the productivity of the community and the capability to address business opportunities. Boosting knowledge circulation improves the global know-how of the community as a whole and attracts members with valuable competencies. Promoting social interaction further supports collaboration and knowledge sharing, besides making life and work in the PVC an attractive experience.

Acknowledgments. This work was funded in part by the European Commission through the ECOLEAD project.

10 REFERENCES

Biasci, F., Bifulco, A., Fantoni, G., Santoro, R. (2006), Collaborative problem solving in design methods: foundation elements for an integrated approach. In Proceedings of the 12th International Conference on Concurrent Enterprising (ICE 2006), Milan, 26-28 June 2006.

Bifulco, A.; Santoro, R. (2005). A conceptual framework for Professional Virtual Communities, in Proceedings of PRO-VE'05 - Collaborative Networks and their Breeding Environments, Springer, pp. 417-424, Valencia, Spain, 26-28 Sep 2005.

Camarinha-Matos, L. M.; Afsarmanesh, H.; Ollus, M. (2005). ECOLEAD: A holistic approach to creation and management of dynamic virtual organizations, in Proceedings of PRO-VE'05 – Collaborative Networks and their Breeding Environments, Springer, pp. 3-16, Valencia, Spain, 26-28 Sep 2005. ´

Camarinha-Matos, L. M.; Afsarmanesh, H. (2007). A comprehensive modeling framework for collaborative networked organizations, Journal of Intelligent Manufacturing, Volume 18, Number 5 / October, 2007, pp 527-615.

Camarinha-Matos, L. M.; Afsarmanesh, H. (2005). Collaborative networks: A new scientific discipline, L.M. Camarinha-Matos, H. Afsarmanesh, J. Intelligent Manufacturing, vol. 16, N° 4-5, pp439-452, ISSN: 0956-5515 , 2005.

Gusmeroli S., Roberto Ratti, Marco Serina. A Knowledge IPR Tool. In Proceedings of the 13th International Conference on Concurrent Enterprising (ICE 2007). Sophia-Antipolis, France, 4-6 June 2007.

Gusmeroli, S.; Ratti R. An Interactive User-centered Business Process Management Services. In Proceedings of eChallenges Conference 2007. Den Hague, The Netherlands, 24-26 October 2007.

Gusmeroli S., Ratti R, Serina M.. A Knowledge IPR Tool. In Proceedings of eChallenges Ratti 2007. Den Hague, The Netherlands, 24-26 October 2007.

Ollus, M.; Approaches and Solutions Supporting Collaboration in Networks. International Cluster Conference: Patterns of Clusters Evolution, Venice, 18-19 January 2007.

Sun Microsystems. Introduction to JSR 168—The Java Portlet Specification. White paper, 2003.

PART 5

ICT INFRASTRUCTURES

ADVANCED COLLABORATIVE BUSINESS ICT INFRASTRUCTURES

Ricardo J. Rabelo

Federal University of Santa Catarina, BRAZIL, rabelo@das.ufsc.br

GSIGMA – Intelligent Manufacturing Systems Group, Department of Automation and Systems

This paper points out the need of advanced collaborative business ICT infrastructures (CBI) for CNOs, the requirements for the development of CBIs, and the technologies and trends considering CNO issues. The CBI devised in the ECOLEAD Project is also presented, showing how most of these requirements and emergent ICTs have been incorporated in it. This CBI – called *ICT-I* – is a distributed, open and security-embedded infrastructure, and it relies on the service oriented architecture paradigm. Its services are to be used under the on demand and pay-per-use models. The assessment of ICT-I, some conclusions and challenges are presented in the end.

1. INTRODUCTION

The adoption of the Collaborative Networks Organizations (CNO) paradigm by organizations has been imposing an increasing and tremendous pressure on the companies´ competitive matrix, directly affecting their market positioning in terms of general quality, diversity and innovation of processes and products, prices, delivery dates, and level of relationship with suppliers and customers.

Nevertheless, in order to support the CNO concept realization, three essential pre-conditions are necessary to exist. The first one is that it requires *collaboration* among involved partners at a level far beyond sending e-mail messages. The second one is the existence of *trust*, considering that partners shall rely on each other (at variable levels). The third pre-condition is that all (or most of) the activities carried out within a CNO should be made via computer networks, i.e. *digital transactions* should be the routine, and not an exception.

Although the expression "working collaboratively" has been largely used by people and several authors, practice shows, however, that embedding this into the companies' daily business life impose drastic changes at all of their levels. Part of the changes is related to the difficulties related the *collaborative business infrastructures* (CBI) that are requested to support those pre-conditions.

In essence, a CBI for CNOs should be transparent, enabling networked organizations to agilely define and set up relations with other organizations seamlessly, and to be adaptive according to the business environment conditions and current organizations' autonomy levels (Camarinha-Matos and Afsarmanesh, 2004). This means having a CBI where businesses and collaboration can be accomplished more effectively, agilely, flexibly and trustworthily. Developing such kind of infrastructure is a key step towards creating an organization culture where collaboration can become part of the process and not only an option of work. More than this, it can help in making managers indeed confident and enthusiastic to use it in the support of their daily networked businesses as long as they realize the value added of such support.

Another fundamental facet about this issue is related to the different natures and sizes of the companies that typically are members of CNOs. In Europe, for example, more than 98% of them are SMEs[1]. As such, most of them have enormous difficulties to have access to the main products of the market as they require high investment in supporting software, hardware and IT experts.

Despite the complexity the development of such kind of CBI represents, the fact is that current solutions neither attend these requirements at all nor offer adequate support to CNO-related business processes. Moreover, they use to be complex to deploy and to use, they require powerful computing environments, they are usually expensive and not open, they require additional packages of security, and they are offered as huge packages of software no matter how much of this will be used. In other words, they preponderantly look to large companies and not to SMEs too.

This is the essential motivation of this paper, which presents the *concepts* of the CBI devised in the ECOLEAD project to cope with these requirements, and which can be affordable to SMEs. This paper is organized as follows. Chapter 1 highlights the need of CBIs for CNO, and presents requirements for that as well as some obstacles towards the development of advanced CBIs. Chapter 2 presents ICTs (Information and Communication Technologies) that have been currently used to support such requirements, and trends and more advanced ICTs that can be applied in the development of advanced CBIs. Chapters 3 and 4 present the developed CBI, which is called *Plug and Play Horizontal ICT Infrastructure*, or simply *ICT-I*. Chapter 5 gives a general overview of the security framework. Chapter 6 provides an analysis of ICT-I, pointing out its features, innovative aspects and limitations. Chapter 7 gives a final overview of the developed ICT-I.

While this chapter introduces the ICT-I from the conceptual point of view, next book chapter describes its implementation, describing the used ICTs and the developed services.

1.1 Functional Requirements for Advanced CBI

CNOs have a different sort of business processes that is not handled by B2B and EIA solutions. Actually, CNO processes complement the processes managed by such solutions. CNO processes use to be interactive/user-centric, asynchronous and not necessarily well structured or defined a priori. The focus is on flexibility and adaptability rather than on execution efficiency. Figure 1 lists just some CNO-related processes (at application level) involved in the life cycle of a CNO of type Virtual Organization (VO), which should then be supported by CBIs.

In order to support such high-level processes at infrastructure level, it can be observed that a CBI for CNOs is much more than supporting the execution of groupware facilities. In fact, a CBI for CNOs should fundamentally provide functionalities associated to five types of elements (Figure 2), enabling:

- *people* to collaborate and negotiate;
- *systems / services* to execute and adapt;
- *knowledge and information* (at *all* levels) to be exchanged and retrieved;
- *computing and human resources* to be discovered and shared;

- *processes* to be interconnected and synchronized.

VO Creation	VO Operation & Evolution	VO Dissolution
• Business Opportunity characterization • Selection of performance indicators • Partner Search • Partner Selection • Negotiation & Risk Analysis • E-Contracting • VO Planning	• VO Launching • VO operational governance • Dynamic VO management • VO performance measurement • Business Process supervision • Collaborative decision-making • VO simulation	• VO inheritance • Partners assessment • IPR Management • Checking contract • Security access cancellation • Legal issues • VBE members rewarding

VO lifecycle

Figure 1 – Example of CNO-related collaborative processes

Security and interoperability are two technological elements that should permeate the CBI, whereas business models can be applied upon the CBI as long as services and resources in general are going to be accessed and also made available to other CNOs' members. Managing this with high efficiency, cleverness and transparency is the challenge to be reached by advanced CBIs.

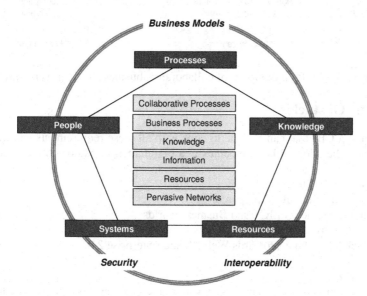

Figure 2 – Requirements for Advanced Collaborative Business Infrastructures

1.2 Technological Requirements for Advanced CBI

A number of business models and ICTs have recently been emerged, and they are being used by some companies already. They represent a clear trend and its impact is tremendous on the way systems have been designed by now. Their consideration in the design of advanced CBIs is of paramount importance as they represent technologies that will increasingly be incorporated into the next generation of eco-systems, which are implemented in a diversity of platforms, equipments and ubiquitous devices.

Figure 3 resumes the characterization of past values and future values in terms of CBIs for CNOs, changing the focus from processing efficiency and full automation, to collaboration flexibility and human intervention. This reflects a scenario where composable and autonomous services of software – deployed in several repositories and seen as utilities – can act with cleverness and flexibility to solve problems and to adapt themselves to changes in the business environment, having the human being as the centre of actions and decisions.

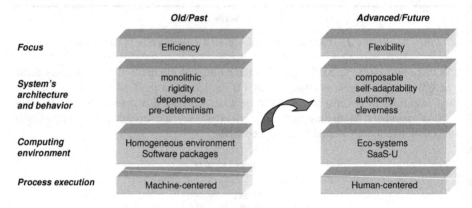

Figure 3 – Shift on the focus of collaborative business ICT infrastructures

1.3 Some Obstacles

Developing a CBI that can be able to cope with all these requirements and that can immediately be adopted by companies is a big challenge. Major obstacles for that involve:
- short ICT life cycle;
- level of companies' preparedness;
- non-alignment of ICT and Business worlds;
- lack of trustworthy environments;
- lack of roadmaps towards Web 2.0 and Enterprise 2.0.

Short ICT life cycle
The fast evolution of ICT technologies with reduced life cycles and the need to cope with technologies with different life cycles and at different stages of the corresponding life cycle has introduced enormous difficulties for developing cost-effective and long-life collaborative tools, especially regarding that in CNO systems of diverse companies should interoperate. However, if on one hand ICT usage is a key enabler element to enhance competitiveness, on the other hand they bring another sort of problems that should be permanently managed by SMEs, which would be difficult regarding their lack of resources and IT skills. Therefore, the project of advanced CBIs should take this into account.

Level of companies' preparedness
A significative underlying motivation of CNO is based on the notion that SMEs can largely benefit from this specially when belonging to strategic alliances like VBE

(Virtual Organizational Breeding Environment (Hamideh and Camarinha-Matos, 2005) and VE (Virtual Enterprise (Goranson, 1999). However, reaching the level of preparedness to indeed work in a CNO is a long and hard way. Hamideh et al., 2004) have depicted the benefits to work collaboratively but also the impact of this in terms of preparedness. The problem is that SMEs have already so many difficulties to have their systems organized, integrated and managed, and expanding this at the inter-enterprise level too is even more complex and demands still more resources and time. Therefore, the project of advanced CBIs should mitigate the usual required efforts spent on this preparedness, namely in terms of systems interoperability and customizations, and of training.

Non-alignment of ICT and Business worlds

A usual complaint from companies and managers about ICTs is that most of them are not only too complex, but they are far from considering the requirements of real business processes. Part of this is caused because ICT people and business people use to work totally separated, leaving the required adaptations and integrations up to software-houses and consultants.

Considering the increasing investments spent with ICT solutions, the fact is that most of SMEs get lost in managing this problem, meaning that they don't know at which extent which ICTs are adding value to businesses nor the medium and long term consequences of their adoption. It can be seen a paradox, but if on one hand ICT is seen as part of the solution to leverage companies competitiveness, on the other hand they face difficulties to find out the most suitable ICTs for them. Actually, the main underlying challenge related to this is to leave managers enthusiastic with ICT in a way they can better reason about how it can bring innovations to their businesses.

It is however important to mention that a new generation of managers is coming, formed by people who were born with Internet and for whom ICT is a routine and not an issue to be feared. They tend to create an additional "entropy wave" to business as they are usually more open-minded and so can introduce deep changes in the traditional way of doing business and so on how business processes should be conducted. This reinforces the need for very flexible and easy-to-use ICT solutions.

Lack of trustworthy environments

Trust building is a cornerstone issue in CNO. When this is to be handled at infrastructure level, it comprises both security and information access. Collaboration should be safe, and authorized partners should only have access to pertinent information that is effectively required for every particular and current business (Mezgar, 2006). This means that there is a life cycle for information access and this should be controlled on the fly, opening the access to the exact and required information for each business as long as transactions are being carried out. All this should be done safely, supported by AAA (*Authorization, Authentication and Accounting*) mechanisms. This is however very much complex to provide, and this lack can mitigate a more intensive and faster adoption of the CNO paradigm by companies. In spite of the existence of several security methods and approaches, there is no solution yet for that envisaged scenario. The security framework developed in ECOLEAD (see Chapter 5) represents an important contribution towards this.

Lack of roadmaps towards Web 2.0 and Enterprise 2.0
Web 2.0 and *Enterprise 2.0* are two relevant movements that have arisen "around" companies and that will impact them deeply, directly or indirectly. Web 2.0 is the business shift in the computer industry caused by the move to the Internet as platform. The idea of Web 2.0 can also relate to a transition of some websites from isolated information silos to interlinked computing platforms that function like locally-available software in the perception of the user. Web 2.0 also includes a social element where users generate and distribute content, often with freedom to share and re-use. In the context of a CBI for CNOs, this imposes important requirements in terms of knowledge search and retrieval as long as the sharing of knowledge and best practices among partners is one of the most powerful evolving mechanisms of a CNO.

Enterprise 2.0 is the general term for the technologies and business practices that liberate the workforce from the constraints of legacy communication and productivity tools like email. It provides business managers with access to the right information at the right time through a web of inter-connected applications, services and devices. Enterprise 2.0 makes accessible the collective intelligence of many, translating to a huge competitive advantage in the form of increased innovation, productivity and agility. Transparency, ubiquity, support for mobility, flexibility, information and knowledge sharing, evolving information systems and folksonomies are features that should be incorporated in advanced systems (Mcafee, 2006).

The problem is that these technologies have been soundly announced as being the future of the companies but there is not any roadmap that helps SMEs to be prepared for that and to benefit from that. Actually, only few companies are able to realize their impact and requirements for their adoption. Advanced CBI for CNOs must hide all this, endowing managers and SMEs with an environment where services, information and knowledge sharing, access and adaptations can be made transparently, seamlessly, intelligently, and in a secure manner.

2. MAIN CONCEPTS AND APPROACHES

This chapter aims at presenting the most important approaches and technologies to deal with the requirements of CBIs for CNOs stressed in chapter 1. It starts mentioning the most important technologies currently being applied, passing by a description about the most relevant trends, and it ends with an explanation of advanced ICTs that can support these trends. In general, each ICT is presented, its basic weaknesses are pointed out, and its usage in a CBI for CNO is identified.

2.1 Current Approaches

Computer Supported Cooperative Work
Computer supported tools for cooperation/collaboration is not a new subject. Since 90ths CSCW (*Computer Supported Cooperative Work*) tools has been a very prominent area providing many tools, both commercial suites and free software packages easily downloaded from Internet. CSCW tools' scope varies quite a lot

from one to another. Some tools only offer specific groupware functionalities whereas others can even treat processes and human interaction in an integrated environment. Despite CSCW advantages, the problem is that this class of systems only gives support for human interaction, when advanced CBI requires much more than this (as already explained).

Workflow systems

Workflow systems are another class of technology that has been growing very much in acceptance by companies nowadays. It is a powerful approach as it allows a tight coordination of flow of activities and can support detailed customizations about the processes to be supervised and executed. They can cover both intra-enterprise and inter-enterprise business processes, besides having capabilities to interact with legacy applications (Chen and Hsu, 2001). Despite its potentialities, the problem is that it works quite well with pre-defined flows of activities associated to each business process. In a CNO scenario, a much higher level of flexibility is necessary during the execution of processes as several collaborative processes are, *per se*, non-structured and/or can't be defined *a priori*. Another drawback is their limitation to work with highly interactive and user-centric approaches, as they were mainly conceived to automate the execution of pre-defined business processes.

Enterprise Application Integration

Although businesses among different companies are generally treated at high-level, it does not mean that "classical" issues are no longer necessary to be dealt with. One of the most relevant issues from the ICT perspective is the access to legacy or corporate systems. In general, these are the systems within which most of the information that flow in the collaborative and B2B transactions comes from. No matter the underlying ICTs used to support this, this issue has been tackled in the scope of the EAI (*Enterprise Application Integration*) area.

EAI can be used for data integration from multiple systems; for process integration in a way to link business processes across applications; for vendor independence in the sense of facilitating the replacement of applications without the need of re-implementing the business rules; and for common front-end of clusters of applications (Lee et al., 2003). In spite of that, current solutions present some limitations when applied to a CNO scenario. One of the major problems is that CNOs require a CBI that supports dynamic and temporary mapping of the information that has to be accessed in every source, in every partners´ database and/or legacy system, for every different business. This also means to manage the fact that each of those sources usually has different formats, semantics, and partners are not necessary previously known to each other. This is very complex as it requires an optimum but flexible design and integration of high-level inter-enterprise business/collaboration processes with (individual) low-level intra-enterprise business/manufacturing processes.

"My" System

Looking at SMEs and the problem of solutions´ customization, the *"my system"* approach is very relevant nowadays. One of the most known cases is *mySAP*[2]. It corresponds to light versions of large packages of software that intends to not only fit the SMEs financial and technical conditions, but also to allow them to only use the most relevant modules' functionalities for their businesses. Adopting this approach, companies keep using large packages anyway, and observations have shown that most of the users of this approach are in fact "large SMEs". Even though, and in what CBIs are concerned, a revision in the literature has revealed the inexistence of something like *"my CBI"*. Besides that, users should either utilize software from the same vendor, or they should learn how to utilize different systems, interfaces and terminologies. Although web-based portal solutions have been used – mostly by large companies – to integrate disparate systems, an ideal solution should provide a CNO with an *integrated* computing environment and supporting infrastructure where intra-enterprise process-based transactions, B2B transactions and inter-enterprises collaborative-based transactions could be carried out seamlessly, no matter which software modules are being used.

Application Service Provider

Another interesting model that has tried to mitigate the impacts of the adoption of modern and more complex systems by companies is the *Application Service Provider (ASP) model* (Dewire, 2002). ASP provides access to applications that are located outside the client environment. In essence, ASPs are a way of companies to outsource some or almost all aspects of their information technology needs, providing a contractual software-based service for hosting, managing, and providing access to an application from a centrally managed facility. For a certain periodical fee, the ASP provides content and other services for users connected through the internet or any other network platform, and the users do not need to be concerned with software versions and upgrades. Although too dependent on the quality of the network and the provider's pricing policy and security infrastructure, ASP became a successful model and it could be useful for SMEs in terms of accessing a CBI remotely. However, companies would keep accessing to and paying for the whole CBI, no matter how much of it would be indeed used, which is not very adequate to CNOs/SMEs.

Component-Based Model

A step forward towards solving the necessity of working with an entire module or system is represented by the *Component-Based Model*. It is a branch of the software engineering discipline, with emphasis on decomposition of the engineered systems into functional or logical components with well-defined interfaces used for communication across the components (Shaw, 1996). Reusability is a key characteristic in this model. A software component should be designed and implemented in a way it can be reused in many different programs. Applying this model at a CBI level has, however, some important restrictions. The most relevant one is the non interoperability among the standard component models, which would mean to force the adoption of an almost proprietary CBI to the CNO members, an unthinkable decision regarding their intrinsic heterogeneity and autonomy.

It is important to point out that a project of a CBI for CNOs has to cope with the need of its fundamental "users", which are the *application clients and users,* and *the developers/providers* of the CBI's functionalities. This means avoiding the common problem in most of infrastructures or development environments, which are either too complex to deploy, to configure and to use by users, or too complex to add new functionalities or changes made by developers.

2.2 Current Trends

Knowledge Search & Sharing
In what *knowledge search* is concerned, Information Retrieval (IR) technique has been the most used supporting approach. In general, its main goal is to provide means for searching information in documents or searching for documents themselves. Traditional implementations, such as *Google*, retrieve documents containing keywords specified in the query. Although such techniques provide some support for semantics, this is not enough to cope with the characteristics of knowledge search in CNOs. From another point of view, one of the trends in the IR area is ontologies, which improves the effectiveness of information search, and helps in knowledge retrieval. However, to deal with CO requirements, a tough reality should be dealt with as partners can be involved in multiple CNOs simultaneously. Each partner has its semantics when publishes information and knowledge, and the involved ontologies are not static, which requires permanent maintenance. This problem is intrinsically complex, but some works have been offering some contributions towards using smart search engines for federated search over highly distributed knowledge sources, as in Tramontin et al. (2007).

Enterprise 2.0 & Web 2.0
As mentioned before, *Enterprise 2.0* and *Web 2.0* will demand another era in terms of information systems and infrastructures. This means that CNOs, as a paradigm vitally linked to computing networks, will need CBIs that are web-driven, using Internet as the core communication mean, allowing an easy and fast configuration, connection and disconnection of partners as long as businesses finish. This is important as traditional infrastructures (or middlewares) are customarily deployed as huge, proprietary and complex packages of software, so going to the opposite direction of CNO needs. In the CNO scenario, where alliances are volatile and the flow of collaboration is sometimes only defined on the fly according to the required (and quite often interactive) business process, more flexible infrastructures are necessary. This means to have something like a *plug and play* infrastructure (Miller et al., 2001), where its existence is even not noticed by users, where interoperability problems are (mostly) hidden, and where is not necessary to have it completely loaded when just few of its functionalities are requested. In resume, this gives rise to lean, on demand and fully standard-based collaborative infrastructures, which allows an "a la carte" and "mouldable" infrastructure for each business.

Service Oriented Architecture
Service Oriented Architecture (SOA) is a more recently paradigm for systems design and integration. It can be defined as an architectural paradigm for components of a system and interactions or patterns between them (Singh et al., 2005). In a SOA-based architecture, all functions – or *services* – are defined using a description language and have evocable interfaces that are called to perform business processes. A *service* is a software element that can both call for other service and be called by another service (www.w3C.org). A service has an interface described in a machine-processable format that is usually platform-independent,

meaning that a client from any device using any operating system in any language can use the service.

From the perspective of a suitable approach for supporting CBIs for CNOs, SOA copes far much with most of the limitations previously mentioned, especially in terms of scalability, modularity and granularity, reusability, independence of platform and technology, and on-demand usability. Despite some open points associated with the implementing technologies so far available to materialize SOA-based systems, SOA is clearly the most relevant current software-engineering approach. According to (Gartner, 2006), 30% of Supply Chain Management (at Intranet level) solutions and 20% at Extranet level already applies SOA-based software, and it is expected that this grows up to 90% by 2010.

Software-as-a-Service & Saas-Utility models
Nowadays the ASP model acquired a more refined vision, where software is no longer seen as a monolithic package to be sold and deployed, but rather as a service to be offered on demand. This has been called the *SaaS* paradigm (*Software-as-a-Service*). In this model, software access is subscription-based, remotely hosted, and delivered over the Internet, without the need of complex implementations and IT infrastructure[3]. This gradual shift in the terminologies is also a direct reflection of the change in the business requirements demanded by customers. The focus of SaaS is more on what the customer wants, rather than what the vendor could give. Anyway, ASP model does not solve some important aspects for CNOs.

SaaS-as-Utility (Saas-U) is seen as an extension of SaaS model. In general, this means to adapt the concept of on-demand application to on-demand service, in a large-scale and ubiquitous environment, where services can be accessed from everywhere and can be composed on the fly to create new applications according to current and variable business rules.

2.3 Advanced Approaches

A number of ICTs has emerged both to offer possible architectural solutions for some of those limitations in the ICTs mentioned above, and to open more advanced perspectives of CBIs for CNOs.

Pervasive computing
Pervasive or Ubiquitous computing integrates computation into the environment or, *computing everywhere*, using "Things That Think" (Singh et al., 2006). It is based on the idea that embedding computation into the distributed environment and everyday objects would enable people to interact with information-processing devices more naturally and casually than they currently do, and in whatever location or circumstance they find themselves (*AAA paradigm – Anywhere, Anytime, Anybody / Any type / Any device*). This is an enabling technology for adaptive infrastructures. Thus, a CBI should act as the "glue" between the needs of a given client application in a given moment and the information pervasive servers can provide in that moment, creating a real-time adaptive and context-aware environment. This technology can allow self-adaptability of advanced CBIs.

Peer-to-Peer
Peer-to-Peer (or just P2P) is a computer network that relies primarily on the

computing power and bandwidth of the participants in the network rather than concentrating it in a relatively low number of servers. Such networks are useful for many purposes. Sharing content files containing audio, video, data or anything in digital format is a very common usage of P2P technology. A pure peer-to-peer network does not have the notion of clients or servers, but only equal *peer* nodes that simultaneously function as both "clients" and "servers" to the other nodes on the network. Therefore, P2P model differs from the client-server model where communication is usually to and from a central server (Parameswaran et al., 2001). Main usages in advanced infrastructures comprise publishing, advertising, searching and exchange / sharing of knowledge, information, applications and services of several types of media from/to heterogeneous & distributed sources (e.g. e-mail, blogs, chats, forums), i.e. among CNO members. This is a technology which can enhance the reliability and hence the efficiency of advanced CBIs.

Grid computing

Grid computing is an infrastructure based on the P2P architecture that allows flexible, secure and coordinated resource sharing among dynamic collections of individuals, resources and organizations. In short, it involves computing resources virtualization. Grid computing offers a model for solving massive computational by making use of the unused resources (*CPU cycles* and/or *disk storage*) of large numbers of disparate computers, often desktop computers (Foster et al., 2001). In a CNO scenario, however, companies are in a collaboration alliance but they usually don't benefit at all from this. In other words, collaboration can go beyond business opportunities and knowledge: it can also involve computing resources. Therefore, CNO members can rationalize the utilization – and even the purchasing – of computing resources as CNO´s members can share this with each other (Pinheiro and Rabelo, 2005). *Virtualization*, a recent concept in the business arena, can be seen as a facet of this scenario, although its application has been so far used at intra-enterprise level. Grid and virtualization are technologies that can enhance the efficiency and resources rationalization of advanced CBIs.

Multi-agent systems

Multi-agent systems (MAS) is a field of research within the distributed Artificial Intelligence area where a system is composed of one or several ("intelligent computing processors") - *agents* - that interact with each other (using a high-level protocol) asynchronously and with variable levels of autonomy, with other sources of knowledge and with other systems, to solve complex problems that are intrinsically dynamic and distributed. Depending on the problem requirements, an agent can even move itself to other computers through the network and execute its mission there. This is a technology which can endow some intelligence to an advanced CBI, which can reason about the information gathered via the three technologies mentioned above for clever actions (e.g. services selection based on QoS criteria and information filtering) at infrastructure level (Acampora, 2007).

3. DEVELOPED CBI: THE ECOLEAD ICT-I

After motivating for the need of advanced CBIs for CNOs and stressing the requirements for that, this chapter presents the *concepts* of the CBI developed in the ECOLEAD project. In this project, this CBI is called *ICT-I*, an acronym for "plug and play horizontal ICT infrastructure". Actually, ICT-I is here described only at conceptual and architectural levels, stressing the devised *Reference Architecture* and the *Reference Services*. The ICT-I itself, derived for the services implemented in ECOLEAD, is detailed presented in the next book chapter.

ICT-I has been designed to cope with most of the identified requirements. Nevertheless, developing a completely transparent, fully interoperable and totally reliable CBI to cope with all CNO requirements is not possible considering the limitations of current ICTs and a good number of related research problems. Moreover, CNO is an emergent area and many related issues are still gaining ground, which means the existence of several open questions. In this sense, the strategy adopted in ICT-I was to design a generic/reference architecture and flexible framework in a way it can evolve as long as newer CNO models and ICTs are introduced and open questions are solved.

ECOLEAD ICT-I intends to cover part of this gap based on the vision of a *plug & play* infrastructure. This means that any VBE/VO/PVC member is provided with adequate tools to be easily *plugged* into the ICT-I / CNO community and to *play* (i.e. to collaborate with other organizations) in a secure, on-demand and pay-per-use way. In order to cope with this need, ICT-I has been fully developed based on open / platform-independent specifications and ICT standards.

Regarding its features and potentialities, ICT-I applies the SOA approach, and *web-services* (WS) is the core technology that has been used to implement ICT-I. An important feature for the desired flexibility and scalability is that ICT-I is not a monolithic piece of software that follows the traditional notion of middleware as a "closed world bus" that allows integration of distributed/heterogeneous parts. Instead, ICT-I is a "pulverized" open bus composed of many distributed services which, on demand and according to the precise needs/services for a given transaction, gives the conditions for CNO members to collaborate and to make businesses. That is why it has been called ICT *infrastructure* and not *middleware*.

ICT-I is a scalable and, to some extent, evolving CBI, as new services can be added and others withdrawn from a logical federation of services providers (including the own CNO members). Different implementations of the same services can co-exist and are accessed following agreed business models, security policies, and according to the current context and performance criteria. ICT-I applies the SaaS-U model. CNO members can have a remote and (mostly) transparent CBI, and they use (and can pay for) only what they need, when they need, without any local deployment. Therefore, ICT-I is *not* a framework for SOA-based developments (like IBM *WebSphere*[4], SAP *NetWeaver*[5] or Oracle *Fusion*[6]), nor an integrated CSCW/Groupware package (like *Lotus*[7] or *PHPCollab*[8]), nor another B2B middleware (like Microsoft *BizTalk*[9]), and not a proprietary services-based platform (like *DBE*[16]). Regarding those SOA frameworks, as they are just frameworks, any of them could be used to develop web-services for CNOs. In ECOLEAD, almost all the developed services have utilized the *AXIS*[10] framework, which is robust, open-source, free and compliant to all the W3C recommendations.

3.1 ICT-I Scope

ICT-I acts as a CNO collaborative bus, allowing different and distributed organizations to interact with each other. As said before, the interaction between CNO members comprehends diverse classes of elements: people, processes, systems, knowledge and resources. ICT-I functionalities are modeled as services (see chapter 4) and high-level applications (ICT-I *clients*) can have access to them via web portals and/or via invoking ICT-I services directly. ICT-I can then be used as the ICT glue to link all those elements, also including CNO members' legacy systems. Figure 4 illustrates this scenario and the ICT-I scope. Services (both from ICT-I and from services-based applications) are registered, deployed and maintained in distributed repositories, which are logically joined in a common area called *Services Federation* (see section 3.4). This distribution is, however, totally transparent to the ICT-I's clients.

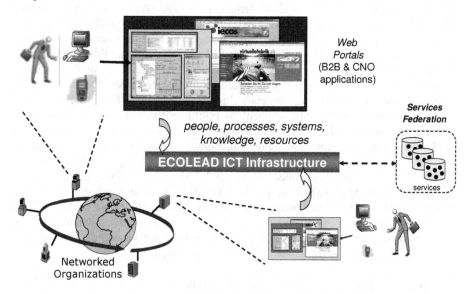

Figure 4 - General ICT-I usage scenario

3.2 Interoperability and Security

Interoperability plays an essential role in any infrastructure where CNO actors and their applications are distributed and heterogeneous. In this context, Interoperability is seen as the ability of a system or a product to work with other systems or products without special effort from the customer or user[11].

Interoperability is a very wide area, comprising since low-level sensors integration till higher levels of inter-organization collaboration. Regarding the core focus of ECOLEAD ICT-I, interoperability aspects are covered only at its essentials, i.e., interoperability issues are tackled by each ICT-I service according to its specific needs, also benefiting from existing software and approaches.

An extremely important enabler for interoperability is the use of standards. Large international initiatives (e.g., OMG, OASIS, W3C and TeleManagement Forum) have been creating specifications with large acceptance by software developers and vendors worldwide. Therefore, to mitigate interoperability problems, the ECOLEAD ICT-I has been fully developed based on ICT standards, independent of computer platforms. Yet, all the current available ICT-I services have been formally specified independent of technology, using the UML methodology, meaning that they can be implemented in any language or environment. However, ICT-I services have been implemented as WS, which is a particular technology. On the other hand, WS have been considered as a standard *de facto* for implementing SOA-based systems, and since recently, newer specifications and initiatives (e.g. WS-I) have overcome initial interoperability problems among different specifications' implementations of WS. An example of this is the WSIF[12], which effectively supports the invocation/interaction among WS deployed in different B2B frameworks.

In the ICT-I design, WSIF is a strategic element to support the ICT-I vision for CNOs. Thanks to it, different CNO members can also share their services among them (following security access rules). This enlarges the collaboration as any company can put available its services, no matter which environment has been used in the implementation of the services. It is to be highlighted that this endows ICT-I services to be integrated to existing organizations' B2B portals, giving to companies a more comprehensive environment where traditional processes and CNO-related supporting services can work seamlessly (Piazza and Rabelo, 2007).

Security is a fundamental element to reinforce trust building in CNO. The security framework that is incorporated in the ICT-I supports authentication, authorization and accounting along the collaborative transactions that are carried out among CNO partners, regarding the different roles and privileges each one has in a CNO. This framework is embedded in the ICT-I. It is flexible and declarative, allowing responsibilities (and eventually delegations) to be dynamically assigned to actors and required security mechanisms settled accordingly (Sowa et al., 2007). It means that the access (their "visibility") to the services (and information) of the federation by users and by other services is prevented considering the CNO actors' privileges. The security framework is described in Chapter 5.

3.3 SaaS-U and related Business Models

Regarding the increasing complexity and powerfulness of B2B frameworks and ERP systems, they have in turn required more powerful computer hosts and sophisticated people to maintain them. Reality has been showing that this is becoming a vicious cycle, which starts to create several difficulties for plenty of CNO members, mostly composed of SMEs. Worse than having to invest to host such systems, companies often use only a very low number of the systems' functionalities but they pay for the whole system, no matter how much or how frequent they are accessed.

ICT-I applies the SaaS-U paradigm (see section 2.2), meaning that its services are accessed remotely, upon request, paid-per-use, based on a contractual software-based service (SLA – service license agreement) for hosting, managing and providing access to its services following QoS levels, no matter where the services providers are and how services have been deployed. This gives rise to several business models to exploit ICT-I, as stressed in Borst et al. (2005), making possible to offer an affordable and 'made to fit' ICT-I for companies.

From the conceptual point of view, this is similar to what *Salesforce.com*'s platform[13] does. The difference is that it offers CRM-related (web) services, which are physically centralized at the Salesforce company. Customers usually pay a fee monthly or pay according to the number of users of a company.

3.4 Services Federation

A fundamental concept in the ECOLEAD ICT-I is the so-called *Services Federation*. A Federation corresponds to groups of devices and software components organized into a single, dynamic distributed system. Members of the federation are assumed to agree on basic notions of trust, administration, identification, and policy. The dynamic nature of a federation of services enables services to be added or withdrawn from a federation at any time according to demand, need, or the changing requirements of the workgroup using it (Sun, 1999).

This concept was adapted to the ICT-I environment, meaning that all CNO-related services are seen as members of a logical entity, the Services Federation. This federation comprises *all* services that can be reached, used and shared among CNO members, involving the ones related to: i) the ICT-I lifecycle; ii) the supporting services for high-level applications (i.e. the ICT-I itself); iii) the CNO life cycle (comprising VBE, PVC and VOM vertical services); and iv) legacy / (intra-organization) (wrapped) systems services. Thus, all existing services can coexist in a virtual logical repository of services and can be accessed transparently and seamlessly according to some rules (see Figure 4).

From the ICT-I point of view, users and applications do not need to know about which services are needed to support a collaborative transaction, where they are, how they should be executed, and which technologies have been used in their implementations. Services are invoked, searched, discovered and properly executed. Providers of such services can be both CNO members and independent software providers/vendors, having their own policies and rules to manage the services repositories. This means that *ICT-I clients* involve not only CNO client applications, but also CNO services providers.

The presented ICT-I is evolving as the Services Federation is a dynamic and self-manageable entity, with new members and services being incorporated to (or modified) and others being withdrawn from it in a transparent way. This also means that a given service may have different implementations available over the network and thanks to smart services search and orchestration mechanisms, the most suitable set of services for a given business transaction can be found out dynamically. This is, however, a challenge issue and some comments about it are given in Section 6.

One of the ICT-I underlying goals is to act as a catalyzer of independent software providers or vendors – private and even from the open source community – that can provide CNO supporting services through the ICT-I. Such community can therefore be seen as a "CNO of services providers", similarly to the Linux community, which add / refine "services" following (standard) rules of quality of software, software development processes (e.g. CMMI), and even the trust level. In this sense, the agreed and involved business models (via SLA) can drive the "quality" of the services or of the repositories a given company can have access to.

The ECOLEAD Services Federation is to be completely open to embrace eco-services for any type of CNO, of domain, with "any" business model (contrarily to *salesforce.com*, which is focused on CRM, it has its particular community of developers, and is not free), using open ICT standards (contrarily to *DBE*, which don't use web-services).

4   ICT-I REFERENCE ARCHITECTURE

In order to provide an open and scalar model, ICT-I has a reference architecture from which instances-of it can be derived for different CNOs. Figure 5 presents the devised *ECOLEAD ICT-I Reference Architecture (ICT-I-RA)*. In theory, it comprises all the possible classes of services than can be useful for any kind of CNO. This generalization has considered the three kinds of CNOs tackled in ECOLEAD: VBE, VO and PVC.

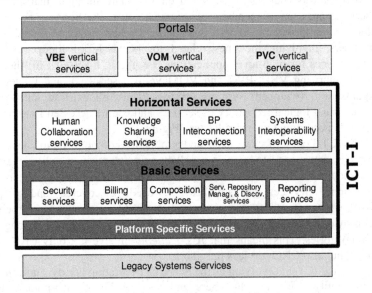

Figure 5 – ICT-I Reference Architecture

4.1   ICT-I Reference Architecture rationale

In the ECOLEAD project, a number of types of CNOs has been comprised, namely VBE, VOM and PVC, for which specific functional needs were identified for each one. Thus, it can be said that such CNOs have *Vertical* needs or, in other words, they require specialized services. On the other hand, they also have some common needs, which help in the execution of any service. For that, ICT-I provides *Horizontal* services, i.e. services independent of any of those three specific applications.

Horizontal services in turn need lower-level services to support their execution, transparently to the application services / CNO actors. These services are seen and called as *Basic* services. They are domain-independent and are essentially used by other services to support the complete and correct execution of a collaborative transaction. Basic services represent the very core of the ICT-I, comprising the discovery, selection and orchestration of services, security, billing and reporting, and some basic interoperability supporting services.

Platform Specific Services is a layer to cope with the fact that, in practice, services (both Basic and Horizontal) require specific tools and/or services when deployed. Therefore, they are intrinsically dependent on the services' implementation.

Legacy system services is another class of reference services. They provide information about activities inside a given company to satisfy vertical services needs. They use to be implemented in heterogeneous platforms and native front-ends, typically representing ERP systems and corporate databases. It shall be pointed out that legacy system services don't belong to ICT-I, but they can belong to the services federation.

As mentioned in section 3.4, when seen as a whole, vertical, horizontal, basic and legacy services compose the Services Federation.

A special and optional element of this architecture is the *Portals*. They act as an integrator front-end (a kind of mega presentation layer, as illustrated in figure 4) to the services themselves, or even to other portals, as a way to invoke services directly by the end-user. Portals are not services.

Per definition, there is not a hierarchy among services. For example, the execution of vertical services requires the combination of services of different nature (considering security aspects, levels of visibility, billing, etc.) no matter the services type (horizontal or basic) and layers they are placed. The effective set of services to be involved and the sequence of their invocation / execution are configured by means of orchestration / composition services, according to the required business processes' rules.

4.2 Derivation of Particular CBIs

A reference architecture is a generic arrangement of modules which represent the most abstract functionalities (or services) that serve as a reference for specializations. In the case of ICT-I-RA, the goal is to be the base for a globally coherent *derivation* of particular ICT-Is (CBIs) for given CNOs. Actually, there are three further stages that have to be passed till building the ICT-I itself.

The first stage of the derivation is the *ECOLEAD ICT-I Reference Framework (ICT-I-RF)*, which is an instance of the ICT-RA. At this stage, the abstract functionalities of ICT-I-RA start to become more concrete and they are already viewed as services. However, they still remain at an abstract level as they are independent of implementation technologies and platforms. This stage and the two others are detailed explained in the next book chapter.

The second stage of the derivation is the *ECOLEAD ICT-I Framework (ICT-I-F)*, which instantiates the ICT-RF's services to particular ICTs. In ECOLEAD, web-services technology and other associated standards (e.g. SOAP and UDDI) have been chosen. Although this particularization, the specification of the services are made in a complete but also abstract way, using the UML standard, which in turn makes the specification of the ICT-I-F still independent of platform. Even though, particular ICT-Is can be further implemented using different technologies (e.g. web-services without SOAP or UDDI) and supporting tools (either open-source or COTS), depending on the envisaged CNO to support.

The third and last stage of such derivation is the implementation and the deployment of the ICT-I's services themselves. As it was already mentioned, this is detailed presented in the next book chapter. Figure 6 illustrates this derivation process in a rough way, picking the case of Human Collaboration services. In the vision applied to it, this is viewed as a CSCW issue. In the derivation done in ECOLEAD, CSCW presents a sort of more specific services, like calendar and file storage. Each of this reference services are completely and formally specified through several UML diagrams, and the services interfaces' description is generated (in the WSDL standard) at the end. In essence, the service name and its WSDL description is the only thing a client application should know to use the ICT-I services.

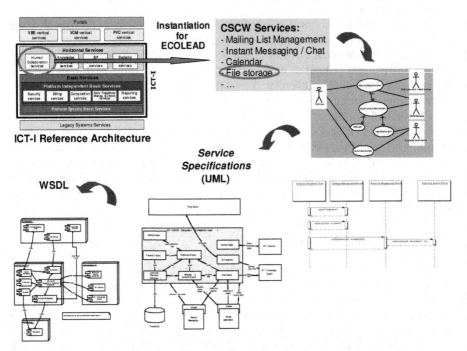

Figure 6 – Derivation Process: from the ICT-I-RA to a CBI

In resume, a CBI derived from the ECOLEAD ICT-I-RA is defined as *an open, distributed, scalable, transparent and security-embedded collaborative service-oriented infrastructure, tailored to support CNOs in the modeling and execution of collaborative tasks, on-demand and paid-per-use.*

4.3 ICT-I Reference Services

This section explains in general the classes of services presented in the ICT-I Reference Architecture.

Horizontal Services

- <u>CNO Actors On-Demand Collaboration Services</u>. For supporting *human collaboration*: mailing, chat, task list, file storage, notification, calendar, wiki, forum, voice and syndication.
- <u>CNO Knowledge Search Services</u>. For supporting *knowledge sharing*, empowering the management of distributed and heterogeneous bodies of knowledge exposed by CNOs. Proper ontology and reconciliation rules have to be used for bridging the semantic gaps among knowledge repositories, allowing seamless retrieval of information.
- <u>Interactive, user-centered BP Management Services</u>. For supporting *business process interconnection*, on top of an existing open-source BPM environment (modeling module and execution engine), ICT-I should provide support to task-oriented, interactive decisional activities to be performed by CNO actors. The forthcoming *BPEL4PEOPLE* standard can also be used for that.
- <u>CNO Data Access Services</u>. For supporting *systems interoperability*, ICT-I needs to offer services to support an easy and secure access to CNO members' databases, which includes the support for defining and configuring them and the information to be shared.

Basic Services

- <u>ICT-I Security Services</u>. These services aim to support confidentiality, integrity, availability and authentication in the communications. This includes the log-in and user management service.
- <u>ICT-I Billing Services</u>. They allow the implementation of different billing models to support the pay-per-use and on-demand service provision.
- <u>ICT-I Services Composition</u>. This service provides facilities to define and execute composed services, preferably using BPEL standard for services composition.
- <u>ICT-I Reporting Services</u>. For supporting the generation of reports to other services (e.g. "detailed billing usage", "services bill summary"), using pre-defined templates in well known formats (e.g. pdf, XML, HTML).
- <u>ICT-I Services Registry and Discovery</u>. For supporting the publishing of the web services in a UDDI repository as well as the search and browsing of services. These services also include the management of the ICT-I life cycle, involving services associated to its deployment, plugging, use, maintenance, unplugging and undeployment.

This description of the horizontal and basic services categories of services is evidently very general since they are detailed described in the next book chapter. The goal here is just to give the core idea of each one, even because the scope and behavior of each service can only be specified when they are designed and implemented.

The derivation process is not a new approach. In the enterprise context, the concept of derivation has been also applied by some more recent relevant initiatives, like VERAM (Zwegers et al., 2003), which acts as a methodology to drive the derivation process of virtual enterprises, from a reference architecture to a particular architecture (therefore, only at abstract level). Another example is ARCON

(Camarinha-Matos and Afsarmanesh, 2006), which extends the virtual enterprise concept to CNOs in a wider reference framework, even though without offering a supporting methodology to derive particular CNOs.

It can be said that ICT-I-RA is positioned at a lower level. It complements those initiatives as it can be seen as a result of an enterprise / CNO derivation process in terms of *supporting infrastructures*. Under this perspective, ICT-I-RA can be used for two different purposes. Firstly, it can be used to derive particular services/functionalities of CBIs for specific CNOs. Secondly, it can be used as a reference, as a "global map", to guide developments for other CNOs.

5. SECURITY FRAMEWORK

Security is a crucial issue in CNOs. Actually, it is seen as a key enabler element to sustain CNO realization as it requires information and knowledge sharing, as well as very intense electronic (collaborative) transactions among partners. This is even more critic as several sensible information needs to be accessed to guarantee the adequate management of CNOs. In a VBE, for example, partners can share best practices and internal benchmarking. In a VO, partners - especially the VO coordinator - should know the status of production of each member and see their production capacity and scheduling.

Regarding this, most of organizations are very skeptic to share information, and this is worse when there is a need to collaborate with unknown partners. Part of the problem is related to the lack of trust, both between organizations and with their systems. Therefore, and from the technological point of view, security is considered a must to reinforce trust building and, as such, it should be managed properly.

Managing security is very complex. Considering that most of organizations in a CNO are composed of SMEs and that VOs are per definition a unique business, the security mechanisms to support the sharing and information access should be flexible and easily configurable. This allows a quickly setup of the visibility of companies' information according to each VO needs and of the partners' roles in every VO. Ideally, this should be dynamically made and adjusted as long as business processes are executed and hence the information access by the involved partners can be controlled accordingly.

However, a number of technical and non technical aspects should be overcome to allow this, like: usual misunderstandings of security management policies by technical staff; a lack of ability to reflect management intentions by IT systems rights (strictly defined static roles); a too long time to transform management decisions into proper configuration of access rights; a too freedom of en-users on their systems environment; hard interoperability problems among different security technologies and mechanisms; and the usual budget restrictions in SMEs. Besides that, most of SMEs have ICT infrastructures that are not fully compliant with security standards and their requirements, and several security tools are not prepared to handle the flexibility and control necessary in CNOs.

Aiming at filling this need, a security framework to cope with CNO requirements

has been devised in ECOLEAD[*] (Sowa et al., 2007). In resume, it gives support for the following actions:
- Flexible and easily configurable multi-level security architecture and mechanisms;
- Infrastructure monitoring facilities;
- Dynamic security for allocation and access rights revoking;
- Quality of service and protection.

It can be said that these actions essentially aim to enable the *trust establishment*. These actions are, in fact, used to support security in several concrete CNO-related issues, such as: the management of password, smart card and mobile id logging-in; the management of trust levels; the creation of a new VO; the control of services access; and the control of switching security contexts.

The security framework is embedded in the ECOLEAD ICT-I. It prevents CNO users both from dealing with the usual complexity to deploy security systems, and from knowing security aspects in details. This is achieved via a transparent security environment, facilitating ICT-I acceptance by VBE members and people.

5.1 Legal Issues

Companies are used to follow rules daily. These rules come from the local company's policies, local state laws, national codes of law, and should follow international agreements such as European Commission directives, international pacts, conventions, and treaties. This impacts companies at variable levels as the nature of every business implicates in specific laws that must be followed.

Legal issues have a huge influence on security aspects. The three security pillars - *confidentiality, integrity, and availability* (CIA) - have to be adapted to concrete laws in terms of how systems' functionalities should be executed (Figure 7).

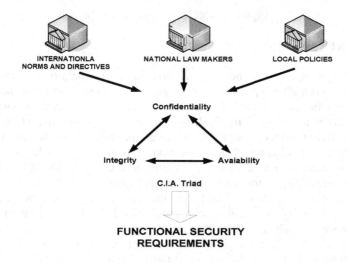

Figure 7 - The impact of legal issues on the security functionalities

---

[*] Development by COMARCH company.

5.2 A Declarative approach for Security

Security is an issue traditionally considered at coding level when programmers have to implement appropriate mechanisms to check user permissions. Declarative security moves main security aspects to the server level. This avoids applications and web pages to have any code about security into them. This approach is the most important underlying aspect in the ECOLEAD security framework towards security transparency. The declarative approach provides means for selecting the security functionality that is effectively required by a given application / service (Figure 8).

Actually, the ECOLEAD security framework can be viewed as a pool of services that are made available as an API. These services are explicitly chosen at configuration time (e.g. when a VO is created). On the other hand, once a given service is chosen and VO roles are assigned to by the VO manager, the information access rights configuration is dynamically and automatically set up, and the required security mechanisms are used.

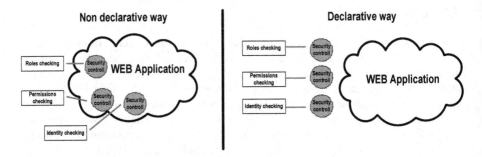

Figure 8 - Declarative security approach

5.3 DRACO Model

The developed security framework supports AAA (*Authorization, Authentication and Accounting*), allowing SMEs to configure the security levels and mechanisms for *each* VO they are involved in. The main element of the security framework is the DRACO (*Dynamic Responsibility Authorization for Collaborative Organizations*) model. DRACO offers flexible ways to define roles in VOs and respective responsibilities (including their delegations) in a way privileges to access information can be dynamically set up. In more concrete terms, DRACO offers:
-   Transparent support for web services (ws) security;
-   Transparent delegation of end-user identity, starting from the web portal, passing by every intermediary web-service involved in the invocation path, and ending with database (Figure 9);
-   Declarative SAML-based authorization at each node of ws-invocation path;
-   Guidelines to mitigate the impact of the adoption of the security model in the companies;
-   Flexible security for allocation and revoking of access rights;
-   Some support for security in mobile computing.

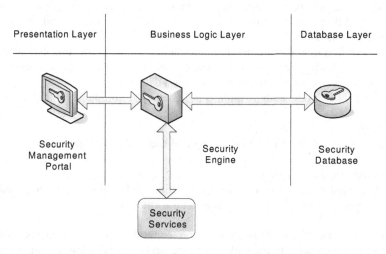

Figure 9 - security management components

Figure 9 also means that some entities (presented in the ECOLEAD vision for CNOs) are directed affected by a security framework. The first one is the end-users, who access services via a web portal and some of them require security (like CSCW tools when some content should be sent out and this should be encrypted). The second one is the companies themselves, i.e. the security required in the transactions involving their systems. The third one is the databases, i.e. how data should be protected, which data may be disclosed, and how security in handled at intra-enterprise level (i.e. internal policies should be coherent with the care a company should take at inter-enterprise level). The last entity is the services providers, which should design their services in a way they are compliant with the required standards and security technologies.

Authentication
DRACO's modules grouped under this services category are responsible for the whole process of getting users' identity, verification of user identity, and the transparent delegation and propagation of the identity to the whole environment.

The concept of transparent delegation is based on the assumption that every single service along the execution path must act in scope of a particular end-user. In order to achieve this, user's identity must be transferred to every involved service. A classical way to support is simply providing the current user's identity in every service call. This approach has some disadvantages, such as the developers must provide user's identity manually every time, and, which is worst, this can be easily tampered. DRACO Security framework provides fully transparent user identity delegation. User's identity is automatically transferred between all components involved in the services execution.

Authorization
DRACO's modules belonging to this service category acts as gatekeepers. Its role is to validate privileges and permissions against the (security) database in a transparent

way. At each access point (portal, web service or database) privileges are validated by security filters. User's identity for authorization modules are taken from the authentication modules.

Authorization modules are involved in four situations: every time user invokes a portal's functionality, or a portal invokes a web service, or a web service invokes another web service, or a web service accesses a database.

In the world of DRACO authorization is designed to be completely transparent.

Accounting
DRACO's modules responsible for storing end-user's actions history.

Secure authenticated channels
DRACO's modules responsible for establishing and maintaining encrypted and digitally signed channels between infrastructural components.

These facilities have consequences on some issues and elements that are involved in the security framework and in the services execution. Figure 10 shows this.

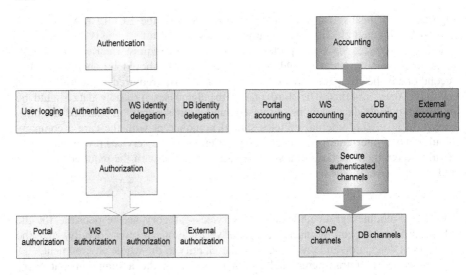

Figure 10 - security management components

Section 5.2 has mentioned that the VO manager (or some authorized person) is responsible for setting up the VO members´ roles and other information. Aiming at facilitating this task, DRACO also provides a user-friendly interface, which is called DRACO's *Console*. Actually, the Console is a service that can be invoked by any application (e.g. VOM system). Figure 11 illustrates one of its graphical interfaces.

Figure 11 - security management console

DRACO development has focused on the main issues related to the support of CNO requirements. Other necessary elements of the security framework have benefit from other reference international initiatives in the security area, namely *WS-Federation[14], Liberty Alliance[15]* and *WS-Trust[16]*.

The main advantage and innovation introduced by DRACO are: *i)* the easy manageable and adjustable access control model based on responsibilities; *ii)* the transparent support for specific needs of evolving and fluctuating structures of VOs (new people and partners can enter in and leave from the structure dynamically); *iii)* the support for most relevant authentication mechanisms (PKI/SPKI, passwords, one-time passwords, biometry); *iv)* the support for multiple forms of responsibility delegation, mapping of responsibilities onto specific application privileges models and; *v)* the application of flexible QoP (quality of protection) policies.

Regarding collaborative processes, four requirements are to be supported by the information security services: *confidentiality, integrity, availability* and *accountability*, no matter if communication is carried out in the traditional client-server model or if mobile codes through the network are involved in. Besides that, it is important to select the suitable mechanisms for every class of transaction as well as for each process phase (normal information exchange phase, contracting and negotiation phase, payment phase, delivery phase, etc.) as security mechanisms use to overhead the network and the client applications themselves.

5.4 Some impacts

In order to attend those requirements, a number of areas (Figure 12) are influenced and hence require a wider vision on how security impacts can be mitigated, regarding that every CNO member is usually very different to each other in terms of systems and security policies.

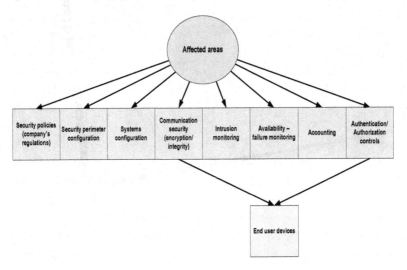

Figure 12 - Areas affected by security

Another aspect that should also be handled by the security framework is the threats that applications can suffer. In fact, web services bring up a new form of attacks that focuses on exploiting XML. The list of potential new vulnerabilities is manifold:

- Parameter tampering – manipulated XML values are used to conduct fraudulent transactions;
- Coercive parsing – corrupted XML/SOAP messages are used to disrupt and disable unprepared and vulnerable services;
- Recursive payload – deeply nested XML documents are constructed to exhaust computing resources;
- WSDL Scanning – Business APIs are probed for sensitive data and vulnerabilities;
- External Entity Attacks – External references can be made to import certain data;
- SOAP Routing Detours – Messages are redirected to malevolent processing intermediaries;
- SOAP with malicious software – SOAP hides and obscures viruses, spywares, and other similar programs;
- SQL injection into SOAP – SQL code is modified and left undetected because it is embedded in XML;

- WS-Security Spoofing – SOAP security contexts are overridden to gain unauthorized data access.

5.5 Authentication – interoperability between different security technologies

Tools for ICT security are very often considered as weakness and brakes to develop quickly new relationships. Heterogeneity of context, tools and technologies is a real obstacle for SMEs. In CNOs, as companies are heterogeneous, this is much worse and very complex to handle.

In order to enable a secure communication among heterogeneous CNO partners, DRACO solution allows companies in establishing trust relationships with partners even if they use different security technologies/domains (e.g. *SPKI*, *X.509* and *Kerberos*). In general terms, this is achieved by means of the generation and assignment of a generic "security token" to each partner. Figure 13 illustrates a CNO (VO) where the organizations are grouped according to security technologies. When a VO is going to be created as an answer to a given collaboration opportunity, this interoperation problem should be transparently resolved.

In the scenario depicted in the figure below, the problem is that each partner has a different security technology. The VO Manager only supports X.509, which means that all partners would have to use X.509tokens/certificates to communicate with it. In addition, these tokens should be issued by an organization that the VO Manager trusts. The main difficulties in this scenario are: (1) locating this organizations that the VO Manager trusts; and (2) defining how the tokens/certificates will be issued.

In the developed security framework, the infrastructure to support the VO is fully based on web services and on its security specifications (such as *WS-Trust* and *Security Assertions Markup Language - SAML*). WS-Trust defines a *Security Token Service (STS)*, which is responsible for issuing standard security tokens that should be understood by all CNO participants. Security tokens are represented by *SAML* assertions and used to establish the trust relationships among the VO partners. Access rights or roles to each partner in the VO are dynamically assigned by the VO Manager, managed by DRACO, and expressed in SAML assertions. This means that the security technologies present are not important to the communications within a VO, as the only security token used in all communications will be the SAML tokens issued by DRACO.

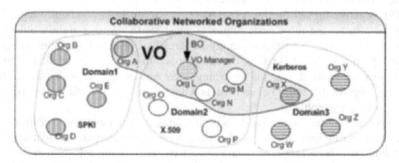

Figure 13 - A VO immersed in different security domains.

5.6 Affected Entities and general assessment

The use of the developed security framework affects three categories of entities associated to a CNO and to the ICT-I: the CNO users, CNO actors, and the CNO services providers.

CNO's users are the people involved in VO activities and who accesses portals and the available high-level CNO-related applications (e.g. VBE management portal, VO management portal, etc.). Impact from their perspective is the necessity to use some specialized security tools (for instance, e-mail message encryption), which can be not that easy to be understood by users. This can also comprise situations where external tools are invoked but they are not fully integrated with ECOLEAD portals, which can break the security chain. Another important factor, especially when considering access to the portal via mobile devices, is the limited capabilities (in terms of memory and processing power) and lack of expandability of some devices, which would then require additional and advanced functionalities that would not be available.

CNO's actors are the organizations participating in a VBE or VO, for example. As it was already mentioned, organizations are usually highly heterogeneous in terms ICTs and security technologies, and most of SMEs are not aware about how important is to adopt ICT standards. This heterogeneity brings hard interoperability problems and can put down a long effort in the changing of the organizations' mentality to work as a CNO. Although DRACO has provided some solutions for that as well as the adopted approach had mitigated the impacts of the introduction of the security framework in the companies, several issues are still unsolved. On one hand this means that CNO members should be aware about this to do not overestimate the level of possible transparency in the systems and ICT-I. On the other hand, they can try to take this interoperability issue into account when designing their systems' architecture and selecting software products or services.

CNO's Software Providers are companies which develops applications and services for CNOs. Similarly to CNO's companies, these providers are usually heterogeneous too in terms of ICTs used, standardization awareness, quality of development process, etc. No matter if they are the own members of a CNO or they are external companies (outsourcing model), they should consider the requirements stressed above so that their services can be compatible with the ICTs used in ECOLEAD, ICT-I and security framework.

The negative impact on the organization environment is potentially high. New forms of attacks and more open networks must lead to paying significantly more attention to operating systems' configuration. This means that more resources should be put on configuration checking, operating systems updating, systems parameters verification, systems hardening, etc.. Another aspect is that the security in every application must be verified and tested in order to eliminate the most common security problems.

In terms of support to mobile devices, it is important to point out their limitations (memory, processing power, modularity) and different built-in features. For exploiting the whole scope of security services (encryption, integrity, methods of authentication) some additional modules must be provided for the above devices.

The Security Framework is not locally deployed. Following the same SaaS-U principles adopted in the ICT-I, security services and facilities are used on demand.

6. GENERAL ASSESSMENT

This chapter provides a general assessment about the ECOLEAD ICT-I, positioning it against other relevant initiatives, highlighting its innovative aspects, and pointing out some of the main open issues and foreseen challenges.

6.1 ICT-I Positioning against other initiatives

ICT-I-RA is evidently not the only one which tries to generalize concepts and services related to enterprises operation. Figure 14 shows the positioning of ICT-I-RA against other reference initiatives. In order to facilitate the comprehension, three different perspectives have been considered, i.e. where these reference initiatives are placed from the process, reference interoperation and Software-as-a-Service (SaaS) paradigm points of view.

From the *process* perspective, ICT-I-RA is placed at a CNO / collaborative level. Any other RA has been found out in the literature which is placed at this level too. At intra-enterprise level there is other RAs, like the *IBM Reference Architecture*, which a direct analogy can be established with if compared to ICT-I-RA: business layer with vertical services, human & process integration with horizontal services, process automation with basic services, and resources virtualization with legacy and basic services. As they are at different business layers, these two RAs complement to each other.

From the *interoperation* perspective, ATHENA project can be considered as the most relevant recent initiative to propose interoperability solution for B2B & at intra-enterprise level. Its reference architecture comprises enterprise models, processes, general services, and information and data that should flow across processes. There are other RAs for interoperability, which cope with other dimensions of interoperability, such as for grid computing and mobile computing. ICT-I-RA does not focus on interoperability. Its services make use of RAs that deal with interoperability according to the approach used in services derivation, implementation and deployment.

From the SaaS perspective, NESSI-RA[17] can be considered one of the most relevant ones. In resume, NESSI sees services as entities that sustain business processes, which should be composed to establish the correct set and flow of services and their execution, that exist and needs to be organized, and that require a computing infrastructure to run. Projects like ECOLEAD, DBE[18] and ABILITIES[19] offer some support just for the three first facets.

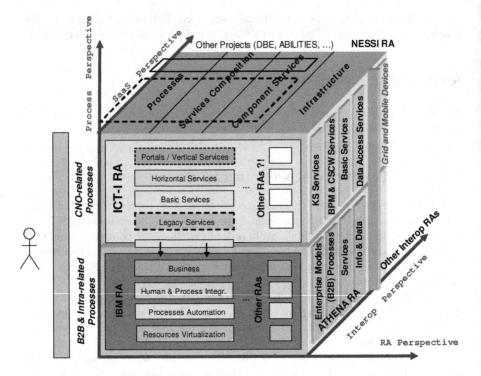

Figure 14 – Positioning of ICT-I-RA against other initiatives

6.2 Innovative Features

Supporting CNOs imply in a different set of functionalities, meaning that ICT-I complements B2B functionalities as well as it adapts and integrates traditional groupware functionalities to a CNO environment. Thanks to the ICT-I framework flexibility and strong utilization of standards, all these functionalities can be integrated in the same computing working environment so that users do not need to see them as separate systems.

From the technological point of view and following current trends, ECOLEAD ICT-I has as main features:

- It is a web/SOA/standard-based integrated platform devoted to CNOs, meaning that users should only have a browser and internet access. No local deployments;
- Suitable and feasible for SMEs;
- It is open and flexible to embrace new services without any interference in the use of the infrastructure, also meaning that ICT-I can intrinsically evolve;
- Services are accessed on demand (SaaS-U paradigm) and can be found out in a clever way, according to the business process flow. This means having almost an 'a la carte' environment to fit each organization's needs.
- Services are paid per use, respecting variable and flexible business models;
- (Some) Services can also be accessed through mobile devices.

- Services and data access are dynamically controlled by a flexible security system.

Regarding its CNO orientation and other features stressed along the paper, it is believed that ICT-I is unique and it clearly goes towards supporting several requirements of Web 2.0 and Enterprise 2.0. Besides that, its conception and features are in line with a number of relevant initiatives, like NESSI and ATHENA.

6.3 Challenges & Impacts

Although a CBI based on the ICT-I RA had been successfully derived for the CNOs and pilots involved in the ECOLEAD project, it can't be said it is finished. Actually, besides the development of other services of the ICT-RF (see next book chapter), there are some open issues and challenges to be faced, some of them associated to the decisions taken in its design. Some of them are generally mentioned below.

Web-service technology, despite its potentialities and increasing acceptance, has some drawbacks (e.g., it is stateless) that should be managed depending on the desired business process's behavior. Dealing with large-scale fault-tolerance platforms is still an open and very complex topic of research so it is expected that future outcomes of this can be incorporated in the ICT-I. Another complex issue is the management of the services federation. Each service provider can determine its own operational and security rules besides having different levels of computing infrastructures to run services, which can create serious troubles and to lead to other class of interoperability problems when several providers were established.

Moreover, the operational policies should deal with the different life cycles of each service that is made available, which is also complex. Services should be easily discovered and immediately integrated/bound to workflow or orchestration systems mechanisms, but this bumps into the different ways and semantics the diverse providers have registered the services, on how the services interfaces (WSDL) are expressed, and if context awareness has to be considered.

All these difficulties represent challenges in the web-related community in spite of several ongoing works. Two interesting research projects that can be mentioned and that are dealing with some of those problems are DBE and ABILITIES, but their results are still not at a level for being now used. These problems are essentially related to the *technological* perspective of the difficulties and impacts the adoption of the CNO paradigm by companies and the use of such kind of CBI to support their collaboration tends to provoke. As mentioned in the introduction, other perspectives, e.g. organizational, cultural, financial, among others are also extremely relevant and must be dealt with properly for the successful realization of the CNO paradigm. These perspectives are, however, out of scope of this book chapter.

7. CONCLUSIONS

This chapter presented an overview of the main issues that advanced collaborative business infrastructures (CBI) for CNOs should consider, and the one developed in the ECOLEAD project (called *ICT-I*), which corresponds to a CBI derived from the *ECOLEAD ICT-I Reference Architecture*.

ICT-I has been conceived based on the service oriented architecture paradigm / web-services technology, providing organizations with a transparent (mostly), platform-independent, easy deployable and configurable, secure-embedded, lean, distributed, scalable, on-demand and pay-per-use CBI. The presented features and its focus on CNO make it somehow unique.

It has been validated within ECOLEAD, close to the 20 developers and 9 pilots of the project, considering three types of CNOs (i.e. ICT-I "clients"): Virtual Organization Breeding Environments (VBE), Virtual Enterprises / Organizations / Teams (VE/VO/VT) and Professional Virtual Communities (PVC).

ICT-I doesn't aim to compete with B2B framework or EAI solutions. Instead, it aims to complement them regarding that supporting CNOs imply in a different set of functionalities, including an adaptation of traditional groupware functionalities to a CNO environment. Interoperability is not its focus, being restricted to the requirements of each service when they are implemented.

The concept of Services Federation is extremely powerful as it allows a seamlessly access of any service of the federation, no matter where services are and how they were deployed. Besides that, depending on the richness of the services and involved business models, several equivalent services can co-exist and can be selected according to performance criteria, business context and business process alignment. New services can be incorporated to the Federation along its life cycle and withdrawn from it, transparently to the clients. However, tough issues should be more researched in order to realize the full concept of Federation. Examples of this include the conception of supporting services for the management of the services federation's life cycle, and of advanced searching mechanisms and semantic-driven services selection and composition over large-scale services repositories.

Although thought as generic as possible, ICT-I-RA can naturally evolve as CNO area is only now gaining maturity. So it is expected that new services, concepts, etc., have to be contemplated by it and in the derivation process, as long as new achievements – of any nature – are made available.

Acknowledgments

This work was mostly supported by the European Commission under the project IST FP-6 IP ECOLEAD project (www.ecolead.org). The Brazilian participation was also supported by the Brazilian Council for Research and Scientific Development – CNPq (www.cnpq.br) in the scope of IFM project (www.ifm.org.br).

8. REFERENCES

1. Acampora, G.; Loia, V. - A Proposal of an Open Ubiquitous Fuzzy Computing System for Ambient Intelligence, in Computational Intelligence for Agent-based Systems, Eds. Raymond Lee and Cincenzo Loia, Springer, pp.1-26, 2007.
2. Afsarmanesh, H.; Camarinha-Matos, L.M. - A Framework for Management of Virtual Organization Breeding Environments. Proceedings PRO-VE'2005 – 6th IFIP Working Conference on Virtual Enterprises, Kluwer Acad. Pub., pp. 35-48, 2005.
3. Afsarmanesh, H.; Marik, V.; Camarinha-Matos, L.M. - Challenges of Collaborative Networks in Europe, in Collaborative Networked Organizations – a research agenda for emerging business models, Ed.s Luis M. Camarinha-Matos and Hamideh Afsarmanesh, Kluwer Acad. Pub., pp. 77-90, 2004.
4. Borst, I.; Arana, C.; Crave, S.; Galeano, N., Technical Report (Deliverable) D62.2 ICT-I Business Models, October 2005.

5. Camarinha-Matos, L. M.; Afsarmanesh, H. - Towards Next Business Models. In Collaborative Networked Organizations: a research agenda for emerging business models, Kluwer Academic Publishers, pp. 3-6, 2004.
6. Camarinha-Matos, L. M.; Afsarmanesh, H. - A Modeling Framework for Collaborative Networked Organizations, in Proceedings PRO-VE'2006 – 7th IFIP Working Conference on Virtual Enterprises, Springer, pp. 3-14, 2006.
7. Chen, Q.; Hsu, M. - Inter-enterprise collaborative business process management. Proc. 17th IEEE Int. Conf. on Data Engineering, pp.253-260, 2001.
8. Dewire, D. T., Application Service Providers - Enterprise Systems Integration, 2nd Edition, pag.449-457. Auerbach Publications, 2002.
9. Foster, I., Kesselman, C.; Nick, J.; Tuecke, S. - The Anatomy of the Grid: Enabling Scalable Virtual Organizations, in Int. J. of High-Performance Computing Applications, pp.200-222, 2001.
10. Goranson, T. - The Agile Virtual Enterprise – Cases, Metrics, Tools, Quorum Books, USA, 1999.
11. Lee, J.; Siau, K.; Hong, S. - Enterprise integration with ERP and EAI, ACM, New York, USA, Vol 46, Issue 2, pp. 54-60, 2003.
12. Mezgar, I. - Trust Building for Enhancing Collaboration in Virtual Organizations, in Proceedings PRO-VE'2006 – 7th IFIP Working Conference on Virtual Enterprises, Springer, pp. 173-180, 2006.
13. Mcafee, A.P. - Enterprise 2.0: the dawn of emergent collaboration, in IEEE Engineering Management Review, Vol 34, Issue 3, page 38, 2006.
14. Parameswaran, M.; Susarla, A.; Whinston, A. - P2P Networking: An Information-Sharing Alternative, in IEEE Computing Practices, pp.31-38, 2001.
15. Pinheiro, F.; Rabelo, R. J. Experiments on Grid Computing for VE-related Applications, in Proceedings PRO-VE'2005 – 6th IFIP Working Conference on Virtual Enterprises, Kluwer Acad. Pub., pp 483-492, 2005.
16. Piazza, A.; Rabelo, R. J. An Approach for Seamlessly Interoperation among heterogeneous web services-based B2B Frameworks [in Portuguese], in Proceedings 8th Brazilian Symposium on Intelligent Automation, pp. 451-458, 2007.
17. Shaw, M.; D. Garlan - *Software Architecture: Perspectives on an Emerging Discipline*. Prentice Hall, Upper Saddle River, NJ, USA, 1996.
18. Singh, M.; Huhns, M.; Service Oriented Computing -Semantics, Processes, Agents, Wiley, 2005.
19. Singh, S.; Puradkar, S.; Lee, Y. Ubiquitous computing: connecting Pervasive computing through Semantic Web, in Int. Journal on Information Systems and E-Business Management, Springer, Vol. 4, N4, pp. 421-439, 2006.
20. Sowa, G.; Sniezynski, T. - Technical Report (Deliverable) D64.1b – Configurable multi-level security architecture for CNOs, in www.ecolead.org, 2007.
21. SUN - JINI Technology Architectural Overview, http://www.sun.com/jini/whitepapers/ architecture.html, Jan 1999, in 30/08/2005.
22. Tramontin, R.; Rabelo, R. J. - A Knowledge Search Framework for Collaborative Networks, in Proceedings PRO-VE'2007 – 8th IFIP Working Conference on Virtual Enterprises, Springer, pp. 573-582, 2007.
23. Zwegers, A.; Tolle, M.; Vesterager, J. - VERAM: Virtual Enterprise Reference Architecture and Methodology, in Global Engineering and Manufacturing in Enterprise Networks (GLOBEMEN), pp17-38, 2003.

---

[1] www.eubusiness.com/topics/SMEs

[2] www.sap.com/solutions

[3] http://www-304.ibm.com/jct09002c/isv/marketing/saas/index.html

[4] www-306.ibm.com/software/websphere/

[5] http://www.sap.com/platform/netweaver

[6] http://www.oracle.com/applications/fusion.html

[7] www.ibm.com/developerworks/lotus/products/notesdomino/

[8] http://sourceforge.net/projects/phpcollab/

[9] www.microsoft.com/biztalk/default.mspx

[10] ws.apache.org/axis/

[11] www.atena-ip.org

[12] http://ws.apache.org/wsif

[13] www.salesforce.com

[14] http://www.ibm.com/developerworks/library/specification/ws-fed

[15] http://www.projectliberty.org

[16] http://docs.oasis-open.org/ws-sx/ws-trust/v1.3/ws-trust.html

[17] NESSI Strategic Research Agenda - Framing the future of the Service Oriented Economy. Version 2006-2-13 (http://www.nessi-europe.com/documents/NESSI_SRA_VOL_1_20060213.pdf); ICT for Enterprise Networking (http://cordis.europa.eu/ist/directorate_d/en_intro.htm).

[18] www.digital-ecosystem.org

[19] http://services. txt.it/abilities

THE ECOLEAD PLUG & PLAY COLLABORATIVE BUSINESS INFRASTRUCTURE

Ricardo J.Rabelo[1], M.Mar Rodrigo Castro[2], Alex Conconi[3], Michele Sesana[3]

[1] *Federal University of Santa Catarina, BRAZIL, rabelo@das.ufsc.br*
[2] *Software AG Spain, SPAIN, mrodrigo@softwareag.es*
[3] *TXT e-Solutions, ITALY, {alex.conconi; michele.sesana}@txt.it*

This chapter presents a distributed and open ICT infrastructure called *ICT-I* that has been implemented in the ECOLEAD project to help members of Collaborative Networks in doing businesses and collaborations more efficiently. ICT-I design relies on the service oriented architecture paradigm, and it has been implemented with web-services. Its services are used on demand and pay-per-use models. It is flexible to support an easy entrance of new services and the withdrawn of others. So far the type of organizations envisaged by the proposed ICT-I are the members of virtual breeding environments, virtual organizations and professional virtual communities. This paper details the ICT-I reference framework and the derived services. A general overview about its main value and assessment is given in the end.

1. INTRODUCTION

Previous book chapter has motivated for the need of collaborative business infrastructures as well as has introduced the concepts that were applied in the design of an infrastructure within the ECOLEAD project. This chapter focuses on the presentation of the related underlined implementation aspects, showing the so-called *plug & play collaborative business ICT infrastructure* (or simply *ICT-I*) derived for the three classes of CNOs in ECOLEAD: virtual organizations breeding environment (VBE), virtual organizations (VO) and professional virtual communities (PVC).

ICT-I acts as a collaborative bus or platform that allows different and distributed CNO members and involved applications to better collaborate with each other. Regarding the CNO requirements for an ICT-I and the envisaged business models associated to current trends on software development, it has been designed as a *distributed* middleware and implemented as a set of services. Besides being devoted to CNOs, its main value-added relies on the fact it is *plug & play*, i.e. once CNO members want to collaborate, they get plugged into the CNO "world" and can further "play" with by accessing the available supporting services, seamlessly. The ICT-I designing principles aimed to build it as a transparent (as much as possible), open and easy-to-use platform, and that can be able to support the requirements associated to CNO in terms of processes, knowledge, computing resources, people and information (Rabelo et al., 06).

From the technological point of view, it has essentially been designed applying the SOA (*Service Oriented Architecture*) paradigm and the SaaS-U (*Software-as-a-Service-Utility*) model. ICT-I is security embedded (Sowa & al., 2007) and it is not locally deployed. Its services are accessed remotely, on-demand and paid-per-use, following a diversity of *business models* (Borst & al., 05). As it was mentioned in the previous book chapter about the ECOLEAD ICT-I, it is an evolving infrastructure as long as its new services can be added and others be withdrawn from the *Services Federation*, a logical aggregation of services providers (Rabelo and Gusmeroli, 2007).

ICT-I implementation is actually the last stage of a derivation process, i.e. an activity where a particular instance is derived from an abstract concept. In this case, the *ECOLEAD ICT-I Reference Architecture* is the most abstract definition of "all" functionalities that can be developed to support "any kind" of CNOs, and that can last as long as ICTs evolve. This Reference Architecture has been detailed described in the previous book chapter.

The first stage of the derivation is the consideration of the *ECOLEAD ICT-I Reference Framework*, which is an instance of the Reference Architecture. At this stage those functionalities are already viewed as *services*, but they are still at an abstract level as they are independent of implementation technologies and computing platforms. This Reference Framework is depicted in section 2.

The second stage of the derivation is the *ECOLEAD ICT-I Framework*, which instantiates those reference services to particular ICTs; in this case to web-services technology. Although this particularization, the specification of the services are made in a complete but also abstract way, using the UML standard, which in turn makes the specification of the ICT-I Framework still platform independent. Even though, particular collaborative business ICT infrastructures can be implemented using different web-services-related technologies depending on the envisaged CNOs to support.

The third and last stage of such derivation is the implementation of the ICT-I's services themselves. In the ECOLEAD project, a set of web-services has been used and a subset of them - from the ICT-I Reference Framework - has been effectively implemented. Therefore, these services represent the ECOLEAD ICT-I itself and they are detailed in section 3 of this book chapter. The implementation of the ICT-I services tried to be the most generic as possible although ECOLEAD has focused on VBEs, VOs and PVCs.

Section 4 concludes this book chapter presenting a general assessment of the developed *ECOLEAD plug & play collaborative business ICT infrastructure*.

2. ICT-I REFERENCE FRAMEWORK

As clarified in the previous section, the reference framework is a possible derivation from the reference architecture. Therefore, the list of particular derived services reflects a view (including the services' names) about the CNO needs in terms of a supporting collaborative infrastructure. In the CNO context, this view means an infrastructure that endows *services* to enable *people* to collaborate and negotiate, *systems* to interoperate and adapt, *knowledge* and resources to be discovered and shared, and *processes* to be interconnected and synchronized. Figure 1 shows this particular view of the ICT-I Reference Framework, which tried to be the as wide as possible to cover the most different types of CNO manifestations as possible.

Looking at the ICT-I Reference Architecture (stressed in the previous book chapter), this figure 1 shows an "explosion" of the Reference Architecture's boxes. For instance, "human collaboration services" in the reference architecture are here seen as a CSCW issue, which in turn could offer groupware, officeware and product development supporting services. As it was said before, this explosion reflects one vision in terms of needs for human collaboration. Other visions can exist for that.

For the ECOLEAD project, only some of these services have been implemented, either from scratch or from adaptations of existing open source tools (see section 3). Services in grey scale represent the developed services, whereas the black ones are supported only at a basic level. Services in white represent those that were not implemented but that can be easily added to the framework in the future.

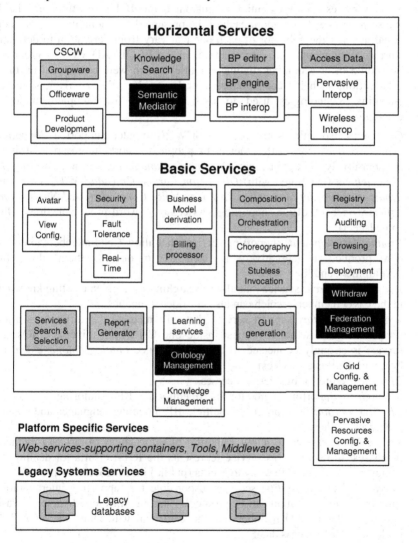

Figure 1 – ICT-I Reference Framework

In the following sections all services are briefly described. Their description is very general as their detailed scope, functionalities and behaviour can only be specified when they are derived for particular CNOs.

2.1 Horizontal Services

The following list corresponds to the horizontal services considered in the ICT-I framework. Horizontal Services can be described as offering general purpose and common services to the business level (i.e. at VOM, VBE and PVC), which represents the high-level CNO-related applications. Although important and useful, horizontal services aren't essential to guarantee the ICT-I functioning. The list below also reflects a vision about each of the presented functionality, i.e. the scope, functionalities and the behavior of each one can vary from derivation to derivation (and further implementation). For instance, in the ECOLEAD view, a groupware service should offer a number of functionalities which were considered useful. In other derivation, such list can be smaller or larger. Yet, the behavior, scope and implementing technologies used to each can vary from implementation to implementation.

- *Groupware:* sometimes referred as CSCW (Computer Supported Cooperative Work) services, they offer means to people to work in group, distributed, collaboratively. They include: *Document Management, News, Mailing List Management* (integrated with) *Discussion Forum, Calendar, Wiki, Information Syndication, Instant Messaging, Task List, Voice Conference,* and *Notification.*
- *Officeware:* back-office-supporting services (e.g. word processor, draw editor, spreadsheet).
- *Product Development:* supporting services that allow CNO members to develop new products collaboratively as well as to manage them along their development and life cycle.
- *Knowledge search:* service that allows searching for a given existing knowledge in the CNO members, which can also consider semantics.
- *Semantic mediator:* support service that will mediate the differences among diverse ontologies that may exist inside one CNO or in diverse CNOs. This service is strongly connected to the basic service *ontology management* (see below in the Basic services).
- *BP editor:* editor of business processes.
- *BP engine:* supporting engine for the BP editor and BP monitoring.
- *BP interoperability:* support for multiple BP modeling languages and business processes models.
- *Access Data:* service to allow gathering of information from CNO members' databases. In resume, this service represents the ICT-I efforts for dealing with legacy systems, i.e. as the way to access (public) information they provide.
- *Pervasive interoperability:* services responsible for supporting interoperability (platforms and communication protocols) among different/diverse pervasive networks which CNO members can have to deal with along the VO/VT life cycle in order to access data.

-    *Wireless interoperability:* services responsible for supporting interoperability among different wireless protocols which CNO applications can have to deal with along the VO/VT life cycle in order to access data.

2.2 Basic Services

Basic Services can be described as domain-independent services that are used mainly by other services. These services represent the core of the ICT-I, comprising services as discovery, selection and orchestration of services, and security. The same considerations about different views and derivations mentioned in section 2.1 about horizontal services are valid to the basic services.

-    *Avatar:* service that can act on behalf of users in some situations (entire or partial business processes) during their absence or busyness, or even in repetitive activities (Zambiasi and Rabelo, 2007).
-    *View configuration:* supporting service through which users can configure the avatar' behaviors and user preferences.
-    *Security:* security services. This service comprises authentication, authorizations and accounting (AAA).
-    *Fault tolerance:* supporting services that can implement fault tolerance mechanisms to recover from faults in the network also during the execution of some transactions/communications. This is one facet of the wider issue Quality of Service (QoS).
-    *Real time:* supporting services that can allow the execution of some services in very well defined / tight time slots. This is another facet of QoS.
-    *Business model derivation:* service that can express the type of business model to be applied to the ICT-I services for billing purposes.
-    *Billing:* to allow services billing.
-    *Composition:* to support web-services composition. Composition can be tackled from different point of views, involving orchestration and choreography, depending on the derivation process. Some standards can be used for that (e.g. *BPEL*).
-    *Stubless invocation:* this service allows seamlessly services invocation without the need of having proxies or other stubs no matter which B2B framework (e.g. *WebSphere, WebLogic, BizTalk, .NET, AXIS*).
-    *Registry:* to publish web-services in given services repositories.
-    *Browsing:* to browse registered web-services in given services repositories.
-    *Deployment:* to aid developers in the web-services deployment. It is also useful to allow a better / more rational (or even replicated) services allocation over distributed services repositories.
-    *Auditing:* to support auditing (from several perspectives, such as quality control, privacy & federation rules, actual amount of accesses versus generated billing) in the services federation.
-    *Withdraw:* to support the unregistering of given services from the services repository.
-    *Federation Management:* global service to support all the issues related to the management of the services federation, basically comprising services & ICT-I life cycles, operational & security rules, and evolving mechanisms.

- *Search & Selection:* to allow the searching and further selection of registered services that fit a set of specifications, which can comprise more intelligent levels (semantics-driven) of searching and selection.
- *Reporting:* to support the generation of reports, usually for billing purposes.
- *Knowledge management:* to support means to manage the knowledge produced in the CNOs along their life cycle.
- *Ontology Management:* to support the use of multiple ontologies expressed in different ontology tools. This service is an essential base for the horizontal service *Knowledge Search*.
- *Learning:* to support the generation of new knowledge out of what is stored in the CNOs' knowledge base (Loss & al, 2007).
- *GUI generator:* to generate (dynamically and automatically) web-based GUIs, also useful for context awareness when on-the-fly adaptations are required (Gesser, 2006).
- *Grid:* general service to allow deployment of grid platforms (e.g. *Globus*) and to configure them in a way to both support high processing and hardware sharing. This aims at extending the collaboration level among CNO members, usually limited to information sharing (Pinheiro and Rabelo, 2005).
- *Pervasive computing:* general service to help in the management of the interoperation with different/diverse pervasive networks in a way to enable high-level systems to access the information provided by these networks for any kind of purpose.

In any case, all these services (Basic and Horizontal) can both call other services and be called by other services. As such, they are both services consumers and providers.

3. ICT-I FRAMEWORK AND IMPLEMENTED SERVICES

This section aims at giving an overview about the implemented ICT-I services. It is important to point out that thanks to the intrinsic flexibility provided by a SOA design and to the derivation processes, ICT-I is not only open, but also a scalable infrastructure. In this way, it is possible to evolve it by providing new services, many different (competing) implementations of the same services, or improving existing ones.

It is also important to highlight that *Interoperability* is not the focus of the ECOLEAD ICT-I. In fact, it is seen as an *enabler* for collaboration. Therefore, particular solutions are restrained only to the essential aspects required to support the services, benefiting from existing results. On the other hand, ICT-I strongly relies on ICT *de facto* standards in order to mitigate interoperability obstacles.

Although not mandatory – considering that a web-service can be implemented in any language and in a diversity of environments – ICT-I's services have been coded in Java, besides using some other basic ICTs, like *XML, SOAP, WSDL* and *UDDI*, and *AXIS, JBoss* and *Jonas* as the main containers.

ICT-I Reference Framework are referred to categories of services that should be implemented applying given technologies. In the current implementation of ICT-I services, horizontal services usually have some direct interaction with their users (via user interfaces) also with the end-users, whereas most of the basic services are directed invoked by other services. In some cases, there is also some interaction with systems administrators. Other implementations of the same service category may present totally different behaviors, depending on the business rules that should be observed in a given derivation. This means that multiple different implementations of the same category of service may exist and hence co-exist in the Services Federation.

In the next sections the implemented services are more detailed described. As said before, they can be implemented in different ways, with a sort of functionalities and associated different behaviors. That's the reason why their description in the next sections is not homogeneous. The complete UML specification and examples of screenshots of all services can be found in (Ratti and Rabelo, 2007), (Rodrigo-Castro and Ratti, 2007) and (Sowa & al., 2007). The security framework, which empowers ICT-I with a very flexible environment allowing dynamic and controlled assignment of access right, s is specifically and detailed presented in another chapter of this book.

3.1 On-demand collaboration services

The on-demand collaboration services represent an integrated suite of the collaboration tools that can be used for mutual communication and information interchange between people inside the CNO. The following collaboration functionalities are included in the implemented version:

- *Instant Messaging / Chat*
- *Discussion Forum*
- *Mailing List Management*
- *Calendar*
- *Wiki*
- *Document Repository / Content Management System*
- *News & Announcement System*

Liferay Portal Server was used as the platform for integrating different collaboration tools. The graphical user interface for all collaboration services is implemented as *portlets* following the *JSR-168 Java Portlet* specification. Their usage enables flexibility and makes it possible to customize the user interface to match particular needs of the different distinct user groups.

Through the advanced integration options, the basic collaboration functionalities are further augmented with knowledge management and data reuse features. The system keeps history records of the ongoing communication and integrates with *Knowledge Search* service to allow finding information easily.

In contrast to other ICT-I basic and horizontal services, the collaboration services are GUI-intensive, meaning that the core part of implemented functionality focuses on the interaction with user through the graphical user interface. Thus, the exposition of the collaboration functionality through the Web Services interface is not always possible / reasonable. The functionality is exposed to other horizontal and vertical services through the Web Services and Java API interfaces.

Architecture
Figure 2 shows the basic architecture of the on-demand collaboration services. It

follows the 3-tier model, which separates the presentation layer, the application logic layer, and data storage layer.

The application logic layer consists of two main parts. One part is represented by the application logic objects for the collaboration services implemented by Liferay.

Components called *connectors* are used to integrate the application logic with Liferay and other external collaboration tools (*Wildfire* for instant messaging and *Asterisk* for voice conferencing). The connectors accommodate interfaces of particular collaboration tools to the needs of the Integration and Adaptation layers. The dependency of the CSCW service related to a particular tool implementation shall be minimized so that the tool can be replaced by other implementation in the future. *Spring* framework is employed as a bean container that is responsible for application objects initialization and their binding. It is based on *IoC* (inversion of control) / dependency injection approach, which promotes decoupling and better reuse of the application components.

The presentation and application logic layers are deployed within the servlet container (usually *Apache Tomcat*) in the form of web applications.

PostgreSQL database is used as the data storage. *Hibernate* is used as ORM (object-relational mapping) tool so that the application can access the database in an object oriented way instead of using SQL statements directly.

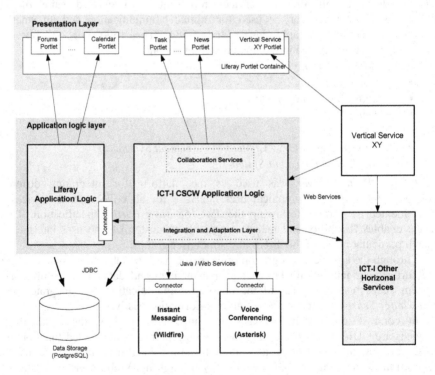

Figure 2 - CSCW services Architecture

Figure 3 shows an example of multi-user chat rooms that can be used for multilateral discussions about specific topics. The chat rooms can be persisted so that a discussion about particular topic can be realized in several sessions over a longer period of time.

3.2 Knowledge search service

Knowledge Search (K. Search) corresponds to a general purpose service that provides support for searching knowledge (and information) available in CNOs in a more precise way (Tramontin-Jr and Rabelo, 2007). This knowledge is the one that is exchanged among CNO partners when they use collaborative tools (forum, chat, wiki, e-mail, files, etc. [see previous section]) and that are further stored in distributed information sources. The knowledge gets shareable only after the user explicitly set it as public.

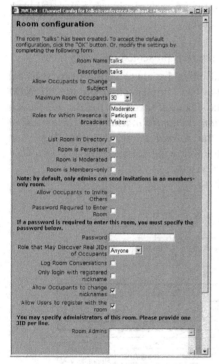

Figure 3 - Chat room configuration and chat room windows

K. search services provide four main functionalities:

1. Ontology management: it is considered a preparatory (off-line) stage for the other functionalities. It should be used by domain experts to build and manage ontologies for representing knowledge in a given CNO. As the process of automatic annotation depends on the instances of the ontologies, this functionality can also be used by CNO-related applications to add or update instance values related to CNO members, like profile information. This functionality is divided into two sub-functionalities: *ontology browsing* and *ontology edition*. While the first one allows users to go through current

ontologies, the edition provides means to add, change or delete elements of the ontology.

2. Document Indexing: system indexes its documents that can be further searched more quickly. Semantic annotations are generated transparently and automatically considering the ontologies used.

3. Simple Search: CNO partners can define semantic queries according to the ontologies adopted by the respective CNO. The results will be related to the contents that have been previously indexed.

4. Federated Search: users taking part in several CNOs perform federated searches by choosing the *context* of the search (among the CNOs they are involved in), defining the semantic query, and then performing the search itself. All the required translations are made transparently according to the ontologies of each involved CNO, and the search results are translated back to the ontologies used in the original query.

Architecture

The K. Search services' implementing architecture is presented in

Figure . K. Search services can be accessed either by client applications (vertical services) or directly by end-users, and they are implemented on top of KIM Platform[1]. KIM covers some of the required features specified for the K. Search functionalities: *automatic semantic annotation*, *semantic indexing* and *retrieval* of content, and query and *navigation* over the *formal knowledge* (ontology and instances). The architecture is composed of the following components:

1. The services themselves (K. search services);
2. A Portlet for general purpose searches;
3. KIM Platform;
4. Client (CNO) applications that access K. Search.

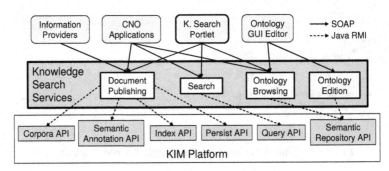

Figure 4 - K. Search architecture

- <u>Document Manager</u>: it implements the functionality *Document Indexing*. This service provides basic CRUD[2] operations on documents using *KIM Corpora* and *Persist* APIs. When documents are created / updated, they are semantically

---

[1] KIM is composed of APIs (Java RMI), some user interfaces, a general purpose ontology and a knowledge base (http://ontotext.com/kim/)

[2] Create, read, update and delete.

annotated and indexed using KIM Semantic Annotation and Index APIs, respectively. When a document is published, the security API is invoked to obtain the user's context (i.e. the CNO he is involved in). This information is transparently attached to the document, which will be further used for filtering during searches.

- <u>Search Engine</u>: it implements the *Simple Search* functionality, using KIM's Query API. It provides four operations:
  - o Search for entities (instances of the ontology);
  - o Search for documents containing semantic annotations related to a given entity;
  - o Search for documents based on semantic queries;
  - o Search for documents using keywords (like a traditional search).
- <u>Ontology Browser</u>: It is implemented on top of KIM's Semantic Repository API.
- <u>Ontology Editor</u>. Implemented on top of KIM's Semantic Repository API.
  The K. Search Portlet is developed as an ordinary JSR-168 portlet.

Figure shows an example of a search, highlighting the correlated terms found out via the (previously defined) ontology.

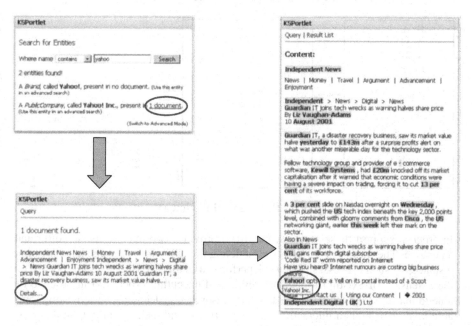

Figure 5: Simplified Mode of the K. Search portlet

3.3 Business Process management service

The goal of this horizontal service is the provision of an advanced user-centered /

interactive Business Process Management service (*iBPM*). The overall idea behind this service is to identify needs for complex business processes management, which may require human interactions (Ratti and Gusmeroli, 2007).

The current state of the art does not provide any tools or standard language able to manage the two separate domains: human and automatic. Currently, what exists is a support for human based activities, supported by the concept of workflow, and the automatic execution activities, namely business processes. Two different languages are widely adopted and recognized as standards: xPDL, for workflow management, and BPEL, for business process execution and orchestration. What is missing is a combination of the two languages, in order to allow the next generation processes, which involves both human and automatic activities. The new language, called CBP (Collaborative Business Process) comprises the two above paradigms.

The analysis performed has highlighted the need of maintaining the semantic and the structure of the two languages as much as possible. For this reason, one language has been chosen as basic (and reference) language, complemented with the tags of the other. So it has been decided to use xPDL as basic language, improved by BPEL constructs which are needed for managing the new approach.

Some semantic elements are still the same in the new schema: for instance, transactions, process and basic xPDL activities with BPEL ones. The inherited tags are not changed through the porting process from one language to the other. Figure 6 shows the "fusion" of the two languages.

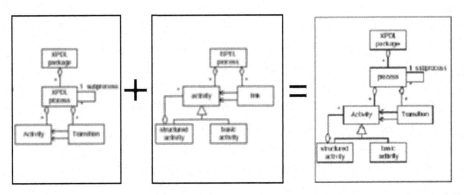

Figure 6 - BPEL and xPDL integration

In order to support these services, the iBPM provides two main tools: an editor and an engine. The former is required for modeling the CBP file, while the latter will run instances of such processes. The work performed in this activity has been focused on the extension of existing tools (for editing and executing processes) in order to be able to manage the new standard. For this reason it was decided to use existing tools able to support human interactions and workflows, and then to build upon them the supporting features for managing BPEL processes.

The selected solutions are two of the mostly used workflow editor and engine: *Jawe*, the editor, and *Shark*, the engine. They are Java client-based applications, which are able to store information inside XML files and to save local data inside any relational database management system. They have been extended using Java as default language in order to save file in CBP and to import BPEL processes.

Architecture

The architecture of the module is very simple. The work performed can be seen as a plug-in of the existing modules for loading BPEL processes and save / load CBP file. In order to provide a more comprehensive usage of the engine, a completely web based module is available for users. This has also been modified during developments stage. The editor will export CBP file, which can be loaded by the engine. Then the external application shall invoke such deployed processes in order to manage the execution of CBP file. Nevertheless, the original BPEL processes will still run under their engine. Figure 7 shows an example of how processes are edited.

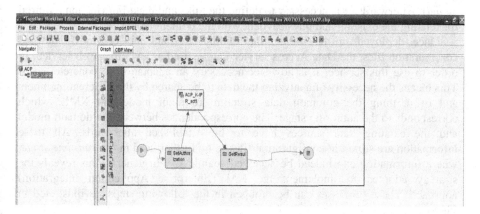

Figure 7 - iBPM editor

3.4 Data Access service

CNO data access facilitates the access to different information sources and databases provided by the different CNO members. It is a software layer, which offers a web service interface for accessing the public data from distinct data sources. It accesses the physical data sources and transforms the physical data into a model that different organizations can understand, providing data abstraction for the VO members. This process is carried out through the steps described below.

First of all, the identification of the domain model that contains the data to be shared between the different organizations should be done. This domain model is known by the organization members and includes the structure and semantic of the information. Data transformation, from the specific data structure of the members to the domain model, is done by the data access middleware.

Interoperability between organizations is facilitated by the use of this service in the data interchange. The incorporation of new members or new services is also made easier, as the meaning and structure of the data is already known. Any data change at low level is transparent to the others ICT-I or client services. Therefore, this data layer provides loose coupling between the services and the underlying databases or information sources.

One very relevant type of data source case is the (relational) databases that belong to the CNO members. A direct access to the companies' database is usually not possible but this can be achieved – once agreed – with the Data Access web service interface. The middleware accesses the given database and transforms the data to XML, according to the pre-defined model. By using this service, organizations are provided with access to the VO members' legacy databases by using the standard http protocol and SOAP messages.

Architecture

There are two different stages for this service: *Authoring* stage and *Run-time* stage. In the first one, it is necessary to analyze the information that is going to be accessed, to understand its meaning and to define its structure (the so-called *domain model*). Afterwards, it is necessary to define the links and meta-information required for relating the existing and physical data with the domain model.

Once deployed in the server, the middleware and the previously defined configuration files, the Data Access service can be used as any other web service. In order to use this service, it is however necessary an adaptation to concrete cases. This means the necessity of analyzing the data to be shared by the different members and of defining the common data structure (domain model) in XML, which corresponds to the authoring stage. The correspondences between the domain model and the existing data sources have to be established afterwards. All these information are stored in configuration files to be further used in the *run-time stage*, where information can indeed be accessed seamlessly. In general, this reveals the strategy adopted to implement the EAI (Enterprise Application Integration) approach. These processes can be grouped in the following steps, as illustrated in Figure 8:

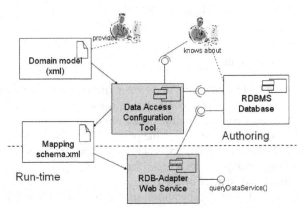

Figure 8 - Data Access services

Two roles can be identified. The first one corresponds to a business expert, who knows about the domain being modeled. The other role corresponds to people with knowledge on the concrete implementation of the information in the data bases. Both roles are necessary to configure this service via the Configuration Tool.

1. Identification and definition of the model that represents the information to be shared by the different members, in XML schemas.
2. Configuration of the adapters to be used. It is necessary to identify the relations between the domain model and each concrete data source. Concrete

parameters for each data source are provided and associated to the suitable adapter. Three types of adapters have been designed: web service adapter, XML files adapter and Relational Database (RDBMS) adapter. The most complex is the last one, and in order to assist the developer in this process a tool is provided. It is a stand-alone tool (*Data Access Configuration Tool*) where the mapping between the DBMS and the *"Domain model schema"* can be done relatively easily.

3. Deployment of the middleware and the configuration files in the corresponding web server. This web server should have access to the data source for which it is configured, and it will offer a Web Service interface.

Figure 9 illustrates a step during the mapping phase, indicating the correspondence between the domain reference model and a given data base model.

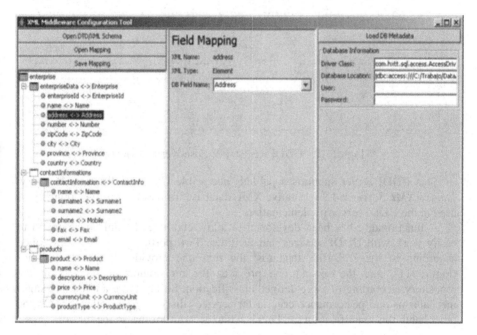

Figure 9 - XML middleware configuration Tool

3.5 Registry and Discovery services

ICT-I Registry and Discovery services provide support for working with the ECOLEAD repository of Web Services. ECOLEAD provides a UDDI v2 (OASIS standard[3]) server in order to register all the developed web services as well as to be able to find and use them in an easy and standard way. The core ICT-I Registry and Discovery includes the following components:

- UDDI Repository: stores the web services' meta information and related information necessary for its characterization;

---

[3]   http://www.uddi.org/

- ICT-I Services Registry: supports registration of the web services in the UDDI server;
- ICT-I Services Discovery: supports the web services finding process.

These services are categorized in two profiles (Figure 10):

(a) for services and applications, it is possible to use these functionalities by the use of the corresponding application programming interfaces (APIs), which are included in the UDDI specification provided by OASIS.

(b) for end-users (developers), it also provides two portlets in a portal for making accessible these web services to users that need to know which services are available.

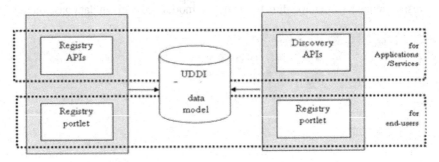

Figure 10 - UDDI Registry & Discovery services

This UDDI server supports a publicly accessible Universal Business Registry. *Tamino XML Server v.4.2.1*, a native XML database from Software AG Company, is used in the UDDI server implementation.

A functionality has been developed to allow end-users (mainly developers) to easily work with UDDI services and facilities. Two portlets have been developed according to the JSR-168 standards: the first one provides browsing facilities (Figure 11), and the second one provides the registration of services in the repository, according to a pre-defined classification. So far, there are not any smart mechanisms and performance criteria for services discovery and selection. On the other hand, this classification can be taken into account for that in the future.

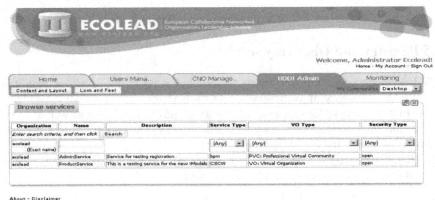

Figure 11 - UDDI Browsing service

3.6 Stubless Invocation

The purpose of a stubless invocation is to allow client applications (e.g. an organization) to effectively use any service of the Services Federation seamlessly, whatever the technology / environment services had been developed and deployed. This goes to the direction of extending the collaboration level among CNO members in a way they can also *share services.* So far there was a hard restriction as current implementations of the web-services specifications by different vendors were not fully compatible hence creating interoperability problems when one tried to invoke another one. Thanks the use of the Apache WSFI (*WS Framework Invocation*) standard specification and its implementation, plus a layer that prevents programmers / client-applications from knowing implementation details and creating proxies manually, the implementation done in the ICT-I makes this automatically and dynamically (Piazza and Rabelo, 2007).

Architecture
Inside this general framework, an entity can be a service provider or consumer. Actually, stubless is not a web service itself. From the consumer view point, Stubless process acts as a *layer* in the form of an API for services invocation support, making the differences among different implementations totally transparent. Using this API, different CNO members can share different services regarding their particular business processes' logics, and without changing the standard way of working with services (registry, publish and invoke). Figure 12 presents the conceptual architecture of the Stubless invocation process.

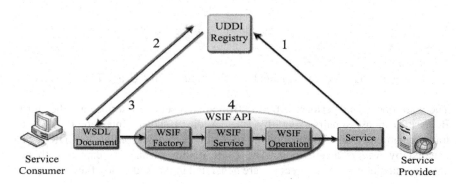

Figure 12 - Stubless Architecture

A stubless invocation is characterized by the following steps:

<u>*Service Provider Side*</u>
1 – Publish a service with the respective WSDL address endpoint
<u>*Service Consumer/Client Side (Stubless invocation)*</u>
2 – Search for a service on a registry
3 – Load the WSDL description of the service
4.1 – Create a WSIF factory for the service
4.2 – Create the WSIF service based on the WSDL document

4.3 – Use the WSIF service to get the operation to be invoked

4.4 – Create the message and invoke the service based on a particular binding. The invocation is handled by the WSIF Provider that is an implementation of a WSDL binding that can run a WSDL operation through a binding-specific protocol (like SOAP, EJB, JMS, JCA and Local Java).

3.7 Billing services

This service operationalizes the pay-per-use model as long as given web-services are accessed/used within previously agreed business models. This service is fed with data from the *Audit Handler* service (*Interceptor* sending *UsageRecords*). The bill is based on a period of Web Services Usage from WSC entities (i.e. Customers). The billing is performed in batch time, with support for simple business models (Data volume and Usage Time). Billing summary reports are automatically generated in HTML thanks to the Reporting Service (see next section). Figure 13 illustrates a bill generated under these two models.

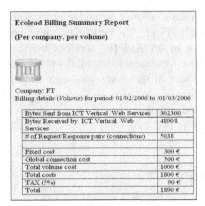
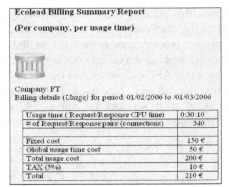

Figure 13a – Volume oriented   Figure 13b – Usage Time oriented

The main operations performed by the Billing web service interface are the storing Request/Responses pairs sent by the Audit Handler Interceptor, and the transformation of this information in start-stop records according to CDR format handled by *Radius* aware tools. The CDR Radius format is adapted with new attributes and new start-stop records are generated in the Radius log files.

3.8 Reporting services

The Reporting Service delivers a Report to a WS Client entity. The report is can be generated in some standard formats and based on predefined templates ('Detailed Billing Usage' or 'Usage Billing Summary'). The Reporting Service mainly offers an operation that computes a bill and delivers it in the HTML format.

3.9 Interception Handler

The scope of this service is to allow interception of messages at SOAP level without disturbing or being intrusive in the web service chain (WS Client <-> intermediates <-> WS Provider). Figure 14 presents a Use Case diagram that explains the high level functions of this Service:

- Intercept and store temporally Requests, Responses and Fault Messages that flow between a WSC and a WSP;
- Send bunches of SOAP messages to a Recording Service offering a function of storing and converting to appropriate format to do accounting and billing.

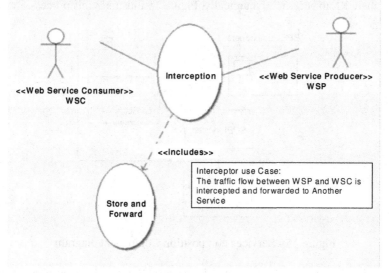

Figure 14 – Use Case Handler service

Interceptor is mainly built on top of the two following objects:

- The *Usage Record* object contains information relative to the SOAP message intercepted,
- The AuditHandler Object (interceptor), instantiated and deployed in the runtime infrastructure where the WSPs are deployed.

The number of items sent each time is a tradeoff between performance penalty (by sending one by one) and accurate/just in time information to the recipient (by sending a too big bunch of items). Handler Interceptor objects can be customizable at launch time or dynamically, at runtime.

3.10 Services composition

This service allows defining how two or more web services can interact. Services composition is a critical part of making web services effective. By using this service, it is possible to set a business process as a flow of executable processes, and to launch this business process by using an engine that interprets it by means of the web services' interfaces. BPEL is the business process language and it is a standard *de facto* for that.

This service is executed at two phases / using two modules: authoring (using the BPEL designer) and runtime (using the BPEL engine). The BPEL designer supports the process of writing how a given set of web services is going to be connected, specifying the conditions of the flow and defining the inputs and the outputs, generating a "BPEL sequence" afterwards. The BPEL engine is the module that interprets and executes the "BPEL sequence". In the current implementation, an extension was added-on for ActiveBPEL engine, which is deployed and installed inside the engine in order to be transparent to the end-user. This functionality consists on the use of the UDDI repository for searching web services and for getting the URL to access it dynamically. Figure 15 illustrates this process.

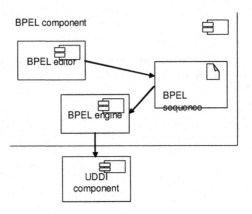

Figure 15 - Services composition Component diagram

A BPEL Editor is needed for the authoring stage. There are different products in the market and Active Endpoints product has been the one used. They have an ActiveBPEL engine (associated to ActiveBPEL™ Designer[4]) that is open-source. The designer is an integrated visual toolset for rapidly creating, testing and deploying composite applications based on the BPEL v1.1 standard. At the runtime stage, then a BPEL engine is required, which is in charge of interpreting and executing the BPEL sequence. To this engine, one module that allows the activation of the searching functionality in a UDDI server has been integrated. During the BPEL sequence execution, the engine checks if the Web Service used in the sequence has been registered in the UDDI server. If it is there, then it reads from the UDDI server the proper URL. This process is totally transparent to the end-user and the system administrator can easily configure this. Figure 16 shows an example of the interface to define a composition.

4. CONCLUSIONS

This paper has presented the Collaborative Business ICT infrastructure (ICT-I) that was developed in the ECOLEAD Project for supporting CNOs in collaborating and doing businesses more effectively. It has been conceived based on the service

---

[4] http://www.active-endpoints.com/products/activebpeldes/index.html

oriented architecture paradigm / web-services technology, providing organizations with a transparent (mostly), platform-independent, easy-to-use, secure-embedded, lean, distributed, scalar, on-demand and pay-per-use ICT-I.

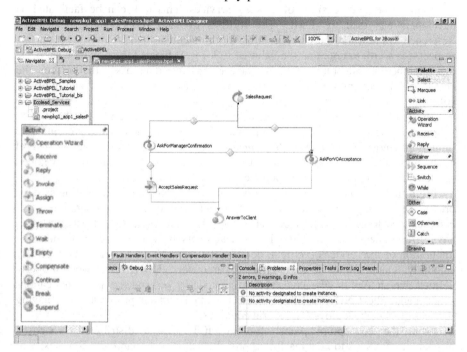

Figure 16 - Services composition editor interface

About the *plug & play* and *transparency* ICT-I features, they are materialized in the following general form. Considering the intrinsic current limitations of existing technologies, *Plug & Play* is concretized in the sense that users can access ICT-I services just using a browser and doing a small configuration of some security issues in the first time they use it. This means that neither local deployments nor intensive configuration operations are required. In the same way, other applications and services can execute ICT-I services just by invoking them. *Transparency* is also supported in the sense that both users and client-applications/services don't need to know anything about ICT-I, i.e. ICT-I services can be discovered, composed and used/executed no matter where they are, how they are and which technology has been used in their implementation, so this is transparent for clients.

It is important to point out the capability of ICT-I to be integrated with B2B functionalities, which are nowadays also getting web-services-based. This means the possibility of having a "complete" and global environment where B2B transactions-based and collaborative-based processes can be glued transparently.

The derivation process allows the instantiation of particular ICT-Is for envisaged CNOs. The services that have been described correspond to the derivation carried out in the ECOLEAD project, and it comprised the requirements of three types of CNOs: Virtual organization Breeding Environments (VBE), Virtual Organizations

(VO) and Professional Virtual Communities (PVC). The implemented services reflect a functional vision upon the Reference Architecture classes of services. As such, different implementations and functionalities can be developed in different derivations and/or extensions of existing services. This task can be facilitated as developers can take the UML specifications of each service presented in the Reference Framework and can specialize and implement them as they wish. In this respect it is worth to note that the value of ICT-I goes beyond the provided services; the reference architecture itself, in fact, is an important asset that makes the development and integration of new services easier, more robust and globally coherent.

The implemented services are actually at prototype level and have been only validated in the scope of ECOLEAD project. This means that services present some limitations, most of that due to their intrinsic complexity. In fact, there are several open and challenging problems around web-services technology and the developed services, and their solving were not the central focus of this work.

From the technological point of view, the chosen web-based technologies have proven to be a good choice in terms of integration and interoperation usual complexities. Regardless the fact that the development environment was settled in advance and hence most of the ICT-I developers have used the same one, the integration of the services (vertical, horizontal and basic) was carried out relatively smoothly. Once all services' interfaces, parameters, UDDI, etc., were properly defined (which used to take a reasonable time to agree on) and set up, all invocations – and hence the CNO processes – were executed without problems even having services physically deployed in several countries.

From the conceptual point of view, ICT-I, as a distributed WS-based infrastructure, seems to be a feasible approach. On the other hand, the complexity of developing web-services-based applications has to be pointed out. In fact, the related standards are capable of coping with relevant interoperability problems, so implementations can be concentrated on the services themselves. However, to become a reasonable expert on web-services, it takes time. The involved platforms, containers, development environments, the several concepts around UDDI, WSDL, SOAP, portlets, etc., are very time consuming to learn and require a relatively solid ICT background to implement services in a good and fast way. Another point refers to the identification of limitations in some specific technologies, e.g., the relative rigidity of LifeRay when more flexible GUIs are required.

From the performance point of view, it could be observed that some services took a relatively long time to execute. On one hand, this was also due to the intrinsic complexity of some services and the required processing time needed by some of them. On the other hand, the "deployment map" of the whole ICT-I (including the services repositories and registration repositories) was set up essentially considering the current partners' convenience and facilities as QoS considerations were not hard taken into account. Anyway, ICT-I is flexible enough to be set-up with any deployment map.

ICT-I will have its development continued. A number of new services and improvements in some already developed is on the way, also trying to take advantage of plenty of outcomes currently being researched and provided by other projects and initiatives.

Acknowledgments
This work was mostly supported by the European Commission under the project IST FP-6 IP ECOLEAD project (www.ecolead.org). The Brazilian participation was also supported by the Brazilian Council for Research and Scientific Development – CNPq (www.cnpq.br) in the scope of IFM project (www.ifm.org.br). Special thanks to Mr. Rui Tramontin and Mr. Carlos Gesser (UFSC), Mr. Philippe Gibert (France Telecom), Mr. Roberto Ratti (TXT), and Mr. Walter Woelfel and Mr. Stanislav Mores (Siemens Austria) for their collaboration in the conception and implementation of the ICT-I services.

5. REFERENCES

Borst, I.; Arana, C.; Crave, S.; Galeano, N. (2005). Technical Report (Deliverable) D62.2 ICT-I Business Models, in www.ecolead.org.

Gesser, C. E. (2006). An Approach for the Dynamic Integration of Web Services in Web Portals. MSc Thesis, Federal University of Santa Catarina, Brazil, in www.gsigma.ufsc.br.

Loss, L; Pereira-Klen, A.; Rabelo, R. J. (2007). Towards Learning Collaborative Networked Organizations. Proceedings PRO-VE′2007 - 8th IFIP Working Conference on Virtual Enterprises, in Establishing the Foundation of Collaborative Networks, Springer, pp. 243-252.

Piazza, A. and Rabelo, R.J. (2007). An Approach for a Seamless Interoperability among Heterogeneous Web-Services Platforms for Collaborative Networked Organizations, MSc Thesis, Federal University of Santa Catarina, Brazil, in www.gsigma.ufsc.br.

Pinheiro, F. R.; Rabelo, R. J. (2005). Experiments on Grid Computing for VE-related Applications. Proceedings PRO-VE'2005 - 6th IFIP Working Conference on Infrastructures for Virtual Enterprises, in Collaborative Networks and their Breeding Environments, Springer, pp. 483-492.

Rabelo, R. J.; Gusmeroli, S.; Arana, C.; Nagellen, T (2006). The ECOLEAD ICT Infrastructure for Collaborative Networked Organizations. Proceedings 7th IFIP International Working Conference on Virtual Enterprises, in Collaborative Networked Organizations and the Services Oriented Economy, Springer, pp. 451-460.

Rabelo, R. J.; Gusmeroli, Sergio (2007). A Service-Oriented Platform for Collaborative Networked Organizations. Proceedings 8th IFAC Symposium on Low Cost Automation, 2007, Havana, Cuba.

Rabelo, R.; Nagellen, T.; Arana, C. (2005). Technical Report Deliverable D61.1a (v2) – Reference Framework for a Collaborative support ICT infrastructure, in www.ecolead.org.

Ratti, R.; Gusmeroli, S. (2007). Interactive User-Centered Business Process Management Services, in Proceedings PRO-VE′2007 - 8th IFIP Working Conference on Virtual Enterprises, in Establishing the Foundation of Collaborative Networks, Springer, pp. 487-494.

Ratti, R., Rabelo, R.J. (2007). Technical Report Deliverable D61.1c – ICT-I Reference Framework, in www.ecolead.org.

Rodrigo, M.; Arana, C.; Rabelo, R. (2005). Technical Report Deliverable D61.3a – First Prototype ICT-I Infrastructure for collaboration, in www.ecolead.org.

Rodrigo, M.; Ratti, R. (2007). Technical Report Deliverable D64.1d – ICT-I Integrated Prototype, in www.ecolead.org.

Rodrigo, M.; Ratti, R. (2007). Technical Report Deliverable D64.1c – ICT-I Integrated

Prototype, in www.ecolead.org.

Sowa, G., Śnieżyński, T. and Wolański, M. (2007). Technical Report Deliverable D61.4b - Security Framework and Architecture, in www.ecolead.org.

Tramontin-Jr., R.; Rabelo, R. J. (2007). A Knowledge Search Framework for Collaborative Networks. Proceedings PRO-VE´2007 - 8th IFIP Working Conference on Virtual Enterprises, in Establishing the Foundation of Collaborative Networks, Springer, pp. 573-582.

Zambiazi, Saulo P.; Rabelo, R. J. (2007). Virtualization of Collaborators in the Manufacturing: a Model based on Agent Bots, Proceedings VIII SBAI - The Brazilian Symposium on Intelligent Automation [in Portuguese].

PART 6

PILOT DEMONSTRATORS

PILOT DEMONSTRATORS

Jean-Michel Ortholand

France Telecom Orange Labs - jeanmichel.ortholand@orange-ftgroup.com

Jean-Louis Leroux

France Telecom Orange Labs – jean-louis.leroux@orange-ftgroup.com

This section of the book is focused on the pilot demonstrators. The first chapter aims at describing the methodology used for demonstration activities of ECOLEAD with a focus on the criteria to identify the scenarios and expected impacts. Furthermore, methodological findings and future directions for sustainability of demonstrators are highlighted.

In the following chapters, each end user's scenario is detailed with its take-up plan and outcomes of metrics to verify the complete and successful achievement according to targets.

1. APPROACH FOR PILOT DEMONSTRATION

1.1 Introduction

Any association or company in charge of deploying a framework to set up a virtual collaborative organization is concerned with the viability of such a project. Even if the legitimacy is confirmed, how to be sure that implemented concepts and tools will accommodate the users' expectations? How to evaluate objectively their taking over and benefits? Many challenges must be faced and require a tried and tested methodology. This section aims to share the ECOLEAD experience with the reader regarding pilot implementations based on research results, to give her/him insights on the methodology carried out as well as significant results.

1.2 Challenges

In large or medium-scale projects with a tremendous organizational impact, a sustained evaluation strategy is required. In this sense, a group of well-identified *testers / evaluators* must be involved from the initial stages. Their selection is done to cover the functional scope of the project. These evaluators must be willing to contribute positively to the evaluations. This implies defining a proper organization for performing their testing activities, to learn the used concepts and tools, to formalize their objectives, and to give feedback which will allow improving the solution. Finally, they have to show their honest motivation to produce findings which relevance and the durability will be useful to the community.

In the ECOLEAD context, the main challenges in leading demonstration activities lie in its European scope: the multiplicity of the stakeholders (developers and end users) which induces differences in interests and objectives.

Regarding design and development teams of the infrastructure and tools, their objective is to implement formalized concepts and processes in a collaborative way in order that the whole solution is integrated and works harmoniously. Each developer of one or several software (S/W) components must take into account the end user's expectations having, at the same time, in mind the original functional objectives. In addition, his/her vision is mainly technical and focused on the boundary of the S/W piece to be implemented.

The diversity of pilots in ECOLEAD is wide. They come from various environments (SMEs, associations, laboratories, etc). Their approach is business-oriented which underlies that their major concerns are in line with their activity. Concretely it means that the use of the solution and its impact evaluation require performing real use cases from beginning to end and defining objective metrics in phase with the business. Every scenario is to be achieved by using several S/W demonstration objects and guided by conceptual and methodological results of the project.

Three focus groups were constituted within the ECOLEAD context. Concepts and mechanisms to manage new Virtual organisations Breeding Environments (VBE) were experienced by ITESM/IECOS, Helice(ISOIN)/CeBeNetwork networks and Swiss Microtech. Virtuelle Fabrik, Supply Network Shannon and ORONA/OIN were in charge of assessing methodologies, models, services and management tools dedicated to the management of a Virtual Organization (VO). Finally, AEISEC, EDINFORM/FEDERAZIONE and Joensuun Science Park assessed foundations proposed for developing the "Professional Virtual Community" concept.

1.3 Methodology

To efficiently cope with stakes, a full ECOLEAD sub-project has been dedicated to demonstration activities. As shown in the illustrated global life-cycle (Figure 1), the evaluation activity encompasses trial and take-up phases.

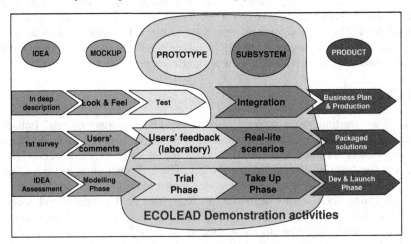

Figure 1: Position of ECOLEAD Demonstration activities in a general project life-cycle

The **trial phase** started once first prototypes have been developed. This activity lasted one year for the specific case of ECOLEAD. The evaluation method is based on several "laboratory" sessions organized by VBE, VOM and PVC stakeholders directly involved in the co-development of CNO solutions. This concurrent demonstration approach resulted in two advantages.

Firstly, initial "demonstration objects" (i.e. combination of early prototypes, conceptual frameworks, templates etc) have been used by end users as soon as they became available and consequently faster improved without waiting for them to reach the full maturity generally expected in a traditional approach. CNO Stakeholders have been invited to indicate possible **areas of improvement** of the experimented ECOLEAD solution, **modifications, additional functionalities** and **new solutions** which best fulfilled their needs. Secondly, end users gave feedback in full objectivity by filling in an **evaluation form** of criteria applied on each one of the tested functionalities and key results.

In the ECOLEAD project, apart from the very specific technical questions raised among developers and end users, the evaluation form collected the qualitative feedback relative to the comprehension easiness, relevance -impact and utility-, usability of the tested material (methodological document, template document, ICT tool…).

After the trial phase, in which software was developed and tested separately outside of any business context, the **take-up phase** consisted in implementing tools in the end user's environment and in qualifying their orchestration. Concept implementations and all mature results were subjected to the test in relevant business scenario. The iterative approach initiated from the beginning of the trials made it possible for each end user (also named pilot) to prepare the take-up phase in advance and to deliver business information to developers in order to be more efficient. Therefore, each pilot has identified several major **business processes** (in relation with the significant ECOLEAD result bundles with information like process description, preconditions, inputs and outputs, milestones) and defined **business scenarios** (as a set of characteristics to pass from current situation to a "to-be" situation, that could be typically creating new CNOs or evolving the existing ones according to emerging paradigms issued from the ECOLEAD project). Furthermore, in order to have a **factual impact evaluation**, pilots were initially requested to describe the expected impact of the solution and then, to evaluate it along the take-up phase.

The impact evaluation in the ECOLEAD context was based on the ITESM methodology where the following topics are addressed: activities, outputs, change/effects, impacts and benefits (cf. Table 1).

Activities	Outputs	Change/Effects	Impacts	Benefits
All necessary activities to implement a tactical decisions making:	Immediate results of activities:	Change in business processes:	Impact on performance measures:	Operational: - Value added per strategy, process and resource
	- People trained	- Flow of activities and information	- Quality	
	- Project designed	- Availability of data, information and knowledge	- Volume - Time	Economical:
- Train	- Project implemented	- Human capital: knowledge, skills	- Cost - Flexibility - Environment	- Profit - Return On Investment
- Design				

- Implement	- Project	and abilities		- Economic
- Evaluate	evaluated	- Technological		Value
		capital: capacity,		Added
		capabilities and		
		usage		**Strategic:**
		- Organization capital:		- Innovation
		practices,		- Excellence
		procedures,		- Customer
		methods and tools		focus

Table 1: Evaluation table

In conjunction with qualitative elements issued from the impact evaluation, a set of **objective metrics** were defined in order to ensure that business scenarios are achieved and expected results met. Choice of criteria must be done with discernment to take into account business perspective like process efficiency, effectiveness (i.e. the actual capability of the proposed demonstration objects to deliver the intended benefits and to achieve the business objectives), and ease of implementation.

2. PUTTING THE METHODOLOGY IN PRACTICE

2.1 The Helice/CeBeNetwork pilot

To illustrate this approach, the take-up of two ECOLEAD partners, the Spanish cluster Helice(ISOIN) and the German network CeBeNetwork, is hereafter detailed. These two aeronautical actors have decided to reinforce their cooperation activities by constituting one pilot context.

The first business process resulting from the preparatory period was the characterization of the two preexisting VBEs and the creation of a new joint VBE. Helice and CeBeNetwork have described its details as follows:

- **Goal:**

  "The goal is to design the organizational and technical framework to support the operation of the VBE according the ECOLEAD VBE Ontology. In parallel, a structure for the cooperation of Helice and CebeNetwork will be analyzed."

- **Current situation:**

  "Helice Foundation acts as a service centre for resources management, business developments and control and management ... collaborates in business developments by putting in contact main contractors and subcontracting companies ... and helps SMEs with the control and management of their processes by ICT infrastructure. Helice promoted the formation of the cluster and motivated the companies to join it.
  As broker of the network, CeBeNetwork organises non-profit events ... All VBE members are invited ... Small workshops are in place to solve interface problems and improve processes commonly. Cooperative meetings serve as well as an opportunity for exchange and discussion. Some ideas for common activities among VBE members have already evolved from those meetings. CeBeNetwork has already offered to provide his capability and contacts to serve as well as initiator for non-aerospace projects.
  The existing organisation and ICT infrastructures do not allow the formation of clusters or VBEs between Helice and CeBeNetwork or other aeronautic organisations in the European context."

- **To-be situation:**

"The challenge is to exploit key skills of the auxiliary companies belonging to the two aeronautic networks and overcome their reduced dimension by promoting joint activities and thus enable them to take on more risks in a more reliable environment, both in regional and European business contexts.

Firstly the take-up aims at designing in a common ontology the characteristics of every network, then provisioning a database according to the model. Secondly the take-up emphasizes the way to manage soft skills like trust, based on different categories like participation on common events."

- **Impact evaluation:**

Activities	Results	Effects	Impacts
- Characterization of actors and their roles - Competency classes definition - Characterization of business processes for each member - Analysis of business challenges - Implementation of approaches and mechanisms for trust and performance management	- Organisational and governance framework - Catalogue of members of the VBE and roles - Catalogue of competencies of the VBE - Methodology for VBE members registration and accreditation - Information about capabilities of each member of the VBE - Methodology to collect performance information - Single value of trust level for every member	- Preparedness oriented methodology to cooperate in the international market - A standardized process for registration of new VBE members - VBE members´ information systematized - Capability to identify partners with suitable trust level for specific needs - Capabilities information available for members - Empowered trust among members - Performance enhancement - Stable framework to further develop and extend the results from the demonstration phases in ECOLEAD to other strategic industrial cases.	- Readiness to cooperation - Increase of validated available information - Increase the formalisation of existing collaborations in supply chain at VO level - Increase cooperation with European VBE such as CeBeNetwork - Number of projects quoted and executed - Multiplying effect by technology transfer and best practices recommendations to other business sectors.

Table 2: Expected impacts (excerpt from Helice/CeBeNetwork take-up)

- **Metrics:**

Table 3 illustrates several business metrics elaborated by Helice and CeBeNetwork to assess tools used to manage the trust criterion and competencies. The values are both quantitative and qualitative, originated from either ECOLEAD tools or surveys.

2.2 Methodological findings

The findings regarding the methodology used for performing demonstration activities are given hereafter.

During the trial phase, iterative approach took advantage of the constant implication and close communication of ECOLEAD partners. Workshops and trainings resulted in a better practical experience and dissemination of tools by pilots inside their organization, a better understanding of business expectations from developers to produce S/W suited to real-life context.

Business Metrics (name and description)	Validity Domain	Initial Value	Expected Value	Current Value
Trust Assessment				
Base trust in HELICE VBE: Average base trust in HELICE VBE	0-5	0	3	3
Base trust in CBN VBE: Average base trust in CBN VBE	0-5	0	3	3.62
Aggregated base trust in the joint VBE: Average base trust in the joint VBE	0-5	0	3	3.3
Increased trust according to economic criteria in the joint VBE: Average economic trust in joint VBE related to the average economic trust in separate VBEs	0-5	0	3	1.1
Increased trust according to technical criteria in the joint VBE: Average technical trust in joint VBE related to the average technical trust in separate VBEs	0-5	0	3	4
Increased trust according to management criteria in the joint VBE: Average management trust in joint VBE related to the average management trust in separate VBEs	0-5	0	3	3.4
Competency management				
VBE members' information systematized: Competence View-Discovery functionality easy use. Tests in this section aim to measure the possibility to identify members' capabilities/resources in a standardized way.	Very Good, Good, Acceptable, Not acceptable	Acceptable	Good	Good
Competence information availability and discovery. The test will define a number of significant search according the different competences /capabilities/resources described in the VBEs. Each indicator will be given as the probability to discover a given characteristic in PCMS of the VBEs. Tests will be done in the separate VBEs and joint VBE and a comparison will be executed.	0-1	0	0.75	0.8
Confidence in information collected because of validation	Very Good, Good, Acceptable, Not acceptable	Not acceptable	Good	Good

Table 3: Business Metrics with intermediate values (excerpt from Helice/CeBeNetwork take-up)

Two main challenges were significantly taken up to facilitate the usage of tools in business contexts.

- The wide variety of current situations required to manage the interoperability with legacy data as well as the integration with the existing

SI –portal. An effort was deployed to specify and provide an interface loose enough to be customized to each environment.

- The willingness to define scope-limited pilots led to select a Service Oriented Architecture (SOA) with demonstration objects assessable unitarily. This approach allowed development teams to improve components safely and to avoid system crash failures.

Along the take-up period, demonstration activities were emphasized on the methodology features to assess business impact, partners' involvement and contribution with actions and occurred under the form of:

- Support for defining with precision instantiatable scenario with evaluation metrics according to templates,
- Proposal of metrics to assess the global solution,
- Setting of tool-dedicated metrics,
- Recommendations on impact evaluation (identification of the take-up-responsible team, typical schedules to plan scenario, elements to define a good metrics –relevance/simplicity/independence/decorrelation).

The follow-up of partners' involvement and motivation has kept the take-up progressing steadily. The variety of pilots has generated difficulties to synchronize take-up progress which have been carefully mitigated thanks to an iterative follow-up and a communication based on continuous progress reports.

Avantages in terms of Business Impact
Target values of business metrics of all scenarios have been reached
Globally, the ECOLEAD solution has met your business expectations
Understanding of the ECOLEAD framework
The ECOLEAD concepts are rather easy to comprehend and to follow
The ECOLEAD terminology is understandable
Adequacy of the ECOLEAD solution to your context
The ECOLEAD solution suits to my business context
The ECOLEAD solution is naturally integrated to my IT infrastructure
Qualities of the ECOLEAD solution
Performance: the ECOLEAD solution doesn't lead to significant inconvenience
Security: the ECOLEAD security complies with business expectations
Scalability: the ECOLEAD solution may extent context dimensions without perceptible constraints or limitations
Simplicity: the ECOLEAD solution is simple to use
Extensibility: a new functionality may be subsequently added without difficulty.
Configurability: the ECOLEAD solution may be tuned to the business context without difficulty
Availability/Support of ECOLEAD resources
ECOLEAD developers are available when necessary
Initialization (ex: data provisioning) of the ECOLEAD environment complies with my supply

Table 4: Statements of overall metrics

Besides business-dedicated metrics, a set of **overall metrics** were defined to evaluate the global solution through simple statements (shown above) that end users were asked to agree on or disagree (with different levels of intensity).

Interviewees were also invited to complete their answers with a free-text comment useful for a deeper qualitative interpretation of results.

3. CONCLUSION

We have seen in this preamble, before entering pilot descriptions, that demonstration management is a key activity which needs to be handled with care, according to the twofold objectives to a full achievement:

1. To offer methodological conditions to reveal all benefits and limits when production elements (material and prototypes) are checked against hands-on experience,
2. To perform actions that guarantee end users carry out actively and correctly their take-ups according to business processes.

Specifically to ECOLEAD project, several lessons emerge from the analysis of empirical results coming from demonstration activities:

1. The solution has widely proved to be popular with the majority of end users regarding the business impacts. Its adequacy has been reinforced during efficient workshops.
2. Scale of the project has highlighted the need to plan a ramp-up stage to become acquainted with concepts, terminologies and tools. Trained leaders must in turn disseminate and adjust their knowledge of principles and practices to their professional environment to have a real local support.
3. Technological choices have allowed addressing the diversity of IT systems without negative effects.
4. Criteria like performance, security and scalability have increased steadily along the take-up stage and convinced demonstrators of the ECOLEAD viability.
5. Stakeholders have got out of the solution many advantages and several positive impacts: new business opportunities, better reactivity, leverage of services between organizations ...

Like ECOLEAD partners, interested CNOs could take advantage of this return on experience materialized by tools and artifacts such as: implementation guides, success stories, scenario descriptions, covering processes, etc.

4. REFERENCES

1.   Nexus Associates, Segal Quince Wicksteed Ltd. and ITESM (1998). "Assessment System for No-Financial Enterprises Support Programs for Mexican SMEs". Project Final Report.
2.   France Telecom Quality Process Referential – Process and Methods Department – 2004
3.   ISO 9001 Certification of Orange Business Services - 2005

Nathalie Galeano[1], Arturo Molina[1], Jean Beeler[2], Francis Monnier[2], Michel Pouly[2], Carmen Aguilera[3], Alberto Olmo[3], Daniel Laessig[4], Berthold Tiefensee[4]

[1]*Tecnológico de Monterrey, MEXICO,* [2]*Swiss Microtech Enterprise Network, SWITZERLAND* [3]*ISOIN, Spain,* [4]*CeBeNetwork, GERMANY*
ngaleano@itesm.mx, armolina@itesm.mx, jean.beeler@bluewin.ch, f.monnier@ravine.com, michel.pouly@epfl.ch, caguilera@isoin.net, aolmo@isoin.net, dlaessig@cebenetwork.com, btiefensee@cebenetwork.com

The experiences of applying ECOLEAD research project results different Virtual organisation Breeding Environment (VBE) are presented in this chapter. Virtual Breeding Environment reference model has been used in IECOS, SMT, ISOIN and CeBeNetork for the improvement of its business processes. These organizations as pilot demonstrators have followed three take-up phases: definition, implementation, and demonstration, allowing an adequate feedback methodology to improve project results. Results, experiences and lessons learned regarding the implementation of ECOLEAD VBE model and tools in these demonstrators are detailed in this chapter.

1. INTRODUCTION

Large research projects that aim to create operational models, mechanisms, methodologies and new tools that improve the operation of any organization must include in their programs implementation and demonstration phases that permit suitable progress during the development process. ECOLEAD as an integrated research project that developed new tools, models and methodologies that foster the creation and management of Virtual Organization Breeding Environment (VBE) as one of its main vertical pillars, planned a demonstration phase where several pilot networks took up the results of the project.

For this purpose, four networks were the demonstrators that implemented and validated the results of the project related to the VBE model: 1) IECOS, a Mexican network in the manufacturing and engineering field, 2) SMT, a Swiss network of screw machining companies, 3) CeBeNetwork, the leader of an engineering supplier network based in Germany in the aerospace industry and, 4) the Aeronautic Cluster of Andalusia, represented by its core technological partner of ISOIN. The latter two networks formed one demonstrator case due to their common interest in quickly create order-dependent Virtual Organizations for the aerospace engineering sector and its geographical proximity.

Results, experiences and lessons learned regarding the implementation of ECOLEAD VBE model and tools in each demonstrator case with IECOS, SMT, ISOIN and CeBeNetwork are described in this chapter. The list of tools demonstrated and taken-up by the different demonstrators are:

- MSMS – Membership & Structure Management System
- PCMS – Profiling & Competency Management System
- ODMS – Ontology & Discovery Management System
- Trust-Man - Trust Management System
- DSS – Decision Support System
- VIMS – Virtual Organization Information Management System
- BAMS – Bag of Assets Management System
- Co-Finder – Collaboration Opportunity Finder
- COC-Plan – Collaboration Opportunity Characterization and Rough Plan
- PSS – Partners Search and Suggestions
- WizAn – Agreement Negotiation Wizard

The structure of each case description follows the demonstration guidelines of the ECOLEAD project, the results are presented in terms of the different phases of the take-up roadmap: definition, implementation, and demonstration.

2. IECOS

IECOS S.A de C.V (Integration Engineering and Construction Systems) is a Brokerage company, created at CIDYT (Centre of Innovation in Design and Technology) of Tecnologico de Monterrey, Mexico. In 2000, IECOS initiated operations, using the Virtual Organisation (VO) model as its operational model. Brokers in IECOS after searching for business opportunities and/or developing new products in specific market sectors, select and integrate competencies of different Mexican SMEs from a pool of companies (know as Virtual Breeding Environment - VBE) as its main manufacturing partners.

IECOS is actually divided into three business units: *IECOS Technology* offering the development of new products, processes and manufacturing systems; *IECOS Supply Services* offering the integration of associated enterprises capable to deliver manufactured products (mainly metal-mechanic and plastic parts) according to the quality, cost and delivery time expected by the customer; and *IECOS Engineering* developing customized solutions in the electronic and mechanical engineering processes.

2.1. IECOS Definition Phase: Activities and Results

During the *definition* phase, IECOS General Director and Tecnológico de Monterrey team worked together to obtain the involvement of network representatives and to identify the main ECOLEAD tools that would improve IECOS operation. Instruction and training meetings were made to disseminate the Virtual organisation Breeding Environment (VBE) concepts and models.

Two preparation meetings were carried out together with IECOS General Director and Supply Services Manager in order to identify the main opportunity areas that could be tackled with ECOLEAD strategic results. These two meetings comprised: a training session in which the ECOLEAD results were explained and a workshop session in which IECOS main problems were identified. The following were the main opportunities areas recognized:

1. The registration of new members and the identification of profiles and competencies is an un-standardized process that should be automated in a formal way.
2. The IECOS management activity is subjectively measured. The definition of performance indicators that measure VBE members' performance within a Virtual Organisations (VOs) and the VBE as a whole are not formally defined.
3. The use of non-standard procedures for VO creation is a weakness that IECOS network has. Brokers manage VO creation according to their intuitive procedures.

With the identification of these opportunity areas, three business processes, with independent objectives, were defined and considered for implementation and demonstration activities. Pilot scenarios were planned and adapted for each business process, and a set of indicators for each scenario were also defined (See Table 1).

Table 1. Results of IECOS Definition Phase

	Scenario 1	Scenario 2	Scenario 3
Business Process	Members Registration and Profiling & Competency Management	VBE Performance Management	VO Creation
Addressed Issue	Requirements for member's registration process standardization and their competencies identification	Indicators & methodologies for measuring members' performance are not formally defined	VO creation process is managed intuitively by each IECOS broker
Main Objective	Improvement of VBE members' registration process	Formalization of VBE performance measurement system	Semi-automation of CO-Characterization process for competencies deployment
Indicators	• Number of Registered Members • Information Availability • Organisation/Structure of Member Information • Degree of understanding on VBE terms	• Number of Evaluated Applicants in IECOS • Information availability about IECOS members' trust levels • Facility to monitor performance/operation of the VBE • Organisation of VO historical information	• Facility to decompose products and services • Facility to design work plans • Partners Selection Process • Organisation of VO information
Tools Used	• MSMS • PCMS • ODMS	• TrustMan • DSS • VIMS	• COC-Plan • PSS • VIMS

2.2. IECOS Implementation Phase: Activities and Results

The focus of *implementation* phase was to create the necessary environment in IECOS (the pilot demonstrator) for taking-up the tools, and to ensure that the tools were ready for its use by end-users. Trial sessions were prepared by ECOLEAD developers were specific training and tests were experienced by networks' end-users, and also developers received feedback according to each demonstrator needs. Besides the trials, IECOS' business processes modelling were also part of this phase identifying the main changes and expected impact in the process concerned by each tool.

The aim of these training and trial sessions was to familiarize IECOS staff with the suitable usage of ECOLEAD tools, and to obtain the corresponding feedbacks about their functionality and usability. These comments and feedbacks have become an efficient source of information for developers to improve their tools. Tecnológico de Monterrey team has also modelled the AS-IS and TO-BE business processes for each scenario.

2.2.1 Scenario 1: Registration of New Members and Profiling & Competency Management System

The first scenario deals with Member Registration. Figure 1 shows the TO-BE model for this business process, three ECOLEAD tools were used in this scenario: MSMS, PCMS and ODMS .The member registration process was improved using the Membership & Structure Management System (MSMS) tool. This allowed a standardized mechanism for applicants to be part of IECOS, to ensure that all the information related to membership applicants is appropriately entered into the respective database and to provide new applicants the needed information regarding the roles they play inside the network. In addition, the Profiling & Competency Management System (PCMS) as semi-automated tool allowed IECOS Supply Services manager to better sort and storage organisations information (profile, skills, capacities, etc.) of IECOS itself, its members and VOs. Finally, the Ontology & Discovery Management System (ODMS) was used for the discovery of new competencies that IECOS may develop for further requirements of new VOs.

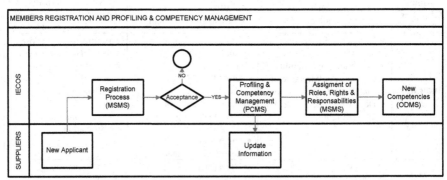

Figure 1. TO-BE Model for Registration of New Members and Profiling & Competency Management

2.2.2 Scenario 2: Performance Management

The main goal to reach in this scenario is to manage and control the performance information within the IECOS network. The innovative tools that were implemented in order to support performance management scenario were: Trust Management

System (TrustMan) to assess IECOS members trust level in relation to five trust perspectives: organisational, social, financial, technological and behavioural (Ratnasingam, 2005), through a set of predefined base trust criteria (Msanjila & Afsarmanesh, 2006). TrustMan aims the creation of an integrated decision making environment through which IECOS Supply Services manager can take faster and at the same time smarter decisions. A Decisions Support System (DSS) has been also included to monitor IECOS performance at different levels: VBE, VBE member and VOs, through a set of graphs, traffic lights and controls charts based on calculated performance indicators. Finally a VO Information Management System (VIMS) tool was implemented in order to facilitate the storage and availability of inheritance information about VOs created within the IECOS network (the VBE).

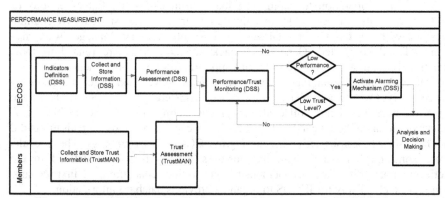

Figure 2. TO-BE Model for Performance Management in IECOS Network

2.2.3 Scenario 3: VO Creation

A VO creation scenario has been planned in IECOS Supply Services (See Figure 3).

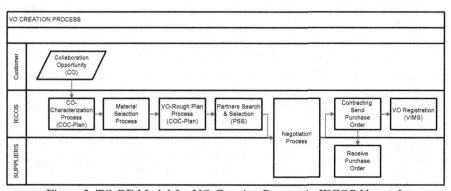

Figure 3. TO-BE Model for VO Creation Process in IECOS Network

One of the innovative tools for this scenario is the Collaboration Opportunity Characterization and Rough Plan (COC-Plan) tool. This tool supports IECOS brokerage process in the decomposition of a business opportunity in terms of required competencies to fulfil the requirements. Afterwards, a VO rough plan is developed to schedule VO tasks. A Partners Search & Suggestion (PSS) tool has been included to semi-automate the configuration of VOs, assisting partners' search and selection through a multiple criteria model (Jarimo & Salo, 2007). This tool matches required competences from the COC-Plan tool with available ones from the IECOS-PCMS in order to find the most suitable partners for a particular business opportunity. Finally, VOs are registered through the VIMS which organize and store information for further use.

2.3. Demonstration Phase: Activities and Results

During the *demonstration* phase, Tecnológico de Monterrey team followed IECOS daily business operation to capture feedback from end-users. Early versions of ECOLEAD tools were available since the demonstration phase started. Live training sessions with IECOS General Director and Supply Services Manager were also prepared and completed. General feedback and comments are related to tools functionalities, usability, bug reports, and opportunities for improvements.

All three tools belonging to the first scenario have been used and taken-up successfully. Over twenty members have been registered in the MSMS. Data from each member has been collected for profile submission in the PCMS. This information had to be adapted to ECOLEAD concepts, since most organisations did not have their processes defined according to ECOLEAD terminology. These results were constantly measured with the business metrics that were defined in the definition phase (See Table 2). Demonstration activities concerning the first scenario were an excellent way for IECOS to organize previous database information.

Table 2. Business Metrics for Scenario #1: Registration of New Members and Profiling & Competencies Management

Business Metrics	Validity Domain	Initial Value	Expected Value	Current Value	Tools Involved
Number of Registered Members	0-90	0	10 members registered in the first quarter. In total 20 members by M44	20	MSMS
Information Availability	None Low Medium High	Low	High availability of the information	High	MSMS PCMS
Organisation and Structure of Members' Information	None Poor Medium Good Very Good	Poor	Very good organisation and structure of members' information	Medium	PCMS
Understanding/ Comprehension of terms in VBE Environment	None Poor Good Very Good	Poor	Very good understanding about terms of the VBE	Good	ODMS

Tools that belong to the second scenario (Performance Management) have also been taken-up. Detailed information from VBE members was needed to assess their base trust level using the TrustMan tool. This tool offers a set of generic trust criteria that can be adapted to any VBE. For this particular case, a meeting was held with IECOS General Director who stated the specific criteria and metrics that apply to IECOS context, consequently the tool was customized using only the trust criteria that suited IECOS business operation. There was also a live personalized training session with the DSS tool, where developers directly showed IECOS end-users the most efficient way to apply tool functionalities in their business, including an example of how to complete a basic balanced scorecard. In this session, different indicators related to IECOS Supply Services were defined. It is planned to continue measuring these indicators after take-up activities in order to analyze long term results.

Table 3. Business Metrics for Scenario #2: Performance Management

Business Metrics	Validity Domain	Initial Value	Expected Value	Current Value	Tools Involved
Number of Evaluated Applicants	0-90	0	5 members evaluated in M45.	5	TrustMAN
Information Availability about IECOS members' Trust Levels	None Low Medium High	Low	High availability of the information	High	TrustMAN
Facility to monitor performance/ operation of the VBE	None Difficult Easy Very Easy	Poor	Very easy to monitor performance / operation of the VBE	Easy	DSS
Organization of VOs Historical Information	None Poor Good Very Good	Poor	Very good understanding about terms of the VBE	Good	VIMS

The tools defined in the third scenario were also taken-up. IECOS Collaboration Opportunities, like a Centrifuge Machine and a Punch for biopsies, were decomposed and characterized using the COC-Plan tool. Competencies were assigned for each component, and this information was sent to the PSS tool, which searched for potential partners automatically in IECOS' own PCMS database.

Table 4. Business Metrics for Scenario #3: VO Creation

Business Metrics	Validity Domain	Initial Value	Expected Value	Current Value	Tools Involved
Facility to decompose products and services	None Difficult Easy Very Easy	Difficult	Very Easy to Decompose Products and Services	Easy	COC-Plan
Facility to Design Work Plans	None Difficult Easy Very Easy	Difficult	Very Easy to design Work Plans	Easy	COC-Plan
Partners' Selection Process	None Difficult Easy Very Easy	Difficult	Very easy to select partners to satisfy a Collaboration Opportunity	Easy	PSS
Organization of VO's Information	None Poor Good Very Good	Poor	Very good understanding about terms of the VBE	Good	VIMS

After the development of each scenario, several surveys were applied to IECOS representatives, where they provided comments and suggestions about the

ECOLEAD solution in general. Among their comments, IECOS end-users stated that the ECOLEAD tools were generally easy to use, and that they represented an excellent long-term solution for the company. However, they also suggested that further training was needed in CNO concepts for many partners who work in the manufacturing industry that do not know these concepts.

2.4 Lessons Learned and Next Steps

The continuous interaction between ECOLEAD team and IECOS regarding project activities has enabled remarkable knowledge transference. IECOS has assimilated ECOLEAD basic concepts and operational model features. For ECOLEAD, this has been a very valuable experience, since it has supported the tools development process and project results.

The implementation and use of VBE tools in IECOS' daily business operations have provided a valuable learning experience for the network. Users learned that it is very important for the VBE administrator to have all members' information readily available in an organized and structured way to facilitate the creation of VOs. End-users also highlighted the importance of interoperability between the tools used in a VBE; since there is information constantly being transferred from one tool to the other. Finally, it is very important to document performance indicators, especially with an eventual expansion of the network, where it would be much too difficult to keep track of members' performances without a standardized system.

One of the main issues that came up during implementation and demonstration activities is that, in order to guarantee the implementation of VBE models and tools, it's necessary to have the complete involvement and commitment of all nodes inside the network. Therefore, there has to be a *culture of collaboration* among the members of a VBE. Several guidelines for VBE culture have been defined which focus on commitment, leadership, self-learning, trust, among others (Romero et al, 2007). In Latin American SMEs, this collaboration culture has not developed yet. It is necessary to define methodologies that can aid in the successful dissemination of this concept (collaboration culture) among the members of an existing or new VBE. This is one of the main issues that need to be addressed in future research that would greatly benefit emerging VBE administrators.

Another issue that is needed for the creation and operation of VBEs is the presence of Information and Communications Technologies (Camarinha-Matos et al, 2004). Although some SMEs in Latin America do have access to the internet, most of them do not use it in daily business. Therefore, for this particular case, two issues need to be addressed. First, large investments in ICT are needed to provide the required infrastructure to implement Collaborative Networks in SMEs that are not familiar with these technologies. Second, promotion and dissemination of the idea of using the available ICT tools to do business are recommended, particularly in the formation of VBEs.

3. SMT

Swiss Microtech (SMT) is a network (founded in 2001) of seven independent SMEs active in the screw machining industry. They produce parts for the automotive, medical, space and telecommunication sectors and export 90% of their production. Four members are competitors and the three others bring complementary competences. Each company keeps its full independence to serve its own customers and alliances (Virtual Organizations) are created to address new markets or orders that are out of reach for single companies. Swiss Microtech started collaborating with a Chinese partner network located in the Guangdong Province to address the Chinese market and find suppliers even for simple and cheap parts as the customers expect a single supplier for a broad range of parts.

3.1. SMT Definition Phase: Activities and Results

As in the previous example, during the *definition* phase, the SMT project team worked together with the network members to identify the main ECOLEAD tools that would improve SMT operation. Information meetings and diverse activities were developed focusing on the identification of SMT main opportunity areas that could be tackled with ECOLEAD strategic results. SMT representatives also attended two meetings coordinated by the developers in order to explain the basic needs of the network. The identification of the SMT business processes that were planned to be improved by the use of ECOLEAD tools gave the following results:

1. The identification of the profiles and competences of SMT and the Chinese partner network is an un-standardized and lacking process that should be realized in a formal way.
2. Technical misunderstandings appeared between the Chinese and Swiss partners because of the different cultural and industrial environment and corresponding implicit knowledge. Notions or terms, which are obvious for one side and are normally not explicitly described, are not clear for the other side and reciprocally. The consequences of these misunderstandings considerably disturb the collaboration.
3. A lot of knowledge and experiences are created within SMT but they are not efficiently shared between the members.
4. The main drawback of collaborative networks is the supplementary delays induced by the participation of many partners. These delays must be shortened as much as possible by using a workflow tool which enables following up the state and the progress of the business processes.

With the identification of these opportunity areas, three business processes, with independent objectives, were defined together with a set of indicators.

Table 5. Results of SMT Definition Phase

	Scenario 1	Scenario 2	Scenario 3
Business Process	Profiles & Competences Management	VBE Knowledge Management	VO Creation
Addressed Issue	Identification of the member's profiles and competences Definition of a common ontology for multicultural VBE's	Sharing of the generated knowledge and experience	VO creation process must be accelerated

Main Objective	Improvement of VBE members' competence registration process and reduction of misunderstandings	The generated knowledge must be shared systematically between all members	Identification of new e-business opportunities Time reduction to set up VO's
Indicators	•Information Availability •Organisation/Structure of Member's profiles & competences •Degree of understanding within the VBE	•Number of issued Bag of Assets items •Information availability for the members	• Identification of interesting tenders on the web • Time reduction to set up VO's
Tools Used	• MSMS • PCMS • ODMS	• BAMS	• CO-Finder • WizAN

3.2. SMT Implementation Phase: Activities and Results

During the *implementation* phase the necessary environment within SMT (the pilot demonstrator) for taking-up the tools (mainly gathering all the necessary data) was created. Trial sessions were prepared by the ECOLEAD developers where specific training and tests were experienced by networks' end-users, and also developers received feedback according to each demonstrator needs. Two common workshops with the developers of PCMS/ODMS tools were also organized at SMT. In parallel SMT' business processes modelling was prepared identifying main changes and impact in the processes supported by each tool.

3.2.1 Scenario 1: Profiles & Competency and Ontology Management Systems

The member registration process was improved using the Membership & Structure Management System (MSMS) tool. This allowed a standardized mechanism for new members joining SMT to ensure that all the information related to membership applicants is appropriately entered into the respective database.

The Profile and Competences Management tool PCMS is used to manage the competences and profiles of both Swiss Microtech and the Chinese partner network. Different levels of aggregation are used within PCMS:

- The network level which describes the competences of the collaborative networked organization as a whole
- The members level which describes the competences of each member
- The VO level which describes the competences of a specific virtual organization

For instance, the following items can be defined at the member level:

Table 6. Items defined at member level in PCMS

Competence	Milling
	Product, dimensions (diameter and length), lot sizes, precision, material etc.
Resources	Machines and human resources
Capability	Actual free capacities
Conspicuity / Evidence	Certifications (ISO 9000, QS 9000, ISO 14000 etc.) Customer evaluations Past experiences (previous quotations/orders)

For Swiss Microtech, the conspicuity data can be used to decide if a request for quotation should be sent to the Chinese partner network or not knowing that each quotation represents a certain amount of work and that receiving requests having a low chance of success negatively affect the motivation. The conspicuity (or factual evidence) will be continuously enriched with successive collaboration experiences. The profiles and competences data can also be used by the sales agents to better target the requests they would send to SMT.

Technical misunderstandings appeared between the Chinese and Swiss partners due to the different cultural and industrial environment and corresponding implicit knowledge. Notions or terms, which are obvious for one side and are normally not explicitly described, are not clear for the other side and reciprocally. The consequences of these misunderstandings considerably disturb the collaboration process. This kind of problem can be avoided through the use of an *ontology*. The Ontology Discovery and Management System tool ODMS supports ontology functions at different levels of abstraction:

- The *meta* level represents meta-concepts like the abbreviation (VBE, VO etc.) used to define other concepts
- The *core* level is used to define common concepts, notions and terms related to collaborative networked organizations
- The *domain* level is used to define common concepts, notions and terms related to a specific activity like metal working or tourism etc.
- The *application* level is used to define usual concepts, notions and terms related to a particular network like Swiss Microtech

At the application level, terms or notions such as commonly used norms and standards (ISO, DIN, etc.), definition of particular machining operations and surface finishing or specifications for raw material (for instance, SMT uses the definitions of the so called German "Stahlschlüssel" handbook to specify steel) can be introduced in the corresponding ontology database and viewed through the tool browser on the web. The notions and terms introduced in ODMS must not be explicitly defined again during the clarification phase of the request for quotation business process, thus considerably reducing the risk of misunderstanding and the time needed to get a quote.

3.2.2 Scenario 2: VBE knowledge Management

Networks that are either competitor based or at least active in the same industrial branch can generate a lot of knowledge when a certain level of trust is reached. This knowledge can be of technical or commercial nature and is not restricted to generalities. Within Swiss Microtech, technical knowledge represents best practices to machine special metals or alloys or to raise the productivity with special tools and fixtures that the members are ready to share with their partners. Commercial knowledge is for instance information concerning the quality of a given customer (delays of payments, alleged problems with the acceptance of parts to reduce the price etc.) The main goal to reach in this scenario is to ensure that these knowledge and experiences generated within SMT are really and efficiently shared between the members. In the past, such knowledge was informally exchanged during meetings but only between the present members. A lot of knowledge that could be shared was lost due to the lack of an appropriate tool. The Bag of Asset Management System

(BAMS) is used in this scenario to overcome these problems as BAMS allows the edition, sharing and recording of this kind of information.

3.2.3 Scenario 3: VO Creation

Developing e-commerce was one of the strategic goals of SMT at its creation time. Manually finding and analyzing tender sites is a time consuming work and the Co-Finder (Collaboration Opportunity Finder) tool could be used to crawl on specific sites to fetch the tenders which could really be interesting for SMT.

On the other hand, the main drawback of collaborative networks is the supplementary delays induced by the participation of many partners. These delays must be shortened as much as possible by using a tool which enables tracking and following up the progress of the business processes workflow. The Agreement Negotiation Wizard (WizAN) is used by the brokers that prepare the quotations involving members of the Swiss and Chinese networks; this tool supports the broker to:

- create and edit the main part of a quotation
- add partners for the quotation preparation
- create Virtual Negotiation Rooms according to the requested topics to be discussed and agreed upon and invite all or some partners to enter the corresponding room
- keep track of the partner's commitments and agreements (e-signatures)
- produce the final quotation

This workflow tool is also important in relation to the ISO 9000 certification of both networks as it ensures clearly defined and repeatable procedures.

3.3. Demonstration Phase: Activities and Results

During the *demonstration* or take-up phase, ECOLEAD tools were taken-up on SMT real-life environment. All four tools belonging to the first and second scenarios have been used and taken-up successfully. Almost all SMT members have been registered in the MSMS and their competences submitted to PCMS. These results were measured with the business metrics previously defined in the definition phase.

Table 7. Business Metrics for Scenario #1: Registration of New Members and Profiles & Competences and Ontology Management

Business Metrics	Validity Domain	Initial Value	Expected Value	Current Value	Tools Involved
Number of registered members	0-x	0	7	7	MSMS
Work and associated costs to manage the VBE competences	Low/ Medium/ High	High	Low	Low	PCMS
Amount of identified and accessible competences	0 – 100%	10%	100%	95%	PCMS
Use of the tool by the different actors	Number of accesses	0	5 per month	1 per month	ODMS PCMS
Share of the implicit SMT definitions	None / Low Medium / High	None	High	Medium	ODMS

Tools that belong to the second scenario (Knowledge Management) have also been taken-up. The Bag of Assets tool has been used and its results were constantly measured with the business metrics previously defined in the definition phase. The evaluation of the economic value of the shared BAMS items is empirically defined by the network coach in a first phase.

Table 8. Business Metrics for Scenario #2: Knowledge Management and Sharing

Business Metrics	Validity Domain	Initial Value	Expected Value	Current Value	Tools Involved
Number of registered bag of asset items	0-xxx	0	10 per member per year	3	BAMS
Economic value of the bag of assets	Sfr.	0	2'000.- per member per year	Not yet available	BAMS

Several tests also started with the tools from the third scenario during the take-up phase. Concerning CO-Finder, the biggest problem was and still is to find tender sites in the field of activity of SMT as many sites, which were identified in 2000, disappeared during the first e-business crash. The WizAN tool has mainly been used within the collaboration with the Chinese partner network.

Table 9. Business Metrics for Scenario #3: VO Creation

Business Metrics	Validity Domain	Initial Value	Expected Value	Current Value	Tools Involved
Time reduction to get an useable quotation from the Chinese network	0-15 days	15 days	7 days	12 days	WizAN
Traceability of the agreed items	None / Low Medium / High	None	High	Medium	WizAN

3.4 Lessons Learned and Next Steps

The proposed ECOLEAD solutions and tools really make the management of SMT easier and more efficient, particularly PCMS/ODMS that has been made available to the sales agents and customers of SMT thus increasing its visibility on the market.

The large amount of knowledge generated within SMT can be systematically shared between the members through the BAMS tool thus allowing SMT to become a true learning organization which increases its success chances in the future. The financial evaluation of theses assets can enhance the motivation of its members. The WizAN tool can reduce the response time within the Swiss-Chinese network and thus increases the benefits of the collaboration. If some of the tools developed within the ECOLEAD project address the needs of large CNO's, the selected ones are useful also for a small, already existing network like SMT. However, it also has to be noted that there are opportunities for improvement, mainly in the user's interface, but we fully understand that the tested prototypes are not (yet) commercial products.

The choice of the "Software as a Service" architecture is particularly relevant as SME are often reluctant to install new software and particularly if it would interfere with the current tools as their IT support resources are limited.

4. ISOIN / CeBeNetwork

As mentioned before, this demonstration scenario is performed together by ISOIN, as the representative of the Aeronautic Cluster of Andalusia and CeBeNetwork, the leader of an aerospace engineering supplier network based in Germany. In order to understand this case, first, the two networks are described.

ISOIN

ISOIN is the core technological partner of the Aeronautic Cluster of Andalusia coordinating innovation activities for the adoption of the advanced CNO (collaborative networked organization) paradigm. The Aeronautic Cluster of Andalusia brings together prime contractors (EADS-CASA, AIRBUS and GAMESA), 93 subcontractors and supporting entities (Universities, Research Centres and Regional Government) in order to increase process efficiency and collaboration opportunities while fostering innovation in a sustainable structure. Most of the companies are located in the provinces of Seville and Cadiz in the South of Spain.

ISOIN coordinates its activities under stable long-term collaboration agreements, mainly under a subcontracting form, operating with a common ICT infrastructure. As the core technological partner of the Cluster, ISOIN acts as a catalyst to promote research initiatives and best practices implementation for the adoption of technological pillars towards the collaborative enterprise paradigm within the aeronautical value network. Its activities in the context of the regional 'Strategic Plan for the evolution of the Aeronautic Cluster of Andalusia' cover:

- Definition of the technological capabilities and readiness for the evolution to the advanced networked structure, as a key factor to achieve world-excellence in the global market.
- Definition, launch and execution of research and development activities to foster innovation in the cluster,
- Provision of suitable infrastructure to match collaboration demand and offer, based on collected competencies and availability.

Strategic projects strengthen the importance of Andalusia as one of the country's main aerospace production regions, such as production of structural components of the A380 program and the final assembly of all-new A400M military aircraft. Besides the final assembly line, the excellence centre in sheet metal production and composites are the key services provided to the aeronautic industry.

The Andalusia Aeronautic Cluster has a consolidated position in the European aircraft Industry, operating since 1930. The network has established collaboration initiatives since its origin, evolving to the current situation (structured as a Foundation, 2002) promoted by the Regional Development Agency to foster collaboration activities and improve the cluster competitiveness in the European aeronautic market. The regional aeronautical sector has dramatically multiplied the number of companies, personnel and turnover, increasing to 125 companies, 6206 employees 850 million Euros in 2006.

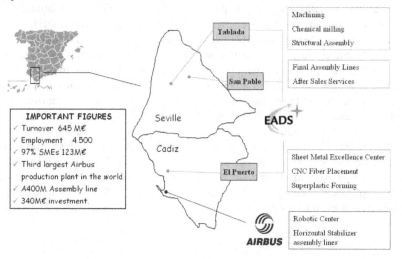

Figure 4. Andalusia Aeronautical Cluster Location

The entities related to the aeronautic sector currently operate under an Extended Enterprise model, with common supporting ICT infrastructure, derived form an ERP model (SAPECMA and SAPORTAL), together with methodologies, services, and tools for facilitating the delivery of supplied parts.

The participation in ECOLEAD is considered a key step towards the collaborative networked business vision, as an effective instrument to enforce this positive evolution and increase its competitiveness in the global market.

CeBeNetwork:

The CeBeNetwork Group was founded by Dr. Frank Arnold and Prof. Dr. Stefan Rill in 1996 in Bremen, Germany and is one of the largest owner operated company's in the European air transportation industry today. In the beginning a classical service company in engineering and engineering similar information technology. Today CeBeNetwork carries out worldwide complex development projects for the European air transport industry and other innovation driven branches. Additional production locations through worldwide cooperation make it possible to target airlines and aircraft producers also in production activities.

CeBeNetwork GmbH Engineering & IT is the core company of the CeBeNetwork Group which was founded as a spin-off of the air transportation industry. The company offers its customers comprehensive performance services and products in the fields of cabin, flight physics, systems and structures. The interdisciplinary teams from the various specialised fields and countries throughout Europe are focused on integrated performance services in product development processes. As strategic supplier of the Airbus Group, CeBeNetwork Engineering & IT takes responsibility for specialized individual activities and the delivery of entire project solutions. Sister companies are situated worldwide in Bristol, UK (CeBeNetwork UK Limited), Toulouse, France (CeBeNetwork France SARL) while

Joint Ventures are founded with the companies Eurogiciel in Toulouse, France (CeBeNetwork Eurogiciel France (CEF) SAS), CADES in Bangalore, India (CeBeNetwork-CADES India (CCI) plc) and the company Global Aviation Services in Lilienthal, Germany (G.A.S.-CeBeNetwork Engineering (GCE) GmbH).

Moreover CeBeNetwork is the leader of an engineering supplier network of currently 39 companies, mostly active in the aeronautical industry and at the same time a strategic supplier to its main customer in the civil aerospace industry. Besides the direct activities through own technical departments in this sector it is the initiator of the network consisting mainly of SMEs. Here the cooperation department builds the umbrella and thus fulfils the role of a broker and coordinator who operates and maintains the network and their projects. The composition of the network plays an important role, an optimized portfolio of competences is only reached if all required customer demands can be fulfilled and every partner feels comfortable and well recognized. Common marketing activities, strategy meetings in terms of innovation and best practices belong to the business tasks as well as the tendering and coordination of the manifold projects.

Figure 5. CeBeNetwork presence

As a 1st Tier partner, it represents the interface to the customer and is the only company in the network which acquired a valid frame contract. As a corollary, the whole responsibility for all partners and the management of the network in a highly efficient way is under the competence of CeBeNetwork. Besides a wide knowledge in nearly all aerospace disciples, it requires knowledge in management tasks such as project management or project controlling and monitoring.

The characterization of CeBeNetwork VBE as a business process within the ECOLEAD VBE Ontology fostered the creation of the organizational and technical prerequisites to support the operation of the CeBeNetwork Cooperation VBE in a more efficient and professional way. The expected benefit is the availability of preparedness and measures to carry out large projects on the national and European level mutually and thus compete with large enterprises.

4.1. ISOIN / CeBeNetwork Definition Phase: Activities and Results

During the *definition* phase, ISOIN and CeBeNetwork teams worked together to align their objectives, and select the ECOLEAD tools that would increase the performance of both networks. Introduction and training workshops were carried out in both networks identifying the multidisciplinary ECOLEAD working group by selecting the representative companies from the diversity of them that formed the cluster.

In ISOIN case, the selected members represent all its stakeholders providing a global feedback during the pilot phase. Selected members had previous experience in the development of projects in cooperation and stated their interest and commitment. They were classified into four main groups:

- Main contractor: EADS-CASA
- Manufacturing and assembly SMEs: INESPASA, AEROSUR and MEUPE. Engineering company: GHESA which has had international experiences in the naval engineering field. The internationalisation of their aeronautical field through cooperation with CeBeNetwork is a cornerstone.
- Supporting entity: Regional Development Agency, responsible for the promotion of the advanced collaborative paradigm in strategic industrial clusters as a driver in the Regional RTD Program for Innovation.

In the case of CeBeNetwork, all members are engineering services suppliers that have the same status within the network and thus are equal members amongst each other. Attributes which differentiates the companies towards each other are the so called "Cluster" affiliation where they are listed. Cluster affiliation depends on the competencies of the companies and is divided into the four fields: Flight Physics, Aero-Structures, Cabin Interior and Aircraft Systems. Larger companies within the network can also be assigned to two or three clusters. The customer is not directly involved in this project as it is the target to optimize and improve the internal processes, workflows and communication.

In summary a mixture of smaller and larger companies were selected to represent the interest of all companies as realistic as possible. Namely these companies are:

- AEROCON GmbH & Co. KG
- P+Z Engineering GmbH
- Euro engineering AEROSPACE GmbH
- AIDA Development GmbH

Specific training activities for the demonstration team were executed: an initial Workshop on Collaborative Initiatives in the Aerospace Industry during the Fair of the Aerospace Auxiliary Industry, and a second Workshop on Best Practices in Collaborative Networked Organisations. The objective was to promote the cooperation in strategic sectors of the regional economy through the introduction of innovative processes and ICT platforms delivered by ECOLEAD.

The working group has worked together with ECOLEAD team in order to identify the suitable industrial scenarios and relevant commitment for a successful adoption and implementation of ECOLEAD result suite:

1. The structured and systematized registration and administration of the corresponding companies and its related information.
2. Identification of collaboration opportunities with other companies to perform larger packages than those that can be performed alone.
3. Optimize the effort of creating a project agreement and the related working mechanisms when a business opportunity is identified.

Two business processes, were defined and considered for implementation and demonstration activities (see Table 10). Pilot scenarios were planned and adapted for each business process, and a set of indicators for each scenario was defined.

Table 10. Results of ISOIN / CeBeNetwork Definition Phase

	Scenario 1	Scenario 2
Business Process	Characterization of the Andalusia Aeronautical VBE, and a joint VBE with CeBeNetwork	VO Creation and launch in the joint VBE
Addressed Issue	Characterization of actors and their roles Characterization of business processes for each member Analysis of joint business challenges and collaboration strategy Analysis and definition of trust criteria Implementation of approaches and mechanisms for trust and performance management Requirements for member's registration process standardization	Rapid selection of the best business opportunity and partners for the VO within the VBE Possibility of breaking down a business into specific macro-processes Effective selection of partners for each macro-process Rapid definition of a rough VO planning Risk and chances management A rapid and easy methodology for negotiation
Main Objective	Design the organizational and technical framework to support the management and operation of the VBE Ease the evaluation and registration of new members and introduce them to the existing VBE Centralized tool to exchange relevant data	To support a VBE broker or a single company to identify collaboration opportunities to perform larger packages than those that can be performed alone. Optimization of the effort and cost reduction during the creation of a project agreement by ICT enabled mechanisms Serious competitor for "large" companies for the accomplishment of multi-disciplinary and transnational projects
Indicators	• Capability of the tool to define the specific VBE profile • Discovery of new competencies semi-automatically in the joint VBE • Transparency and validity of partners company data • Aggregated base trust in the joint VBE • Proactive behaviour of partners in terms of information forwarding	• Percentage of reduction of time to find and contact partners • Percentage of issues that might be agreed in a negotiation through WizAN • Percentage of time saved in the preparation of the documents to formalise an agreement • Share of high volume projects with involvement of more than one partner
Tools Used	• MSMS • BAMS • PCMS • TrustMan	• COC-Plan • PSS • TrustMan • WizAN

4.2. ISOIN / CeBeNetwork Implementation Phase: Activities and Results

The main objective in this implementation phase was to prepare the required environment to implement the advanced collaborative practices within the networks and the evaluation of the expected benefits further to the adoption of tools and methods for consolidating advanced collaboration schemes. The following activities were carried out during this phase:
- Tools customization according to specific demands for specific scenarios
- Implementation of prototypes into CeBeNetwork and ISOIN ICT infrastructures for separate VBEs
- Feeding databases with real data from both networks
- Link CeBeNetwork and ISOIN systems towards a joint VBE
- Feeding a common database
- Training workshops with partners at local sites
- CeBeNetwork and ISOIN joint workshop with aligned activities in Seville
- Take up and tests
- Tools evaluation and impact analysis

A familiarisation workshop was conducted in each of the clusters in order to introduce ECOLEAD concepts and its approach to enterprise collaboration. The objective of the workshops was to analyse the existing and emerging cooperation models, the business opportunities they support, along with the ECOLEAD results to support networked organisations. They brought together representatives from the aeronautic companies in the network and public bodies supporting the collaborative paradigm, the aim to meet the various expectations and demands from in the enterprise collaboration domain.

Representatives of the Andalusia Network (ISOIN and three partner companies) participated in the trial session on January 2007 as well as two partner companies of CeBeNetwork. Only the first release of services and tools was tested in this meeting. A second trial day was developed on May 2007, in order to test the advanced tools provided by the developers.

During the take-up, two tests were performed:

1) **In each separated VBEs.** In order to measure the business/process and technical improvements provided by the use of the ECOLEAD-VBE tools, in relation to the traditional approach.

2) **In the joint VBE.** The VBE prototypes were used in order to develop the product taking advantage of the new and complementary competences available in the joint VBE. Furthermore, the negotiation process among distant entities is facilitated by the available VBE tool.

A qualitative evaluation was provided by the companies to describe the impact of the collaboration services in their business processes.

4.2.1. Scenario 1: Characterization of the Andalusia Aeronautical VBE, and a joint VBE with CeBeNetwork

The objective of this scenario was to design the organizational and technical framework to support the operation of the ISOIN VBE and CeBeNetwork VBE according to the ECOLEAD VBE Ontology and tools.

Competences in both networks are complementary, as the Andalusian network is focused on manufacturing and CeBeNetwork's main operation are engineering activities. In order to take advantage of this synergy, a structure for the cooperation of both networks as the form of a joint VBE was analyzed. The goal is the analysis of common business challenges at international level, identifying shared objectives in the short, medium and long terms, and thus fostering a deeper collaboration between Helice and CeBeNetwork.

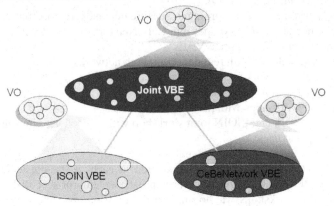

Figure 6. Joint VBE scenario: ISOIN & CeBeNetwork

The following tools are the basis to coordinate and maintain an emerging network of companies which are each specialized in their way: MSMS, BAMS, PCMS, TrustMan.

In the case of member registration, MSMS is the first tool to be used. The integration of the tool enables transparency of the basic company data amongst the VBE members itself.

Bag of Assets provides a number of elements that are interesting and useful for VBE Members (and for VBE as a whole) such as the general sharable information provided in some documents, software tools, lessons learned, etc. The main components of the Bag of Assets include Documents, Software Tools and the VBE Ontology. The VBE Bag of Assets therefore refers all valuable elements that different VBE participants use and share with others, provided that they are approved by the VBE administrator. The main purpose of the VBE related assets is to speed up and improve the process of a VO creation, which is the main task of a VBE.

A characterization of partners, business processes and information about members of the VBE is required to implement a partner search when necessary. Profile and Competency Management System (PCMS) supports the management of the company profiles and competencies. It allows comparing entities with other entities, analyzing and convincing that an entity is suitable for involvement into some specific joint activities / operations and help to rapidly associate potential partners with the business processes required.

Finally, TrustMan system is used for the selection of partners. It allows a trust assessment based on the performance information gathered from various activities, stored and maintained in the VBE. It defines mechanisms through which the VBE members can verify and foresee trustworthiness level of the others, evaluating not only technical and financial capabilities, but the quality required for the main contract.

4.2.2. Scenario 2: VO Creation and launch in the joint VBE.

The goal is to develop and implement the required infrastructure to support the creation and launch of a VO structure to perform larger workpackages than those that can be performed by single SMEs. The use of VO creation and Launch tools support the selection of partners in the VBE, optimize the effort of creating a project agreement and the related working mechanisms when a business opportunity is identified.

A reference collaborative project was identified as suitable scenario to build the take-up: Design and manufacturing of the Loading Assy-Passageway for the C-295 Aircraft. This scenario comprises the description of the collaborative product, partner search and VO Launch using the following tools: COC-Plan, PSS, TrustMan and WizAN.

Figure 7. Collaborative Project: Loading Assy-Passageway for the C-295 Aircraft

In current situation, activities in the Andalusia cluster are coordinated under stable long-term collaboration agreements, mainly under a subcontracting form, covering all the processes in the supply chain. Production is lead by the main contractors, conducting R&D, design, production, commercialization and maintenance. The majority of companies in the cluster are auxiliary SMEs, providing structure assemblies, sheet metal working, composites and the production of small runs. Within the subcontracting process, orders are sent to specific companies through the existing ICT tools.

When a company identifies a business opportunity and needs to cooperate with another one, the selection of the company is based on the mutual trust obtained in years of coexistence in the same sector and in the same place. Therefore, there have not been cooperation agreements with companies that do not belong to the cluster, and no specific tools have been used in the process of reaching an agreement.

It is expected to evolve from the current competitive approach in the subcontracting process to a collaborative paradigm among companies, in which collaboration opportunities can be rapidly identified. Besides, an efficient selection of partners according to the competencies needed is a basic issue and finally, it is expected to reach an environment in which the launch of a VO is a very quick and automated process, supported by the companies that form the VO.

In this scenario two assistance services were used for the dynamic VO creation. On one hand, the Collaboration Opportunities Identification Tool (Co-Finder) for identifying business opportunities, and on the other hand the Collaboration Opportunity Characterization and Rough Planning Tool (COC-Plan) and the Partner Search and Suggestion Tool (PSS) for the selection of the most interesting business opportunities according to the network partners interests and competencies.

Finally, a contract negotiation tool (WizAN) based on ICT technologies, allows to save time in the implementation of the contracts, to support the definition of responsibilities, risks, etc. in contractual terms.

4.3. ISOIN / CeBeNetwork Demonstration Phase: Activities and Results

Tools were tested with the aim of providing feedback in terms of methodology, functional requirements and technical evaluation of the joint experience in comparison with the results obtained without the ECOLEAD methodology and tools. During the demonstration phase, the ISOIN representative provided comments and suggestion through several surveys. The following table summarizes some general results:

Table 11. Business Metrics for ISOIN

Business Metrics	Validity Domain	Expected Value	Reached Value	Tools Involved
Capability of the tool to define the specific VBE profile	None / Low / Medium / High	High	High	PCMS
Discovery of new competencies semi-automatically in the joint VBE	None / Low / Medium / High	Medium	High	PCMS
Number of competency classes registered in ISOIN VBE	0-10	4	5	PCMS
Number of competency classes registered in JOINT_VBE	0-20	4	11	PCMS
Aggregated base trust in the joint VBE	None / Low / Medium / High	Medium	Medium	TrustMan
Average base trust in ISOIN_VBE	0-5	3	3.5	Trustman
Average base trust in JOINT_VBE	0-5	3	2.8	Trustman
Increased trust according economic criteria: Average economic trust in the JOINT_VBE related to the Average economic trust in separate VBEs	0-5	2/3	2.3 / 2.8	Trustman
Increased trust according technical criteria: Average technical trust in the JOINT_VBE related to the Average technical trust in separate VBE	0-5	3/4	4.2/4.5	Trustman
Increased trust according management criteria: Average management trust in the JOINT_VBE related to the Average management trust in separate VBE	0-5	3/4	3.8/4.1	Trustman
Percentage of reduction of time to find and contact partners	1-100	15%	20%	PSS
Preparedness of members to react to a collaboration opportunity immediately	None / Low / Medium / High	Medium	Medium	Wizan
Traceability and Bindingness of partners on partial agreements	None / Low / Medium / High	Medium	High	Wizan
Acceleration of negotiation process by	None / Low /	Medium	Medium	Wizan

achieving partial agreements	Medium / High			
Interchange of documents per internal project contract between partners	None / Low / Medium / High	Medium	High	Wizan
Secure and eased communication with potential VO partners	None / Low / Medium / High	High	High	Wizan

CeBeNetwork came up with a large extend of solutions obtained by the careful examination of the tools and of the VBE Ontology. In order to lay out those results briefly, it might be useful to have a look at the table below:

Table 12. Business Metrics for CeBeNetwork

Business Metrics	Validity Domain	Expected Value	Reached Value	Tools Involved
Capability of the tool to define the specific VBE profile	None / Low / Medium / High	High	High	PCMS
Discovery of the new competencies semi-automatically in the joint VBE	None / Low / Medium / High	Medium	High	PCMS
Number of competency classes registered in CBN VBE	0-10	5	6	PCMS
Average base trust in CBN_VBE	0-5	3	3.6	Trustman
Aggregated base trust in the joint VBE	Strongly less trustworthy / Less trustworthy / Average trustworthy / More trustworthy / Strongly more trustworthy	Average trustworthy	Average Trustworthy	TrustMan
Increased trust according economic criteria: Average economic trust in the JOINT_VBE related to the Average economic trust in separate VBEs	0-5	2/3	2.3 / 2.6 CBN	Trustman
Increased trust according technical criteria: Average technical trust in the JOINT_VBE related to the Average technical trust in separate VBE	0-5	3/4	4.2/4.4 CBN	Trustman
Increased trust according management criteria: Average management trust in the JOINT_VBE related to the Average management trust in separate VBE	0-5	3/4	3.8/2.6 CBN	Trustman
Time savings for including (new) members into the VBE	0-50%	20%	25%	MSMS
Time savings for including new supporting institutions into the VBE	0-50%	20%	25%	MSMS
Secure and common platform for exchanging relevant information through BAMS functionality	None / Low / Medium / High	Available	High Availability/ Operative	MSMS
Functionality of Rewarding members with free of charge offers	None / Low / Medium / High	Available	High Availability/ Operative	MSMS

4.4 Lessons Learned and Next Steps

The Andalusia Aeronautic Cluster aims to be an international reference model by providing a collective response through cooperation to the strategic challenges of the sector. ISOIN considers that the tools could be applied in real cases in the cluster operation to that end; however, further customisation is needed.

In relation with the specific tools that have been used by both networks the main conclusions that arise are:

- The member registration service is the first tool to be used in the chain of ECOLEAD developments by potentially new VBE members. It is easy to understand and can be used right from the start without comprehensive explanations or a deeper consciousness of the network structure. The rewarding mechanism motivates members to actively contributing relevant information and this way plays a significant role on the overall VBE management. Depending on the interests of the members, rewards can be customised according to specific demands.

- BAMS provides a secure and centralised platform to exchange relevant data within the VBE in a structured way. Through its integration with the member rewarding tool it represents a significant tool beneficial for every VBE member.

- PCMS allow a good capability to define the specific VBE profile. The flexibility of the tool enables a detailed and customised definition of resources and its implementation in the cluster is foreseen as a valuable instrument to facilitate competence discovery, and thus joint business opportunities, among distant clusters. This point is crucial for the operation of the network, since the structured and systematized registration and administration of the corresponding companies and its related information is considered an important task. Using the PCMS gains in time and efforts are expected.

- TrustMan is useful at a first approach to evaluate partners which are not known. They are the basis to coordinate and maintain an emerging network of companies which are each specialized in their way.

- WizAN reduces time and resources to identify the final partner, it increases effectiveness in terms of time and resources to react to a business opportunity, facilitating the negotiation of the different issues related to a proposal and reducing the time and effort required to formalize a VO.

CeBeNetwork, as one of the facilitator within the ECOLEAD project, takes the extension of the current VBE to the European level for granted. The contribution, which is to be brought by the harmonization and development of the software tools on a collaborative basis, fosters the security of the ICT in addition to serving to the management of the future VBEs. The software tools such as TrustMan, PCMS, WizAN, and MSMS have proved themselves as being successfully developed for the sake of an assured VBE furnished by the well defined member organisations.

5. CONCLUSIONS

With ECOLEAD tools being used with real data from the IECOS, SMT, ISOIN and CeBeNetwork, it is clear that the proposed ECOLEAD solution benefits the management of actual and future VBEs. However, it also has to be noted that there are opportunities for improvement in order to launch commercials products. This lead to several tasks that are needed to further convert the prototypes into final products, but one of the important issue is that real end users have taken-up and validated the tools and this give a real feedback for improving them considering a real business environment.

ECOLEAD project was a successful project as well as for IECOS, SMT, ISION and CeBeNetwork. In the case of ISOIN and CeBeNetwork, by collaborating in several tasks both companies/networks learned to understand each others needs and demands which might become relevant in future projects during the European-wide expansion and harmonisation process within the aircraft industry. The close collaboration and thus exchange of information about approaches in problem solving, best practices etc extended the scientific as well as the practical background of each partner. Moreover business contacts were made where both organisations are benefiting in the way that first common projects between ISOIN partners and CeBeNetwork are already running and further ones are planned. The developed tools help to structure these projects in terms of common wording and problem consciousness which are significant factors for a successful partnership.

7. ACKNOWLEDGEMENTS

The information presented in this chapter is part of the results of the ECOLEAD Project (European Collaborative Networked Organisations Leadership Initiative), funded by the European Community, FP6 IP 506958. The authors wish to acknowledge the support of ITESM (specially Juan Pablo Cotes, David Romero, and Teddy Charris); IECOS, SMT, ISOIN and CeBeNetwork representatives and ECOLEAD partners and developers during take-up activities.

6. REFERENCES

1. Camarinha-Matos, L.M. and Afsarmanesh, H. (2004). "Support Infrastructures for New Collaborative Forms", in Collaborative Networked Organizations: A Research Agenda for Emerging Business Models, Kluwer Academic Publishers, pp. 175-192.

2. Jarimo, T. and Salo A. (2007). "Optimal Partner Selection in Virtual Organisations with Capacity Risk and Network Interdependencies", [to appear] in IEEE Journal of Systems, Man, Cybernetics.

3. Msanjila, S. and Afsarmanesh H. (2006). "Assessment and Creation of Trust in VBEs", in Network-Centric Collaboration and Supporting Frameworks, Camarinha-Matos, L.M., Afsarmanesh, H., and Ollus, M. (Eds.), in International Federation for Information Processing (IFIP), Vol. 224, New York: Springer Publisher, pp. 161-172.

4.   Ratnasingam, P. (2005). "Trust in Inter-organizational Exchanges: A Case Study in Business to Business Electronic Commerce", in Journal of Decision Support System, Vol. 39, pp.525-544.

5.   Romero, D.; Giraldo, J.; Galeano, N., and Molina, A. (2007). "Towards Governance Rules and Bylaws for Virtual Breeding Environments", in Establishing the Foundation of Collaborative Networks, Camarinha-Matos L.M., Afsarmanesh, H., Novais, P. and Analide, C. (Eds.), in International Federation for Information Processing (IFIP), Vol. 243, New York: Springer Publisher, pp. 93-102.

VO MANAGEMENT PILOT CASES
Virtuelle Fabrik, Orona, SNS

Joseba Arana[1], Luis Berasategi[1], Iñaki Aranburu[2],
Stefan Bollhalter[3], Bruno Landau[3], Matthias Oswald[3],
Cathal Heavey[4], Eugene O' Regan[4], Paul Liston[4], PJ Byrne[4]

[1]*IKERLAN Technological Research Centre, SPAIN*
jmarana@ikerlan.es, lberasategi@ikerlan.es
[2]*ORONA EIC, SPAIN*
iaranburu@orona.es
[3]*Virtuelle Fabrik AG, SWITZERLAND*
stefan.bollhalter@virtuelle-fabrik.com, bruno.landau@virtuelle-fabrik.com,
matthias.oswald@virtuelle-fabrik.com
[4]*Supply Network Shannon/Enterprise Research Centre, University of Limerick, IRELAND,*
cathal.heavey@ul.ie, eugene.oregan@ul.ie, paul.liston@ul.ie, pj.byrne@ul.ie

Dedicated tools for the monitoring and control of Virtual
Organisations have been developed under the ECOLEAD research
project. This chapter reports on the application of these tools to real
life Virtual Organisations. Specifically, the tools concerned are
VOMod, SID, DI3, MAF and DSS, and the three participating
networks are Virtuelle Fabrik (Switzerland), Orona (Spain) and SNS
(Ireland). The following sections of this chapter detail the working
scenarios in which the tools were used, the contribution which each
tool made to the successful operation of the Virtual Organisations,
and the feedback from the participants based on their experiences of
working with the software.

1. INTRODUCTION

The future competitiveness of European companies will depend to a great extent on
their ability to collaborate. Many companies have already recognized that, in order
to rival competitors in lower cost economies, they must cooperate with
complementary companies and offer extended solutions to their customers. To this
end, an increasing number of companies are affiliating themselves with Virtual
Breeding Environments (VBEs) and participating in Virtual Organisations (VOs).

The topic of providing the necessary information technologies to facilitate this
integrated mode of operation has been considered in research for at least a decade
(Strader et al. 1998). However, despite this work, there are still many obstacles
prohibiting this collaborative business model from being adopted on a larger scale

(Corvello and Migliarese 2007). Recognising the practical difficulties faced by industrial companies when operating in VOs, the ECOLEAD research project was undertaken to examine the underlying obstacles and to provide understandable frameworks for sustained collaboration. Beginning with the base theories of collaboration, this research group developed tools and technologies to facilitate the successful management of a network of independent companies.

One of the key aspects of this project was the development of relevant Virtual Organisation Monitoring and Control tools and methodologies. When designing these tools particular attention was paid to the defining characteristics of VOs. For instance, ease of access and affordability (Camarinha-Matos 2003) were important requirements, due to the IT capability and scale of the companies typically involved in VOs. Similarly, the speed at which the VO can respond to a business opportunity is recognised as a key determinant of success (Camarinha-Matos and Afsarmanesh 2007) since such opportunities are often short-lived due to the fast pace of modern marketplaces. These key requirements of usability and accessibility were determined to be best served by the internet and accordingly a suite of web-based applications was developed. In this chapter the tools which are considered from this suite are those that support the management activities of Virtual Organizations. These tools are briefly described as follows:

- **VOMod** (VO Model Wizard): The VOMod environment maintains information about the Virtual Organization and its structure. The VO manager models the structure of a particular VO starting from a preconfigured general VO template and following a predefined VO meta-model.
- **SID** (Supporting Indicator Definition): The SID is responsible for keeping Indicator information. Like the VOMod, the SID also consists of an administrative part (database, web application) and a handler, based on Web service interfaces, interacting with the other components.
- **DI3** (Distributed Indicator Information Integrator) The DI3 component consists of a configurable broker that interacts with a set of information-retrieval components. These components fetch data at various VO member locations.
- **MAF** (Monitor and Finance): The MAF component provides a dashboard for visualizing the information retrieved and stored among the other components of the framework.
- **DSS** (Decision Support System): The Decision Support System for Virtual Organizations (DSS) is dedicated to provide decision support services to the VO manager given the inputs from other components.

Figure 1 (Hodík et al. 2007) below displays the main elements of each tool and indicates how the tools interact with each other.

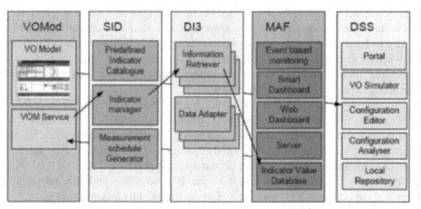

Figure 1 Component diagram of VOPM

Three real world networks were selected for the initial implementation and testing of the above software. These were 1.) Virtuelle Fabrik, a Swiss-German network of primarily engineering companies 2.) Orona, a Spanish based network that manufactures elevators and associated equipment, and 3.) SNS, an Irish based network of engineering and electronic sub-component manufacturing SMEs. Each of these networks is dealt with in a dedicated section in this chapter and each section is subdivided as follows:

- **Network Overview**: Gives background information on the network.
- **Definition Phase**: Introduces each of the test bed scenarios.
- **Implementation Phase**: Discusses the application of the concepts and tools developed in the ECOLEAD project to the specific VO instances.
- **Demonstration Phase**: Demonstrates the results achieved by the network through the use of the ECOLEAD tools.
- **Lessons Learned and Next Steps**: Details the lessons learned by the test network and outlines what they consider to be the most beneficial next steps for furthering the work.

2. VIRTUELLE FABRIK

2.1 Network Overview

Virtuelle Fabrik AG (VF) is a project management and sales provider for the Virtuelle Fabrik community with over 50 companies, which was founded in 2001. Situated in the north-eastern part of Switzerland, it serves three regional clusters, one in north-western Switzerland, one in eastern Switzerland and one in southern Germany. The network consists of highly qualified engineering, design and manufacturing companies, procedure technicians, management consultants and various service companies. VF operates with high quality industrial products mainly combining SMEs and also subsidiaries of bigger companies.

Offering a wide variety of services covering most parts of the value chain, customers receive ideal solutions out of one source for their complex tasks. The customers' added value lies within the VF internal idea of a build to order factory. A structure to efficiently identify opportunities and enable cooperative behaviour is the key to success. VF acts as one factory, where the customer can profit from the know-how of many, while still having to communicate with one. Like this, demanding and quality-orientated customers receive tailored solutions matching their needs, in a cost and time efficient way.

The primary role of VF is to be the general contractor for the benefit of all members of the network concerning complex activities, i.e. to offer project management and systems integration as a service. In order to ensure this, VF serves the integrated industrial capabilities and capacities of the network. Key staff of the member companies are involved in all parts of the processes. Key factors are trust, the transparent organisational structure, the ICT structure and the individual and integrated capabilities. VF vows for quality as stated in its mission statement:

- VF is the leading collaborative network enterprise in achieving optimal use of industrial know-how.
- VF accelerates the use of information as a production factor. The net yield for the customers results from within and outside of the network.
- VF makes ideas into marketable products. It takes over the total process from the idea to the product or steps from this process as a built to order factory.
- VF offers all necessary structures and aids for the fast structuring of business systems. It offers the access to entrepreneur teams and organises the financing.
- The backbone of VF is a coordinated organisation and information infrastructure; this is a mandatory standard for all groups. Thus knowledge and information is brought in place timelessly and purposefully to the application.
- Success in the market is realised by the activities of every individual partner of VF.

Principal Industries
VF offers a wide product range from innovation consulting, designing, construction and prototyping, industrialisation, manufacturing, distribution and life cycle services for systems, facilities and machines in the fields of electric, electronic and mechanical components. Main industries where VF is involved in are: precision mechanics, medical engineering and tool making. In the field of precision mechanics, the core competency lies in the processing of complex components such as the development of prototypes. The latter will also be the starting point of the case study outlined in this chapter.

The future of the dynamic network VF
The future of the industry lies in dynamic networks with defined system leadership for reasons among others as stated below:

- The volatility of the market requires flexible structures.
- The order complexity requires cross-company structures.

- The increasing global price competition and transparency requires a tightened focus on core competencies of the network itself and its members.

For this reason, VF builds up the structure to quickly and efficiently identify market opportunities. Each member is independent and offers different services to cultivate its markets autonomously. VF can act and react with its given authority enabling it to offer customers value added services thanks to the dynamic network: more products, quicker and cost effective realised ideas, a bigger knowledge pool and higher capacities The conceptual and methodological results of the ECOLEAD project were tested and implemented into the VF structure enabling the dynamic network. Beside the theoretical foundation the ICT infrastructure proved fundamental for the success. The following sub-sections describe the identification and evaluation process of the ICT infrastructure in form of the web tool suite for VO management discussed above and in parts 3 and 5 of this book.

2.2 Definition Phase

The collaboration between VF and the German *Centre of Research and Development ZF Friedrichshafen AG* (ZF) evolved in 2001 with the goal to support the development and manufacturing of an advanced mechanical power divider for a leading car manufacturer. The development of the prototype proceeded very harmoniously and successfully, leading to the agreement to develop another prototype, but this time on an electronic basis to allow optimal control over the vehicle no matter what surface.

The goal was to develop and manufacture an electro dynamic gear (EDG) where coupler, starter motor and transmission are combined. The idea is to let the starter motor have such a strong motor so that in the end a hybrid gear is generated. The partners chosen to be part of this temporary Swiss and German based VO were *Innotool AG, Greminger AG, ALWO SMA AG* and *Schuler Konstruktionen GmbH & Co. KG (Schuler GmbH)*. Each VO member contributed with their core competencies: Schuler GmbH contributing with the engineering side, ALWO SMA AG with turning tasks, Greminger AG with EDM[1] and grinding and Innotool AG with milling and turning. The management of the VO lied within the responsibility of VF, which also served as the connection point between the VO members and the customer ZF. Each member is distinguished by a dedication to high quality, precision and a large knowledge pool, all of which are SMEs with sales volume ranging from € 1.5 million to € 13.5 million.

Project timeline: ECOLEAD
The EDG project kicked-off in February 2003, when VF made ZF an offer over three prototypes. After ZF accepted, development and manufacturing were completed in August 2003 and delivered. Over the years of 2004, 2005 and 2006 ZF had repeatedly ordered variations, additional parts and modifications. During this period the VO was managed by traditional means.

---

[1] Electrical discharge machining (EDM) is a machining method primarily used for hard metals.

In 2007 VF decided to fully trial the ECOLEAD management tools suite with the real case scenario EDG. Initial trials succeeded and resulted in offering and delivering further prototypes in the same year. Furthermore, VF decided to improve the prototype suite in order to fully implement it into the VF structure. **Table 1** shows the process that ensured identification, evaluation and optimisation:

Table 1 VF Scenario Descriptions

	Theoretical foundation: methodologies and concepts		
	Scenario 1	**Scenario 2**	**Scenario 3**
Business Process	VO management	VO performance measurement	VO Management e-services
Issues Addressed	• VO modelling • VO performance measurement modelling • VO monitoring	• Definition of VO performance • Performance measurement processes • Monitoring of the VO processes	• Efficient VO modelling and performance measurement • Intuitive, comprehensive VO management with the tool suite
Main Objective	Methodology for the implementation of the VO management	Methodology for the realisation of VO performance measurement	Provision of an integrated e-services software prototype for VO efficiency
Indicators	• Coordination effort • Substitution of tools • Amount of interaction needed • Partner satisfaction VO performance measurement modelling	• Controlling effort • Machinery utilisation • Delivery reliability • Partner satisfaction	• Partner satisfaction
Tools Used	• VO Mod • SID • DSS	• DI3 • MAF	• All tools

The three scenarios identified are defined by the business processes VO management, VO performance management and the integrated VO management. The latter combines scenarios one and two. This definition is the combined ECOLEAD achievement of the concepts and methods with VF specifications.

The addressed issues and main objectives are in line with the theoretical foundation translated into the needs of VF VOs. The indicators chosen reflect two perspectives: the first is to show potential value-added to VF after the use of the suite and the second the development respectively the improvement itself. The tools used inform which tools of the suite were needed in which process.

2.3 Implementation Phase

The EDG project served as a pilot case to implement and test the ECOLEAD VO management tool suite. As shown above the main objectives in this pilot business case was the support in VO modelling, VO performance measurement, VO monitoring and VO management e-services. Although VF had identified these business processes together with ECOLEAD methodologies and concepts, VF had to align the network environment in order to cope with the ECOLEAD processes and ensure viable test results given the identified indicators. After the definition phase described in **Table 1**, VF matched the ECOLEAD theoretical results with the activities in the network. This means

- alignment of ontologies and taxonomies,
- optimisation of governance structures and principles,
- optimisation of competency profiles,
- documentation of the business cases' collaboration processes,
- to ensure the correct use of the tool suite and
- to ensure the correct reporting on tool suite issues.

Prior taking up the EDG project, VF had successfully adapted the structures as well as the principles and instructed the relevant member representatives. In this manner, the network was able to communicate on the same level, exchange knowledge and ECOLEAD based issues correctly and, beneficial for each member and the network itself, improve the competency identification.

Initially, the list above had been implemented for the four members enrolled in the EDG project. However, parts of the ontology and taxonomies spilled over to the whole network. Furthermore, the governance structures and principles, the competency profiles and the documentation found its way through the whole network.

In order to assess the processes and the respective issues, the tools were split up into a VO cockpit to govern the VO in an efficiently. All tools were enrolled successfully into the EDG project and the VF network structure. The following four main categories reflect the analysis:

1. *VO modelling*

    VO modelling should enable a more efficient way of creating well structured processes within a VO. Complex collaboration processes have a lot of influential variables which need to be managed in a transparent way. Consequently, ECOLEAD management methodologies and tools were implemented into this EDG project management.

    a. The *VO Mod Wizard* tool offers a Meta model to manage a VO in a dynamic environment. It includes relevant data concerning customer, partners and basic project information as the work breakdown structure, budget allocation and used key performance indicators

2. *VO performance measurement*

VO performance measurement is one of the primary functions of VO management. An aggregated overview of the important transactions and interactions is needed. The efficient gathering of data from all participants of the VO namely, Schuler GmbH, Innotool AG, Greminger AG, ALWO SMA AG, and of course VF, is one of the key functions in this process.

    a.   The *SID* (Supporting Indicator Definition) supports the VO manager in the selection of performance indicators to be used in the monitoring of the VO. The *DI3* (Distributed Indicator Information Integrator) tool empowers a network to gather the necessary information about the project. Through a combination of these tools, the VO manager can collect data to gain a clear picture of the VO's performance.

3. *VO monitoring activities and finance*

Full monitoring of the activities and financial evolution of the VO were tried out in the EDG case. The VO monitoring allows the VO manager to act and react based on facts as given by the VO members.

    a.   The *MAF Platform* (Monitor and Finance) allows the VO Manager to monitor the status, model, changes and exceptions for the project in all its aspects. The *DSS* (Decision Support System) component supports the VO manager to visualise running projects. The manager is supported by tools, for example rescheduling time tables after unexpected shifts and finding alternatives when required.

4. *Integrated VO management with VO management e-services*

An integrated trial of the full VO management e-services in the real VO for the project EDG is the highlight of this pilot case. This trial showed the impact for VO Management in terms of efficiency, speed and an overview of the progress of all relevant data of a VO. The primary indicator is partner satisfaction, since it integrates points 1 through 3.

Figure 2 below shows an example of performance measurement set out by the MAF system. It shows a part of the tasks as defined by the work breakdown structure. The figure informs about the relation between task completeness in % to the task fund usage.

The tools should empower VF in improving different collaboration processes. Through real-time data it will be easier to govern running VOs. The model also increases the independence from individual and intangible knowledge and skills. Much effort has been done to understand the different tools' functionality. The different end-users, i.e. the VO members for the EDG project, have been given demonstrations and have used the tools since beta versions were made available. The results of this pilot case are presented below. Ultimately, the tool suite should enable end-users to improve VO performance just as it has done for the VF and the project EDG.

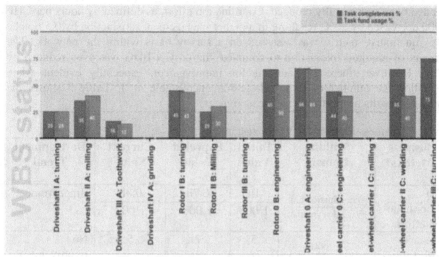

Figure 2 MAF work breakdown structure

2.4 Demonstration Phase

Within ECOLEAD, VF had the possibility to get a better understanding about the different collaboration processes from the opportunity identification to metamorphosis. Through the contribution in different meetings and workshops a new kind of comprehension was realised. In the discussion with the community of experts all around Europe best practices were distributed. Resulting models and methodologies proved as a useful assistance in the structuring and optimisation of collaboration processes.

In the range of tools VF reached a powerful impact through the universal real-time concept. Current software improvements are strongly driven by ECOLEAD activities towards process maturity. The three scenarios outlined in **Table 1**, VO management, VO performance measurement and VO management e-services have been taken up. The results are shown below.

The VO cockpit has left the theoretical sphere and shifted towards the practical implementation. The *VO Mod Wizard* serves as the primary cockpit grid and connects the other tools. The *SID, DI3* and *MAF Platform* constitute powerful tools when challenging various aspects in the arising processes for the EDG. The *DSS* combines the know-how of the other tools and enables the project manager to quickly perceive the situation of the VO in terms of progress, actual situation, changes in the plan, potential changes and their impact. The structuring of collaboration processes leads to shorter cycle times and smaller administration expenses. The two tables below show detailed results as defined for the analysis of the tools implementation. It is important to understand that the current values are due to restrictions, because the empirical data does not allow valid statistical evidence. Therefore, in order to better understand the values, the current development of the metrics has been included in the tables.

The business metrics concerning the VO management show positive results as provided by Table 2. The coordination effort and the interaction between partners needed were successfully reduced. Coordination effort, as defined by hours per CHF 1000 decreased by 20%, resulting in a higher management satisfaction by 0.5 points. This qualitative metric was assessed on a survey basis within the network. The amount of required interaction to complete the project EDG was even reduced by 30%. However, there is potential for improvement, especially evident when regarding the number of tools. These remained stable at 5. **Table 3** shows the indicator results for performance measurement.

Table 2 Business Metrics for VO management

Business Metrics	Validity Domain	Initial Value	Expected Value	Current Value	Development Trend
(1) Coordination effort	$\frac{\sum \text{coordination time}}{\text{VO sales volume}}$	$\frac{1h}{1'000}$	$\frac{0.7h}{1'000}$	$\frac{0.8h}{1'000}$	Improvement
(2) Substitution of tools	$\frac{\sum \text{tools}}{\text{VO}}$	5	2	5	No improvement
(3) Amount of Interaction needed	$\frac{\sum \text{face-to-face interactions}}{\text{VO}}$	~ 50	~ 30	~ 35	Improvement
(4) Partner satisfaction	5 very satisfied 4 satisfied 3 no change 2 unsatisfied 1 very unsatisfied	3	4	3.5	Slight improvement

Table 3 Business Metrics for performance measurement

Business Metrics	Validity Domain	Initial Value	Expected Value	Current Value	Development Trend
(1) Controlling effort	$\frac{\sum \text{controlling time}}{\text{VO sales volume}}$	$\frac{0.4h}{1'000}$	$\frac{0.2h}{1'000}$	$\frac{0.35h}{1'000}$	Improvement
(2) Machinery utilization	$\frac{\text{Actual hours used}}{\text{Available hours}}$	~ 0.85	~ 0.9	~ 0.85	No visible improvement
(3) Delivery reliability	$\frac{\text{Unproblematic deliveries} * 100}{\text{Total deliveries}}$	80%	85%	80%	No visible improvement
(4) Partner satisfaction	5 very satisfied 4 satisfied 3 no change 2 unsatisfied 1 very unsatisfied	3	4	4	Improvement

The business metrics concerning the VO performance measurement show at first less success. Partner satisfaction, however, clearly went up by one level, shifting from neutral to satisfied. Like above, satisfaction was measured by means of surveys. The reason for this mainly lies in the fact that the ECOLEAD toolset is capable of identifying upcoming problems efficiently and effectively. Beside numerical representation graphical supports the interpretation of the performance measured. Analogously, controlling efforts were slightly reduced, whereas capacity and delivery reliability issues have not yet been improved. Reasons for this are amongst other things the generally high allocation and delivery reliability coefficients due to an industry-wide good economic situation.

The maturity level of the connection between the tools and the know-how of the end-users in using the tools are fundamental in achieving collaboration excellence. The business metric concerning VO management e-services, partner satisfaction, was found qualitatively with surveys. The EDG partners and the customer ZF were included in the survey and it resulted in a half point rise, from 4 to 4.5. Much progress has been done, know-how has been built up and the work must continue in the same direction in order to achieve the optimal level of collaboration within networks such as VF in tackling complex projects like EDG.

2.5. Lessons Learned and Next Steps

ECOLEAD and VF supplement each other. The ECOLEAD framework helped VF identify its structure, main functionalities and potential. The theoretical foundation with the CNO terminology and VO methodology and concepts combined with the findings on dynamic VOs enabled VF to enhance process recognition, coordination and control. VO management and performance measurement improved evidently. Likewise, VF helped develop a viable toolset in order to efficiently manage and monitor VOs in general.

These results are taken into account when defining lessons learnt from the project. As an industrial partner, VF always intended to direct ECOLEAD activities towards practical solutions. The major benefit will be generated through coherent applications that are easy to implement, intuitive to use and fit for a broad band of cases. The key to proceed in this direction are ECOLEAD methodologies and tools that enable the people in charge to practice structured and ongoing real-time communication to govern VOs.

The static and time-consuming management of VO projects has been replaced by dynamic and time-efficient operational processes. The next step consists of formulating strategic break-through elements evolving from CNO research. ECOLEAD has helped operational management concerning VO management, performance measurement and VO management e-services within the scenarios, as defined above. Strategic management scenarios are the next step when going beyond.

3. ORONA INNOVATION NETWORK

3.1. Network Overview

Mondragón Corporación Cooperativa (MCC) is a business group made up of 264 companies and entities organized in three areas: Financial, Industrial and Distribution, together with the Research and Training sectors.

Mondragón Corporación Cooperativa leads the Industrial Sector in the Basque Country and is 7th in ranking in Spain, with sales of 13,266 million euros in its Industrial and Distribution activities, 12,332 million euros of administered assets in its financial activity and a total workforce of 81,880 as at the end of 2006. Within MCC, the Orona Group is currently a consolidated business that ranks as the leading Spanish company in the lift industry and an outstanding supplier of technology and materials on the international scene.

Commitments to the future, generation of wealth and employment are the mainstays of a workforce of over 3,000 people scattered throughout Spain and more than 85 countries - in agencies - who offer products and services locally to their customers. The enterprise architecture of the Orona Group is determined by its lines of activity: Orona services, Orona industrial and associated companies

The Orona Group has been incorporating major companies from the sector into its organizational relations and associations, both on a national and international level, that have helped to consolidate its leadership in Elevation on the domestic market, and as an outstanding supplier of technology and products worldwide. Consequently, some years ago Orona participated in the creation of MCC's Elevation and Urban Mobility Systems Association, jointly with the Electra Vitoria S.Coop.

The development of new products for the elevation sector draws on knowledge from many technological fields based on interdisciplinary expert knowledge with high levels of specialization. It is neither practical nor feasible for Orona to maintain all these necessary skills in-house. Accordingly, in 2002, Orona promoted the creation of an Innovation Network of highly specialized experts, working in a Collaborative Networked Organization of multi-company and multidisciplinary communities that focused their activity on the discovery of new technological opportunities and the transformation of these opportunities into innovative product ideas for short-distance transportation. Nowadays, the network comprises several industrial companies, universities, RTD centres and consultancy organizations with highly qualified know-how in technological renewal of the sector. This association is largely a response to the competitive threat of the biggest manufacturers of elevators in the world.

The Orona Innovation Network (OIN) started out with a stronger relationship between ORONA and a small number of primary nodes which shared a vision at the conception stage, and evolved into a broader network (see **Figure 3**).

Furthermore, it should be noted that this organization is open to evolving over time, according to developments in the market and changes in technology.

The ORONA Innovation Network pilot case is a very good demonstrator in order to test the concepts, methodologies and tools developed in the ECOLEAD project. The main reasons for endorsing this claim are as follows:

1. OIN network objectives and activities focus on innovation and New Product development. These are the main areas on which most advanced European companies focus in order to maintain their competitiveness to deal with the global market.
2. OIN network members have a vast wealth of industrial experience.

3. The potential growth of the network is high.
4. The experience of OIN in the ECOLEAD project could be translated in the future to other collaboration network experiences within the MCC group.

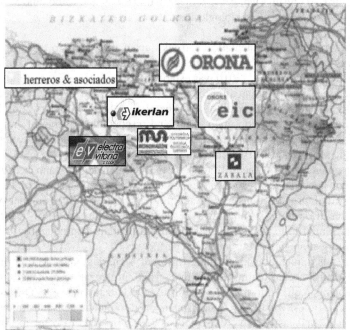

Figure 3 Orona Innovation Network partners

3.1 Definition Phase

The objectives that Orona Innovation Network had set out prior to its participation in the ECOLEAD project included many of the aspects taken into account in the framework defined within the project.

From this point of view, one of the first decisions taken once the scenarios for the planned take-up activities were decided upon was to establish two levels of application of the results.

The first level of application corresponds to a theoretical foundation whose aim is to deploy the conceptual development of ECOLEAD in the Orona Innovation Network.

In this sense, the scenario known as 'OIN Roadmap' attempts to establish a reference model for the Orona Innovation Network where the role of all the elements identified as pillars in ECOLEAD model was defined. Furthermore, another important objective of the scenario is to set up the mechanisms needed to make the right integration possible between different Virtual Organizations and Professional Virtual Communities.

The development of this scenario and its implementation were identified as a priority by the different managers of Orona Innovation Network. On the one hand, to rely on the deployment of ECOLEAD pillars to the network allows the Technical Committee – a committee created to manage the network with representatives of all the partners – to specifically identify the activities to be taken into account in launching Virtual Organizations. On the other hand, establishing a steady model allows Orona Innovation Network not to be restricted to the implementation and use of the ECOLEAD results while the project is underway and to be able to make use in the future of other methodologies and tools developed in other areas of the project.

To carry out the implementation and take-up of this scenario the need to run a real deployment process covering the definition of a roadmap of the network activities for the period 2006-2010 was established.

The second level of application concerns the use of the results attained for the Virtual Organization Management itself. The aim of the Orona Innovation Network was to facilitate the definition, monitoring and rescheduling of the different Virtual Organizations launched via the network for technology and product development in the strategic scope 2006-2010 defined in the roadmap.

The management of the different Virtual Organizations launched from the network consumes many resources, taking into account that some of the up and running Virtual Organizations rely on the participation of a great number of people and the result (which is not always successful in the area of technological innovation) could affect other Virtual Organizations and consequently the product and marketing strategies of our industrial partners.

Within this application level, three different scenarios have been defined. The "VO-Modelling" scenario aims to help the Virtual Organization manager in defining all the elements required to manage the Virtual Organization. The "VO-Monitoring" scenario seeks to establish the mechanisms needed to pursue activities in the Virtual Organization. And lastly, the "VO-Analysis" scenario tries to offer to the Virtual Organization manager the tools required to respond to any untoward events that may occur during the life of the Virtual Organization.

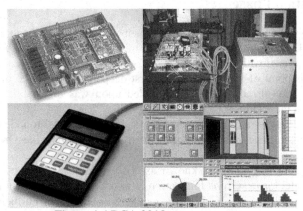

Figure 4 ARCA 2010 components

To proceed with a demonstration of the results of the ECOLEAD project in these scenarios, the Orona Innovation Network has selected the Virtual Organization known as 'ARCA 2010' as a basis for realization of the take-up, created in order to design and develop reliable programmable electronic systems with high availability. The concept of availability is considered to be the relationship between the time of operation without faults and the total time also taking into account the time of replacement. The Virtual Organization will develop the technology platform that includes the controller, the maintenance terminal, controller testing and control supervision (see Figure 4).

A unified vision of these four scenarios described above is shown in Table 4. In this table, besides the issues addressed and the main objectives, the tools implemented and the indicators used to validate the take-up are also shown.

Table 4 Scenarios for the Orona Innovation Network

	Scenario 1	Scenario 2	Scenario 3	Scenario 4
Business Process	OIN Roadmap	VO Modelling	VO Monitoring	VO Analysis
Issue Addressed	Need to formalize a reference model for innovation activities	Need for standard formalism to define activities, budgets and indicators for all partners in the VOs	Need for standard procedures to collect and monitor indicators. Reduce interaction.	Need to perform analysis and decisions so as to deal with deviations. Better decisions.
Main Objective	Implementation of a process to define mid-long term innovation activities	Formalization of VO modelling rules and tools	Formalization of VO monitoring rules and tools	Formalization of VO analytical rules and tools
Indicators	• Formalize process • Knowledge strategy defined • PVCs created • Roadmap defined • VO launched	• Number of task leaders to access • VO Manager satisfaction • VO task leader satisfaction • Interaction needed • Technology Committee Satisfaction	• Number of monitoring steps • VO Manager satisfaction • VO task leader satisfaction • Interaction needed • Technology Committee Satisfaction	• Number of periodic analyses • VO Manager satisfaction • VO task leader satisfaction • Interaction needed • Technology Committee Satisfaction
Tools Used		• VO-Mod • SID	• VO-Mod • DI3 • MAF	• VO-Mod • DSS

3.2 Implementation Phase

3.2.1 Scenario 1: OIN Roadmap

The first step for adapting the results of the ECOLEAD project to the special characteristics of our innovation-oriented CNO was to analyse the different concepts developed in the course of the project and to contrast them with the activities currently being carried out within the Orona Innovation Network. This step identified environments related to the Virtual Breeding Environment itself and the different types of Virtual Organizations and Virtual Communities required.

The first aspect taken into account to establish the comparison between ECOLEAD concepts and the ongoing practices of the Orona Innovation Network was the correspondence of the network with the concept of Virtual Breading Environment defined in the project. The main characteristic in the case of the Orona Innovation Network was the existence of a roadmap that laid down the strategic and overall goals of the Virtual Breading Environment in terms of business, product, technology and partnership, as well as the way in which these four axes co-evolve within the network over time. Therefore, the Orona Innovation Network roadmap has been identified as the cornerstone for governing the Virtual Breading Environment and improves the likelihood of network strategic plans being implemented effectively.

Another important aspect analysed was the correspondence of the Professional Virtual Community concept with the groups established in the network to develop the monitoring of the market and technology and to generate opportunities, ideas and product concepts.

In this sense, several Professional Virtual Communities were created based on the competences needed to establish a good knowledge of the market, product and technology evolution. Furthermore, starting with the information and business opportunities detected in the Professional Virtual Communities, the virtual teams that had been created *ad hoc* looked after the definition of product concepts and resulting technological platforms to feed the Orona Innovation Network roadmap.

The technology platforms that demonstrate the suitability of selected novel technologies to be incorporated in the future generation of products and the future innovative new product concepts for short-distance transportation were identified during the road-mapping process. The objective was then to launch the relevant Virtual Organizations. Consequently, the network constituted two types of Virtual Organizations to successfully tackle the development of technology platforms and new products: Virtual Organizations for Technology Platform Development (VO-TPD) and Virtual Organizations for New Product Development (VO-NPD).

The main aim of the Virtual Organizations for Technology Platform Development is to attain the level of competence required to serve as the technological basis to develop future short-distance transportation products.

It is important to point out that to develop one of the Technological Platforms identified in the roadmap, one Virtual Organization was defined; accordingly, this Virtual Organization could contain several related projects. The Virtual Organizations will be made up of company members that are internal or external to the network. This could contribute towards the best added value regarding the gaps identified between the technology being used at present and that established as an objective for future product concepts. Each Virtual Organization has clearly defined its objective and scope based on a specific demonstrator close to the identified product concept. This demonstrator will be useful for assessing the results and transferring them to the product development process.

The Orona Innovation Network roadmap establishes the level of detail and also the risk of each of the Virtual Organizations mapped. Accordingly, it will be needed to distinguish between the Virtual Organizations launched to develop platforms for clearly visualized short-term product concepts and those initially launched for less visible long-term concepts. The latter will entail more risk and will usually respond to a demonstration of the feasibility of new product concepts being incorporated into the roadmap.

On the other hand, the Virtual Organizations defined for New Product Development constitute a response to product concepts that contain less risky technological elements of development either because of the objective itself or because they have been dealt with previously in specific Technology Platform Development Virtual Organizations. In these cases, the creation of the Virtual Organizations by the Virtual Breading Environment responds to the objective of launching a new product on the market.

In the same way as for technology development, it is usually needed to launch several coordinated projects within a unique Virtual Organization in order to develop a whole product concept.

With all the elements identified, the next step to be carried out in this scenario was to define a global process so as to establish the synchronized behaviour among the different environments (see Figure 5).

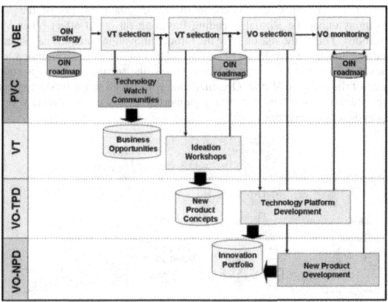

Figure 5 Orona Innovation Network ECOLEAD-based roadmap process

In a simplified way, the process defined is as follows:
1. VBE Technology Committee defines the market, product and technology strategy.
2. VBE Technology Committee decides the PVCs to launch for business opportunity identification.
3. PVCs perform their activities and define the business opportunities portfolio.
4. Virtual Teams are created in order to obtain the innovation portfolio based on new product concepts.
5. VBE Technology Committee decides and launches the new Virtual Organization for technology and product development.

Finally, in order to perform the take-up of this methodological scenario, a first definition of the roadmap process has been carried out in order to define the concept-lift 2010 and to identify the Virtual Organizations needed.

3.2.2   *Scenarios 2, 3 and 4: VO modelling, monitoring and analysis*

In any case, success in the development of the strategies defined in the roadmap depends to a great extent on the effective management of the various Virtual Organizations. This efficient management should be extended to all phases of the Virtual Organization life cycle: initiation and set-up, operation, evolution and dissolution.

In the case of the Orona Innovation Network, the product concepts planned in the roadmap and defined by the Virtual Breading Environment are supported by the results of the activities of one or more Virtual Organizations for new product development, each one supported by the results of the development of one or more Virtual Organizations for technology platform development. This dependence chain implies that any unexpected incident in the development of any of the Virtual Organizations under the Virtual Breading Environment could affect other Virtual Organizations. This is the reason why the Orona Innovation Network has taken into account monitoring on two levels. The first related to the own development of the activities considered in the Virtual Organizations; the second took into account an aggregate of the different Virtual Organizations with regard to the roadmap planned. This second level is defined as being supported by an explicit review process defined in detail (see Figure 6).

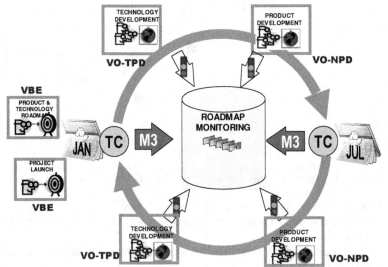

Figure 6 Virtual Organizations' monitoring and control from VBE

This review process establishes:

- The roadmap analysis by the Technology Committee at the beginning of a year, as well as the decision to launch new Virtual Organizations.
- Monitoring of the existing Virtual Organization (VO-TPD and VO-NPD) several times in the course of the year.

- An intermediate review midway through the year.

With the aim of supporting the management of the Virtual Organization during the ECOLEAD demonstration phase, these three different scenarios must nevertheless be integrated into one single general process that enables the controlled progress of the activities inside the Virtual Organization and the evolution to deal with unexpected events.

The first VO-Modelling scenario is in charge of initiating and defining the Virtual Organization.

By means of the VO-Mod (VO Model Wizard) tool, the following aspects have been established for the 'ARCA 2010' Virtual Organization selected in the pilot.

- Topology of the Virtual Organization: To enter all the information about the 'ARCA 2010' partners.
- Definition of the Work Breakdown Structure of the Virtual Organization 'ARCA 2010': Designing tasks and assigning them to the partners defined in the previous process.
- Definition of budget elements: Collecting resources for the partners and assigning them to WBS tasks

By means of the SID (Supporting Indicator Definition) tool, the following have been carried out:

- Identification of the standard indicators and metrics to be used.
- Definition based on these standard indicators of the specific indicators and metrics for 'ARCA 2010' Virtual Organization.
- Definition of provision rules to specify when indicator values should be transferred and stored.

The second 'VO-Monitoring' scenario is in charge of facilitating the collection of metrics from task leaders, the calculation of the indicators defined and the display of the status of the Virtual Organization related to those indicators defined.

By means of the DI3 (Distributed Indicator Information Integrator) tool, a request for the different indicators is sent towards the task leaders. Every task leader of 'ARCA 2010' has periodically input the required values related mainly to the fulfilment of planned objectives and incurred accumulated cost of their task.

The MAF (Monitor and Finance) tool has been used by the manager of 'ARCA 2010' to display the status starting from the received information related to indicators and also from their own perception (see Figure 7). Some aspects that this tool has enabled the manager to verify are:

- VO status details: KPIs status overview, completeness and budget
- Work Breakdown status
- Work Breakdown deviation
- Work Breakdown Gantt analysis
- Work Breakdown historical details

The third VO-Analysis scenario has been used in 'ARCA 2010' progress to respond to the needs of rescheduling that the Virtual Organization manager of 'ARCA 2010' has been obliged to overcome, due to non-fulfilment of objectives, shortage of resources or divergence in terms of planned expenditure.

By means of DSS (Decision Support System) tool, the Virtual Organization manager of 'ARCA 2010' can deal with the crucial analysis to carry out the rescheduling. In this sense, some of the functionalities used are:

- Management of VO configurations to create/view/edit/analyse/delete alternative configurations for 'ARCA 2010'.
- Overview of the VO schedules related to different configurations.
- What-if-analysis to simulate the future VO performance
- Rescheduling and reconfiguration of 'ARCA 2010'.

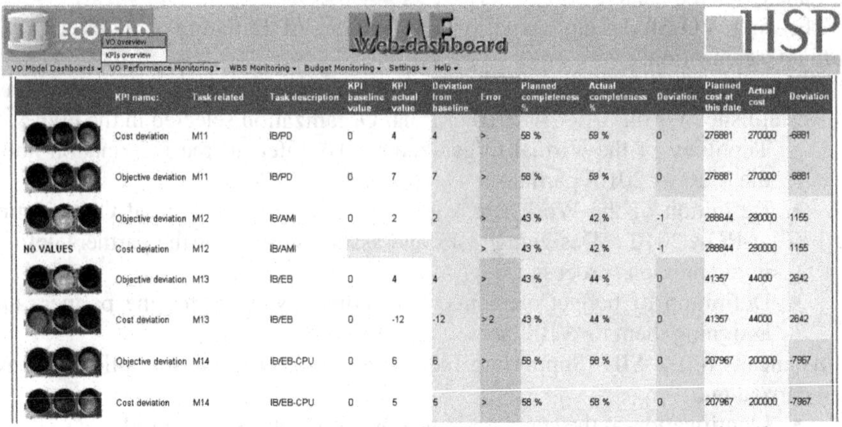
ECOLEAD
VO overview
KPIs overview
MAF Web-dashboard
HSP
VO Model Dashboards VO Performance Monitoring WBS Monitoring Budget Monitoring Settings Help
KPI name: | Task related | Task description | KPI baseline value | KPI actual value | Deviation from baseline | Error | Planned completeness % | Actual completeness % | Deviation | Planned cost at this date | Actual cost | Deviation
Cost deviation M11 IB/PD 0 4 4 > 58 % 59 % 0 276881 270000 -6881
Objective deviation M11 IB/PD 0 7 7 > 58 % 59 % 0 276881 270000 -6881
Objective deviation M12 IB/AMI 0 2 2 > 43 % 42 % -1 288844 290000 1155
NO VALUES Cost deviation M12 IB/AMI > 43 % 42 % -1 288844 290000 1155
Objective deviation M13 IB/EB 0 4 4 > 43 % 44 % 0 41357 44000 2642
Cost deviation M13 IB/EB 0 -12 -12 > 2 43 % 44 % 0 41357 44000 2642
Objective deviation M14 IB/EB-CPU 0 6 6 > 58 % 58 % 0 207967 200000 -7967
Cost deviation M14 IB/EB-CPU 0 5 5 > 58 % 58 % 0 207967 200000 -7967

Figure 7 MAF Web Dashboard – Check the current VO status details

The integration of the three scenarios and their synchronized progress has constituted an important challenge during the implementation and use of the tools described. The use of methodologies and tools developed in the ECOLEAD project for Virtual Organization Management makes the management of the ongoing Virtual Organizations within the Orona Innovation Network viable.

Finally, it must be said that in the course of implementing the Virtual Organization Management process in the Orona Innovation Network we had to distinguish clearly between two types of monitoring: the one established for the real-time monitoring of the Virtual Organization activities and the one established to assess the performance and inheritance factors at the end of the life cycle.

The first type of monitoring allows us to determine the running of the Virtual Organization in terms of the plans set out and to take the action required to overcome divergences in terms of time, cost or objectives. This is the one solved using the scenarios described.

The second type of monitoring allows us to draw conclusions about the performance of the processes defined for technology platforms and new product development, the suitability of the consortia and, in general, about any other aspect taken into account during the process for creating new Virtual Organizations.

3.4. Demonstration Phase

Firstly it is important to point out that the establishment in a network like Orona Innovation Network of formalized processes and common tools is not an easy task and demands continuous supervision and redefinition of the mechanisms that have been implemented. Despite these difficulties, the results obtained are promising. The results obtained in this scenario have been very successful. From the network point of view, the use of ECOLEAD elements and the process defined seem to be a very important basis for development in the future.

Knowledge strategy has been defined, four PVCs for technology-watching have been created, a complete roadmap of market, product and technology has been defined and four Virtual Organizations have been organized.

Table 5 shows some of the results obtained during the take-up which are related to the first scenario.

The results obtained in this scenario have been very successful. From the network point of view, the use of ECOLEAD elements and the process defined seem to be a very important basis for development in the future.

Knowledge strategy has been defined, four PVCs for technology-watching have been created, a complete roadmap of market, product and technology has been defined and four Virtual Organizations have been organized.

Table 5 Business indicators for Scenario 1: OIN-Roadmap

Business Metrics	Validity Domain	Initial Value	Expected Value	Current Value
Formalize process	Yes / No	No	Yes	Yes
Knowledge strategy defined	Yes / No	No	Yes	Yes
PVCs created	N/A	2	N/A	4
Roadmap defined	Yes / No	No	Yes	Yes
VO launched	N/A	3	N/A	4

As regards scenarios 2, 3 and 4 implemented for Virtual Organization Management, the following business metrics were attained during the final phase of the take-up (see Table 6, Table 7 and Table 8 respectively).

Table 6 Business indicators for Scenario 2: VO-Modelling

Business Metrics	Validity Domain	Initial Value	Expected Value	Current Value
Number of task leaders to access	0-50	0	5-15	8
VO manager satisfaction	0-10	5	8	7
VO task leader satisfaction	0-10	4	8	6
Interaction needed	0-10	10	3	6
Technology Committee satisfaction	0-10	6	8	7

Table 7 Business indicators for Scenario 3: VO-Monitoring

Business Metrics	Validity Domain	Initial Value	Expected Value	Current Value
Number of monitoring steps	0-20	0	5	3
VO manager satisfaction	0-10	4	8	6
VO task leader satisfaction	0-10	4	8	6
Interaction needed	0-10	10	3	7
Technology Committee satisfaction	0-10	6	8	7

Table 8 Business indicators for Scenario 4: VO-Analysis

Business Metrics	Validity Domain	Initial Value	Expected Value	Current Value
Number of periodic analysis	0-20	0	5	3
VO manager satisfaction	0-10	5	8	6
VO task leader satisfaction	0-10	5	8	6
Interaction needed	0-10	10	3	8
Technology Committee satisfaction	0-10	4	8	6

These indicators, taken at the end of the take-up phase, show that although there are some improvements in all aspects related to the qualitative measure of satisfaction, these are not as great as originally anticipated. Further use and development of associated tools and the software will help increase the values shown.

As regards other indicators, we can say that eight task leaders use the systems, the interaction needed between Virtual Organization manager and task leaders has been reduced in the three scenarios, and also two periodic analyses have been carried out.

Moreover, the satisfaction of the Technology Committee has increased because of the real possibility noted of standardizing the use of the tools created in ECOLEAD to manage the existing Virtual Organizations.

Summarizing, it can be said that the overall innovation process defined in the first scenario and the experience carried out with the Virtual Organization Management tools used in the second, third and fourth scenarios will help Orona Innovation Network to facilitate the following:

- Increase in efficiency and quality in terms of the identification of technological opportunities and maturing of product ideas.
- Metamorphosis needed to easily change the network to the appearance of emerging technologies, strategies and social needs.
- Growth of the innovation network because of the ability to expand with the introduction of new members.
- Increase in operational efficiency, due to ECOLEAD mechanisms for handling Virtual Organizations.

3.5. Lessons Learned and Next Steps

By way of a conclusion of the experience of the Orona Innovation Network within the ECOLEAD project, it is possible to point out the validity of the concepts, models, methodologies and tools developed in the project to apply them to Collaborative Networked Organizations that focus on innovation and new product development.

Special mention regarding this point must be made of the importance in these kinds of networks to bear in mind a master roadmap that sets out the priorities in the development of competences, technology and new products.

This roadmap is the cornerstone for assuring consistency between the different activities launched as Virtual Organizations and the strategic objectives of each partner. Another worthwhile aspect of the roadmap is that it is a very good tool for reinforcing trust among partners, as it establishes the expected contribution of each partner in the future.

Another lesson learned is the importance of a good coordination among all the basic pillars - Virtual Breading Environment, Virtual Organizations and Professional Virtual Communities - in these kinds of network. Only this coordination assures the effective management and synchronization of processes involved in the development of opportunities, ideas, technologies and new products needed in any kind of innovation network.

The use of the methodologies and tools developed for Virtual Organization Management of course provides very good support for standardizing the way in which different partners deal with their respective tasks, and also makes it easier to add new partners to the network.

To summarize, it can be said that participation of the Orona Innovation Network in the ECOLEAD project is expected to have a significant impact on the industrial competitiveness of its members.

Furthermore, we are confident that the application of the results of ECOLEAD in Orona Innovation Network will help to improve its overall objectives defined as:

- Sharing the cost and risk of research
- Pooling scarce expertise and co-specialization
- Performing pre-competitive research
- Gaining new competences through learning and collaboration in the network
- Increasing trust and reducing transaction cost among members
- Creating innovative products

However, participation in the Orona Innovation Network in the ECOLEAD project, apart from the framework defined in the first scenario, has been confined to the use of the tools created for the Virtual Organization Management. The next challenge for the future will be to analyse and apply the other methodologies and tools created for Virtual Breading Environments and Professional Virtual Communities management.

Finally, the aim of the Orona Innovation Network is to spread the results, the experience and the lessons learned via its participation in ECOLEAD to other CNOs inside the Mondragon Corporación Cooperativa group.

4. SNS

4.1. Network Overview

Supply Network Shannon (SNS) was set up in 1998 and incorporated as a limited liability company the following year. Located in the Shannon region of Ireland (see **Figure 8**), SNS is a network of over 40 companies, primarily engaged in the engineering and electronics sub supply sector, supplying various larger multi-national companies located within the area. This region has a strong basis for Electronics and Engineering work with approximately 80 such companies primarily involved in an array of operating sectors, including the supply of electronic assemblies and components, metal fabrication, plastic components and packaging materials. Most of the firms in SNS are classified as SMEs.

SNS is governed by a board consisting of executives from member companies and representatives from various government agencies, including Enterprise Ireland (a state agency responsible for entrepreneurial growth). The activities of SNS are discussed and acted upon, typically at the monthly meetings of the steering committee. This group delegates the duties through various sub-committees. SNS also has strong research links with the University of Limerick, including the Enterprise Research Centre. This is part of a proactive campaign of participation in joint research.

At a practical level, SNS fosters co-operation between its members by the provision of information, forums and facilities in the following areas of shared interest:
1. Business issues such as supply chain management (SCM)
2. Technical issues relevant to engineering and electrical manufacturers and ICT usage
3. Training and promotion between partners for shared activities.

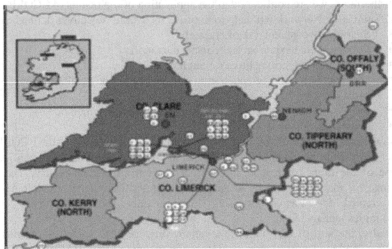

Figure 8 Supply Network Shannon main locations of activity in the Shannon Region

Additionally, SNS helps its members to look beyond their current areas of expertise and interest by becoming a partner in various projects which broaden the scope of their knowledge and capabilities. These projects include work in:
1. Environmental issues, such as balancing company commitment to waste management and effective cost reduction.
2. All-Ireland collaboration at SME level. This is done in conjunction with similar bodies in Northern Ireland, such as Invest Northern Ireland.
3. The fostering of closer bonds between members and local multinationals. An example of how this is achieved is the annual "Meet the Buyer" seminars, where SMEs are given the opportunity to make presentations to various multinationals. This breeds awareness of the SME's work, which may not otherwise be known by the multinational and therefore possible future work for the SME. With large multinationals such as Dell located in the region, this task is an important duty of SNS.

Already, SNS is seeing the benefits, as well as the potential difficulties, of networking and have pursued a proactive campaign of involvement in third party research into the area of collaboration in a series of formalised research projects. In its present guise, SNS could be seen as an emerging Virtual Breeding Environment, where the group has shown a commitment to collaborate on projects where possible. However, in order for members of this group to routinely use the VO approach to conducting their business, improvements in several key areas were required. One of these areas was the need to provide a means of standardised ICT support to coordinate and monitor collaborative activities. This requirement drove initial interest for SNS in the ECOLEAD initiative and encouraged their involvement in the development and testing of associated tools and methodologies.

4.2. Definition Phase

On being accepted as a partner in the ECOLEAD program, SNS was requested to suggest suitable existing networks which demonstrated high levels of collaboration. After samples of possible networks were reviewed, the Vigitek network was selected as an appropriate test case for the purposes of the ECOLEAD work.

The Vigitek Virtual Organisation is a five stage process of Electronic Component manufacture, where Vigitek is the end customer. This VO is a network of four companies and is intrinsically a Supply Chain partnership. The companies involved are:

- RTR Electronics (Materials collation, testing and distribution);
- Ryan Prototyping (Mechanical manufacture);
- Bright Solutions (Surface mount manufacture), and;
- Ship Co. Ltd (PCB manufacture).

The main tasks of this network are the manufacture, test and repair of PCB boards. All of the companies in the Virtual Organisation could be classified as either Micro or Small businesses since the number of employees per firm falls in the range of 1 to 40 employees (these values are adjusted seasonally through the use of contract labour). The principal characteristics of this VO and the reasons for its creation are outlined in the following points:

- RTR Electronics supplies customized electronic components and associated services to a number of companies in the Mid-West Region in Ireland.
- RTR Electronics has a long term relationship with Vigitek (a Limerick based producer of print inspection equipment) to whom it supplies short production run customized electronic components. Delivery of these components requires that RTR brings together companies in a VO to meet theses need.
- RTR electronics would be classified as a micro enterprise and does not have in-house capabilities to supply all services to Vigitek.
- RTR Electronics competitive edge is its ability to meet short deadlines for its customers, being flexible in relation to providing customized products and production runs with short turn around times. It is not primarily cost that it is competing on, i.e., it cannot compete with low cost countries.

In relation to this VO, Vigitek would request from RTR a component for a product that Vigitek are developing. RTR would develop a prototype for this using several companies, in this case Ryan Prototyping, Bright Solutions, Ship Co LTD and various suppliers. Once this prototype has been developed and tested Vigitek may order varying production volumes. These may be a once off purchase order run or a supply contract where RTR would be required to delivery the components over several months where products are being shipped daily or monthly. **Figure 9** below illustrates the main tasks of each partner in the network.

The major issues with the scenario described above relate to the management of an SME based supply chain where each partner has their own limitations and priorities with regard to work scheduling and WIP storage. The difficulty from a VO managerial perspective lies in matching these individual concerns with the needs of the overall VO. **Table 9** summarises this issue and outlines the consequent performance indicators. The ECOLEAD tools used to address this problem are also detailed.

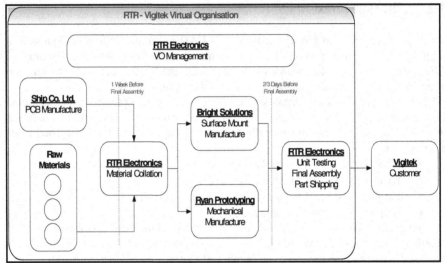

Figure 9 The partners of the Vigitek Virtual Organisation

Table 9 Vigitek VO Scenario

	Scenario
Business Process	Vigitek VO Management
Issue Addressed	Current approach to management of the VO is informal and not conducive to process improvement
Main Objective	To implement a standardized approach to VO supply chain management.
Indicators	• Amount of time dedicated to management of VO • Ability to identify and react to quality issues in any of the VO partners • VO manager satisfaction. • VO member commitment to participate in future VOs
Tools Used	• VOMod • SID • DI3 • MAF • DSS

The various tools created by the ECOLEAD developers (as summarised at the beginning of this chapter) provide the capability to store the relevant information in relation to a Virtual Organisation and also give the end users key functionality in the areas of:

1. Development of structured Virtual Organisation;
2. Virtual Organisation Control and Management;
3. Virtual Organisation Monitoring and Analysis.

After initial review of the software and discussions with the companies, it was felt that the tools which specifically dealt with Virtual Organisation monitoring and control issues were of most relevance to this scenario (i.e. VOMod, SID, DI3 & MAF) and that the Decision Support tool (DSS) may not be necessarily used by firms of this profile. However despite this, it was decided to demonstrate all aspects of the software to the VO as it was felt that this was an apt opportunity to demonstrate the main principles of the tools so that they would be considered for potential use in the future. The activities conducted when gathering case information, populating the tools, and implementing this software in the VO scenario are described in the next section.

4.3 Implementation Phase

Once it was decided what specific SNS network would be used (Vigitek), several steps were taken in order to bring the software to a developed stage near take-up.

1. After initial demonstrations to the end-user companies at various locations, a request for case-specific data was made from the developers to the end-user representative. The various elements of data were then inputted to the relevant software in order to ensure the software was ready for test. The data that was submitted related to:
   a. Company information of all partners within the VO.
   b. Budgetary breakdowns of associated assembly projects and the related work breakdown structures.
   c. Key Performance Indicator information used to evaluate the performance of the VO, i.e. the metrics used to calculate the VO performance
2. On completion of the various elements of software, through various conference meetings and email forums, a series of guided functional demonstrations of the software were conducted by the relevant developers with representatives of the end-user networks.
3. Intended end-users were then shown the completed software for testing. This was done in conjunction with further development of the tools on the basis of feedback from the end-users. The tools were tested in relation to the normal business activities of the network. This stage also included the provision of regular feedback to developers for future development.
4. Using predefined business metrics, the software was evaluated under two key criteria – the actual usability of the software and its applicability to the network itself.

This last evaluation step (4) is discussed further in the Demonstration Phase in the next section, but first, the details of the implementation and use of the tools at the various stages of the Vigitek Virtual Organisation are outlined in the following points. These points also highlight some of the areas where the ECOLEAD tools have been recognised to replace older methodologies. Previously, VO management would have been done in an ad-hoc fashion, with each partner using their own specific means of performance measurement (which would have only reflected their own performance primarily and not that of the entire VO).

1. Vigitek (a Limerick based producer of print inspection equipment) places an order for a specific amount of finished PCBs to RTR. RTR, being the primary contact, then initiates a Virtual Organisation from its associated partners in the SNS network. The structure and associated details of this Virtual Organisation is captured using the **VOM** tool (see **Figure 10**), where partner details and the associated Work Breakdown Structures are stored (amongst other details). Previously, this would have been done via separate tools and most details would have been omitted. The **VOM** tool now provides a centralised collection point for this information.

2. On receipt of the PCB boards from Ship Co. Ltd. to RTR, the goods are organised into specific batches and prepared for distribution to the various manufacturing partners. At the point of departure, the KPI performance measurement capabilities of the software are initiated. The KPIs are selected and configured for collection using both the **SID** and the **DI3**, a process which is co-ordinated with the other partners within the Virtual Organisation. This is done for mutual agreement on procedure of data collection from various internal storage points. This functionality can then be used as a real-time performance measurement technique, with the *Alert Rules Monitor* alerting the VO manager of possible problems. As the network of companies is primarily a linear Supply Chain, the two overall performance indicators needed to be recorded and shown would be (through the combination of various measurements):

   a. Quality of Goods Received
   b. Time of Goods spent at each point of production

   The **MAF** tool acts as a means to communicate these results in an easily understandable manner to RTR, being the primary partner. Once the relevant stock has been collected, it is distributed to either:

   c. Bright Solutions – At this point, surface mounting of specific components and subsequent testing of this work is carried out. This is the typical route of the majority of the boards.
   d. Ryan Prototyping – From time to time, RTR will need a "once-off" prototype PCB. Ryan Prototyping facilitates this need.

3. Once the PCB boards are returned from either sub-contractor, they are then returned to RTR for final assembly and testing. Once again, the **MAF** displays the relevant KPI values and alerts RTR if any of the performance indicators falls below a designated threshold via the Alert Monitor e.g. if goods are delayed or of inadequate quality. If this occurs, the relevant party then contacts the origin of this measurement and solves any potential problems immediately for subsequent deliveries. Without this functionality, this information may have gone unnoticed for a longer period, which would be highly detrimental given the short lead times stated by the customer.

4. On completion, the finished goods are then transported (via courier) to Vigitek for use in its own product range. At this point, the second purpose of

the KPI measurements (i.e. to evaluate the VO as a whole and not just on a real-time basis) would be used to identify areas of concern and form the basis for improvement in future guises of this specific VO.

5. While the network is easily controllable due to its size and the familiarity between the relevant partners, deviations from the planned operation can occur. While the **MAF** will alert the VO partners of any such deviations (which can be subsequently fixed quickly), it is quite possible that changes of a larger scale will be needed to be implemented. If that is the case, the **DSS** tool would be utilised in order to reschedule the relevant Work Breakdown Structure of the project. This is done in a highly accessible manner, with events such as delays at specific points being easily captured and their subsequent effects on the entire project plan, with a revised Work Breakdown structure, shown. This can be either

   a. Viewed for possible examination

   b. Or through the use of the simulation capability, adapted as the new WBS.

As stated before, many of the processes in the above procedure would have been carried out by each partner separately. Using the ECOLEAD software, many of the processes now benefit from the sharing of information and the fact that the tools directly answer VO specific needs.

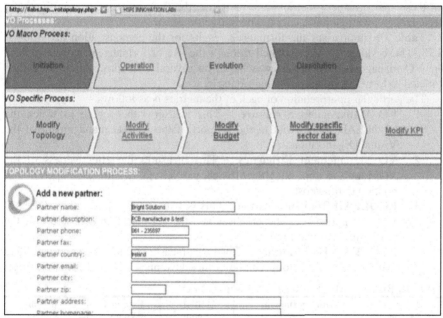

Figure 10 Addition of new Virtual Organisation partner

4.4 Demonstration Phase

This section demonstrates the effectiveness of the ECOLEAD VO management tools by comparing current situation with that prior to the use of the ECOLEAD tools. Previously the management of VOs in RTR Electronics was carried out manually and informally, with communication and monitoring being done via email, phone and fax in a non-standardized manner. The details of VOs were not formally recorded for later analysis thereby making it difficult to instigate process improvement initiatives. The ECOLEAD methodology and tools provide a framework for more structured and efficient management of these VOs. The VOMod allows a recording of the VOs, which did not exist in the company. Monitoring of the VO is provided by three different tools. The SID provides a catalogue of generic performance indicators, while the DI3 tool allows for data capture in relation to these indicators. The MAF tool then provides an easily understandable means of displaying the information back to the network. RTR Electronics found merit in the approach of ECOLEAD for the management of VOs. Specifically it found from a business perspective it would give competitive advantages by:

- Facilitating better control of VOs to meet customer demands;
- Helping to sell solutions to RTR customers like Vigitek, who see the use of such tools as another example of the suppliers' commitment to providing a robust solution.

It is obvious that these two criteria are also paramount to other SNS member companies, who are not in a position to make low cost the selling point of their goods or services and so must rely on their ability to produce high quality goods in short lead times. It is crucial for these companies maintain their credibility in regard to these performance metrics as many of their customers are multinational organizations with global access to alternative suppliers.

Table 10 summarises the formalised results for the demonstration activities at SNS. These values were calculated through the use of formalized interviews with the VO managers. Each metric was based on several questions, which were then collated to form the value for the metric itself.

The particular interpretation of each of the metrics is as follows:

1. **VO Management Structure** – This measures the degree to which the ECOLEAD tools assist in the support of the general management of the Virtual Organisation.
2. **VO Management Efficiency** – This measures the effectiveness of the VOM tools in improving the efficiency of Virtual Organisation operation in relation to time/cost.
3. **ECOLEAD Tool Integration** - This is a measure of how the ECOLEAD tools integrated with the practises and the current IT infrastructure of the test Virtual Organisation.
4. **ECOLEAD Tool Validity** – This is the measure of how the candidates feel that the ECOLEAD tools can be further developed and used commercially.

Table 10 Business Metrics Results for Vigitek VO.

Business Metrics	Validity Domain	Initial Value	Expected Value	Current Value
VO Management Structure	**Level of Improvement**: None/Low/Medium/High	No Management Structure	High	Medium
VO Management Efficiency	**Level of Improvement**: None/Low/Medium/High	No distinct means of measurement	High	Low
ECOLEAD	Yes/No	N/A	Yes	Yes (but with

Tool Integration				improvements)
ECOLEAD Tool Viability	Yes/No	N/A	Yes	Yes (but with improvements)

While most of the values were positive, it must be noted that these were given on the basis that future development of the tools in order to customize them to be suitable to the Irish SME environment tested (i.e. most of the participating companies were micro-firms with 1-10 employees). These companies would have different requirements and resource levels from other European networks containing larger companies. The scale of the companies allows for closer relationships to be established which already facilitates effective business co-operation and the sharing of key information, thus making some of the functionality of the tools somewhat unnecessary. Another consideration that was felt that would need to be considered was the fact that the software is focused on project based network activities. The Vigitek network is primarily a supply based network with different characteristics to a project based network e.g. longer duration and less emphasis on Work Breakdown Structures. Therefore, it is important that these considerations must be taken into account when viewing the evaluation. This is especially true when reading the ECOLEAD tool **Integration** and **Viability** criteria, which would suggest that specific catering for the network would have to be done (this is explained in more detail in the next section).

4.5 Lessons Learned and Next Steps

During the implementation and demonstration phases, SNS member companies, as well as the Vigitek VO companies were shown the tools, given a demonstration of their main functionality and asked for their feedback. This included the demonstration of any incremental changes to the software due to correspondence with the developers. This feedback generated a forum for improvements and also gave an insight to the more relevant issues as regards collaboration, especially at SME level. Some of the issues highlighted were specific to the SNS network itself and would have to be considered in future guises of the software i.e. the need to cater for clusters with companies of a specific profile.

On a whole, the underlying concept of the tools was recognised and received good comment. The fact that the project met a need for such a suite of tools was noted and that it is hoped that the positive aspects of this work are carried on to future development of such tools and methodologies.

As regards the individual tools, some of the observations made by the end-users:

- While the accessibility of web-based tools was praised increased standardisation of the interfaces would improve usability of the tools.
- The companies in the SNS VO have very limited IT resources therefore reduction in the resources required to deploy the VOM tools needs to taken into consideration.
- The tools should provide controlled access to customers of VOs to allow them to monitor its execution.

From a wider perspective SNS has benefited from its involvement in the ECOLEAD initiative in a number of ways. Firstly, new methodologies and technologies have been introduced to the network. While some will not be directly used by SNS, others will be taken up and developed into the processes of the network. Secondly, the forum of discussion has given all participants opportunity to discuss the more salient topics with regards inter-firm collaboration and its future. This has also been aided by the participation of academic research personnel and bodies. There is a realisation that there is much more work to be done in this area but this project has definitely been a positive step.

Based on their interaction with the ECOLEAD tools to date, SNS believe that the next logical steps for this research are to apply the refined tools from this pilot implementation to a broader range of VOs. In addition to ascertaining the wider applicability of the tools and the ease with which this software can be integrated into existing IT environments, this would provide an opportunity to discover further desired functionality that would promote take up of the finished products.

5. CONCLUSION

The ECOLEAD project has yielded a suite of software designed specifically for an important and expanding mode of operation in the European manufacturing sector, which is the Virtual Organisation concept. The success of these VOs is heavily dependent on the close collaboration of their member companies and the need for careful management of these relationships has given rise to new requirements in terms of manufacturing support tools and methodologies. The ECOLEAD project has aimed to satisfy these requirements and, in this chapter, the experiences gained through implementing the resulting software in three distinct VO scenarios have been outlined.

Each of the three pilot cases returned positive reviews of: 1) the underlying concepts and objectives of the tools; 2) the usability of the developed software; 3) the applicability of the developed software; and 4) the possibility of even greater benefits with future development. The variety of responses was attributable to the different environments, the differing scales of the constituents of the VOs, and the different types of business undertaken by the VOs. Many of the further opportunities for improvement, as identified by the test cases, could be readily achieved through customisation of the existing software and none were seen as unsurpassable obstacles to the successful implementation and use of the ECOLEAD software.

Acknowledgments. This work was funded in part by the European Commission through the ECOLEAD project. The authors thank the contribution of their partners in the consortium.

6. REFERENCES

1. Camarinha-Matos, L. M. (2003). Infrastructures for virtual organizations - where we are, *Proceedings of Emerging Technologies and Factory Automation*, Vol. 2, 405-414
2. Camarinha-Matos, L. M. and H. Afsarmanesh (2007). A framework for virtual organization creation in a breeding environment, *Annual Reviews in Control*, 31 (1), 119-135.
3. Corvello, V. and P. Migliarese (2007). Virtual forms for the organization of production: A comparative analysis, *International Journal of Production Economics*, 110 (1-2), 5-15.
4. Hodík, J., W. Mulder, L. Pondrelli, I. Westphal and R. Hofman (2007). ICT services supporting virtual organization management, in D. Pham, E. Eldukhri and A. Soroka, eds., *Proceedings of Innovative Production Machines and Systems: Third I*PROMS Virtual International Conference*, Whittles Publishing, 2-13 July.
5. Strader, T. J., F.-R. Lin and M. J. Shaw (1998). Information infrastructure for electronic virtual organization management, *Decision Support Systems*, 23 (1), 75-94.

PVC PILOT CASES

Tatiana Glotova[1], Sabine Ziem[2], Ilkka Kakko[3], Mika Lavikainen[4]

[1]*Joensuu Science Park FINLAND, tatiana.glotova@carelian.fi*
[2]*AIESEC International, NETHERLANDS, sabinez@ai.aiesec.org*
[3]*Joensuu Science Park, FINLAND, ilkka.kakko@carelian.fi*
[4]*Joensuu Science Park, FINLAND, mika.lavikainen@carelian.fi*

Authors give evaluation of applicability of ECOLEAD methodological and ICT results on the example of two pilot PVC cases. One PVC case is represented by a community of ICT professionals in Joensuu Region, Finland, the other one is based on a global alumni community AIESEC and focuses on Human Resource Management experts. Authors discuss the challenges and solutions for the establishment of successful PVCs, describe the phases, where ECOLEAD results were applied in the PVCs, and suggest the future PVC concept development and integration of supporting tools with other available on the market solutions.

1. INTRODUCTION

PVCs are one representation of Collaborative Networked Organizations (CNOs). The idea of gathering individual professionals into collaborative networks is not new. ICT enabled the virtual dimension of these networks, making them global in their scale. This new dimension requires developing new concepts and new management paradigms for networked organizations.

Professional Virtual Communities (PVCs) are very diverse by their nature. The application of ECOLEAD concepts in each case is different and this should be taken into consideration when planning a new PVC. In the following sections we describe two different cases which were pilot PVCs in ECOLEAD project.

One of the PVC pilots gathers alumni of AIESEC, a non-profit, non-commercial, non-government global organization, run by students and recent graduates, to encourage the formalization of generally loose networks in the area of Human Resources Management and Development (HRMD).

The other one is ICT PVC in Joensuu Region, Finland, where ICT professionals and international business development experts were gathered in order to enable new business opportunities and to extend the existing ICT professionals network to the international level.

PVCs can be considered as creative organizations, where individuals work on the tasks interesting for them personally. According to (CNO book, p.127) the key characteristics of a creative organization include:

- Continuous reassessment of tasks and assignments through interaction with others during iterative processes;
- Communication network for tasks control based on expertise and commitment;
- Open and extensive communication;
- Network-type of structure;
- Commitment and relevant expertise are the key factors for success;
- Leadership for inspiring, motivating and aligning people.

These characteristics are relevant for the PVCs since they operate as networks of independent individuals, who are assigned to particular tasks based on their competences, motivation and through the interaction with other participants; leadership is self organized within the community and commitment is crucial.

Motivation

Motivation of PVC members to interact with each other and to establish collaborative activities is a key issue for the PVC sustainable development. The pilot cases have shown that the motivation factors include at least:

- Trust within the community
- Transparency
- New contacts
- New opportunities
- Finding international collaboration for Research and Development activities
- Possibility to work with tasks that are personally interesting
- Improving and widening personal skills and competences
- Financial expectations or opportunities
- 24 hour access from anywhere in the world

Challenges

Both individuals and organizations are challenged by the CNOs' era. There is a role for the traditional organization, but individual professional's responsibility and ownership of knowledge are increasing. Potentially, the new organizational structures will reflect these changes (CNO book, p.129).

Main challenges for the individuals:

- to find a place in the new economic environment
- to constantly improve skills and acquire new knowledge
- to establish professional and personal networks
- to be trustful and trusted
- to find a niche in the market offering a unique competence
- to be never absolutely sure about the future

Main challenges for companies:

- to compete with professional networks
- to become very flexible
- to increase the speed and quality of development
- to keep individual professionals in the company
- to attract talent into the company

In the next sections we shall describe two ECOLEAD pilot PVC cases followed by the conclusions and references.

2. ICT PVC IN JOENSUU REGION, FINLAND

2.1 Brief description of the pilot network

One pilot case of ECOLEAD PVC concept is ICT PVC in Joensuu region, Finland. It was originally created within ICT Development Program and was administrated by Joensuu Science Park Ltd (JSP). Another source of origin of the PVC is netWork Oasis (www.network-oasis.com), which is an essential part of JSP's innovation environment. It is a collaborative working, learning and development environment which is designed to increase the productivity of knowledge workers. netWork Oasis is a combination of physical, virtual and hybrid space and on the other side it is a platform for various networks of diverse people – experts, working in netWork Oasis. netWork Oasis represents an unique breeding environment for emerging PVCs (Kakko, Glotova, 2007).

ICT PVC, as one of those emerging PVCs, is concentrating on creating new commercial software products, which are MES (Manufacturing Engineering Systems), PLM (Product Life-Cycle Management) and SCM (Supply Chain Management) systems, their integration to business ERP's (Enterprise Resource Planning) and internalization of their research and development activities. The target industry is plastic and metal production companies having discrete manufacturing processes. During the ECOLEAD project the knowledge scope of the original PVC was extended to include experts on international collaborative projects and therefore make it possible for the PVC to enter EU market.

ICT PVC members
ICT PVC involves the following members:
- People from SMEs working in IT sector in Joensuu Region, Finland
- IT experts and management of Joensuu Science Park
- Researches and students of the University of Joensuu
- Researches and students of the North Carelian University of Applied Sciences
- Future collaboration with researchers from Lappeenranta University of Technology and VTT (Technical Research Centre of Finland)
- International experts

The core group in the PVC is twenty people, and the total number of the PVC is around fifty professionals, with possibility to widen the PVC even further.

2.2 Definition Phase

Identification of the main tools
The tools, used in the ICT PVC before joining ECOLEAD project included:
- FlexLab and netWork Oasis, provided by JSP, as a neutral physical space for collaboration.
- TULO Laboratory was used as a piloting environment.
- E-mails for asynchronous, and chats, mobile phones for synchronous collaboration.

Tools that had been highly appreciated but not available for the ICT PVC included:

- Shared document editing
- VT management tools
- Review and acceptance process tools.

From the tools developed by ECOLEAD Consortium the highest expectations were towards Collaborative Problem Solving e-services (C-PS) and Advanced Collaboration Platform (ACP), in particular:

- ACP platform:
    o General collaboration tools: Forum, Wiki, Chat
    o PVC Knowledge & IPR management
    o Economic Human Competency evaluation
    o PVC Governance and Collaboration rewarding
    o Social & Business networking
- C-PS e-services:
    o Planned Collaboration
    o Ad Hoc Collaboration

Identification of the business processes

Business orientation of this PVC is to develop software tools and sell them to the customers. The first pilots were implemented during the ICT Development Program and further development in order to commercialize the solutions was going on during the ECOLEAD demonstration phase. The main focus of the solutions is:

- To have production systems based on modularized, standardized architecture provided by ICT-supplier network.
- To implement customer production processes and workflows into the system following ISA 95 standard.
- To decrease human errors.
- To provide a possibility of having a shorter production and development cycle.

There were some challenges for the whole ICT PVC, besides the general challenges for individuals and companies, mentioned above. One problem was how to make the PVC self-organized without the support of JSP. Our solution was to teach the members of the PVC how to work in a peer-to-peer mode and establish a set of common values such as trust and open-minded attitude.

Initially there were no consistent methods for PVC creation, governance and evolution used. When the PVC first started to emerge from the members of ICT Development Program, it was rather unmanageable and unstructured. In this case no one was willing to take responsibility to organize any activities. ECOLEAD methodologies helped us to establish governance principles for the PVC.

Close geographical location of the members means that face-to-face meetings are the most common way to work, with exchanging documents via e-mails. Therefore, it was expected from the very beginning that ICT tools developed in ECOLEAD will not replace face-to-face interactions, but rather complement these activities and enhance knowledge management in this PVC. Another challenge concerning the ICT tools was to inspire the members using them, as many of the members are ICT professionals and their expectations of benefits using the tools were much higher than average. Constant dialog with the developers of Advanced Collaboration Platform helped to improve the quality of the ICT solution.

The competitiveness of the ICT PVC on international market was one of the key challenges, while PVC's international experience was limited and no international experts were included. ECOLEAD methodologies on PVC life-cycle management were used to lead the PVC through the evolution phase, to extend the knowledge scope and to get the international partners and cross-border projects.

Identification of scenarios for the business processes
Scenario 1: ICT PVC formalization and operation
- Formalization
- Operation, Governance, Extension and Promotion

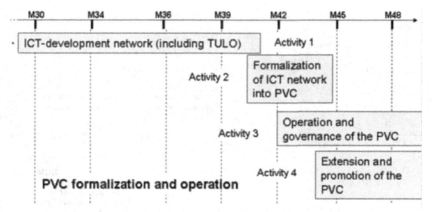

Figure 1 ICT PVC Formalization and operation scenario

The first scenario aims at the formalization of the ICT PVC. The former network of ICT experts was coordinated by ICT Development Program and had some common frame-agreements, but they were not comprehensive and they were designed to support certain projects, not the network itself. In addition, the former network was more or less self-organized and loose without common comprehensive rules. ICT Development network has acted as an entity to identify market needs and cover some of those needs with the competences of regional ICT professionals. As a result of these activities the network has generated new customer oriented collaborative projects. After the ICT professionals had experience of collaborative working across organisational barriers it was necessary to get the network to operate by its own as a PVC without any external incubator or coordinator.

To formalize the network (Figure 1) JSP utilized ECOLEAD methodologies such as "PVC reference framework" and "Value system and metrics for PVCs" and went though the following stages:
- PVC identification
- PVC scenario planning, mission creation and formalization
- PVC operation and governance principles creation
- PVC extension to European level plans.

Scenario 2: VTs creation and operation within ICT PVC

This scenario aims at creating new VTs within ICT PVC, which are able to create new products. Projects represented on Figure 2. were originally related to the ICT Development Program. TULO Laboratory was created within the first project focusing on MES and it created a piloting and integration environment for new systems that will be developed in this PVC. TULO Laboratory combines development and research efforts of researchers from local educational institutes, representatives of industrial companies and IT-professionals of the PVC. PLM and SCM projects are related to the first project, though business case and therefore VTs are different for each of them.

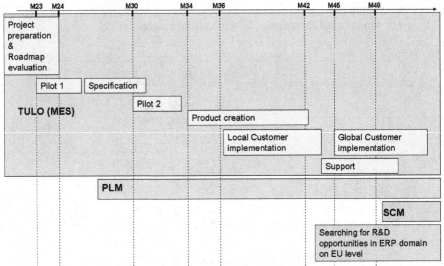

Figure 2 VTs creation and operation within ICT PVC

Other projects are not depicted on the Figure 2 as they were not initially planned in the scenario, but rather emerged in the later phases of PVC operation and required an extension of the knowledge scope of the ICT PVC.

Identification of business metrics/indicators

Scenario name: ICT PVC formalization and operation

Quantitative Business metrics, which were included in the ICT PVC formalization and operation scenario, were defined as:

- Number of registered in the PVC members (with signed agreement) and number of ACP portal users
- Position of the PVC in the Knowledge-Business-Social triangle
- Number of documents uploaded in the Knowledge IPR directory
- Number of VTs created in the PVC

The quantitative expectations and the results after applying ECOLEAD methodologies and tool will be discussed in the section 2.4. The summary of the expected results, effects, impacts and benefits in the qualitative sense:

1) Using ECOLEAD methodologies to formalize the ICT network into PVC.

Results: Network is prepared to change into real PVC with necessary documents and rules. PVC created using ECOLEAD PVC-models and governance principles, and tools provided with the ACP

Effects: PVC running without external incentives

Impacts: PVC is able to establish new businesses and projects themselves according to the members' competences

Benefits: Independent decision making, better communication between the members. Easier and faster project creation without unnecessary bureaucracy

2) Using ECOLEAD methodologies in operation and governance of the PVC

Results: Operational and manageable PVC with common rules and processes.

Effects: Availability of a "library" of competences. Methods and tools to cope in different tasks and situations

Impacts: Enables the management of the PVC, more effective development of new ideas.

Benefits: Less time used for idea-to-project/product generation. Better communication in the PVC, better knowledge of the competences in the network.

3) Using ECOLEAD methodologies in extension and promotion of the PVC

Results: Larger PVC, more widely spread knowledge about the PVC, its competences and references. ECOLEAD network is used for the extension of the ICT PVC.

Effects: Widened scope of competences of the PVC. Spreading the knowledge about the PVC and what kind of services / products it can provide.

Impacts: New business opportunities, more jobs. Sharing human and knowledge resources.

Benefits: Members get more pleasurable tasks related to their interests and competences. New business for the members. New social contacts in personal network.

Scenario name: VT Establishment and operation within ICT PVC

Quantitative Business metrics for the second scenario, VT Establishment and operation, include:

- Number of VT's members, minimum, maximum and average
- Total financial value of the projects generated by VT contribution
- Number of projects running at a time

The results, effects, impacts and benefits, which were expected from the activities with application of ECOLEAD results are:

1) Road-Mapping

Results: Collaborative planning of the activities is done using ECOLEAD C-PS methods and tools.

Effects: Planning is done in a way that is more suitable for distributed collaborative implementation in the following stages.

Impacts: Less need for face-to-face meetings, asynchronous collaboration allowed, more professionals might be included.

Benefits: Road-Mapping might be done not only in face-to-face meetings, but in physically distributed teams.

2) Pilots

Results: VTs created using ECOLEAD collaboration models and governance principles, and tools provided with the ACP.

Effects: The right competencies are chosen from the PVC.

Impacts: More focused VTs, better and faster solutions, more efficient PVC.

Benefits: Easier and faster VT establishment for rapid prototyping, for example, like in Pilot case.

3) Product creation and customer implementation

Results: Local expertise is involved for product creation and customer implementation via C-PS tool and ACP.

Effects: Less time is spent on product creation. Possibility to involve customer's end users in the early stages of product creation.

Impacts: Governance is done more effectively in distributed teams.

Benefits: Increase in productivity and profit ability; no need for travelling; more efficient allocation of resources; IPR issues are easier to handle.

4) Support

Results: PVC is able to re-create the VT in case the support is needed, or provide the knowledge from that VT, as it is inherited in the PVC.

Effects: Networked support availability 24/7 at any place.

Impacts: Sustainable customer satisfaction.

Benefits: Getting feedback and ideas for further development of the network; new orders / business possibilities; knowledge is managed in a more structured way.

Table with the results of the activities:

Table 1 – Results of the activities

	Scenario 1	Scenario 2
Business Process	ICT PVC formalization and operation	VT's establishment and operation within ICT PVC
Addressed Issue	PVC establishment and governance principles; Tools to be used in the PVC	Methodologies to work in VTs, ICT tools for distributed collaboration, IPR protection
Main Objective	Creation self-governing PVC from the loose network of professionals using ECOLEAD methodologies and ICT tools	Enabling effective VTs creation and operation processes
Indicators	- Number of registered in the PVC members (with signed agreement) and number of ACP portal users - Position of the PVC in the Knowledge-Business-Social triangle - Number of documents uploaded in the Knowledge IPR directory - Number of VTs created in the PVC	- Number of VT's members, minimum, maximum and average - Total financial value of the projects generated by VT contribution - Number of projects running at a time
Tools Used	Advanced Collaboration Platform (ACP)	Advanced Collaboration Platform (ACP) Collaborative Problem Solving e-services (C-PS)

2.3 Implementation Phase

Description of the creation of the necessary environment in the pilot demonstrator for taking-up the tools

Set up steps

In the ICT PVC the initial core team of the PVC was the same as the main actors of ICT Development Program and some JSP professionals. They had a community of individuals from a number of companies and research institutions forming a VT and working on the same project. This community was not officially defined as a PVC, though acted as such. With the help of ECOLEAD methodologies the core team established the "First" ICT PVC, which involved mostly local ICT companies' employees.

General line of development

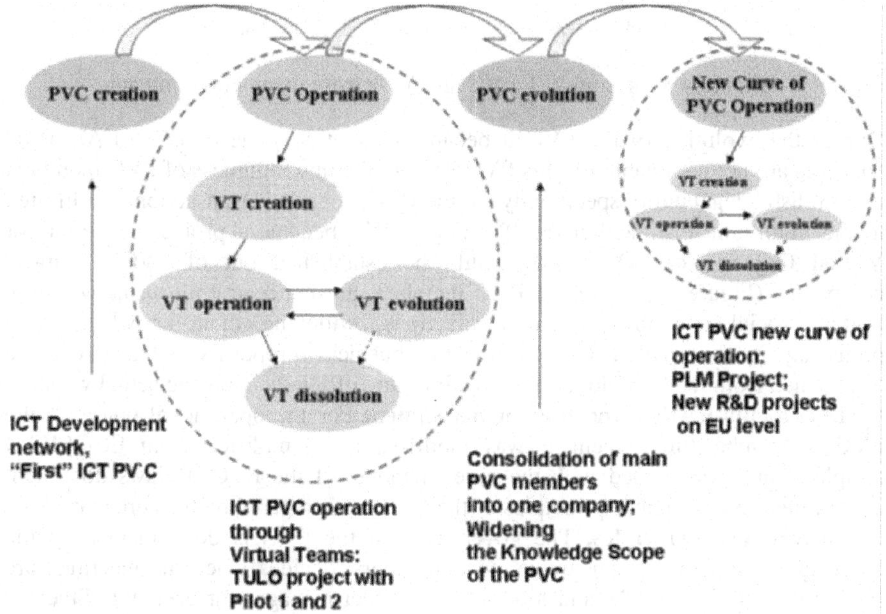

Figure 3 ICT PVC Life-Cycle

One of the challenges of this PVC was that it could not find an easy way to internationalize itself. Another big challenge came up when the main members (representing three different companies) of the PVC decided to merge into one company.

At this step PVC core team started to deploy ECOLEAD methodologies and decided to widen the knowledge scope of the PVC in order to extend it beyond the borders of the new consolidated company (Figure 3).

The vision of the PVC remained the same as the initial one, as it included internalization aspect already, but the knowledge scope had to be extended in order to involve new members with complementing competences for internalization of PVC and its R&D projects.

Evolution of the PVC

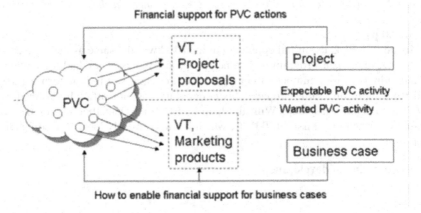

Figure 4 VTs from ICT PVC and VOs from members' companies

During the evolution of the PVC it became clear, that some of ECOLEAD PVC concepts are not applicable for this PVC. Due to the unwillingness of PVC members to establish a legal entity specifically for the PVC, economic transactions are limited to the minimum level within the PVC. ICT PVC became a project generator for Virtual Organizations (VO) that would be established out of PVC members' companies (Figure 4). Therefore PVC members are concentrating on networking, finding social and professional connections, widening their knowledge and preparing international R&D projects or business proposals, while VOs are established from their employer organizations and officially carry the actual work.

Documents needed and documents signed. For the operational phase of the PVC a Membership agreement was modified and simplified from ECOLEAD templates and was signed with the core members of the PVC. Bylaws document containing the governance principles of the PVC was prepared by the core team.

Governance principles. The governance of the PVC is done mainly by the Steering Committee, which invites new members, decides when the meetings are held, helps to create a VT and to choose a project manager for each VT. Steering Committee is also responsible for finding the funding for the PVC activities, such as planning new projects and supports the finding of new business opportunities for the PVC.

Membership management. Steering committee is responsible for:
- Inviting new people to PVC,
- Creating the criteria for invitation, which is based on references,
- PVC maintenance, organizing meetings
- Organizing and holding negotiations, when a new VT is needed by inviting around 20 members to negotiations and choosing some of them for the VT.

Knowledge management. There are several types of knowledge processed in the community:
- tacit, during the discussions and meetings

- explicit (source code, specifications, project proposals and plans, financial documents)

According to different access rights there are three main categories of knowledge assets in the ICT PVC. We may categorise them as Public (available outside the PVC), Restricted (or Semi-public, available only for PVC members), and Confidential (or Private, available for Steering Committee, property of one member, or between two members, or bigger amount of members, depending on a document itself). The "Document IPR management" system at the ACP allows users to set different access rights for different groups of ACP users according to the ACP IPR management specification, which is pretty coherent with the categories initially used in the PVC.

Business processes management. Steering Committee is responsible for choosing from the business opportunities presented by individual PVC members. Steering Committee is selecting the VT members after the preliminary negotiations. VT manager is appointed during the negotiations and he will take care of the activities during the VT operational phase.

ICT Support. Members of the ICT PVC were provided with the opportunity to use Advanced Collaboration Platform (ACP) and Collaborative Problem Solving e-services (C-PS) developed within ECOLEAD. The following tools were taken up:

- Collaborative Problem Solving tools (C-PS)
  - o Planned Collaboration
  - o Ad Hoc Collaboration
- Social and Business Networking functionalities (ACP)
- Collaboration primitives of the portal: wiki, chat, forum, etc. (ACP)
- PVC Governance and Collaboration Rewarding (ACP)
- Economic Human Competency Evaluation (ACP)
- PVC Knowledge & IPR management (ACP)

In addition members of ICT PVC are using other existing tools for networking and in their business activities. To mention some of the tools, for example, FaceBook (www.facebook.com) is quite common for networking and discussing about issues not directly related to business, creating groups, using forum, social credits, etc. Google Docs (docs.google.com) and Google Calendar (www.google.com/calendar) are used by some of the PVC-members as tools for implementing collaborative tasks.

Identification of the main changes and impact in the process concerned by each tool
ICT PVC formalization process was influenced very much by the ECOLEAD results. Without the main idea of operating as PVC, the companies, where core ICT PVC members are employed, would merge and act as one entity. But thanks to ECOLEAD PVC concept, the evolution phase enabled widening the knowledge scope and involving new members. The benefits such as new business and research opportunities for new and old members became evident during the evolution process. Without the PVC concept this would not happen and the opportunity most probably would have been lost completely. The main impacts of PVC operation are expected to become most visible after several years of PVC operation.

ICT tools developed in ECOLEAD enabled creation of systematized competence profiles of the PVC members. In particular, the following tools were used in this process in ACP:

- Economic Human Competency Evaluation
- PVC Governance and Collaboration Rewarding

Every PVC user can search other users, view the list of all users, information, evaluations and rate of a particular user and evaluate user's competencies. Collaboration Primitives of the portal (wiki, chat, and forum) are very standard and every ICT PVC member is familiar with using them.

"PVC Governance and Collaboration Rewarding" supports creation of virtual teams, viewing the activity metrics in "PVC triangle" or chromo-framework in Knowledge-Business-Social dimensions for the requested period of time. This enables better understanding of ones own activities and position and community as a whole. Dynamic advices of how to improve one or another dimension are included in the tool.

"Economic Human Competency Evaluation" increases the capacity of PVC collaborations. It simplifies searching for the needed people by their professional skills and wishes, contacts and virtual teams and thereby increases the possibility of collaborations of different VTs.

"PVC Knowledge & IPR management" supports uploading and downloading of the office and project documents, and chat sessions. IPR management provides transformation of all the documents in PDF format automatically during the document uploading; this is an additional data integrity measure. The possibility to set access right permissions on group level is a confidentiality treatment.

Collaboration Problem Solving tools (CP-S), in particular, Planned and Ad-Hoc collaboration, took some time for understanding. Usage of CP-S tools may cause inefficient distribution of time resources for the first time. There are many levels of hierarchy for project execution in Planned Collaboration, which causes difficulties and requires additional study and training. The best way of utilizing Ad Hoc collaboration is not obvious for the first-time users, its integration with Planned Collaboration and the whole ACP portal is needed. Though the idea of Planned and Ad-hoc collaborations is interesting and very promising, the implementation and user interface should be considered in more details.

For the ICT PVC members the portal was not so effective for collaboration in the beginning. One reason was that the PVC members were in the same region, though virtual collaboration was still needed. The other reason was that they had to study and practice a lot how to work with the ACP portal. After using all ACP functionalities they found that portal has a lot of interesting ideas and benefits for easy and fast collaboration, like competencies evaluation, planned collaboration and IPR document management. Members of the PVC produces a valuable amount of good suggestion for further portal development and improvement.

Identification of tools' application areas and the expected results
Scenario 1: ICT PVC formalization and operation
Advanced collaboration platform (ACP)
ACP supports ICT PVC's everyday functioning, human competency evaluation, collaboration rewarding and governance, and provides IPR protection for the uploaded documents. The ACP portal is used on the everyday basis as a main portal of the community for social and business networking, including forum, chats, wiki with the possibility to share documents and exchange files.
Expected results

- Heterogeneous community of IT-professionals has a supporting virtual environment
- Competence management makes the process of finding the right persons faster
- Social involvement of PVC members
- IPR tracking support
- Collaboration rewarding for additional inspiration to participate in different PVC activities

Collaborative Problem Solving support e-services (C-PS). PVC members use CP-S, in particular ad hoc collaboration, for creating tasks for their VT members, using shared calendar and setting up reminders. Ad-hoc collaboration tool is used occasionally, when needed for collaboration within PVC.

Expected results

- More spontaneous and more frequent collaboration
- IPR-tracking during collaboration

Scenario 2: VTs' creation and operation within ICT PVC

Advanced collaboration platform (ACP). ACP enables search for the most relevant competences for the VT. Frequency of use:

- During the project preparations and planning, when a new VT is needed, ACP is used as often as possible (from several hours to daily basis, depending on suitability for project)
- Economic and human competency evaluation and collaboration rewarding is done after the VT dispersion or after the collaboration

Expected results

- Competence management tools to support VT creation taking into account combinations of competences of VT members
- Collaboration rewarding of the VT members after the VT project has ended
- Social and Business Networking tool helps to create unique and unexpected combinations of competences
- Smoother project planning, increased collaboration on project preparation phase and, as a result, better project plans
- IPR tracking support

Collaborative Problem Solving support e-services. CP-S tools are utilized during the creation of VT (ad-hoc collaboration) and operation phase of the VT (ad hoc and planned collaboration). Frequency of use:

- During the project preparations and planning C-PS is used on everyday basis
- Everyday basis for planned collaboration during the VT operation, and ad hoc on demand
- IPR-tracking tool is used during the collaboration sessions

Expected results

- Software tool that would concentrate on "network problem solving"
- Making better project plans with the help of planned collaboration
- More effective distribution of tasks and time within a project based on competences
- IPR-tracking during collaboration

2.4 Demonstration Phase

Description of what scenarios and tools were taken up

During the ECOLEAD project the ICT PVC realized two scenarios, described in the previous sections:

- Scenario 1: ICT PVC formalization and operation
    - o Formalization
    - o Operation, Governance, Extension and Promotion

The addition to the initial scenario was the evolution phase of the ICT PVC, described in 2.3. The need for change was noticed during the early staged of PVC operation, and did not have any significant impact on the changes in tools take up.

- Scenario 2: VTs' creation and operation within ICT PVC

This scenario was followed in general, though it included even more VTs creation than it was planned in the beginning because of the changes in Scenario 1 and PVC evolution.

The following tools developed by ECOLEAD were taken up in the ICT PVC:

- ACP platform
    - o PVC Governance & Collaboration rewarding
    - o Economic Human competency evaluation
    - o PVC Knowledge & IPR management
    - o Portal functionalities (forum, chat, wiki)
    - o Social & Business networking
- C-PS e-services
    - o Planned Collaboration
    - o Ad Hoc Collaboration.

Results presentation according to the business metrics:

Table 2 – Metrics for Scenario 1: ICT PVC formalization and operation

Business Metrics	Initial Value (before ECOLEAD)	Expected Value	Current Value	Tools involved
Number of registered members	0	8 members registered in the first quarter (by Dec 2007). 20 members by June 2008.	8 with signed PVC agreement 23 ACP portal users	**ACP platform:** Portal functionalities; Economic Human competency evaluation
KBS Position of the PVC	None	Balanced	Balanced with slightly Social dimension dominating (according to the ACP governance tool)	**ACP platform:** Economic Human competency evaluation; PVC Knowledge & IPR management; **C-PS e-services:** Planned Collaboration
Number of documents	0	2-3 per week	6-8 in different collaborative	**ACP platform:** PVC Knowledge &

			processes and under generic PVC files	IPR management
in Knowledge IPR				
Number of VTs	0	2-5 running at any time	6 running during the take up	**ACP platform:** PVC Governance & Collaboration rewarding; Economic Human competency evaluation; **C-PS e-services:** Planned Collaboration; Ad Hoc Collaboration

Table 3 – Metrics for Scenario 2: VT Establishment and operation within ICT Development PVC

Business Metrics	Initial Value (before ECOLEAD)	Expected Value	Current Value	Tools involved
Number of VT's members	0	3-15 depending on the task or VT purpose	4-6 in different VTs	**ACP platform:** PVC Governance & Collaboration rewarding; Economic Human competency evaluation; **C-PS e-services:** Planned Collaboration; Ad Hoc Collaboration
Total financial value of the projects generated by VT contribution	n/a	€1,5mln by end of 2008 total € 800.000 – **estimated** value when the PLM project starts	€ 20.000 for PLM preparation	**C-PS e-services:** Planned Collaboration
Number of projects	0	3 projects	4 projects	**C-PS e-services:** Planned Collaboration

2.5 Lessons Learnt

The main benefits and limitations of the take-ups

The whole concept of PVC was new for ICT experts in the Joensuu Region and it took time to learn what it means and what it might bring for the community. The main benefits, which the community got from implementing the PVC concept, are:

- International contacts, which are valid for the community, motivated for collaboration and are beneficial for the PVC activities
- Creation of the PVC rose interest in international business and collaboration
- The PVC's evolution phase combined third parties that would not normally collaborate.

- Written principles of governance and organization of the whole collaboration process.
- Documented guidelines for building CNOs, practical experience and ICT tools, especially this is valuable for JSP.
- Widened the knowledge scope in the area of CNOs, especially important for JSP.
- Tool-box for the future use in PVC, including ECOLEAD solutions and open-source.

The transformation from the network of individuals to the formal PVC requires time, and the time for the take up was rather limited. There was no legal base for the PVC-type of communities, thus making the transformation process even more complicated. Some of the benefits, mentioned above, are already noticed, but the long-term changes and impacts will be visible months or even years after the project.

One of the limitations of the take ups in general is that the plans for take ups were structured in advance and therefore some real benefits were left out of scope of the project, for example, combination of ECOLEAD and open source tools available in the market.

Other limitations of take-ups for the PVCs concern mostly the following issues:

Potential PVC members might not have resources to implement completely new PVC. They might be reluctant to put resources into financially uncertain tasks (PVC implementation). In addition they might not want to invest on membership fees as long as there is no clear evidence of the profitability of the PVC.

Legally it is problematic to create working PVC because the economic transactions ought to go through the PVC and in this case the PVC should be a legal entity. Some light version of PVC that is not as restraining as the original ECOLEAD declared PVC might be one of the possible solutions.

PVC templates (Membership agreement and Bylaws document) provided by ECOLEAD seem to be very comprehensive and too strict and complicated for the potential PVC members, therefore some modifications and customisations are needed for every new PVC. The idea is to get the PVC members to work together with a simpler case like collaborative project proposal and to develop more business oriented solutions through these kinds of lighter activities.

The ACP platform is not anymore of the highest IT-industry standard, because the development of open-source solutions (Google tools, facebook, skype, etc.) has been extra-ordinary since the launch of ECOLEAD project. We expect ACP to be further developed and to become more user-friendly in the near future. We are keeping in touch with the developers to report and fix the current problems. The ACP is a challenge in particular for the ICT PVC because they are ICT-professionals and have their own "ways" to communicate virtually. This can be turned to the benefit for the whole ECOLEAD while receiving professional comments and development ideas.

Involvement of international members is crucial in order to enable virtual communication. Otherwise all communication can be done physically or with the existing tools, like instant messengers, Voice over IP technologies, etc. In this case the ACP will be just tested and not used in real life.

In addition to ECOLEAD ICT support, the ICT PVC found out other free online tools to support their social and knowledge dimensions, such as

- Google Groups (groups.google.com) for social interaction

- Skype (www.skype.com) for voice calls and instant messaging.

The inconvenience is that user has to register to all different tools and remember all his usernames and passwords, and add all his PVC collaborators to every tool. These solutions were not available when ECOLEAD project started, but were developed recently.

3. AIESEC PVC CASE

AIESEC was established in 1948 as a non-profit, non-commercial, non-governmental global organization, managed and operated by students and recent graduates with the aim to provide them with an international platform to discover and develop their leadership potential. AIESEC members form strong social bonds across national borders during their time in AIESEC. These bonds are maintained when they become alumni upon leaving the organization, and are enforced through physical events and interaction on the online platform www.myaiesec.net, coordinated by AIESEC or the alumni directly. Alumni are staying in touch via personal contacts, semi-formal groups at the level of alumni clubs, groups, etc.

The above described organizational setup was recognized as a great environmental opportunity for piloting the take-up of ECOLEAD tools to build sustainable professional virtual communities for AIESEC alumni leveraging on the existing social ties and harvesting their economic potential.

This involves the creation of a PVC in the area of Human Resources Management and Development (HRMD), which has been integrated into AIESEC global ICT infrastructure www.myaiesec.net

HR PVC members come from the following groups:

- Alumni of AIESEC with interest or professional background in HRMD
- AIESEC members with interest in HRMD
- Partners of AIESEC upon invitation for specific initiatives

3.1. AIESEC Definition Phase: Activities and Results

3.1.1 Business imperative for choosing the PVC topic

For every organization that reaches a certain size, effective Human Resources Management and Development (HRMD) practices become a necessity for continued performance. For this reason it is a valuable area to explore further for those AIESEC alumni that have it as professional focus and those who consider it as complimentary to their primary professional focus. AIESEC alumni are typically in managerial roles which also makes this area important for them. The AIESEC network and AIESEC alumni network is a trusted network, and for that reason enables business cooperation on a virtual level much faster, in HRMD and in other areas. In addition the ability of AIESEC as an organization to bring together diverse perspectives and expertise on the topic is a unique advantage of the HR PVC.

There is opportunity for the involvement of AIESEC partner organizations as partners of the HR PVC, either through financial sponsorship or by providing relevant content. Through their involvement in this PVC and the activities thereof, there is a more accessible audience for initiatives developed by VOs and VTs within the PVC.

For organizations that specialize in the creation of knowledge and educational material on Human Resource management, the HR PVC provides an excellent ground for testing new and existing materials in a multi-cultural environment and for receiving diverse feedback on these products in focus groups.

For the economic gain of AIESEC, the HR PVC provides an excellent way for these and other organizations to market their products as well as a way to access talent.

3.1.2 Identification of the main tools

As it was to be expected from the organizational environment of AIESEC alumni, the Social & Business networking module was the first tool to be picked up by the PVC members, before the Ad Hoc Collaboration, PVC Governance, Knowledge & IPR management as well as Economic Human Competency evaluation and an advanced networking module were employed.

The final ECOLEAD tool to be tested was the advanced SBN.

In order to facilitate the step-by-step creation and evolution of the PVC, three core business processes were identified and the related scenarios planned for and executed. This served as a guiding light for AIESEC as initiating organization to promote the process and provide the necessary resources to PVC members.

Scenario #1: PVC creation

Establishment of PVC – identification, design and set-up
This phase comprises of all the pre-operational activities aimed at the establishment of the HR PVC. It included the identification, design and set-up of the HR PVC in order for it to become operational. By defining the business model, this business process specifies the business logic and the rationale behind the establishment of the HR PVC.

The use of this key ECOLEAD result enabled a clear sequential structure for the planning and execution of this subsystem. This result also contains models that can be applied to the AIESEC business environment to facilitate decision-making and analysis needed.

Scenario #2: PVC Governance and Life cycle management

Operational Phase – start-up, ramp-up, operation, evolution and metamorphosis
The scenario presents the creation of the PVC within a wider community linked by social factors. The trial aimed at exploring mechanisms for forming sustainable virtual structures based on the social and professional backgrounds capable of collaborating in the PVC sense. The HRMD PVC was launched and designed with the members of the PVC using ECOLEAD results. The business, knowledge and social dimensions of PVC were explored in the trial. While social mechanisms for virtual collaboration have been an established process in AIESEC, integration of business and knowledge dimensions were new processes. The trial involved different generations of alumni.

The ECOLEAD implementation guidelines for PVC business models were used, as well as the specifications of different types of PVC business models for reference during the expected evolution of the PVC.

The different stakeholders of the PVC were defined and detailed as outlined above. These stakeholders include AIESEC as an organization, its alumni, its partners and prospects, its members etc.

The business model decided upon was a simple and flexible one, with limited initial investment, but with close measurement of activity in order to inform future initiatives of a similar nature.

With the use of existing technical tools as well as the ECOLEAD tools, the only investment required to launch the HRPVC was the consolidation of freely available resources by a moderator and a limited marketing campaign to AIESEC alumni (with membership open to all recognized AIESEC alumni). This also implied that no investment from sponsors would be solicited and that the option of "core" and "light" members was not to be implemented at that stage.

The reference business models and the overall conceptual framework gave a paradigm for deciding upon these elements of the business model as well as a more integrated study of stakeholders and their needs.

Scenario #3: Virtual Team (VT) formation

This scenario was a trial creation of VTs within the PVC: formation of social links among members, identification of business ideas and harvesting the knowledge potential of the participants. The trial aimed at showcasing extension of social and business networks; the ability of the PVC to come up with the collaborative business ideas and evaluated resources shared among the members. PVC participants were closely involved in defining the targets and processes for trial which increased accountability.

As social links among members were formed, business ideas were identified and the knowledge potential of the participants was harvested, a VT was formed within the PVC. During this phase the HR PVC showcased the extension of social and business networks; abilities of the PVC to come up with the collaborative business ideas and evaluated resources shared among the members.

VT formation could only commence once the HR PVC was in the operational phase (Phase 3, Business process #2).

In order to track the achievements of the execution of the business processes, clearly measurable metrics were established and related to the scenarios described above. Table 2 below provides an overview of the practical implementation of ECOLEAD tools when establishing the HRPVC.

Table 1 – Results of HRPVC definition phase

	Scenario 1	Scenario 2	Scenario 3
Business Process	PVC creation	Governance and Life cycle management	VT formation
Addressed Issue	identification, design and set-up of the HR	Creation of the PVC within a wider community linked by social factors	formation of social links among members, identification of business ideas and harvesting the knowledge potential of the participants
Main Objective	defining the business model to specify the business logic and the rationale behind the establishment of the	exploring mechanisms for forming sustainable virtual structures based on the social and professional backgrounds capable of collaborating in the PVC sense	showcase the extension of social and business networks; abilities of the PVC to come up with the collaborative business

	HR PVC		ideas and evaluation of resources shared among the members
Indicators	1. Number of initial subscriptions to PVC 2. Number of applicants for moderator position	1. Number of virtual teams initiated (groups created) 2. Number of network connection requests sent and received 3. Number of forums created 4. Number of forum posts created 5. Number of files uploaded 6. Number of files commented on 7. Number of news items created 8. Number of news items commented on	1. Number of successful projects run by the virtual team
Tools Used	• PVC conceptual framework • Business model, value system and metrics for PVC • Social & Business networking • C-PS e-services: Ad Hoc Collaboration	• PVC conceptual framework: *PVC Governance and Life Cycle Management* • Business model, value system and metrics for PVC: *PVC Governance and Life Cycle Management* • Organisational and operational models for PVC: *Customisation and implementation of governance principles* • Elements of the ACP platform	• Economic Human Competency evaluation • Advanced SBN

3.2. AIESEC Implementation Phase: Activities and Results

The business environment of the HRPVC is that of AIESEC as a non-profit, non-commercial, non-governmental global organization, run by students and recent graduates, specifically the business environment as it relates to the alumni of AIESEC.

The relation of the HRPVC to the business environment is Virtual Breeding Environment Entangled, its typology is Established Single Discipline PVC and the specific knowledge scope is Human Resource Management and Development.

The HRPVC is an entity that is under the control of the parent organization – AIESEC. It exists independently from the individual AIESEC members and AIESEC alumni, but it does not function without the support and the active involvement of AIESEC. As it is under the control of the parent organisation, it will not be registered as a separate legal entity, and any monetary gains of its activities will be invested into AIESEC in the same way that a donation or grant would be invested.

Upon establishing the pilot, participation in the HRPVC was open freely to all AIESEC alumni. If partner organizations were to be participating in the HR PVC in the future, they would contribute a fee and the income gained from this would be invested into AIESEC and into funding the activities of the HR PVC. Occasionally, AIESEC is interacting as an organization, with the groups that have formed in the HR PVC in some form of value exchange, for example when receiving advice from HRPVC members on AIESEC's own HRMD processes. This led to a pilot project, in which HRPVC members consulted AIESEC International on the cross-cultural implications of the organization's online competency assessment tool.

The base principles for the governance elements of the HRPVC were adapted from ECOLEAD templates in consultation with members of the ECOLEAD consortium. These structures are not only reflecting the current needs of the HRPVC, but also take into account further potential needs for evolution of the HRPVC.

- Empowerment
  - o Initially – everything is done by the Assembly of Members, with the moderator driving and coordinating the PVC.
  - o After 1 year – due to the increase in size of the PVC, the Assembly of Members still take the decisions and deliver the results, the team leaders are there to coordinate the team to deliver the result, moderator for day to day management and structuring of knowledge on the site etc, the supervisory group to ensure the PVC is meeting it's objectives set, and the advisory group to offer insights from their many years of experience in the field on a consultant basis as needed. This therefore ensures that the Assembly of Members are empowered, but under the guidance and frameworks laid out to support them.
  - o After 2 years - the Assembly of Members still take the decisions and deliver the results, the team leaders are there to coordinate the team to deliver the result, moderator for day to day management and structuring of knowledge on the site etc. As the PVC has reached the stage where it has administrative needs – in terms of marketing, management of membership, gaining sponsorship, training members, organising events etc, the administrative body take this burden from the Assembly of Members, to leave them to make decisions and deliver the results. The Board of Directors hold legal responsibility for the PVC, so provide guidance and strategic direction, but leave most of the decision making to the Assembly of Members. the supervisory group to ensure the PVC is meeting it's objectives set, and the advisory group to offer insights from their many many years of experience in the field on a consultant basis as needed. This therefore ensures that the Assembly of Members are empowered, but under the guidance and frameworks laid out to support them.

The above is reflected in the following initial structure implemented in the HRPVC.

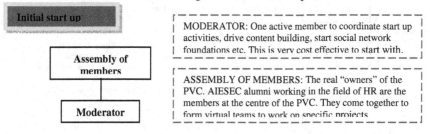

Figure 5: Initial start up phase structure

This structure should encourage the individual empowerment of the PVC members to create a vibrant PVC with the help of a moderator. As the PVC evolves, it is expected to require more and more sophisticated structures:

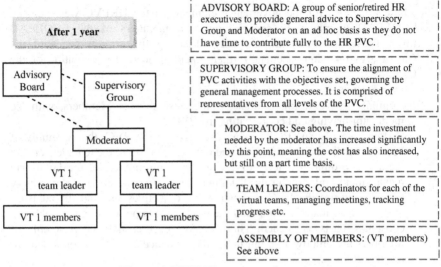

Figure 6: HRPVC structure after one year

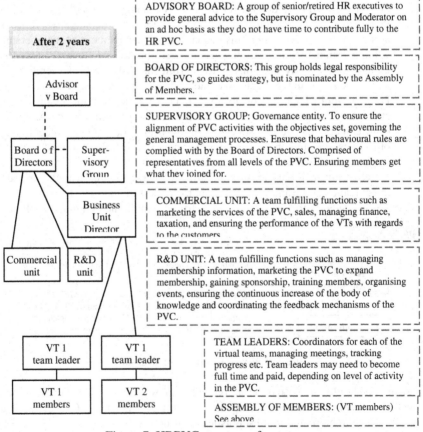

Figure 7: HRPVC structure after two years

Besides the above structural requirements, the following additional factors were taken into account in order to establish the PVC:

- Voluntary Approach

From the set up phase, all members of the HR PVC are volunteers. It has shown to be a point of attraction for AIESEC alumni to the PVC, as AIESEC itself is an organization run on volunteer basis: many feel an emotional connection with the PVC at the start when joining. Members choose how much time to spend working on the PVC and in which areas to ensure their experience suits their expectations and objectives for joining.

- Self organisation

Members come together and organise themselves for the projects they are working on, they decide amongst themselves which role each member will play, and assign a team leader to coordinate the activities of the team and ensure the team is steered towards achieving the results and objective of the team.

- Peer assessment

If members agree, periodic peer assessments take place, after the completion of a project, for an award or for quality control. Each member is assessed by 5 other members and rated on various criteria common to all assessments, including: contribution to project; level of commitment; level of drive; meeting deadlines; punctuality for meetings etc. The ratings from their peers are then combined so the member being assessed sees only the aggregate scores.

- Sustainability

The members of the PVC will work towards and in accordance with
  o human life
  o the capabilities that the natural environment has to maintain the living conditions for people and other species (eg. clean water and air, a suitable climate)
  o the aspects of the environment that produce renewable resources such as water, timber, fish, solar energy
  o the functioning of society, despite non-renewable resource depletion
  o the quality of life for all people, the livability and beauty of the environment

- Code of Ethics

Once the PVC starts to function, members agree on a code of ethics as adopted from the sponsoring organization. The code covers:
  o The ethical principles all members adhere to
  o The practices in day-to-day work, interactions and decision-making at all organizational layers
  o The enforcement mechanisms to align the practices and conducts with the values. `

The PVC enhances the value of the existing online platform for alumni because it is designed in such a way that the objectives of the PVC itself is as much as possible equal to the ones of the individuals that belong to it. The members are empowered, during the PVC operation, to contribute to the evolution and refinement of the PVC objectives according to their personal expectations and it acts as an enabler of profitable business activities for its members.

The following pages contain a concise overview of the results achieved in the end phase of the pilot for all three scenarios with their associated business metrics. The business metrics helped to keep execution of the scenarios on track and to take corrective action when needed.

Table 5. Business Metrics for Scenario #1: PVC creation

Business Metrics (name and description)	Validity Domain	Initial Value	Expected Value	Current Value	Tools used
Number of initial subscriptions to PVC	0-n	0	100	115	Social & Business networking module
Number of applicants for moderator position	0-n	0	5	23	Social & Business networking module

Table 6. Business Metrics for Scenario #2: PVC Governance and Life cycle management

Business Metrics (name and description)	Validity Domain	Initial Value	Expected Value	Current Value	Tools used
Number of virtual teams initiated (groups created)	0-n	0	1	1	Ad Hoc Collaboration, PVC Governance, Economic Human Competency evaluation
Number of network connection requests sent and received	0-n	0	100	15	Social & Business networking module
Number of forums created	0-n	0	15	35	Social & Business networking module
Number of forum posts created	0-n	0	100	>100	Social & Business networking module
Number of files uploaded	0-n	0	20	35	PVC Knowledge & IPR management
Number of files commented on	0-n	0	20	0	PVC Knowledge & IPR management
Number of news items created	0-n	0	15	1	Social & Business networking module
Number of news items commented on	0-n	0	15	1	Social & Business networking module

Table 7. Business Metrics for Scenario #3: VT formation

Business Metrics (name and description)	Validity Domain	Initial Value	Expected Value	Current Value	Tools used
Number of successful projects run by the virtual team	0-n	0	1	1	Social & Business networking module, Ad Hoc Collaboration, PVC Governance, Economic Human Competency evaluation

3.3. AIESEC Lessons learned and next steps

For AIESEC as an organization the learning through ECOLEAD has been substantial. Even though some of the theoretical concepts sometimes required considerable investment in time, they did direct AIESEC into a new direction in terms of online collaboration and encouraged AIESEC alumni to break their old paradigms about the benefits of virtual networking.

It has to be said that even though the trust between the individuals in the AIESEC alumni network is by definition relatively high compared to other networks, it takes continued effort to encourage commitment and active collaboration between these individuals. Due to the nature of the fast moving labor market and the resulting instabilities for the individuals, fluctuations in participation have been frequent. This might be something that changes as the value proposition of the HRPVC gains strength through increasing levels of participation.

Another key to the flourishing of the HRPVC is continuous education and reiteration of the ECOLEAD concepts and tools. In the future this will play a considerable part of the necessary activities, especially considering the relatively slow absorption of the concepts by the network.

Moving forward, AIESEC and its alumni network is going to add a number of PVCs with different focus areas to the existing HRPVC, and consider the integration of the advanced tools into its existing global ICT infrastructure to further the opportunities provided to both alumni and AIESEC as organization.

4. CONCLUSIONS

The whole idea of the PVC is very innovative and represents a model for future collaboration between individuals, public sector, research organizations and SMEs. More real business experiences are needed to deploy the concept further and spread it globally. The take up cases demonstrated good applicability of the results of ECOLEAD project in the professional networks.

In some cases, as in ICT PVC, the PVC concept can help to create stronger and more competitive companies. The close collaboration between real businesses and researches from universities is especially valuable achievement for this PVC.

In AIESEC, ECOLEAD concepts have led to consider the business aspects of virtual connections – in the past only the social and to a lesser extent the knowledge aspects were considered.

The biggest challenge for the demonstrations was, that creation and maintenance of the sustainable PVC is much more time and money consuming then previously expected. Another big challenge was caused by the tool-box provided for the use in real business cases. The integration of developed solutions with open-source products, involving such development methods as rapid prototyping and agile software development, are vital in the fast-changing modern ICT environment.

The methods developed within ECOLEAD and the whole idea of PVCs, as one of the representations of CNOs, are the biggest benefits for the future developments in this area. The individuals, who learnt about CNO models and got some experience working in them, are able to spread their knowledge further. Still more research is needed when there are more real cases. The models of how to administrate and maintain PVCs from the real business point of view should be developed and adapted for a number of particular cases, best practices gathered and presented in an appropriate for the business world form.

Acknowledgments. This project would not be possible without the support of ECOLEAD Consortium and inspiration from all the interested parties.

6. REFERENCES

1. Camarinha-Matos, L.M.; Afsarmanesh, H. (2004). Collaborative Networked Organizations: A research agenda for emerging business models. Springer Science + Business Media, Inc.

2. Facebook PVC discussion group http://www.facebook.com/group.php?gid=5921954526

3. Kakko I., Glotova T. (2007). "Breeding Environments for Open Innovation". Proceedings of the 13th International Conference on Concurrent Enterprising, Sophia-Antipolis, France. Published by: Centre for Concurrent Enterprise, Nottingham University Business School, UK, 2007: 19-26.

4. netWork Oasis (http://www.network-oasis.com/)

PART 7

FURTHER STEPS

A REFERENCE CURRICULUM FOR EDUCATION IN COLLABORATIVE NETWORKS

Luis M. Camarinha-Matos [1], Hamideh Afsarmanesh [2],
Tiago Cardoso [1], Edmilson Klen [3]

[1] *New University of Lisbon, PORTUGAL – cam@uninova.pt, tomfc@uninova.pt*
[2] *University of Amsterdam, THE NETHERLANDS – hamideh@science.uva.nl*
[3] *Federal University of Santa Catarina, BRAZIL - erklen@gsigma.ufsc.br*

A proposal for a reference curriculum for teaching Collaborative Networks at university level is introduced. This curriculum is based on the experience of the authors in teaching and disseminating corresponding concepts in the context of several international projects as well as on the findings of a survey conducted worldwide. A set of teaching units and the corresponding content are introduced. Guidelines for the application of the curriculum are given. A set of experiments and projects are also suggested as a support for the accompanying hands-on lab work. Finally, one concrete experience of application of the proposed curriculum is described.

1. INTRODUCTION

Education plays a vital role in facilitating the dissemination and broad acceptance of virtual organizations (VO) and other forms of collaborative networks (CNs). The practical development and exploitation of new collaborative network forms such as virtual organizations / virtual enterprises, VO breeding environments, professional virtual communities (PVC), virtual laboratories, virtual institutes, etc., is hindered by the lack of an organized and widely accessible body of knowledge on the related supporting concepts, models, technologies, processes, and methodologies. Although considerable progress has been achieved in recent years, most of the underlying knowledge in this area is possessed only by a limited number of researchers and engineers. In fact, the study of collaborative networks is still absent from most of the traditional university programs (Camarinha-Matos, Cardoso, 2004).

Nevertheless the situation is changing. As reported in previous works (Camarinha-Matos, Cardoso, 2004), (Garita, 2004), (Gloor et al., 2006), (Klen et al., 2005) several universities worldwide already offer courses on related topics and this number is increasing rapidly. As shown by a survey conducted in the scope of the ECOLEAD project most of these courses are however somewhat unbalanced, giving only partial views and, in many cases, biased by the scope of the department offering the course.

As the area is growing as an autonomous discipline, i.e. gaining its own "identity" (Camarinha-Matos, Afsarmanesh, 2005), it is becoming clear that there is a need to elaborate more comprehensive, less biased, programs. Similarly to what has happened with other disciplines in the past, it is necessary to establish a "reference curriculum" in order to:

-    help extending the focus / coverage of early initiatives;
-    help launching new training initiatives.

The main contribution of this chapter is a proposal for such a reference curriculum for a university-level course on collaborative networks. A preliminary version of the curriculum was first applied and evaluated in a number of cases (e.g. at New University of Lisbon, 1st ECOLEAD Summer School, Polytechnic University of Valencia, BEST Summer School in Lisbon) and also discussed in conferences and in the context of the IFIP Working Group 5.5 on Virtual Enterprises and e-Business and SOCOLNET – Society of Collaborative Networks (Camarinha-Matos, 2006), (Klen et al., 2005).

The version included in this article integrates the received feedback and acquired experience with the previous draft and represents a more consolidated proposal. Nevertheless, like with any other emerging discipline, this curriculum certainly needs to be periodically updated and improved. In addition to the curriculum itself, a number of practical experiments and projects are suggested to support the hands-on lab work of the students. Finally, the experience of applying this curriculum at the New University of Lisbon is reported.

2.   FORECASTING THE NEEDS

In order to identify the level of interest and opinions about the teaching of Collaborative Networks, as well as the already existing initiatives, from the perspective of educators, a survey involving some prestigious Institutes around the world was performed in the context of the ECOLEAD project (Camarinha-Matos et al., 2005).

From the beginning it was clear that conducting an extensive survey for an emerging area would be a very resource consuming task. On one hand, in order to cover a significant number of geographical regions, the number of universities and other educational institutes would grow dramatically. On the other hand, even when focusing on a limited number of institutions, there is a major difficulty regarding the identification of which departments and which academic staff to contact. Being CNs a multi-disciplinary area, it is natural that teaching initiatives emerge in different departments. In order to determine the universe of institutions to contact for this initial study the following steps were followed:

1. *Select a preliminary group of top universities.* As a starting basis the list of the top 500 universities according to the "**Academic Ranking of World Universities**", organized by the Institute of Higher Education, Shanghai Jiao Tong University, was considered. Taking into account the limited resources available to perform this survey it was not feasible to consider this full list. Therefore, only a subset (66) of the list was selected:

-    The top universities per geographical region (5 from each of the following continents: America, Europe, Asia, Oceania, and 4 for Africa), plus

- An additional group of 42 institutions selected randomly from the remainder of the list.

The decision regarding the size of the target group was solely based on the estimated effort required and the available resources.

2. *Select other universities from web search.* In addition to the institutions selected in the first step, some other universities were added to the list when it was possible to identify, by a simple search on the web, that they already offer teaching initiatives on CNOs.

3. *Include other universities from analysis of conference publications.* Complementarily to the web search, a few other universities were selected via a brief analysis of the proceedings of past PRO-VE conferences.

As a result of this selection process, a total of 82 institutions were considered as the target "population" for this survey.

The next step was the identification of potential participants from selected institutions, i.e. which professors at those institutions to contact. For the cases of courses found on the web or through publications in conference proceedings, the contact persons were directly identified. The other cases required and extensive and focused manual search through the web sites of the selected institutions (focusing mainly on engineering and management departments). As a result, a total of 1024 academic staff was contacted from the 82 institutions out of which (only) 76 replies were received. The received answers included contributions from 44 institutions (i.e. about 54 % of our target universe of institutions). Table 1 below summarizes the participation per country.

Table 1 – Respondents per country

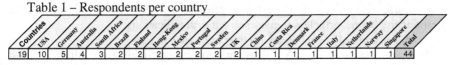

Countries	USA	Germany	Australia	South Africa	Brazil	Finland	Hong-Kong	Mexico	Portugal	Sweden	UK	China	Costa Rica	Denmark	France	Italy	Netherlands	Norway	Singapore	Total
	19	10	5	4	3	2	2	2	2	2	2	2	1	1	1	1	1	1	1	44

The following diagrams illustrate some of the results of this survey. More details can be obtained in (Camarinha-Matos et al., 2005).

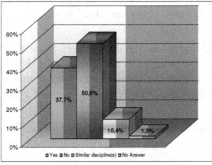

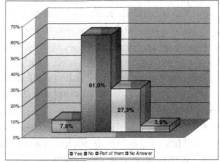

Figure 1 - Is there a dedicated discipline on CNs in your Institution?

Figure 2 - Do you consider the concepts in the CNs area already consolidated?

These percentages need to be read with some caution. They do not represent a percentage of the full universe of high education institutions but rather a percentage of the respondents to the survey, i.e. people that are involved in the area or likely to be motivated for its importance. Nevertheless, under this constraint, these numbers give an indication that several CNs teaching initiatives already exist.

The answers to this question clearly confirm the need to invest more on the consolidation and structuring of knowledge in the area.

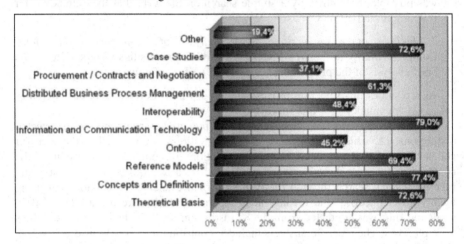

Figure 3 - Which subjects should be included in a CN basic course?

Fig. 3 summarizes the list of topics suggested by the respondents to include in a basic course. This diagram is certainly affected by the options offered in the questionnaire but nevertheless it gives some useful indications:

- ICT is certainly associated with the core issues in CNs.
- Case studies are very important to create motivation, illustrate the applicability of the concepts, and help identifying requirements.
- The theoretical foundation (including theoretical basis, concepts and definitions, reference models, and ontologies) is fundamental in a training program.
- Interoperability, although somehow important, is not perceived as too critical. The same with procurement, contracts and negotiation.

Based on the results of this survey and additional search on the web, the second phase of this study was devoted to identify and collect information about existing teaching initiatives. The existence of quite distinct initiatives made it clear that it would not be reasonable to compare them all together. Therefore, three main kinds of courses were identified:

- Formal university courses fully dedicated to the subject. This case typically includes a one-semester course that is offered as part of a formal university program.
- Short courses dedicated to the subject or long courses that include a short module on CNs.
  In this category, either the course is not fully dedicated to the "Virtual Enterprise" or "Virtual Organization" paradigms or it is a short course or summer course.

- On-line / Web-based courses.

Among these categories, the most significant kind of courses to analyze for the purposes of this work is the first one – the University initiatives fully focused on CNs and related manifestations.

Most of the identified initiatives (88%) are offered either at the undergraduate or Master level. It is also important to notice that there is quite a large heterogeneity in terms of the structure of the university courses. Some universities consider a model of 3 years (bachelor) plus 2 years (master), while others offer a 2-year master degree after a 5-year university course. The two notions (and levels) of master are necessarily different. In other countries there is a single degree for engineering courses (5 or 5.5 years). PhD courses, due to their specificity, are to a large extent out of the scope of this study. In many universities the PhD program does not include a formal training program but rather research work only. The ongoing implementation of the Bologna model in Europe is likely to lead to a more uniform structure.

Table 2 shows the main initiatives identified for formal university courses. This is certainly not a full survey, but it nevertheless offers a good set of base information.

Table 2 – Examples of formal university courses

#	Course name	Location / Institute	Duration
1	Virtual Enterprises	New University of Lisbon Portugal	1 semester
2	Virtual Organizations	ITCR Costa Rica	1 semester
3	Enterprise Integration Systems	UFSC Brazil	1 semester
4	Information Systems / Virtual Organization	City University of New York USA	1 semester
5	Agile Virtual Enterprise	Universität der Bundeswehr München	1 semester
6	Management and Information Systems	University of York UK	1 semester
7	Seminar in Virtual Collaboration	University of Nebraska at Omaha USA	1 semester
8	Organizational Networks and Communication	Helsinky University of Technology	1 semester
9	Managing in a Virtual Environment	Claremont Graduate University	1 semester
10	Virtual Organisation Management	The University of Queensland	1 semester
11	Information Systems	Edith Cowan University	1 year
12	Information Based Manufacturing	New Mexico State University	1 semester
13	Coordination and Control in the Virtual Organization.	The FOX School of Business and Management	1 semester
14	Virtual Organisations	City University of Hong-Kong	1 semester
15	e-Business Technologies	University of Porto	1 semester

In terms of focus of each course, the first indicator is the course's name. Here, many differences can be noticed. While some courses take a general / horizontal point of view, some others choose one particular perspective about these new paradigms, like the enterprise integration or the agility characteristic. On the other hand, two other main perspectives can be identified in the course names analysis: management and organization.

Based on the information collected during this survey and some additional web search, a number of example curricula were collected. This collection includes curricula from both formal university courses and also from some of the short courses / modules. These materials, together with the experience acquired in several training actions conducted by various R&D projects in which the authors were involved, were the basis for the preparation of the current curriculum proposal.

3. OBJECTIVES OF THE CURRICULUM

The following generic and specific objectives are considered in this proposal:

Generic objectives. A reference course on CNs shall:
-   Provide an intuitive introduction to the paradigm of CNs, with illustrations based on case studies, and discuss why collaboration is becoming a key competence for organizations and professionals.
-   Provide a good understanding of the various technical and scientific components involved in CNs.
-   Develop systems integration competencies (holistic perspective).
-   Contribute to help the student develop planning and problem solving capabilities in the context of integrated and distributed collaborative systems.
-   Develop the capacity to attack problems whose specification is incomplete, leading to focus on creativity and search for new systems and solutions.
-   Clarify and exemplify the multi-disciplinarity of the CNs paradigm.
-   Develop an understanding and a critical perspective regarding the impacts of ICT in modern society.

Specific objectives. As specific objectives the course shall help the student understand the various underlying topics in CNs and the way they are inter-related, which include:
-    (Business) process modeling skills and familiarization with related tools, such as workflow tools.
-   The basic functionalities of an interoperable infrastructure for collaborative networks.
-   A capability to plan a CNs infrastructure fitted to target scenarios.
-   The issues of integration / interoperability among different technologies.
-   Skills to specify coordination mechanisms.
-   The role and limitations of standards in supporting collaboration.
-   The basic focus of the most typical manifestations of collaborative networks.
-   The main strategies and mechanisms for safe communications and distributed information and knowledge management.
-   The socio-economic impacts of the introduction of new technologies and new paradigms in the companies.
-   A general perspective of the trends and expectations in CNs.

Clearly many of these objectives are not achievable if only presented through the theoretical material suggested in the curriculum. Their achievement also depends on many other factors such as the practical work (lab experiments), the support materials and case studies, and even the pedagogic approach. As the survey work also showed, there is a lack of support materials for teaching CNs. At least in terms of materials available through the web, only a few support texts and slides could be found (in several cases, in languages other than English). In our study, direct enquiries to the persons that have organized courses, also did not produce more information either. One of the major difficulties observed so far is the lack of well prepared examples / case studies and laboratory experiments that could provide some practical experience and, at the same time, fit within the time limits of a single course.

From the didactic and course *delivery* perspectives it would be interesting to exploit new approaches based on collaborative networks and e-learning. However this will require considerable resources to develop. A preliminary study regarding pedagogic approaches for training and education through distance learning, although limited to the extended enterprise, is done by the GEM project (Haugen et al., 2002).

4. SYLLABUS

4.1 Units

In order to cope with the mentioned requirements and objectives, the following main units are proposed for a reference curriculum on Collaborative Networks:

UNIT 1: **MOTIVATION FOR THE PARADIGM**

This first unit aims at creating a motivation for the course through a brief presentation of application areas, illustrated by concrete examples in industry, services, government, etc. A brief historic overview of the industrial organizational paradigms leading to collaborative networks as well as a summary of current technological and organizational trends is presented. For each example an attempt to identify the main involved problems (e.g. organizational forms, processes, cooperation, and collaboration forms) is made, calling the attention for the potential contributions from other disciplines. The socio-economic importance of each case is also briefly highlighted.

UNIT 2: **BASE CONCEPTS OF COLLABORATIVE NETWORKS**

After the motivation phase, the base concepts are introduced. Considering the large variety of collaborative networks, a categorization of the various forms is made and a taxonomy is introduced in order to give students a global perspective of the area. The main types of collaborative networks, namely the long term strategic alliance as well as the dynamic (short term) opportunity driven collaborative network is addressed. The various actors involved in a collaborative network as well as the roles they can play are identified. Finally the life cycle of a collaborative network is discussed in terms of its main phases.

UNIT 3: **VO BREEDING ENVIRONMENTS**

The concept of Virtual organization Breeding Environment (VBE) is elaborated and justified. Illustrating examples are provided. The components, structure and life cycle of this organizational form as well as its involved actors and roles are identified and characterized. Main processes, working & sharing and governance principles are discussed. The architecture and supporting functionalities for a VBE management system as well as the corresponding information and knowledge bases are introduced in a step by step approach. The issues of management of competencies, VBE assets, and trust, as well as the value systems are analyzed in terms of modeling, support functionality, and practical use.

UNIT 4: **VIRTUAL ORGANIZATIONS**

The concept of Virtual Organization (VO) previously introduced is briefly revisited and the conditions for its emergence are discussed. Particular emphasis is devoted to the creation of dynamic VOs in a VBE context. The life cycle – creation, operation, evolution, and dissolution – of the VO is analyzed and the supporting information / knowledge and functionalities are discussed together with the involved actors and roles. Special attention is devoted to the consortia formation, negotiation, distributed business process planning and supervision, performance management, dissolution and inheritance, and business modeling. The relationship to other more classic networks such as supply chains is made. Examples in various domains are analyzed.

UNIT 5: **VIRTUAL COMMUNITIES**

The concept of Virtual Community (VC) previously introduced is briefly revisited and compared with the concept of VO. A typology of VC is suggested and a particular attention is devoted to Professional Virtual Communities. The components, structure, and life cycle of PVCs are discussed and modeling options introduced in comparison with the VBE. Architectural options for a PVC management system and supporting functionalities are analyzed. The creation of Virtual Teams within a PVC and their management are studied. Governance principles, main processes, intellectual property issues, and social computing issues are discussed.

UNIT 6: **BASE INFRASTRUCTURES**

The establishment of adequate communication channels and protocols is a basic pre-requisite for the operation of collaborative networks and interoperation among its components and subsystems. Therefore the main logical components of a communications infrastructure are introduced. Various implementation approaches are discussed, including agent-based and service-oriented approaches. The security issues deserve special attention and the various mechanisms and technologies are discussed in terms of their benefits and limitations. Emerging computing models, mobile and pervasive computing are briefly studied in terms of their contribution to collaborative networks.

UNIT 7: **INFORMATION MANAGEMENT**

Information management in a distributed, multi-ownership context is discussed and mechanisms for information sharing, information exchange, and access rights definition and enforcement are introduced. The role of standards is discussed and main standards briefly characterized. Various information management approaches are also discussed, with particular emphasis on the federated information management systems. Different implementation approaches are also discussed.

UNIT 8: **SPECIAL INFORMATION EXCHANGE STANDARDS**

A number of standards particularly relevant for collaborative networks are introduced and analyzed. Among them: EDI (Electronic Data Interchange), which in historical terms represents one of the first tools for cooperation among enterprises, is introduced and briefly characterized. The interaction between EDI and ERP systems is discussed. The EDIFACT standard is presented and current XML-based implementations mentioned. The STEP standard for the exchange of technical product data is described and its applicability in virtual enterprises is discussed. Support technologies as well as PDM systems are identified. Other emerging standards for information and knowledge exchange are pointed out.

UNIT 9: **COORDINATION MECHANISMS**

Various modalities of collaboration are discussed and the corresponding coordination needs introduced. The concept of coordination is highlighted. Process-based coordination and the corresponding distributed business process modeling, planning, scheduling, and execution are particularly focused. Languages for business process modeling are introduced. Workflow / process execution engines are discussed and standard architectures for inter-organization workflow are analyzed. Finally challenges in flexible coordination are raised and the students are motivated to suggest approaches.

UNIT 10: **MANAGEMENT OF COMMON ONTOLOGIES**

Considering the complexity of the collaborative network environments, a number of benefits are gained through provision of the ontology for these networks. Development of common ontology for collaborative networks enhances: i) common understanding of their related entities and concepts, ii) classification of their knowledge in order to facilitate the knowledge interoperability both among the network participants and among different networks, as well as iii) the development of a management system for collaborative networks and the needed databases and data/knowledge access functionality. Approaches for a common ontology are presented and mechanisms required for ontology customization and management are addressed.

UNIT 11: **e-COMMERCE AND e-MARKETS**
Although these issues are not part of the Collaborative Networks, they share a number of common issues. Therefore the concepts of e-Commerce and e-Market are introduced and the differences and commonalities in relation to collaborative networks highlighted. The involved organizational issues are discussed and

supporting architectures and technologies introduced. Finally the contact points between these areas and collaborative networks in a new digital ecosystems context are discussed.

UNIT 12: **NON-TECHNOLOGICAL ISSUES**

The success and effectiveness of implementation of the collaborative networks depend on a number of other important issues besides the technological solutions. In this unit social, ethical, legal, and organizational issues are addressed and current trends pointed out. New business models and their applicability are discussed, namely through the introduction of examples. Marketing and sustainability of the network, intellectual property management, systems of incentives, etc. are other relevant issues.

Alternatively each of these topics can be introduced in parallel and along the other units.

UNIT 13: **REFERENCE MODELS**

The concept of reference model and its need is introduced. Modeling frameworks are presented and discussed. Example reference models are introduced and methods for models evolution and derivation of particular models are briefly discussed. A reference modeling framework for CNs will be presented, addressing its specific dimensions and elements. Some CN reference models, for example for VBEs and VOs are presented.

UNIT 14: **EMERGING COLLABORATIVE FORMS**

In this last unit, and after a brief summary of the various collaborative forms studied in previous units, a discussion of possible new models and generalizations is made. As a starting basis, new forms of collaborative e-government, e-science, virtual institutes, Virtual laboratories, etc, are discussed. Other generalizations include: networks of sensors, networks of machines, etc. Afterwards students are encouraged to suggest other application areas and identify the innovative collaborative forms needed.

4.2 Curriculum

Based on the above units, Table 3 shows the proposed reference curriculum.

Table 3 – Reference curriculum for Collaborative Networks

UNIT	TOPICS
1. MOTIVATION FOR THE PARADIGM	▪ Practical examples of collaborative networks. ▪ Historic overview. ▪ Technological and organizational trends. ▪ Discussion of the usefulness / benefits and current limitations of CNs
2. BASIC CONCEPTS OF COLLABORATIVE NETWORKS	▪ Categories of CNs. ▪ Actors and roles. ▪ Life cycle and related key processes.
3. VO BREEDING ENVIRONMENT	▪ Concept and examples. ▪ Components, structure, actors and roles. ▪ Competencies and assets.

	▪ Processes and governance principles. ▪ VBE management system. ▪ Trust and value systems.
4. VIRTUAL ORGANIZATIONS	▪ Concepts, organizational models and operational rules. ▪ Life cycle. ▪ VO creation process and functionalities. ▪ VO management functionalities and performance measurement. ▪ VO dissolution and inheritance.
5. VIRTUAL COMMUNITIES.	▪ Concepts and typology. ▪ Components, structure, and life cycle. ▪ Professional virtual communities (PVC). ▪ PVC management system. ▪ Virtual teams. ▪ Governance principles and social computing.
6. BASE INFRASTRUCTURES.	▪ Computer networks basics. Base Internet technologies. ▪ Components of a communication infrastructure. ▪ Implementation approaches: agent-based, service-oriented, etc. ▪ Security mechanisms and technologies. ▪ Emerging computing models.
7. INFORMATION MANAGEMENT	▪ Information management requirements. ▪ Mechanisms for information sharing and exchange. ▪ Access rights definition and enforcement. ▪ Federated /distributed information management.
8. SPECIAL INFORMATION EXCHANGE STANDARDS	▪ Importance of standards in collaborative networks. ▪ EDI and EDIFACT. ▪ Interaction with legacy systems. ▪ XML and its role. ▪ STEP and PDM. ▪ Other standards.
9. COORDINATION MECHANISMS	▪ Collaboration modalities. ▪ Concept of coordination. ▪ Distributed-business process modeling and planning. ▪ Distributed scheduling and re-scheduling. ▪ Languages for business process modeling. ▪ Workflow and process execution engines. ▪ Challenges in flexible coordination.
10. MANAGEMENT OF COMMON ONTOLOGIES	▪ Glossary and specification of base entities and concepts. ▪ Core level common ontology for collaborative networks. ▪ Ontology engineering approaches. ▪ Learning ontology from unstructured sources. ▪ Semi-automatic customization of common ontology to specific domain/application
11. e-COMMERCE AND e-MARKETS	▪ Concepts of e-Commerce and e-Market. ▪ Relationships to collaborative networks. ▪ Support institutions. ▪ Support systems. Portals. Negotiation. ▪ CRM. Logistics.
12. NON-TECHNOLOGICAL	▪ Social, ethical, legal, and organizational issues. ▪ Contractual issues.

ISSUES.	<ul><li>New business models.</li><li>Collaboration sustainability mechanisms.</li><li>Intellectual property management.</li></ul>
13. REFERENCE MODELS	<ul><li>Concept of reference model.</li><li>Modeling frameworks.</li><li>Examples of reference models.</li><li>Derivation and evolution methods.</li></ul>
14. EMERGING COLLABORATIVE FORMS	<ul><li>Summary of studied collaborative forms.</li><li>New application examples: collaborative e-government, e-Science, Virtual Institutes, Virtual Labs, etc.</li><li>Networks of machines, networks of sensors.</li><li>Other emerging cases.</li></ul>

4.3 Sequence of topics

The proposed curriculum does not imply a rigid sequence of topics although some dependencies among subjects can naturally be identified, as shown in Fig. 4. The "Non-technological issues" can either be introduced towards the end, or they can be "merged" with the other topics and be addressed when the VO Breeding Environment (Afsarmanesh, Camarinha-Matos, 2005), the Virtual Organization / Virtual Enterprise (Goranson, 1999), and the Virtual Communities are introduced. Another approach is to emphasize technological aspects in the first phase, giving students the background to start the laboratory work, and postpone the other issues to a later stage.

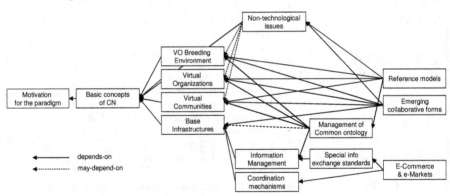

Figure 4 - Main dependencies among subjects

Taking the indicated dependencies into account, various alternative schedule sequences can be considered. Two examples are illustrated in Fig. 5.

Option A corresponds to introduce the main concepts and organizational forms before the technological aspects. This option can be adequate if the experimental lab work does not start in parallel with the theoretical lectures.

Option B might be more adequate for those cases in which theory and practical work have a parallel schedule. For instance when the course plan includes a theoretical lecture and a practical lecture every week, as it is common in some universities. This option might be more motivating for students that want to have "hands-on" experience from the beginning.

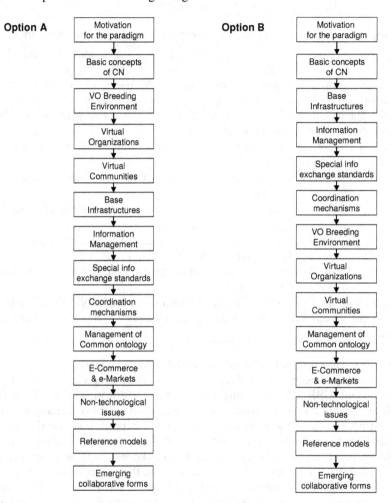

Figure 5 - Examples of sequences of topics

5. LAB WORK

Experimental work aimed at giving students some practical experience can be organized as projects. Instead of small disconnected experiments to be performed by students, the basic idea of a "project" is to have more ambitious lab works in which various groups of students design and develop components to be integrated in a collaborative platform. In this way, the working method to be adopted by the students will be collaborative, giving them more real understanding of the issues involved in a collaborative network. These projects are supposed to be developed along several sessions, typically along <u>one semester</u>.

Examples for students with a background in ICT

Example 1: *Infrastructure to support a central Certification Breeding Environment*

<u>Scenario</u>. Consider you want to build one house from scratch. You start buying the land and contacting an architect to elaborate a project design for your house. After the project is elaborated and you got the necessary licenses, the house construction starts and things go on normally but, as it seams to be usual, instead of the planned 12 months you realize that the key came to your hands only two years after the construction started.

The main reason for the delay was the need of getting several certifications along the construction process, namely:

- Construction certification – got in the City Hall, needed for the construction to start, ...
- Electrical Certification – needed to guarantee the electrical installation, ...
- Communications Infrastructure Certification – needed to guarantee the quality of the communication infrastructure, ...
- Usage Ability Certification – final certification needed for you to be able to live in the new house.

Sad with all the time lost, you decide to propose to your city council the creation of a Centralized Website where people could apply for any kind of certification services.

<u>Objectives</u>. This work aims at designing and developing a platform to support public certification processes for buildings, i.e. the support of a Certification Breeding Environment (CBE). Based on this framework, a Certification Virtual Organization could be created for each needed specific certification process. Taking into account the distinct phases of the software lifecycle this lab project will be divided into 4 phases: Analysis, Design, Development and Tests. For the analysis phase, the students should identify the system goals and skeleton, i.e., who are the actors, which modules will compose the system, what are their functionalities or features – the Use Cases. In this specific context, a discussion has to take place in order to clearly identify the goals of the infrastructure to be developed – the Certification Breeding Environment, namely:

- Register Certification entities, as well as their capacities / certification fields that the entities are able to certify.
- Find, within the CBE, entities that are able to provide specific certifications.
- Create a Certification Business Process – CBP, composed of a graph of certification Services associated to specific certification entities from the CBE.
- Execute and Monitor the execution of specific CBPs.
- ...

In terms of the CBE platform, it must contain modules responsible for:

- Storage and management of the service provision members.

- Provide an interface to the certifying entities.
- Provide an interface for clients who need to access certification services.
- Provide an interface for the creation of Certification Value Added Services, through the creation of workflow specification of CBPs.
- ...

Working Method. Students will be divided in groups to discuss the needs and constraints for this infrastructure. Each group makes a presentation of their work in the third lab session and proposes a final System Architecture, as well as the development technology to use. After all the proposals are discussed, the class will decide a common final System Architecture and the development technology to use. Each group of students will then be given a specific set of modules from the architecture to design, develop, integrate and test. In other words, each group will contribute with a distinct piece of the global system. Nevertheless, all groups have to be aware of what is going on with the other groups – the difficulties they are facing, the results they are producing, etc., in order to facilitate the final integration and improve the overall performance.

Example 2: *Infrastructure to support a PVC of Engineering consultants*

> *Scenario.* A group of engineers from different specialties and living in different geographical regions / countries are organized as a PVC to provide consulting services. The PVC interacts with potential customers through a web portal. Customers will see this community as a service market.
> Basic services can be combined into higher level services (value added services) in order to better respond to market opportunities, implementing, in this way, a kind of "learning system". Therefore, it shall be possible to use the output of a service as input for another service.
> The coordination of a value-added service execution is also supported by the platform that keeps track of the status of evolution, exceptions, etc.

Objectives. This work aims at designing and developing a platform to support a Professional Virtual Community devoted to offer engineering consulting services. The typical phases of Analysis, Design, and Development shall be carried out. For the analysis phase the students shall be organized around a forum, playing different roles, in order to identify and characterize:
-   The needs from the end-users point of view.
-   The possibilities offered by current ICT tools and systems.
-   The opportunities for commercial exploitation.

The next phase shall involve the design of the system's architecture, with a clear identification and specification of the various needed modules, as well as their interactions.

During the implementation, each group of students (2 or 3) will develop a specific module and will be responsible for the integration of this module with the other modules.

Some initial questions to motivate the work:
-   Which basic functionalities are needed to interact with potential customers?
-   Which basic functionalities are needed to support the organization of a value-added service?

- Is it feasible to have shared information spaces? How to deal with information visibility and access rights?
- How to keep track of the execution status of services?
- How to model the support information structures?

Working method. Each group of students will be given a specific task in order to add value to the common goal, just like in a virtual community. In other words, each group will contribute with a distinct piece of the global system. Nevertheless, all groups have to be aware of what is going on with the other groups – the difficulties they are facing, the results they are producing, etc., in order to facilitate integration and improve the overall performance. During the initial analysis phase, students are supposed to also identify existing platforms and tools that will facilitate the development.

Example for students with other backgrounds

Example 3: *P2P Social Networking tools to support PVCs*

<u>Scenario</u>. Imagine the following situation: you, together with your classmates, are part of a Professional Community which basically consists of the students of the course. You are together in a Community because you have similar interests and goals as for instance to learn about Collaborative Networks, to develop your competencies and to work collaboratively. Now, imagine further: the relation among the members of this Community will mainly be mediated through the use of computers. There will be face-to-face interactions, but these will not be the predominant ones. The tools used for these interactions will be the ones used for P2P social networking: Skype, MSN, Orkut, blogs, videologs, emails, SMS, GoogleSpreadsheets, etc. Now the question is: can you work together and collaboratively according to this social and organizational structure taking advantage of the internet-enabled society?

<u>Objectives</u>. The students will form a Virtual Team to work collaboratively in order to put together a project proposal to be submitted (hypothetically) to a Funding Agency call. The expertise aggregation should allow the elaboration of a proposal in the field of Collaborative Networks. In this sense, students have to take into account the current topics and the Open Calls for project proposals. Guidelines and rules to elaborate the proposal are the ones provided by the funding agency.

Some initial questions to motivate the work:

- How can the work be distributed among the members of the Virtual Team?
- Which governance principles are going to be used / adopted?
- How can conflicts be handled?
- How can the quality of work be measured?
- How to deal with Intellectual Property Rights?
- How to deal with trust issues?
- How can the tasks be monitored with transparency?

Working method. Students will have two face-to-face meetings mediated by the course assistant namely: the first and the last lab sessions. In the first one, the experiment will be explained and the roles will be pre-defined according to the background and competencies of each participant. Also during the first session, a brainstorming on the project idea and the definition of start-up tools will take place.

In the last lab session, a round table will be organized to discuss and evaluate the procedure, the achievements as well as the strong and weak points of the experiment. All other lab sessions will be carried out remotely. Students will interact either from home, office or from the University premises. The remote lab sessions will be monitored by the course assistant. The first remote session will be used to agree on the set of tools to be used as well as on the topic to be developed for the project proposal. If other interesting tools are identified *a posteriori*, they might be suggested and included in the set if the participants agree on.

Ideally, students should try to discuss issues related to the experiment using only the identified tools (and not informal personal chats, for instance). With this lab project, students will be exercising and practicing concepts and models related to: working and sharing principles, governance, trust, management, IPR and transparency in a CN environment.

6. APPLICATION

Summer course. Part of the ideas suggested in this curriculum was tested in an ECOLEAD Summer School held in Helsinki in 2006.

Figure 6 – ECOELAD Summer School in Helsinki

Experience at UNL. An instantiation of the proposed curriculum has been included in the Electrical and Computer Engineering program of the Faculty of Sciences and Technology of the New University of Lisbon. This is an integrated MSc program (5 years) and the CN course is entitled "Virtual Enterprises". Although the course is, for historic reasons, entitled Virtual Enterprises, it covers all CN-related subjects proposed in this curriculum.

This course is located in the summer semester of the 4th year of the master program. Previous to this course, students have gone through several other courses that provide important ICT background to facilitate the understanding of the Virtual Enterprises curriculum. The following diagram illustrates these main subjects that constitute relevant background for the CN course (Fig. 7).

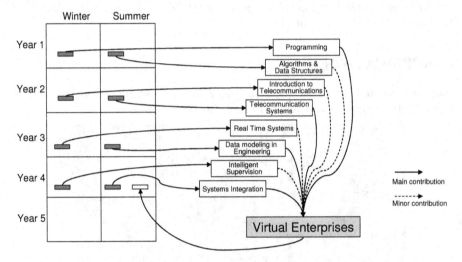

Figure 7 - Virtual Enterprises course and supporting courses

In the first occurrences of this course (till 2006), the course included 14 theoretical lectures of 2 h each, and 14 lab sessions of 3 h each. With the recent adaptation of the program to follow the Bologna model, the lab sessions were reduced to 2 h each. The course spans along 14 weeks; in each week there is one theoretical lecture and one lab session.

Given the nature of the program where this course is included, a strong emphasis on the ICT aspects was naturally adopted. The implementation of such a course with a strong laboratorial component faced a number of obstacles, namely:

- Complexity of the area;
- Lack of tradition of teaching these subjects;
- Lack of appropriate didactic materials;
- Dilemma between the option of increasing the number of students per lab session (limited by the available lab resources) or increasing the number of times each lab session is repeated (limited by the university policy regarding hiring new teaching assistants). But in spite of these obstacles, the adopted approach was to keep a strong laboratorial component in order to give students a sound hands-on experience.

Although this course is offered as elective (optional), the number of registered students has been growing every year, as shown in Fig. 8.

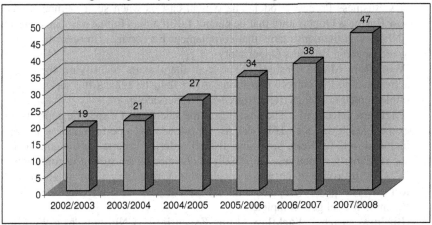

Figure 8 - Evolution of registered students for the Virtual Enterprises course

In the last 3 years, due to the number of students, the lab sessions had to be duplicated, with half of the students attending each turn. As lab work, a different project, based on the examples provided in section 5, has been successfully implemented every year. At the end of the semester it has been possible to demonstrate a working integrated system composed of modules developed by different groups of students.

As an indicator of success, in the year 2004, the project example n° 2 described in section 5 (students with ICT background) was adopted. The developed work was submitted to the Microsoft competition "**Imagine Cup**" and won the 1st position in the national competition, taking a group of students to the world finals in Brazil. The developed system was called "Collaborative Networked Environment – CNE" and the central aim of the infrastructure was to put together various consultants, as described before. Follows a brief description of CNE usage:

1. [**Consultant Registration**] - Other than personal data, each consultant provides a set of services he is able to offer to the virtual community. As more consultants register, the

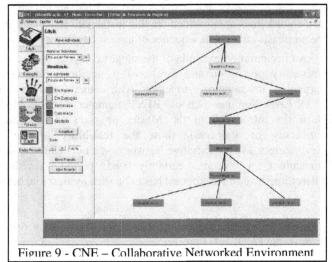

Figure 9 - CNE – Collaborative Networked Environment

resulting community gets bigger, as well as the provided services increase.

2. **[New Business Process Model Creation]** – Each member of CNE can start a new Business Process Model. The typical case is when such member finds a new Business Opportunity that he cannot fulfill alone. In that case, he comes to CNE to find the consultants that complement his services, in order to respond to that specific Business Opportunity.

3. **[Workflow Model Design]** - The consultant starts identifying the needed activities and the correct transitions. After that, he selects the services to be implemented in each activity from the CNE-services-pool.

4. **[Partners Selection]** – The next step is the selection of a specific consultant to execute each service. This task is supported by a performance supervisor included in the system, providing distinct ordering criteria for the consultants' set available for each service. Finally each selected consultant is contacted by the system, asking if he wants to join this Virtual Team that is about to be formed. The process repeats until all the services have an executor and the Business Model gets complete.

5. **[Business Process Workflow Model Execution]** - CNE includes a Workflow Engine responsible for this task, sending a message to each consultant when the time for his service to start comes. When each consultant finishes the specific service, he sends back a message to the engine, eventually including relevant files, and the process is repeated for the next consultant(s) on the workflow graph.

6. **[Execution Monitoring]** - CNE also provides an execution monitor, enabling all the consultants involved in a common Business Process to see the state of its execution (as shown in Fig. 9).

7. CONCLUSIONS

The proposed curriculum is aimed to provide a basis for a *reference*. Specific courses can be derived from this general reference curriculum, taking into account the specific context where the course will be introduced and the target students. Some guidelines are provided for this instantiation, namely in terms of where to put the emphasis and which sequence of topics to follow.

An instantiation example of the suggested syllabus was implemented at the New University of Lisbon and results of its application were briefly reported. This particular instantiation, together with other specific teaching actions (e.g. ECOLEAD Summer School, BEST Summer School, Module on Collaborative Networks introduced in the Master program on Logistics of the Polytechnic University of Valencia), show the feasibility of the proposed curriculum. Nevertheless, as Collaborative Networks is a new and very dynamic field, a training curriculum for this area certainly needs periodic revisions and improvements. Therefore, the current proposal has to be seen as an initial basis.

Acknowledgments. This work was funded in part by the European Commission through the ECOLEAD project.

8. REFERENCES

Afsarmanesh, H., Camarinha-Matos, L. M., 2005). A framework for management of virtual organization breeding environments. In Collaborative Networks and their Breeding Environments (L.M. Camarinha-Matos, H. Afsarmanesh, Ed.s), pp. 35-48, Springer, Boston.

Camarinha-Matos, L. M., 2006. Towards an education curriculum on Collaborative Networks, IFIP Newsletter, March 2006.

Camarinha-Matos, L. M.; Afsarmanesh, H., 2005. Collaborative networks: A new scientific discipline, *J. Intelligent Manufacturing*, vol. 16, N° 4-5, pp439-452.

Camarinha-Matos, L. M.; Afsarmanesh, H., Ollus, M., 2005. ECOLEAD: A holistic approach to creation and management of dynamic virtual organizations. In Collaborative Networks and their Breeding Environments (L.M. Camarinha-Matos, H. Afsarmanesh, Ed.s), pp. 3-16, Springer, Boston.

Camarinha-Matos, L. M.; Cardoso, T., 2004. Education on Virtual Organizations: An Experience at UNL. In Virtual Enterprises and Collaborative Networks (L. M. Camarinha-Matos, Ed.), pp 579-588, Springer: Boston.

Camarinha-Matos, L. M.; Cardoso, T.; Klen, E.; Afsarmanesh, H., 2005. A study of VO, VBE and PVC curricula, Deliverable D71.2, ECOLEAD project, March 2005, www.ecolead.org.

Garita, C., 2004. A case study of VO education in Costa Rica. In Virtual Enterprises and Collaborative Networks (L. M. Camarinha-Matos, Ed.), pp 589-596, Springer: Boston.

Gloor, P.; Paasivaara, M.; Schoder, D.; Willems, P., 2006. Correlating performance with social network structure through teaching social network analysis. In Network-centric collaboration and support frameworks (L.M.Camarinha-Matos, H. Afsarmanesh, M. Ollus, Ed.s), pp 265-272, Springer: Boston.

Goranson, H.T., 1999. The Agile Virtual Enterprise – Cases, metrics, tools (Quorum Books).

Klen, E., Cardoso, T., Camarinha-Matos, L. M., 2005. Teaching Initiatives on Collaborative Networked Organizations, in *Proceedings of 38th CIRP - International Seminar on Manufacturing Systems*, May 16-18, Florianópolis-SC, Brazil.

Haugen, J., Hussein, B. A., Solbjørg, O., Andersen, B., 2002. Pedagogic Approaches for Training and Education (Distance Learning) in the Extended enterprise, GEM deliverable D2.1, Dec 2002. http://www.sintef.no/static/tl/projects/gem/documents/D2.1.pdf

EMERGING COLLABORATION FORMS AND FURTHER RESEARCH NEEDS

L. M. Camarinha-Matos
New University of Lisbon, PORTUGAL
cam@uninova.pt

Several international research initiatives and a growing number of practical implementations are helping the consolidation and expansion of the collaborative networks paradigm. New forms of collaboration are emerging in various domains and further research needs are identified. A summary of these trends is presented.

1. INTRODUCTION

A considerable progress in collaborative technologies and systems could be observed in the last five years. Enabling tools and frameworks have been complemented with a better understanding of the collaborative networks paradigm and its implementation requirements. The acquired experiences with earlier application cases drive the development of improved functionalities and governance models.

A variety of collaboration forms are being developed in practically all domains, turning collaborative networks into a pervasive phenomenon. In some cases those developments tend to adopt a terminology that is specific of that domain; often the involved actors in a given domain are not fully aware of the developments in the mainstream research on collaborative networks. For instance, the grid community adopted the term "virtual organization" but focused mainly on the resource sharing perspective, paying little attention to the other aspects involved in collaboration. The European enterprise interoperability community, which was initially focused on the intra-enterprise aspects, is moving towards inter-enterprise collaboration.

On the other hand, there is still some divorce between the engineering and management schools, in spite of the need for a holistic approach. And yet the collaborative networks discipline is steadily consolidating (Camarinha-Matos, Afsarmanesh, 2005). The ECOLEAD project is an example of a large initiative contributing to this consolidation. But dozens of other international initiatives are contributing to advance different aspects of the discipline. As the area progresses new research challenges become, naturally, evident.

Therefore, this chapter intends to illustrate and summarize such trends and identify important future research needs.

2. EMERGING COLLABORATIVE FORMS

As mentioned above, new collaborative forms are emerging in various sectors as a result of the new possibilities offered by technology, the increasing awareness about those possibilities, and the accumulated experiences with the "classic" collaborative networked organizations (CNOs). In some cases these CNOs can be considered as particular cases of previous forms that just emphasize one or two particular characteristics. Other cases show a larger number of specificities and may be considered as new classes of CNOs. The following table (Camarinha-Matos, 2007) shows a number of such forms and their most relevant or distinctive features. Several other features, common to many collaborative forms, may be present as well but the purpose here is to emphasize the ones that are more relevant for each case.

Table 1: New collaborative forms

New collaborative form	Some relevant / distinctive features
1) Joint resource management (e.g. grid / dispersed manufacturing networks, computer grid)	- Pool of resources. - Separate ownership from management – joint (centralized?) management. - Implies continuous awareness of capacities, status, etc. - Needs proper business models (how to pay the owners). - Specialized scheduling policies and access rights management.
2) Collaborative virtual lab	- Combination of organizations and largely autonomous people. - Remote access to (shared) equipment. - Protocols for experiments. - Special visualization techniques and data mining. - Access rights management. - Intellectual property.
3) Inter-modal collaboration (e.g. integrated transportation systems)	- Service composition / multiple service providers. - Tracking, geo-referencing. - Automatic identification. - Link to payment system (bank network).
4) Collaborative e-government / network of governmental organizations	- Provision of integrated services to the citizen (combining lower level services from different organizations). - Very flexible workflow / service composition (e.g. building a house, changing address, etc.). - Service / process planning / "discovery" (adaptation to the situation of each citizen). - Security / privacy. Need for "intermediaries" for service composition assistance.
5) Energy networks management	- Network of producers. Consumers also as (potential) producers (solar energy, wind energy, etc.). - Continuous adaptation to fluctuating demand. - Specialized decision making (for distribution of price, losses, load, etc).
6) (Occasional) crisis management	- Very short window of opportunity. - Large diversity of entities (public, NGOs, private). - Highly incomplete and rapidly changing information. - Geographical dependence. - Limited communications infrastructures.

	- Competing operational coordination bodies.
7) Customers involvement networks (kind of living lab)	- Network of manufacturers and customers. - Levels of disclosure of information / levels of involvement. - Guarantee of benefits for both sides. - Communication with customers (non-experts) and impact in product design (by experts). - Regional aspects / preferences / culture. - Involvement of other regional actors (besides the customers) at the end of the chain.
8) Virtual institutes	- Involvement of professors from different institutions to prepare / deliver a course. - (Usually) remote delivery of courses. - Strong support on multi-media and authoring tools. - Intellectual property and business model – a critical issue for sustainability. - Relationship individual (professor) and organization (university) and intellectual property. - Possible combination with virtual lab / remote access to equipment. - Specialized delivery / interaction platforms. - Course management services.
9) Permanent crisis / social care (e.g. supporting homeless)	- Mostly information exchange, some coordination. - Permanent cases (daily) and sporadic (small crisis, e.g. one family needing immediate intensive care). - Mostly based on volunteers – large heterogeneity of qualifications. - Geographic referencing.
10) Collaborative gaming	- Gaming over the net. - Potentially large groups / multiple instances. - Variable levels of "membership". - Formation of teams, organization of competitions. - Rewarding mechanisms. - Additional socialization mechanisms. - Collective intelligence / collective strategy. - Advanced GUI and other user interfaces.
11) Collaborative innovation	- Creation / innovation process (understanding, modeling, drivers). - Support for joint work / tools sharing. - Brainstorming, argumentation, synthesis, etc. - Value identification, intellectual property, rewarding. - Safety / protection mechanisms. - Trust management.
12) Context awareness service provision (i.e. providing services that depend on the context, e.g. location of a mobile customer)	- The actual contributors for a service depend on the actual context of the customer. - Mobile computing, geo-referencing. - Limited communication (in some cases). - Services built on the fly – planning, discovery. - GIS support. - Contexts may be continuously changing (mobile customer). - Identification (of the user), roaming infrastructure. - Business model / payment model.
13) Machine and sensor networks (e.g. networks of robots)	- Intelligent machines or sensorial nodes. - More structured interactions. - Handling errors. - Planning and reasoning techniques. - Machine learning.

As illustrated by these examples, the Collaborative Networks paradigm is spreading to new sectors and application cases. It is, however, necessary to wait until enough experiences are realized so that a proper characterization and classification of these collaborative forms can be made.

Furthermore, as a result of the maturation of a number of new fields, as illustrated in Fig. 1, it is likely that new collaboration forms and new ways of work will also emerge in the near future.

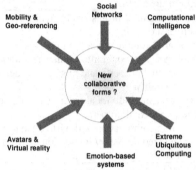

Figure 1 - New synergies in support of collaboration

The integration of concepts and mechanisms originated in these areas may lead to improved collaboration support. For instance, affective computing / emotions-based systems seem quite promising in better supporting geographically distributed communities. Computational intelligence modeling and reasoning mechanisms are likely to induce more advanced decision-support systems for collaborative networks.

3. ACHIEVEMENTS AND FURTHER CHALLENGES

During the last decade a large number of R&D projects have made substantial progress, not only in terms of development of support platforms and tools, but also contributing to a better conceptual understanding and characterization of the area (Camarinha-Matos et al, 2005a), (Camarinha-Matos, 2007). ECOLEAD, an integrated project including 28 partners from 15 countries, with a duration of 4 years, is an example initiative that addressed several key issues of collaborative networks under a holistic perspective (Camarinha-Matos et al., 2005b). The following tables (Tables 2-6) illustrate the current issues and results in various focus areas of CNOs. Further research challenges are also identified. These tables are not complete but only intended to give a synthetic overview of the current state of the art and exemplify further research needs.

Table 2: Status on VO Breeding Environments

Focus area: VO Breeding Environment		
Current issues and results	*Example projects*	*Examples of further challenges*
VBE Reference framework including: - Elements	ECOLEAD, (Virtuelle Fabrik)	▪ Better understanding of collaboration drivers, including principles of interactions, notions of ecosystem and

- Typologies - Life cycle - Governance rules - Working and sharing principles	LogNET-LOGICA, VIRTUE PlaNet	leadership, self-organization and behavioral models, models of complexity, etc. ■ Refined working and sharing principles configurable to different application
Value systems and Trust: - Value system concept and elements (conceptual framework, preliminary formalization, benefits network) - Objective trustworthiness evaluation - Basic mechanisms for trust building	ECOLEAD e-Hubs EVCM	domains together with practical instantiation procedures. ■ Business, marketing and branding methods and support services. ■ Legal frameworks and advanced support services (e.g. practical e-notary services, intelligent negotiation wizards). ■ Ontology construction dealing with distributed and dissimilar views
VBE management system, typically comprising: - Membership management - Support information management - Ontology construction and management - Knowledge discovery / data mining - Trust management - Competency management - Bag of assets management - Decision support system	ECOLEAD AerViCO PlaNet	bridging. ■ Trust management, providing advanced functionalities for trustworthiness analysis, assessment, and forecasting, based on computational intelligence and qualitative reasoning approaches. ■ Sound theoretical background modeling support for value systems and methods to determine the added-value of each partner, analysis of alignment of value systems, etc. ■ Advanced competency management
Network analysis mechanisms such as: - Global network analysis - Profit / benefit analysis and estimation methods - Business models	CODESNET, ECOLEAD, PRIME, (MYCAREV ENT), DIMA (Swiss Microtech)	focusing on discovery of new competencies, competency gap analysis, and identification of (emergent) composite competencies. ■ Analysis and data mining of historic performance data, which has a raising potential as collaboration history data are being collected.
VO creation framework comprising: - VO creation process - Actors, roles, and functionalities	ECOLEAD SIMCT MAPPER	■ Assessment of members' readiness for collaboration based on other factors than the traditional competency-capacity matching.
VO creation services - Collaboration opportunity finding - Brokering - VO rough planning - Partners' search and suggestion / selection	ECOLEAD, CDVEs	■ Development of advanced graphical visualization methods for key performance indicators of the VBE. ■ Bag of assets management including traditional documents and knowledge items as well as services and corresponding access and composition methods.
Negotiation and contracting - Negotiation framework, negotiation rooms - Contract models - Templates - Negotiation protocols (agent-	ECOLEAD LEGAL-IST e-LEGAL SESAM TrustCOM	■ New simulation tools to support decision making, what-if analysis, study of emerging behaviors, self-organizing patterns, etc. ■ Policies and mechanisms for monitoring and enforcement of the

based)		VBE governance principles and rules (including warning systems).
- e-Notary and electronic institutions		▪ Advanced support for finding collaboration / business opportunities.
Electronic Service Markets	NASCEM	

Table 3: Status on VO management

Focus area: VO Management		
Current issues and results	*Example projects*	*Examples of further challenges*
VO governance principles and models, supporting diverse: - Management styles - Management levels and actors	ECOLEAD PANDA	▪ Advanced support for planning VO governance models. ▪ Simulation and assessment environments to analyze VOs. ▪ Support for more fluid customer involvement with VO creation and operation.
Collaborative process specification and modelling: - (Distributed) business process modelling - Process supervision - Exception handling	ECOLEAD INTERPROD ArKOS ECOSELL AerViCO PANDA	▪ New network-centric performance indicators focused on collaboration. ▪ Mechanisms and tools to determine added-value of each partner, distribution of benefits and losses.
Performance management mechanisms: - Network-oriented performance indicators (collaboration performance indicators) - Performance measurement - Distributed data acquisition	ECOLEAD, (SCOR) Tool-East PMS-EVE GPM-SME	▪ Risk management tools for VOs. ▪ Advanced manufacturing models for diverse distributed collaboration modalities. ▪ Models and mechanisms to generate aggregated performance indicators (e.g. at the dissolution phase). ▪ Policies and mechanisms for VO inheritance and transfer of responsibilities.
Preliminary decision support systems: - Conflict resolution - Risk management - Financial decision making	ECOLEAD GPM-SME	▪ New process / workflow models coping with ad-hoc collaboration, complexity and evolvability.
Principles of VO inheritance: - Lessons learned - Aggregated performance indicators - Transfer of liabilities / responsibilities - Benefits / losses / assets distribution	ECOLEAD	▪ Real-time (virtual) enterprise – the "old" concepts of intelligent supervision acquire new "life" in the context of collaborative networks being necessary to revisit this body of knowledge and extend it, possibly in combination with RFID and sensor networks.

Table 4: Status on Professional Virtual Communities

Focus area: Professional Virtual Communities		
Current issues and results	*Example projects*	*Examples of further challenges*
PVC conceptual framework, including: - Main concepts	ECOLEAD CSDN	▪ Since this is an emerging concept, it is necessary to progress further in the organizational models, leadership and

- Actors and roles - Life cycle - Typologies - Business drivers and interaction with other organizational forms - Main processes		coordination principles. ■ Specific value systems and appropriate IPR are needed, both for pure PVCs and PVCs embedded in VBEs. ■ The legal framework needs to be further developed as well as the interactions with other organizational forms (interactions of the PVC as a whole or interactions of its individual members).
Basic PVC business model, analyzing: - Value objects and metrics - Business strategy - Legal, social, ethical, and societal issues	ECOLEAD CSDN	
PVC organization and processes - Legal / informal structures - Governance principles and processes - Value-adding processes	ECOLEAD	■ New "life support" institutions (e.g. new forms of social security) need to be developed to cope with the volatility of the working conditions. ■ Appropriate ethical codes need to be developed, namely for PVCs spreading over different geographical regions. ■ Advanced process models adjusted to new collaboration / working modalities.
PVC management system, including: - Membership management - Documents and knowledge management - Basic collaboration tools - Virtual teams creation	ECOLEAD AREITO network OASIS	■ Advanced competency management (similarly to VBEs). ■ Advanced collaboration platforms supporting mobility / pervasive computing, multiple virtual rooms, etc.
Virtual Teams management Collaborative problem solving - Negotiation, argumentation, consensus building, task decomposition and distribution, … - Conflict / dispute resolution	ECOLEAD (ECOLEAD) (SciencePeer) (Modelling Space)	■ New affective computing / emotion-based models and support tools for collaboration environments. ■ Collaborative problem solving integrating mechanisms for distributed brainstorming, argumentation, avatars management and virtual reality, delegation, etc. ■ Mechanisms for determination of members' added-value and distribution of benefits and losses.
Collaborative engineering platforms (for collaborative or concurrent engineering as a particular case of PVC) - Design tool sharing and encapsulation - Shared access to computational facilities, experiments, labs and prototyping facilities - Collaboration support - Knowledge sharing and collaborative learning - Digital manufacturing - Joint IPsharing and protection - Standards for technical	e-COLLEG VIVACE ACTIVe3D-Build	■ Advanced trust and reputation management mechanisms focused on professional collaboration. ■ Practical negotiation, e-contracting, and virtual team creation support. ■ Better understanding of the collaboration drivers (behavioral models, self-organizing principles). ■ Handling multi-cultural issues in collaborative product / service design. ■ Measuring added-value and benefits of collaboration on design. ■ Methods for collaborative learning in design. ■ Computer-aided creativity support.

product data exchange (e.g. STEP).		

Table 5: Status on ICT infrastructures

Focus area: ICT Infrastructures		
Current issues and results	*Example projects*	*Examples of further challenges*
Service Oriented Architecture (SOA) orientation established as the main approach for integration of distributed services	ECOLEAD ITSIBus ATHENA INPREX	▪ In spite of the growing importance of SOA approaches, there is a need for better standardization and design methodologies. Other aspects include: Services' semantic annotation (focused on collaboration), dynamic ("on the fly") service combination, intelligent planning, search, and integration of services, soft matching methods, etc.
Security infrastructures including: - Basic security mechanisms - Authentication mechanisms - Responsibility policies	ECOLEAD TRUSTCOM DyVOSE	
Distributed workflow / business process modeling and execution engines	WIDE CrossFlow	▪ Sustainable business models for the infrastructures (one of the main current obstacles for the development of the area).
Distributed information exchange and sharing mechanisms: - Federated systems - Standards for information exchange - Web-based document management systems	PRODNET II MASSYVE	▪ Absorption of emerging computing paradigms. ▪ Grid computing has been trying to be a kind of "bandwagon" that collects / integrates ideas from other areas but still offers a limited conceptualization of VO and corresponding business model. Nevertheless it includes some potentially useful mechanisms for resource management and
Interoperability principles and approaches for integration of legacy systems	ATHENA ITSIBus INTEROP ECOLEAD	collaboration between the two communities could be useful.
Base collaboration services: - CSCW - Document management - Forum, chat, billing, etc.	ECOLEAD	▪ As the area of mobile computing, WiMax, new mobile devices and infrastructures is developing, it is necessary to identify / create new opportunities for new pervasive collaborative environments.
Agent-based approaches: - Agent-based enterprise modeling - Agent-based infrastructures - Agent-based simulation - Mobile agent infrastructures	TeleCARE, SteelNet Global Automation Platform	▪ RFID (radio frequency identification) may enable better real-time management in production and logistic networks for which a holistic approach is needed. ▪ The Multi-Agent Systems area continues to be promising from a conceptual perspective but there is a need for more robustness in development environments for widely distributed systems.

Table 6: Status on the theoretical foundation for collaborative networks

Focus area: Theoretical Foundation		
Current issues and results	*Example projects*	*Examples of further challenges*
On a modeling basis: - Identification of modeling approaches and tools developed in other disciplines but with potential applicability in CNOS - Initial attempts to combine different modeling approaches - Preliminary consolidation of concepts	ECOLEAD, THINKcreative VOSTER	• More rigorous and formal models of the base concepts. • Development of base theories of collaborative networks. • Exploration of soft modeling and qualitative reasoning in addressing complex decision-making problems in CNOs. Examples include, value systems, trust, risk management, readiness and preparedness to join a CNO, etc.
Modeling framework: - Some attempts to extend enterprise modeling frameworks (e.g. Zachman, CIM-OSA, GERAM) to CNOs - Some attempts to extend supply chain frameworks (e.g. SCOR) to CNOs - ARCON, a comprehensive framework covering both the Endogenous Elements of a CNO (Structural, Componential, Functional, and Behavioral dimensions) and the Exogenous Interactions (Market, Support, Societal, and Constituency dimensions)	GLOBEMEN ECOLEAD	• Validation of the ARCON framework. Namely in the case of emerging collaborative forms. • Revision and extension of ARCON. • Elaboration of reference models for specific cases / classes of CNOs. • Further development of the behavioral dimension, namely exploration of the emergence and self-organization principles. • Identification and characterization of the mechanisms that motivate and sustain collaborative behaviors.
Reference modeling: - Preliminary attempts to define reference models for virtual organizations - First stage of ARCON reference model for collaborative networks	VOSTER ECOLEAD	

The following sections illustrate some of the challenges in the context of specific application areas.

4. CASE 1: PRODUCT / SERVICE FOCUS AND CUSTOMER INVOLVEMENT

During the 1990s there was a considerable effort worldwide focused on product and process modeling. A major stream was represented by the activities around the

STEP standard. Logically, contemporary research on virtual enterprises also embedded a strong focus on the exchange of product models and related technical data among the participants in the collaborative network. In the current decade, however, the product / service do not appear to be explicitly in the center of attention of many projects. For instance, ECOLEAD quite intensely focused on the organizational and governance aspects of the collaborative network and the product or service got somewhat less attention.

It is now important to refocus the research attention, revisiting the aspects of distributed product / service design and development, and consequently align the corresponding process models, governance and organizational structures of the collaborative networks.

Current trends in mass customization have highlighted the need to take into account the preferences, specificities, and constraints as well as the assets of the target market regions. In fact there are plenty of examples of failed cases of manufacturing projects due to the lack of proper customization, especially related to intangible products and services. To access different markets, large companies possess enough resources to install local branches, able to address the local specificities. SMEs and micro enterprises however, can only compete for such markets through collaboration. Furthermore, in addition to the need for involvement of local enterprises, it is important to extend the collaboration process to selected customers and lead users - a form of focused living lab environment. In fact, the classical corporate boundaries have recently begun to blur and the value chain is loosing its attributes, and being replaced by a web of fluid and flexible relations. In this context, customers are becoming an important part of the value creation, offering new possibilities to increase operational efficiency as well as to define strategic uniqueness through innovation.

The role of the customer is changing from a pure consumer of products and services to a partner in the value creation process, i.e. consumers become pro-sumers and co-designers (Hippel, 2002), (Reichwald et al., 2005). Empirical studies find that innovation by customers tends to be concentrated on lead users of the products. In some cases the innovation comes from expert users (e.g. sports users can suggest / design completely new products fitting their specific needs), in which case the process goes far beyond simple customization to even radical "first" product type innovation. Many publications have analyzed a diversity of case studies and the related economics of co-innovation. Several of these empirical studies show that innovating users often choose to freely reveal their innovations to other users and to manufacturers as well. Some reasons for this behavior (Hippel, 2002) include: 1) Often not practical to benefit from intellectual property via either licensing or secrecy (even if innovators should wish to do this). 2) Much intellectual property does not qualify for protection. 3) Gains can be obtained by reputation. 4) Other gains can be achieved through earlier market realization of solutions to users' needs. It is however unclear the evolution of this situation if more and more customers get involved in the process.

A large number of empirical studies are reported in the literature on involvement of customers in the innovation process (Reichwald et al., 2005). Most of this work however merely covers the descriptions / enumerations of cases, adding only little contribution to the needed systematic definition of processes, structures, and drivers involved. Fig. 2 (inspired from Berger *et al*, 2005) summarizes the main characteristics of many of these cases found in literature.

The current challenge is to enable *collaborative innovation* involving a network of SMEs (manufacturers, designers, etc.), interfacing different entities and customers. Unlike previous works focused on interactions between one company and its customers, it is necessary to address the much more challenging scope of customer involved networked collaboration and co-innovation, as shown in Fig. 3.

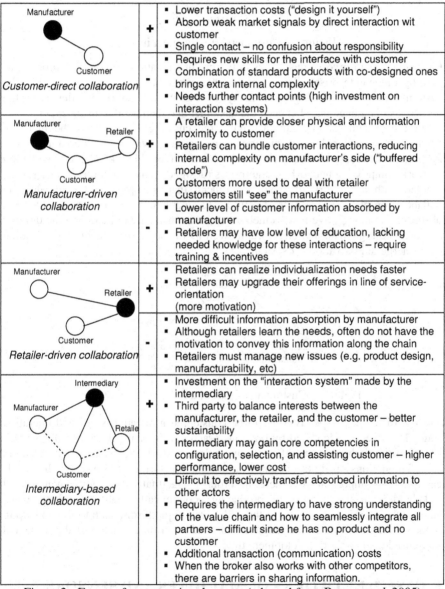

Manufacturer ● — ○ Customer *Customer-direct collaboration*	**+**	• Lower transaction costs ("design it yourself") • Absorb weak market signals by direct interaction wit customer • Single contact – no confusion about responsibility
	-	• Requires new skills for the interface with customer • Combination of standard products with co-designed ones brings extra internal complexity • Needs further contact points (high investment on interaction systems)
Manufacturer ● Retailer ○ Customer ○ *Manufacturer-driven collaboration*	**+**	• A retailer can provide closer physical and information proximity to customer • Retailers can bundle customer interactions, reducing internal complexity on manufacturer's side ("buffered mode") • Customers more used to deal with retailer • Customers still "see" the manufacturer
	-	• Lower level of customer information absorbed by manufacturer • Retailers may have low level of education, lacking needed knowledge for these interactions – require training & incentives
Manufacturer ○ Retailer ● Customer ○ *Retailer-driven collaboration*	**+**	• Retailers can realize individualization needs faster • Retailers may upgrade their offerings in line of service-orientation (more motivation)
	-	• More difficult information absorption by manufacturer • Although retailers learn the needs, often do not have the motivation to convey this information along the chain • Retailers must manage new issues (e.g. product design, manufacturability, etc)
Intermediary ● Manufacturer ○ Retaile ○ Customer ○ *Intermediary-based collaboration*	**+**	• Investment on the "interaction system" made by the intermediary • Third party to balance interests between the manufacturer, the retailer, and the customer – better sustainability • Intermediary may gain core competencies in configuration, selection, and assisting customer – higher performance, lower cost
	-	• Difficult to effectively transfer absorbed information to other actors • Requires the intermediary to have strong understanding of the value chain and how to seamlessly integrate all partners – difficult since he has no product and no customer • Additional transaction (communication) costs • When the broker also works with other competitors, there are barriers in sharing information.

Figure 2 - Forms of customer involvement (adapted from Berger *et al*, 2005)

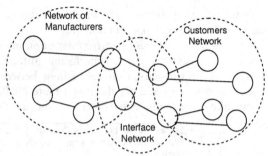

Figure 3 - Customers' involvement in a CN

Early attempts to involve customers in the product creation / innovation process, as tried by single enterprises (Salkari et al., 2005) while having the merit of putting the customer in the center, ignored many of the interaction difficulties (e.g. the knowledge/ language gap) between the customer and the manufacturing experts.

Future systems should aim at giving the customer, as well as the involved enterprises a new role, i.e. making them partners within a co-creation / co-innovation network, as illustrated in the diagram on Fig. 4. The co-innovation network comprises a network of enterprises (designers, manufacturers, brokers, etc.) merged with a network of (lead) customers, that is supported by an adequate collaboration platform and infrastructure. The interaction gaps that represented big obstacles for an effective involvement of the customers, are to be overcome through an adequate organizational structure, as well as the supporting technology, leading to a synergetic innovation ecosystem.

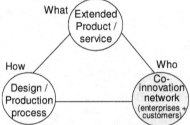

Figure 4 - Customers as part of a co-creation network

Clearly, different perspectives are to be considered at creation stage and operation stage. However, as identified by previous practices, the main current challenges for an effective establishement of a co-innovation network are related to its creation stage. The notions of digital factory / digital manufacturing and corresponding tools can play an important role here in order to facilitate the involvement of all stakeholders in the process of producing economically viable solutions. Once adequately integrated / adapted to the collaboration platforms, such tools can help in reducing the problems of the language gap and contribute to support the more and more needed ultra-short development times.

5. CASE 2: NETWORKS OF MACHINES AND SENSORS

The growing diffusion of computational power and sensorial systems in manufacturing equipment, combined with the integration of real-time and computational intelligence functionalities, are giving machines an increasing level of intelligence and autonomous decision making capabilities.

On the other hand, the participation of enterprises in dynamic (and temporary) networks requires agile adaptation to each new scenario, namely in terms of its manufacturing capabilities, processes, capacities, etc. The processes of change have been addressed mostly at the level of business process re-engineering and information technology infrastructures. Little attention however has been devoted to the changes needed at the manufacturing system level although the shop floor suffers a continuous evolution along its life cycle. A non-agile shop floor seriously limits the global agility of a manufacturing company even if its higher levels are agile. A particularly critical element in a shop-floor evolution process is the control system. Current control/supervision architectures are not agile because any shop floor changes require programming modifications, which imply the need for qualified programmers, usually not available in manufacturing SMEs.

The above needs and the new levels of intelligence and autonomy of equipments suggest that a collaborative networks approach can be adopted in the design of new manufacturing systems. The potential similarity between the dynamic adaptations at shop-floor level and the formation of consortia regulated by contracts in networked enterprise organizations was first identified in (Barata, Camarinha-Matos, 2003), work that also made a first feasibility demonstration. The problems a company faces in order to join a consortium are, to some extent and at some abstraction level, similar to the shop floor dynamic adaptation / re-configuration problem. The proposed approach is therefore to use the mechanisms and principles developed to support the enterprise integration into dynamic enterprise networks as inspiration for a new generation of agile shop-floor systems and the design of new mechatronic components.

Sensor networks are also becoming more relevant in practical applications. For instance, in environmental protection, a large number of sensors measuring environmental parameters such as temperature, pressure, concentration of chemicals, etc., and with embedded computational power can be organized in a network of cooperative autonomous sub-systems. In manufacturing sites and other large facilities (e.g. airports, ports, and large public buildings) networks of sensors can be implemented for monitoring of errors, attacks, optimization of energy consumption, etc. Each sensor in the network can do some amount of computation and communicate the raw and/or processed data to a central computing facility or intermediate integration nodes for further processing and integration with other data.

Although the interactions among nodes in these contexts tend to be more structured that in the case of networks of organizations, it is expected that structural, functional and behavioral models of inter-organizational networks can inspire new solutions here. Artificial intelligent techniques and particularly computational intelligence (soft computing, genetic computing, etc.), machine learning, federated systems, planning, and decision making are expected to provide the base implementation tools. Like in inter-enterprise networks, the outcome of machines and sensors networks is more than the sum of its parts. For instance, a complex pick-and-place skill may become available when a robot and a flexible gripper work together. This skill results from a proper combination of more elementary skills provided by the two individual manufacturing components. Therefore, principles of emergence, both in terms of manufacturing / perception skills and behavior need to be properly identified, understood, and modeled.

6. CASE 3: ACTIVE AGEING SUPPORT

It is widely recognized that Europe's population is ageing and with ongoing improvements to health and welfare, life expectancy is progressively increasing. It is foreseen that by 2020, people over the age of 60 will constitute 25% of the number of people in Europe. It is thus timely for Europe to reassess the understanding of such terms as ageing and retirement, and questioning the assumptions as to work, happiness, leisure, community involvement etc. with respect to old age.

The current understanding of elderly as a dependent stage of life no longer coincides with the way society is developing at the outset of the 21st century. The concept of *"active ageing"* provides a more appropriate understanding of the later phase of life given both social and technological trends and outlook for the future. One significant challenge is thus to enable older people to continue participating in and contributing to economic and social life – where they wish to do so – and to reduce social isolation and exclusion.

Many senior citizens across Europe, as they reach the age of retirement, desire to remain engaged in economically and socially productive activities. Indeed, their knowledge and experience is a critical asset to the future development of European society. In fact, this desire to remain active and to use their professional skills for the benefit of the wider community is the driving force behind the emergence of what has now become recognized as the *"silver economy"*. However, many elderly citizens, following retirement, quickly become marginalized as they feel discarded by a society which often fails to recognize their worth, and to appreciate and benefit from it. They are often seen as a cost burden rather than a resource, capable of value creation. This feeling of exclusion creates a vacuum in the life of the elderly citizens which can affect their health and well being. The critical challenge for society in this aspect of the active ageing process is to create an ICT-supported environment in which elderly citizens do not feel excluded, but rather have a chance to use their knowledge and expertise in a meaningful way by making a valued contribution to the communities in which they live.

Taking advantage of current technology, a number of initiatives have been launched in several regions to establish virtual communities that try to help elderly to remain active and involved. These communities although playing a beneficial role, namely in terms of "socialization", are quite limited in several other important aspects, e.g.

(a) They lack modeling the evolution of the elderly's behavior and adapting to the emotional state of the elderly, and therefore cannot provide any effective support (so much as needed in this phase of life).

(b) They lack adequate mechanisms for interaction with the economic system and therefore face big difficulties in making use of the potential contributions of retired professionals, even when they would be wiling to volunteer such contributions.

To exploit these issues and elaborate a strategic roadmap focused on innovative solutions and ensuring a balanced post-retirement life-style, a new European project (ePAL - extending Professional Active Life) was launched recently. As a guiding case study in the ePAL project, an existing virtual community of retired professionals is used. Members of this community provide, on a voluntary basis, help in assessing the viability plans and initial business plans for launching small and micro enterprises. One such specific network that will participate in the ePAL has been created in the region of Andalusia in Spain and consists of approximately 300 retired professionals.

In general, small start-up companies cannot support the costs of such specialized analysis help. The governmental organizations also can only give partial help. On the other hand consulting companies can usually provide analysis methodologies that help with the problem diagnosis of such entrepreneurial projects, but often do not provide much advice on how to find suitable solutions to the identified problems. Applying their life time gained experience, expertise, and wisdom, retired professionals in interaction / collaboration with public institutions, can provide a valuable help contributing to the development of the economic tissue in their region and otherwise. However, in order to be effective, this process requires involvement of a variety of actors including: the target beneficiaries, i.e. the small and very small enterprises, the (regional) entities involved in supporting the economic developments (governmental organizations, chambers of commerce, etc.), consulting companies specialized in SMEs, and other support institutions, e.g. financial institutions.

Each member of the retired professionals' community has specific knowledge in a particular field, while often an adequate solution for the problems of every start-up company requires a proper combination from multiple fields. Therefore, virtual teams of elderly professionals can be engaged on providing the assessment and advice to each specific case. On the other hand, the retired elderly may not have the possibility or even interest in doing the necessary field work (e.g. the problem diagnosis and identification, characterization of the situation, etc.) and therefore it is necessary to create synergies with other (economic) actors that perform that role.

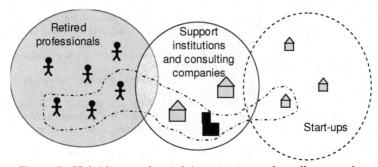

Figure 5 - Hybrid network to advice start-ups and small companies

At present there is a "gap" between the "potential" valuable help that can be provided by elderly professionals and the need for assistance and consultancy raised by the economic system, especially in the context of scarce resources at SMEs and start-ups. The challenge is for ICT-supported specialized virtual communities that (i) *reduce the geographical barriers* – supporting limited mobility, (ii) *allow flexibility* - not necessarily synchronous collaboration, (iii) *enhance establishing links with other retired professionals in similar circumstances* – finding new " (*electronic*) *pals*", and (iv) *facilitate the integration and interaction with other stakeholders* in the socio-economic system.

7. CONCLUSIONS

The discipline of collaborative networks and particularly the collaborative networked organizations are going through an expansion and consolidation process, as shown by the large amount of conceptual results, support tools, and developed pilot demonstrations and applications during the last years.

As the area progresses, and especially as a result of the enlarging application base, new research challenges are being identified. Collaborative networks are nowadays applied in a large variety of sectors, including industrial manufacturing, services, logistics and transportation, energy management, education, agribusiness, government, research, elderly care, etc. Three examples presented in this chapter illustrate some of the challenges faced in these diverse application areas. The paradigm is becoming a pervasive phenomenon with a great potential. Further research and development shall materialize this potential.

Acknowledgments. This work was funded in part by the European Commission through the ECOLEAD project. The author thanks the contribution of his partners in the consortium.

8. REFERENCES

Barata, J.; Camarinha-Matos, L. M. (2003). Coalitions of manufacturing components for shopfloor agility, Int. Journal of Networking and Virtual Organizations, Vol. 2, N° 1, pp 50-77.

Berger, C.; Moslein, K.; Piller, F.; Reichwald, R. (2005). Cooperation between manufacturers, retailers, and customers for user co-design: Learning from exploratory research. In: European Management Review, 1, pp 70-87.

Camarinha-Matos, L.M., (2007). Collaboratived Networked Organizations in manufacturing. Proceedings of IFAC Conference on Cost Effective Automation in Networked Product Development and Manufacturing, Monterrey, Mexico, 2-5 Oct 2007.

Camarinha-Matos, L. M.; Afsarmanesh, H. (2005). Collaborative networks: A new scientific discipline, J. Intelligent Manufacturing, 16, N° 4-5, pp 439-452.

Camarinha-Matos, L. M., H. Afsarmanesh, M. Ollus (2005). Virtual Organizations: Systems and Practices. Springer, Boston.

Camarinha-Matos, L. M.; Afsarmanesh, H., Ollus, M., 2005. ECOLEAD: A holistic approach to creation and management of dynamic virtual organizations. In Collaborative Networks and their Breeding Environments (L.M. Camarinha-Matos, H. Afsarmanesh, Ed.s), pp. 3-16, Springer, Boston.

Hippel, E.(2002). Horizontal innovation networks – by and for users. MIT Sloan School of Management.

Reichwald, R.; Seifert, S.; Walcher, D., Piller, F. (2005). Customers as part of value webs: Towards a framework for webbed customer innovation tools. Technische Universitaet Muenchen.

Salkari I, Heilala J, Simons M. (2005). Challenges of innovative operations development in project oriented manufacturing industry - case operations strategy. 12th International EurOMA Conference on Operational and Global Competitiveness. Budapest, 19-22 Jun 2005. Diamond Congress Ltd., 1305–1312.

Author Index